A History of the Germans of Roberts Cove, 1880-2007

A History of the Germans of Roberts Cove, 1880-2007

Reinhart Kondert

With genealogical materials
by Lawrence and Mary Cramer

Foreword by
Fr. Keith L. Vincent

Center for Louisiana Studies
University of Louisiana at Lafayette
2008

Back Cover Image Courtesy of Lawrence Cramer

Center for Louisiana Studies
University of Louisiana at Lafayette
© 2008 by Center for Louisiana Studies
P.O. Box 40831
Lafayette, LA 70504-0831
http://cls.louisiana.edu

All rights reserved
ISBN (paper): 1-887-366-82-2
This book is printed on acid-free paper.

Library of Congress Cataloging-in-Publication Data

Kondert, Reinhart.
A history of the Germans of Roberts Cove, 1880-2007 / by Reinhart Kondert ; with updated genealogical materials by Lawrence Cramer ; foreword by Keith L. Vincent.
    p. cm.
Includes bibliographical references and index.
ISBN 1-887366-82-2 (alk. paper)
1. German Americans--Louisiana--Roberts Cove--History. 2. Roberts Cove (La.)--History. 3. Roberts Cove (La.)--Social life and customs. 4. Roberts Cove (La.)--Ethnic relations. 5. Roberts Cove (La.)--Genealogy. I. Cramer, Lawrence. II. Title.

F379.R63K66 2008
305.893'1073076356--dc22

2008025078

To the descendants of Roberts Cove's founding fathers:
Their history has enriched us all.

Table of Contents

Foreword ix

Introduction xi

Chapter I
    From Geilenkirchen to Acadia Parish 1

Chapter II
    The Establishment of Economic and Religious Security, 1882-1900 13

Chapter III
    The Golden Age of Roberts Cove, 1900-1917 29

Chapter IV
    World War I and Its Aftermath, 1917-1956 43

Chapter V
    The Revival of the Ethnic and Historical Consciousness
    of Roberts Cove (1950s to the Present) 53

Chapter VI
    Recent Developments, 1987-2007 61

Notes 77

Appendices 93

Bibliography 483

Index 491

Foreword

Hidden treasure lies just three miles from busy Interstate-10. This is no ordinary country church. Its turreted steeple could be at home in a German village. The massive live oaks a few feet away would astound in Europe, but the gingerbread architecture of the pilgrimage chapel they shade would not be out of place. Signs 500 feet before and after the church say "Roberts Cove," but this is all: no post office, gas station/grocery store/café, bar or school? Only the Church of St. Leo IV and an enormous tranquility?

The greater part of Roberts Cove is hidden. Nine or ten miles away there are people who "belong" to the Cove, despite what their addresses might suggest. Throughout Louisiana and other states are thousands—not all with German names—for whom this is more than an ancestral home. At the Feasts of Corpus Christi or All Saints or St. Nicholas—to name but a few times for reunion—you can find many of them coming home. The hymn "Maria zu lieben" or "Großer Gott, wir loben Dich" starts, and you see what makes this community unique: it is a little piece of Germany in French Acadiana. And for over a century it has kept its Germanic identity while much larger communities lost theirs.

Secrets too well kept pass into oblivion. For this reason the Catholic community of St. Leo IV welcomes this latest study by Dr. Reinhart Kondert of the University of Southwestern Louisiana.. We welcome the retelling of our story, the intelligence of the account, the rare materials and scholarship that have been made accessible to the layman, and the opportunity given to contribute clarifications for the manuscript.

The Roberts Cove German Centennial of 1980 and the St. Leo Parish Centennial of 1985 brought this hidden treasure to regional and even national attention. May this study enjoy the same honor and the extended family of Roberts Cove take renewed commitment to the heritage Dr. Kondert describes.

Keith L. Vincent
Pastor, St. Leo IV Church
Roberts Cove, Louisiana, 1987

Introduction

Deep in the heart of South Louisiana's Cajun Country lies the small "German" community of Roberts Cove.[1] This settlement was founded in the early 1880s by a handful of Catholic immigrants seeking to escape the "Prussianization" of Germany and the turmoils of Chancellor Otto von Bismarck's *Kulturkampf* (the struggle between his administration and the country's Catholics). In their search for a new homeland, the prospective colonists were directed to the prairie regions of Catholic Louisiana. There in Acadia Parish they prospered as innovative pioneers in the rice culture. To preserve their ethnic cohesiveness, the settlers established their own church and school. Through these institutions, they passed on to future generations the language and culture of their fatherland. For over forty years, they flourished as Germans in a sea of French Acadians.

The coming of World War I brought dramatic changes to this peaceful existence. As the United States entered the war against Germany, citizens throughout the land, including those in Louisiana, began to suspect the Germans in their midst as being treasonous foreigners. Many states passed legislation severely restricting the actions of their German inhabitants. Louisiana's anti-alien laws were among America's harshest. The Germans of Roberts Cove were forced to limit their reliance on those institutions which had served so well to protect their cultural inheritance. Use of the German language in church, at school, and in public conversations, at least during the war years, was greatly restricted.

The imposition of these wartime restrictions severely retarded the future ethnic vitality of the Roberts Cove community. The hatreds and suspicions generated by the war lingered for many years. Neither the inhabitants of Roberts Cove nor the residents of the surrounding regions would have welcomed a return to the conditions of the past, and the Germans generally recognized that a turning point in their history had been reached. They would have to lose their Germanic ways and become fully integrated into the American mainstream.

For a number of decades after the war, the citizens of Roberts Cove gave less thought to the maintenance of their German identity. The generations since the Great War had dispersed, intermarried with "outsiders," and lost all but a vague recollection of their Teutonic heritage. The German language was spoken by only a few of the oldest inhabitants still residing in Roberts Cove. For all intents and purposes, it appeared that the Germanic identity of this small community had been washed away by time and circumstances.

Introduction

However, just when it seemed that the Germanic identity of Roberts Cove had disappeared, concerned individuals launched efforts to keep alive the memory and customs of the community's Teutonic past. The Church of St. Leo was a catalyst in this effort at cultural revival. In the early 1950s, Father Gerard Wolbers of St. Leo's Church began interviewing the last of the original colonists. It was also Father Wolbers who emphasized the singing of German songs, who revived the St. Nicholas celebration, and who introduced a German architectural style in the new church constructed in 1954. Then, in the late 1950s, Charles Zaunbrecher, native priest of St. Leo's and descendant of a Roberts Cove pioneer, began a crusade to rejuvenate the ethnic and historic consciousness of the Cove's inhabitants. He emphasized the need to keep alive the community's Germanic past, and to that end, encouraged the descendants of the original settlers to host annual family reunions to commemorate the achievements and the traditions of their forefathers. Beginning in 1956 on a rather modest scale, these reunions over the years have become joyous celebrations attended by hundreds, even thousands, of the Cove's inhabitants and friends. They are Louisiana's version of the Germanic *Oktoberfest* in which gratefulness for the bounty of the land and the joy of sharing a common past are combined.

Equally important in these efforts at cultural rejuvenation were the steps taken by St. Leo's. The Roberts Cove church has always been in the forefront of keeping alive traces of the community's Germanic ancestry, and, at about the same time that the family reunions were started, and perhaps even earlier, the congregation began to sponsor special holiday celebrations emphasizing Germanic customs. Particularly during St. Nicholas Day and Christmas, and on many lesser occasions as well, German foods, songs, prayers, and other traditions of the homeland were perpetuated. Together with the family gatherings, these church practices seem to have reversed the tide of cultural disintegration. The Germanic roots of the Roberts Cove community, at least for the time being, seem to be on firm footing.[2]

The success that the inhabitants of Roberts Cove had in first retaining and then recapturing their cultural inheritance was unique among Louisiana's German settlers. Many other Germanic communities had been established in this state in the nineteenth century.[3] None of these, however, was able to retain its ethnic identity. All of them were swallowed up by the tide of Americanization, including the once populous and powerful German element of New Orleans, which once supported dozens of German churches, schools, and newspapers. By the turn of the twentieth century, however, virtually all of these cultural institutions had disappeared.[4] Only at the Roberts Cove settle-

Introduction

ment was there still an active German school and church through two decades of the twentieth century.

The ability of the Roberts Cove settlement to retain at least some aspects of its German culture into the present age has aroused the interest of a number of individuals. In 1980 David Treen, then governor of Louisiana, attended the centennial celebration of the community's founding. Numerous other important dignitaries, especially from the Catholic church, joined almost 6,000 individuals, mostly direct descendants of the community's founders, in paying homage to their German forefathers and the colony they established.

Scholars have also directed their attention to the birth and development of the Roberts Cove settlement, particularly the community's cultural retentions. These areas of scholarly interest were first explored in 1969 by Stanley Joseph McCord through a 300-page doctoral dissertation on this colony's history and culture.[5] Almost half of McCord's work is dedicated to the study of the German dialect which is still spoken by the community's oldest inhabitants. McCord also carefully investigated the settlement's economic growth by consulting Acadia Parish's land conveyance records. His careful scrutiny of these documents indicates that most of the original settlers were already quite well off by the turn of the century.

McCord's scholarly investigation piqued the author's interest in this small German enclave in the middle of French Acadiana. I arrived in Lafayette as a history instructor at the University of Southwestern Louisiana the very year in which McCord's study was completed. In the course of my own subsequent research on Louisiana Germans, I encountered his work. I became convinced that McCord's findings, as well as those that I have arrived at after several years of independent research, needed to be brought before a larger audience—an audience not of scholars but of laymen who might benefit from the knowledge of this community. Above all, I became determined to reveal the history of Roberts Cove to the descendants of the community's founders, many of whom are surprisingly ignorant of their historical background. It is to these individuals that I dedicate this book.

Chapter I

From Geilenkirchen to Acadia Parish

A proper accounting of the history of Roberts Cove must begin with a discussion of the homeland. What region of Germany were the emigrants from? What conditions prevailed in the mother country to cause them to leave? Why did they choose to settle in southern Louisiana? All of the original immigrants who settled in Roberts Cove were natives of the district of Geilenkirchen-Heinsberg (hereinafter called Geilenkirchen), in the westernmost part of Germany. The area is located a few miles north of the historic city of Aachen and about forty-five miles west of the city of Cologne. Geilenkirchen lies so far to the west that the region is surrounded on three sides by Holland. The names of some of the cities from which the founders originated were Geilenkirchen, Hastenrath, Kreuzrath, Waldenrath, Langbroich, and Millen. The overall area is located in the state of North-Rhine Westphalia and is considered to be a part of the Rhineland.[1]

The Rhineland region of Germany has traditionally borne the brunt of the country's wars. A glance at the history of that region indicates that three particularly destructive wars were fought in this portion of the Rhineland: (1) the Thirty Years' War, 1618-1648; (2) the wars of Louis XIV, 1676-1713; and (3) the wars of the French Revolution and Napoleon, 1794-1815.

The Thirty Years' War was one of the most devastating in all of Germany's history. Like all religious wars, it was fought with special ferocity. In fact, historians maintain that Germany was physically ruined by the war and that her political development was retarded by two hundred years.[2] Geilenkirchen did not become a theater of the war until 1635, and, for the next decade and a half, the region was occupied by both Catholic and Protestant forces. In those days, supply lines for the armies were non-existent; soldiers foraged, pillaged, stole, and lived off the land as best they could, leaving in their wake large-scale devastation. The detrimental effects of this war were felt for many years by the residents of the Geilenkirchen area, and deprivation and starvation were a part of daily life for decades thereafter.

Just when the inhabitants of the region were beginning to recover from the ravages of Europe's last and most destructive religious war, disaster struck again when the armies of Louis XIV invaded Holland in 1676. This so-called "Dutch War" later expanded into the Geilenkirchen region, and French troops plundered and burned many German villages. The French occupation continued for a number of years, and the local Germanic population endured numer-

Chapter One

ous indignities. But, in the end, Louis XIV's forces withdrew without having accomplished their goal of conquering the Dutch. Although two additional major wars were fought by the armies of Louis XIV (the War of the League of Augsburg [1688-1697] and the War of the Spanish Succession [1701-1713]), neither caused as much damage in Geilenkirchen as the previous Dutch War.

Though the Geilenkirchen region was spared the ravages of these conflicts it was again devastated during the French Revolution. The wars unleashed by this great uprising brought turmoil to the European continent for over twenty years. Geilenkirchen, because of its proximity to France, and because of its location in the strategic Rhineland, was a major military theatre. Indeed, French troops occupied the area between 1794 and 1815, and Geilenkirchen became a virtual appendage of the French state, paying French taxes and submitting to French military conscription for the entire twenty-one years. After Napoleon's defeat in 1815, Geilenkirchen was ceded to militaristic Prussia as part of the province of Jülich, and military conscription, as a result, was retained.[3]

It is difficult, if not impossible, to determine with precision the effect that this history of warfare had on the residents of the Geilenkirchen district. One can only conclude that the many years of strife imprinted upon the collective psyche of the local population the lingering fear that wars and upheavals could return at any time. A more direct impact, particularly on the minds of the young men of the region, was a hatred for military service. The traditional revulsion for forced military conscription seems to have been one of the motivating factors for their emigration to Louisiana in the early 1880s.

Military conscription in Geilenkirchen had again become a major issue because of the Wars of German Unification. Between 1864 and 1871, Prussia under its iron chancellor Otto von Bismarck, fought three wars of "German unification." Actually, they were wars of conquest by which Prussia annexed the remainder of Germany to itself. As Prussian subjects, the young men of Geilenkirchen were forced to serve in these wars. Although we do not know how many men from Geilenkirchen served in these wars, or how many fell victim to them, we do know that these wars revived the local population's hatred of conflict and the attendant conscription. In 1878, when emigration to the United States was first proposed, at least some of the prospective colonists voiced approval out of a desire to escape the militarized Prussian system.[4]

Another important factor that led to the exodus of thousands of Germans, especially those of the Catholic religion, was the *Kulturkampf*,[5] the political battle fought between Chancellor Bismarck and Germany's Catholics in the 1880s. For various reasons, Bismarck feared the existence of his country's Catholics, particularly the Catholic Center Party which tended to be indepen-

From Geilenkirchen to Acadia Parish

dent-minded and difficult to control. The members of this party and those individuals it represented in the *Reichstag* (lower house of the legislature), were apt to look to the pope for guidance and support. It was probably this Catholic trait that Bismarck liked least, for it meant that his own power and that of the emperor were proportionately diminished.

To counter the influence of the nation's Catholics, Bismarck pushed through the German parliament a series of anti-Catholic measures referred to as the "May Laws." These deprived Catholics of both civil and religious liberties. For example, one law forced people to be married in state courts in which religious ceremonies were, of course, barred. Another law reduced greatly the number of seminaries where future priests were to be trained, and a third law actually expelled the Jesuits from the country. Although these measures were all eventually repealed by 1887 because of their immense unpopularity, their immediate effect was to cause many Germans to question whether they should remain in their country.[6]

The Catholics of Geilenkirchen undoubtedly asked themselves that very question on the eve of their departure from their native land. Several Roberts Cove inhabitants subsequently cited their disapproval of Bismarck's policies toward Catholics as one of the reasons for their emigration. Probably every one of the colonists who eventually settled in Roberts Cove had his or her own individual reason for wanting to begin life in a new land. But, without military conscription and the *Kulturkampf,* it is doubtful that personal motives alone would have been sufficient cause to leave their homeland.[7]

To the general and the personal motives must be added the encouraging role played by Father Peter Leonhard Thevis. He was the single most important force behind the immigration from Geilenkirchen. The influence exercised by him on a host of individuals from his native district of Geilenkirchen persuaded many Germans to emigrate. Most receptive to his arguments to begin a new life abroad were members of his own family. Because of the importance of Father Thevis to the founding of Roberts Cove, it is essential that the basic contours of his life and career be outlined.

Father Thevis was born on February 27, 1837, in the village of Langbroich. Because of his religious nature, he decided very early to become a man of the cloth. He was ordained a priest in 1862 in the Archdiocese of Cologne. It was here that he later met Archbishop Jean-Marie Odin of New Orleans. Odin regularly made trips to Germany to find priests for churches in New Orleans where thousands of German Catholics resided in the middle of the nineteenth century. On one of his recruitment expeditions to Germany in 1867, Arch-

Chapter One

bishop Odin met Father Thevis and persuaded the latter to accompany him to New Orleans.[8]

Once in New Orleans, Father Thevis took on the duties of assistant pastor of the Church of the Holy Trinity, one of the oldest, most venerable houses of worship in the entire city. Later, in 1867, Father Thevis inherited the job of pastor due to the untimely death of his predecessor. As pastor of this important German church, Father Thevis gained considerable influence over New Orleans' leading German Catholics.[9]

Father Thevis was a man of immense drive and energy, and he wasted little time in making his presence felt in his adopted city. For example, he founded the German School of the Holy Trinity for young children. He also brought the Benedictine sisters from Covington, Kentucky, to teach the lower grades, and an instructor from Germany for the upper grades. The school proved to be a huge success and remained in existence for many years.

An equally ambitious but ultimately less successful venture was the founding of the newspaper, *Das Echo von New Orleans.* The newspaper was founded in 1870, the same year as the school, but it did not survive the year. Only twenty editions of New Orleans' first and only German Catholic newspaper were published. Why Father Thevis embarked upon this risky enterprise when so many German newspapers had already failed is difficult to ascertain. Probably, he simply overestimated its potential for success since it was to become the only tabloid of its kind. At any rate, his intentions were admirable in that he wished to offer to his readers an unadulterated Catholic view of the world and provide advice on how to accommodate oneself to that world.[10]

As it turned out, Father Thevis' newspaper was much more than a religious sheet. In the medium which he created, he openly, and sometimes brazenly, expressed his political views. On a regional and national level, Thevis was fervently anti-Reconstructionist, considering it to be a "party-swindle."[11] In the larger arena of world politics, he was consistently pro-German. The Franco-Prussian War was the hottest issue of the day; and, needless to say, Father Thevis came out decidedly in favor of a German victory in this conflict of arch-rivals. In his unequivocal support for Prussia and the other German states, Father Thevis earned the enmity of the majority of the Catholic clergy and laity of New Orleans since most were of Gallic background. His German nationalism and the complaints that it engendered forced his superiors in the office of the archdiocese to order a suspension of the newspaper.[12]

During its short lifespan between May and September 1870, *Das Echo von New Orleans* also gave expression to Father Thevis' views on German immigration. His opinions on this topic were ultimately of great importance for

From Geilenkirchen to Acadia Parish

the founding of Roberts Cove. As one might assume, this pastor of one of the city's leading German churches, this highly religious and nationalistic man, would use his journalistic skills and influence to attract German Catholics to his adopted land. *Das Echo von New Orleans* devoted more attention to expansion of German immigration to the New World than any other issue. In an article entitled a "Chronicle of German Communities in the South,"[13] one of the many pro-immigration pieces, Thevis strongly upheld the necessity of attracting Germans to the South, where their industry and ingenuity were needed to develop the war-ravaged region.[14]

Father Thevis' profound interest in German Catholic immigration had already led to the establishment of the Fabacher community in Acadia Parish. This German colony, which preceded the birth of Roberts Cove by a decade and helped to inspire the founding of the latter, was the brainchild of Joseph Fabacher, a wealthy businessman and a parishioner of Father Thevis' church who was so inspired by his pastor's views on immigration that he founded a German settlement in South Louisiana. Later, we know that close ties were established between the two settlements because Anton Frey, a prominent resident of New Orleans and a close relative of the Freys who settled in Fabacher, donated forty acres of land for the location of a school at the Roberts Cove community. And, according to Christian Hensgens, one of the Cove's early inhabitants, we also know that Joseph Fabacher provided material assistance to the colonists who arrived later in 1881 aboard the *S.S. Mississippi*.[15]

The relationship between these neighboring German colonies is important enough to merit a brief summary of the early history of the Fabacher community. As has already been indicated, the Fabacher settlement was founded in 1870. Although the colony received its name from Joseph Fabacher, Zeno Huber played as important a role as the colony's namesake. He, too, was a native of Germany who had settled in New Orleans and who now wanted to help in the establishment of a new German settlement. Fabacher and Huber had together toured the prospective settlement area and had determined the location for the new community on the basis of its promise as a flourishing agricultural area. Located about ten miles northwest of Crowley between two bayous, this region had the added attraction of lying on or near a projected railroad line which would connect Vermilionville with Orange, Texas. Using the fertility of the soil and rail service as inducements for settlement, the two men persuaded roughly sixty Germans from New Orleans and other recent immigrants from Germany to set down their roots in this part of Louisiana.[16]

Although many of the Germans from New Orleans returned to that city shortly after Fabacher was founded—life in the wilderness was much more difficult than they expected—the community survived. But its continued existence was jeopardized by construction of the rail line considerably to the south of the settlement. Despite this disappointment and other setbacks, the Fabacher colony remained and flourished, as a result of the intensive cultivation of rice. Joseph Fabacher, who encouraged the colonists to engage in the rice culture after he himself successfully experimented with growing the crop, is credited by one contemporary source with "cultivating the first large field of rice ever grown in Southwestern Louisiana," with "introducing rice culture into this section of the state," and with bringing "the first machine for threshing to this corner of the state."[17] Only one year after they were established, a local newspaper, the Opelousas *Journal*, stated that the Germans of Fabacher were living in a "perfect democracy." These farmers, the *Journal* went on to say, "do more and better work than our laborers. They are more economical, saving and thrifty ... and make money and property where we would starve or remain in poverty." The newspaper predicted a rosy future for the settlement.[18]

Nine years later, a report in the *St. Landry Democrat* seemed to bear out the optimism of the Opelousas *Journal*. On September 18, 1880, the former newspaper indicated that the Germans of the Fabacher settlement were anticipating a rice crop of 4,600 barrels. "This rice in the 'rough,'" the *Democrat* went on to say, "will net about four dollars per barrel. So we have a small neighborhood where they used to produce absolutely nothing for sale, now producing a revenue of 16,000 dollars." This productivity, averred the newspaper, had increased the value of these marshlands to the extent that before too long "they cannot be bought for any reasonable price."[19]

For many years thereafter, the Fabacher colony, now called Ritchie, continued to attract the favorable attention of outside observers,[20] despite the fact that as a German community the settlement was rapidly losing its identity. The process of assimilation and absorption into the American cultural mainstream seems to have occurred by the turn of the century, certainly no later than the end of the First World War.[21]

These early reports of success on the Fabacher colony spurred Father Thevis into action on his own colonization plan. Within a few years of his arrival in New Orleans, he returned to his native land and discussed with his relatives the possibility of founding a community in southern Louisiana. He probably informed them of the Fabacher colony's success to offer encouragement to those who had doubts about such a venture. While in Germany, Father Thevis also visited the religious shrines of Bavaria in order to model his own shrine of St. Roch along the lines of Europe's most beautiful.[22]

From Geilenkirchen to Acadia Parish

Several years later, probably in 1878, a vanguard of two Germans sailed for Louisiana to more closely examine the prospects of founding a colony in that state. They were to have met Father Thevis in New Orleans and then have continued on an inspection tour of prospective settlement sites. Their rendezvous in the Crescent City was delayed by two years, however. Yellow fever once again broke out in the city, and the two German travelers were advised to remain in the Northeast with relatives until the time came when it was safe for them to continue their journey.[23]

The two Germans from Geilenkirchen, both of them close relatives of Father Thevis, finally reached New Orleans in January 1880, and immediately set off for Rayne, Louisiana. Father Thevis had arranged for this advance party of prospective colonists to meet with Anton Frey, an enterprising businessman and real estate developer of New Orleans with investments in that region. Frey hoped to be able to convince Father Thevis and his German guests to set down their roots in Acadia Parish. Thevis led the Germans to Roberts Cove, lying about three miles northwest of Rayne. Its proximity to Rayne, to which the Southern Pacific Railroad had only recently completed a rail line, was crucial for its assured access to the markets of the larger cities to the east and west. This fact was made abundantly clear to the prospective immigrants, and it must have been the single greatest factor causing them to choose Roberts Cove as their future homesite. Furthermore, the Germans were informed that land in this region was abundant and cheap, relatively high, easy to clear, and fertile. The local Acadians had prospered for years cultivating small patches of rice and raising cattle. Intensive cultivation of the land might yield unexpected riches.[24] On January 12, 1880,[25] the visiting Germans decided to establish themselves in this area, a date that may be used as the birthdate of the Roberts Cove settlement.

Who were the two individuals in this vanguard who arrived at this historic decision? They were John Gerhard Thevis, nephew of Father Thevis, and Herman Grein. These two individuals might be considered the official founders of Roberts Cove, while Father Thevis may be looked upon as the moving force behind the entire venture.[26]

Although the decision to establish a colony had been made in January 1880, it was not until a year later that the first immigrants actually settled at Roberts Cove. Meanwhile, the two Germans in the advance party returned to New Orleans with Father Thevis, for it was not feasible for them to remain alone at Roberts Cove. Both worked at a New Orleans brewery for several months until late 1880, when Herman Grein returned to Germany to find a bride and come back with her and other family members to Roberts Cove. He

Chapter One

did not find a bride, but he was accompanied on his return to New Orleans by ten immigrants from the home district of Geilenkirchen.

The ten individuals to make the initial trip to the New World for the purpose of settling at Roberts Cove were Joseph and Josepha Vondenstein and their five children, Heinrich and August Leonards, and Johanna Piepers. These ten arrived in New Orleans in March 1881. On March 22, Johanna Piepers and Peter Joseph Thevis, Father Thevis' brother who had arrived independently in New Orleans, were married by Father Thevis in the Church of the Holy Trinity. Herman Grein and August Leonards served as witnesses. Several days later all thirteen Germans, the two in the original vanguard and the eleven who now joined them (including Peter Thevis), continued their journey to Roberts Cove and became the settlement's first permanent inhabitants.[27]

Gerhard and Peter Joseph Thevis almost immediately purchased land upon their arrival, indicating that they were individuals of some means. They jointly bought 387 acres for $967.50. Later in the year, Herman Grein homesteaded 155 acres. The land that was purchased lay on the north bank of nearby Bayou Wikoff. Grein's homesteaded acreage was adjacent to the Thevis property on the east side.[28] The relative ease with which these properties had been acquired showed that land was indeed abundant and inexpensive as Anton Frey had promised. One month after the initial settlers arrived, the Achten family joined the fledgling community. The members of this family consisted of husband Joseph, his wife Josepha, and their three children Matthew, Anna, and Johanna Catherina. They had arrived in New Orleans on April 27, 1881, on board the *S.S. Frankfurt* and had proceeded from there to Roberts Cove.[29]

Seven months passed before the next contingent of Germans arrived. These newcomers arrived in direct response to an appeal by Father Thevis, who had journeyed to Langbroich in the summer of 1881, to visit his brother Jacob, the father of Gerhard. While on this vacation visit, Father Thevis met with several residents of the area and distributed advertising literature describing in glowing terms South Louisiana's terrain and climate and the opportunities which existed there. Some of these tracts and pamphlets had probably been given to Father Thevis by the New Orleans German Society, since that organization had traditionally been involved in the recruitment of German immigrants to Louisiana. Some promotional literature from a local realty company was probably also in his possession.[30]

Father Thevis emphasized the religious issue in this recruitment effort. As one of the oldest inhabitants of Roberts Cove later put it, Father Thevis told them that there was "no religion" in the region they would settle, meaning that there was no organized religion, and that the colonists would have a free hand in providing for their spiritual sustenance. The fact that Germany's Catholics were still suffering from the negative repercussions of the *Kulturkampf* weighed heavily on the minds of the potential recruits. This fact, brought home through the impassioned pleas of a respected friend and relative, was sufficient justification for most of those who decided to emigrate at this time. Other factors were undoubtedly present (economic hardship, continuing abhorrence of military conscription, etc.) but the lack of religious freedom in Germany was the determining one.[31]

Eventually, eight families and two bachelors responded to Father Thevis' exhortations to settle in Louisiana. The eight families were Hubert Wirtz, his wife, and three children; Lambert Schlicher, his wife, and one child; Christian Hensgens, his wife, and five children; Peter Gossen, his wife, and four children; Jacob Thevis, his wife, and four children; Nicholas Zaunbrecher, his wife, and six children; Franz Reiners, his wife, and two children; and John Gielen, his wife, and six children. The two bachelors were Joseph Leonards and Johann P. Schlicher. In all, these newcomers comprised forty-nine individuals and constituted the bulk of the Roberts Cove community.[32]

There is an interesting story about the twenty-two year old bachelor Joseph Leonards. His name was recorded on the custom rolls as Joseph Zaunbrecher. This false name was given purposefully in order to deceive German authorities. As a young man of military age, Joseph Leonards was not allowed to leave his country. On the day of his departure for the New World, he had worked in the fields near the Dutch border. That night he slipped across the border and joined his relatives. To better conceal his identity, he carried the surname of his brother-in-law Nicholas Zaunbrecher throughout the overseas journey. In this one particular instance, we know that the distastefulness of military service was a causative factor for immigration.[33]

Joseph Leonards and his forty-eight companions, however, did not actually depart their homeland until late 1881. It took all summer to make the necessary preparations for their trip. They had to sell all of the belongings that they could not carry with them, book passage on an appropriate steamliner, and say farewell to their friends and relatives. They even made a pilgrimage to pray for a safe voyage across the sea. Finally in October they were ready. Their itinerary called for them to travel to Semplevelt, Holland, and from there they would proceed by train to Antwerp, Belgium. Here, they boarded an English Channel ferryboat, and later took a train to Liverpool. At this English port they boarded the *S.S. Mississippi* to begin their five-week voyage across the Atlantic.[34]

Chapter One

The crossing took somewhat longer than usual since the ship they boarded was a cargo vessel with scheduled stops at Spain and then Cuba before reaching New Orleans. During the course of this journey, the travelers endured considerable boredom but no real hardships. Food was plentiful but not at all what the Germans were accustomed to, and once their German bread gave out their trip became infinitely more difficult. One thing that the immigrants learned on board this confining vessel was cooperation. In a sense, they were like one big family, sharing such joys and responsibilities as preparing communal meals, washing clothes, watching and entertaining the children, and praying together. This community spirit which was instilled during the voyage stood them in good stead when they reached Roberts Cove, and helps to explain why the colony fared so well later. After what seemed like an interminable time at sea, the *S.S. Mississippi* docked at New Orleans on November 17, 1881.[35]

Awaiting them were Father Thevis and Anton Frey, the well-to-do inhabitant of New Orleans who owned large tracts of land near Roberts Cove and who later donated some of his land to that fledgling community. Frey informed the arriving immigrants of the availability of cheap land, and he apparently offered to sell them some of his for $3.00 an acre. On the same day, the German colonists boarded a train for Rayne where Joseph Achten was waiting to lead them to the Cove. Two ten-year-old boys, incidentally, remained behind to receive instruction for communion from Father Thevis. These two boys, Lorenz Zaunbrecher and Daniel Thevis, later rejoined their friends.[36]

At Rayne there was a short delay. The hard rains of November 17 had flooded the local roads, making them impassable. Furthermore, since no bridges then existed locally, it was impossible to ford the area's bayous and streams. The colonists were thus forced to spend their first night in Louisiana in a Rayne hotel. The following day they proceeded to Roberts Cove, and with their arrival the community's population was augmented from eighteen to about sixty-five.[37]

Problems, and perhaps a few real hardships, awaited the new arrivals, who immediately confronted the necessity of finding shelter and food. Undoubtedly, the eighteen colonists who were already there provided some help, but the exact nature of their accommodations and precisely how they nourished themselves remain unknown. The settlers probably came with enough money to procure the lumber for their dwellings from hardware stores in Rayne. Food was probably also purchased in Rayne, at least until the first gardens and crops were harvested. Few records, oral or written, about these early times exist. One can imagine, however, that many difficulties and some suffering must have been endured.

From Geilenkirchen to Acadia Parish

Courthouse records do shed light on some aspects of life in the first year of the settlement's existence. Professor Joseph McCord, through land conveyance documents, has reconstructed the manner in which land was purchased and at what price. The records reveal the names of the purchasers and therefore inform us as to the relative well-being of the colonists. It is known, for example, that Nicholas Zaunbrecher was one of the wealthiest settlers, since he was able to purchase 213 acres of land from Isaac E. Clark of Fabacher for $640 cash. This transaction was completed on November 28, 1881, only ten days after the arrival of the colonists at Roberts Cove. On January 9, 1882, Peter Gossen, Christian Hensgens, and Hubert Wirtz each bought 100 acres from Anton Frey and Franz Reiners purchased 50 acres from the same man. The cost of the land varied from $3.25 to $4.50 an acre. Only Peter Gossen paid cash for his acreage. The others made small down payments and contracted notes to pay for the remainder later. From the land conveyance records McCord has concluded that only six of the eleven families were able to purchase land. In addition, one single man bought land and another, Herman Grein, homesteaded on government land. Finally, the land conveyance documents confirm that close ties were quickly established between the newcomers of Roberts Cove and their German neighbors to the north at the Fabacher settlement.[38]

The second year of the settlement witnessed the arrival of twenty-one additional Germans. These twenty-one brought the colony's population to about eighty-five and represented the final large contingent of immigrants to come from Germany. The considerable growth of the colony that was registered later came through natural increases from within, although a few of the settlers from the nearby Fabacher community, as well as some Germans from elsewhere, did subsequently join the Roberts Cove community. The individuals who came in the spring, 1882, were Hubert Theunissen, his wife Maria Catherina, and their two children; three single men, Henry Joseph Spaetgens, Arnold Jacobs and Johann Ronkartz; and a married man who came by himself, Gerhard Joseph Heinen. The latter arrived to check on conditions at the colony before bringing his family. He remained at Roberts Cove for about half-a-year, returned to Germany, and came back the same year with his wife Maria Josepha and their five children. Accompanying Joseph Heinen was his brother Peter William Heinen.[39]

In the first two years of the settlement's establishment, the survival, let alone the expansion of Roberts Cove, seemed far from certain. An indication that the years 1881-1882 were extremely demanding was the number of deaths that were recorded by the community. Deaths actually exceeded births

Chapter One

in these two years and caused the colony to decrease in size. Fortunately, the ratio of births to deaths in these two years was an aberration caused by the unusually trying circumstances of the settlement's founding. In future years births always outnumbered deaths.

The first infant to be born in the colony was Peter Joseph Vondenstein, who saw the light of day on July 26, 1881. The following year two more children were born. A daughter was born to Christian Hensgens and his wife Regina in December; and a son to Lambert Schlicher and his wife Marie the previous May. Those who suffered losses were the Theunissen, Gielen, Gossen, and Thevis families. The family of Hubert Theunissen witnessed the demise of two of its children.

One child died during the crossing, and the second passed away on June 25, 1882. Magelena Gielen died in childbirth on September 25, 1882, and the infant succumbed three weeks later. In October Peter Gossen died at age sixty-seven, and the following month Magdelena Gertrude Thevis, wife of Jacob, expired, becoming the fifth fatality in the colony's first two years of existence.[40]

With the difficult founding years behind them, the colonists experienced primarily growth and success. The remaining eighteen years of the nineteenth century would be some of the most lively and creative in the colony's history. They were years in which the inhabitants secured their material and spiritual welfare. The settlement was like a flower which through proper nourishment blossomed into full glory.

Chapter II

The Establishment of Economic and Religious Security, 1882-1900

The development of the Roberts Cove colony in the last eighteen years of the nineteenth century was remarkable. Within those eighteen years, the colonists adapted to the agricultural conditions of the region. Primarily through their native intelligence, perseverance, and hard work, they wrested from the plains of Acadia Parish a prosperous standard of living through the rice culture. At the same time, they saw to it that their cultural inheritance would be preserved through the establishment of a German church and school.

The colony's survival, however, hinged upon its economic fortunes, and success at farming was not automatic. Several years of trial and error were required before the colonists prospered. Before cultivating rice, the settlers tried cotton and corn, but neither crop succeeded. Some of the Germans in the early years consequently were forced to work in the salt mines of Avery Island to support themselves.[1] Success at farming was difficult because the colonists had no examples to follow. There was very little established agriculture in the region. The French Acadians of the region lived primarily off their cattle and the small plots of "providence" rice and other garden grains and vegetables. Following this example could lead to self-sufficiency, but it would never make them wealthy farmers.

Yet, the Roberts Cove settlers eventually made the transformation to large-scale rice farming. The Germans were actually rather lucky in this regard because they happened to come along at the right time in the development of this crop. New methods of growing this crop were being tried in several areas of South Louisiana, and this experimentation coincided with an increasing appearance of mechanized farm machinery. Capitalizing upon these new technologies, the Germans were able to flourish. They added their natural industriousness and ingenuity to these developing conditions and emerged as well-established farmers.

One of the important ingredients that was added to the rice culture in the 1880s was a more systematic method of irrigation. Prior to this time, rice was grown primarily in two ways. The first way had existed since the French colonial era and ironically, had been first used quite effectively by Louisiana's original German Coast colonists.[2] Their manner of irrigating rice was to direct water by way of ditches from the Mississippi River to the lower-lying swamp-

Chapter Two

lands inland. This method could not be used when the land along the bayous and streams was higher than those bodies of water. This was the case in the high plains of Roberts Cove.

The second method of cultivating rice was to sow the seeds in depressions or lower sections of land and then hope that the rains would be sufficient to keep those low-lying areas flooded. This manner of growing rice was quite haphazard and undependable. The Acadians of southern Louisiana had used this method for years, and it was they who called their crop "providence rice" since it was up to Providence for this type of rice to flourish. Obviously, the amounts of rice grown in these two ways were quite limited.

In the 1880s old techniques began to change as experimentation in the rice culture took hold. Farmers in the prairie regions of Louisiana began to build levees around higher sections of land to trap the water for longer periods of time, in a sense, creating artificial lakes. The waters from these shallow lakes would then be diverted to the adjacent rice lands, but plentiful rainfall was necessary for this system to work. Another innovation was the construction of canals from permanent bodies of water to the rice fields. This method of irrigation became feasible through the simultaneous introduction of the steam pump, which lifted the water from the lakes into the canals in sufficient volume to flood the nearby rice fields. Important in all of this was the fact the soils in southwestern Louisiana were compact enough to retain the waters without too much seepage. Below the topsoils usually existed a hard claypan which was impervious to water loss. By the 1890s water pumps and irrigation canals were in general use in southwestern Louisiana.

The man credited with introducing the first steam pump in 1885 in southern Louisiana was W.W. Duson. The introduction of this device helped increase the state's output from 40 million pounds in 1880 to about 100 million pounds in 1890, making Louisiana the nation's leading rice producer by 1890. Another machine introduced around this time which benefited rice farmers was the rice binder. It was an implement devised by Midwestern farmers who were then migrating to the South in large numbers. These farmers had gained considerable experience in the use of machinery in the wheat fields of Kansas, Iowa, and other places. They brought their skills and machinery with them and adapted them with ease to rice farming. The same machines used in the harvesting of wheat could be used to harvest rice. The first rice binder was introduced in 1884, and within six years, there were over one thousand of these implements in use in Acadia Parish alone. The machine's popularity stemmed, in part, from its ability to operate in soggy rice fields. The same

The Establishment of Economic and Religious Security, 1882-1900

hardpan which prevented excessive seepage prevented the machinery from bogging down once the water was drained from the fields.[3]

The German farmers of Roberts Cove eagerly adopted the newer methods of farming then coming into use. They were among the first in Acadia Parish to avail themselves of these new developments. Nicholas J. Zaunbrecher, however, was also an innovator, developing novel solutions to local farming problems. He was one of the first rice farmers of his area to make use of an artificial lake. This lake became a familiar feature of the countryside after its introduction in 1884.

Nicholas Zaunbrecher was also the first farmer in his region to ship his rice to market by way of the Crowley Switch to New Orleans.[4] Shipment by rail constituted a major advance over the primitive overland transportation methods that preceded it.

To ship his rice to New Orleans in earlier times, Zaunbrecher had to overcome several hurdles. The crop had to be carried by wagon to Bayou Plaquemine Brulée. Since no bridge spanned that stream, the rice had to be unloaded, transferred to boats, and then loaded onto wagons again on the opposite side. This was such a tedious, time-consuming process that Zaunbrecher and his fellow agriculturalists were determined to construct a bridge across the bayou as quickly as possible. By 1886 a bridge was completed, and credit for this accomplishment was duly recorded by the local newspaper, the Rayne *Signal*. The newspaper reported that Mr. Zaunbrecher's bridge would greatly facilitate "travel from Prairie Hayes via Roberts Cove to Rayne." Needless to say, all the farmers of the region were benefited by this service.[5]

The improvement of local roads remained a general concern of Roberts Cove farmers. At various times in the 1890s, Germans served as road supervisors and as road committeemen. Among the Germans who participated actively in such functions were Lorenz Zaunbrecher, Hubert Wirtz, Henry Zaunbrecher, William Zaunbrecher, Theodore Heinen, and Joseph Leonards. Their service was occasionally recognized in the press. The Crowley *Daily Signal* reported that Franz Reiners gave repeated assistance to travelers crossing Cole's Gulley on the public road near his home, and quite often, he could be seen spading and performing other maintenance chores on his road to make it passable during bad weather. The paper concluded by saying "old men [he was only fifty-one] sometimes have a more public spirit than younger ones."[6]

Improving the local roads naturally helped to make the cultivation of rice more profitable, particularly since the area's farmers had no choice but to transport their rice great distances, due to lack of storage and no milling facilities. The fact that all local rice had to be shipped to New Orleans quite often

Chapter Two

meant that there was little profit left. This problem of distant market places was greatly alleviated when Rayne opened its own rice mill in 1887. Although the Germans did not appear to have actively involved themselves in this project, they did become some of the mill's first customers, and, only a few years after the mill was built, they became officers and stockholders of this and other rice processing plants.

They probably did not become involved in the original venture of 1887 simply because they lacked sufficient capital or chose rather to put their money into purchasing lands and generally expanding their farm businesses.[7] Indeed, Professor Stanley Joseph McCord has shown that land acquisitions were very common at an early date and that most of the German farmers were well off by the turn of the century. Below, I will summarize his findings. McCord's conclusions were based on the land conveyance records and the homesteading records found in the St. Landry Parish and Acadia Parish courthouses.

These records reveal that only six of the original colonists purchased land on their arrival, and one had homesteaded. Between 1882 and 1886, nine other Roberts Cove inhabitants acquired property by homesteading government lands: Lambert Schlicher obtained 162 acres in late 1882, and his brother Johann P. Schlicher acquired the same amount of acreage the following year also in the area west of Roberts Cove. August Leonards filed a homestead claim for 114 acres in Roberts Cove in December 1883. In 1884, Joseph Gossen, Joseph Leonards, Jacob Thevis, Peter Thevis, Hubert Wirtz, and Nicholas Zaunbrecher filed claims, presumably for quarter sections. Only one of the claims was in the Cove, the rest being to the west and north of the settlement.[8]

Due to growing prosperity, a number of Germans began to purchase land in 1886. Some of these purchased were quite sizeable. In February 1886, for example, Peter J. Thevis bought from his nephew Gerhard 196 acres of land, bringing his share of the original joint purchase to 330 acres and leaving the nephew only 56 acres. Two years later, Peter J. Thevis bought 653 additional acres five miles northwest of Roberts Cove, making him the owner of almost one thousand acres. In 1886 Joseph Leonards and Nicholas Zaunbrecher added to their holdings by each purchasing 80 acres to the north of Crowley. Hubert Theunissen became a landowner for the first time when he bought 50 acres that same year in the Cove.

Additional purchases were not far off. In 1887 Joseph Heinen acquired 140 acres in Roberts Cove and added another 100 acres the next year. In 1888 William Zaunbrecher became the first second-generation German to purchase land when he bought 42 acres to the west of the settlement. Also in that year, John Ohlenforst, a new member of the community who had just arrived with

The Establishment of Economic and Religious Security, 1882-1900

his family from Milwaukee, purchased 201 acres. Joseph Spaetgens and Lambert Schlicher bought 40 acres of land in 1889 for $400 and $365, respectively. The prices they paid indicate a remarkable increase in the value of the land. Only a year or two before land had sold for less than $5.00 an acre but was now bringing twice that amount. The rice boom had been largely responsible for this inflationary spiral.[9]

The rice boom probably reached its peak in 1890 and 1891. One indication that this was so was the fact that Joseph Heinen was able to buy 264 acres of land in the Cove for $2,200 cash. This purchase showed how prosperous some of the German farmers had become. Another sign of the boom was the extraordinary number of land transactions in 1891. This year was probably the best of all for the inhabitants of Roberts Cove. In all, ten land transactions were recorded. Thereafter purchases declined as the rice boom faded. The years 1893 and 1894 were particularly bad for rice farmers,[10] and the Germans showed that they were affected by this trend by making few land purchases in those two years. Thereafter, purchases increased and continued to climb until the end of the century, and despite the temporary reverses, the general trend was for ever greater prosperity.[11]

The most prosperous of the families were the Zaunbrecher, Heinen, Thevis, and the Gossen. Their success can partly be accounted for by the fact that these families arrived with relatively large amounts of capital. Nicholas Zaunbrecher, for example, came to this country with $4,000. Although much of it was expended in the first two years when both cotton and corn were cultivated, he, nevertheless, was able both to purchase some land with the balance and to invest it in improvements, such as his artificial lake. After 1885, Nicholas Zaunbrecher consistently made profits from his farm enterprises, and by the turn of the century was the owner of 1,500 acres of land. His eldest son, William, was also successful, accumulating roughly 800 acres of land.[12]

Joseph Heinen was also a man of some means upon his arrival in the United States, having $2,000 in cash. He built that nestegg into a large fortune by the turn of the century, amassing 1,900 acres for himself and an additional 260 acres for his son.

Meanwhile, the Thevises—Peter Joseph and Gerhard—purchased almost 400 acres of land for about $1,000. Within fifteen years, Peter Joseph Thevis owned more than 1,000 acres, while his brother Jacob and his nephew Gerhard each owned about 500 acres.

The Gossen family was also industrious. Peter Gossen had come to this country with about $1,500, but shortly after his arrival, he had spent about $500 of that for 100 acres. Peter Gossen died in 1882 and left his capital and

Chapter Two

farm to his three sons. Two of these three acquired another 160 acres before the end of the century.[13]

Perhaps more noteworthy were the accomplishments of those immigrants who came with little or no capital. Christian Hensgens, for example, arrived with only $300, one-third of which he later used for a down payment on a farm and the remainder was kept in reserve to support his wife and family. Yet, by 1896, he and his partner, Xavier Dischler, were able to buy an additional 322 acres. Dischler, an Alsatian, came to the Roberts Cove area in 1886 as a sharecropper, as did Joseph Leonards. Leonards established a homestead in 1884, but worked as a hired hand for five years. By 1899 he had added an additional 210 acres to his holdings. Finally, Leo Habetz came to Roberts Cove in 1892 with the reputed sum of seventy-five cents. Yet, by 1895, he had bought an 80-acre farm and had added 80 acres by 1900. The entire community shared in their success, for virtually every family that settled in the Cove flourished to one degree or another.[14]

The prosperity of these German farmers attracted the attention of Louisiana's German-immigration proponents. The German press of New Orleans was particularly interested in the activities and the status of the state's German colonists. One German tabloid which devoted much space to the progress of Germans in Louisiana was *Der Südliche Pionnier* (The Southern Pioneer). The following brief report on the Roberts Cove colony was found in the May 31, 1893, issue:

> Today the colony consists of roughly 30 families with over 150 souls. The heads of these families, in addition to those already mentioned (Peter Joseph, Gerhard, Aloysius and Jacob Thevis) consist of: Heinrich Achten, Johann Gielen, Heinrich and Joseph Gossen, Leo Habets [sic], Franz Reiners, Theo Scheuffens, Heinrich J. Spaetgens, H.J. Theunissen, Hubert Wertz [sic], Lambert Schlicher, Lorenz Zaunbrecher, among others, whose post office is in Rayne. With few exceptions, most of the colonists settled on government land, and all of them are today well off. Their prosperity can be seen in the good condition of their farms, in their magnificent cattle, and also by the fact that some still store rice from last year's harvest and by their total independence from bankers, salesmen, and speculators. The colony possess a good school, as well as a church and rectory.[15]

The report obviously intended to paint the settlement in the best colors possible. It exaggerated the number who homesteaded on government land

The Establishment of Economic and Religious Security, 1882-1900

to give the impression that free government land was abundantly available to prospective immigrants, and it also stated that the region's climate was unusually salubrious. As evidence of its healthy climate, the article cited the case of Theodore Scheuffens, formerly afflicted with chest ailments, but able to plant by himself twenty-five acres of rice and ten acres of corn since his arrival in Acadia Parish. The colonist personally was convinced that had he remained in Germany he would almost certainly have perished.[16]

The German Society shared the interest of the Crescent City press in the Roberts Cove settlement. The Society had come into existence in 1847 to provide assistance to German immigrants landing at the port of New Orleans. Prior to the Civil War, New Orleans was the chief port of entry for immigrants entering the United States. Many hundreds of thousands of these were Germans, and the German Society provided virtually all of them with temporary shelter, money, or advice. Most of the German immigrants continued their journey up the Mississippi River to the farms and cities of the Mid-West. Those who chose to stay in Louisiana were helped by the Society in finding jobs either in the city or among the German communities scattered around the state.

After the Civil War the New Orleans German Society had to redirect its purposes, for its primary function was no longer providing succor to incoming Germans. Most immigrants, including Germans, were now entering the United States through the northern ports, especially New York, from which rail connections to the American interior were readily available. Because of the declining numbers of Germans passing through Louisiana, the German Society in the 1880s redirected its efforts to recruitment of German immigrants. An important incentive for prospective colonists was the existence of established German communities, and thus the prosperous Roberts Cove settlement captured the attention of immigration societies like the one in New Orleans.[17]

In 1895, J. Hanno Deiler, president of the New Orleans German Society, wrote a pamphlet describing Louisiana's German colonies, including Roberts Cove. The Roberts Cove sketch indicated that the settlement had been founded by Father Leonhard Thevis in 1880 and that the friends and relatives who responded to his call to establish the colony had fortunately been able to settle on free government land. This information was misleading since most of the Germans had bought their lands. Deiler, however, was perhaps unaware of that fact, though he probably would not have mentioned it even if he had known. He continued his depiction of the colony by emphasizing its material prosperity, its cultural cohesiveness, and its religious harmony. Indeed, he referred to the settlement as the "baptized colony of St. Leo" consisting exclusively of 160 "German souls" who "possess their own beautiful church and German school."[18]

Despite the distribution of such glowing accounts of German colonization, immigration groups such as *Der Südliche Pionieer* and the New Orleans German Society attracted few Germans to the state. Roberts Cove, the most successful German colony in the state, did gain some additional German colonists, but those who joined the settlement after the 1880s did so primarily because they had friends or relatives in the community. For example, Joseph Schaffhausen and Leo Habetz joined the colony in 1892, and August Habetz, the latter's brother, came in 1896. These three Germans were from the Geilenkirchen region of Germany and had known some members of the Roberts Cove settlement before their emigration. John Berken and his family arrived in 1894. He and his wife and their four children came on the advice of his brother-in-law, John Cramer. The latter was a German who had lived in Lafayette with his family and who moved to the Roberts Cove settlement in 1902. Other Germans, such as the Bunt, Meyer, and Huesers families, joined the Roberts Cove community around this time. They too had settled first in Lafayette and were drawn subsequently to the German colony to the west. Still others were Germans from the Midwest and settlers of the Fabacher colony who were attracted to the Cove by its more vibrant German culture. Among the 33 families, both midwesterners and Fabacher colonists were the Ohlenforsts, Freys, Knippings, Jansens, Bollichs, Dischlers, Kleins, Schneiders, Olingers, Schatzles, Neus, Stamms and Kopmiers.[19]

As the continuing influx of Germans suggests, the Roberts Cove colony by 1900 was a highly successful German settlement. But economic prosperity was merely one facet of the community's attractiveness to immigrants recoiling from culture shock. Roberts Cove was socially, economically, and culturally a self-contained unit. These settlers had reestablished their own cultural institutions and thereby preserved their ethnic identity. The two institutions which were most important for the settlement's cultural survival were the German church and school, both of which had been established within five years of the colony's founding.[20] Both church and school were served in the beginning by Benedictine monks (the school was later administered by Benedictine sisters). The significance of these two institutions for Roberts Cove was so great that a detailed discussion of their origin and development is in order.

One of the reasons that the Roberts Cove Germans emigrated from Germany was to find religious liberty. Devoutly religious, the German immigrants traveled first to Poupeville, and then to Rayne, to participate in religious ser-

The Establishment of Economic and Religious Security, 1882-1900

vices before they established their own church.[21] The Poupeville and Rayne churches, however, were distant—three and six miles, respectively—from Roberts Cove, and their services were not conducted in German. A Jesuit priest would occasionally come from Grand Coteau to say Mass, but this arrangement was also unsatisfactory.[22] What the colonists clearly needed was their own church.

Due to a number of factors largely beyond their control, the German immigrants got their wish by 1885. The settlers' desire to establish their own church was connected with the *Kulturkampf* in Germany, which placed Germany's Catholics on the defensive. The Jesuits, for example, had actually been expelled from the country in 1872. Other orders, such as the Benedictines, had been threatened with the same fate and had begun to make plans to leave the country. The Benedictine monastery of St. Boniface in Munich sent one of its monks to the United States to prepare for that eventuality. This monk, Father Aegidius Hennemann, went to the St. Meinard Abbey in Indiana, in an unsuccessful attempt to find land on which to relocate the home monastery. Two years later, in 1878, Father Hennemann traveled to Arkansas and remained there for five years serving as vicar general to the bishop of Arkansas. Having found no appropriate site in Arkansas, he carried his quest to New Orleans when he transferred to the Crescent City in 1883.[23]

Once in Louisiana, Hennemann's inquiries led him to Roberts Cove. Father Thevis received Father Hennemann in New Orleans and immediately informed him of the existence of the German community in Acadia Parish and the possibility that a suitable location for the St. Boniface monastery might be found there. Father Hennemann became convinced that he had at long last found what he was looking for. He traveled to Roberts Cove, met with W.W. Duson, and purchased 640 acres of land from Paul Manouvrier, the realtor's father-in-law, for $2,500. On this section of land were located several buildings which could be converted to schoolhouse, church, and rectory. Indeed, Father Hennemann agreed that the buildings would be placed at the service of the Roberts Cove community for those very purposes. He and an accompanying monk, Brother Johann Kögl, would serve as the settlement's first pastor and school teacher. In the meantime, plans would be formulated for the transfer of the St. Boniface monastery from Germany to the new site, and for the possible establishment of a seminary.[24]

Father Hennemann's ambitious plans for the relocation of the St. Boniface monastery for the establishment of a church and school for the local German inhabitants, and for the creation of a seminary to train priests were not realized. Upon returning to New Orleans for some business, he discovered that

Chapter Two

the Monastery of St. Boniface no longer wished to relocate, a German court having intervened on behalf of the Benedictines. This information came as a crushing blow to the monk who had spent seven years trying to find the monastery a new home. Already weak from the tuberculosis that he had contracted earlier in Arkansas, Father Hennemann died in December 1883, in New Orleans.[25]

Father Hennemann's will stipulated that the purchased property at Roberts Cove go to his friend Father Thevis. The latter agreed to assume the property and its debt with the hope that something could still be done with the land that would benefit his friends and relatives in the Cove. He contacted the Abbey of St. Meinard in Indiana, the institution which had earlier hosted Father Hennemann. Perhaps its leader, Abbot Fintan, could be persuaded to take on the responsibility of developing the property in the Cove.[26]

Abbot Fintan agreed to come to Louisiana and study the possibilities. In November 1884, he inspected the property with Father Thevis. He was impressed enough with it to decide that his institution would purchase it, if for no other reason than to relieve Father Thevis of the debts he had assumed as owner. But Abbot Fintan refused to consider establishing a sister institution on the property, as Father Thevis had hoped. At any rate, in December 1884, the Abbey of St. Meinard Indiana became the new owner of 640 acres in the Cove at a cost of $3,042.[27]

Because a decision regarding the ultimate disposition of the land was postponed, Abbot Fintan placed the property temporarily at the disposal of the German colonists, to serve their spiritual needs, as Father Hennemann had intended all along. Abbot Fintan accordingly agreed that the land and its buildings could serve as the foundation for a new parish. He even provided the clerics that would be needed for the newly established parish. In March 1885, Abbot Fintan returned from Indiana with two colleagues who would serve as the spiritual leaders of the newly founded religious community, Father Sylvan Buschor and Brother Clement Seichler, both of whom were fluent in German.[28]

One of Father Buschor's duties as the new pastor was the naming of the church, which was officially incorporated on March 27, 1885. He decided to call the parish St. Leo's, in honor of both St. Leo the Great (440-461) and the contemporary pope, Leo XIII (1878-1903), an opponent of Bismarck's anti-Catholic *Kulturkampf.* It was one final way in which Roberts Cove's German Catholics could strike back at the German chancellor.[29]

Unfortunately, the new name created an immediate problem for the German colonists. The feast day for St. Leo the Great occurs in April, a time which

The Establishment of Economic and Religious Security, 1882-1900

conflicted with the farming activities of the parishioners. The month of April was traditionally one of the busiest in the farmers' schedule, for it fell right in the middle of the rice planting season. They consequently would not be able to dedicate any of their time to honor their patron saint. Father Buschor found a solution. Still determined to honor the contemporary pope, Leo XIII, he examined carefully the Church's Calendar of Saints and discovered another St. Leo, Leo IV (847-855), whose feast day was July 17. Mid-summer was a much more relaxed time of the year when the rice fields, now well established, did not need much attention.[30]

Hand-in-hand with the founding of a new church came the establishment of a new church-school. The children of the settlement had been educated in a haphazard manner since 1881. A temporary school had been set up on forty acres of land donated to the colony by Anton Frey of New Orleans, and, presumably, the settlers themselves had served as teachers. In 1883 Father Hennemann temporarily established a German school on the property he purchased from Paul Manouvrier. One of the buildings on that property served as the schoolhouse, and the teacher for a short while was Brother Johann Kögl, Hennemann's colleague from the St. Meinard Abbey in Indiana. Instruction in the school was discontinued in April 1883, shortly after it began, for unknown reasons. Between 1883 and 1885, the colonists apparently again assumed the responsibility of educating their children, perhaps conducting classes in the original structure on the forty-acre site.[31]

The community's educational problems were resolved with the arrival of Father Buschor and Brother Seichler in 1885. They agreed to serve as the community's teachers, but they needed a schoolhouse. No structure existed near the church building where Mass was held and where the living quarters of the two clerics were also located. To solve this problem, the colonists decided to move the building which had served as the school during Father Hennemann's short ministry. The idea to move an old building rather than build a new one, something which could be done much more cheaply and quickly, came from a previous experience. The German immigrants had helped move St. Joseph Church from Poupeville to Rayne back in 1882[32] and three years later were confident of being able to accomplish a similar feat in Roberts Cove. The task of moving the school was completed without incident on July 20, 1885, and, to celebrate this achievement, Father Buschor sponsored a picnic (to which he contributed a barrel of beer). Instruction in the school began that fall (with time being taken for harvest), and early the following year the church services were also held in the schoolhouse, which was pressed into service as a chapel because the old church-rectory could no longer accommodate the burgeoning congregation.[33]

Because of the parish's growth two additional clerics were assigned to the St. Leo parish in 1888. Father Buschor had begun to serve some of the outlying communities and needed assistance. Coming to Roberts Cove in 1888 essentially to administer the church in that community were Father Felix Rumpf and his aide Brother Francis Bessler.[34] Father Rumpf carried to Roberts Cove the news that the Benedictines of St. Meinard were again contemplating the establishment of a sister monastic institution and/or a seminary on their property in Acadia Parish. In 1889, Abbot Fintan once more visited the Roberts Cove colony to examine the possibilities. He was impressed and recommended to the archbishop of New Orleans that a seminary be established at the Cove. The archbishop, however, felt that Roberts Cove was not close enough to New Orleans and thus suggested another location proposed by Father John Bogaerts, a 2,000-acre wooded tract near Gessen, Louisiana. Abbot Fintan concurred, and without seeing the property, bought it for $8,000. Gessen consequently became the new home of St. Joseph's Benedictine Seminary instead of Roberts Cove. But Gessen was much too swampy an area for the seminary to flourish, and, in 1901, it was moved to Covington, Louisiana, where the seminary is still located today.[35]

Following establishment of the seminary at Gessen in 1889, St. Leo parish became a mission under the jurisdiction of St. Joseph's instead of St. Meinard's. The colonists expected the transfer to bring some semblance of order to their religious affairs, but for the next several years, the Benedictine Order debated the establishment of a monastery at Roberts Cove and thus was unable to determine St. Leo's ultimate purpose. Adding to the disorder was the frequent rotation of religious personnel at St. Leo's. The resulting confusion is recounted below: Father Luke Gruwe, the prior of St. Joseph's initiated an effort to bring a more substantial religious establishment to St. Leo's, by asking his superior, Abbot Fintan, to resume efforts to bring to St. Leo's either a monastery, or perhaps even a rest home for retired college teachers. All of Father Gruwe's efforts failed. While St. Leo's future religious role was being debated by church authorities, the church itself was facing it own problems of religious continuity. Father Buschor again temporarily ministered to the religious needs of the Germans. In 1891 Father Buschor retired and was replaced by Father Ziegenfuss. The following year Father Ziegenfuss went to St. Joseph's and Father Rumpf returned.[36]

Understandably, these transfers aroused concern among St. Leo's parishioners, who now wondered whether the Benedictines were serious in their

The Establishment of Economic and Religious Security, 1882-1900

efforts to administer the church. Twice, the colonists thought that St. Leo's would become the home of a monastery and twice they were left bewildered and disappointed. In seven years they had been served by four priests, and the frequent reshufflings left confusion in their wake.

Disheartened, the Germans pleaded with Father Luke Gruwe to bring to their church greater stability and direction. Father Luke consequently appeared at the community in 1892 to personally take charge and offer encouragement. He called a meeting of the male parishioners and promised more constancy in his order's support of the parish. The Benedictines of St. Joseph's, he argued, would be more inclined to lend consistent help if the parishioners, on their part, would agree to improve the parish's physical facilities. What was most needed, according to the prior, was a more spacious church. If St. Leo's parish would build a new church, he would see to it that German Benedictines would serve as its ministers, thereby preserving the Germanic identity of Roberts Cove for at least a couple of generations. This promise would be honored as long as the community would retain its social and cultural cohesiveness.

The meeting between the men of Roberts Cove and the prior of St. Joseph's monastery was one of the most significant events in the community's history, for it assured that the community would remain Germanic well into the twentieth century. In exchange for the church's guarantee of cultural preservation, the men of the colony agreed on the spot to build a new church by pledging five percent of the profits from their rice crops toward construction of a new house of worship. It was estimated that this would raise about $1,500, a sizeable amount which would be sufficient not only to build the church but also to purchase the necessary furnishings. Furthermore, the men promised to help with the labor and to provide the lumber for the structure. Finally, since only half the men of the colony attended the meeting with Father Gruwe—some of the others were kept away by high water—the actual sum that might be raised toward the construction of the church could grow significantly if those who were absent would join in this venture.[37]

The actual construction of the church began the following year and took place under the supervision of Father Rumpf who had returned as St. Leo's pastor in January 1892. The committee which oversaw the planning and building of the church consisted of the pastor and the following men from the community: Joseph Heinen, Christian J. Hensgens, Peter Joseph Thevis, and Nicholas Zaunbrecher, who signed a contract with the builder on November 8, 1893. The latter agreed to build the church in three months for $550. The frame structure was to rest on a brick foundation, be sixty feet long, thirty feet wide, and twenty-two feet high. The tower, which would crown this rectangular frame, was to rise to a height of fifty-four feet and eleven inches, be ten feet square, and be topped by an octagonal roof and a six-foot cross. The church was finished sometime in early 1894. On January 25, 1895, Lawrence Zaunbrecher and Gertrude Hensgens had the honor of being the first couple to be married in the church, and by an ironical twist of fate, they were the last couple to be buried from this church before it was replaced by a new house of worship in 1954.[38]

Construction of a new church brought more than just a new physical presence to the Roberts Cove community. The church became a symbol of unity. Cooperation among the colonists had brought it into being, and the church continues to foster among its members a spirit of familial unity. The church also became the vehicle through which the German settlers preserved their society and culture. It became the central meeting place for the scattered farmhouses that existed in and around the Cove. Even as the offspring of the colony's founders were forced to stray farther and farther from Roberts Cove in search of land, or in search of employment, they felt bound to the community by the church. Sunday Mass at Roberts Cove became not only an important religious event; it became the occasion for regular family gatherings and reunions. It was here that the strong ties of kinship and culture could be maintained and periodically renewed. Without the physical presence of the church, the social and ethnic cohesiveness of the Roberts Cove community could not have been retained.

The school was a perfect complement to the church for the retention of language and culture. It kept the German language, and to a degree knowledge of German history and literature, alive through the second and third generations. Until 1897, the school was administered by the pastor and his assistants. Instruction was in High German despite the settlers' usage of a Low German dialect. The pupils' education was also hampered by the priests' occasional preoccupation with other matters or lack of familiarity with the subject matter. These problems were resolved by Father Placidus Zarn who served as pastor of Roberts Cove from 1897 to 1907. Through his efforts, Benedictine sisters were brought from Indiana and employed as teachers at the school. And, to induce them to remain at Roberts Cove, he arranged for construction of a new convent and schoolhouse.[39]

By the end of the nineteenth century, the Roberts Cove community was in a position to be well satisfied with itself. All of the German colonists had acquired land and were prospering to some extent. They had established both a school and church to be staffed by German-speaking Benedictine monks and nuns. These institutions guaranteed that the religion and language of their

The Establishment of Economic and Religious Security, 1882-1900

forefathers would be passed on to their children and grandchildren. In every respect, the Roberts Cove settlement appeared to be a vibrant and flourishing ethnic community whose future seemed assured.

For another fifteen years this relatively happy state of affairs continued. But the coming of World War I altered forever the equation by which the colony had constructed its material and spiritual foundations.

Chapter III

The Golden Age of Roberts Cove, 1900-1917

The years between the turn of the century and America's entry into World War I saw the Roberts Cove community enjoy to the fullest measure its material prosperity and its identification as a Germanic entity. In these years the colonists expanded their farming operations, became active in politics, and generally participated more fully in the American way of life. Yet, at the same time, their loyalty to their nationality, their community, their church remained as strong as ever. The special virtues of the American Constitution and the political system it created allowed the settlers of Roberts Cove, as it permitted Germans in every region of the nation, to live freely as Germans in America. They functioned as German-Americans in the fullest sense of that term. They enjoyed the benefits of this great country without having to sacrifice their cultural essence. Yet, even in these "golden years," a creeping, almost imperceptible process of Americanization of the colonists and their community was taking place. Even without the pressures of Americanization brought by the war, the Roberts Cove community would eventually have lost its exclusive identification as a Germanic colony.

The first steps toward accommodation to the American way of life began years before. The immigrants were fully cognizant of the dynamics of American politics, and the necessity of functioning within the system thus became obvious very early. The most effective method of operating within the new nation was to become a citizen of that nation. Consequently, many of the Germans had decided to become naturalized shortly after their arrival in the country. Herman Grein and August Leonards applied for citizenship in 1881. The following year Hubert Wirtz and Lambert Schlicher followed suit; and in 1883 Joseph Achten, Christian Hensgens, Peter J. Leonards, Johann P. Schlicher, and Nicholas J. Zaunbrecher did likewise. Among the largest group to file for citizenship, in 1884, were Johann Gielen, Joseph Gossen, Arnold Jacobs, Joseph Heinen, William Heinen, Joseph Spaetgens, Franz Reiners, and Hubert Theunissen. In 1885 William J. Zaunbrecher became a citizen, and in 1886 Matthew Achten and Theodore Scheuffens added their names to the citizenship rolls. Within five years of their establishment, twenty inhabitants had completed the naturalization process.[1]

Chapter Three

All of the new citizens were eager to vote; or, should we say, the area's politicians were eager for them to vote, as is evident from the correlation between elections and naturalization ceremonies. It seems that a large number of the colonists became "naturalized" and thereby gained the right to vote by simply making a public declaration of allegiance shortly after arriving. This public declaration of loyalty, according to William Gossen who was ten years old when he arrived and who remembered the event, was also made by minors and occurred just before an election. Assuming that he was a citizen by his declaration of loyalty, William later exercised his rights to vote by casting his ballot for Grover Cleveland in 1896 while farming in Texas. But, when he subsequently returned to Louisiana, he discovered that he was not officially a citizen. Judge William Campbell, a candidate for district attorney, hurriedly brought him and several others to the Lafayette Parish Courthouse, where they filed the necessary papers and voted shortly thereafter for the patronizing politician.[2]

The Germans of Roberts Cove readily took not only to voting but also to actually running for office. Several entered local and state politics. Joseph Leonards was elected a member of the parish school board in 1904. That same year, he and Lawrence Zaunbrecher were chosen to the parish Democratic committee.[3] In 1908, several members of the community sponsored a reception for the Democratic gubernatorial candidate in Crowley.[4] Also in 1908, William Heinen and Lawrence Zaunbrecher were elected members of the Democratic executive committee and were included in the eighteen-member delegation sent to the state Democratic convention in support of William Jennings Bryan's presidential candidacy.[5] Four years later, Lawrence Zaunbrecher returned to the state convention.[6] Other members of the community held lesser positions (deputy sheriff, poll commissioner, etc.) throughout these years.[7]

One of the most active and successful politicians from the Roberts Cove community was William Joseph Zaunbrecher. As indicated, he served as delegate to the state Democratic convention in 1908, and in the same year was elected to the Acadia Parish Police Jury. Eight years later he gained a seat in the state house of representatives.[8] Also in 1916, a short biography of William J. Zaunbrecher appeared in *A History of Who's Who in Louisiana Politics*, which indicates, its glaring factual errors notwithstanding, that he had become a relatively well-known state politician. The pamphlet portrayed Zaunbrecher as having arrived in this country as a penniless and helpless immigrant who rose to wealth and fame by his own considerable efforts, but it neglected to mention that William was the son of Nicholas Zaunbrecher, probably the wealthiest of the Roberts Cove immigrants. Such misinformation was almost certainly in-

The Golden Age of Robert's Cove, 1900-1917

tentional, for the publication was designed to convince prospective voters that here was a man of worthy credentials. The depiction of William Zaunbrecher is so interesting that it bears extensive quotation:

> ... Zaunbrecher came to America from Germany, when a boy of 14 years, with hardly any knowledge of the English language, and no one to push along his career in the new and strange country. Yet this plucky boy has surmounted the obstacles, overcame lack of capital by earning and saving for himself, and is known as one of the large landowners of his parish, as well as one of its substantial farmers and business men. From obscurity, a stranger in a strange land, he has now come into the ownership of 1300 acres of the best land in Acadia Parish, and is a director in the State Bank of Rayne, Louisiana, from which place he was elected to a seat in the General Assembly. Surely this is another instance of German pluck, if not preparedness. His preparedness was only such as a friendless boy could provide for himself, but the results accomplished shows pretty conclusively that it was substantial.[9]

As a state representative, William Zaunbrecher understandably interested himself in agricultural matters. Acadia Parish was primarily agricultural in makeup, and he personally was a farmer and cattleman. One of the first issues that captured his time and attention was the tick eradication program. His support of the program earned him the gratitude of his area's farmers, even though a small minority opposed the practice of dipping their cattle in poisonous solutions. His support of this law showed that he was in the forefront of the cattle business and that he was willing to take political risks.[10]

While a member of the house of representatives, William Zaunbrecher also became involved in the anti-prohibition movement. In opposing prohibition, he was only following the instincts of most Germans. Even more then than now, the drinking of beer was a German national pastime. The Germans of Roberts Cove were no exception in their devotion to this brew, and, as is evident to anyone who has ever attended one of their recent family reunions, their beer consumption has in no way diminished.[11] Yet, the availability of these alcoholic beverages, now taken for granted, was interrupted on at least two occasions earlier this century, prompting Germans to mobilize their political clout against prohibition. Thus, while a member of the Acadia Parish Police Jury in 1910, Zaunbrecher sponsored a resolution to repeal an ordinance providing a reward for information leading to the arrest and conviction of anyone selling alcoholic beverages.[12]

Chapter Three

William Zaunbrecher's success as a politician symbolizes how well the Germans had adapted themselves to the American system. They were able to take advantage of the opportunities around them working as German-Americans without losing their identity in the process. Their participation in the political arena was a sign of their cultural maturation. They were secure in their new surroundings and did not want to isolate themselves from the outside world, but they were open to change.

Nowhere was this spirit of openness, this ability to adapt, grow, and diversify, more visible than in the colonists' farming operations. As the rice industry continued to decline in the early years of the twentieth century, the German farmers adjusted by diversifying their agricultural endeavors and by intensifying their efforts to better market their rice.[13]

To come to grips with the rice depression,[14] the Germans of Acadia Parish formed, in May 1910, the Southwest Louisiana Rice Farmers' Union. Meeting in Crowley, they agreed to pool their crops, mill the rice, and sell it directly through their marketing association to German communities in cities such as Chicago, Milwaukee, and St. Louis. On November 5, 1910, the Southwest Louisiana Rice Farmers' Union was formally constituted and immediately went into business.[15]

But the organization did not function quite as successfully as hoped, and many Union members soon joined larger organizations. In March 1912, for example, William Heinen, regional manager of the Southern Rice Growers' Association, presided over a meeting of fellow Germans in which they agreed to market their rice through the Southern Association. During the meeting, some Germans, even such formerly harsh critics of the Southern Association such as Lawrence Zaunbrecher, promised to induce their countrymen to join. Four months later, William Zaunbrecher actually assumed the duties of an Association director. By joining the Association the Roberts Cove Germans demonstrated not only their adaptability, but also their pragmatism and business acumen, for they gained economic power by joining forces with other Louisiana and Texas rice farmers.[16]

The Roberts Cove Germans also demonstrated their adaptability by diversifying into the hardware, ice making, and real estate businesses in Rayne and Crowley. A detailed picture of the business activities of these settlers, and a general view of their material well-being appeared in an agricultural pamphlet published in 1907 by W.W. Duson. This remarkable tract, entitled *Deutsche Landwirte von Südwest Louisiana* (German Farmers of Southwest Louisiana), was written in German and provides the historian with one of the more fasci-

The Golden Age of Robert's Cove, 1900-1917

nating, though somewhat slanted, evaluations of the Germans of Roberts Cove in the early twentieth century.[17]

The pamphlet began by assessing the more prominent of the colonists, particularly in terms of their wealth. Rice farmer Joseph Heinen, depicted as "one of the most substantial and successful farmers of the region,"[18] had amassed more than 2,000 acres of rice land, owned at least 200 head of cattle, and owned large numbers of shares in the Rayne City Bank. In addition, Joseph Heinen's two sons, Wilhelm and Theodore, each possessed large farms, the former owning 1,000 acres, the latter, 170. Together, the Heinens were perhaps the most successful of Acadia Parish's German families.[19]

Not far behind were the Zaunbrechers. Nicholas Zaunbrecher, "one of the most successful German farmers who had made much money in the rice culture,"[20] owned 1,232 acres of farmland valued at almost $50,000. Each of his four sons had flourished as well. William Joseph, though in the prime of his life, had retired and lived entirely off his investments. His leisure had allowed him to go into politics, and when not politically involved, to dabble in his garden. Carl, the pamphlet indicated, had just purchased his first piece of property from the earnings of the previous year's rice crop. The other two sons, according to the tract, also prospered,[21] though the youngest son, August, apparently still worked with his father, since he had not married.[22]

The Gossens were equally prosperous. Joseph Gossen owned over 500 acres of land and possessed stock in the Commercial Bank of Rayne and in the Stamm Hardware Store. Furthermore, Gossen, together with Joseph Leonards, owned and operated the Rayne Ice Factory. Joseph's two brothers, Wilhelm and Heinrich, were not quite as successful, being relatively small landowners possessing 160 and 140 acres respectively.[23]

Joseph Gossen's partner, Joseph Leonards, had come to this country with virtually nothing. He had fled German military conscription and had joined his fellow-immigrants in Holland after slipping into that country under the cover of darkness. He brought with him only that which he could carry. Yet, by 1907, he had apparently acquired over 800 acres of land. In addition, he owned fifty percent interest in the Rayne Ice Factory, was a large stockholder in the Commercial Bank of Rayne, and possessed small tracts of real estate in Rayne and Crowley.[24]

Although the economic well-being of many other farmers of the Cove area were discussed in slightly lesser detail than the individuals mentioned above, the overall message conveyed by the Duson publication was pervasive German prosperity. Indeed, the pamphlet concluded its description of the Germans with the somewhat amusing statement that "Germans who have amounted to nothing are so rare that one would have to search for them with a lantern in the light of day."[25] Although this comment might be construed as being exaggerated, it nevertheless affords a factual representation of the Cove's inhabitants.

Publication of Duson's pamphlet in 1907 suggests that it was timed to coincide with the promotional efforts of the New Orleans German Society and the Louisiana Bureau of Agriculture and Immigration. In the early twentieth century, these two organizations combined forces to make yet another effort to attract German colonists to Louisiana. The Bureau of Agriculture and Immigration was headed by Charles Schuler, who personally wrote a number of German-language tracts lauding the virtues of farmlife for dissemination throughout Germany.[26] The New Orleans German Society participated in this promotional venture by issuing literature written by Reverend Louis Voss, who described, as advantageously as possible, the state of Louisiana and its German communities. Voss' 1907 work, entitled *Louisianas Einlaudung an Deutsche Landwirte und Kolonisten* (Louisiana's invitation to German farmers and colonists), was almost an exact transcription of Deiler's previous publication (*Louisiana, A Home for German Settlers*). Once again, the community of St. Leo was referred to as a "baptized, blossoming, exclusively German colony of approximately 160 souls."[27] But, once more, despite wide distribution in this country and abroad, Voss' pamphlet failed to ignite the interests of Germans in colonizing Louisiana.

Indeed, the entire promotion effort—that involving Duson, the agricultural and immigration agency, and the New Orleans German Society—was an exercise in futility. Germans, wherever they might be, were no longer interested in immigrating to this country, at least not in significant numbers. The German migrations of the nineteenth century could probably never be duplicated. According to the records of the New Orleans German Society itself, only a handful of Germans from South America, South Africa, and Germany immigrated to Louisiana due to Voss' advertisement,[28] and none settled at the Cove. Duson's pamphlet, which was given some exposure in the midwestern states, was equally unsuccessful, attracting only one German visitor to the Roberts Cove community. This individual, John Kretzer (or Kreiter), was impressed with the prosperity of the German settlement and indicated a desire to settle there. His name, however, did not become known in the colony, suggesting that he did not actually move to Roberts Cove.[29] The only German family that definitely joined the Cove community at this time was that of John Bischoff, who came not because of official promotions but because of the

The Golden Age of Robert's Cove, 1900-1917

bonds of friendship. He had met William Heinen and Lawrence Zaunbrecher in Germany and had been persuaded by them to settle at the Cove.[30]

The failure to attract German newcomers to the Roberts Cove region, at least in any significant numbers, did have certain unsettling implications for the future. The colony's ethnic identity would ultimately be jeopardized without the influx of new "German" blood. Without new settlers from the homeland, the gradual Americanization of the community would be facilitated, though the inevitable process of acculturation probably did not bother the Germans too much in these early years. Their cultural autonomy seemed secure as long as the Benedictines presided over their spiritual and educational concerns. After all, this clerical order had promised to remain in charge of the community's church and school for two generations, if the colonists on their part worked hard to remain true to their Germanic heritage.

Despite the understanding between the colonists and the Benedictines to cooperate at preserving the Germanic identity of the Roberts Cove community, "cracks" in this understanding began to appear even in these "golden years." Although the settlement's Germanic identity was not seriously threatened, the colony's ability to resist "Americanization" was weakened by a series of developments that took place between 1900 and 1917. Together, these developments constituted the first challenges to the community's ethnicity and pointed to the serious erosions of the settlement's ethnic autonomy that would subsequently occur.

The first development that redounded to the detriment of the community was the replacement of Father Placidus Zarn, who had been recalled to St. Joseph's Abbey, with Father Leo Schwab in 1907. Zarn's departure was viewed with displeasure by the Benedictine sisters who, it will be recalled, had come to the Cove ten years earlier at his request. The close ties that existed between Father Zarn and the sisters occasioned the precipitous decision on the part of the nuns to also leave the Cove. The official reason given for their departure was lack of personnel, but as one of the community's residents later revealed, it was the change in administration and the apparent loyalty of the sisters to Father Zarn that caused the Benedictine nuns to move from the Cove.[31]

The departure of the Benedictine sisters did not mean an end to the German school. The school was retained and henceforth directed by private instructors. Yet, their departure probably did mean that the quality of instruction in German diminished, and the caliber of education overall declined. The entire process of teaching the children of Roberts Cove became less systematic and less organized, undoubtedly accelerating the tendency of many Cove inhabitants to send their children to local parochial schools. Some had already

Chapter Three

been doing this because their farms were too distant from the Cove to begin with. The population had been spreading out for some time so that many colonists found it more convenient to send their children to the schools in Crowley or Rayne. Furthermore, many of the settlement's children attended the public schools to complete their education after finishing the seven or eight grades afforded by the colony school. Finally, a few of the children, particularly those destined for the priesthood, were enrolling in seminaries[32] and colleges. All of these ties with the outside world naturally brought gradual "Americanization" and change.

Another development that was far less significant, but symptomatic of the decreasing role that the Benedictine Order was prepared to play in the Cove, was the sale of most of the original section of land purchased by Father Aegidius Hennemann. No longer was there any chance whatsoever of establishing a monastic institution, seminary, or rest home among the Germans at Roberts Cove. Lacking interest in the site, the Benedictines had rented most of the land since 1896, and in 1902, they sold to Joseph Heinen 600 acres of the original 640 for $20 an acre. The remaining 40 acres retained by the Benedictines is the present location of St. Leo's Church and cemetery. Although Heinen paid $4,000 down and promised to pay the remainder in two equal notes over the next two years, he did not receive immediate use of the land because of a property dispute with Jacob Thevis. The following year the dispute was resolved through a court-appointed surveyor. Heinen, who completed paying for the land in 1906, kept about 250 acres for his own use and divided the remainder between his two sons, Theodore receiving roughly 60 acres, Wilhelm the remaining 290 acres. Interestingly enough, the elder Heinen, in concluding the original transaction with the Benedictines, demanded that the purchase-sale agreement be written in German so that he might more easily read it. Consequently, two copies of the contract were written, one for Joseph Heinen in his native tongue, and the other in English as the official copy.[33]

Joseph Heinen's insistence on having his act of sale written in German may have reflected the fear of the older generation that they were losing contact with the language of their homeland. This fear was a sure sign that gradual "Americanization" was setting in. Others in the German community went to even greater pains to retain contact with the language and customs of their German homeland by traveling to the fatherland itself. In August 1901, for example, Christian and Regina Hensgens and Joseph Heinen and several members of his family visited Germany for part of the summer.[34] Joseph Heinen went again in 1914, as did Joseph Gossen, his wife, and daughter.[35] Joseph Heinen, because of illness, remained in Germany and died there in 1916.[36] It

The Golden Age of Robert's Cove, 1900-1917

is interesting to note that Joseph Heinen's daughter Anna, the only one of his children born in this country, refused to visit the homeland of her father because, as the Crowley *Daily Signal* reported, she "considered herself an American and did not want to visit Germany."[37] Her attitude, however, was atypical, and only one member of the Roberts Cove community completely broke his ties with the German colony prior to World War I. Johann Schlicher, who had taken a Protestant wife and moved to Crowley, seemed determined to disassociate himself from the German settlement. The lingering ties to the fatherland are also evidenced in the lack of enthusiasm in the colony for America's war effort against the Central Powers. Johann's son William was the only individual from the Roberts Cove community to serve overseas in the armed forces during World War I.[38]

Another manifestation of the weakening of German culture in the Roberts Cove community was the growing use of English in the Sunday sermons in 1899, when at least one sermon per month was delivered in English. This may suggest that at least a few of the Cove's inhabitants were more comfortable in that language than in German, although it is possible that one English sermon a month may have been introduced as a teaching device to instruct students and parents in the use of English.[39] In 1900 another concession to the mainly English-speaking residents of Roberts Cove was made when half of the proceedings during a school picnic were conducted in English. It is possible that English was used during that event to cater to the non-German speaking guests invited to participate. But, the greater likelihood is that it was done for the primarily English-speaking residents themselves.[40]

The first intrusions into their cultural heritage perhaps caused the Germans of Roberts Cove to form an organization to preserve their "threatened" heritage—the *Deutsche Gesellschaft,* or German Society, founded in 1909. The German Society of New Orleans may have encouraged the Roberts Cove Germans to form this society, which grew out of a meeting held in Crowley on November 27. The German-Americans who assembled there pledged their support for an organization which would foster the "immigration of Germans," that would "keep alive an interest in the German language and literature," and "encourage social contact among German-Americans."[41]

The establishment of this organization was brought one step closer when the individuals who had earlier gathered in Crowley placed the following advertisement, in German, in the local newspaper.

> Crowley, December 28, 1909. German Society, Acadia Parish, Louisiana. In order to give all Germans an opportunity to partici-

Chapter Three

pate in the next session of the German Society, we have decided to gather on Sunday on the 2nd of January at 1:30 p.m. in the Hall of the Knights of Columbus for the purpose of choosing officials and directors and to determine the days for future gatherings.

It is therefore absolutely necessary that every single individual appear in order to express his views and defend them accordingly.[42]

The announcement indicated that membership was open to all individuals who were able to speak the German language. All others who were in sympathy with the Society's goals could become honorary members.

Forty-eight individuals responded to the call for the *Gesellschaft's* organizational meeting. Several of the Cove's inhabitants were elected as officers or directors, including Joseph Leonards, vice-president, and William Gossen and Leo Habetz, directors. It was unanimously agreed that one of the Society's most important objectives was the introduction of the German language in public schools. This was seen as the most effective way of "keeping alive" the German language and its literature. There was also general agreement, though no specific dates were set, to meet regularly in the future for the purpose of fostering social and cultural intercourse among the Society's members.[43]

It is extremely difficult to gauge the success of the German Society in meeting its stated goals. Subsequent social gatherings were held in Crowley and at St. Leo's Church. These events were widely attended not only by the Society's members but also by its friends and supporters. Many of the midwestern German-Americans who had been drawn south by the rice culture attended these socials, as did the increasingly Americanized Fabacher "Germans." The St. Leo Day celebrations, held on the church grounds at the Cove, seem to have been one of the more popular social events sponsored in these years by the local German Society.

Though social and cultural intercourse were undoubtedly fostered by these gatherings, the Society clearly failed to achieve its other stated objectives. German immigration into Acadia Parish was not appreciably increased, nor did the Acadia Parish School Board introduce the German language into its school curriculum. These failures may be owing to the short lifespan of the Society, which was disbanded when this country entered World War I. Possibly more would have been accomplished without the disruption of the war.[44]

The founding of the *Deutsche Gesellschaft* reveals that the Germans of Roberts Cove were still acutely aware of their own ethnic identity. Slight erosions of their heritage and culture might have taken place, and could even have been viewed by some as threats to their separate existence, but the fact

The Golden Age of Robert's Cove, 1900-1917

that the Society was founded at all signified that the German community was strong and vibrant.

Certainly this was the view of many non-Germans who could look more objectively at the German colony. The Crowley *Daily Signal*, for example, went to considerable trouble and expense to purchase the German *Fraktur* type to accommodate the Germans of the region. The newspaper hoped to be able to use its new type to attract a larger German readership, and it obviously thought that there were enough German readers to justify the additional cost. Less than two months after the establishment of the German Society, the newspaper began to print the obituaries of the area's Germans in *Fraktur*. Beginning on February 25, 1910, these obituaries, such as Maria Heinen's, always emphasized the Germanic origin of the deceased. As was usual, the obituaries tended to stress the excellent qualities of those who had passed away—perhaps so because they were viewed as qualities possessed by the Germans as a people. Furthermore, any general reference to the Cove settlers was virtually always a reference to them as hardworking and industrious "Germans."[45]

All such positive allusions ceased after 1917. The outbreak of World War I captured the attention of this country's Germans long before it did the rest of the population. The Cove's German inhabitants were no exception. The terrible bloodshed that even the earliest battles exacted on the German combatants naturally evoked the interest and concern of their countrymen throughout the world. The German Society of Acadia Parish called two special gatherings of its members to respond to the hardships that the war brought to their homeland. Both meetings were advertised in the Crowley newspaper. The pleas for the members of the Society to assemble were printed in German and read as follows:

> ATTENTION! All members of the German Society of Acadia Parish and vicinity are hereby invited to attend a special meeting which will take place on Sunday October 4 at 3:00 p.m. in the fire station of Crowley. The Fatherland is in need and in danger. The bloody conflict reverberates on all sides. In order to lessen the need and the misery of those who were left behind and have fallen on the battlefield, we too want to do our best to offer help. All Germans and Austrian-Americans who want to help in this work are invited to participate intimately in our assembly.[46]

> ATTENTION! All members of the German Society as well as all other Germans, Austrians, and those who are sympathetic are

Chapter Three

hereby invited to attend a meeting in the fire station on November 1 at 3:00 p.m.⁴⁷

The actions taken by the participants of the first meeting were recorded in the Crowley *Daily Signal* later in October. What the participants of the second meeting discussed, or whether the meeting even took place, is not known since no follow-up report was made by the newspaper. The announcement for the first meeting was printed in German only, whereas the second meeting was announced in both German and English in the hopes of attracting a larger audience to the subsequent gathering. The results of the first assembly were, as the local newspaper reported, "a surprise to even the most optimistic of the old members."⁴⁸ Those who had gathered initially in support of their fatherland collected $150 for the German Red Cross. All who were present agreed to work at persuading their friends and neighbors to become more understanding of the German cause and to encourage them to make contributions to that nation's Red Cross.⁴⁹

The efforts of the German Society's members to work on behalf of their mother country was not viewed with any particular alarm by their American friends. At least until this country's entrance into the war, the tone of the reaction of Americans toward the activities of their German compatriots was usually sympathetic. German-Americans were still considered as trusted, industrious citizens. Heinrich Habetz, for example, was described in the Crowley *Daily Signal* as being a member of "that sturdy race whose representatives turned so many U.S. prairies into rich fields and whose coming to Acadia Parish has enriched our country with so many exemplary farms."⁵⁰ This flattering appraisal, it should be noted, appeared in July 1916, two years after the European war had started. It was also the year in which William Zaunbrecher was elected to the state house of representatives.

Some of the actions of the Cove's Germans were even treated with humor. When Conrad Hensgens was asked by a reporter of the Crowley newspaper in January 1915 whether the German military was in need of his service, he replied that his eleven cousins serving in the German army were more than sufficient.⁵¹ Another incident involving a German from the Cove found its way into the local newspaper later that year. On finding that his horse and buggy had been stolen, the local German reportedly reacted to the theft by "praying for his enemies, der Kaiser, his friends, and self."⁵² Both reports suggest that there was still an easy-going relationship between the Germans and their American neighbors in the first two years of the war.

The Golden Age of Robert's Cove, 1900-1917

The mood of the American people started to become less tolerant in mid-1916. However, it was not yet directed against the nation's Germans, but rather toward Pancho Villa and Mexico. July 4 was dubbed "Preparedness Day,"[53] and, later in the year, Louisiana's National Guard was put on a war footing. These actions were a harbinger of the xenophobic attitudes that emerged the following year. Meanwhile, the presidential elections of November 1916 inflamed the patriotic fervor of Americans. Woodrow Wilson was viewed as the war-candidate, whereas his Republican opponent, Charles Evans Hughes, tended to be associated with pacifism and neutralism. The Germans of Roberts Cove recognized the personal implications of their conflicting positions and acted accordingly. Although they normally voted Democratic, they opted for Hughes by a margin of twenty-six to nine. The German vote, however, had little impact upon the outcome of the balloting in strongly Democratic Acadia Parish, which gave Woodrow Wilson 1,137 votes, but only 208 to Charles Evans Hughes. Roberts Cove, in fact, was the only ward in Acadia Parish that went Republican.[54] Wilson went on to win the national election and subsequently led the country to war.

Thus, as 1916 ended and the new year dawned, ominous clouds drifted on the horizon for America's German citizens. The more perceptive of the country's Germans might have been aware of their precarious position. Few could have guessed, however, that with this country's entrance into the war that an entire era was ending. The German people and culture were everywhere placed on the defensive, nowhere more so than in Louisiana.

Chapter IV

World War I and Its Aftermath, 1917-1956

With the United States' entrance into World War I, Americans came to view their German neighbors in a dramatic new way. Whereas before the war Americans considered Germans as industrious and respected members of society, the former now looked upon the latter as untrustworthy, possibly treasonous foreigners in the country's midst. Germans everywhere were consequently placed on the defensive. Their institutions—German schools, churches, newspapers, and other cultural organizations—were forced to disband, and these closures almost inevitably proved to be permanent.

The setbacks experienced by German minorities throughout the land were shared by the Roberts Cove colonists, who first became targets of American anger and suspicion on the eve of World War I.[1]

On March 17, 1917, an ominous editorial appeared in the Crowley *Daily Signal* openly criticizing German-Americans and their German-language press. The Crowley editor also questioned their patriotism because some members of the German community had voiced support of the Central Powers and expressed ambivalent attitudes toward the role that the United States should play in the war and called for stern measures against this potential fifth column.

> ... let us prepare to deal with disloyalty and treason, from whatever source they emanate, so drastically that all of our energies may be devoted to the outside enemy. From this time on, until again peace reign in the world, the citizen or alien in this country, whatever his propaganda or unpreparedness is an enemy, and if there is no law to punish him as such, congress should enact one.[2]

Caught up in the now pervasive local anti-German backlash, the Acadia Parish sheriff, on April 14, reminded the local citizenry that "any act, however slight, tending to give aid or comfort to the enemy is treason."[3] He also repeated the U.S. Justice Department's admonition to resident aliens "to obey the law: keep your mouth shut."[4] The Germans of Roberts Cove, therefore, would have to tread carefully when it came to war-related matters, particularly because the sheriff had suggested that the Justice Department's exhortation should apply not only to enemy aliens but to foreign-born citizens as well. In other words, no distinction would be made between those Germans who had become naturalized and those still classified as aliens.[5]

In the same issue of the newspaper in which the sheriff issued his veiled warnings against the area's Germans, he published a list of instructions on how to catch spies, implying that spies were abundant in Acadia Parish because of the large number of Germans. He also cautioned citizens not to trust any of the area's foreign-born Germans because "prominent persons in the community"—a pointed reference to the wealthy farmers of Roberts Cove—were often spies. The sheriff, however, also cautioned his constituents to remain within the bounds of the U.S. Constitution when apprehending suspected spies. Rumor and innuendo were not legitimate evidence of suspicious or treasonous activity, and no one could take the law into his hands to punish the suspected spies. All traitors, or those suspected of questionable loyalty, were to be reported to law enforcement officials.[6]

The public, however, generally ignored the sheriff's warnings. A totally fictitious, but obviously popular story, printed in the Crowley *Daily Signal* on April 7, 1917, made a mockery of the sheriff's call for restraint:

> Two Germans at Iota the other day who interfered with a recruiting officer and insulted the United States Flag were severely dealt with by an American who is reported to be Jesse Reed of that place. Mr. Reed beat up both Germans, made them salute the flag and had them on their knees begging for mercy. Mr. Reed said he would beat to death the next German traitor whom he heard abusing the president and insulting the flag. His action was highly approved by the citizens of the community.[7]

Though this story proved to be completely groundless, the local press showed no qualms about spreading such fabrications, and the public proved equally willing to accept uncritically such anti-German rumors.

Throughout the war, German actions were viewed with suspicion. Behavior which in the past would have been considered innocent or gone unnoticed now attracted undue attention. In reporting the public drunkenness and arrest of a Roberts Cove German, for example, the local press embellished the narrative with the rumor that the drunkard had uttered pro-German remarks while being taken into custody. But the anti-Americanism accusation proved groundless, and the German was released without charge.[8]

Roberts Cove Germans endured other forms of wartime harassment and were routinely blamed for vandalism. For example, an American farmer residing near the Cove complained that his farm was being repeatedly vandalized,

World War I and Its Aftermath, 1917-1956

and after each complaint, a different German was taken in for questioning. Each time the German suspect was released without charges being filed. The "American's" farm, it was ultimately discovered, was actually vandalized by a disgruntled family member.[9]

This episode was overshadowed by the Stamm Hardware Store incident in Rayne. Johann Stamm, the proprietor, arrived in the Cove with his father Ferdinand in 1895 and was one of the few Germans of the area who early left farming to establish a business of his own. Though a pillar of the community, Johann Stamm was rumored to be abetting the enemy by making guns for the kaiser at night.[10] Nothing during the war proved more ridiculous than this story, which symbolized perfectly the climate of suspicion that existed in those tragic years.

It is perhaps surprising, considering the readiness of the American population to believe the worst of their German neighbors, that only three area Germans were actually arrested and interrogated for making "treasonous" remarks. Viewed from the contemporary perspective, the reasons for their detention seem ludicrous. John Frey was detained briefly for having compared President Woodrow Wilson unfavorably with Emperor William II. He reputedly remarked that he would rather serve in the German, rather than in the American, army, and that William II could probably do a better job running the country than the incumbent American president.[11]

Like Frey, Ferdinand Olinger and Joseph Schaffhausen seem to have been arrested on rather flimsy charges. Olinger was questioned and detained after having expressed doubts about the reasons for this country's entrance in the war. He indicated that he wished to remain neutral and refused, consequently, to contribute to the American Red Cross. Schaffhausen complained somewhat too loudly about compulsory military conscription in this land, an institution which had caused his forebears and other Roberts Cove pioneers to emigrate from Germany to this country. After a short detention, both men were released on bail. Olinger subsequently purchased $1,000 in War Savings Stamps to "correct" the error of his ways.[12]

A small number of the German-Americans from the Cove found it "expedient" to make large donations to the Red Cross or to invest heavily in War Bonds or Stamps, for it was in this manner that they could best demonstrate their loyalty to their adopted nation and thus avoid difficulty with their neighbors and local law enforcement officials. The harassment of the Germans of Roberts Cove declined significantly as the war progressed when it was discovered that the citizens of that community were making sizeable purchases of various kinds of U.S. War Bonds. William Heinen even received public ac-

Chapter Four

claim when it was revealed that he had sold over $20,000 in War Bonds to his neighbors at the Cove.[13] Probably most of the Cove's residents purchased the bonds because they genuinely supported the American cause. A small minority may have made the investments to protect them from future harassment. In a sense, they were "buying" their safety.

The anti-German sentiments of the American population of Acadia Parish, displayed on occasion through the criticism, harassment, and even detention of the Germans of that region, was not a development unique to the people of that area. The fear and suspicion of all things German was a nationwide phenomenon. In state legislatures throughout the country, and in the United States Congress itself, laws were passed which stringently controlled the actions of the nation's Germans. Xenophobia generated by the war led various law-making bodies to pass legislation so severe that the ethnic and cultural vitality of America's German minorities were irreparably damaged.[14]

Nowhere were the Germans of the United States dealt with more severely than in Louisiana. According to Frederick Luebke, an expert on the treatment of Germans during World War I, Louisiana's legislature passed the harshest anti-German laws in the entire nation.[15] It is not exactly clear why Louisiana's legislators felt compelled to deal so severely with the state's German inhabitants when the latter constituted such a small and relatively harmless percentage of the overall population. The time when the Germans might have posed a potential threat, or possibly even acted as a "fifth column" within the internal political structure of the state had long since passed. The once mighty German community of New Orleans was completely "Americanized" by the beginning of World War I, and the Germans in other parts of the state were far too few in number and disinclined to mount anti-American activities. The only cohesive, culturally viable German colony in the state was Roberts Cove, but its inhabitants could hardly have justified the anti-German laws that the Louisiana legislature enacted.[16]

The legislature was called into special session shortly after the U.S. declaration of war to deal with the crisis at hand. In this special meeting and in the regular session the following year, a total of five separate measures were passed to control the activities of the state's German aliens. It is interesting to note that in the deliberations that led to the passage of these laws, William Zaunbrecher, the only foreign-born member of the legislature, played a relatively inconspicuous role. Although one might have expected this Roberts Cove German to have acted vigorously to protect the rights of his constituents, friends, and relatives, he was in fact severely constrained in what he could do by the political milieu of his day. To vindicate his now doubted patriotism,

World War I and Its Aftermath, 1917-1956

William Zaunbrecher voted in favor of each anti-German bill, with full knowledge that he was restricting the freedoms of his German constituents.[17]

The five measures which were enacted into law by the Louisiana general assembly included: House Act No. 20 which required the registration of all aliens;[18] House Act No. 14 which made it illegal for aliens of enemy lands to own explosives or firearms;[19] House Act No. 259 which forbade the teaching of the German language in all public and private schools from the elementary to the university level;[20] Senate Act No. 42 which made it unlawful for anyone to use the language of a nation at war with the United States in public discussion of the United States' entrance and role in the war, the American flag, its emblems, and colors;[21] and Senate Act No. 175 which prohibited the selling of anything made in Germany, advertised in German, distributing anything printed in German, or anything in print which favored Germany.[22]

Senate Act 175 and House Act 259 must have been considered particularly odious to Representative Zaunbrecher and his German constituents at Roberts Cove. These laws were specifically directed against the state's German element—an element, which we have noted, no longer comprised a significant proportion of the state's overall population. In 1910, foreign-born Germans numbered only 9,000, roughly seventeen percent of Louisiana's 52,000 foreign-born residents and .005 percent of the total populace (1,656,388).[23] Louisiana's lawmakers, clearly victims of the anti-German hysteria then sweeping through the United States, had grossly over-reacted to the potential threat posed by Louisiana's Germans. William Zaunbrecher obviously recognized that fact but was powerless to oppose the over-reaction.

The laws passed by the Louisiana legislature remained in force until 1921, but the climate of suspicion and animosity generated by the war lingered far longer. It was recognized by Germans and Americans alike that a turning point had been reached and that the congenial pre-war atmosphere would never return, a fact that became painfully clear to the Roberts Cove community in 1919, when a violent, cross-cultural confrontation took a German life on August 1.[24] August Zaunbrecher was mortally shot by one Leonard Stark during a confrontation on Zaunbrecher's property. After accusing Stark of stealing some dirt, Zaunbrecher pulled out a shotgun and informed the American that he was making a citizen's arrest. Stark then dismounted from his horse, went to the rear of his animal, pulled out a pistol from behind the saddle and shot his accuser. Although the German farmer fired twice at Stark, only Zaunbrecher was hit in the back during this exchange of gunfire. Zaunbrecher died two days later. In the intermittent moments of consciousness that he experienced in those two days, the Cove inhabitant claimed that his opponent had fired first and that he had only responded.[25]

In the ensuing trial, Stark was charged with manslaughter, though the Zaunbrecher family privately believed him guilty of murder. The lesser charge, however, offered greater potential for conviction because lingering anti-German antipathy had generated widespread public sympathy for Stark. The defendant was nevertheless acquitted following a lengthy trial.[26]

During the trial, the German community kept very quiet. No known public expressions of resentment or dissatisfaction were voiced by the Cove's inhabitants. However, there was one incident which occurred two weeks before the trial which was attributed to the Germans and which was considered a form of protest on their part. Two witnesses for the defense, on their way from Crowley after speaking on behalf of Stark, were followed by five men in a car and were later accosted. One of the witnesses avoided apprehension. Neither person was seriously injured, and the five assailants, one of whom was black, were never identified. Although no connection between the Stark trial and this event was ever officially made, sufficient evidence exists to suggest that one probably spurred the other.[27]

The Zaunbrecher killing was not an isolated case of post-war Germanophobia. Anti-German sentiment manifested itself in several forms which, taken individually, seem insignificant but, taken as a whole, paint a telling story. For example, the Roberts Cove community withdrew from public involvement. William Zaunbrecher, the state representative in 1916-1918, chose not to run for reelection after only one term. No one from the Cove, for the first time in many years, came forward as a candidate for the Acadia Parish Democratic Committee in 1918 or 1919. Until 1922, no obituary of any inhabitant of the Cove included the deceased's place of birth.[28] William Zaunbrecher's death in that year was given copious coverage in the local press. He was praised as one of Acadia Parish's most important people, but his Germanic origins were hardly mentioned.[29]

The suppression of Zaunbrecher's Germanic origins is revealing. Because of the new political and social realities, residents of the Cove could no longer pass themselves off as Germans or German-Americans. They could only achieve acceptance as "Americans." Although they could still claim to be of German descent, they deemphasized their national or cultural origins. This emphasis on Americanization pressured those in the Cove community who had not yet acquired citizenship to take the necessary steps to become naturalized. In May 1922, the few remaining "Germans" of the Cove completed the process of naturalization as American citizens.[30]

World War I and Its Aftermath, 1917-1956

It was also in 1922 that the German School at St. Leo's Church ceased operations. The teaching of German had only briefly been reintroduced in 1921 when it again became legal to offer instruction in that language. However, it almost immediately became apparent to church officials and the private instructors hired after the war that the teaching of the German language was no longer as viable an option because of growing apathy among both students and parents. Consequently, most education in German was terminated. Some private instruction among individuals, however, continued into the 1930s.[31]

The school itself remained open, but only temporarily. In 1923 the school was taken over by the Sisters of the Most Blessed Sacrament in Lafayette. Enrollment was meager—only twenty-five to thirty students for grades one through eight; and interest in the school continued to wane. Enrollment in the next thirty years gradually declined as more of the Cove's inhabitants recognized that the overall educational needs of their children could be better served in the communities of Rayne and Crowley. In 1951 the Sisters permanently closed the school. By then the number attending had dropped to fifteen, and instruction was offered only to grade four. The cessation of most teaching in German in 1922 and the closing of the school altogether in 1951 were the most obvious indications that the Roberts Cove community was being drawn into the mainstream of American life. The former development in particular signaled the beginning of the end of the settlement's Germanic ethnicity.[32]

Another important thread of historical continuity in the Roberts Cove colony was broken in 1930, when the Benedictines severed their connection with the St. Leo community, as a result of the retirement of the church's last Benedictine pastor, Father Leo Schwab. The church members immediately petitioned St. Meinard Abbey for a replacement but were turned down. This came as an unexpected blow to the parishioners who still labored under the assumption that as long as their community remained in existence they would be supplied ministers by the Benedictines.[33]

Their pleas were ignored by the Benedictines, ostensibly because the Roberts Cove community was no longer a "Germanic" settlement since German was no longer being taught in the colony's school. Hence their obligation to supply the community with German pastors, an obligation the Benedictines had incurred in the 1890s, was no longer binding. In any event, the previous agreement between the Benedictines and the Germans of Roberts Cove in light of World War I, became meaningless. St. Leo's parish was placed under the jurisdiction of the Diocese of Lafayette after 1930, but heedful of the settlement's Germanic past, the diocesan bishops agreed to supply German priests to St. Leo's well into the future.[34]

Chapter Four

Despite the presence of German priests after 1930, the settlement's decline as an ethnic community was irreversible. Numerous economic factors, which emerged after World War I and continued to operate throughout the interwar era and beyond, accelerated the disintegration of the community's social and cultural cohesiveness. After the war, for example, many of the Cove's farmers turned to cattle ranching. Some, like William Heinen, had already introduced cattle on their farms prior to the war, but ranching had been merely a sideline. After 1918, however, livestock production began to rival rice cultivation in economic importance. A number of local farmers had accumulated substantial herds by the time of World War II, including the Heinen, Gossen, Leonards, Thevis and Zaunbrecher families.[35] Ranching required a considerable amount of land, and, as the cattle culture spread, land became more and more scarce. The younger, aspiring farmers of the community were thus forced to seek their fortunes in agriculture elsewhere. Still others were compelled to look outside of agriculture to establish their professions and careers. Those who left their homes lost touch with their "Germanic" roots and tended to become more thoroughly Americanized.[36]

Two other disruptive influences of the interwar era were the Great Depression and the discovery of oil in the surrounding parishes. The former caused the bankruptcy of a few farmers who were forced to seek their livelihood away from the Cove. Though a positive force in the local economy, the discovery of oil, also drew Germans away from the colony to the South Louisiana oil communities where lucrative jobs were available. The effect, once more, was the loss of the German heritage of those who became separated from the home community.[37]

Also weakening Roberts Cove's Germanic heritage was the increasing tendency of the younger generations to find spouses outside their own community. "Mixed" marriages prior to World War I were extremely rare. Almost without exception, members of the German settlement married one another.[38] But, by the time of the third generation, this practice diminished greatly because the now extensive network of blood relationships made it almost impossible to find a mate within the Roberts Cove community. Mixed marriages in the interwar period accelerated tremendously not only to avoid in-breeding, but also because of the "dispersion" of community members brought on by economic factors. Germans leaving the Roberts Cove community to find jobs elsewhere tended to find their mates in their adopted homes. In marriages between Cove residents and outsiders, and especially in those cases where the outsider was the wife, the children were usually brought up as Americans speaking only English and only vaguely aware of interest in their Germanic background. The German spouse would often lose the use of the German language through disuse in a matter of a few short years.[39]

Exogamous marriages, the anti-German laws of World War I, and the exodus of young Germans from Roberts Cove sapped the colony's cultural vitality. Yet, Roberts Cove never totally lost its Germanic identification. In the last several decades, the settlers of Roberts Cove have experienced a revival of their Germanic ethnicity. This revival has obviously taken place within certain limitations. A return to the German language and culture is, needless to say, impossible. Americanization is far too advanced to make the latter probable. However, many of the community's inhabitants are showing an increased awareness of their settlement's Germanic background and are trying to reestablish connections with relatives in the land of their forefathers. And, with the help of St. Leo's Church, some Germanic customs and practices are being perpetuated among the children of the community.

Chapter V

The Revival of the Ethnic and Historic Consciousness of Roberts Cove (1950s to the Present)

The inhabitants of the Roberts Cove community began in the 1950s to exhibit a growing desire to become more keenly aware of their ethnic and cultural roots. Many of the settlers realized that the colony's unique Germanic heritage was disappearing and that the younger generations would soon have only the vaguest knowledge, or no knowledge at all, of their ethnic and historic backgrounds. The possibility that the Roberts Cove community might lose altogether its connections with its Germanic past led to a variety of efforts by individuals and groups to revitalize the community's Germanic heritage. Through annual family gatherings, through church sponsored festivities at which Germanic customs were perpetuated, and through group-trips to Geilenkirchen, Germany, the inhabitants of Roberts Cove have effectively recalled the memory of their Germanic past and have done much to restore the ethnic consciousness of the settlers.

According to Charles J. Zaunbrecher, the ethnic revival began when several individuals in the Zaunbrecher family initiated talks about the possibility of holding family reunions to revive the memory of the colony's founders. The first reunion occurred in 1956 when Joseph Zaunbrecher, William Zaunbrecher and William Gossen gathered their families for a special celebration.[1] Most of the Cove's remaining families were eventually drawn into subsequent gatherings. Because of their popularity, the reunions, originally planned as biannual affairs, became annual events by the 1960s. These now traditional family reunions, which have retained their original purpose, are held on the grounds of St. Leo's Church on the first Sunday in October and are an occasion for great merriment. In recent times it has become customary for reunions, scattered throughout the year, to be sponsored by several of the Cove's families. Attendance at these get-togethers is always large, often running into several hundreds.[2]

Anyone who has attended one of these family gatherings at Roberts Cove recognizes that he is attending an unusual event, an event designed to instill in the participants a consciousness of their community's past. The community's Germanic characteristics are strongly emphasized. German foods are served, some German songs are sung, however imperfectly, and even part of the church services are performed in the German language. Needless to say, copious amounts of beer, the German national beverage, are consumed, and in recent years, relatives from the German fatherland have participated in these festivities.

The greatest of these family gatherings occurred in October 1980, the centennial celebration of the founding of the Roberts Cove colony. This event was advertised extensively in the regional newspapers,[3] and numerous dignitaries, both lay and clerical, were invited to attend. The gathering took place on October 5, a brilliant fall day. Bishops Jude Speyer, Maurice Schexnayder, and Gerard Frey, all of German ancestry, were in attendance. Governor David Treen of Louisiana also came. Father Ignatius Fabacher, a descendant of Joseph Fabacher, founder of the Fabacher German colony established in 1870, was another special guest. The oldest living relatives of the original settlers were also honored. Casper Berken, who at eighty-nine years of age was not only one of the oldest living descendants of the original settlers, but the only one actually born in Germany, was shown special consideration as a living monument. The celebration was a tremendous success, attracting more than six thousand relatives to the Cove.[4]

This centennial celebration was of such special importance not only because of the magnificent attendance and the widespread publicity that it received, but because of the Germanic emphases that were placed on all of the activities surrounding this event. The very name of the reunion indicates to what extent the organizers of this event wanted it to be a German celebration. In newspapers and other media, as well as on the bumper stickers that were printed for this special occasion, the gathering was advertised always as the "German" centennial of Roberts Cove. This observer, who attended the gathering, noted that all of the centennial proceedings did indeed have a Germanic flavor. Throughout the day's activities, Germanic customs and ways were stressed. Even a band playing "German" polkas and German "beer-drinking music" was engaged to emphasize the Teutonic heritage of the Roberts Cove community. Consequently, it probably did as much to revive the ethnic and historic consciousness of those present as all previous family reunions combined.[5]

The inhabitants of Roberts Cove and all of their relatives who regularly return to St. Leo's Church to pay homage to the memory of their Germanic ancestors may very well have been inspired in their ethnic revival by the simultaneous and ongoing Acadian cultural revival. Indeed, the search for one's roots and the attendant restoration of pride in one's ancestors have been national phenomena experienced by virtually every American ethnic minority. This has been a refreshing historical development which has contributed enormous information and understanding of America's nationalities and minorities. The "Germans" of Acadia Parish can take special pride because they were in the vanguard of the national ethnic revival movement, having organized their initial efforts to "resurrect" their past in the 1950s, fully one decade before parallel efforts by other groups.

Indeed, it could be argued that the Germans of Roberts Cove had never really forgotten their debt to their Germanic forefathers. Even in the interwar era when the forces for ethnic disintegration were at their strongest, the Cove's inhabitants were constantly reminded of their Germanic past by the muted Germanic customs and traditions of many of the community's elders. Some Cove residents retained portions of their Germanic heritage as late as the fifties and sixties. By the 1970s and 1980s, the old Germanic ways were again prized, but, what the Germans of Roberts Cove have accomplished was not so much a revival of their ethnicity as an even stronger appreciation of their diminishing heritage.

Father Charles Zaunbrecher, perhaps more than any other person, spearheaded this "ethnic revival" movement. Zaunbrecher grew up in the Cove and appreciated intensely the richness of his community's history and culture. He has dedicated much of his life to the rejuvenation of the Cove's Germanic traditions and to the perpetuation of its founders' memory. As a Catholic cleric, he is particularly concerned with retention of the religious practices of his German forebears. It is partially due to his efforts, as well as those of Clara Habetz, organist at St. Leo's for fifty-two years, that German hymns are still performed at many special religious festivities. It is also Father Zaunbrecher who seems to have been the ultimate guiding spirit behind the family reunions and the special historic celebrations, such as the Centennial.[6]

Father Zaunbrecher arrived at his personal mission of reviving the ethnic and religious history of Roberts Cove early in his religious career. Upon returning from Rome after completing his studies in 1958, he began to consider revitalization of his home community's religious and ethnic heritage as part of his religious calling. In fact, Roberts Cove's "ethnic revival" may actually have begun with the sermon he delivered before his friends and relatives at St. Leo's Church on July 17, 1959, in which he maintained that their Germanic heritage was worth perpetuating. Coming at a time when a number of the parishioners were already imbued with a heightened sense of their special heritage, because of Father Wolber's previous efforts at ethnic rejuvenation in the early 1950s, the sermon helped to galvanize his fellow Germans into action. It is possible that without this timely admonition from this youthful and enthusiastic priest, the incipient efforts to begin holding family reunions might have died out.[7]

Chapter Five

In countless other ways, Father Zaunbrecher has helped to revitalize the history and ethnic consciousness of Roberts Cove. He has amassed hundreds of documents which recount the historic growth and development of Roberts Cove and St. Leo's Church. He has graciously placed these documents at the disposal of professional historians to enable them to write scholarly works on the Roberts Cove community and its inhabitants. He has personally composed large numbers of articles on the German colony for newspapers and magazines, recounting the history and traditions, particularly religious traditions, of his people.[8]

But perhaps his greatest contribution has been the compilation of an extensive genealogical history of the thirty-seven German families who have lived in Roberts Cove at one time or another.[9] To make his compilation as complete and reliable as possible, Father Zaunbrecher has made at least 17 trips to Germany. Most of these trips were to the district of Geilenkirchen, where lie the roots of most of the families who settled in Acadia Parish. His elaborate genealogical reconstruction has been made readily available to those groups involved in the Cove's history to allow them to take their rightful place in the overall history of their community. The most numerous descendants, incidentally, of those families who originally founded Roberts Cove, according to Father Zaunbrecher's genealogical records, are the Hensgens, the Zaunbrechers, and the Heinens, in that order.[10]

It was also through his genealogical research ventures that Father Zaunbrecher helped his community to physically bridge the gulf of space and time between Roberts Cove and the fatherland. In June 1981, Father Zaunbrecher and thirty-two like-minded relatives and friends who desired to establish direct contacts with the land of their forebears traveled to Geilenkirchen and met its people and discovered, on a first-hand basis, where and under what conditions their ancestors had lived. This journey to the fatherland received considerable publicity in Germany, and the travelers who participated were ceremoniously welcomed by city officials of Geilenkirchen. At a public gathering held in honor of the visitors, Josef Dahlen, one of the city fathers, delivered a thirty minute recitation of the history and background (beginning with Roman times) of Geilenkirchen and its environs.[11] The entire trip was highly successful, not only because it established cordial relations with important officials of the homeland, but also because of the close ties that developed with relatives still living in Geilenkirchen, and because of the valuable genealogical and historical information that was brought back from the mother country.[12]

The ties forged between the parent and daughter communities in 1981 merely renewed trans-Atlantic links maintained by earlier generations between Roberts Cove and Geilenkirchen. Connections between relatives on both sides of the Atlantic were maintained even during the interwar period when the ethnic consciousness of the Roberts Cove community was at a low point.[13] Since World War II, communications between relatives have expanded greatly. Today it is not at all uncommon for German visitors to be found at any given family reunion,[14] and by the same token for a Cove descendant to be traveling in Germany. These ties, maintained by correspondence and cemented by transatlantic visits, appear to be quite viable. Maintenance of these ties, in turn, nurtures the Cove's Germanic identity, thus insuring its survival.

Trips to Germany, family reunions, and centennial celebrations have contributed to the ethnic revival at Roberts Cove. However, none of these activities has been as effective in perpetuating Germanic traditions as those sponsored by St. Leo's Church. These are activities most often related to religious holidays and frequently carried out for the benefit of the children of the community. During religious occasions such as marriages, funerals, St. Leo's Day, Mardi Gras, Corpus Christi Day, All Souls' Day, Christmas, and, above all, St. Nickolas's Day, German prayers, songs, recitations, and other Germanic practices, are being perpetuated among the parishioners of the church. By sponsoring these events on a regular basis, the Church has managed to remain the most important unifying force for not only its own parishioners but also for all the dispersed descendants of the original settlers. St. Leo's Church acts as a magnet which regularly draws its scattered flock back to its fold.

It is in association with religious events that specific aspects of the German culture are perpetuated. A few of the religious customs that began in Germany which are still practiced through the church are weddings and funerals. At the burial of a Cove descendant, for example, the traditional German funeral hymn, "Das Schicksal" (Destiny), is sung by the choir and those in attendance. On Palm Sunday, some of the farmers still bury "blessed palms" in the fields to guarantee a rich harvest. Mardi Gras (Fasching) is celebrated with the preparation of traditional pastries, and at Christmas-time such old German songs as "Stille Nacht," "Ihr Hirten Erwacht," and "Ihr Kinderlein Kommet," are sung by the church congregation.[15]

The most popular of the religious holidays, and the one most clearly involving the practices of the German homeland, is St. Nickolas's Day, near the beginning of the Advent season. St. Nickolas's feast day was a major religious event in southern Holland and in Geilenkirchen, just as it was throughout Catholic Europe. Because St. Nickolas was identified as the patron saint of children, the Germans of Roberts Cove eagerly continued this custom which

Chapter Five

afforded the best opportunity of passing on their happy memories of Geilenkirchen to their children.[16]

This festive spiritual event is actually observed on December 5, the eve of St. Nickolas's Day, when the church choir gathers with the pastor at the church. One of the choir members dresses up in liturgical robes to represent St. Nickolas, the renowned bishop of Myra in Asia Minor. The bishop wears a cope (cape), mitre (pointed hat), and crosier (staff). The choir members dress in red sweaters and black trousers. St. Nickolas and the choir members as well as the pastor of St. Leo's then set out for a number of homes where the children of the community have gathered. Within the last few decades, two additional members have been added to this procession: Santa Claus and Black Peter (Schwarze Peter), the former to bring this festivity more in line with modern traditions, the latter to bring the celebration more in line with old Dutch practices. In the modern adaptation of this tradition, Black Peter, dressed as a small child with blackened face, accompanies St. Nick simply to serve as his helper in distributing the goods.[17]

St. Nickolas's arrival is heralded at the designated homes by the ringing of bells and the singing of carols in both English and German. The singing continues as the bishop walks among the children asking them whether or not they have been good. An answer in the affirmative merits the handout of sweets and other goodies. A negative response, or an answer to the effect that the child has been bad, might cause Black Peter to hand out sticks.[18] But, not surprisingly, the children have always been so good that only treats are distributed. In fact, Black Peter no longer even carries sticks (or switches). Refreshments are then served to all present, and the procession then moves on to the next home. The celebration of St. Nickolas' Day is so popular that it appears in little danger of dying out.[19]

By sponsoring such events as St. Nickolas' Day, St. Leo's Church performs an invaluable service to its parishioners, both in accentuating the spirituality of the church community, and in perpetuating Old World customs which enrich the lives of its membership. And the church community extends far beyond the ecclesiastical parish boundaries, for St. Leo's continues to serve as the focal point for the greater family of Cove descendants. Cove descendants from far and wide attend Church functions, even those primarily designated for the broader community. St. Leo's Church has, and will continue, to play the central role in perpetuating the Germanic traditions of the Roberts Cove community and in keeping alive the memories of its founders.

Thus, as the Roberts Cove community approaches the 1990s, the prospects that it will retain at least some semblance of its Germanic character

The Revival of the Ethnic and Historic Consciousness of Robert's Cove (1950s to the Present)

remain good. Two events of the mid-1980s have highlighted the continuing interest shown by the Roberts Cove inhabitants toward their past: In May 1984, the St. Leo's grounds were the site of a most exceptional gathering of fifteen former German prisoners-of-war. The majority of these German POW's had previously been detained in Louisiana camps and wished to return to the sites of their former imprisonment. Some of the returning Germans had, in fact, worked on farms in and around Roberts Cove. Their visit to Roberts Cove gained exceptional significance because of the popular support it received from the local "German" populace, and because of the broad coverage given to the event by the local, state, and national news media. This gathering of the POW's at Roberts Cove provided the community the opportunity to tell its ethnic story to a national audience. Father Zaunbrecher, who coordinated the day's activities and who led the former prisoners through German prayers, songs, and even a sermon partially delivered in German, was interviewed at length by NBC news personality Douglas Kiker. In this interview, Father Zaunbrecher enthusiastically recounted the Germanic roots of the Roberts Cove community. Although the priest's views were not actually aired by NBC, the day's proceedings at Roberts Cove were subsequently given national exposure.[20]

The second, more recent, event was the centennial celebration of the founding of St. Leo's Church. This event, held on July 17, 1985, at St. Leo's Church, was officially recognized by Bishop Gerard Frey, who praised the Cove parishioners for "one hundred years of dedicated service to God and his people...."[21]

To make this occasion even more memorable, St. Leo's parishioners presented two special gifts to the church. One was a special Casavant Frères Pipe Organ, bearing custom German markings and dedicated on June 9, 1985. A centennial recital was performed on July 17, 1985, by Brother Robert LeBlanc of St. Joseph's Abbey in St. Benedict, Louisiana, to call attention to this donation. Also, at the time of the organ-dedication, the Gangelt coat-of-arms, featuring the lion, was adopted as the emblem for St. Leo IV parish. This logo was adopted not only because it fit the name Leo (Latin for "lion"), but also because it emphasized the Germanic background of the parish and some of its families, such as the Gossens.

Father Keith Vincent of St. Leo's presented the second gift to his parishioners—a special commemorative booklet recounting the history of St. Leo's Church from its founding. This richly illustrated, fifty-six page pamphlet emphasized the strong Germanic character of the church and its founders. To give special distinction to this small Catholic congregation, it was decided by

Chapter Five

the pastor and his parishioners on July 17, 1985, that Roberts Cove's church would henceforth always be referred to as St. Leo IV Catholic Church to remember and honor the church's close ties to its long-time patron saint Pope Leo IV (847-855).[22]

As we move through the 1980s, it can be stated that the future ethnic vitality of Roberts Cove appears in all respects to be bright. Even as this book is being written, the Cove's Germanic traditions are being revived and strengthened. The most recent example of this revival is the centennial celebration of St. Leo's Choir on March 22, 1987. To honor this event, a special edition of German hymns was published, and the role of organist Clara Habetz was highlighted. Furthermore, German hymns and other Germanic customs were once again evident at the recent St. Leo's Day celebration of July 19, 1987.

As long as the activities of St. Leo's Church to perpetuate Germanic customs are continued and the efforts of certain individuals to prolong the memories of the area's Germanic past are sustained, the ethnic consciousness of the Roberts Cove community will survive. This fact should gladden the hearts of St. Leo's roughly 500 parishioners[23] and the thousands of "German" relatives scattered throughout the region. Their pride in their roots has enriched us all.

Chapter VI

Recent Developments, 1987-2007

It is with great pleasure that I undertake the assignment of adding another chapter to my book on the "Germans" of Roberts Cove. Since its original publication some twenty years ago, many new and exciting developments have occurred within this community that continue to bear witness to the astounding vitality of these people. Above all, the events that have unfolded since July 1987, the date on which my earlier work ended, confirm the undying interest that these remarkable people have in their Germanic past and their Catholic faith. These two loyalties—to their history and their Church—are the interconnected themes that form the basis of the recounting of the Roberts Cove community's newest historical chapter.

In 1996, St. Leo's Church opened its new Church Annex, which began as an idea by Father Keith Vincent ten years before. In a letter to his parishioners on November 1, 1987, Father Vincent reminded the members of his church community that they had originally voted to add a Hospitality Center (later renamed the Church Annex) on Pentecost Sunday 1986. This structure, he said, would be "a homey place extending from the church—ready to welcome people right where they naturally gather. Its location and flexibility will make it easy to use for after-Mass visiting, coffee, Scripture study, small religious or social meetings, and at weddings or funerals." Father Vincent went on to report that since fund-raising had begun one year prior, $45,000 had already been generated thanks to the generous support of hundreds of parishioners, friends, and patrons. Received gifts ranged in size from $5 to $2,000, and were supplemented by significant bequests from the wills of Fathers Stanley Begnaud and Alois Reznicek. Pastor Vincent suggested that "with continued generosity from parishioners and friends, the coming year can see us reach $75,000: our minimum goal for the beginning of construction." An early start of construction would, he continued, "allow our generous supporters, our older people, to begin enjoying the Hospitality Center facilities without great delay."[1]

For a number of reasons, fund raising efforts slowed down significantly and actual construction of this new facility did not begin until eight years later. Ground was broken for the St. Leo IV Annex on March 6, 1995. Father Francis Bourgeois, the new pastor of St. Leo's Church, reported on this wonderful event in a letter to his parishioners on March 27, 1995, with the headline, "Dear Brothers and Sisters of the St. Leo Family: Our Dream is Com-

Chapter Six

ing True! What a Day For Rejoicing!" He went on to point out that "one of the shovels used for the groundbreaking was the same one used by Bishop Maurice Schexnayder, D.D. in 1953 for the groundbreaking ceremonies of the present church." The Parish Annex, he declared, would consist of "an activity room, two offices, restrooms, kitchenette, covered carport entrance and drive-through and display space" and would cost slightly over $200,000. This low cost was made possible by a favorable bid made by E.L. Habetz, a descendant of one of the early German families who settled in the Roberts Cove region. Roughly half of the amount needed had been raised, declared Father Bourgeois, but further generous donations would be required for the project to be completed in a timely fashion. Included in Father Bourgeois' letter was a list of those who had made contributions thus far, as well as a schematic drawing of the 1,900 square-foot facility.[2]

Participating in the groundbreaking ceremonies on that joyful Monday were building committee members Lawrence Habetz, Julian Didier, Mary Jo Olinger, Louis Cramer, Lawrence Cramer, Jerry Leonards, Parish Council President Shirley Leonards, Father Francis Bourgeois, Edmund Habetz of E.L. Habetz Builders, Inc., and Robert Barras of Barras Architects Inc., as well as other interested church members and officials. Presiding over these ceremonies were Father Bourgeois, who delivered the opening prayer, and Father Don Leger, Dean of Churches of Acadia Parish and pastor of St. Joseph's Church in Evangeline. The groundbreaking ceremonies were given prominent coverage in the local newspapers. Accompanying the news stories of this exciting event were pictures of building committee members and visiting dignitaries wielding shovels, ready to symbolically turn the ground for the planned Church Annex.[3]

What was so meticulously planned and ardently hoped for came to pass in July the following year. On July 14, 1996, a special Sunday service at 11:00 a.m. was held to celebrate the feast day of patron saint Leo IV and to formally announce the completion of the much anticipated Church Annex building. As Dawn Ohlenforst of the Rayne *Acadian Tribune* reported, "a tangible feeling of excitement was in the air as parishioners filed past several visiting priests and clergymen to receive Communion in the small, colorful church that was filled to capacity with well-wishers." Those present were "filled with a sense of pride" as they assembled to "celebrate the Thanksgiving and Dedication Ceremonies of the new St. Leo IV Parish Annex." This celebratory occasion was considered noteworthy enough for Lafayette Bishop Edward O'Donnell to personally preside over this special service. The joyful voices of St. Leo's Church Choir added to the festive nature of this dedicatory celebration. Also attending and helping

Recent Developments, 1987-2007

with these ceremonies were seminarian Thomas Habetz, Fathers George Heffner, William "Bill" Ohlenforst, Francis Bourgeois, current pastor of St. Leo's, Deacon Mitchell Guidry, Monsignor Glen Provost, and Sisters Clare Cramer, Margaret Ohlenforst, and Marie Habetz. Finally, making this event even more meaningful were the special contributions of the St. Leo IV altar servers, the Sodality of Mary who devote themselves to the memory of Mary, and a group of Angel Flower Girls which consists of the daughters of parishioners. These "angel" girls wore white robes and white headpieces, and carried white gladiola stalks as they seated themselves in the front pews of the church. During the service, all those who played a significant part in bringing the Annex to completion were thanked, with special acknowledgment going to Robert E. Barras architect, E.L. Habetz contractor, and building committee members Jerry Leonards chairman, Louis Cramer, Julian Didier, Lawrence Habetz, and Mary Jo Olinger. After the dedication services and Mass, the attending church members and dignitaries proceeded to the Annex Hall to enjoy food, fellowship, and German hymns sung by the church choir. With the conclusion of this special dedication and thanksgiving service, the arduous efforts begun by Father Keith Vincent and a key group of committed parishioners ten years before were brought to a glorious conclusion.[4]

The mid-1990s were years of tremendous activity and creativity for the greater Roberts Cove community. Not only were the attentions of this community focused on the completion of the Church Annex, but other projects of a broader historical and cultural nature were also conceived and acted upon. The two most important developments in this regard were the construction of the German Heritage Museum and the hosting of annual Germanfests. Both of these events began to take shape at the same time as history-conscious members of the Roberts Cove family began to think of ways to better preserve and commemorate their Germanic roots. Each of these endeavors deserves the most careful and extensive coverage possible. In telling the story of these two important projects in Roberts Cove's most recent history, I wish to point out that it may not always be possible to give credit to all those who took part. Any omissions of names and institutions is unintentional, and I apologize from the outset if anyone is overlooked.

Let us begin by recounting the story of the founding of the German Heritage Museum. The concept to create a separate physical structure to house cultural keepsakes started in the mid-l990s when a crew of ladies, led by Josephine "Josie" B. Thevis and Dorothy "Dot" O. Leger, began to assemble pictures, artifacts, and other items of historical interest and place them on exhibit in St. Leo IV's Parish Hall for the early Germanfest celebrations. As these displays grew in complexity and sophistication, it was clear that they needed a permanent home. The first public mention of the necessity for a German cultural museum was most likely made in a letter sent out in 1997 to Germanfest sponsors, workers, participants and other interested parties by Louis Cramer, who was then president of the Germanfest Association. A group of enthusiastic supporters then got together to begin implementing a plan for the establishment of such a building. According to Paul Kedinger of the Rayne *Acadian Tribune*, this initial group of museum advocates "nursed the idea through its early infancy, determined to see it eventually become reality," and consisted of Marie Habetz, her grandson Joshua Hoffpauir, Kay Habetz, and Louis Cramer. These museum supporters at first entertained the thought of moving a house near St. Leo's on the church grounds to serve perhaps as a temporary museum structure. However, those plans proved unfeasible and the focus shifted back to a new facility.[5]

Momentum for the construction of a new museum picked up in 1999 when museum supporters gathered in St. Leo's Church Hall on June 6 to view an architectural drawing of the proposed structure, sketched by fourth-year LSU architectural student Joshua Hoffpauir. About the same time, Kay and Marie Habetz, along with the full museum committee, reported that the permanent museum should officially be called the Roberts Cove German Heritage Museum. Also about that time serious efforts began to obtain funding for this enterprise. Initially it was thought that grant applications to various agencies of the federal government might secure the necessary funding. Congressman Chris John and Senators John Breaux and Mary Landrieu were contacted to assist in locating federal funds for the project. Federal assistance was not forthcoming, and eventually, local financial institutions provided the necessary loans for the museum. These included the Bank of Commerce in Rayne, Evangeline Bank in Crowley, Farmer's State Bank of Church Point, First Bank of Crowley, and Rayne State Bank. These banks loaned over $300,000 for the construction of this highly anticipated and much needed cultural facility.[6]

Actual construction of the German Heritage Museum began in mid-summer 2001 on land donated by St. Leo's Church, thanks to the efforts of Father Francis Bourgeois. He helped secure diocesan support for this venture after the Acadia Parish Police Jury provided $35,000 in seed money to allow for site preparation. The police jury funds originated from the governor's Office of Rural Development. With financial support guaranteed through loans from these various institutions, full-scale construction concluded by September 2002. On September 16, the building committee members and others who had played an important role in bringing this project to fruition were on hand to officially commemorate this most significant of achievements. On this festive occasion Marie Habetz was recognized for spearheading the initial efforts to establish this wonderful monument to the region's German culture. Lawrence Cramer, a member of the building committee, offered Marie special commendations and a plaque, and praised her for "maintaining the determination to make the dream come true," to which Ms. Habetz replied: "I didn't do it alone, I first had family and then friends." Several members of the building committee, which Marie Habetz had chaired, were present to pay tribute to her and to share in the pride of their common accomplishment. Additional members of the building committee in attendance were Lawrence Habetz, Vincent Zaunbrecher, Loretta Kurta, Herbie Gossen, and Gerard Olinger. Committee members not present were Dr. Philip Fabacher, Raymond Hensgens, Shirley Leonards, and Jerome Ronkartz.[7]

Also attending the opening ceremony of the German Heritage Museum were a number of additional honorees and dignitaries. Among those separately honored were the original "dreamers," as they were referred to by Paul Kedinger, who formed the nucleus of those who anticipated the eventual completion of the present structure. These "dreamers" included Clara Habetz, Joshua Hoffpair, Louis Cramer, Kay Habetz, and Marie Habetz. Fittingly, among the honorees that were invited to attend, "cut the ribbon," and herald in the opening and dedication ceremony were the three oldest citizens of Roberts Cove. Three special guests were asked to "oversee" the "christening" of the heritage museum—Clara Habetz (already serving in other capacities), Felicitas Cramer, and Johnny Heinen, Sr. (who was not able to participate). The two elderly ladies snipped the red, gold, and black ribbon in front of a group of proud onlookers. It was appropriate that Congressman Chris John, a descendant of the original Cove founders, was witness to this event. Lastly, even the financial backers who helped to underwrite the construction of this important cultural edifice were singled out for their contributions. Those present representing their institutions were Mike McBride of Evangeline Bank, Steve Mire of First Bank, and Louis Nugent and Charles Scanlan of Rayne State Bank. The Bank of Commerce in Rayne and Church Point's Farmers State Bank also provided funding but were not represented at this time.[8]

To close out our discussion of the opening of the German Heritage Museum on September 16, 2002, we must mention the role of perhaps the two most important people present—the two ladies who would become the museum's curators—Dot Leger and Josie Thevis. Both had for many years served as the unofficial caretakers of many of the important historical artifacts and keepsakes that represented the community's Germanic past. They would continue to serve in those roles in a more official and permanent capacity. During the opening ceremonies, Congressman Chris John provided these two ladies with an official American flag which would henceforth be displayed at the museum. It was these two insightful and hardworking women who envisioned the various purposes that the heritage museum might serve. They anticipated that this 3,000-square-foot structure might be divided into a lobby, reception room, gift shop, genealogy rooms, and storage area. Furthermore, they hoped the heritage museum might be divided into separate thematic categories, such as a space for religious items highlighting the Germanic observance of Christmas and St. Nicholas Day and other rooms that might feature the area's agricultural industry, containing antique farming tools. These "visions" have all become reality in the new structure. Finally, I might add, in completing my discussion of the present topic, that both individuals have been extremely helpful in making the museum available for meetings with the various persons who have been involved in updating other parts of this book, the genealogy section in particular. They were also most gracious and supportive by providing this author with important and much needed information for making current the present volume.[9]

One of the most remarkable of all of the developments in the recent history of the Roberts Cove community—on par, both historically and culturally, with the founding of the German Heritage Museum, and in some respects even more significant because of the ongoing commitments required by literally hundreds of people—was the decision made by a group of highly motivated people to stage the annual Germanfest. This festival, reminiscent of the famous Oktoberfests held yearly in Munich to celebrate the end of the harvest season, is a monumental undertaking requiring the coordinated efforts of huge numbers of inspired supporters both within and beyond the Roberts Cove-St. Leo Church family. Germanfest is held annually on the grounds of St. Leo's Church on the first weekend of October and showcases the cultural creativity of these people, highlighting in particular the Germanic and agricultural beginnings of the Roberts Cove community. So many people are involved in these enormous enterprises that it is impossible to name them all.

According to Louis Cramer, the initial president of the Germanfest Association, the concept of having a Germanfest developed from the practice of inviting Catholic youth organizations to host programs for St. Leo's parishioners and other interested parties in which they enacted some of the activities of the German colonists who settled in Roberts Cove at the turn of the century. The interest in these programs was so great that it led to the decision to form a steering committee to plan bigger events of a similar nature. Out of

Recent Developments, 1987-2007

these early deliberations developed the idea of staging a full-fledged festival that might be opened to a paying public-at-large which would help defray the costs of such an event. This committee began its meetings in November 1994, and through its dedicated efforts, and that of hundreds of others, was able to successfully stage the first Germanfest the following year. The happy faces of the members of this steering committee appeared in a special souvenir edition of the Germanfest program inserted into both of Rayne's local newspapers on September 28, 1995. Shown in this picture was the steering committee—Mary Ann Leonards, Kay Cramer, Kay Habetz, Lawrence Habetz, Louis Cramer, Gwen Thevis, and Susan Olinger. Not pictured was Mike Leonards. Included in the caption identifying the members of this committee was the revealing statement that the members of this committee had "logged over 1,000 hours in meetings" preparing for this event. Apparently these hours were well spent since the first Germanfest proved to be an unqualified success.[10]

It was hoped that this and later Germanfest celebrations would keep alive for the Roberts Cove-St Leo IV Church extended family's Germanic heritage alive and, at the same time, reveal this unique culture to a much larger audience through participating in the annual October festival. When advertising the first Germanfest in its pages, the Rayne *Independent* aptly described this festival's purpose "to educate and promote the German culture in the surrounding area." The newspaper then went on to describe the activities that were to take place during this event. There were to be, according to the *Independent*, "five main areas of German cultural activities." These included "food, folklore, crafts, music, and dancing." In elaborating on these and other activities that were to take place during this first Germanfest, the newspaper was, in fact, revealing the essential program of events that would be followed in all of the subsequent Germanfest celebrations, because it proved so successful. Indeed, the very first Germanfest is estimated to have attracted over 20,000 participants. All later Germanfests pulled in roughly equal numbers of festival-goers with only bad weather dampening spirits and numbers.[11]

All twelve Germanfests that have taken place since 1995 are each, in their own way, unique. However, the first Germanfest must take pride of place because it established the parameters by which all of the others were measured. It demonstrated what the combined efforts of a large number of dedicated people could accomplish. Through its many triumphs it inspired the later Germanfest volunteers to emulate the achievements of their predecessors. The emphasis on folklore, German music and dancing, native costumes worn in the German homeland, as well as German foods such as sausage, sauerkraut, Zuckerplatzchen, Apfelkuchen, and other desserts, has contributed to making

Chapter Six

these October festivals hugely popular. Furthermore, highlighting the histories of individual families and emphasizing the farming backgrounds of the original Roberts Cove settlers provides additional appeal, especially to historically-minded visitors.

A perfect example of the way in which succeeding Germanfests preserved the original attractions and organization of the first, and at the same time have learned to adapt to the needs of the increasingly younger and more sophisticated audiences, can be seen in the description offered by the Rayne *Acadian Tribune* of the 2006 Germanfest. In an article entitled "Celebrate German Style!," the newspaper, in its special souvenir edition of October 5, promoted the upcoming twelfth celebration of this event by stating that this festival "will not only feature traditional Cove German foods such as sausage, potatoes, sauerkraut, and desserts but will also highlight German cultural activities, folklore, music, dancing, and other great food and drinks." The newspaper continued, "Festival goers can also enjoy the Roberts Cove German Heritage Museum which will exhibit artifacts from many ancestors, including handwork such as embroidery, crochet, doilies, tatted, knitted, smocked, etc. An 'angelic room' which will exhibit angel statues, wall-hangings...and a non-electric hand tool display will be of interest to men." Also featured, according to the *Tribune*, were rice-threshing demonstrations, reenactments of the threshing dinner, sack sewing, and shock assembly. To attract a broader South Louisiana audience, the festival organizers invited popular Cajun chef John Folse to show how "German communities and their food had influenced Louisiana's culture and food." His demonstrations at the Germanfest were taped and later aired on his television show, "A Taste of Louisiana with Chef John Folse."

Other activities illustrating the wide variety of amusements provided by the 2006 Germanfest were "music from the German bands Alpenfest [performing at this festival since 1995] and Alpenmusikanten...along with the Germanfest Folk Singers and German dancers. A delightful attraction will be Kinder Auftrit, a local children's dancing and singing group." And, to draw younger adults, "a local group called the 'Tailgators' will be performing" on Saturday evening. Still other events of interest were "an Antique Tractor Club displaying their antique tractors, the Blacksmith Association demonstrating old time blacksmith skills, Kinder Land, a kid-friendly festival with free games and activities...and the Louisiana Purchase Barber Shop Quartet," which performed their songs while strolling through the grounds. Not mentioned in this newspaper article, but yet another highly popular musical attraction, was the volunteer piano-accordianist Bob Chaney, who entertained willing listeners with his stirring renditions of polkas, waltzes, and other forms of German music. Finally, at the gift shop one could purchase "hand-crafted gifts, German hats, pins, T-shirts, German cookbooks, aprons, stems, canned fruits and vegetables, and much more." Indeed, there was something for everybody at this and earlier Germanfests. It was this great variety of attractions, adapted as necessary to changed conditions, that have guaranteed the continued popularity of Roberts Cove Germanfests in their South Louisiana homeland.[12]

The spirit of several of the Germanfests was dampened by the deaths of important individuals who were crucial not only in the inception and production of these festivals, but whose contributions penetrated far into the depths of the Roberts Cove community and who were also, in a sense, the heart and soul of St. Leo IV Church. Two of these people were Father Charles Zaunbrecher and Clara Habetz. Both were honored and given plaques in the 1995 Germanfest while still alive, and their singular roles in Roberts Cove's history were again given special tribute in later Germanfests shortly after their deaths—Father Zaunbrecher in 1996 and Clara Habetz in 2006. The lives of both deserve to be recalled at some length in the pages below.

Father Charles Joseph Zaunbrecher was born in 1931 to Charles Zaunbrecher and the former Bertha Dischler. He died in the early morning hours of June 19, 1996, in Our Lady of Lourdes Hospital in Lafayette. His funeral services were held at St. Michael's Church in Crowley on June 20 and he was interred at St. Leo's Church cemetery in Roberts Cove on June 21. Father Zaunbrecher's grave, along with the graves of the original immigrants who emigrated from Germany, received special recognition at the 1996 Germanfest by being decorated with a balloon bouquet consisting of an arrangement of orange, yellow, and black flowers which were placed at their headstones. Kay Cramer remarked that Father Zaunbrecher's grave deserved to be included with the old graves because of his importance to Roberts Cove's history and because "tradition is important to us."[13]

Father Charles received his elementary education at St. Leo's in Roberts Cove and St. Joseph's in Rayne. Later, he studied religion at St. Joseph's Seminary in St. Benedict, Louisiana. From there he went on to major in philosophy at Notre Dame Seminary in New Orleans. He completed his theological studies at North American College at Vatican City State and at the Gregorian University in Rome. In December 1957 he celebrated his first Mass in Rome at the Altar of St. Leo IV in St. Peter's Basilica. Later, he was honored to perform a Mass of Thanksgiving in Roberts Cove in July 1958. His first religious posting was to Kaplan and he later became pastor of St. Jules Church in Lafayette. Thereafter, he served in the Diocese of Lafayette as director of the Office of

Chapter Six

Religious Education, vicar of the West Acadian Deanery, vicar of the Lafayette City Deanery, and vicar of the South Lafayette Regional Deanery.[14]

Fortunately for us, he became interested in genealogy and history—especially that of his own forefathers. He began to trace the roots of the original settlers of Roberts Cove and compiled valuable genealogies and histories of Roberts Cove's founding fathers. His intense interest in his ancestry led him to sponsor annual family reunions, beginning in the late 1950s. These early gatherings grew into ever larger celebrations, and increasingly attending these celebrations were relatives from the old country. Father Zaunbrecher had the habit of checking telephone directories and other official records for the name Zaunbrecher, and on one occasion discovered that there was a Peter Joseph Zaunbrecher, who was also a priest, in Essen, Germany. They began to correspond, discovered that they were related, and realized their families came from the Nierstrass-Gillrath region of north Germany. In 1961 Father Zaunbrecher made the first of many trips to Europe and invited relatives to the Zaunbrecher family reunion the following year. To make a long story short, after many additional family reunions, correspondences, cross-ocean visits among relatives, and genealogical publications, the full-fledged ethnic-historical revival of the Roberts Cove community began. Out of this revival emerged the Germanfests and my own publication of the history of the Germans of Acadia Parish in 1988 and the present updating of this history. For all of this we are indebted to Father Charles Joseph Zaunbrecher.[15]

Clara Habetz, like Father Zaunbrecher, was an indispensable pillar of the Roberts Cove community. Through her long life and her deep commitment to her church and people, she has left an indelible mark on the countless individuals who were lucky enough to know her. She had an infectious personality and made all around her believe they could accomplish great things. She participated in virtually all of the important developments that have occurred in the life of St. Leo IV Church and the Roberts Cove family in the last seven decades. I myself was fortunate enough to have met with her and several others as we were preparing to expand the genealogy and history of Roberts Cove for an upcoming publication. She always gave good advice and encouragement for our work. The two of us particularly enjoyed practicing our German on each other and laughing when we made mistakes or struggled for the right expression. She will be missed by all who knew her. But, rather than mourn her passing, we should rejoice in the knowledge that she had a long and fruitful life. She died on August 22, 2006, almost ninety-two years old.

Her eventful life, filled with numerous accomplishments, deserves to be recalled at some length. Maria Clara Habetz was born in 1914 to Wilhelm

Recent Developments, 1987-2007

Habetz and the former Franziska Theunissen, the fourth of twelve children. The household was fairly strict, where only German was spoken. This was a rule imposed by her father, who according to Clara, declared to the children: "You speak English at school, but at home you will speak only German." After completing her education, she determined not to follow the "normal" path of getting married and having children. She decided to dedicate her life to the church, but not through the traditional way of becoming a nun. At age twenty-one she began her long devotion to her beloved church by becoming church organist—a position she held until just before the time of her death. Then, in 1940, she began a long stint as priest housekeeper, and from 1942 to 1990 served as a church sacristan. Along the way, she was involved in numerous other activities in support of her Catholic church. For over seventy years she was a member and occasional secretary of St. Leo's Altar Society. She was also active for many years in the Acadia Parish Serra Club which encouraged young men to adopt the priesthood as their vocation, and she was a charter member of St. Leo's #2168 Catholic Daughters of the Americas. Her involvement with the CDA gave her particular satisfaction as it enabled her to work with children ages five through ten. One of her singular accomplishments, born out of her gifts as a musician and her knack for working with children, was preparing the young for their popular singing and dancing performances at the Germanfests, known as the Kinder Auftritt. Her work with children probably gave her as much pleasure as anything else she ever did.

She was honored many times during her lifetime. In 1970 she received the Papal Award, "Benemerenti," given by Pope Paul II for her outstanding service to the church. The "Bishop Medal," bestowed upon her by Bishop Flynn in 1991, was for meritorious work on behalf of the Catholic church. In 1985 a new Casavant pipe organ was installed in St. Leo's Church. This event coincided with her fiftieth year as organist for the parish. A special recital was performed in her honor followed by the unveiling of a marble plaque that dedicated this organ to Miss Habetz. In 1998 she was named the "Woman of Achievement" by the Rayne *Acadian Tribune.* She was a member and president of the Roberts Cove Home Demonstration Club and had also served as president of the Acadia Parish Council and received from this organization the Fifty-Year Membership Award and the Key Award. All of these, and many other distinctions, have enshrined Clara Habetz as one of the truly outstanding individuals of all of South Louisiana, and her long life was a particular testament to the energy and creativity of the "German" community of Roberts Cove.[16]

Let us now turn our attention to other important developments that have recently occurred within the Roberts Cove-St. Leo Church community. One of

Chapter Six

these was an event that began on a very negative note but that ended as an uplifting experience for St. Leo's parishioners. This was the 2004 rededication of St. Leo IV's famed Pilgrimage Chapel which had been destroyed by Hurricane Lili in early October 2002. This fierce storm severely damaged not only this historic chapel, but also brought great harm to the main church, the parsonage, the church hall, and a warehouse. It forced the cancellation of that year's Germanfest which was only a few days away. The St. Leo's church community considered it an important task to restore the chapel to its previous condition since it had played such an important role in St. Leo's religious history.

The rededication ceremonies took place on July 18, 2004. The beautifully restored Pilgrimage Chapel—in German it is referred to as the *Wallfahrtskappelle*—was blessed at an 11:00 a.m. Mass. The presiding priest was Father Thomas Habetz, pastor of St. John the Evangelist Church in Mermentau. Participating also were Father Francis Bourgeois of St. Leo's Church and visiting priests Fathers George Hefner and Paul Thibodeaux. Also taking part in various capacities, and shown in a picture appearing in the July 22, 2004, edition of the *Acadian Tribune*, were Daniel Reynolds, Michael Legnion, Zachary Benoit, John Leonards, John Reynolds, chapel reconstruction committee head Ambrose Olinger, Sisters Margaret Ohlenforst and Clare Cramer, and alter boys Stephen Benoit and Paul Thibodeaux. This blessing coincided with the feast of St. Leo's Day, and in charge of that part of the festivities was Josette Dupuis.

To the parishioners of St. Leo's Church, the reconstruction of their beloved chapel was considered absolutely essential. First built in 1890, it became a part of the family life and services of the St. Leo's Church community. It served as a continuing reminder of the traditions and customs of the original settlers, and it contained many cherished memories for numerous churchgoers who had prayed within its confines through the years. A particularly meaningful portion of the Pilgrimage Chapel was the completely restored altar depicting the Sorrowful Mother holding Christ and adorned with the following moving quotation on the pedestal supporting the statue (translated in English from the Latin): "Great as the sea is my sorrow."[17]

It was fitting that Ambrose Olinger was placed in charge of the chapel's reconstruction, as he was also a surviving member of the building committee which had overseen the construction of St. Leo's Church in 1954. Olinger recognized that the rebuilding of this treasured symbol would be no easy task. He described the chapel upon viewing it shortly after its destruction as "a pile of rubble on the ground." Although the destruction seemed total, important elements of the chapel were left intact, including the structure's doors, windows,

Recent Developments, 1987-2007

and many of the stained glass panels that were refitted into new frames. Also left mostly intact was the statue of Mary holding Jesus in her lap, with only a few fingers missing from the statue of Jesus. Everything was totally rebuilt or repaired under the careful supervision of Ambrose Olinger and his crew of skilled craftsmen from the nearby city of Crowley.[18]

The successful restoration of the Pilgrimage Chapel and the repairs to the main church and other structures that were completed in 2004 were a necessary and fitting prelude to the fifty-year re-consecration of St. Leo IV Church that followed two years later. With the damages caused by Hurricane Lili no longer visible, the ceremonies of July 16, 2006, could be appreciated in all their glory, especially by Ambrose Olinger who had played such an important role in the original construction and reconstruction efforts of 2004 of St. Leo's Church. The original consecration of St. Leo's took place on July 17, 1956, officiated by then Bishop Maurice Schexnayder and aided by numerous other religious and lay dignitaries. The fifty-year re-consecration was overseen by Father Francis Bourgeois and took place concurrently with the July 16 feast day of the church's patron saint Leo IV. Other individuals on hand and lending their support were Matt Rimmer, president of the St. Leo Church Council, and Jerry Gossen, son of Joseph Gossen, the contractor who had built St. Leo's over fifty years before. A pictorial display was placed in the parish hall to help commemorate this historical event and dinner was served to bring these festive proceedings to a most satisfying conclusion.[19]

To close our discussion of recent events, let us examine the important place of ongoing "heritage tours" in Roberts Cove's history. These are trips to the mother country undertaken by a cadre of dedicated and historically-conscious descendants of the original settlers who do not wish to forget the memory of their forefathers. These pilgrimages to the German homeland began in 1965 and have been repeated at roughly five-year intervals, with the most recent one taking place in 2005. These tours began under the inspiration and guidance of Father Charles Zaunbrecher. For thirty years, between 1965 and 1995, he led contingents of South Louisiana "Germans" back to their cultural roots, visiting the exact locations where their forefathers had been born, worked, worshiped and died. Dr. Philip Fabacher took on the "mantel" of heritage tour leader after the death of Father Zaunbrecher in 1996. He has capably filled the void left by Father Zaunbrecher by leading two successful tours—in 2000 and 2005—and because of his own deep interest in history and genealogy, might well be designated the next "family" historian for South Louisiana's "Germans."[20]

Chapter Six

The four tours that have occurred in the last twenty years since the publication of my book bear further discussion. The 1990 tour led by Father Zaunbrecher was one of those lesser attended, with only seventeen individuals participating. Its significance was also somewhat diminished by the fact this was not so much a trip to the Geilenkirchen homeland as it was an excursion to see some of the important sites of Germany, Austria, and Switzerland. Only one stop of ancestral significance was made, and that was the visit to the pilgrimage town of Kevelaer where some of the original Roberts Cove colonists worshiped.

Better attended and more "historically" important was the trip of 1995. Thirty-eight excited travelers accompanied Father Zaunbrecher on his last heritage tour. Its principal purpose was to visit the sites and to meet with the relatives of the ancestral motherland. The tour began in the city of Geilenkirchen, the original home of many of the travelers' forefathers. Here they were greeted by the mayor and other dignitaries, told about the history of that region, and given a chance to meet with and be entertained by distant relatives such as Gerry and Gerta Zaunbrecher of the Geilenkirchen-Nierstrass area. In fact, one day out of the three-day stop in the Geilenkirchen region was set aside to visit with individual families in that region who were thought to be related to tour participants.

Some of the Zaunbrechers, Leonards, and Gossens who made this trip visited Fine Zaunbrecher and Maria Zitzen; the Heinen descendants visited Joseph and Elizabeth Heinen; the Hensgens visited Karsten Heinrichs and grandparents; other Leonards and Gossens visited with Hans Otto and Gesela Leonards; and the Thevis and Berkens travelers visited with their relatives. These were wonderful "family reunions" in which many lasting friendships were made. There was even a special train prepared for the visitors which had been converted into a "living" museum and provided them a tour of many of the villages that were the homes of their forefathers. At the end of their village tour they were welcomed by a band and regaled with much food, music, and dancing. All in all, the 1995 heritage tour was a memorable experience and a huge success, and, indeed almost as an afterthought, included visits to some of the beautiful sites of Austria, Italy, Switzerland, and Holland.

The 2000 heritage tour was the first led by Philip Fabacher and was called "The Reverend Charles Zaunbrecher Memorial Trip to Europe" to honor the memory of the founder of these pilgrimage trips. Thirty travelers accompanied Dr. Fabacher on this tour of the homeland and other places of interest. As in 1995, the emphasis was to visit the locations meaningful for those in attendance. The travelers attended even more of the villages where their ances-

Recent Developments, 1987-2007

tors lived. Relatives were once more visited and their hospitality was enjoyed. Yet again, many rich memories were made. The travelers brought with them a commemorative poster of the 2000 Germanfest celebration and offered it to the mayor of Geilenkirchen as a token of their common heritage. And in turn, the visitors were given a festive reception at the city hall and a tour of the local *Heimatsland* (homeland) Museum. An additional nearby site of interest visited was Aachen—the ancient capital of the emperor Charlemagne—where a Mass was held and German songs familiar to St. Leo IV parishioners were sung. The 2000 heritage tour expanded its travels through the German homeland by visiting locations such as the Wasnau region where they traveled to the town of Busenberg, the ancestral home of the Fabachers, Rupperts, Kleins, and Wilferts. Also visited were locations in France where related members of the Frey family were looked up. Perhaps the highlight of the entire tour was an event not directly related with its actual "ancestral" purpose. This was a trip to Rome which included an audience with Pope John Paul II during this "Jubilee Year" of 2000. Once more, all who participated were deeply enriched by their opportunity to experience first hand the land and culture of their ancestors.

The 2005 heritage tour held special significance because it commemorated the 125th anniversary of the founding of Roberts Cove. It was attended by twenty-four people and led by Philip Fabacher, and it lasted from June 14 to July 1. Specific villages again were visited that held special meaning for some of the attending families. The villages toured that were especially important were Gangelt, home of the Gossens; Schwierwaldenrath where the Thevis, Zaunbrecher, and Heinen families originated; Nierstrass, the home of other Zaunbrechers; the town of Putt, where some of the Leonards came from; Hastenrath, the home of the Hensgens, Spaetgens, and Scheufens; and Braunsrath, from where the Reiners originated. In each of these villages, relatives waited to welcome and entertain their American "cousins." According to the calculations once made by Father Charles Zaunbrecher, most of these villages, being as close as they were, could fit inside the area of Roberts Cove (that area encompassed by the five bridges that would have to be crossed to get to Roberts Cove). One new area visited was the region of Hebelermeer. This part of Germany was especially important for the Berken, Cramer, Hueser, and Meyer families, for it was this region that was the home of their ancestors. They visited the town of Twist which served as the city hall of this extended area—it is spread out somewhat like Roberts Cove. Here they were welcomed and given a plaque with the name Hebelermeer inscribed on it in remembrance of their 2005 visit. The 2005 heritage tour, as all of the others, deeply impressed those

Chapter Six

who participated and left most of them with the wish that they would again return to the land of their founding fathers.[21]

In the final analysis, it might be said of these heritage tours as a whole that they have been tremendously successful enterprises that have helped the Roberts Cove community to keep alive a continuing reverence for the land and the culture of their ancestors. In that respect, they play the same role as the German Heritage Museum and the Germanfests. The continued popularity of these tours is a further tribute to the remarkable historical consciousness of these people. There seems little doubt that there will be many more of these tours to come.

The occurrences of the last twenty years are an outstanding record of achievement testifying to the great energy and spirit that resides within the extended St. Leo-Roberts Cove family. They are a group of people who do not want to forget their ancestors and the German culture which the original settlers brought with them. With the establishment of the German Heritage Museum, the annual Germanfest celebrations, and the heritage tours, they have safeguarded the legacy of their forefathers while at the same time paying tribute to their Catholic church. They have melded their loyalties to family and faith in a most successful way, since virtually all ethnic related activities are blessed by the church and take place on church grounds. There is nothing on the horizon that suggests that these loyalties will diminish. There are many signs that these bonds to their ancestors and their church will remain strong. Indeed, plans for the 2007 Germanfest are already fully underway even as these pages are being written. We can be grateful to past and present generations of the Roberts Cove family for keeping alive their connections to the past. For all of their efforts we are deeply appreciative, and we look to the future with eager anticipation.

Notes

Introduction

[1] Roberts Cove received its name from Benjamin Robert, the original owner of a Spanish land grant on Bayou Plaquemine Brulée's south side. The "cove" is formed by Bayous Wikoff and Plaquemine Brulée. This region was also referred to as "Roberts Prairie" by the early German settlers. Briefly in 1883-85, the fledgling German community was called "Hennemann" after the Benedictine priest who ministered to the religious needs of the colonists in 1883. And, finally, in the early years, Roberts Cove was also referred to as "German Cove" by the settlement's neighbors. After World War I, that name was dropped when all things German gained unpatriotic connotations. These variations of the Roberts Cove name appear on a number of manuscripts in the Fr. Charles Zaunbrecher Collection of Documents Relating to the History of Roberts Cove. Father Zaunbrecher has graciously allowed me to copy many of his manuscripts on the history of Roberts Cove.

[2] Interview with Father Charles Zaunbrecher, October 22, 1985, Milton, Louisiana; interview with Father Keith Vincent, pastor of St. Leo's Catholic Church, June 19, 1987, Roberts Cove, Louisiana.

[3] These communities are described in J. Hanno Deiler, *Louisiana, Ein Heim für deutsche Ansiedler* (New Orleans, 1895); and Louis Voss, *Louisianas Einladung an Deutsche Landwirte und Kolonisten* (New Orleans, 1907).

[4] On the strength of the German culture and institutions in New Orleans in the nineteenth century, see Robert T. Clark, "The German Liberals in New Orleans, 1840-1860," *Louisiana Historical Quarterly* 20 (1937): 137-151; Robert T. Clark, "The New Orleans German Colony in the Civil War," *Louisiana Historical Quarterly* 20 (1937): 990-1015; Robert T. Clark, "Reconstruction and the New Orleans German Colony," *Louisiana Historical Quarterly* 23 (1940): 501-524; Arthur H. Moehlenbrock, "The German Drama on the New Orleans Stage," *Louisiana Historical Quarterly* 26 (1943): 361-627; John Frederick Nau, *The German People of New Orleans, 1850-1900* (Leiden, Germany, 1958); J. Hanno Deiler, *Geschichte der New Orleanser deutschen Presse* (New Orleans, 1901); J. Hanno Deiler, *Geschichte der deutschen Gesellschaft von New Orleans* (New Orleans, 1897); and J. Hanno Deiler, *Zur Geschichte der deutschen Kirchengemeinden im Staate Louisiana* (New Orleans, 1894). The decline of these institutions is discussed in William Konrad, "The Diminishing Influence of German Culture in New Orleans Life Since 1865," *Louisiana Historical Quarterly* 24 (1941): 127-167.

[5] Stanley Joseph McCord, "A Historical and Linguistic Study of the German Settlement at Roberts Cove." (Ph. D. dissertation, Louisiana State University, 1969).

Chapter I

[1] See the booklet entitled *German Centennial, 1880-1980*, Zaunbrecher Collection. The centennial booklet cited above contains a detailed map of the Geilenkirchen area and includes the location of the towns from which the Roberts Cove colonists originated.

Notes

[2] That is the contention made in R.R. Palmer and Joel Colton, *A History of the Modern World*, 6th ed. (New York, 1984), 145.

[3] The impact of these wars on Geilenkirchen is discussed in Werner Reinartz and S. Corsten, "Von der Frankenzeit bis zur Gegenwart," *Unsere Heimat* (Geilenkirchen, Germany, 1963), 84-96. The effects of these wars on Geilenkirchen is also discussed in the lengthy greeting given by one of the city fathers to Father Charles Zaunbrecher and thirty-four Roberts Cove residents on their 1981 visit to the city of Geilenkirchen. See "Begrüssung von Josef Dahlen," in Zaunbrecher Collection.

[4] McCord, "A Historical Study of Roberts Cove," 60-61.

[5] The term means "struggle of civilizations."

[6] The precise impact of the *Kulturkampf* on overall German immigration is unclear. Fewer Catholics, as a percentage of the total number of immigrants, left Germany in the 1870s than in the 1850s, for example. See Georg Timpe, *Katholisches Deutschtum in den Vereinigten Staaten von Amerika* (Freiburg, 1937), 51-53. On the other hand, the *Kulturkampf* may have contributed to a climate of unease and suspicion in Germany and may help to account for the massive emigration of Germans in 1881-1882, when many of the "May Laws" were still in effect. In 1881-1882, over 450,000 Germans entered the United States. This is the largest number that ever left Germany in a two-year period. See Wilhelm Mönckmeier, *Die deutsche überseeische Auswanderung: Ein Beitrag zur deutschen Wanderungsgeschichte* (Jena, 1912), 18.

[7] Bill Voelker, "Kulturkampf Drove Germans to Acadia," in Zaunbrecher Collection.

[8] "The Reverend Peter Leonhard Thevis," in the Zaunbrecher Collection. See also Roger Baudier, *The Catholic Church in Louisiana* (1939; reprint ed., New Orleans, 1972), 558; and Deiler, *Deutsche Kirchengemeinden*, 68.

[9] Deiler, *Deutsche Kirchengemeinden*, 68-69.

[10] "The *Echo of New Orleans*," in Zaunbrecher Collection.

[11] *Das Echo von New Orleans*, July 31, 1870.

[12] Deiler, *Deutsche Kirchengemeinden*, 108-109.

[13] *Das Echo von New Orleans*, July 31, 1870.

[14] Ibid., May 1-September 11, 1870. Described was the community of Gretna.

[15] See "Family of Hensgens Adds Germanic Touch to Life in Acadia," Crowley *Daily Signal: Golden Anniversary Edition, 1899-1949. An Album of Acadia Parish and Neighboring Communities*, 99.

[16] Mary Alice Fontenot and Paul B. Freeland, *Acadia Parish, Louisiana: A History to 1900* (Baton Rouge, 1976), 177; William Henry Perrin, ed., *Southwest Louisiana Biographical and Historical* (New Orleans, 1891), Part I, 228-231; Deiler, *Louisiana, Ein Heim für deutsche Ansiedler*; "Joseph Fabacher's Obituary" in New Orleans *Times-Picayune*, March 4, 1897; Reinhart Kondert, "The Germans of Acadia Parish," *Louisiana Review/Revue de Louisiane* 6 (1977): 21-22; and "Fabacher Family Records and Genealogy," in Philip Fabacher Collection. Philip Fabacher of Iota (a great-

Notes

great-grandson of Joseph Fabacher) has amassed a large collection of records on his well-known ancestor and other family members and has shared some of this information with me.

[17] See newspaper article entitled "Medical Student [Philip Fabacher] Traces Family History from 16" in the Zaunbrecher Collection. A short biography of Joseph Fabacher is also found in Perrin, *Southwest Louisiana, Biographical and Historical*, Part II, 262-263.

[18] As quoted in Clark, "Reconstruction and the New Orleans German Colony," 513-514.

[19] Opelousas *St. Landry Democrat*, September 18, 1880.

[20] Two agencies interested in the fate of the Fabacher community were the Louisiana Agricultural Commission and the German Society of New Orleans. Both organizations remained in touch with the German settlement in the late nineteenth century. See William H. Harris, *Louisiana: Products, Resources and Attractions* (New Orleans, 1881); and Deiler, *Louisiana, Ein Heim für deutsche Anseidler*, 46-47.

[21] That the Fabacher Colony seems to have lost its identity rather quickly is attested to by the numerous name changes that the colony experienced. After Joseph Fabacher returned to New Orleans in 1879, the community became known as Trilby. Then in 1905 the colony became known as Gassler, a name it received from Reverend Francis Gassler, the settlement's priest. In 1926, after a disastrous fire destroyed the church at Gassler, the center of the settlement was shifted to Mowata where a new church was constructed. This site tended to become the headquarters for a group of German Protestants who settled in that area in the early twentieth century (the Loewers, for example). Another offshoot of the Fabacher settlement was the Catholic community of Frey which received its name from the numerous members of that family who settled there and which was located near the original Fabacher settlement. Today that area is also known as Ritchie. The Freys, as we have seen, developed close connections with the Roberts Cove settlement and intermarried readily with the Germans of that community. See Kondert, "The Germans of Acadia Parish," 24; and Charles Zaunbrecher, "German Colonists of Roberts Cove, Louisiana: Their Ancestors, Children and Grandchildren," Zaunbrecher Collection.

[22] Baudier, *The Catholic Church in Louisiana*, 658. The following reason is given by Baudier for Father Thevis' decision to build a shrine to St. Roch: "Seeing with dismay the toll of death in the city, Father Thevis prayed to St. Roch to intercede for the congregation among whom he labored. He promised St. Roch that if the congregations were spared he would construct a shrine in honor of the saint with his own hands. Though many in Holy Trinity were stricken, there was not one death, according to Father Thevis."

[23] There is conflicting evidence as to when these two Germans actually left for the United States. The "Recollections of William Gossen and Gertrude Thevis Klein," 1954, give the dates of 1876 and 1877. Father Zaunbrecher, on the other hand, believes the two Germans left in 1878. The latter date seems the most probable since it coincides with the outbreak of a yellow fever epidemic in New Orleans. The two visiting Germans apparently stayed with relatives in Milwaukee. See Zaunbrecher Collection; McCord, "A Historical Study of Roberts Cove," 66-67; and T.E. Kaiser, "Yellow Fever in 19th Century New Orleans." (M.A. thesis, Tulane University, 1941), 33.

[24] Velma Lea Hair, "The History of Crowley, Louisiana," *Louisiana Historical Quarterly* 27 (1944): 1173-1175. Some of the land around Roberts Cove belonged to an enterprising realtor, W.W. Du-

Notes

son and to his father-in-law, Paul Manouvrier. The latter sold 640 acres to Father Aegidius Hennemann. This land made up the bulk of the holdings for St. Leo's Church. Other property, as well, was later sold by Manouvrier to the German colonists. See "Notes About St. Leo," Zaunbrecher Collection.

[25] The visiting Germans were amazed at Louisiana's unusually mild winter climate. January 13, 1880, was unseasonably warm, and, according to a popular story still told today, Herman Grein turned to Gerhard Thevis and asked: "What have we gotten into? If it's this hot in January, what will it be like in July?" In his native German, he might have said something like this: *"wie sind wir hier hineingeraten? Wenn es hier so heiss im Januar ist, wie wird es erst im Juli sein?"* This story appeared most recently in the "German Centennial Newsletter No. 1," Zaunbrecher Collection.

[26] There is confusion whether there were two or perhaps three Germans present at Roberts Cove in this initial visit. By one account, a third person, Peter Thevis, was present at the original visit. See "German Centennial Newsletter No. 1," for the first version and "Notes about St. Leo," for the second. Both manuscripts are found in the Zaunbrecher Collection.

[27] See "Recollections of Gertrude Thevis Klein and William Gossen;" "Notes about St. Leo;" and "German Centennial Newsletter, No. 1," all located in the Zaunbrecher Collection. See also McCord, "A Historical Study of Roberts Cove," 70.

[28] McCord, "A Historical Study of Roberts Cove," 70-71, 264.

[29] United States Customs Bureau, "Passenger Lists of Vessels Arriving in New Orleans, 1820-1902," Microfilm Reel No. 63, Special Collections Louisiana Room, Edith Garland Dupré Library, University of Louisiana at Lafayette, Lafayette, LA.

[30] "History of St. Leo," Zaunbrecher Collection.

[31] "Reminiscences of William Gossen," as printed in the Crowley *Daily Signal, Golden Anniversary Edition,* September 1, 1949, 111.

[32] "Die Deutsche Katolische Colonie St. Leo bei Rayne, Parish Acadia," Zaunbrecher Collection; "Letter to Descendants of the Original Passengers of the *S.S. Mississippi,*" November 7, 1981, ibid.; and United States Customs Bureau, "Passenger Lists of Vessels Arriving in New Orleans, 1820-1902," Microfilm Reel No. 64, Special Collections Louisiana Room, Edith Garland Dupré Library, University of Louisiana at Lafayette, LA.

[33] Letter from Father Charles Zaunbrecher to author, May 11, 1977.

[34] "History of St. Leo," Zaunbrecher Collection.

[35] One of the biggest hardships during the crossing was the unpalatable food offered onboard. This did not become a serious problem until the immigrants exhausted their own food supplies. One of the favorite "simple meals" that the colonists consumed during the crossing was their own homemade black bread spread with lard. Mrs. Jacob Thevis was most seriously inconvenienced when the black bread gave out because she "could not digest the bread the ship furnished." This information is gathered from the "Recollections of Gertrude Thevis Klein and William Gossen," 1954,

Notes

Zaunbrecher Collection. See also Hermann-Josef Lentzen, "35 Amerikaner auf den Spuren ihrer Ahnen: Schmalz, Apfelmus und Scharzbrot Serviert," June 27, 1981, newspaper article in ibid.

[36] "Recollections of Gertrude Thevis Klein and William Gossen," 1954, Zaunbrecher Collection.

[37] Ibid. See also McCord, "A Historical Study of Roberts Cove," 79.

[38] McCord, "A Historical Study of Roberts Cove," 79-80.

[39] "German Centennial Newsletter," Nos. 1 and 2, Zaunbrecher Collection.

[40] McCord, "A Historical Study of Roberts Cove," 81-83; Rayne *Tribune*, March 2, 1929; Deiler, *Deutsche Kirchengemeinden*, 124.

Chapter II

[1] Florence Boudreaux, "German Customs Still Retained in Roberts Cove," *Attakapas Gazette* 3 (1968): 16.

[2] Reinhart Kondert, "Les Allemands en Louisiane de 1721 à 1732," *Revue d'Histoire de l'Amérique française* 33 (1979): 51-65.

[3] Mildred K. Ginn, "A History of Rice Production in Louisiana to 1896," *Louisiana Historical Quarterly* 23 (1940): 550-563. In reminiscences published in the Crowley *Daily Signal* in 1949, William Joseph Gossen credited the Abbot brothers with making important advances in rice production. The brothers referred to were Miron, Martin, and Lafe. See Crowley *Daily Signal, Golden Anniversary Edition*, 111.

[4] Crowley *Daily Signal, Golden Anniversary Edition*, 111.

[5] Ibid.; McCord, "A Historical Study of Roberts Cove," 88-90; Rayne *Signal*, August 28, 1886. Nicholas Zaunbrecher was also given credit for using the first binder and steam powered thresher in his area, but that assertion proved false. See Gin, "History of Rice Production," 560; and Eunice *News*, August 26, 1965. Nevertheless, Nicholas Zaunbrecher was one of the first farmers in Southwest Louisiana to use a steam-powered thresher and was given credit by local newspapers for being one of the region's most enterprising rice growers. See Rayne *Signal*, August 7, September 25, and October 9, 1886. Joseph Fabacher, it will be recalled, was also credited with agricultural innovations. About a decade before Nicholas Zaunbrecher was displaying his ingenuity in rice farming, Fabacher was introducing oxen-powered threshers in his community.

[6] Crowley *Daily Signal*, February 10, 1900; and McCord, "A Historical Study of Roberts Cove," 90-91.

[7] Ginn, "History of Rice Production," 562; and McCord, "A Historical Study of Roberts Cove," 92.

[8] McCord, "A Historical Study of Roberts Cove," 92-93.

Notes

⁹ Ibid., 94-96.

¹⁰ Ginn, "History of Rice Production," 567.

¹¹ McCord, "A Historical Study of Roberts Cove," 96-97, 265-271.

¹² Ibid., 97-98; W.W. Duson, *Deutsche Landwirte von Südwest Louisiana* (Crowley, LA., 1907), 3-5.

¹³ Duson, *Deutsche Landwirte*, 3-7

¹⁴ Ibid.

¹⁵ *Der Südliche Pionieer*, May 31, 1893. This paper was founded by Hugo Lehmann in 1893. It discontinued publication after only one issue. It had come into existence through the financial support of W.W. Duson and his brother C.C. Duson. The first and only issue dealt with Acadia Parish and the German colony of Roberts Cove. After the Duson brothers withdrew their backing, Lehmann turned to the German Society of New Orleans for financial assistance. It offered some aid but not enough for the paper to remain in existence. Lehmann appears to have been an incompetent businessman and journalist. See Deiler, *Die New Orleanser Deutsche Presse*, 38; and Konrad, "The Diminishing Influence of the German Culture in New Orleans," 133.

¹⁶ *Der Südliche Pionieer*, May 31, 1893. In reference to Scheuffens' good health, the newspaper remarked that had he "remained in Germany he would no longer be over there but up there" (heaven?).

¹⁷ Reinhart Kondert, "The New Orleans German Society, 1847-1927" (paper read before the Southwestern Social Science Association, Fort Worth, TX, March 23, 1984). See also, Deiler, *Geschichte der deutschen Gesellschaft von New Orleans*; and Louis Voss, *History of the German Society of New Orleans* (New Orleans, 1927).

¹⁸ Deiler, *Louisiana, Ein Heim fur deutsche Ansiedler*, 44.

¹⁹ McCord, "A Historical Study of Roberts Cove," 119; and "German Centennial Newsletter No. 1," Zaunbrecher Collection.

²⁰ The size of the Roberts Cove settlement was estimated at 160 inhabitants in 1895. See Deiler, *Louisiana, Ein Heim fur deutsche Ansiedler*, 44.

²¹ They even helped to move the church building from Poupeville to Rayne a few months after they arrived. "Recollections of Gertrude Thevis Klein and William Gossen," Zaunbrecher Collection.

²² Baudier, *The Catholic Church in Louisiana*, 448.

²³ Deiler, *Deutsche Kirchengemeinde*, 128-129.

²⁴ "Notes About St. Leo," Zaunbrecher Collection; Albert Kleber, *History of St. Meinard Archabbey, 1854-1954* (St. Meinard, IN, 1954), 343; and Baudier, *The Catholic Church in Louisiana*, 452.

²⁵ Deiler, *Deutsche Kirchengemeinden*, 128-129.

Notes

[26] Kleber, *History of St. Meinard*, 452.

[27] Ibid., 360-361. See also *Ozone Pelican*, January, 1908, 3, No. 1, in Zaunbrecher Collection.

[28] Kleber, *History of St. Meinard*, 344-345.

[29] "Life of St. Leo IV," Zaunbrecher Collection; and Interview with Father Charles Zaunbrecher, January 3, 1983.

[30] Mary Alice Fontenot, "German Settlement Is 100 Years Old," Zaunbrecher Collection; McCord, "A Historical Study of Roberts Cove," 110-111; and Boudreaux, "German Customs Still Retained in Roberts Cove," 16.

[31] Interview with Father Charles Zaunbrecher, May 11, 1977.

[32] "Recollections of Gertrude Thevis Klein and William Gossen," Zaunbrecher Collection.

[33] McCord, "A Historical Study of Roberts Cove," 111-112.

[34] Kleber, *History of St. Meinard*, 345.

[35] Ibid., 361-364; and McCord, "A Historical Study of Roberts Cove," 112-113.

[36] McCord, "A Historical Study of Roberts Cove," 113-114.

[37] Ibid., 114-115. See also "History of St. Joseph's Catholic Church," Zaunbrecher Collection.

[38] Ibid., 115-116; and "Specifications and Contract of St. Leo's Church, November 8, 1893," Zaunbrecher Collection.

[39] McCord, "A Historical Study of Roberts Cove," 116-118.

Chapter III

[1] McCord, "A Historical Study of Roberts Cove," 100-101.

[2] "Reminiscences of William Joseph Gossen," Crowley *Daily Signal, Golden Anniversary Edition*, 111. Gossen was seventy-eight years old at the time of his interview in 1949. Renaturalized, along with William Gossen, were Henry Zaunbrecher, William Heinen, Doris Heinen, and others.

[3] Crowley *Daily Signal*, January 30, 1904.

[4] Ibid., April 1, 1908.

[5] Ibid., May 16, 1908.

[6] Ibid., April 13, 1912.

Notes

[7] McCord, "A Historical Study of Roberts Cove," 126. Politics has exerted its fascination on some of the descendants of Roberts Cove into more recent times. William Gossen was mayor of Rayne from 1950 to 1958 and from 1962 until his death in 1974. Joseph Gielen served as mayor of Crowley from 1954 to 1978. This information was gained in telephone conversations with the mayors' offices of Rayne and Crowley on December 14, 1976, and November 30, 1984.

[8] Crowley *Daily Signal*, February 5, 1916. Zaunbrecher ran in the Democratic primary and was the second highest vote-getter in a field of four candidates. Since there were two vacancies, he gained the right to one of the two contested seats. Out of a total of 6,282 votes cast, Zaunbrecher received 1,713. Those knowledgeable about Louisiana politics, or Southern politics for that matter, recognize that the winner in a Democratic primary automatically won his position by virtue of the weakness of the Republican party.

[9] Dave H. Brown, *A History of Who's Who in Louisiana Politics in 1916* (New Orleans, 1916), 81-82.

[10] McCord, "A Historical Study of Roberts Cove," 128-129.

[11] Father Charles Zaunbrecher proudly announced that the Centennial Celebration had been a "56-keg celebration." He went on to declare that the money spent for the beer "could have bought 800 acres of land in 1880." See "German Centennial Newsletter No. 3," Zaunbrecher Collection.

[12] Crowley *Daily Signal*, May 28, 1910. In the same year, the voters of Acadia Parish repealed prohibition by a slim margin of 70 votes out of a total of 2,200. At the Roberts Cove ward, the results were lopsidedly in favor of the repeal of prohibition. There the vote was 39 to 4 to abolish prohibition. See ibid., November 12, 1910.

[13] William Heinen introduced some of the first registered bulls into Acadia Parish. He must be considered one of the pioneers of the cattle industry in his region. See McCord, "A Historical Study of Roberts Cove," 137.

[14] Some of the Germans of Roberts Cove feared that the abundant rice harvests and the attendant depressed prices that resulted would drive many Americans out of the rice culture altogether. This was the feeling of Joseph Heinen, for example. See ibid.

[15] Crowley *Daily Signal*, May 21, 1910, and November 5, 1910.

[16] Ibid., March 3, 1907, July 13, 1912, and March 16, 1912. See also McCord, "Historical Study of Roberts Cove," 138-139.

[17] An English translation of Duson's pamphlet is found in the Zaunbrecher Collection.

[18] W.W. Duson and Bro., *German Farmers of Southwest Louisiana*, Zaunbrecher Collection.

[19] Ibid.

[20] Ibid.

[21] Ibid.

Notes

[22] McCord, "A Historical Study of Roberts Cove," 135.

[23] Duson, *German Farmers of Southwest Louisiana*, Zaunbrecher Collection.

[24] Ibid.

[25] Ibid.

[26] For example, see the following pamphlets by Charles Schuler published by the Louisiana Agriculture and Immigration Bureau in 1907: *Ackerbau Gelegenheiten in Tangipahoa Parish, Louisiana; Karte von Louisiana; Schweinezucht in Louisiana; Tensas Parish im Staate Louisiana;* and *Ouachita Parish im Staate Louisiana: Was die Gegend den deutschen Ansiedlern bietet*. For a more thorough discussion of Louisiana's efforts to attract immigrants earlier in the nineteenth century, see E. Russ Williams, "Louisiana's Public and Private Immigration Endeavors, 1866-1893," *Louisiana History* 15 (1974): 153-173.

[27] Louis Voss, *Louisianas Einladung an Deutsche Landwirte und Kolonisten* (New Orleans, 1907), 20.

[28] In a later book, Voss enumerated the Germans who arrived in Louisiana as a result of the advertising efforts of 1907. See Louis Voss, *History of the German Society of New Orleans: With an Introduction Giving a Synopsis of the History of the Germans of the United States, with Special Reference to Those in Louisiana* (New Orleans, 1927), 70-72.

[29] Crowley *Daily Signal*, February 24, 1907; and McCord, "A Historical Study of Roberts Cove," 132.

[30] McCord, "A Historical Study of Roberts Cove," 132. John Bischoff is not mentioned in Father Zaunbrecher's exhaustive genealogical study of the settlers of Roberts Cove. See Charles Zaunbrecher, "German Colonists of Roberts Cove, Louisiana," Zaunbrecher Collection.

[31] "History of St. Joseph's Catholic Church," and "Some Pastors of St. Leo," Zaunbrecher Collection. See also Baudier, *The Catholic Church in Louisiana*, 549. Father Zarn, according to Father Keith Vincent, the present pastor of St. Leo's, was related to the Neu family. Several members of this family became Benedictine sisters.

[32] At least eleven priests have come from the original thirty-one families: Daniel Thevis, Aloysius Olinger, Clement Habetz, Daniel Habetz, Carl Schutten, William Ohlenforst, Charles Zaunbrecher, Ronald Bollich, Gerard Young, Martin Leonards, and Michael Schatzle. The first five are deceased. See "German Centennial Newsletter No. 1," Zaunbrecher Collection.

[33] McCord, "A Historical Study of Roberts Cove," 124-125.

[34] Crowley *Daily Signal*, August 24, 1901.

[35] Ibid., May 30, 1914.

[36] McCord, "A Historical Study of Roberts Cove," 140.

[37] Crowley *Daily Signal*, June 1, 1900.

Notes

[38] Ibid., January 23, 1930; McCord, "A Historical Study of Roberts Cove," 142.

[39] Crowley *Daily Signal*, April 8, 1899.

[40] Ibid., June 23, 1900.

[41] Ibid., November 27, 1909.

[42] Ibid., January 1, 1910.

[43] Ibid.

[44] McCord, "A Historical Study of Roberts Cove," 143-144.

[45] Crowley *Daily Signal*, February 25, 1910.

[46] Ibid.

[47] Ibid., September 26, October 3, 1914.

[48] Ibid., October 10, 1914.

[49] Ibid.

[50] Ibid., July 22, 1916.

[51] Ibid., January 16, 1915.

[52] Ibid., December 18, 1915.

[53] Ibid., June 24, July 4, 1916.

[54] Ibid., November 16, 1916; McCord, "A Historical Study of Roberts Cove," 147-148.

Chapter IV

[1] A good discussion of World War I and its impact on the German people and culture in the United States is found in Frederick C. Luebke, *Bonds of Loyalty: German-Americans and World War One* (Dekalb, IL., 1974); and Carl Wittke, *German-Americans and the World War* (Columbus, 1936).

[2] Crowley *Daily Signal*, March 17, 1917.

[3] Ibid., April 14, 1917.

[4] Ibid.

[5] Ibid.

Notes

[6] Ibid.

[7] Ibid., April 7, 1917.

[8] Ibid., March 2, 1918. See also McCord, "A Historical Study of Roberts Cove," 153-154.

[9] McCord, "A Historical Study of Roberts Cove," 154.

[10] Interview with N.J. Gossen, December 7, 1977, Rayne, Louisiana.

[11] Interview with Father Charles Zaunbrecher, April 14, 1975, Lafayette, Louisiana.

[12] Ibid. See also Crowley *Daily Signal*, July 13, 1918; and McCord, "A Historical Study of Roberts Cove," 154-155.

[13] Crowley *Daily Signal*, June 29, 1918.

[14] Luebke, *Bonds of Loyalty*; and Wittke, *German-Americans and the World War*.

[15] Luebke, *Bonds of Loyalty*, 252. See also U.S. Army, Office of Judge Advocate General, *Compilaton of War Laws of the Various States and Insular Possessions* (Washington, D.C., 1919), 45. For the impact of these laws and the anti-German attitudes on Louisiana's schools, see Jean M. Palmer, "The Impact of World War One on Louisiana's Schools and Community Life," *Louisiana History* 7 (1966): 323-331.

[16] It is possible that the legislature perceived the Germans as being more numerous and thus a greater threat than they actually were.

[17] Interview with Father Charles Zaunbrecher; and McCord, "A Historical Study of Roberts Cove," 151.

[18] State of Louisiana, *Official Journal of the House of Representatives, 1st Extra Session, 1917* (Baton Rouge, 1917), 43.

[19] Ibid., 37.

[20] State of Louisiana, *2nd Regular Session, 1918*, 336.

[21] Ibid., 802-803.

[22] Ibid., 872-873.

[23] *U.S. Bureau of the Census: Statistics for Louisiana: Thirteenth Census of the United States Taken in the Year 1910* (Washington, D.C., 1916), 583, 588.

[24] Interview with N.J. Gossen.

[25] Ibid. See also Crowley *Daily Signal*, August 9, 1919.

Notes

[26] McCord, "A Historical Study of Roberts Cove," 156-157; and Crowley *Daily Signal*, November 30, 1919.

[27] Crowley *Daily Signal*, November 15, 1919.

[28] Interview with Father Charles Zaunbrecher; and McCord, "A Historical Study of Roberts Cove," 158.

[29] Crowley *Daily Signal*, March 18, 1922.

[30] Ibid., May 13, 1922.

[31] McCord, "A Historical Study of Roberts Cove," 159. Father Vincent reports that private instruction of German continued beyond the 1920s. Sister Crescentia of the Cove taught Cecile Zaunbrecher High German as late as 1930.

[32] Ibid., 159-160.

[33] Ibid., 160-161; and "Some Pastors of St. Leo," Zaunbrecher Collection.

[34] Albert Kleber, *History of St. Meinard Archabbey, 1854-1954* (St. Meinard, Ind., 1954), 392; and "Some Pastors of St. Leo," Zaunbrecher Collection. According to Father Vincent, all five of St. Leo's priests from 1930 to 1976 spoke German.

[35] Ellis Arthur Davis, ed., *The Historical Encyclopedia of Louisiana* (Baton Rouge, 1940), 896-1275.

[36] McCord, "A Historical Study of Roberts Cove," 162-163.

[37] Ibid., 163.

[38] In the early years of the Roberts Cove community it was almost unthinkable to marry someone from outside the community. On rare occasions when that occurred the couples involved were frequently ostracized by the other German settlers. Joseph Dischler apparently suffered severe criticism for marrying a French girl. Another early inhabitant of the settlement indicated that there was also considerable pressure placed on the young people against dating non-Catholics. See Florence Boudreaux's paper on customs, Zaunbrecher Collection.

[39] McCord, "A Historical Study of Roberts Cove," 164.

Notes

Chapter V

[1] See "1976 Supplement to the Zaunbrecher Family Tree," Zaunbrecher Collection. Father Vincent contends that an important thread of continuity in keeping alive the Cove's German culture in the 1930s and 1940s was H. Leo Habetz, Sr.'s frequent trips to Germany, as well as the several visits by some of the Cove's children to Germany after World War II.

[2] "1982 Edition: Hensgens Family Tree," Zaunbrecher Collection.

[3] Some of the newspapers which advertised the Roberts Cove Centennial were: Lafayette *Daily Advertiser*, September 28, 30, 1980; Baton Rouge *Morning Advocate*, August 25, 30, and September 28, 1980; Rayne *Acadian Tribune*, September 11, 28, and October 2, 1980. All of these articles are found in the Zaunbrecher Collection. A collection of records on the Roberts Cove German Centennial is also found in the Archives of the Diocese of Lafayette. The diocesan archives has been designated as the main repository of all records pertaining to the Centennial.

[4] "German Centennial Newsletters, Nos. 1, 2, and 3;" "Principal Celebrants of the Centennial Eucharist;" Rayne *Free Press*, October 5, 1980; *Morning Star*, October 16, 1980; Rayne *Independent*, October 9, 1980; Rayne *Acadian Tribune*, October 9, 12, 16, 1980; Lafayette *Daily Advertiser*, October 6, 1980; and Crowley *Daily Signal*, October 6, 1980. The foregoing newspaper references are but a few of the clippings in the Zaunbrecher Collection and the Archives of the Diocese of Lafayette.

[5] These are my own recollections of that day's events. See also Interview with Father Charles Zaunbrecher, October 5, 1980, and January 3, 1983.

[6] Interview with Father Charles Zaunbrecher, April 14, 1975, and January 3, 1983. See also "Fr. Zaunbrecher Sets Anniversary Fete;" and "Some Pastors of St. Leo," both in Zaunbrecher Collection. Father Vincent has suggested that Clara Habetz and the St. Leo's Choir have played a more important role in cultural retention than previously thought. The role played by Clara Habetz is especially important. Recently, on March 22, 1987, the choir celebrated its centennial by issuing a new edition of German hymns, thus assuring continuity in the Cove's Germanic hymnal traditions.

[7] Interview with Father Charles Zaunbrecher, January 3, 1983.

[8] See, for example, "Experiences of St. Nicholas' Visit Recounted by Fr. Charles Zaunbrecher," Sunday Rayne *Acadian Tribune*, December 8, 1974, Zaunbrecher Collection, and a number of additional articles that have appeared in the Catholic newspaper, the *Morning Star*, found in the Archives of the Diocese of Lafayette.

[9] The most complete compilation was issued in honor of the Roberts Cove Centennial. It is a thirty-nine page booklet entitled "German Colonists of Roberts Cove, Louisiana: Their Ancestors, Children and Grandchildren (A Project of the German Centennial of Roberts Cove—1880-1980)," Zaunbrecher Collection.

[10] Interview with Father Charles Zaunbrecher, January 3, 1983; and "German Centennial Newsletter, No. 2," Zaunbrecher Collection.

Notes

[11] Josef Dahlen, "Begrüssung an Pater Zaunbrecher und Gäste," June 1981, Geilenkirchen, Zaunbrecher Collection.

[12] While in Germany, Father Zaunbrecher and his fellow visitors traveled to the city of Cologne to gather information from the genealogical archives museum located there. Here, also, they received an official welcome from the director of the museum. See "Begrüssung von Grete Esserheim," June 27, 1981, Köln; and Hermann-Josef Lentzen, "35 Amerikaner auf den Spuren ihrer Ahnen: Schmalz, Apfelmus und Schwarzbrot Serviert," June 27, 1981, both of which are in the Zaunbrecher Collection.

[13] McCord, "A Historical Study of Roberts Cove," 165.

[14] A number of relatives and friends from Germany were present at the Centennial celebration, for example.

[15] McCord, "A Historical Study of Roberts Cove," 167-168; and "German Hymns Sung at Roberts Cove," Zaunbrecher Collection.

[16] Boudreaux, "German Customs Still Retained in Roberts Cove," 16.

[17] Ibid., 16-17. See also Kathleen Toups, "St. Nickolas Visits Roberts Cove," *Morning Star*, December 22, 1982; Charles Zaunbrecher, "In Roberts Cove: A Special Celebration," *Morning Star*; and Eva Vincent, "St. Nickolas Visits Roberts Cove." The three foregoing news articles are in the Zaunbrecher Collection.

[18] Father Zaunbrecher reported that when he was a child, the younger children often received whippings from the older ones during the St. Nickolas Day celebration. Apparently, this type of roughhousing sometimes got out of hand and was for that reason discontinued as part of the St. Nickolas Day festivities. According to Father Vincent, it was Father Wolbers (1952-1955) who brought a solemn character to the St. Nicholas celebration. See also "Experiences of St. Nickolas' Visit Recounted by Fr. Charles Zaunbrecher," Zaunbrecher Collection.

[19] Boudreaux, "German Customs Still Retained in Roberts Cove," 17-18; McCord, "A Historical Study of Roberts Cove," 168.

[20] Interview with Professor Matthew Schott, May 21, 1984, Lafayette. Dr. Schott was the organizer of this unusual visit by the German prisoners-of-war and plans to publish a history of the entire Louisiana experience of the Germans, both as prisoners-of-war and as subsequent visitors.

[21] Bishop Gerard Frey to St. Leo Church, June 20, 1985, St. Leo's Church Archives, Roberts Cove, LA.

[22] Keith L. Vincent, *A Century of Catholic Life, 1885-1985: St. Leo IV Catholic Church, Roberts Cove, Louisiana, St. Leo IV Day 17 July 1985*, ibid. The St. Leo IV parish at Roberts Cove is the only one with that name in the world, according to Father Vincent and Father Zaunbrecher.

[23] "St. Leo IV Parish, Roberts Cove, Louisiana: 1987 Parish Census," Ibid.; interview with Father Keith Vincent, June 19, 1987, Roberts Cove, LA.

Notes

Chapter VI

[1] Father Keith Vincent, letter, November 1, 1987, in "First Year Report St. Leo's Church of Roberts Cove Hospitality Building Fund," St. Leo IV Church Archives, made available to the author by Mary Ann "Rusty" Leonards. (hereinafter cited as Church Archives).

[2] Father Francis Bourgeois, letter, March 27, 1995, ibid.

[3] Lisa Soileaux, "Groundbreaking Ceremonies are held in St. Leo Church Annex Addition," Rayne *Acadian Tribune*, March 9, 1995.

[4] Dawn Ohlenforst, "A new 'form' of worship," Rayne *Acadian Tribune*, July 18, 1996; *Acadiana Catholic*, August 1996.

[5] Paul Kedinger, "Dream becomes reality," Rayne *Acadian Tribune, Eighth Germanfest Souvenir Edition*, October 3, 2002; and Paul Kedinger, "German Heritage Museum in planning stage," Rayne *Acadian Tribune, Fifth Germanfest Souvenir Edition*, September 30, 1999.

[6] Paul Kedinger, "German Heritage Museum in Works," Rayne *Acadian Tribune, Visitors & Tourist Guide*, March 21, 2002; and Paul Kedinger, "German Heritage Museum Opens," Rayne *Acadian Tribune*, September 9, 2002.

[7] Ibid.; and Kedinger, "Dream becomes reality," Rayne *Acadian Tribune, Eighth Germanfest Souvenir Edition*, October 3, 2002.

[8] Ibid. See also Rayne *Acadian Tribune, Eleventh Germanfest Souvenir Edition*, September 29, 2005, which reported on the installation of a large and beautiful new sign that was placed in front of the museum to better advertise its location.

[9] Rayne *Acadian Tribune, Eighth Germanfest Souvenir Edition*, October 3, 2002. See also Rayne *Acadian Tribune, Visitors & Tourist Guide*, April 26, 2007, which ran a special feature on the German Heritage Museum and work that these two ladies have done on behalf of this museum and the culture of Roberts Cove's Germans. Also, one should not overlook the significance of the support staff, such as Sherry Rimmer and Shirley Leonards, who help make this museum such a smoothly functioning facility.

[10] The Rayne *Independent, Germanfest Edition*, September 28, 1995; and Rayne *Acadian Tribune, First Roberts Cove Germanfest Edition*, September 28, 1995. See also "Germanfest: a capsule history," Rayne *Acadian Tribune, Second Roberts Cove Germanfest Souvenir Edition*, October 3, 1996; and "In Memory of Miss Clara," Rayne *Acadian Tribune, Twelfth Germanfest Souvenir Edition*, October 5, 2006. The number of people involved in staging a Germanfest is legion. Louis Cramer, president of the Germanfest Association, in his public invitation to potential visitors to the fourth Germanfest in 1998, declared that "some 600 volunteers...work to stage" this event.

[11] Rayne *Acadian Tribune, Fourth Germanfest Souvenir Edition*, October 1, 1998; and The Rayne *Independent, Germanfest Edition*, September 28, 1995. Not all Germanfests have been unqualified successes. Unrelenting rains in the 1996 Germanfest reduced attendance considerably, but not the enthusiasm of those who did attend, according to Dawn Ohlenforst, the managing editor of the Rayne *Acadian Tribune*. See her article "Germanfest declared success," in the October 10,

Notes

1996, issue of that newspaper. The eighth Germanfest planned for the year 2002 had to be cancelled altogether because of Hurricane Lili, which struck on October 3, just a few days before that year's celebration was to have taken place.

[12] Rayne *Acadian Tribune, Twelfth Germanfest Souvenir Edition,* October 3, 2006.

[13] Rayne *Acadian Tribune,* October 10, 1996. His death was announced on June 20 and a complete obituary came out on June 27 in the same paper.

[14] Ibid.

[15] Rayne *Acadian Tribune, Second Roberts Cove Germanfest Souvenir Edition,* October 3, 1996.

[16] "Funeral for Clara Habetz set Thursday," Rayne *Acadian Tribune,* October 24, 2006; and "In Memory of Clara Habetz," in Rayne *Acadian Tribune, Twelfth Germanfest Souvenir Edition,* October 5, 2006.

[17] See "Famed Chapel Rededicated," Rayne *Acadian Tribune,* July 22, 2004; and "Blessing and Re-Dedication of *Wallfahrtskappelle,*" Church Archives.

[18] Paul Kedinger, "Congregation rebuilds prize chapel destroyed by Hurricane Lili, Rayne *Acadian Tribune, Ninth Germanfest Souvenir Edition,* October 3, 2003.

[19] "50th Anniversary Celebration St. Leo IV Church," The Rayne *Independent,* July 20, 2006; and "Roberts Cove Church reaches milestone: St Leo IV parishioners to mark Fiftieth year of consecration Sunday, July 16," in Rayne *Acadian Tribune,* July 3, 2006.

[20] Philip Fabacher has had a long-standing interest in history and genealogy. Over twenty years ago he provided me with many important details on the history of the Fabacher and other families. This information was incorporated into my original book on the history of the Germans of Roberts Cove and helped make it a better publication. I am still indebted to Dr. Fabacher for his unselfish support of my research those many years ago. I thank him for the support he provided me in the past, and I laud him for the responsibilities he has taken on as an organizer of the "German Heritage Tours," as well as his involvement in other Roberts Cove endeavors.

[21] All of the heritage tours are discussed at length in the special edition of The Rayne *Independent* that was prepared for the 2006 Germanfest. See The Rayne *Independent, Germanfest Edition,* October 5, 2006. Included in the articles describing these tours are first-hand recollections of tour participants, itineraries, and lists of the travelers.

Appendices

*Genealogical Materials
Furnished by*

Lawrence and Mary Cramer

Chronology of Settlement in Roberts Cove

Appendix I

A. *Roberts Cove colonists listed according to places of origin in Germany:*

1. State of North Rhine-Westphalia (formerly called "Rhineland"), in the area around the towns of Gangelt and Geilenkirchen: Achten, Gielen, Gossen, Grein, Habetz, Heinen, Hensgens, Jacobs, Janssen, Knipping, Leonards, Ohlenforst, Reiners, Ronkartz, Schaffhausen, Scheufens, Schlicher, Spaetgens, Stamm(?), Theunissen, Thevis, Vondenstein, Wirtz, Zaunbrecher.

2. State of Lower Saxony, in the area around the towns of Meppen and Hebelermeer: Berken, Bunt, Cramer, Huesers, Meyer.

3. Elsewhere in Germany: Dischler (Wolxheim, Alsace); Jabusch (through New York, from East Prussia[?]); Moeder (through Milwaukee, from Bavaria?); Neu (through Indiana from near Switzerland); Olinger (through Indiana from near Luxembourg); Schatzle (through Indiana from ?).

B. *Chronology of Settlement in Roberts Cove:*

January 13, 1880: Gerhard Thevis (single), **founding father**; Herman Grein (single), **founding father.**

Later, 1880: Peter Thevis (single, later returned to Germany). Peter Thevis, Gerhard Thevis, and Herman Grein had earlier gone to Milwaukee in the mid-1860s.

Early 1881: Heinrich Achten (with family); August Leonards (single, later returned to Germany), Joseph Vondenstein (with family).

November 17, 1881: This group arrived in New Orleans aboard the *S. S. Mississippi*. Families are listed according to the age of the head of family, eldest to youngest: Peter Gossen (with family); Johann Gielen (with family); Jacob Thevis (with family; son Gerhard already here); Christian Hensgens (with family); Franz Reiners (with family); Nicholas Zaunbrecher (with family); Hubert Wirtz (with family); Lambert Schlicher (with family); Johann Schlicher (single); Joseph Leonards (single, came as part of the Zaunbrecher family).

1882: Hubert Theunissen (with family); Theodor Scheufens (with family); Joseph Heinen (with family, except daughter Maria); Peter Heinen (single);

Chronology of Settlement in Roberts Cove

Johann Ronkartz (single); Joseph Spaetgens (single); Arnold Jacobs (single).

September 5, 1885: Dr. Henry Leonards (single; graduated from Heidelberg University, June 1885. Moved to Texas, September 1887).

1886-1887: Xavier Dischler (with family, in stages).

1888: Wilhelm Ohlenforst (with family); Theodor Ohlenforst (single). (Both came earlier to Milwaukee, in the early 1860s).

1890: Maria Heinen (came to join family).

1892: Leo Habetz (single); Joseph Schaffhausen (single); Joseph Knipping (with family).

1894: Joseph Habetz (single); Elizabeth Habetz (single); August Habetz (single); Henry Habetz (single); Joseph Janssen (single); Herman Berken (with family; went earlier to Lafayette in 1892); Bernard Meyer (single; went earlier to Lafayette, 1892); Gerhard Bunt (single; went earlier to Lafayette, 1887); Robert Jabusch (with family; went earlier to New York in ?).

1896: Heinrich Habetz (father of family already here); and son Wilhelm Habetz (single); Ferdinand Stamm (with family; went earlier to Milwaukee); Heinrich Huesers (with family; went to Lafayette in 1892).

1897: Rosa Neu (single; came to be housekeeper for her uncle, Father Placidus Zarn, pastor of St. Leo).

1902: Herman Cramer (with family; went earlier to Lafayette in 1884 and to Mowata in 1895).

1906: Joseph Neu (single; came to join sister Rosa).

1908: Ferdinand Olinger (with family; went earlier to Indiana); Florenz Schatzle (with family; went earlier to Indiana).

1910: Jacob Neu (with wife; joined part of family already at Roberts Cove; went earlier to Indiana); Anna Neu (single; accompanied her brother Jacob Neu).

Ca. 1910: Joseph Moeder (single; went earlier to Milwaukee).

Appendix II

Alphabetical Listing of Colonists' Families

The following individuals were the original immigrants that settled in the community of Roberts Cove between the years 1880 to 1910. In this appendix, there are four generations listed for these original immigrants. The number on the left side of each name reflects their generation. The number two (2) are children of the immigrant; the number three (3) are grandchildren of the immigrant; and number four (4) are great grandchildren of the immigrant. There were extensive attempts to get accurate updates of all descendants; however, due to loss of contacts and the number of descendants now living elsewhere, some descendants and their complete information may not be included.

There are many marriages within the German families of Roberts Cove. If there is a marriage with another person within an immigrant's family, their names are identified with a number [ ] as a reference to another location within that immigrant family.

1. Achten, Heinrich
2. Berken, Herman
3. Bunt, Gerhard
4. Cramer, Herman
5. Dischler, Xavier
6. Gielen, Johann
7. Gossen, Peter
8. Grein, Herman
9. Habetz, Heinrich
10. Heinen, Joseph
11. Heinen, Peter
12. Hensgens, Christian
13. Huesers (Hüsers), Johann Heinrich
14. Jabusch, Robert
15. Jacobs, Arnold
16. Janssen, Joseph
17. Knipping, Joseph
18. Leonards, August
19. Leonards, Dr. Henry
20. Leonards, Joseph
21. Meyer, Bernard
22. Moeder, Joseph
23. Neu, Jacob & Anna
24. Ohlenforst, Johann Wilhelm
25. Ohlenforst, Theodor
26. Olinger, Ferdinand
27. Reiners, Franz
28. Ronkartz, Johann
29. Schaffhausen, Joseph
30. Schatzle, Florenz
31. Scheufens, Theodor
32. Schlicher, Johann Lambert
33. Schlicher, Johann Peter
34. Spaetgens, Heinrich Joseph
35. Stamm, Ferdinand

Alphabetical Listing of Colonists' Families

36. Theunissen, Hubert
37. Thevis, Jacob
38. Thevis, Peter
39. Vondenstein, Joseph
40. Wirtz, Hubert
41. Zaunbrecher, Nicholas

Guide to symbols in genealogy

2 = Second generation
3 = Third generation
4 = Fourth generation

+ = indicates marriage
* = indicates remarriage

1. Achten, Heinrich Joseph:
Heinrich Joseph Achten b: 6/19/1834 d: 8/5/1902 from Breberen, was the son of Hubert Achten (1803-?) From Buscherheid and Barbara Koulen/Kuhlen. He married on 9/15/1865 Maria Josepha Piepers (8/20/1833-5/14/1904), daughter of Matthias Piepers and Agnes Kreckelberg. (Maria Josepha Piepers was the sister of Johanna Katherina Piepers who married Peter Joseph Thevis).

2	Matthias Joseph Achten	b: 4/13/1865		d: 1912
	+Eveline Lacasse	b: 1870	m: 11/7/1887	d: 1937
3	Maria Gertrude Achten	b: 11/16/1888		d: 1970
	+Joseph Kraeger	b: 1880	m: 1907	d: 1918
	*2nd Husband of Maria Gertrude Achten:			
	+William Boudreaux	b: 1870	m: 1921	d: 1962
	*3rd Husband of Maria Gertrude Achten:			
	+Louis Bennan	b: 1887	m: 1964	d: 1969
3	Maria Josepha Achten	b: 4/15/1891		d: 1936
	+Charles Preble	b: 1871	m: 1912	d: 1958
3	Johanna Achten	b: 10/11/1895		d: 1980
	+Clayeus Thibodeaux	b: 1899	m: 1914	d: 1934
3	Henry Joseph Achten	b: 10/10/1897		d: 1961
	+Anna Fuselier	b: 1902	m: 1916	d: 1972
3	John Joseph Achten	b: 1901		d: 1951
	+Woodley Wells	b: 1913	m: 1934	
3	William Joseph Achten	b: 1903		d: 1988
	+Elise Street	b: 1902	m: 1934	d: 1940
	*2nd Wife of William Joseph Achten:			
	+Pearl Oliver	b: 1918	m: 1954	
3	Christian Achten	b: 1906		d: 12/7/1965
	+Bertha Darcey	b: 1910	m: 1928	d: 1933
	*2nd Wife of Christian Achten:			
	+Hazel Mae Crews	b: 1908	m: 1936	d: 1970
2	Maria Sofia Achten	b: 6/4/1866		d: Bef. 1881
2	Arnold Achten	b: 1/8/1868		d: 1868

Achten

2	Christian Achten	b: 12/18/1868		d: Bef. 1881
2	Maria Agnes Achten	b: 10/31/1870		d: Bef. 1881
2	Anna Maria Achten	b: 5/16/1872		d: 11/25/1943
	+Joseph Schneider	b: 2/10/1862	m: 1/25/1888	d: 6/26/1940
3	Franz Joseph Schneider	b: 3/3/1888		d: 4/10/1952
	+Odelia Green	b: 10/21/1897	m: 1916	d: 12/19/1977
4	Henry Joseph Schneider	b: 7/22/1917		d: 9/30/1987
	+Ruth Baker	b: 2/17/1919	m: 10/9/1952	d: 1/27/1995
4	James Dallas Schneider	b: 10/6/1919		d: 11/26/1988
	+Rose Helen Zaunbrecher	b: 11/5/1915	m: 2/24/1941	d: 2/22/1993
4	Mary Ellen Schneider	b: 5/5/1921		d: 2/23/1982
	+Martin Thevis	b: 2/20/1913	m: 1/24/1940	d: 4/26/1989
4	John Dillard Schneider	b: 9/15/1922		d: 1/6/1998
	+Juanita Agnes Launey	b: 10/19/1927	m: 12/15/1946	
4	Anthony Lee Schneider	b: 1/21/1924		d: 2/24/2005
	+Olga Mae Killmer	b: 6/4/1924	m: 12/12/1959	
4	Anna Louise Schneider	b: 1925		d: 1925
4	Janette Cecilia Schneider	b: 8/2/1926		d: 3/22/1979
	+Gilbert Neil Pousson	b: 4/20/1920	m: 6/23/1946	d: 7/14/1986
4	Lawrence Elmo Schneider	b: 2/28/1928		
	+Gisela Ruoff	b: 12/26/1929	m: 8/11/1951	
4	Frank Joseph Schneider	b: 6/28/1930		
	+Germaine Frances Hensgens	b: 12/14/1935	m: 10/25/1955	d: 2/2/1996
4	Catherine Schneider	b: 6/28/1933		
	+Raymond A. Hensgens	b: 7/22/1932	m: 10/20/1951	
4	August Ray Schneider	b: 1/1/1942		
	+Patricia Ann Trahan	b: 1/30/1941	m: 11/24/1960	
3	Aloysuis Louis Schneider	b: 10/5/1890		d: 12/13/1944

Achten

	+Ezora Ledoux	b: 1896	m: 1912	d: 9/6/1972
4	Annie Mary Schneider	b: 9/25/1913		
	+John Paul Dischler	b: 1915	m: 1936	d: 1992
4	Henriettta Schneider	b: 11/8/1914		d: 1/26/1986
	+Velton Cart	b: 8/2/1914		d: 12/6/1984
4	Stella Madeline Schneider	b: 5/23/1916		d: 4/28/2007
	+Floyd Killmer	b: 1918	m: 10/25/1948	d: 4/24/2004
4	Joseph Frank Schneider	b: 12/19/1919		d: 6/11/1985
	+Evelyn Reed	b: 7/18/1924		d: 5/9/1998
4	Helen Marjorie Schneider	b: 10/30/1921		d: 3/4/1990
	+Joseph Leo Schultz	b: 9/18/1914	m: 5/30/1943	d: 1/26/1996
4	Clara Elizabeth Schneider	b: 2/17/1925		d: 11/22/2003
	+Clinton Adams	b: 1/30/1925	m: 12/23/1947	d: 3/3/2006
4	Dorothy Rita Schneider	b: 1933		d: Deceased
	+Steve Kalacki			
4	Louis Schneider, Jr	b: 12/10/1929		d: 9/4/1956
3	Matthias Joseph Schneider	b: 9/7/1892		d: 4/26/1964
3	Francisca Louisa Schneider	b: 4/8/1895		d: 1980
	+Martin Joseph Schatzle	b: 1891	m: 1917	d: 1967
4	Joseph Florenz Schatzle	b: 1917		d: 1993
	+Margaret Klein	b: 2/1/1921	m: 10/8/1947	
4	Sophie Schatzle	b: 1919		
	+Gerhard Cramer	b: 1917	m: 1946	d: 1978
4	Victoria Annie Schatzle	b: 12/9/1921		
	+Gerhard Joseph Leonards	b: 10/21/1916	m: 11/27/1940	d: 2/20/1973
3	Josepha Maria Schneider	b: 9/19/1897		d: 2/1/1981
	+Hubert Donahue Burton	b: 1893	m: 1915	d: 9/3/1927
4	Joseph John Burton	b: 1917		d: 2004

Achten

	+Josephine Marie Ronkartz	b: 1920	m: 1941	
4	Louis Burton	b: 1918		d: 10/20/1998
	+Gertrude Hensgens	b: 1917	m: 1940	d: 1986
4	Martha Frances Burton	b: 11/15/1920		d: 1999
	+John Gerhard Thevis	b: 7/28/1914	m: 12/31/1940	d: 1983
4	Frank Winston Burton	b: 9/6/1922		d: 7/22/1950
4	Margaret Burton	b: 1925		
4	Mary Susie Burton	b: 1/9/1916		d: 10/6/1999
	+Gaston Hebert	b: 1/1/1914	m: 12/28/1938	d: 2/4/1974
4	Hubertina Burton	b: 5/27/1927		
3	William Joseph Schneider	b: 11/2/1899		d: 4/17/1964
	+Victoria Habetz	b: 1899	m: 1943	d: 9/9/1965
3	Maria Barbara Schneider	b: 9/7/1902		d: 3/22/1984
	+Albert Clarence Fabacher	b: 11/10/1896	m: 11/30/1920	d: 7/2/1986
4	Lucille Fabacher	b: 6/24/1922		
	+Gustave John Gravot	b: 7/23/1911	m: 12/31/1939	d: 7/29/1964
4	Rita Magdelena Fabacher	b: 2/4/1924		
	+Decheil Joseph Castille	b: 10/2/1920	m: 11/16/1941	
	*2nd Husband of Rita Magdelena Fabacher:			
	+Stanley Goryzcki	b: 8/12/1919	m: 8/12/1965	d: 7/25/1979
4	Francis Nathaniel Fabacher	b: 2/6/1926		d: 1/23/1991
	+Jeanette Hebert	b: 9/30/1928	m: 11/30/1947	
4	Philip Joseph Fabacher	b: 11/10/1928		d: 9/11/1944
4	Clarence Albert Fabacher	b: 3/17/1931		
	+Mary Agnes Zaunbrecher	b: 2/21/1930	m: 2/4/1956	
3	Maria Schneider	b: 5/20/1904		d: 7/24/1988
	+Charles Joseph Joseph	b: 4/27/1906	m: 7/10/1930	d: 1/23/1996
4	Greta Patricia Joseph	b: 12/19/1931		

Achten

	+Edison James Ortego	b: 3/2/1932	m: 9/3/1955
	*2nd Husband of Greta Patricia Joseph:		
	+Cary Lee Gaskell		m: Aft. 1966
	*3rd Husband of Greta Patricia Joseph:		
	+Bryant Paul Anacher, Sr.		m: Aft. 1966
4	Felicita Louise Joseph	b: 11/13/1935	
	+John "Al" Gibson	b: 5/7/1934	m: 11/19/1960
4	Joseph Charles Joseph	b: 8/14/1939	
	+Darlene Soderstrom	b: 3/30/1938	m: 1/2/1959
3	Bernadine Schneider	b: 7/14/1906	d: 1998
	+William Hoffpauir	b: 4/1/1895	m: 4/29/1949 d: 5/18/1966
3	George Schneider	b: 5/19/1908	d: 1/28/1970
	+Clara Manual	b: 2/28/1910	m: 1930 d: 3/10/1994
4	Theresa Juanita Schneider	b: 12/3/1931	d: 1/21/1932
4	John Ray Schneider	b: 8/20/1934	
	+Linda Rougeau	b: 7/22/1938	m: 8/24/1957
4	Julia Ann Schneider	b: 8/2/1938	
	+Daniel B. Slade	b: 7/10/1933	m: 9/24/1957
4	George Clarence Schneider	b: 8/2/1942	
	+Patricia Ann Manuel	b: 4/26/1946	m: 6/9/1962
4	Clara Marie Schneider	b: 6/2/1945	
	+Elmo Charles Smith	b: 9/24/1937	m: 10/24/1963 d: 5/1/2006
3	Anna Victoria Schneider	b: 10/11/1910	d: 2/18/1990
2	Johanna Katharina Achten	b: 6/18/1874	d: 1/24/1929
	+Johann Bernard Meyer	b: 1872	m: 1/21/1896 d: 1964
3	Anna Helena Meyer	b: 9/2/1896	d: 10/19/1988
	+Danial Joseph Theunissen	b: 1/19/1892	m: 1918 d: 7/2/1985
4	Maria Catharine Theunissen	b: 12/16/1918	d: 10/14/1989

Achten

	+Ralius Paul Dupuis	b: 4/14/1924	m: 1949	d: 6/21/1993
4	Joseph Peter Theunissen	b: 1921		d: 1956
	+Eva Gertrude Leblanc	b: 1923	m: 1947	
4	Annie Louise Theunissen	b: 3/21/1923		d: 3/16/1991
	+John Daniel Klein	b: 12/30/1924	m: 2/5/1947	d: 8/6/1964
4	Joseph Hubert Theunissen	b: 1925		d: 1993
	+Audrey Hope Billeaudeau	b: 1929	m: 1949	d: 1992
4	Mathilda Theunissen	b: 10/15/1929		
	+Paul Jasper Johnson	b: 6/11/1922	m: 1/19/1950	
4	Hilda Helena Theunissen	b: 10/15/1929		
	+James Curney Haure	b: 1930	m: 10/1952	
4	Louise Augusta Theunissen	b: 12/27/1932		
	+Raymond William Leonards	b: 1/19/1929	m: 12/27/1952	d: 4/22/1992

*2nd Husband of Louise Augusta Theunissen:

	+Frank E. Landry, Jr.	b: 12/9/1920	m: 5/20/1994	
4	William Richard "Preacher" Theunissen	b: 11/30/1935		d: 1993
	+Anna Mae Simon	b: 1937	m: 1954	
4	Frances Margaret "Poochie" Theunissen	b: 6/15/1939		
	+Edward Joseph Benoit	b: 3/28/1939	m: 5/19/1960	

*2nd Husband of Frances Margaret "Poochie" Theunissen:

	+Melford Primeaux	b: 1935	m: 1979	
3	Herman Joseph Meyer	b: 1899		d: 1919
3	Henry Joseph Meyer	b: 1901		d: 1983
	+Elna Lafleur	b: 1906	m: 1927	d: 1994
4	Ben Anthony Meyer	b: 1/9/1929		
	+Virginia Rita Falcon	b: 3/11/1930	m: 4/17/1951	d: 4/16/1994

Achten

4	Clara Marjorie Meyer	b: 8/12/1930		
	+Louis J. Simar	b: 11/18/1934	m: 8/5/1961	
4	Gerald James Meyer	b: 4/18/1933		d: 8/10/1951
4	Sylvia Marie Meyer	b: 1/30/1936		
	+Jay Istre	b: 4/21/1935	m: 11/8/1955	
	*2nd Husband of Sylvia Marie Meyer:			
	+Claude D. Cochran	b: 12/13/1935	m: 9/4/1991	
4	Anna Lois Meyer	b: 11/7/1937		
	+Francis Ray Lormand, Sr.	b: 3/23/1935	m: 11/23/1961	
4	Doris Mildred Meyer	b: 1/20/1940		
	+Robert Guilbeaux	b: 2/21/1939	m: 6/4/1960	
	*2nd Husband of Doris Mildred Meyer:			
	+Farol Wade Guidry	b: 5/14/1934	m: 4/4/1969	
4	Henry Joseph Meyer, Jr.	b: 2/5/1942		d: 6/25/2004
4	Lee Leonard Meyer	b: 3/3/1944		
	+Shirley Broussard	b: 9/20/1951	m: 10/28/1967	
4	Harold Phillip Meyer, Sr.	b: 12/7/1946		
	+Carol Lejeune	b: 7/15/1952	m: 12/7/1968	
4	Gerald Meyer	b: 1947		d: 1951
4	Ronald William Meyer	b: 1/18/1949		
	+Jessie Lynn Hawkins	b: 5/5/1948	m: 8/2/1969	
	*2nd Wife of Ronald William Meyer:			
	+Loretta Mae Elliot	b: 12/3/1948	m: 10/25/1976	d: 10/25/1999
3	Josephine Meyer	b: 1903		d: 1993
	+Heinrich Leonard Habetz	b: 3/3/1874	m: 1943	d: 6/9/1958
4	Johanna Habetz	b: 10/6/1944		
	+Carrol Wayne Sittig	m: 6/29/1968		
4	Henry Clemens Habetz	b: 3/5/1947		d: 2003
4	Leonard Paul Habetz	b: 9/2/1950		
	+Brenda Rose Dartez	m: 2/28/1970		

Achten

3	Mathias Joseph Meyer	b: 1905		d: 1979
	+Maria Catherine Scheufens	b: 1912	m: 1932	d: 1988
4	Charles Joseph Meyer	b: 2/8/1933		
	+Agnes Ruth McCown	b: 10/19/1938	m: 5/25/1956	d: 2005
4	Arnold Remy "Ray" Meyer	b: 5/23/1934		d: 11/13/2006
	+Geneva Viola Louviere	b: 12/10/1935	m: 6/4/1959	
4	John Allen Meyer	b: 3/7/1936		d: 7/17/2005
	+Sandra McCown	b: 1/15/1947	m: 4/11/1969	
4	Louis Theodore Meyer	b: 11/26/1937		
	+Jean Pitre	b: 8/29/1942	m: 12/29/1962	
4	Edwin Frank Meyer	b: 9/21/1939		
	+Bobbie Jane Caswell	b: 4/19/1941	m: 6/15/1963	
4	Johanna Catherine Meyer	b: 2/19/1941		
	+Leland Cormier	b: 8/19/1936	m: 7/15/1962	
4	Clyde Joseph Meyer	b: 4/15/1942		d: 3/17/2003
	+Alice Faye Miguez	b: 2/16/1948		
4	Frances Jane Meyer	b: 8/24/1943		
	+Clyde Coble	b: 5/8/1942	m: 3/8/1972	
4	Matthias Joseph Meyer, Jr.	b: 5/25/1946		d: 9/29/1995
	+Dolores Ann Richard	b: 9/17/1945	m: 5/10/1966	
4	Steven James Meyer	b: 11/16/1947		
	+Eloise Joan Richard	b: 1/15/1950	m: 2/14/1969	
	*2nd Wife of Steven James Meyer:			
	+Sharon Gayle Galley	b: 1953	m: 1973	
4	Michael Lawrence Meyer	b: 4/1/1951		
	+Susan Matt	b: 10/30/1952	m: 10/17/1970	
4	Thomas Larry Meyer	b: 7/6/1953		

Achten

	+Bridgett Ann Hoffpauir	b: 8/31/1955	m: 8/16/1975	
	*2nd Wife of Thomas Larry Meyer:			
	+Sarah Frances Kennedy	b: 1/2/1958	m: 4/19/1990	
3	Maria Gebina Meyer	b: 1908		d: 1929
3	Gerhard Aloysuis Meyer	b: 1910		d: 1975
	+Antoinette Dischler	b: 1911	m: 1933	d: 1998
4	Melvin Meyer	b: 1941		
	+Audrey Dommert	b: 1940	m: 1975	d: 1996
3	John Kasper Meyer	b: 1912		d: 7/25/1987
	+Anna Marie Habetz	b: 6/28/1910	m: 6/7/1937	d: 5/9/1990
4	Leonard John Meyer	b: 1/31/1938		d: 3/2/1938
4	Leonard "John" Meyer	b: 3/28/1939		
	+Pearl Ann Watson	b: 11/1939	m: 11/26/1966	
4	Henry Leonard Meyer	b: 9/25/1940		
	+Jo Ann Zaunbrecher	b: 7/22/1944	m: 7/15/1964	
4	Mary Ann Meyer	b: 2/2/1942		
	+John Herman Reiners	b: 10/19/1938	m: 4/8/1961	
4	Margaret Mary Meyer	b: 7/31/1943		
	+Charles Herbert Simpson	b: 9/1942	m: 5/12/1964	
4	Joseph Bernard Meyer	b: 8/27/1944	d: 8/23/1989	
	+Betty Ann Gould	b: 4/1946	m: 4/28/1966	
4	Kathleen Marie Meyer	b: 11/19/1947		
	+Larry John Viator	b: 2/1947	m: 6/6/1970	
4	Marie Antoinette Meyer	b: 12/19/1950	d: 6/8/1951	
4	James Anthony Meyer	b: 10/22/1955		
	+Patricia Ann Meche	b: 9/1962	m: 10/26/1991	
3	Maria Frances Meyer	b: 1914	d: 1986	
	+Leonard Alphonse Habetz, Sr.	b: 5/12/1916	m: 1/8/1941	d: 4/9/1974

Achten

4	Henry Bernard Habetz	b: 12/19/1941	d: 1/7/1986	
	+Laura Sonnier	b: 1/2/1943	m: 11/28/1963	d: 8/11/2006
4	Leonard Alphonse Habetz, Jr.	b: 6/23/1943		
	+Carolyn Spell	b: 9/23/1940	m: 6/5/1965	
4	Alberta Habetz	b: 2/21/1945		
	+Johnny Winn Barlow	b: 8/9/1953	m: 2/2/1974	
4	Charles Joseph Habetz	b: 9/6/1946		
	+Katherine Link	b: 1/22/1948	m: 4/27/1968	
4	Lucille Marie Habetz	b: 4/2/1948		
	+Norman Jean Borne, Jr.	b: 9/15/1946	m: 6/12/1976	
4	Catherine Helen Habetz	b: 6/25/1949		
	+Hugh Fred "Pudgy" O'Connor, Jr.	b: 3/31/1938	m: 8/21/1982	d: 3/4/2002
4	Henrietta Louise Habetz	b: 7/28/1951		
4	Ralph Mark Habetz	b: 2/16/1953		
	+Katherine Sudwischer	b: 1/16/1957	m: 7/15/1983	
4	Frances Adelieth Habetz	b: 8/10/1954		d: 10/30/2004
	+Dan R. Hooten	b: 2/4/1944	m: 12/4/1982	d: 1/2002
4	Claire Marie Habetz	b: 9/22/1957		
4	Pauline Margaret Habetz	b: 1/5/1960		

2. Berken, Johann Herman:

Johann Herman Berken b: 6/26/1847 d: 8/3/1917 from Hebelermeer was the son of Johann Bernard Berken. He married Angela Adelheid Cramer on 11/21/1871 b: 5/14/1849 d: 10/2/1913 from Hebelermeer, daughter of Johann Kasper Cramer. (The Berken and Cramer immigrant couples are double brother-sister-in-laws, see Cramer family. They are also the uncles/aunts of Johann Bernard Meyer. See Meyer family).

2		Euphemia Maria Berken	b: 7/16/1873		d: 1892
2		Helena Adelheid Berken	b: 1/4/1877		d: 1895
		+Gerhard Bunt	b: 1867	m: 1894	d: 1930
3		Fina Maria Bunt	b: 1895		d: 1895
2		Anna Helena Berken	b: 4/24/1880		d: 9/8/1968
		+Peter Joseph Reiners	b: 1/11/1874	m: 2/14/1900	d: 5/13/1936
3		Frank Reiners	b: 9/8/1901		d: 9/25/1987
		+Anna Maria Thevis	b: 1905	m: 1924	d: 1973
	4	Joseph Reiners	b: 4/9/1925		d: 11/16/2005
		+Harriette Louise Klein	b: 10/13/1931	m: 11/9/1949	
	4	Alois Reiners	b: 7/25/1926		d: 3/19/1999
		+Lucille Gossen	b: 11/11/1928	m: 11/25/1953	
	4	Elizabeth Reiners	b: 10/16/1928		d: 4/17/2000
	4	Helen Reiners	b: 9/20/1932		
		+Sylvester Frey	b: 7/20/1930	m: 1/20/1954	
	4	Anthony Reiners	b: 11/18/1933		
		+Pauline Habetz	b: 4/14/1934	m: 9/19/1957	
3		John Herman Reiners	b: 1904		d: 1904
3		Maria Adelheid Reiners	b: 1907		d: 1907
3		Adelheid Reiners	b: 11/24/1907		d: 12/15/1975
3		John Herman Reiners Sr.	b: 6/27/1915		d: 11/1/1991
		+Willie Mae Reed	b: 2/16/1916	m: 11/10/1937	d: 7/17/1945
	4	John Herman Reiners Jr.	b: 10/19/1938		
		+Mary Ann Meyer	b: 2/2/1942	m: 4/8/1961	

Berken

	4	William Joseph Reiners Sr.	b: 8/7/1940		d: 11/28/1999
		+Elizabeth Thevis	b: 3/1/1942	m: 11/11/1961	
	4	Rose Marie Reiners	b: 3/28/1942		
		+Stephen Joseph Zaunbrecher	b: 9/2/1940	m: 6/26/1962	
	4	Mary Magdalene Reiners	b: 3/31/1944		
		+Lawrence Aloyious Cramer, Sr.	b: 9/12/1941	m: 6/11/1963	
	4	Anna Marie Reiners	b: 7/17/1945		d: 7/17/1945
		*2nd Wife of John Herman Reiners Sr.:			
		+Agnes Ancelet	b: 8/17/1925	m: 7/26/1971	
3		Anna Helena Reiners	b: 1918		d: 1918
3		Anna Maria Reiners	b: 1918		d: 1918
3		Helena Veronica Reiners	b: 3/9/1919		
		+Camile Richard	b: 11/7/1914	m: 8/28/1940	d: 5/10/1999
	4	Joseph Richard	b: 7/6/1941		
		+Rose Marie Robicheaux			
	4	Theresa Marie Richard	b: 10/9/1942		
		+Wilbert Thevis, Sr.	b: 8/27/1940	m: 1/24/1961	
2		Gebina Berken	b: 1884		d: 1964
		+Henry Schultz, Sr.	b: 8/16/1884	m: 1909	d: 6/20/1954
3		John Herman Schultz	b: 1/4/1911		d: 4/22/1963
		+Ida Regina Hensgens	b: 9/23/1909	m: 1/13/1937	d: 1/26/1980
	4	Charles Herman Schultz	b: 10/23/1937		
		+Geraldine Elaine Trumps	b: 5/20/1937	m: 11/9/1957	d: 12/4/1998
	4	John Herman Schultz	b: 9/6/1939		
		+Marjorie Ann Robicheaux	b: 10/19/1943	m: 11/10/1973	
	4	Mary Frances Schultz	b: 1/13/1942		

Berken

	+Thomas Michael Wall	b: 12/4/1947	m: 7/17/1971	
4	Patrick Leo Schultz	b: 2/16/1944		d: 9/1/1968
3	Xavier Lawrence Schultz	b: 9/1/1912		d: 10/21/1975
	+Maria Gesina Cramer	b: 5/20/1914	m: 1/17/1934	d: 8/29/2000
4	Gerald Andrew Schultz	b: 1/1/1935		d: 3/26/2002
	+Loretta Lorraine Klein	b: 5/8/1937	m: 6/30/1955	d: 1/15/2005
4	John Lawrence Schultz	b: 2/8/1937		
	+Cora Lee Cormier	b: 9/21/1941	m: 6/21/1959	
4	Leroy Edmond Schultz	b: 3/24/1940		
3	Joseph Leo Schultz	b: 9/18/1914		d: 1/26/1996
	+Marjorie Helen Schneider	b: 10/30/1921	m: 5/30/1943	d: 3/4/1990
4	Kenneth Leo Schultz	b: 12/7/1945		
4	Raymond Louis Schultz	b: 3/6/1951		d: 6/10/1960
4	Jo Ann Schultz	b: 9/24/1953		
	+Patrick Calais	b: 7/8/1934	m: 6/18/1981	
4	Pamela Ann Schultz	b: 11/17/1959		
	+Theodore Michael Allen	b: 12/13/1942	m: 2/28/1981	
3	Henry Schultz, Jr.	b: 9/21/1918		d: 11/1/1983
	+Annie Vondenstein	b: 6/15/1919	m: 1/8/1941	
4	Carol Jean Schultz	b: 3/28/1944		
4	Barbara Schultz	b: 6/11/1949		
	+Ronald Lee Miller	b: 1/10/1949	m: 6/15/1969	
4	Donald Schultz	b: 10/16/1947		
	+Carla Claire Gilmore	b: 12/20/1954	m: 7/12/1980	
4	Patricia Schultz	b: 1/31/1955		d: 9/18/1998
	+Raymond Kenneth Fielder, Jr.	b: 11/4/1959	m: 6/23/1979	

*2nd Husband of Patricia Schultz:

Berken

		+Thomas Winfred Bruner	b: 4/23/1956	m: 2/20/1993	
2		Bernard Berken	b: 10/5/1887		d: 1898
2		Johan Casper Berken	b: 7/6/1891		d: 1/30/1984
		+Thecla Lambertina Thevis	b: 1900	m: 6/18/1919	d: 1981
	3	Herman Aloysius Berken	b: 3/5/1920		d: 2/18/1992
		+Elvina Bourque	b: 1930	m: 1950	d: 2000
	4	Donald Berken	b: 7/2/1951		
		+Charlotte Sonnier	b: 8/18/1951	m: 6/3/1972	
	4	Brenda Berken	b: 12/12/1953		
	4	Clara Berken	b: 10/6/1955		
		+Doug Welch	b: 3/13/1952	m: 2/28/1976	
	4	Elizabeth (Betty) Berken	b: 4/10/1957		
		+Duncan Wells	b: 4/3/1956	m: 11/18/1978	
	4	Richard Berken	b: 5/28/1958		
		+Sharron Conway	b: 4/22/1957	m: 6/16/1979	
	3	Lawrence Herman Berken	b: 8/10/1921		d: 9/11/1996
		+Barbara Leona Hensgens	b: 5/6/1924	m: 1/30/1946	
	4	Charlotte Berken	b: 2/15/1948		
		+Kenneth Conner	b: 4/23/1948	m: 1/25/1969	
	4	Stephen Berken	b: 5/5/1949		
		+Melanie Boutte	b: 7/21/1953	m: 12/16/1972	
	4	Clarence Berken	b: 12/12/1959		
		+Karen Berry	b: 12/21/1954	m: 1/6/1973	
	4	Martha Berken	b: 3/26/1955		
		+Homer Stevens II	b: 4/9/1954	m: 8/3/1974	
	4	Rachel Berken	b: 12/1/1957		
		+Thomas (Tom) Andrus	b: 5/12/1951	m: 9/4/1976	
	4	Kevin Berken	b: 3/16/1961		
		+Shirley Folcka	b: 2/15/1960	m: 12/14/1990	

Berken

4	Mary Gayle Berken	b: 3/18/1963		
	+Jay Womack	b: 7/8/1965	m: 2/28/1987	
	*2nd Husband of Mary Gayle Berken:			
	+Todd Moses	b: 11/30/1965	m: 6/12/1999	
3	Elizabeth Josephine Berken	b: 11/8/1922		d: 11/27/1995
	+Charles Klein	b: 8/8/1922	m: 11/20/1946	
4	James Klein	b: 10/21/1947		
4	Gerald Klein	b: 7/14/1949		
	+Patricia Bergeron	b: 10/2/1951	m: 6/25/1971	
4	Robert Klein	b: 7/22/1951		d: 7/22/1951
4	Alvin Klein	b: 3/28/1953		
	+Margie Bowles	b: 10/15/1956	m: 12/5/1975	
4	Jane Klein	b: 10/7/1955		
	+Stan Gates	b: 5/9/1954	m: 10/10/1981	
4	Dorothy Klein	b: 9/27/1958		
	+Wayland LaFargue	b: 5/4/1958	m: 5/2/1981	
4	Robert Klein	b: 2/27/1960		
4	Harold Klein	b: 1/10/1962		
	+Gwen ?	b: 3/10/1955	m: 6/20/1998	
3	Christina Marie Berken	b: 3/26/1924		
	+Simon Hornsby	b: 5/7/1925	m: 10/7/1950	d: 7/10/1978
4	Gregory Hornsby	b: 9/6/1952		
	+Brenda Short	b: 6/17/1955	m: 3/3/1973	
4	Anthony Hornsby	b: 8/6/1954		d: 10/9/2005
	+Jeanette Ardoin	b: 7/2/1954	m: 2/16/1980	
4	Cynthia (Cindy) Hornsby	b: 10/9/1955		
	+Kelly Landry	b: 2/26/1959	m: 6/3/1989	
4	Diane Hornsby	b: 11/6/1956		
	+Greg Ronkartz	b: 9/5/1958	m: 6/28/1980	
4	Larry Hornsby	b: 1/24/1958		
	+Sandra Broussard	b: 3/13/1959	m: 6/23/1979	

Berken

4	Barry Hornsby	b: 5/31/1959		
	+Tammy Benoit	b: 10/31/1961	m: 12/12/1980	
4	Jude Hornsby	b: 8/13/1960		
	+Monica Romero	b: 1/16/1965	m: 4/28/1984	
4	Wayne Hornsby	b: 6/7/1962		
	+Jody Bertrand	b: 4/2/1960	m: 6/28/1991	
3	Vincent Joseph Berken	b: 12/17/1925		d: 4/22/2005
	+Marie Louise Thevis	b: 1938	m: 10/24/1956	
4	Deborah Berken	b: 7/25/1959		
	+Jude Clement	b: 5/10/1958	m: 2/10/1979	
4	Mary Berken	b: 9/7/1960		d: 12/13/2001
	+Mark Vail	b: 4/29/1958	m: 1/9/1982	
4	Judy Berken	b: 4/4/1962		
	+Bryant Fletcher	b: 8/22/1961	m: 11/27/1982	
4	Sharon Berken	b: 10/20/1963		
	+Edward Cassiere	b: 10/17/1958	m: 8/11/1990	
4	John Berken	b: 2/5/1966		
	+Virginia Greene	b: 9/6/1966	m: 11/12/1988	
4	Elaine Berken	b: 11/15/1967		
	+Jason Quebedeaux	b: 10/11/1972	m: 8/16/2003	
3	Gertrude Angela Berken	b: 9/27/1927		
	+Robert Leger	b: 12/31/1927	m: 4/14/1951	d: 7/9/2003
4	Robert Leger	b: 2/25/1952		
	+Debbie Marshall	b: 1/30/1956	m: 10/22/1977	
4	Pamela Leger	b: 5/28/1953		
	+Anthony (Tony) Harmon	b: 12/30/1951	m: 7/28/1973	
4	Carolyn Leger	b: 3/19/1955		
	+Bill Chontas	b: 6/29/1948	m: 9/20/1986	
4	Sandra Leger	b: 8/6/1958		
	+Glenn Epps	b: 11/13/1949	m: 5/16/1980	
4	Richard Leger	b: 1/17/1963		

Berken

		+Angela Johnson	b: 9/23/1965	m: 9/26/1992	
3		Mary Agnes Berken	b: 11/30/1929		
		+Jesse Harrington	b: 10/1/1926	m: 6/21/1952	
	4	Annette Harrington	b: 10/28/1953		
	4	Anne Harrington	b: 9/21/1955		
	4	Aileen Harrington	b: 5/29/1959		
		+Jimmy Prevost	b: 12/22/1959	m: 8/9/1980	
	4	Andrea Harrington	b: 2/23/1963		
		+Shawn Hunt	b: 10/24/1967	m: 7/27/1996	
3		Louise Anna Berken	b: 1932		d: 1942
3		Josephine Thecla Berken	b: 7/14/1934		
		+Anthony Thevis	b: 3/23/1928	m: 5/10/1955	d: 4/29/1992
	4	Gwendolyn (Gwen) Thevis	b: 11/9/1963		
	4	Stephanie Thevis	b: 8/11/1969		
		+Gaylon Thibodeaux	b: 1/11/1965	m: 11/16/1990	
	4	Trudy Thevis	b: 11/27/1973		
		+Brian Ronkartz	b: 2/26/1975	m: 5/30/1998	
3		Reinhard John Berken	b: 8/4/1938		d: 10/3/2001
		+Thelma Abshire	b: 10/26/1940	m: 1961	d: 4/6/2007
	4	Yvette Berken	b: 10/19/1963		
	4	Reinhard (Ron) Berken	b: 12/17/1966		
		+Cindy Nordyke	b: 2/7/1964	m: 10/25/1991	
	4	Reginald (Reggie) Berken	b: 8/19/1970		
		+Trisha			
	*2nd Wife of Reinhard John Berken:				
		+Brenda Credeur	b: 1949	m: 11/6/1982	
	4	Alex (Petie) Berken	b: 9/24/1968		d: 2/18/2003
	4	Thad (Mushy) Berken	b: 4/24/1971		
	4	Wendy Berken	b: 7/6/1973		
		+John LaPointe		m: 4/16/2004	

Berken

4	Eric Berken	b: 6/1/1977			
4	Julie Bertrand	b: 5/2/1967			
	+Wayne Morton				
3	Rita Helena Berken	b: 3/23/1941			
	+Jesse Hoffpauir	b: 1/1/1941	m: 2/4/1961	d: 10/5/2002
4	Michael Hoffpauir	b: 9/28/1962			
	+Deborah Denise Brown	b: 9/16/1970	m: 7/21/2001		

3. Bunt, Gerhard (George):

Gerhard (George) Bunt b: 1867 d: 1930 from Hebelermeer was the son of Heinrich Bunt and Hermana Scheever/Scheuven. He first married in 1892 Maria Rosinski b: 1868 d: 1893. His second marriage in 1894 was with Helena Adelheid Berken (1877-1895) (see Berken family). His third marriage in 1897 was to Anna Helena Wilkens (1874-1932), daughter of Bernard Heinrich Wilkens and Anna Helena Albers.

  2 John Henry Bunt   b: 1893   d: 1986
      +Esther Ruth   b: 1894   m: 1917   d: 1971
      Borcherding
    3 John Henry Bunt Jr. b: 1918
      +Bettye Dusky   d: 1984
*2nd Wife of Gerhard (George) Bunt:
     +Helena Adelheid Berken b: 1877   m: 1894   d: 1895
  2 Fina Maria Bunt   b: 1895   d: 1895
*3rd Wife of Gerhard (George) Bunt:
     +Anna Helena Wilkens b: 1874   m: 1897   d: 1932

4. Cramer, Johann Herman:

Johann Herman Cramer b: 1843 d: 1918 from Hebelermeer was the son of Johann Kasper Cramer. He married in 1873 to Anna Gesina Berken b: 1853 d: 1936, the daughter of Johann Bernard Berken. (The Cramer and Berken immigrant couples were double brother/sister-in-laws, see Berken family. They were also uncles/aunts of Johann Bernard Meyer, see Meyer family).

2		Casper Cramer	b: 1874		d: 1961
2		Bernard Cramer	b: 1876		d: 1933
		+Anna Katharina Vondenstein	b: 1884	m: 1905	d: 1968
	3	Maria Josephine Cramer	b: 1906		d: 2000
		+Nicholas Martin Zaunbrecher	b: 1893	m: 1927	d: 1975
	4	Wilma Anna Zaunbrecher	b: 12/6/1928		
		+Huey Patrick Regan	b: 9/7/1930	m: 4/25/1950	
	4	William Joseph Zaunbrecher	b: 7/16/1931		d: 4/1/1990
		+Laurea Marie James	b: 11/15/1939	m: 12/10/1963	d: 9/17/1992
	4	Clarice Ann Zaunbrecher	b: 9/26/1933		
		+Rodney William LeJeune	b: 11/27/1930	m: 4/15/1953	
	4	Otto Bernard Zaunbrecher	b: 8/22/1935		
		+Sylvia Jean Armstrong	b: 9/18/1943	m: 2/8/1964	
	4	Elaine Marie Zaunbrecher	b: 11/25/1937		d: 10/25/2001
		+Carl Barry Leger	b: 8/25/1936	m: 2/1/1958	
	4	Mary Jo Zaunbrecher	b: 1/27/1940		
		+Carl Jerome Foreman	b: 2/29/1940	m: 11/28/1964	

Cramer

4	Wanda Ann Zaunbrecher	b: 12/2/1941		
	+Shelton Eugene Launey	b: 2/9/1937	m: 11/4/1961	
3	Anna Gesina Cramer	b: 1908	d: 2/25/2000	
	+Herman Joseph Habetz	b: 11/16/1901	m: 1/30/1929	d: 2/6/1966
4	Lawrence Joseph Habetz	b: 12/27/1929		
	+Marie Legnon	b: 12/27/1933	m: 2/10/1957	
4	Leonard Joseph Habetz	b: 4/11/1932		
	+Deanna Dean Hoffpauir		m: 6/29/1957	
4	Clementine Anna Habetz	b: 10/27/1934		
	+Huey Pierre Kirsch	b: 9/17/1935	m: 6/7/1958	
4	Bernadine Anna Habetz	b: 2/7/1937		d: 7/6/1994
4	Bernard Joseph Habetz	b: 11/19/1939		
	+Patricia Ann Molbert	b: 10/8/1939	m: 11/17/1962	d: 7/15/2004
4	Albert Joseph Habetz	b: 2/10/1942		
	+Brenda Faye Ruppert		m: 5/29/1965	
4	Robert Joseph Habetz	b: 2/1/1944		
	+Priscella Vera Keigley	b: 10/13/1946	m: 7/15/1967	
4	Josephine Anna "Joann" Habetz	b: 1/28/1947		
	+Fredrick Ledoux	b: 8/9/1947	m: 9/4/1971	
4	Anna Agnes Habetz	b: 10/15/1949		
	+Thomas Michael Jones	b: 2/9/1949	m: 6/21/1969	
3	John Herman Cramer	b: 1909	d: 1980	
	+Gertrude Felicitas Habetz	b: 5/25/1914	m: 2/23/1938	

Cramer

4	Anna Margaret Cramer	b: 12/31/1938		
	+William "Billy" Zaunbrecher	b: 5/31/1938	m: 12/16/1963	d: 8/19/1997
4	Bernard Cramer	b: 9/25/1942		d: 9/25/1942
4	Patricia Marie Cramer	b: 2/21/1947		d: 2004
4	Carolyn Chementine Cramer	b: 7/6/1950		
4	Ignatius John Cramer	b: 4/5/1952		d: 7/23/1982
	+Kathleen Marie Gros		m: 7/11/1975	
3	Maria Leona Cramer	b: 6/11/1912		d: 7/1/1981
	+Henry Leonard Habetz, Jr.	b: 5/11/1912	m: 2/3/1937	d: 9/16/1985
4	Leonard Jerome "Jack" Habetz	b: 4/16/1938		
	+Sylvia Dawn Bigelow	b: 7/3/1940	m: 1/4/1964	
4	Donald Bernard Habetz	b: 9/25/1940		d: 10/24/2004
	+Patricia Anne Istre	b: 3/27/1940		
4	Edmund Leonard Habetz	b: 11/6/1949		
	+Cheryl Anne Hoffpauir	b: 1/15/1948	m: 5/1/1971	
4	Allan Norbert Habetz	b: 9/7/1952		
	+Gwendolyn Marie Truax	b: 1/6/1952	m: 9/21/1973	
4	Kenneth Michael Habetz	b: 11/13/1955		
	+Penny Anne Hargroder	b: 8/3/1958	m: 11/7/1980	
3	Adelheid Helen Cramer	b: 1914		d: 2/24/2007
3	William Joseph Cramer, Sr.	b: 1917		d: 2000
	+Fannie Mary Primeaux	b: 8/10/1922	m: 1943	d: 11/22/1995
4	Jerri Cramer			
	+Les Dolph			

Cramer

	4	Jimmy Dale Cramer			
		+Vicki Denison			
	4	Jolene Cramer			
		+Charles Raymond Williams			
	4	William Joseph Cramer, Jr.			d: 7/18/1989
		+Anna Bouillion			
3		Joseph Bernard Cramer	b: 1920		d: 1992
3		Theodora Lucy Cramer	b: 9/26/1922		
		+Lawrence Nicholas Zaunbrecher	b: 4/12/1925	m: 6/20/1955	
	4	Elwin Zaunbrecher	b: 8/19/1957		
	4	Eugene Zaunbrecher	b: 1/10/1964		
3		Henry Norbert Cramer	b: 1925		
		+Carrie Amelia Leleux	b: 1922	m: 1950	
3		Mary Cecilia (Sister Lucy) Cramer	b: 1927		d: 1965
2		Everhard Cramer	b: 1/8/1879		d: 6/27/1961
		+Anna Maria Thevis	b: 6/13/1880	m: 1907	d: 9/30/1957
3		Gesina [Anna] Cramer	b: 10/2/1908		d: 4/18/2002
		+Leonard August Habetz	b: 8/28/1903	m: 1934	d: 11/22/1978
	4	Margaret Mary Habetz	b: 9/24/1935		
		+Wesley Bouillion	b: 2/26/1936	m: 11/13/1955	d: 11/8/1990
	4	Geraldine Habetz	b: 5/25/1937		
		+Sherman Trahan	b: 2/26/1939	m: 3/17/1962	
	4	Louise Habetz	b: 1/6/1939		
		+Johnny Meche	b: 12/25/1939	m: 11/4/1961	
	4	Edward Habetz	b: 2/7/1941		
		+Marlene Miller	b: 1/10/1946	m: 11/3/1962	
	4	Daniel Habetz	b: 1/3/1943		
		+Judy Savoy	b: 12/19/1943	m: 11/2/1962	
	4	Gerhard Habetz	b: 12/31/1944		

Cramer

	+Brenda Gale Guidry	m: 11/12/1966		
	*2nd Wife of Gerhard Habetz:			
	+Gloria Higginbotham	b: 8/2/1945	m: 4/17/1985	
4	Charles Habetz	b: 5/22/1946		
	+Patty Beard	b: 3/31/1949	m: 10/11/1970	
4	Robert Habetz	b: 5/13/1948		
	+Amber Thomas		m: 4/4/1969	
4	Rose Marie Habetz	b: 4/20/1950		d: 9/1951
3	Jacob Cramer	b: 4/7/1910		d: 1/28/1973
	+Mary Magdalena Habetz	b: 1/5/1906	m: 1/7/1936	d: 12/30/1995
4	Anna Marie "Sr. Mary Clare" Cramer	b: 10/16/1936		
4	Angelina Cramer	b: 1/5/1938		
	+Ralph Gonthier	b: 8/7/1934	m: 6/20/1964	d: 6/25/2001
4	Leonard "Jake" Jacob Cramer	b: 2/17/1939		
	+Catherine Gossen	b: 8/4/1939	m: 11/9/1961	
4	Barbara Anna Cramer	b: 12/18/1940		
	+Stephen Dubose	b: 8/4/1938	m: 6/25/1960	
4	Alberta Cramer	b: 8/16/1942		d: 12/11/1993
	+Leland Paul "T-Boy" Hebert	b: 11/7/1943		m: 2/16/1963
4	Bernadette Cramer	b: 11/7/1943		
	+Douglas Guidry	b: 7/16/1942	m: 8/29/1964	
4	Anthony Edward Cramer	b: 2/20/1945		
	+Rhena Vienne	b: 11/11/1946	m: 4/23/1966	
4	Michael John Cramer	b: 10/14/1946		
	+Yvonne Prather	b: 11/11/1946	m: 9/4/1965	
4	Theresa Cramer	b: 6/21/1948		
	+Lawrence Doucet	b: 2/13/1947	m: 1/31/1970	d: 12/21/1993

Cramer

4	Loretta Cramer	b: 1/10/1952		
	+Glenn Michael Boudreaux	b: 12/27/1948	m: 1/8/1977	
3	Herman Aloyious Cramer	b: 12/5/1911		d: 11/10/1966
	+Josephine Leonards	b: 3/26/1919		d: 1/23/2002
4	Lawrence Aloyious Cramer	b: 9/12/1941		
	+Mary Magdalene Reiners	b: 3/31/1944	m: 6/11/1963	
4	Louis Edward Cramer	b: 2/10/1943		
	+Katherine Carlson	b: 7/4/1945	m: 6/3/1973	
3	Gertrude Cramer	b: 10/2/1913		d: 7/8/1996
3	Adeline "Addie" Cramer	b: 8/30/1915		
	+William "Raymond" Habetz	b: 8/30/1913	m: 8/17/1950	d: 2004
4	May Rose Habetz	b: 1/3/1954		
	+Anthony Bourgeois	b: 1/1/1955	m: 8/17/2000	
3	Gerhard Cramer	b: 8/22/1917		d: 11/28/1978
	+Sophie Schatzle	b: 1919	m: 1946	
4	Jacquline Cramer	b: 10/24/1948		
	+Darrell LeBlanc	b: 3/26/1946	m: 1/11/1966	
4	Mary Frances Cramer	b: 12/22/1950		d: 4/6/1957
4	Elizabeth "Betty" Cramer	b: 7/13/1952		
	+Michael Bellard	b: 5/8/1949	m: 10/14/1972	
4	Cynthia Cramer	b: 6/23/1956		
	+Cody Miller	b: 6/4/1950	m: 6/13/1981	
4	Josie Cramer	b: 11/3/1958		
	+Benny Stelly			
3	Marie Rose Cramer	b: 3/11/1920		
	+Leo Mouton	b: 4/19/1919	m: 2/12/1941	d: 12/9/1981
4	Johnny Mouton	b: 1/6/1942		d: 10/10/2005
	+Virlee Mier	b: 12/24/1941		

Cramer

4	Edwin Mouton	b: 10/17/1944		
	+Ann Burnett	b: 11/27/1943	m: 2/8/1964	
4	James Mouton	b: 7/30/1946		
	+Judy Bearb	b: 12/11/1946	m: 4/15/1967	
4	Genevieve Mouton	b: 2/16/1949		
	+Ronald Melancon	b: 12/21/1949	m: 6/14/1969	
4	Patricia Mouton	b: 2/13/1951		
	+Leonard Breaux	b: 1/25/1949	m: 3/7/1970	
4	Mary Jo Mouton	b: 4/30/1953		
	+Patrick Boudreaux	b: 1/18/1949		d: 6/14/1977
4	Gregory Mouton	b: 3/12/1955		
	+Sherry Myers	b: 8/13/1957	m: 8/17/1974	
4	Dianna Mouton	b: 9/4/1957		d: 9/4/1957
4	Linda Mouton	b: 11/17/1959		
2	Herman Cramer	b: 3/10/1882		d: 10/3/1970
	+Maria Odelia Thevis	b: 1886	m: 1909	d: 1984
3	Anna Marie Cramer	b: 1910		d: 2005
3	Maria Gesina Cramer	b: 5/20/1914		d: 8/29/2000
	+Xavier Lawrence Schultz	b: 9/1/1912	m: 1/17/1934	d: 10/21/1975
4	Gerald Andrew Schultz	b: 1/1/1935		d: 3/26/2002
	+Loretta Lorraine Klein	b: 5/8/1937	m: 6/30/1955	d: 1/15/2005
4	John Lawrence Schultz	b: 2/8/1937		
	+Cora Lee Cormier	b: 9/21/1941	m: 6/21/1959	
4	Leroy Edmond Schultz	b: 3/24/1940		
3	Adelheid Walburga Cramer	b: 1920		d: 1937
2	Henry Cramer	b: 1885		d: 1972
2	Adelheid Cramer	b: 1889		d: 1982
2	Anna Maria Cramer	b: 1893		d: 1980
	+Peter Joseph Thevis	b: 1889	m: 1912	d: 1969
3	John Gerhard Thevis	b: 7/28/1914		d: 1983

Cramer

	+Martha Frances Burton	b: 11/15/1920	m: 12/31/1940	d: 1999
4	Robert John Thevis	b: 1/1/1942		
	+Sadie G. Frey	b: 2/20/1944	m: 6/29/1963	
4	Sandra Ann Thevis	b: 1/9/1944		
	+Thomas E. Myatt	b: 2/20/1944	m: 11/19/1967	
4	Michael Joseph Thevis	b: 3/20/1945		
	+Glynda Gayle Truax	b: 3/30/1946	m: 4/20/1968	
4	Kathleen Marie Thevis	b: 9/12/1946		
4	Mary Antoinette Thevis	b: 12/6/1950		
	+Richard F. Coignard	b: 9/15/1949	m: 5/15/1971	
4	Stephen Anthony Thevis	b: 6/13/1954		
4	Patrick Gerard Thevis	b: 9/1/1955		
4	Marian Elizabeth Thevis	b: 10/18/1959		
3	Annie Gesina Thevis	b: 1917		
	+John Conrad Hensgens	b: 1919	m: 1946	d: 1992
4	John Conrad Hensgens II			
	+Becky Collins			
3	Joseph Herman Thevis	b: 1919	d: 2003	
	+Helen Marie Zaunbrecher	b: 1924	m: 1946	
4	Lucille Thevis	b: 5/16/1948		
	+Al Hebert	b: 7/24/1948	m: 1/19/1969	
4	Philip Thevis	b: 1/7/1950		
	+Katie Guidry	b: 12/14/1950	m: 6/3/1972	
4	Wayne Thomas Thevis	b: 11/7/1951		
	+Glenda LeJeune	b: 3/5/1952	m: 11/4/1972	
4	Brenda Thevis	b: 2/4/1954		
	+Carl Hebert	b: 8/21/1953	m: 7/15/1973	
4	Claudette Thevis	b: 6/23/1957		
	+Roger Blackburn		m: 6/18/1977	
4	Nicholas Thevis	b: 12/27/1960		
	+Monica Daily	b: 1/1/1964	m: 8/3/1985	

Cramer

3		Mary Agnes Thevis	b: 7/14/1921	
		+Paul Doucet	b: 8/17/1919	m: 1945
	4	Mary Theresa Doucet	b: 9/13/1946	
		+Edward Anthony Caruso	b: 3/31/1946	
	4	Richard Paul Doucet	b: 1/12/1948	
	4	David Wayne Doucet	b: 10/24/1951	
		+Susan Bishop		m: 4/15/1988
	4	Lucy Ann Doucet	b: 3/29/1954	
		+Conrad John Tworek	b: 8/29/1946	
	4	Ronald Joseph Doucet		b: 9/12/1957
		+Nacoma Beth Rasberry		m: 1/25/1975
	4	Anthony James Doucet	b: 1/15/1959	
		+Claire Leckelt		m: 3/1989
	4	William Louis Doucet	b: 1/21/1962	
2		Rosa Cramer	b: 1895	d: 1992

5. Dischler, Franz Xavier:

Franz Xavier Dischler b: 2/1/1838 d: 9/10/1911 from Wolxheim, Alsace, was the son of Franz Joseph Dischler b: 10/4/1798 d: ? and Francesca Widt b: 1799 d: ?. He married in 1866 to Carolina Neiderst b: 11/1841 d: 2/3/1917 from Irmstett, Alsace.

2		Joseph Dischler	b: 1866		d: 1921
		+Katharina Hensgens	b: 1872	m: 1893	d: 1955
3		Maria Regina Dischler	b: 1894		d: 1977
		+Lambert Ronkartz	b: 1891	m: 1919	d: 1978
	4	Josephine Marie Ronkartz	b: 1920		
		+Joseph John Burton	b: 1917	m: 1941	d: 2004
	4	Joseph John Ronkartz	b: 1922		d: 1989
		+Rose Marie LeBlanc	b: 1926	m: 1946	d: 1989
	4	John William Ronkartz	b: 1925		d: 2000
		+Effie Katherine Rogers	b: 1933	m: 1950	
	4	Jeanette Juliana Ronkartz	b: 1929		
		+Ronald Gene Robinson	b: 1931	m: 1950	d: 1953
	4	Louise Regina Ronkartz	b: 1932		
		+Daniel Hilarion Troyanowski	b: 1928	m: 1954	d: 1981
	4	Jerome Lambert Ronkartz	b: 1933		
		+Jo Ann Zaunbrecher	b: 1934	m: 1956	
3		Joseph Dischler, Jr.	b: 1895		d: 1959
		+Louise Marie Fontenot	b: 1897	m: 1920	d: 1993
	4	Lorraine Dischler			
		+Leon Rine			
	4	Mary Belle Dischler			
		+Elmo Simon			
	4	Jo Ann Dischler			

Dischler

	+Edmond Dupre, Jr.			
4	Richard Dischler			
	+Sylvia Robinson			
3	Maria Gertrude Dischler	b: 1897		d: 1965
	+Ludwig (Louis) Leonards	b: 8/31/1899	m: 1922	d: 10/30/1978
4	Philomena Hedwig Leonards	b: 1923		
	+John Francis Ohlenforst	b: 1921	m: 1947	d: 1997
4	Blaise Philip Leonards	b: 3/21/1927		
	+Bernadine Marie Habetz	b: 6/9/1927	m: 10/27/1948	
4	Edwin Joseph Leonards	b: 9/21/1928		d: 4/21/2007
	+Genevieve Augusta Frey	b: 11/11/1932	m: 7/9/1951	
4	Eleanor Marie Leonards	b: 7/15/1930		
	+William Anton Braun	b: 10/24/1922	m: 10/26/1950	
4	Dorothy Clara Leonards	b: 4/1/1932		
4	Marcella Marie Leonards	b: 2/3/1934		
	+Andrew Lawrence Ohlenforst	b: 10/6/1928	m: 1/19/1955	d: 10/3/1983
4	Louis Anthony Leonards	b: 1/14/1936		
	+Patricia Ann Spell	b: 1/21/1938	m: 12/28/1960	
4	Leonard Lawrence "Buck" Leonards	b: 6/30/1937		
	+Barbara Ann Link	b: 9/17/1938	m: 11/27/1958	
4	Sylvia Jean Leonards	b: 2/24/1941		
	+Johnny Mack Frugé	b: 10/4/1939	m: 11/17/1962	
3	Charles Barromeo Dischler	b: 1898		d: 1986
	+Clara Julia Olinger	b: 1900	m: 1922	d: 1975

Dischler

4	Barbara Catherine Dischler	b: 1923		d: 1993
	+William "Bill" Reed	b: 1920	m: 1952	
4	Charles Leo Dischler	b: 1924		
	+Carrie Mae Harmon	b: 1929	m: 1949	
4	Cecilla Madelene Dischler	b: 1926		
	+Daniel Landry	b: 1925	m: 1950	
4	Julia Theresa Dischler	b: 1928		
	+Sherril Thompson	b: 1928	m: 1957	d: 2002
4	Alvin Joseph Dischler	b: 1929		
	+Theresa Martarona	b: 1933	m: 1958	
4	Clarice Josephine Dischler	b: 1932		
	+Charles William Stewart	b: 1928	m: 1972	d: 1995
4	Ferdinand Louis Dischler	b: 1933		
	+Wanda George	b: 1933	m: 1956	
4	Robert Louis Dischler	b: 1935		d: 2003
	+Donna Sue Fast	b: 1941	m: 1964	
4	Thomas Anthony Dischler	b: 1938		
4	Marjorie Ann Dischler	b: 1940		
	+Robert Walker	b: 1940	m: 1959	
4	Michael Anthony Dischler	b: 1942		
	+Barbara Hazelton	b: 1948	m: 1973	
4	Carol Bertha Dischler	b: 1945		
	+Lawrence Leonards	b: 1946	m: 6/7/1969	
3	Anthony Conrad Dischler	b: 1900		d: 1986
	+Maria Helena Zaunbrecher	b: 1896	m: 1923	d: 1952
4	Antonia Maria Dischler	b: 1926		

Dischler

	+John Clyde Leger	b: 1923	m: 1949	
4	Martin William Dischler	b: 1927		
	+Marcella Comeaux	b: 1928	m: 1949	
4	Pauline Bertha Dischler	b: 1929		d: 2006
	+Francis Charles Roy	b: 1929	m: 1949	d: 1993
4	Monica "Mona" Dischler	b: 1934		
	+Ronald James Gossen	b: 1929	m: 1953	
4	Helena Marie Dischler	b: 1936		
	+Kenneth Jack Mantle		m: 1961	
	*2nd Husband of Helena Marie Dischler:			
	+Frank Robles	b: 1927	m: 1976	
3	Regina Josephine Dischler	b: 1902		d: 1997
	+Edward John Olinger	b: 1896	m: 1922	d: 1983
4	Ambrose Joseph Olinger	b: 1923		
	+Margaret Leonards	b: 1923	m: 1946	
4	Beatrice Aloysia Olinger	b: 1925		
	+August Joseph Leonards	b: 1924	m: 1947	d: 1988
4	Irene Regina Olinger	b: 1927		
	+Ashton Simon Petijean	b: 1914	m: 1951	d: 1979
4	Rose Marie Olinger	b: 1930		
	+John N. John III	b: 1929	m: 1950	d: 1983
4	Hilary Anthony Olinger	b: 1934		
	+Melba Dean Roy	b: 1937	m: 1955	
4	Mary Jo Olinger	b: 1938		
4	Ray Edward Olinger	b: 1942		
	+Johnnie Ruth Prather	b: 1941	m: 1966	
3	Annie Marie Dischler	b: 1904		d: 1977
	+Joseph August Zaunbrecher	b: 1906	m: 1925	d: 1981

Dischler

4	Edna Augusta Zaunbrecher	b: 1926		
	+Claures Joseph Broussard	b: 1928	m: 1957	
4	Leo Charles Zaunbrecher	b: 1927		
	+Stella Minnie Low	b: 1936	m: 1956	
4	Gerald Joseph Zaunbrecher	b: 1929		d: 1988
	+Shirley Mae Stark	b: 1937	m: 1956	d: 1994
4	Harold Joseph Zaunbrecher	b: 1929		d: 1999
	+Pauline Margaret Dupre	b: 1936	m: 1960	
4	Ferdinand Vincent Zaunbrecher	b: 1932		
	+Janet Louise Summers		m: 1960	
	*2nd Wife of Ferdinand Vincent Zaunbrecher:			
	+Jean Pascoe		m: 1980	
4	Genevieve Marie Zaunbrecher	b: 1934		
	+Gordon Edward Tate	b: 1934	m: 1963	d: 2004
4	Joyce Marie Zaunbrecher	b: 1935		
	+Howard Joseph Melancon	b: 1937	m: 1972	
4	Dorothy Ann Zaunbrecher	b: 1937		
4	Hilary Charles Zaunbrecher	b: 1939		
	+Suzanne Gayle Phillips	b: 1946	m: 1983	

Dischler

4	Donald Louis Zaunbrecher	b: 1942		
	+Josephine Ann Busse	b: 1944	m: 1976	
3	Bertha Marie Dischler	b: 1905		d: 1990
	+Charles Joseph Zaunbrecher	b: 1905	m: 1929	d: 10/25/1972
4	Dolores Marie Zaunbrecher	b: 1930		
	+Phillip Jacob Joseph Habetz	b: 3/19/1930	m: 1956	
4	Fr. Charles Zaunbrecher	b: 1931		d: 1996
4	Vincent William Zaunbrecher	b: 1933		
	+Genevieve Parrino	b: 1930	m: 1955	
4	Jane Frances Zaunbrecher	b: 1934		d: 1990
	+Wilvin LeLeux	b: 1935	m: 1958	
4	William "Billy" Zaunbrecher	b: 5/31/1938		d: 8/19/1997
	+Anna Margaret Cramer	b: 12/31/1938	m: 12/16/1963	
4	Stephen Joseph Zaunbrecher	b: 9/2/1940		
	+Rose Marie Reiners	b: 3/28/1942	m: 6/26/1962	
3	Marie Dischler	b: 1908		d: 1993
	+Anton Joseph Zaunbrecher	b: 1912	m: 1936	d: 1991
3	Francis Nicholas Dischler	b: 1910		d: 1983
	+Genevieve Clark	b: 1914	m: 1938	d: 1968
4	Kathleen Ann Dischler	b: 1941		
	+Daniel Peter Wilfrath	b: 1941	m: 1967	
4	Gretchen Solanges Dischler	b: 1943		
	+Dalton John Istre	b: 1940	m: 1961	d: 1997

Dischler

	4	Nicholas Dischler II			
		+Tanya Firmin			
	4	Helen Manette Dischler	b: 1952		
		+Steven Paul Breaux	b: 1952	m: 1974	
		*2nd Husband of Helen Manette Dischler:			
		+Paul Keith Lopez	b: 1955	m: 1989	
2		Xavier Dischler	b: 7/5/1867		d: 4/25/1945
		+Rosa Wilfert Schultz	b: 1879	m: 10/2/1906	d: 1958
	3	Maria Lena Dischler	b: 1909		d: 1984
		+Frank Edward Huffman	b: 1909	m: 1947	
	3	Antoinette Dischler	b: 1911		d: 1998
		+Gerhard Aloysius Meyer	b: 1910	m: 1933	d: 1975
	4	Melvin Meyer	b: 1941		
		+Audrey Dommert	b: 1940	m: 1975	d: 1996
	3	Francis Xavier Dischler	b: 1913		d: 1925
	3	John Paul Dischler	b: 1915		d: 1992
		+Annie Mary Schneider	b: 1913	m: 1936	
	4	Jacqueline Dischler	b: 1936		
		+Dan Bouligny	b: 1932	m: 1960	
	4	Shelby Dischler	b: 1937		
		+Bob O'Rear	b: 1930	m: 1966	
	4	Douglas Dischler	b: 1943		
		+Cathy Hebert	b: 1952	m: 1979	
	4	Priscilla Dischler	b: 1947		
		+Gary Gotreaux	b: 1945	m: 1968	
	3	Margaret Rose Dischler	b: 1919		d: 10/26/2006
2		Maria Dischler	b: 1868		d: 1957
		+Albert Lafrantz	b: 1872	m: 1894	d: 1947
	3	Charles Albert Lafrantz	b: 12/15/1893		d: 1/2/1962
		+Emelia Anna Bieber	b: 3/21/1903	m: 11/7/1924	
	4	Kathryn Marie Lafrantz	b: 12/7/1925		d: 4/5/1968

Dischler

		+Charles Edward Keenan	b: 10/17/1921	m: 7/3/1945	d: 5/18/1968
	4	Mary Ellen Lafrantz	b: 2/2/1927		
		+Donald Ledford Stephens	b: 5/26/1925		
		*2nd Husband of Mary Ellen Lafrantz:			
		+Lyle T. Hinckley			
	4	Helen Virginia Lafrantz	b: 11/22/1929		
		+Wilbur Hugo "Bill" Grueninger	b: 5/11/1925	m: 9/22/1946	
2		Charles Joseph Dischler	b: 6/5/1871		d: 12/14/1966
		+Bertha Wilfert Schultz	b: 1879	m: 3/1/1897	d: 1949
3		Louis Charles Dischler	b: 1898		d: 1960
		+Beulah Ledoux	b: 1903	m: 1925	d: 1993
	4	Louis Charles Dischler, Jr.	b: 1927		
		+Genevieve Rozas	b: 1929	m: 1950	
	4	Donald Dischler	b: 1929		
		+Anne Hundley			
	4	Anna Lou Dischler	b: 1931		
		+Joseph Fisher	b: 1931		
	4	Emma Lou Dischler	b: 1931		
	4	Richard Dischler	b: 1934		
		+Dolores Duplechin	b: 1936	m: 1956	
3		Anna Mathilda Dischler	b: 1900		d: 1989
		+Placidus Joseph (Sam) Heinen	b: 1899	m: 1921	d: 1974
	4	Dorothy Heinen	b: 1922		
	4	Henry Heinen	b: 1923		
		+Versie Fontenot		m: 1947	d: 1970
		*2nd Wife of Henry Heinen:			
		+Lilly Landreneaux		m: 1973	d: 1981
	4	Helen Heinen	b: 1925		d: 9/16/1991

Dischler

	+Frank E. Landry II	b: 12/9/1920	m: 11/1946	
4	James Heinen	b: 1928		
	+Bonita Rider		m: 1955	d: 1995
4	Lillian Heinen	b: 1931		
	+Norman "Bill" Barron		m: 1951	d: 2001
4	Beatrice Heinen	b: 1933		
	+John Burke Young	b: 1932	m: 1955	
4	Louis Heinen	b: 1935		
	+Marie Francois	b: 1945	m: 1977	
3	Ferdinand Edward (Frank) Dischler	b: 1901		d: 1993
3	Maria Magdelena Dischler	b: 1903		d: 1969
	+Adolph Joseph Frey	b: 1895	m: 1921	d: 1976
4	Daniel Frey	b: 1922		
	+Lillian Fruge	b: 1921	m: 1947	
4	Louis Frey			
4	Edmund Frey	b: 1926		
	+Alberta Heinen	b: 1932	m: 1950	
4	Harold Frey	b: 1928		d: 1982
	+Anna Doise	b: 1931	m: 1952	
3	Henry Vincent Dischler	b: 1905		d: 1921
3	Lawrence William Dischler	b: 1910		d: 1991
	+Annie Marie Hensgens	b: 1914	m: 1933	d: 1995
4	Winona Frances Bertha Dischler	b: 1934		
	+Robert Cartwright	b: 1931	m: 1957	d: 1998
4	Carolyn Ann Dischler	b: 1940		
	+Herman F. "Freddie" Morgan, Jr.	b: 1936	m: 1958	
3	James Dischler	b: 1915		d: 1983
	+Marie Heloise Guillory	b: 1919	m: 1945	d: 2002

Dischler

	4	James Charles Dischler	b: 1950		
		+Paula Schatzle	b: 1951	m: 1972	
	4	Robert Dischler	b: 1952		
	4	Thomas Dischler	b: 1954		
		+Dee Laughlin	b: 1955	m: 1975	
3		Bertha Odile Dischler	b: 1918		d: 1998
		+John Patrick Carroll	b: 1917		d: 1992
	4	Patrick James Carroll	b: 10/3/1944		
		+Linda Thibodeaux	b: 9/29/1944	m: 9/15/1964	
		*2nd Wife of Patrick James Carroll:			
		+Saida Elizabeth Hannie	b: 10/30/1945	m: 4/7/1982	
	4	Allen Charles Carroll	b: 9/29/1946		
		+Patricia Ann Begnaud	b: 1/7/1947	m: 6/3/1967	
	4	Kathleen Odile Carroll	b: 1/25/1950		
		+Frank Beaullieu Randol	b: 9/2/1946	m: 9/18/1973	
2		Sophia Dischler	b: 1873		d: 1893
		+Joseph Hubert Schaffhausen	b: 1855	m: 1893	d: 1938
2		Louis Dischler	b: 1874		d: 1874
2		August Dischler	b: 1877		d: 1938
2		Victor Dischler	b: 1878		d: 1878
2		Anna Dischler	b: 1879		d: 1893
2		Maria Magdelena Dischler	b: 1880		d: 7/31/1914
		+Anthony Joseph Bollich, Sr.	b: 3/23/1870	m: 1899	d: 10/7/1958
3		Louise Marie Bollich	b: 8/25/1901		d: 12/12/1992
		+Leo Paul Frey	b: 10/21/1898	m: 1921	d: 10/4/1982
	4	Lucette Magdeline Frey	b: 12/5/1923		d: 4/26/1995
		+Gilton George Lejeune	b: 4/26/1923	m: 12/20/1945	d: 10/2/1997

Dischler

4	[2] Antoinette Louise Frey	b: 1926		
	+[1] Raymond Joseph Bollich	b: 1925	m: 1946	d: 2004
4	Vernell Marie Frey	b: 1932		
	+Earl Joseph Hebert	b: 1929	m: 1958	d: 2005
4	Shirley Theresa Frey	b: 1934		
	+Maurice Benoit	b: 6/14/1931	m: 1962	d: 8/14/1986
3	Henry Joseph Bollich	b: 1902		d: 1975
	+Theresa Margaret Hensgens	b: 1906	m: 1939	d: 1995
4	Henry Joseph Bollich, Jr.	b: 1947		
	+Cathy Collins	b: 1952	m: 1973	
3	Marie Magdelena Bollich	b: 1904		d: 1995
	+Nicholas Joseph Gossen	b: 1901	m: 1922	d: 1990
4	Marie Antoinette Gossen	b: 12/18/1923		
	+William Charles Puissegur	b: 4/21/1922	m: 11/5/1937	
4	Edna Louise Gossen	b: 7/10/1925		
	+Winfred Joseph Plattsmire	b: 8/3/1921	m: 10/19/1948	d: 1996
4	Raymond Nicholas Gossen	b: 4/3/1927		
	+Henrietta Theresa Habetz	b: 6/1/1928	m: 2/3/1949	
4	Lucille Clara Gossen	b: 11/11/1929		
	+Alois Andrew Reiners	b: 7/25/1926	m: 11/25/1953	d: 3/19/1999
4	Robert Anthony Gossen	b: 10/1/1933		d: 11/3/2006
	+Jeanne Ann Privat	b: 3/15/1937	m: 5/6/1956	
4	Helen Marie Gossen	b: 8/14/1936		

Dischler

		+Clarence Charles Arsement	b: 9/15/1932	m: 10/15/1956	
	4	Catherine Rose Gossen	b: 8/4/1939		
		+Leonard Jacob Cramer	b: 2/19/1939	m: 11/9/1961	
3		Anthony Joseph Bollich, Jr.	b: 1906		d: 1983
		+Rose Doucet	b: 1917	m: 1938	d: 1988
	4	Shelby Michael Bollich	b: 10/24/1941		d: 12/3/1990
		+Marianne Jeffries	b: 4/3/1941	m: 4/15/1963	
	4	Frank Harvey Bollich	b: 3/12/1945		
		+Joan Marie Cadez	b: 10/9/1947	m: 9/20/1969	
3		August Xavier Bollich	b: 1908		d: 1993
		+Bernice Josephine Fontenot	b: 1914	m: 1937	
3		Deceased Infant Bollich	b: 1910		d: 1910
3		John Bollich	b: 1912		d: 6/6/1914
3		Deceased Infant Bollich	b: 1914		d: 1914
2		Ludovica (Louise) Dischler	b: 9/12/1882		d: 8/22/1939
		+Franz Joseph Bollich	b: 12/15/1880	m: 1904	d: 6/24/1974
3		Franz Xavier Joseph Bollich	b: 10/29/1904		d: 2/9/1990
		+Barbara Marie Zaunbrecher	b: 10/26/1903	m: 1926	d: 11/8/1992
	4	Loretta Elaine Bollich		b: 11/7/1927	
		+Burnis Cooper	b: 10/19/1917	m: 9/11/1945	d: 6/26/1991
		*2nd Husband of Loretta Elaine Bollich:			
		+Louis C. Gaspard		m: 5/20/2000	
	4	Clara Louise Bollich	b: 3/23/1929		
		+Durland Joseph Miller	b: 8/25/1924	m: 11/24/1949	d: 2/10/2002
	4	Gerald Francis Bollich	b: 3/9/1930		
		+Delia Marie Breaux	b: 10/1/1931	m: 10/24/1953	d: 11/29/2003
	4	Donald Joseph Bollich	b: 3/26/1931		

Dischler

	+Willie Dean Vidrine	b: 7/31/1934	m: 11/21/1953	
4	Lawrence Charles "Larry" Bollich	b: 6/21/1932		
	+Jacqueline Marie Brown	b: 8/2/1932	m: 4/12/1958	
4	Austin William Bollich	b: 7/15/1933		
	+Sylvia Ann Stelly	b: 11/16/1934	m: 11/8/1953	
4	Elmo Edward Bollich	b: 1/20/1935		d: 12/18/2005
	+Elrena Mary Manuel		m: 2/11/1956	
4	Elaine Marie Bollich	b: 1/20/1935		
	+Carl Edward Turk	b: 2/1/1928	m: 6/5/1956	d: 11/23/1986
4	Sylvia Ann Bollich	b: 6/21/1936		
	+John Luke Emery Lintzen	b: 3/22/1936	m: 4/8/1961	d: 1/13/1976
4	Gregory Augustine Bollich	b: 11/28/1938		
	+Patricia Ann Sittig	b: 7/16/1940	m: 9/2/1961	
4	Barbara Ann Bollich	b: 9/22/1942		
	+James Allen LeJeune	b: 9/19/1942	m: 10/27/1962	
4	Diane Louise Bollich	b: 2/10/1947		
	+Gary Layne Elkins	b: 12/13/1947	m: 7/3/1971	d: 6/17/2001
4	Judy Ann Bollich	b: 5/9/1949		
	+Kenneth Lee Joseph Hollier	b: 10/13/1949	m: 1/27/1973	
3	Annie Caroline Bollich	b: 1906		d: 2004
	+Henry Joseph Zaunbrecher	b: 1901	m: 1925	d: 1993
4	Vera Marie Zaunbrecher	b: 11/6/1926		
	+Frank Conrad Jabusch	b: 1924	m: 1947	
4	Stella Josephine Zaunbrecher	b: 5/5/1928		

Dischler

	+James William Doucet	b: 1928	m: 1951	d: 3/2005
4	Leroy Francis Zaunbrecher	b: 8/1/1929		d: 10/2003
	+Sammie Jane Meaux	b: 1931	m: 1950	
4	James Anthony Zaunbrecher	b: 8/3/1931		
	+Helen Joy Martin	b: 1934	m: 1954	
4	Louise Frances Zaunbrecher	b: 9/1/1933		
	+Aubry Decuir Caffery	b: 5/21/1923	m: 6/1/1957	d: 7/5/1999
4	Lorraine Marie Zaunbrecher	b: 1/9/1935		d: 11/1962
	+Dr. John Joseph Gordon	b: 1926	m: 1956	d: 2004
4	Suzanne Zaunbrecher	b: 5/21/1936		
	+Howard Allen "Boochie" Duncan	b: 1927	m: 1958	d: 2004
4	Dennis Henry Zaunbrecher	b: 12/1938		d: 1991
	+Gerry Broussard	b: 1938	m: 1961	
4	Leonard Anthony Zaunbrecher	b: 8/31/1943		
	+Charlotte Joan Sittig	b: 1942	m: 1964	
3	Albert Joseph Bollich	b: 6/14/1908		d: 4/19/2001
	+Frances Julia Frey	b: 7/24/1909	m: 12/2/1932	d: 9/26/1994
4	Geraldine Helen Bollich	b: 12/11/1933		
	+Alfred Benjamin Horaist	b: 1/5/1931	m: 7/4/1953	
4	Wayne Henry Bollich	b: 6/17/1936		
	+Katherine Olinde	b: 8/14/1941	m: 4/6/1960	
4	Byron Charles Bollich	b: 9/3/1940		
	+Sharon Delana	b: 3/21/1941	m: 6/22/1963	

Dischler

4	Reginald Anthony Bollich	b: 2/4/1944		
	+Martha Thaller	b: 3/29/1944	m: 5/14/1966	
	*2nd Wife of Reginald Anthony Bollich:			
	+Dorothy Compton	b: 10/6/1944	m: 9/28/1991	
3	Charles Joseph Bollich	b: 2/17/1910		d: 8/2/1995
	+Dorothy Elizabeth Alpha	b: 8/11/1907	m: 1932	d: 5/3/2002
4	Joel Lynn Bollich	b: 6/21/1940		
	+Edne Anne Carrier	b: 1940		
	*2nd Wife of Joel Lynn Bollich:			
	+Elizabeth Ann Edwards Bush	b: 9/24/1956	m: 1985	
3	Clare Catherine Bollich	b: 5/4/1913		d: 5/13/1914
3	Edward Peter Bollich	b: 1915		d: 1982
	+Margaret Catherine Mays	b: 1921	m: 1940	
4	Catherine Bollich	b: 12/6/1941		
	+James Guilbeau	b: 4/12/1938	m: 1/27/1962	
4	Edward Peter Bollich II	b: 11/22/1946		
	+Mary Ann Guidroz	b: 9/15/1937	m: 11/21/1987	
4	Michael Bollich	b: 9/18/1951		
	+Debbie Baca			
	*2nd Wife of Michael Bollich:			
	+Mary Mcfinger	b: 1/15/1970	m: 5/18/2000	
3	Marcella Rose Bollich	b: 6/14/1916		d: 9/11/1996
	+Lawrence Aloysuis Frey	b: 5/9/1915	m: 1937	d: 5/1/2001
4	Barry Lawrence Frey	b: 4/18/1938		
	+Laura Leger	b: 11/19/1939	m: 6/6/1959	
4	Quintin Francis Frey	b: 6/16/1943		
	+Judith Clement	b: 3/25/1947	m: 8/31/1968	
3	Leonard Joseph Bollich	b: 4/3/1919		d: 8/18/1944

Dischler

		+Perry Ann Major	b: 1922	m: 1943	d: 1972
3		Thelma Louise Bollich	b: 11/29/1921		d: 3/4/2004
		+Hersey Charles Lejeune	b: 5/14/1924	m: 1945	d: 1/18/1971
	4	Vaughn Charles Lejeune	b: 9/1/1946		
		+Judith Lynn Hoffpauir	b: 3/1/1944	m: 12/26/1971	
	4	Brice Francis Lejeune	b: 8/28/1951		
		+Judith Gomilla	b: 11/14/1952	m: 5/15/1979	
	4	Arlene Louise Lejeune	b: 8/15/1952		
		+Michael John Albarado	b: 1/25/1950	m: 12/2/1972	
	4	Dean Jude Lejeune	b: 11/26/1957		
		+Debra Richard	b: 9/9/1960	m: 11/17/1990	
3		[1] Raymond Joseph Bollich	b: 1925		d: 2004
		+[2] Antoinette Louise Frey	b: 1926	m: 1946	
	4	Carden Joseph Bollich	b: 7/29/1949		d: 7/31/1949
	4	Keith Leo Bollich	b: 5/28/1951		d: 6/2/1951
	4	Kevin Jude Bollich	b: 9/24/1956		
	4	Kent Gerard Bollich	b: 5/2/1963		d: 7/31/1963

6. Gielen, Johann:
Johann Gielen b: 1828 d: 1896 from Birgden was the son of Johann Christian Gielen b: 1796 d: ? from Langbroich and Johanna Maria Janssen. He married in the 1860s to Maria Magdelena Krausen b: 1841 d: 1882 from Dusseldorf.

2		Maria Katharina Gielen	b: 1864			d: 1948
		+William Watson Robinson	b: 1853	m: 1885		d: 1930
3		Martin Aurelien Robinson	b: 1885			d: 1888
3		Helena Catherine Robinson	b: 1888			d: 1980
		+Sydney Ross Shoemate	b: 1882	m: 1919		d: 1962
3		Renold Roland Robinson	b: 1891			d: 1962
		+Mallie Hayes	b: 1895	m: 1919		d: 1966
3		Viola Gertrude Christina Robinson	b: 1894			d: 1954
		+Joseph Luther McClelland	b: 1884	m: 1911		d: 1969
3		Jeanette (Nettie) Robinson	b: 1896			d: 1976
		+William Madison Amy	b: 1894	m: 1921		d: 1984
3		Arden Robinson	b: 1899			d: 1978
		+Irma Lee Stakes	b: 1906	m: 1929		d: 1968
3		Nellie Robinson	b: 1901			d: 1967
		+Daniel Hopkins	b: 1901	m: 1931		d: 1968
3		Harry Ulrich Robinson	b: 1905			d: 1991
		+Hazel Belle Miller	b: 10/14/1913	m: 1953		d: 12/4/1989
2		Johann August Gielen	b: 1866			d: 1886
2		Maria Johanna Gielen	b: 1868			d: 1955
		+James Edward Winchester	b: 1857	m: 1889		d: 1901
3		Edward James Winchester	b: 1895			d: 1/18/1957
		+Ruth Alice Robinson	b: 1900	m: 2/13/1917		d: 1940
	4	Beatrice Ruby Winchester	b: 11/18/1918			d: 9/14/1995
		+Leonard Lejeune	b: 10/28/1916	m: 4/13/1938		d: 8/23/1986
3		William Stuart Winchester	b: 6/20/1889			d: 3/1/1963
		+Joyce "Susie" Phoebe Robinson	b: 4/17/1902	m: 3/15/1922		d: 1997

Gielen

	4	Wilma Vienna Winchester	b: 12/8/1922		
		+Walter Creigh Hall	b: 4/18/1914	m: 4/5/1939	d: 1/5/1950
		*2nd Husband of Wilma Vienna Winchester:			
		+R.A. Bethea, Jr.	b: 3/26/1923	m: 5/3/1958	d: 3/8/2005
	4	Willa Fay Winchester	b: 2/10/1925		
		+Joseph Salvador Faia	b: 11/19/1915	m: 9/29/1945	d: 5/11/1995
		*2nd Husband of Willa Fay Winchester:			
		+C.L. Patterson	b: 1911	m: 9/8/1997	d: 2/22/2002
	4	William Mason Winchester	b: 3/24/1929		
		+Shirley Inez Hicks	b: 9/19/1930	m: 9/2/1953	
	4	James Edward Winchester	b: 2/8/1938		d: 3/21/1958
		+Nettie Lee Trahan	b: 1/17/1936	m: 5/15/1956	
2		Joseph Arnold Gielen	b: 1873		d: 1945
2		John Daniel (Pete) Gielen	b: 1874		d: 1956
		+Fedora Green Robinson	b: 1889	m: 1909	d: 1943
	3	John Daniel Gielen	b: 1912		d: 1952
		+Juliette Mary John	b: 1913	m: 1938	d: 2004
	4	John Daniel Gielen III	b: 10/18/1938		
		+Peggy Regina Angelle	b: 11/19/1940	m: 12/21/1959	
	4	Mary Anne Gielen	b: 1/19/1943		
		+Stephen Anthony Stefanski	b: 3/15/1942	m: 10/1/1966	
	4	Lazar John "L.J." Gielen	b: 4/19/1945		
		+Carol Jane "Chee Chee" Breaux	b: 3/8/1946	m: 8/27/1966	
	3	Arnold Joseph Gielen	b: 1914		d: 1997
		+Eloise Mamie Mouton	b: 1916	m: 1936	
	4	Marvin William Gielen, Sr.	b: 1937		
		+Geneva L. O'Hara		m: 1959	
		*2nd Wife of Marvin William Gielen, Sr.:			

Gielen

	+Linda S. Palmer	b: 1952	m: 1997	
4	Arnold Joseph Gielen, Jr.	b: 1941		d: 2005
	+Darlene Marie Pinter	b: 1938		
4	Gretchen Louise Gielen	b: 1949		
	+Bendal Layne Turner	b: 1947		
	*2nd Husband of Gretchen Louise Gielen:			
	+Lester Joseph Hebert	b: 1931		
3	Hildred Mae Gielen	b: 1916		d: 1963
	+Willard Coleman Edgar	b: 1915	m: 1938	d: 1995
4	Helen Edgar			
4	Patsy Jean Edgar	b: 1940		
	+Robert Lathan Drane			
3	Mildred Helena Gielen	b: 1916		d: 1997
	+Raoul Dudley Breaux	b: 1913	m: 1940	d: 2001
3	Roy Wilbur Gielen	b: 1918		d: 2000
	+Catherine Irene O'Neill	b: 1924	m: 1945	d: 1979
4	James Henry Gielen	b: 1955		
	+Rhonda Black	b: 1961		
4	Alan Roy Gielen	b: 1961		
	+Linda Marie Acevedo	b: 1959		
3	Freda Josephine Gielen	b: 1921		d: 1996
	+Roy Michael Strong	b: 1919	m: 1945	d: 1984
4	Pamela Strong			d: Deceased
	+Michael Potier			
4	Sandra Strong			
	+George Judice			
	*2nd Husband of Sandra Strong:			
	+Don Higginbotham			
4	Michael Strong			
4	Susan Strong			
	+David Bertrand			
3	Henry Herbert Gielen	b: 1927		d: 1951

Gielen

	+Donna Jane Underwood	b: 1929	m: 1950	
2	Marie Caroline Gielen	b: 1878		d: 1955
	+Elly Hiller			d: 1905
3	Charles Hiller	b: 1901		d: 1901
3	Arnold James Hiller	b: 1902		d: 1963
	+Thelma Estelle Hopkins	b: 1904		
	*2nd Husband of Marie Caroline Gielen:			
	+Joseph Honore Fuselier	b: 1877	m: 1908	d: 1963
3	Edward Franklin Fuselier	b: 1910		
	+Catherine Lena Cuccio	b: 1905		d: 1977
2	Catherine Bertha Gielen	b: 1882		d: 1882

7. Gossen, Johann Peter:

Johann Peter Gossen b: 8/13/1815 d: 10/7/1882 from Gangelt was the son of Henricus Johann Gossen b: 11/19/1778 d: 10/24/1867 and Maria Josepha Bautz b. 1783 d: 1815. He married on 5/4/1852 to Maria Agnes Killen b: 3/3/1830 d: 1/2/1898 from Hastenrath. Maria Agnes Killen is the daughter of Johann Arnold Killen b: 1800 d: 1857 and Anna Maria Paulssen. (Maria Agnes Killen was a half-sister of Maria Josepha Killen, who married Wilhelm Joseph Vondenstein, see Vondenstein family).

2	John Henry Gossen	b: 3/8/1854		d: 2/8/1918
	+Anna Katherina Arimond	b: 8/28/1860	m: 2/5/1884	d: 11/7/1893
3	Maria Agnes Gossen	b: 1885		d: 1929
	+Henry Joseph Husers	b: 3/25/1885	m: 12/23/1908	d: 12/26/1935
4	Anna Margaret Husers	b: 3/20/1910		d: 1/30/1929
	+Earl Stakes	b: 1904	m: 1927	
4	Maria Elizabeth Husers	b: 6/11/1911		d: 1987
	+Foster Joseph Istre	b: 1905	m: 1929	d: 1963
	*2nd Husband of Maria Elizabeth Husers:			
	+Boyd Joseph Mayers	b: 1910	m: 1965	d: 1984
4	Hubert Henry Husers	b: 10/6/1913		d: 1988
	+Mary Lois Perry	b: 1922	m: 1938	
4	Josephine Agnes Husers	b: 7/19/1915		d: 2000
	+Wilbur Abel Laine	b: 1914	m: 1937	d: 1998
4	Maria Gebina Husers	b: 12/24/1916		d: 2000
	+Placid Edwin Istre	b: 1914	m: 1939	d: 1988
4	Anthony Bernard Husers	b: 1919		d: 1919
4	Martin Albert Husers	b: 8/3/1920		d: 7/3/1940
4	Maria Cecilia Husers	b: 1/31/1923		
	+Thomas Dodd Jenkins	b: 1922	m: 1943	d: 1997
3	Hubert Joseph Gossen	b: 12/28/1887		d: 2/9/1920
	+Mary (Mamie) Hurly	b: 1881	m: 2/16/1916	d: 1/15/1963
4	Mary Agnes Gossen	b: 12/18/1916		d: 1999
	+Clarence Kosub		m: 11/14/1936	
	*2nd Husband of Mary Agnes Gossen:			

Gossen

	+Alvin W. Young	b: 12/24/1913	m: 12/6/1969	
4	Hubert Henry Gossen	b: 3/11/1918		d: 1992
3	Josepha Elizabeth Gossen	b: 1891		d: 1975
	+Hubert Leo Spaetgens	b: 5/9/1894	m: 1915	d: 8/10/1981
4	Henry Joseph Spaetgens	b: 1916		d: 1996
	+Bertha Ewing	b: 6/26/1923	m: 1/7/1941	
4	John Hubert Spaetgens	b: 1919		d: 1919
4	Anna Marie Spaetgens	b: 1920		
	+Joseph M. Broussard	b: 2/12/1919	m: 11/28/1945	
4	William Leo Spaetgens	b: 1922		
	+Ruby Marie Faulk	b: 1/22/1937	m: 2/1/1958	
4	Anthony Leonard Spaetgens	b: 1924		
	+Mae Joyce Hoffpauir	b: 8/7/1926	m: 1/11/1947	
4	Lawrence Anthony Spaetgens	b: 1926		
	+Carol Jean Linscombe	b: 1/28/1937	m: 8/29/1956	
4	Charles Joseph Spaetgens	b: 1928		
	+Barbara Ann Perry	b: 8/28/1934	m: 6/18/1956	d: 1989
	*2nd Wife of Charles Joseph Spaetgens:			
	+Virginia Gautreaux		m: Aft. 1989	
	*3rd Wife of Charles Joseph Spaetgens:			
	+Ethel Broussard	b: 1931	m: 1994	
4	Allie Agnes Spaetgens	b: 1931		
	+James Calvin Caillier	b: 1/20/1931	m: 4/4/1951	d: 1993
2	Anna Catherine Gossen	b: 1858		d: 1935
	+Ludwig Gielen	b: 1847	m: 1881	d: 1900
2	Peter Joseph Gossen	b: 10/1/1862		d: 8/24/1945
	+Theresa Zaunbrecher	b: 1869	m: 1/4/1890	d: 1933
3	Marie Agnes Gossen	b: 1891		d: 1893
3	Maria Helena Gossen	b: 1893		d: 1894
3	William Joseph Gossen	b: 1894		d: 1974

Gossen

	+Edmae Servat	b: 3/6/1906		d: 11/17/1985
	*2nd Wife of William Joseph Gossen:			
	+Della Marie Petitjean	b: 1898	m: 1916	d: 1947
4	Louetta Josephine Gossen	b: 1917		
	+Louis Clarence Butaud	b: 1913	m: 1936	
4	Edward Joseph Gossen	b: 4/8/1920		d: 5/1/2003
	+Bobbie Louise Hains	b: 1/22/1924	m: 6/8/1946	
4	Richard Nicholas Gossen	b: 9/10/1922		
	+Sarah Ann Tobey	b: 6/28/1923	m: 1/26/1942	
4	Francis Allen Gossen	b: 5/8/1928		d: 8/7/1989
	+Lois Trahan	b: 7/13/1928	m: 5/5/1948	d: 6/22/1964
	*2nd Wife of Francis Allen Gossen:			
	+Billie Jean Long	b: 2/28/1944	m: 3/6/1965	
	*3rd Wife of William Joseph Gossen:			
	+Beulah Marie Hebert	b: 1905	m: 1959	d: 1972
3	Maria Josepha Gossen	b: 1895		d: 1990
	+William Livingston Larcade	b: 1891	m: 1918	d: 1951
4	Harold William Larcade	b: 1/16/1920		d: 8/31/1997
	+Louise Isabel Marchant	b: 8/18/1905	m: 10/20/1950	d: 1/19/1985
	*2nd Wife of Harold William Larcade:			
	+Stella Dupont	b: 10/1/1923	m: 1991	d: 5/4/2001
4	Rita Leona Larcade	b: 10/19/1923		d: 1/18/2005
	+James Howard Booksh, Jr.	b: 1/19/1922	m: 2/4/1947	
3	William Leo Gossen	b: 1897		d: 1897
3	Maria Helena Gossen	b: 1898		d: 1982
	+Austin Peter Landry	b: 1891	m: 1916	d: 1922
4	Vincent Joseph Landry	b: 1917		d: 1968
	+Ruby Mae Dubus	b: 12/19/1918	m: 1938	

Gossen

4	Cecilia Elizabeth Landry	b: 7/31/1919		d: 1998
	+Samuel David Wilder	b: 11/7/1914	m: 1937	d: 2002

*2nd Husband of Maria Helena Gossen:

	+Adolph Paul Frank	b: 1896	m: 1925	d: 1959
3	Peter Joseph Gossen, Jr.	b: 1902		d: 1981
	+Sadie Marie Breaux	b: 1904	m: 1924	d: 1990
4	Gerald Gossen	b: 1/8/1927		
	+Alberta Broussard	b: 1928	m: 1947	
4	Ronald James Gossen	b: 11/17/1929		
	+Monica Anne Dischler	b: 8/29/1934	m: 3/15/1954	

*2nd Wife of Ronald James Gossen:

	+Peggy L. Dufour	b: 1929	m: 2/18/1993	
4	Peter Joseph Gossen III	b: 1933		
	+Dorotha Jim Alverson	b: 1935	m: 1956	
4	Stephen Drozin Gossen	b: 7/20/1939		
	+Judith Martin	b: 12/1939	m: 6/6/1959	

*2nd Wife of Stephen Drozin Gossen:

	+Kathryn Lagarde	b: 4/22/1949	m: 1/26/1980	
3	Henry Joseph Gossen	b: 1904		d: 1998
	+Rita Aline Hebert	b: 1907	m: 4/28/1925	d: 1990
4	Lois Elaine Gossen	b: 7/24/1926		
	+Harrison Freeman Bennett, Jr.	b: 11/22/1920	m: 3/2/1947	d: 3/9/1973
4	Conrad Joseph Gossen	b: 11/2/1930		d: 2/6/2007
	+Barbara Roussel	b: 4/12/1933	m: 10/8/1952	
4	Peggy Ann Gossen	b: 3/1/1935		
	+George Bradford Ware	b: 1/13/1931	m: 2/1/1958	
4	Frederick Joseph Gossen, Sr.	b: 11/21/1940		
	+Annette Marie Larriviere	b: 12/2/1941	m: 8/10/1963	

Gossen

3	Marie Elizabeth (Sister Ann Pauline) Gossen	b: 1907		d: 1989
2	Maria Josepha Gossen	b: 12/17/1865		d: 1/18/1948
	+Joseph Peter Leonards	b: 5/5/1859	m: 3/9/1887	d: 6/16/1924
3	William Leonards	b: 12/18/1887		d: 11/29/1888
3	Henry Leo Leonards	b: 7/17/1889		d: 3/18/1960
	+Mary Olinger	b: 8/18/1891	m: 7/3/1912	d: 4/3/1978
4	Joseph Ferdinand Leonards	b: 1913		d: 1979
	+Alice Patin	b: 1914	m: 1935	d: 2004
4	Ferdinand Joseph Leonards	b: 1914		d: 1914
4	Ferdinand Joseph Leonards	b: 1915		
	+Edna Mae Devillier	b: 1918	m: 1941	
4	Edmund Alois Leonards	b: 1/25/1917		d: 1/28/2006
	+Norma "Cookie" Ziegler	b: 1923	m: 1947	d: 1996
4	Leo Charles Leonards	b: 1918		d: 1984
	+Mary Lee Dumesnil	b: 1930	m: 1950	
4	Rheinoldt John Leonards	b: 1920		d: 2003
4	Clara Marie Leonards	b: 1922		
	+Joseph Clemens Wilfert	b: 1914	m: 1944	d: 2001
4	Henrietta Marcella Leonards	b: 1923		d: 1984
	+John Norbert Gayle	b: 1918	m: 1946	d: 1961
4	Alois Jerome Leonards	b: 1924		d: 1925
4	Theresa Hilda Leonards	b: 1925		d: 1926
4	Sister Mildred Gertrude Leonards	b: 1928		
4	Anthony Phillip Leonards	b: 1930		

Gossen

		+Mary Theresa Carrothers	b: 1934	m: 1953	d: 1979
		*2nd Wife of Anthony Phillip Leonards:			
		+Pamela Marie Mouton	b: 1955	m: 1977	
	4	Sister Benedicta Leonards	b: 1934		d: 1986
3		Maria Agnes Leonards	b: 11/12/1890		d: 7/24/1926
		+William Nicholas Hensgens	b: 12/26/1887	m: 1911	d: 10/4/1955
	4	Maria Josepha Hensgens	b: 1911		d: 1998
		+Gilbert James LeBlanc	b: 1909	m: 1934	d: 1999
	4	Maria Catherine Hensgens	b: 2/8/1913		
		+Leo Ferdinand Heinen	b: 4/11/1909	m: 1/25/1933	d: 12/27/1959
	4	Regina Gertrude Hensgens	b: 1915		d: 2003
		+John Baptiste Duplechin	b: 1907	m: 1938	d: 1963
	4	Charles Nicholas Hensgens	b: 12/22/1916		d: 9/29/1995
		+Leola Landry	b: 9/17/1917	m: 11/9/1938	d: 6/2/1999
	4	Agnes Helen Hensgens	b: 1918		d: 1999
		+Sterling Morris Boudreaux	b: 1914	m: 1938	d: 3/1993
	4	Christine Hensgens	b: 1919		d: 8/9/2006
		+Thomas Alvin Chisholm, Jr.	b: 1918	m: 1940	d: 1991
	4	Annie Dorothy Hensgens	b: 1922		d: 2001
		+Cecil Joseph Hundley	b: 1922	m: 1949	d: 2002
	4	Louise Cecile Hensgens	b: 1/24/1924		
		+Gerard Lumodon Foley	b: 12/10/1920	m: 4/2/1945	d: 4/9/2005

Gossen

4	Nicholas Louis Hensgens	b: 1925		
	+Doris Cecile Landry	b: 1927	m: 1946	
3	Charles Joseph Leonards	b: 2/3/1892		d: 9/23/1945
	+Maria Walburga "Gammy" Thevis	b: 1893	m: 1915	d: 1994
4	Gerhard Joseph Leonards	b: 10/21/1916		d: 2/20/1973
	+Victoria Ann Schatzle	b: 12/9/1921	m: 11/27/1940	
4	Josephine Anna Leonards	b: 2/16/1920		d: 3/14/1992
	+Anthony Joseph Ohlenforst	b: 1916	m: 1/31/1940	d: 1974
4	Agnes Elizabeth Leonards	b: 11/5/1921		
	+William Henry Habetz	b: 5/18/1918	m: 2/13/1946	
4	Margaret Mary Leonards	b: 7/15/1923		
	+Ambrose Joseph Olinger	b: 6/26/1923	m: 11/27/1946	
3	Lawrence Joseph Leonards	b: 2/24/1893		d: 8/5/1945
	+Elizabeth Augusta Zaunbrecher	b: 1/11/1898	m: 2/1917	d: 10/14/1924
4	William Joseph Leonards	b: 12/12/1917		d: 8/24/2000
	+Barbara Rose Bollich	b: 1913	m: 11/20/1940	d: 5/11/2002
4	Josephine Marie Leonards	b: 3/26/1919		d: 1/23/2002
	+Herman Aloyious Cramer	b: 1911	m: 11/13/1940	d: 11/10/1966
4	Rita Helen Leonards	b: 12/27/1920		
4	Norbert Nicholas Leonards	b: 9/12/1922		d: 4/13/1945
4	Vincent Karl Leonards	b: 9/24/1924		d: 12/30/1998
	+Thelma "Tillie" Zaunbrecher	b: 7/30/1926	m: 1949	

*2nd Wife of Lawrence Joseph Leonards:

Gossen

	+Maria Anna Zaunbrecher	b: 11/1/1903	m: 6/15/1926	d: 9/5/1984
4	Raymond William Leonards	b: 1/29/1929		d: 4/22/1992
	+Louise Augusta Theunissen	b: 12/27/1932	m: 12/27/1952	
4	Benno Joseph Leonards	b: 6/16/1931		
	+Arilda Gertrude Heinen	b: 3/16/1934	m: 11/15/1958	d: 5/8/1973

*2nd Wife of Benno Joseph Leonards:

	+Margaret Funk	b: 7/14/1930	m: 3/16/1974	
4	Johanna Augusta Leonards	b: 12/15/1932		d: 5/5/1993
4	Henry Jerome Leonards	b: 9/13/1934		
	+Wilma Thecla Hensgens	b: 11/10/1937	m: 1958	d: 5/21/2006
4	Dennis Louis Leonards	b: 5/24/1936		
	+Phyllis Helen Robichaux	b: 11/18/1939	m: 1/14/1961	
4	Wilfred Charles Leonards	b: 7/3/1937		
	+Elaine Credeur	b: 11/12/1941	m: 7/1964	
4	Mary Ann Leonards	b: 12/10/1938		
4	Lidwina Josephine Leonards	b: 7/20/1940		d: 3/9/1941
4	Catherine Mary Leonards	b: 7/19/1944		
	+Dale Bernard Huesers	b: 3/20/1938	m: 5/9/1964	
3	Maria Theresa Leonards	b: 6/7/1894		d: 11/30/1894
3	August Leonards	b: 9/25/1896		d: 5/3/1962
	+Dorothy Beatrice Frey	b: 1905	m: 1923	d: 1991
4	August J. Leonards, Jr.	b: 1/26/1924		d: 2/26/1988
	+Beatrice Aloysia Olinger	b: 8/13/1925	m: 1947	
4	Antoinette Leonards	b: 9/5/1926		d: 4/16/2000

Gossen

	+Ira L. Miller	b: 7/3/1923	m: 1947	
4	Anthony Leonards	b: 12/20/1928		d: 12/20/1928
4	Alberta Leonards	b: 3/25/1930		d: 6/17/1975
	+Elmen Bergeron	b: 6/22/1923	m: 1947	d: 8/28/2000
4	Patricia Leonards	b: 6/29/1933		
	+Adam Johnson	b: 3/5/1929	m: 1952	
4	Lloyd Phillip Leonards	b: 11/30/1935		
	+Constance Ledoux	b: 1/28/1937	m: 1957	
3	William Joseph Leonards	b: 1/6/1898		d: 5/21/1898
3	Ludwig (Louis) Leonards	b: 8/31/1899		d: 10/30/1978
	+Maria Gertrude Dischler	b: 1897	m: 1922	d: 1965
4	Philomena Hedwig Leonards	b: 1923		
	+John Francis Ohlenforst	b: 1921	m: 1947	d: 1997
4	Blaise Philip Leonards	b: 3/21/1927		
	+Bernardine Marie Habetz	b: 6/9/1927	m: 10/27/1948	
4	Edwin Joseph Leonards	b: 9/21/1928		d: 4/21/2007
	+Genevieve Augusta Frey	b: 11/11/1932	m: 7/9/1951	
4	Eleanor Marie Leonards	b: 7/15/1930		
	+William A. Braun	b: 10/24/1922	m: 10/26/1950	
4	Dorothy Clara Leonards	b: 4/1/1932		
4	Marcella Marie Leonards	b: 2/3/1934		
	+Andrew Lawrence Ohlenforst	b: 10/6/1928	m: 1/19/1955	d: 10/3/1983
4	Louis Anthony Leonards	b: 1/14/1936		
	+Patricia Ann Spell	b: 1/21/1938	m: 12/28/1960	
4	Leonard Lawrence Leonards	b: 6/30/1937		
	+Barbara Ann Link	b: 9/17/1938	m: 11/27/1958	

Gossen

4	Sylvia Jean Leonards	b: 2/24/1941			
	+Johnny Mack Frugé	b: 10/4/1939	m: 11/17/1962		
	*2nd Wife of Ludwig (Louis) Leonards:				
	+Ella Cobena	b: 1903	m: 1968	d: 1982	
3	Maria Anna Leonards	b: 1/20/1901		d: 3/22/1975	
	+William Frederick Zaunbrecher	b: 12/19/1899	m: 1/18/1922	d: 12/6/1972	
4	Paul William Zaunbrecher	b: 6/10/1923		d: 9/20/1982	
	+Cecilia Augusta Habetz	b: 12/6/1921	m: 2/13/1946		
4	Richard Andrew Zaunbrecher, Sr	b: 11/30/1924			
	+Verna Mary Johnson	b: 12/18/1925	m: 6/19/1946		
4	Felix Leo Zaunbrecher	b: 12/30/1926			
	+Hilda Mary Broussard	b: 5/17/1929	m: 1/27/1948		
4	William Zaunbrecher	b: 4/13/1928		d: 4/13/1928	
4	Mary Agnes Zaunbrecher	b: 2/21/1930			
	+Clarence Albert Fabacher	b: 3/17/1931	m: 2/4/1956		
4	Theresa Marie Zaunbrecher	b: 9/28/1931			
	+Jean Edwin Broussard	b: 1/24/1926	m: 11/26/1953		
4	Josephine Ann Zaunbrecher	b: 8/6/1934			
	+Jerome Lambert Ronkartz	b: 2/16/1933	m: 8/20/1956		
4	William Francis Zaunbrecher	b: 9/18/1935		d: 9/18/1935	
4	Willietta Dorothy Zaunbrecher	b: 9/6/1938			
	+Urban Anderson Phillips	b: 10/8/1933	m: 8/29/1959	d: 5/18/1998	

Gossen

4	Francis Martin "Bud" Zaunbrecher	b: 11/11/1943			
	+Hannah Casselman		m: 1963		
	*2nd Wife of Francis Martin "Bud" Zaunbrecher:				
	+Judy Craighead	b: 1945	m: 2/9/1973		
	*3rd Wife of Francis Martin "Bud" Zaunbrecher:				
	+Christine Schroeder	b: 7/25/1937	m: 10/19/1983	d: 11/23/1984	
	*4th Wife of Francis Martin "Bud" Zaunbrecher:				
	+Bertha Jane Doucet	b: 10/26/1941	m: 3/8/1990	d: 5/20/2007	
3	Philip Joseph Leonards	b: 5/26/1908		d: 8/12/1973	
	+Marie Johanna Frey	b: 1/27/1910	m: 1928	d: 12/31/2005	
4	Gerald John Leonards	b: 1933		d: 1989	
	+Shirley Mae Nickel	b: 1935	m: 11/1957		
4	[2] Elaine Lorraine Leonards	b: 6/10/1938			
	+[1] Herbert Joseph Gossen	b: 7/20/1936	m: 6/1958		
2	William Joseph Gossen	b: 5/14/1871		d: 8/25/1963	
	+Anna Maria Zaunbrecher	b: 10/10/1878	m: 1/7/1901	d: 1955	
3	Nicholas Joseph Gossen	b: 1901		d: 1990	
	+Mary Magdelena Bollich	b: 1904	m: 1922	d: 1995	
4	Marie Antoinette Gossen	b: 12/18/1923			
	+William Charles Puissegur	b: 4/21/1922	m: 11/5/1937		
4	Edna Louise Gossen	b: 7/10/1925			
	+Winfred Joseph Plattsmir	b: 8/3/1921	m: 10/19/1948	d: 7/22/1996	
4	Raymond Nicholas Gossen	b: 4/3/1927			
	+Henrietta Theresa Habetz	b: 6/1/1928	m: 2/3/1949		
4	Lucille Clara Gossen	b: 11/11/1929			
	+Alois Andrew Reiners	b: 7/25/1926	m: 11/25/1953	d: 3/19/1999	

Gossen

4	Robert Anthony Gossen	b: 10/1/1933		d: 11/3/2006
	+Jeanne Ann Privat	b: 3/15/1937	m: 5/6/1956	
4	Helen Marie Gossen	b: 8/14/1936		
	+Clarence Charles Arsement	b: 9/15/1932	m: 10/15/1956	
4	Catherine Rose Gossen	b: 8/4/1939		
	+Leonard Jacob Cramer	b: 2/19/1939	m: 11/9/1961	
3	Henry Peter Gossen	b: 1903		d: 1982
	+Julia Rosa Olinger	b: 1904	m: 1929	d: 1991
4	Henrietta Ann Gossen	b: 1929		
	+Julian A. Didier	b: 1928	m: 1949	
4	Gilbert William Gossen	b: 1931		
	+Florence Rita Gonsoulin	b: 1935	m: 1955	
4	Ralph Aloysius Gossen	b: 1934		
	+Marcella Elizabeth Habetz	b: 1942	m: 1962	d: 1973
	*2nd Wife of Ralph Aloysius Gossen:			
	+Marjorie Marie Devillier	b: 1937	m: 1977	
4	[1] Herbert Joseph Gossen	b: 7/20/1936		
	+[2] Elaine Lorraine Leonards	b: 6/10/1938	m: 6/1958	
4	Donald Charles Gossen	b: 1941		
	+Henrietta Breaux	b: 1948	m: 1967	
4	Flavia Diane Gossen	b: 1943		d: 1946
3	Catherine Louise Gossen	b: 1905		d: 1996
	+Theodore Ignatius Heinen	b: 1902	m: 1927	d: 1962
	*2nd Husband of Catherine Louise Gossen:			
	+Raoul Hebert	b: 1907	m: 1966	

Gossen

3	Charles Joseph Gossen	b: 1907		d: 1992
	+Helen Marie Dawson	b: 12/6/1914	m: 1944	d: 10/1/1987
4	Timothy Gossen	b: 1952		
3	Clara Josepha Gossen	b: 1909		d: 2000
	+Eugene Joseph Caillouet	b: 1905	m: 1943	d: 1979
3	Agnes Elizabeth Gossen	b: 1911		d: 1987
	+Elbert Arnold	b: 1911	m: 1938	d: 1966
4	Arleen Arnold	b: 1939		
	+Ralph Stutes		m: 1957	
4	Wade Arnold	b: 1940		d: 1941
4	Ione Arnold	b: 1943		
	+Henry Reed		m: 1964	

8. Grein, Herman Joseph:
Herman Joseph Grein b: 1840 d: 1914 from Millen was the son of Johann Theodor Grein and Maria Katharina Gertrude Gielen b: 1802 d: 1858. After the death of Johann Theodor Grein, Maria Katharina Gertrude Gielen married Johann Gerhard Habetz b: 1814 d: 1868. Herman Joseph Grein is a half brother to Heinrich Habetz. See Habetz family.

William (Wilhelm) J. Zaunbrecher (1867-1922).
Courtesy of Leona Zaunbrecher.

A pioneer farmstead at Robert's Cove.

Rev. John Daniel Thevis.

Father Leo Schwab's Silver Jubilee
June 15, 1909

Two men in front: Karl F. Zaunbrecher, Albert Haines. *Small boys sitting (left to right)*: N. Joseph Gossen, Henry P. Gossen, Nicholas C. Zaunbrecher, Willliam E. Heinen, Placidus J. Heinen, John J. Heinen, Gerhard J. Thevis, Henry J. Zaunbrecher, William C. Heinen, Anthony C. Dischler, William S. Winchester, H. Joseph Thevis, Louis Leonards, Leonard J. Thevis, Daniel A. Thevis, J. Frank Reiners. *Boys kneeling (starting with boy behind two ladies with hats)*: Ralph Schone, unidentified, Anthony D. Olinger, P. Joseph Gossen, Jr., Joseph Schone, Henry J. Meyer, William F. Zaunbrecher, William J. Zaunbrecher, H. Joseph Meyer, William I. Thevis, Charles B. Dischler, Joseph Zaunbrecher, Joseph A. Heinen, Peter J. Theunissen, Leo Schone, Joseph Dischler, Jr., August Leonards. *Men in last two rows (left on drum)*: Hubert J. Gossen, Joseph Dischler, Sr., Nicholas Hensgens, Joseph Reiners, Albert Frey (w/o hat), William J. Reiners, Frank Perkins (w/o hat), W. Joseph Scheufens, John Prejean, Conrad Hensgens (with beard), Martin Schatzle, Edward J. Winchester, Henry Vondenstein (w/o hat), Lawrence J. Leonards, Ed Prejean (w/o hat), Theodore (Doris) Heinen, H. Leon Leonards (w/o hat). *Right of drum*: J. Bernard Meyer (3rd from drum), P. Joseph Leonards (dot on forehead), Joseph M. Neu (4th from end), P. Leonard Thevis (3rd from end), Florenz Schatzle, Sr. (at end). Courtesy of Leona Zaunbrecher.

Maria Regina Tellers and Christian Joseph Hensgens at the time of their wedding, 1871. Courtesy of Alberta Hensgens Lyons.

John Gerhard Thevis.
Courtesy of Rev. Keith Vincent.

Herman Joseph Grein.
Courtesy of Rev. Keith Vincent.

The Ancestral Home of the Zaunbrecher Family, Nierstrass, West Germany.
Courtesy of Rev. Charles Zaunbrecher.

Interior of the 1894 church, taken ca. 1900.
Courtesy of Leona Zaunbrecher.

Rev. Aegidius Hennemann.

Rev. Sylvan Buschor.

Gertrude Klein and William Gossen. The last two surviving pioneers from the Geilenkirchen area.

Franz Xavier Dischler.
Courtesy of Rev. Keith Vincent.

Nicholas Joseph Zaunbrecher's Family, ca. 1888

Back row: Wilhelm (1867-1922), Lorenz (1870-1954), Helena Leonards Zaunbrecher (1844-1926), Theresa (1869-1933), future wife of Joseph Gossen. *Middle row*: Karl (1876-1950), Henry (1875-1944), Nicholas Joseph (1846-1918), Anna (1878-1955), future wife of William Gossen. *In front*: August (1883-1919). Courtesy of Leona Zaunbrecher.

Nicholas Joseph Zaunbrecher and Maria Helena Leonards, ca. 1908.
Courtesy of Leona Zaunbrecher.

Rev. Leo Schwab.

Rev. Peter Leonard Thevis.

St. Leo IV School, 1908-1909
(Students in Sunday dress.)

First row: Anthony C. Dischler, Joseph Schone, Louis Leonards, H. Joseph Thevis, H. Joseph Meyer, Henry J. Zaunbrecher, (post), John. J. Heinen, William C. Heinen, N. Joseph Gossen, Gerhard J. Thevis, William F. Zaunbrecher, Placidus J. Heinen. *Second row (three girls on steps)*: Clara Olinger, Olive Schone, Thecla Thevis. *Third row*: Henry J. Meyer, Anthony D. Olinger, Charles B. Dischler, William S. Winchester, (post), William I. Thevis, Edward J. Olinger, Peter J. Theunissen, Joseph Bickert, John Bickert, (post), Marie C. Thevis, Victoria G. Habetz, Marie Leonards, Augusta Zaunbrecher. *Fourth row*: Joseph A. Heinen, Leo Schone, Joseph Dischler, Jr., Nicholas M. Zaunbrecher, (post), August Leonards, Helen Zaunbrecher, Helen Meyer, Marie (Mae) Habetz, Gertrude Dischler, Waalburga Thevis, Edward J. Winchester, Peter Schneider. Courtesy of Leona Zaunbecher.

St. Leo IV School, 1910-1911
(Students in everyday clothes.)

First row (left to right): N. Jolseph Gossen, William C. Heinen, William F. Zaunbrecher, William I. Thevis, John J. Heinen, Theodore I. Heinen (sitting), Henry J. Zaunbrecher (sitting), William E. Heinen (sitting), Gerhard J. Thevis, Placidus J. Heinen, H. Joseph Thevis, Anthony C. Dischler. *Second row (3 girls on steps)*: Josephing Meyer, Annie Zaunbrecher, Gertrude Thevis. *Third row*: William S. Winchester, Edward J. Olinger, Anthony D. Olinger, (post), J. Frank Reines, Thecla Thevis, Marie Leonards, Clara J. Olinger, Marie C. Thevis, (post), Charles B. Dischler, Louis Leonards, Henry J. Meyer. *Fourth row*: Joseph A. Heinen, Peter J. Theunissen, August Leonards, Augusta Zaunbrecher, Gertrude Dischler, Professor Peter Schneider, (post), H. Joseph Meyer. *Fifth row*: Rev. Leo Schwab. Courtesy of Leona Zaunbrecher.

Rev. Felix Rumpf.

Rev. Placidus Zarn.

9. Habetz, Heinrich:

Heinrich Habetz b: 9/10/1843 d: 7/7/1916 from Millen was the son of Johann Gerhard Habetz b: 1814 d: 1868 and Maria Katharina Gertrude Gielen b: 1802 d: 1858, widow of Johann Theodor Grein, see Grein family. Heinrich Habetz married on 1/22/1870 to Maria Katharina Hermanns b: 4/8/1849 d: 7/8/1918, who is the daughter of Johann Leonard Hermanns b: 1816 d: 1866 and Katharina Gertrude Schaps b: 1825 d: 1876.

2		Maria Katharina Habetz	b: 1870		d: 1870
2		Herman Joseph Habetz	b: 11/9/1871		d: 1/7/1896
2		Heinrich Leonard Habetz	b: 3/3/1874		d: 6/9/1958
		+Anna Margaretha Ohlenforst	b: 1874	m: 2/20/1895	d: 2/9/1918
3		Maria Katharina Habetz	b: 12/5/1895		d: 1/1/1896
3		"Maria" Katharina Habetz	b: 1/27/1897		d: 6/1/1988
3		Gertrude "Victoria" Habetz	b: 6/7/1899		d: 7/16/1965
		+Willie Joseph Schneider		m: 1943	
3		Herman "Joseph" Habetz	b: 11/16/1901		d: 2/6/1966
		+Anna Gesina Cramer	b: 1908	m: 1/30/1929	d: 2000
	4	Lawrence Joseph Habetz	b: 12/27/1929		
		+Marie Legnon	b: 12/27/1933	m: 2/10/1957	
	4	Leonard Joseph Habetz	b: 4/11/1932		
		+Deanna Dean Hoffpauir		m: 6/29/1957	
	4	Clementine Anna Habetz	b: 10/27/1934		
		+Huey Pierre Kirsch	b: 9/17/1935	m: 6/7/1958	
	4	Bernadine Anna Habetz	b: 2/7/1937		d: 7/6/1994
	4	Bernard Joseph Habetz	b: 1/19/1939		
		+Patricia Ann Molbert	b: 10/8/1939	m: 11/17/1962	d: 7/15/2004
	4	Albert Joseph Habetz	b: 2/10/1942		
		+Brenda Fay Ruppert		m: 5/29/1965	
	4	Robert Joseph Habetz	b: 2/1/1944		
		+Priscilla Vera Keigley	b: 10/13/1946	m: 7/15/1967	

Habetz

4	Josephine Anna "Joann" Habetz	b: 1/28/1947		
	+Frederick J. Ledoux	b: 8/9/1947	m: 9/4/1971	
4	Anna Agnes Habetz	b: 10/15/1949		
	+Thomas Michael Jones	b: 2/9/1949	m: 6/21/1969	
3	Anton "Heinrich" Habetz	b: 12/10/1903		d: 4/18/1935
	+Theresa Hensgens	b: 5/22/1906	m: 2/3/1926	d: 6/26/1995
4	James Leonard Habetz, Sr.	b: 12/13/1927		d: 2/18/1996
	+Mary Dean Breaux	b: 1/1/1929	m: 1/18/1950	d: 3/31/1989
4	Henrietta Theresa Victoria Habetz	b: 6/1/1928		
	+Raymond N. Gossen	b: 4/3/1927	m: 2/3/1949	
4	Leonard Conrad Habetz	b: 2/12/1931		d: 2/20/2006
3	Mary Magdalena Habetz	b: 1/5/1906		d: 12/30/1995
	+Jacob Herman Cramer	b: 4/7/1910	m: 1/7/1936	d: 1/28/1973
4	Anna Marie "Sr. Mary Clare" Cramer	b: 10/16/1936		
4	Angelina Maria Cramer	b: 1/5/1938		
	+Ralph Gonthier	b: 8/7/1934	m: 6/20/1964	d: 6/25/2001
4	Leonard "Jake" Jacob Cramer	b: 2/17/1939		
	+Catherine Gossen	b: 8/4/1939	m: 11/9/1961	
4	Barbara Anna Cramer	b: 12/18/1940		
	+Stephen Edmund Dubose	b: 8/2/1938	m: 6/25/1960	
4	Alberta Gertrude Cramer	b: 8/16/1942		d: 12/11/1993
	+Leland Paul Hebert, Jr.	b: 11/6/1943	m: 2/16/1963	
4	Bernadette Rose Cramer	b: 11/7/1943		
	+Douglas Guidry	b: 7/16/1942	m: 8/29/1964	

Habetz

4	Anthonly Edward Cramer	b: 2/20/1945		
	+Rhena Joan Vienne	b: 11/11/1946	m: 4/23/1966	
4	Michael John Cramer	b: 10/14/1946		
	+Yvonne Alice Prather	b: 11/11/1946	m: 9/4/1965	
4	Theresa Marie Cramer	b: 6/21/1948		
	+Lawrence Wayne Doucet	b: 2/13/1947	m: 1/31/1970	d: 12/21/1993
4	Loretta Clementine Cramer	b: 1/10/1952		
	+Glenn Michael Boudreaux	b: 12/27/1948	m: 1/8/1977	
3	Rt. Rev. Msgr. Leonard "Clement" Habetz	b: 1/21/1908		d: 9/16/1968
3	Anna Marie Habetz	b: 6/28/1910		d: 5/9/1990
	+John Kasper Meyer	b: 1912	m: 6/7/1937	d: 7/25/1987
4	Leonard John Meyer	b: 1/31/1938		d: 1/31/1938
4	Leonard "John" Meyer	b: 3/28/1939		
	+Pearl Ann Watson	b: 11/1939	m: 11/26/1966	
4	Henry Leonard Meyer	b: 9/25/1940		
	+Jo Ann Zaunbrecher	b: 7/22/1944	m: 7/15/1964	
4	Mary Ann Meyer	b: 2/2/1942		
	+John Herman Reiners	b: 10/19/1938	m: 4/8/1961	
4	Margaret Mary Meyer	b: 7/31/1943		
	+Charles Herbert Simpson	b: 9/1942	m: 5/12/1964	
4	Joseph Bernard Meyer	b: 8/27/1944		d: 8/23/1989
	+Betty Ann Gould	b: 4/1946	m: 4/28/1966	
4	Kathleen Marie Meyer	b: 11/19/1947		
	+Larry John Viator	b: 2/1947	m: 6/6/1970	
4	Marie Antoinette Meyer	b: 12/19/1950		d: 6/8/1951
4	James Anthony Meyer	b: 10/22/1955		
	+Patricia Ann Meche	b: 9/1962	m: 10/26/1991	

Habetz

3	Heinrich "Leo" Leonard Habetz, Jr.	b: 5/11/1912		d: 9/16/1985
	+Mary Leona Cramer	b: 6/11/1912	m: 2/3/1937	d: 1981
4	Leonard Jerome "Jack" Habetz	b: 4/16/1938		
	+Sylvia Bigelow	b: 7/3/1940	m: 1/4/1964	
4	Donald Bernard Habetz	b: 9/25/1940		d: 10/24/2004
	+Patricia Istre	b: 3/2/1940	m: 8/24/1963	
4	Edmund "E.L." Leonard Habetz	b: 11/6/1949		
	+Cheryl Anne Hoffpauir	b: 1/15/1948	m: 5/1/1971	
4	Allan Norbert Habetz	b: 9/7/1952		
	+Gwendolyn Marie Truax	b: 1/6/1952	m: 9/21/1973	
4	Kenneth Michael Habetz	b: 11/13/1955		
	+Penny Hargroder	b: 8/3/1958	m: 11/7/1980	
3	Felicitas Gertrude Habetz	b: 5/25/1914		
	+John Herman Cramer	b: 1909	m: 2/23/1938	d: 1980
4	Anna Margaret Cramer	b: 12/31/1938		
	+William "Billy" Louis Zaunbrecher	b: 5/31/1938	m: 12/16/1963	d: 8/19/1997
4	Bernard Cramer	b: 9/25/1942		d: 9/25/1942
4	Patricia Marie Cramer	b: 2/21/1947		d: 2004
4	Carolyn Clementine Cramer	b: 7/6/1950		
4	Ignatius John Cramer	b: 4/5/1952		d: 7/23/1982
	+Kathleen Marie Gros		m: 7/11/1975	
3	Leonard "Alphonse" Habetz, Sr.	b: 5/12/1916		d: 4/9/1974
	+Frances Meyer	b: 7/30/1914	m: 1/8/1941	d: 8/13/1986
4	Henry Bernard Habetz	b: 12/19/1941		d: 1/7/1986
	+Laura Sonnier	b: 1/2/1943	m: 11/28/1963	d: 8/11/2006

Habetz

4	Leonard "Alphonse" Habetz, Jr.	b: 6/23/1943		
	+Carolyn Spell	b: 9/23/1940	m: 6/5/1965	
4	Alberta Habetz	b: 2/21/1945		
	+Johnny Winn Barlow	b: 8/9/1953	m: 2/2/1974	
4	Charles Joseph Habetz	b: 9/6/1946		
	+Katherine Link	b: 1/22/1948	m: 4/27/1968	
4	Lucille Marie Habetz	b: 4/2/1948		
	+Norman Jean Borne, Jr.	b: 9/15/1946	m: 6/12/1976	
4	Catherine Helen Habetz	b: 6/25/1949		
	+Hugh Fred "Pudgy" O'Connor, Jr.	b: 3/31/1938	m: 8/21/1982	d: 3/4/2002
4	Henrietta Louise Habetz	b: 7/28/1951		
4	Ralph Mark Habetz	b: 2/16/1953		
	+Katherine Sudwischer	b: 1/16/1957	m: 7/15/1983	
4	Frances Adelieth Habetz	b: 8/10/1954		d: 10/30/2004
	+Dan R. Hooten	b: 2/4/1944	m: 12/4/1982	d: 1/2002
4	Claire Marie Habetz	b: 9/22/1957		
4	Pauline Margaret Habetz	b: 1/5/1960		
	*2nd Wife of Heinrich Leonard Habetz:			
	+Agnes Estilette	b: 1883	m: 1922	d: 1940
	*3rd Wife of Heinrich Leonard Habetz:			
	+Josephine Meyer	b: 1903	m: 6/29/1943	d: 1993
3	Johanna Habetz	b: 10/6/1944		
	+Carrol Wayne Sittig	b: 1945	m: 6/29/1968	
4	Kye Christopher Sittig	b: 11/4/1969		
	+Kenya Trahan	b: 1/8/1969		
4	Jude Christian Sittig	b: 12/13/1971		
	+Anne Schneider	b: 9/7/1975		
3	Henry Clemens Habetz	b: 3/5/1947		d: 8/8/2003

Habetz

3		Leonard Paul Habetz	b: 9/2/1950		
		+Brendel Rose Dartez	b: 1951	m: 2/28/1970	
	4	Traci Paulette Estella Habetz	b: 11/13/1970		
		+Nathan Joseph Leblanc		m: 6/25/1993	
2		Clement Habetz	b: 1875		
2		Elizabeth Gertrude Habetz	b: 11/19/1877		d: 1941
2		Joseph August Habetz	b: 8/30/1880		d: 12/21/1972
		+Anna Martha Ohlenforst	b: 1883	m: 12/11/1902	d: 1937
3		Leonard August Habetz	b: 8/28/1903		d: 11/29/1978
		+Gesina Cramer	b: 1908	m: 11/28/1934	d: 2002
	4	Margaret Mary Habetz	b: 9/24/1935		
		+Wesley Boullion		m: 11/13/1955	d: 11/11/1980
	4	Geraldine A. Habetz	b: 5/25/1937		
		+Sherman J. Trahan		m: 3/17/1962	
	4	Louise Gertrude Habetz	b: 1/6/1939		
		+Johnny Wade Meche		m: 11/4/1961	
	4	Edward Joseph Habetz	b: 2/7/1941		
		+Marlene Miller		m: 11/4/1962	
	4	Daniel Leo Habetz	b: 1/3/1943		
		+Judy Savoy		m: 11/10/1962	
	4	Gerhard Raymond Habetz	b: 12/31/1944		
		+Brenda Gale Guidry		m: 11/12/1966	
		*2nd Wife of Gerhard Raymond Habetz:			
		+Gloria Higginbotham		m: 6/1985	
	4	Charles Herman Habetz	b: 5/22/1946		
		+Pattie L. Beard		m: 10/11/1970	
	4	Robert John Habetz	b: 5/13/1948		
		+Amber Thomas		m: 4/4/1969	
	4	Rose Marie Habetz	b: 4/20/1950		d: 9/1/1951

Habetz

3	Marie Henrietta Habetz	b: 4/15/1905		d: 10/12/1987
	+Stephen Matthew Foytlin	b: 1900	m: 10/22/1940	d: 1967
4	Mary Magdalene Foytlin	b: 10/25/1943		d: 12/1/1943
4	Stephen August Foytlin	b: 2/26/1945		
	+Rebecca Jane Amie		m: 11/19/1969	
4	Joseph John Foytlin	b: 3/16/1949		
	+Romona St. Amand		m: 5/3/1969	
3	John Ferdinand Habetz	b: 12/27/1906		d: 8/24/1963
	+Anna Gertrude Thevis	b: 1908	m: 1/21/1931	d: 1982
4	Vincent John Habetz	b: 10/17/1931		d: 9/5/2001
	+Louella Rita Dronet Greene		m: 9/26/1970	
4	Theresa Margaret Habetz	b: 6/25/1933		d: 6/24/1999
4	Lawrence "Jerome" Habetz	b: 8/12/1935		d: 10/20/2004
4	Florence Marie Habetz	b: 3/15/1939		
	+Paul Edward Russell	b: 6/4/1935	m: 3/28/1959	d: 5/7/1995
4	Annie Louise Habetz	b: 7/29/1942		
	+Elby Joseph Pellerin	b: 1/23/1939	m: 5/4/1963	
3	William Andrew Habetz, Sr.	b: 2/4/1909		d: 4/17/1979
	+Clothilde Borne	b: 1912	m: 6/6/1939	d: 1998
4	William Andrew Habetz, Jr.	b: 8/13/1940		
	+Jeanette Marie Richard		m: 10/20/1972	
4	Harold Joseph Habetz, Sr.	b: 11/26/1942		
	+Barbara A. Mouton		m: 10/12/1963	
	*2nd Wife of Harold Joseph Habetz, Sr.:			
	+Priscilla A. Savoie		m: 7/27/1974	
4	Martha Anna Habetz	b: 4/23/1944		

Habetz

	+Paul Pierret, Jr.		m: 2/20/1976	
4	Doris Marie Habetz	b: 5/31/1945		
	+Isaac Miller, Jr.		m: 3/8/1973	
	*2nd Husband of Doris Marie Habetz:			
	+Henry Purvis Carmouche III		m: 7/3/1980	
4	Louetta Gertrude Habetz	b: 12/15/1946		d: 7/15/1993
	+Robert L. Richard		m: 11/30/1968	
4	Mary Alice Habetz	b: 4/22/1949		
	+Michael James Pastor		m: 11/16/1974	
4	Mildred Jane Habetz	b: 2/5/1951		
	+Roland Leo Matte		m: 5/31/1972	
4	Milton James Habetz	b: 2/5/1951		
	+Jeanette Bourque		m: 6/17/1972	
	*2nd Wife of Milton James Habetz:			
	+Karen Ruth Faulk		m: 7/23/1983	
4	Janet Louise Habetz	b: 3/18/1956		
	+Joey Paul Fontenot		m: 9/18/1978	
3	Herman Joseph Habetz	b: 5/29/1911		d: 1/25/1991
3	William "Raymond" Habetz	b: 8/30/1913		d: 2004
	+Maria Adelheid Cramer	b: 1915	m: 8/17/1950	
4	May Rose Habetz	b: 1/3/1954		
	+Anthony Bourgeois			
3	Anna Franziska Habetz	b: 3/12/1916		d: 8/21/2005
3	Gertrude Mathilda Habetz	b: 3/12/1916		d: 6/18/1994
3	Wenzel Henry Habetz	b: 5/24/1918		
	+Marie Menard	b: 1930	m: 11/8/1947	
3	Helen Walburga Habetz	b: 5/22/1921		
3	Josepha Habetz	b: 5/22/1921		d: 5/22/1921
3	Rita Martha Habetz	b: 6/14/1923		d: 2001
3	Benedict George Habetz	b: 3/21/1926		d: 2/20/1996

Habetz

		+Rita Barbier	b: 1942	m: 9/11/1962	
	4	Christine Ann Habetz	b: 12/16/1963		
		+Greg P. Benoit		m: 1985	
	4	George John Habetz	b: 1/29/1965		
		+Judy Peacock		m: 1987	
3		Paul Anton Habetz	b: 10/27/1928		d: 10/29/1928
2		John Heinrich Habetz	b: 5/2/1885		d: 8/7/1956
		+Elizabeth Marie Kreuser	b: 9/18/1892	m: 2/18/1928	d: 4/10/1983
3		Hildagard Habetz	b: 3/26/1929		d: 3/26/1929
3		Philip Jacob Joseph Habetz	b: 3/19/1930		
		+Dolores Marie Zaunbrecher	b: 1930	m: 11/8/1956	
	4	Jules Henry Habetz	b: 10/17/1957		
		+Claudia Anne Henley		m: 1/7/1978	
	4	Christian John Habetz	b: 8/18/1960		
		+Melissa "Kim" Richard		m: 2/5/1983	
	4	Celeste Claire Habetz	b: 9/14/1961		
		+Paul Louis Lalande		m: 3/6/1987	
	4	Damian Charles Habetz	b: 9/26/1963		
		+Dinah Libby		m: 2/14/1987	
	4	Frederick Joseph Habetz	b: 10/20/1964		
		+Joan Rachelle Leleux		m: 11/24/1984	
	4	Jacqueline Ann Habetz	b: 10/23/1966		
		+Douglas Henry Valdetero		m: 1/6/1989	
	4	Constance Marie Habetz	b: 6/1/1968		
		+Kenneth Shane Leger		m: 7/17/1992	
3		Hilda Catherine Elizabeth Habetz	b: 4/20/1931		
		+Jerome Victorien Simoneaux	b: 1933	m: 5/30/1955	
	4	Joselin Marie Simoneaux	b: 3/5/1956		

Habetz

		+Benson Decuir		m: 1/7/1974	
		*2nd Husband of Joselin Marie Simoneaux:			
		+John Adam Landry		m: 7/5/1986	
	4	Gregory Paul Simoneaux	b: 10/17/1957		
		+Jennifer Zaunbrecher		m: 5/24/1980	
	4	Michael Simoneaux	b: 5/26/1959		d: 5/26/1959
	4	Nickolas John Simoneaux	b: 4/19/1960		
		+Carol Mccall		m: 11/2/1985	
	4	Mary Claire Simoneaux	b: 7/9/1962		
		+Gregory B. Baronet		m: 10/20/1984	
	4	Peter Joseph Simoneaux	b: 5/28/1964		
		+Daphne Morgan		m: 4/24/1987	
	4	Paul Joseph Simoneaux	b: 5/28/1964		
		+Kimberly Savoie		m: 8/10/1985	
3		Pauline Ann Elizabeth Habetz	b: 7/14/1934		
		+Anthony Francis Reiners	b: 1934	m: 9/19/1957	
	4	Charles Brian Reiners	b: 2/9/1967		
		+Shelly Beth Cloud		m: 11/30/1990	
	4	Patrick Lawrence Reiners	b: 1/28/1968		
		+Stephanie Seidel		m: 2/20/1993	
	4	Charlotte Elaine Reiners	b: 3/8/1972		
		+Lance Cope		m: 7/22/1995	
2		Joseph Wilhelm Habetz	b: 8/24/1887		d: 12/9/1968
		+Maria Josefa "Franziska" Theunissen	b: 3/9/1889	m: 1/18/1911	d: 3/13/1980
3		Pirmin Hubert Habetz	b: 11/3/1911		d: 8/22/1970
		+Catherine Frances Hensgens	b: 10/26/1916	m: 1/8/1936	d: 11/15/1997

Habetz

4	Laurentia Frances (Sr. Lawrence) Habetz	b: 1/21/1937		
4	Pirmin Joseph (Junior) Habetz	b: 6/4/1938		
	+Mary Lou Hebert		m: 5/16/1959	
4	Patricia Clara Habetz	b: 2/22/1940		
	+Bennett Augustine		m: 11/7/1959	
4	Marcella Elizabeth Habetz	b: 4/16/1942		d: 5/22/1973
	+Ralph Gossen	b: 1934	m: 5/5/1962	
4	Patrick Conrad Habetz	b: 2/28/1944		
	+Margie Granger		m: 4/11/1964	
4	Kathleen Gertrude Habetz	b: 9/7/1945		
	+Cecil Compton		m: 8/21/1965	
3	Msgr. Daniel Habetz	b: 2/10/1913		d: 9/27/1977
3	Maria "Clara" Habetz	b: 10/4/1914		d: 8/22/2006
3	Sr. Anna "Maria" Habetz	b: 7/31/1916		
3	William Henry Habetz	b: 5/18/1918		
	+Agnes Leonards	b: 1921	m: 2/13/1946	
4	Carl William Habetz	b: 9/5/1951		
	+Deborah M. Darbonne		m: 1/12/1971	
4	Ronald Hubert Habetz	b: 4/2/1953		
	+Colleen A. Kennedy		m: 2/2/1974	
	*2nd Wife of Ronald Hubert Habetz:			
	+Deanna Faye Darbonne		m: 11/19/1993	
4	Marilyn Agnes Habetz	b: 1/28/1955		
4	David Wayne Habetz	b: 2/14/1956		
	+Andrea E. Bruce		m: 4/5/1975	
4	Janelle Mary Habetz	b: 10/30/1958		
	+Ted Bruce		m: 4/21/1979	

Habetz

4	Richard Joseph Habetz	b: 11/26/1959		
	+Darlene Tugwell		m: 1/22/1983	
4	Gregory Anthony Habetz	b: 9/1/1961		d: 9/5/1991
	+Deanna Faye Darbonne		m: 12/18/1982	
4	Loretta Ann Habetz	b: 12/29/1965		
	+Johnny Ray Darbonne, Jr.		m: 11/25/1989	
3	Joseph Peter Habetz	b: 3/8/1920		d: 7/25/2006
	+Rita Ohlenforst	b: 3/29/1924	m: 1/2/1946	d: 5/6/1999
4	Flavia Ann Habetz	b: 11/1/1946		
	+Glenn John Eldridge		m: 11/27/1969	
4	Michael Anthony Habetz	b: 1/5/1948		
	+Cynthia Scott		m: 7/25/1970	
4	Bruno Joseph Habetz	b: 6/20/1950		
	+Debra Judice		m: 5/24/1975	
	*2nd Wife of Bruno Joseph Habetz:			
	+Mary Katherine Derouen		m: 10/27/1984	
	*3rd Wife of Bruno Joseph Habetz:			
	+Linda Leeper		m: 10/9/1992	
4	Tedmund Daniel Habetz	b: 1/4/1953		
	+Kay Voohries		m: 2/29/1980	
4	Joline Rita Habetz	b: 8/3/1955		d: 8/3/1955
3	Cecilia Augusta Habetz	b: 12/6/1921		
	+Paul Zaunbrecher	b: 1923	m: 2/13/1946	d: 9/20/1982
4	Timothy Daniel Zaunbrecher	b: 12/12/1946		
	+Judy Cluchey	b: 9/20/1947	m: 5/29/1971	
4	Godfrey William Zaunbrecher	b: 2/21/1948		
	+Annagail Mitchell	b: 1948	m: 7/27/1968	

Habetz

*2nd Wife of Godfrey William Zaunbrecher:
+Gail Cemer b: 2/21/1952 m: 2/20/1981
*3rd Wife of Godfrey William Zaunbrecher:
+Kathleen Rae Reiftroffer m: 2000

4 Gwendolyn Marie Zaunbrecher b: 1/8/1950 d: 1/8/1950
4 Gerard Joseph Zaunbrecher b: 1/24/1952
+Marsha Ann Sanchez b: 6/1/1952 m: 1/10/1976
3 Hilda Helena Habetz b: 8/23/1923 d: 10/23/1924
3 Anton Theodore Habetz b: 6/7/1925 d: 2/12/2004
+Jose "Joyce" Lynn Leleux b: 1937 m: 2/24/1960
4 Josette Marie Habetz b: 2/25/1961
+Ray Anthony Dupuis m: 1/23/1982
4 Monica Lynn Habetz b: 1/28/1962
+Charles Miller m: 8/10/1985
4 Martin Anthony Habetz b: 12/14/1962
+Tammy Sue Castille m: 4/9/1983
*2nd Wife of Martin Anthony Habetz:
+Jennifer Hildalgo m: Aft. 1983
4 Nicholas William Habetz b: 11/14/1964
+Cynthia Ann Dartez m: 7/10/1987
4 Barbara Ann Habetz b: 11/29/1965
+Carl Stephen Cramer b: 9/10/1967 m: 6/13/1987
4 Dennis Joseph Habetz b: 11/1/1967
+Antoinette "Toni" Lavergne m: 5/12/1990
4 Dewayne Paul Habetz b: 11/7/1968
+Tasca White m: 11/7/1992
*2nd Wife of Dewayne Paul Habetz:
+Michelle Renee Henry m: Aft. 1992

Habetz

    *3rd Wife of Dewayne Paul Habetz:
    +Christa Leger   m: 7/22/2006
4   Alois Philip Habetz   b: 11/7/1969
    +Gaylin Ann Vice
4   Rev. Thomas Edmund Habetz   b: 11/5/1971
4   Hilary Wayne Habetz   b: 8/28/1973
3   Bernardine Marie Habetz   b: 6/9/1927
    +Blaise Philip Leonards   b: 1927   m: 10/27/1948
4   Sylvester Guy Leonards   b: 8/29/1949
    +Eugenie Marie Forstall (Cassie) Colomb   b: 10/14/1951   m: 7/13/1974
4   Blandina Gayle Leonards   b: 9/7/1950
    +Michael Zaunbrecher   b: 8/23/1950   m: 6/22/1972
4   Ludwig Joseph Leonards   b: 1/31/1952
    +Eula Theresa Devall   b: 9/8/1956   m: 6/22/1974
4   Ignatius William Leonards   b: 9/6/1953
    +Janet Ester Lawrence   b: 4/13/1951   m: 10/27/1979
4   Gwendolyn Louise Leonards   b: 1/24/1956
    +Frank Dale Zaunbrecher   b: 10/8/1952   m: 6/9/1973
4   Daniel Lawrence Leonards   b: 3/16/1957
    +Rita Elaine Lejeune   b: 7/10/1958   m: 11/19/1977
4   Caroline Anne Leonards   b: 9/5/1958
    +Eddie James Fontenot   b: 9/2/1958   m: 11/18/1978   d: 9/27/1984
    *2nd Husband of Caroline Anne Leonards:
    +Ellis Michael Trahan   b: 11/20/1959   m: 10/26/2002
4   Joan Dione Leonards   b: 6/8/1960

Habetz

	+Robert Joseph Douget	b: 7/18/1957	m: 6/10/1978	
4	Marie Elaine Leonards	b: 12/10/1961		
	+Ronald James Fontenot	b: 1/9/1956	m: 7/19/1983	
4	Paul Brent Leonards	b: 2/21/1966		
	+Connie Marie Rabalais	b: 3/10/1966	m: 8/10/1990	
3	Martin Habetz	b: 5/20/1929		d: 5/20/1929
3	Bertha Catherine Habetz	b: 10/31/1930		
	+Gerard Owen	b: 1917	m: 8/4/1957	d: 12/27/1987
4	Eileen Owen	b: 10/30/1957		
4	Yvette Owen	b: 12/5/1960		
	+Sergio Garcia		m: 6/17/1983	

10. Heinen, Gerhard Joseph:

Gerhard Joseph Heinen b: 9/6/1845 d: 11/7/1916 from Schierwaldenrath was the son of Anton Joseph Heinen b: 4/8/1803 d: 1/30/1867 and Anna Maria Mertens b: 12/8/1806 d: 12/16/1897. He married on 6/30/1868 to Maria Josepha Jöris b: 7/6/1843 d: 2/20/1910, daughter of Christian Joseph Jöris b: 2/2/1813 d: 6/16/1874 and Maria Elizabeth Schmitz b: 6/5/1817 d: 9/5/1882.

2		Maria Walburga Heinen	b: 5/1/1869		d: 1/25/1959
		+Wilhelm Joseph Zaunbrecher	b: 10/3/1867	m: 11/19/1892	d: 3/11/1922
3		Martin Nicholas Zaunbrecher	b: 11/10/1893		d: 3/26/1975
		+Maria Josephine Cramer	b: 1/6/1906	m: 1/11/1927	d: 2000
	4	Wilma Anna Zaunbrecher	b: 12/6/1928		
		+Huey Patrick Regan	b: 9/7/1930	m: 4/25/1950	
	4	William Joseph Zaunbrecher	b: 7/16/1931		d: 4/1/1990
		+Laurea Marie James	b: 11/15/1939	m: 2/10/1963	d: 9/17/1992
	4	Clarice Ann Zaunbrecher	b: 9/26/1933		
		+Rodney William Lejeune	b: 11/27/1930	m: 4/15/1953	
	4	Otto Bernard Zaunbrecher	b: 8/22/1935		
		+Sylvia Jean Armstrong	b: 9/18/1943	m: 2/8/1964	
	4	Elaine Marie Zaunbrecher	b: 11/25/1937		d: 10/25/2001
		+Carl Barry Leger	b: 8/25/1936	m: 2/1/1958	
	4	Mary Jo Zaunbrecher	b: 1/27/1940		
		+Carl Jerome Foreman	b: 2/29/1940	m: 11/28/1964	
	4	Wanda Ann Zaunbrecher	b: 12/2/1941		

Heinen

	+Shelton Eugene Launey	b: 2/9/1937	m: 11/4/1961	
3	Maria Helena Zaunbrecher	b: 4/14/1896		d: 8/19/1952
	+Anthony Conrad Dischler	b: 9/2/1900	m: 1923	d: 1986
4	Antonia Maria Dischler	b: 1926		
	+John Clyde Leger	b: 1923	m: 1949	
4	Martin William Dischler	b: 1927		
	+Marcella Comeaux	b: 1928	m: 1949	
4	Pauline Bertha Dischler	b: 1929		d: 1/22/2006
	+Francis Charles Roy	b: 1929	m: 1949	d: 1993
4	Infant Dischler	b: 1931		d: 1931
4	Monica Ann "Mona" Dischler	b: 1934		
	+Ronald James Gossen	b: 1929	m: 1953	
4	Helen Marie Dischler	b: 1936		
	+Kenneth Jack Mantle		m: 1961	
	*2nd Husband of Helen Marie Dischler:			
	+Frank Robles	b: 1927	m: 1976	
3	Elizabeth Augusta Zaunbrecher	b: 1898		d: 1924
	+[1] Lawrence Joseph Leonards	b: 2/24/1893	m: 2/1917	d: 8/5/1945
4	William Joseph Leonards	b: 12/12/1917		d: 8/24/2000
	+Barbara Rose Bollich	b: 1913	m: 11/20/1940	d: 5/11/2002
4	Josephine Marie Leonards	b: 3/26/1919		d: 1/23/2002
	+Herman Aloyoius Cramer	b: 1911	m: 11/13/1940	d: 11/10/1966
4	Rita Helen Leonards	b: 12/27/1920		
4	Norbert Nicholas Leonards	b: 9/12/1922		d: 4/13/1945
4	Vincent Karl Leonards	b: 9/24/1924		

Heinen

		+Thelma "Tillie" Zaunbrecher	b: 7/30/1926	m: 1949	
3		William Frederick Zaunbrecher	b: 12/19/1899		d: 12/6/1972
		+Maria Anna Leonards	b: 1/20/1901	m: 1/18/1922	d: 3/22/1975
	4	Paul William Zaunbrecher	b: 6/10/1923		d: 9/20/1982
		+Cecilia Augusta Habetz	b: 12/6/1921	m: 2/13/1946	
	4	Richard Andrew Zaunbrecher, Sr	b: 11/30/1924		
		+Verna Mary Johnson	b: 12/18/1925	m: 6/19/1946	
	4	Felix Leo Zaunbrecher	b: 12/30/1926		
		+Hilda Mary Broussard	b: 5/17/1929	m: 1/27/1948	
	4	William Zaunbrecher	b: 4/13/1928		d: 4/13/1928
	4	Mary Agnes Zaunbrecher	b: 2/21/1930		
		+Clarence Albert Fabacher	b: 3/17/1931	m: 2/4/1956	
	4	Theresa Marie Zaunbrecher	b: 9/28/1931		
		+Jean Edwin Broussard	b: 1/24/1926	m: 11/26/1953	
	4	Josephine Ann Zaunbrecher	b: 8/6/1934		
		+Jerome Ronkartz	b: 2/16/1933	m: 8/20/1956	
	4	William Francis Zaunbrecher	b: 9/18/1935		d: 9/18/1935
	4	Willietta Dorothy Zaunbrecher	b: 9/6/1938		
		+Urban Anderson Phillips	b: 10/8/1933	m: 8/29/1959	d: 5/18/1998

Heinen

4	Francis Martin "Bud" Zaunbrecher	b: 11/11/1943		
	+Hannah Casselman		m: 1963	
	*2nd Wife of Francis Martin "Bud" Zaunbrecher:			
	+Judy Craighead	b: 1945	m: 2/9/1973	
	*3rd Wife of Francis Martin "Bud" Zaunbrecher:			
	+Christine Schroeder	b: 7/25/1937	m: 10/19/1983	d: 11/23/1984
	*4th Wife of Francis Martin "Bud" Zaunbrecher:			
	+Bertha Jane Doucet	b: 10/26/1941	m: 3/8/1990	d: 5/20/2007
3	Henry Josph Zaunbrecher	b: 11/19/1901		d: 1993
	+Annie Caroline Bollich	b: 4/10/1906	m: 1/20/1926	d: 2004
4	Vera Marie Zaunbrecher	b: 11/6/1926		
	+Frank Conrad Jabusch	b: 1924	m: 1947	
4	Stella Josephine Zaunbrecher	b: 5/5/1928		
	+James William Doucet	b: 1928	m: 1951	d: 3/2005
4	Leroy Francis Zaunbrecher	b: 8/1/1929		d: 10/2003
	+Sammie Jane Meaux	b: 1931	m: 1950	
4	James Anthony Zaunbrecher	b: 8/3/1931		
	+Helen Joy Martin	b: 1934	m: 1954	
4	Louise Frances Zaunbrecher	b: 9/1/1933		
	+Aubrey DeCuir Caffery	b: 5/21/1923	m: 6/1/1957	d: 7/5/1999
4	Lorraine Marie Zaunbrecher	b: 1/9/1935		d: 11/1962
	+John Joseph Gordon	b: 1926	m: 1956	d: 2004
4	Suzanne Zaunbrecher	b: 5/21/1936		

Heinen

	+Howard Allen "Boochie" Duncan	b: 1927	m: 1958	d: 2004
4	Dennis Henry Zaunbrecher	b: 12/1938		d: 1991
	+Gerry Broussard	b: 1938	m: 1961	
4	Leonard Anthony Zaunbrecher	b: 8/31/1943		
	+Charlotte Joan Sittig	b: 1942	m: 1964	
3	Maria Anna Zaunbrecher	b: 11/1/1903		d: 9/5/1984
	+[1] Lawrence Joseph Leonards	b: 2/24/1893	m: 6/15/1926	d: 8/5/1945
4	Raymond William Leonards	b: 1/29/1929		d: 4/22/1992
	+Louise Augusta Theunissen	b: 12/27/1932	m: 12/27/1952	
4	[5] Benno Joseph Leonards	b: 6/16/1931		
	+[4] Arilda Gertrude Heinen	b: 3/16/1934	m: 11/16/1958	d: 5/8/1973
	*2nd Wife of [5] Benno Joseph Leonards:			
	+Margaret Funk	b: 7/14/1930	m: 3/16/1974	
4	Johanna Augusta Leonards	b: 12/15/1932		d: 5/5/1993
4	[3] Henry Jerome Leonards	b: 9/13/1934		
	+[2] Wilma Thecla Hensgens	b: 11/10/1937	m: 1958	d: 5/21/2006
4	Dennis Louis Leonards	b: 5/24/1936		
	+Phyllis Helen Robicheaux	b: 11/18/1939	m: 1/14/1961	
4	Wilfred Charles Leonards	b: 7/3/1937		
	+Elaine Credeur	b: 11/12/1941	m: 7/1964	
4	Mary Ann Leonards	b: 12/10/1938		

Heinen

4	Lidwina Josephine Leonards	b: 7/20/1940		d: 3/9/1941
4	Catherine Mary Leonards	b: 7/19/1944		
	+Dale Bernard Huesers	b: 3/20/1938	m: 5/9/1964	
3	Charles Joseph Zaunbrecher	b: 1905		d: 10/25/1972
	+Maria Bertha Dischler	b: 1905	m: 1929	d: 1990
4	Dolores Marie Zaunbrecher	b: 1930		
	+Philip Jacob Joseph Habetz	b: 1930	m: 1956	
4	Fr. Charles Zaunbrecher	b: 11/8/1931		d: 6/19/1996
4	Vincent Zaunbrecher	b: 1933		
	+Genevieve Parrino	b: 1930	m: 6/14/1955	
4	Jane Zaunbrecher	b: 1934		d: 1990
	+Wilvin Charles Leleux	b: 1935	m: 1958	
4	William "Billy" Louis Zaunbrecher	b: 5/31/1938		d: 8/19/1997
	+Anna Margaret Cramer	b: 12/31/1938	m: 12/16/1963	
4	Stephen Joseph Zaunbrecher	b: 9/2/1940		
	+Rose Marie Reiners	b: 3/28/1942	m: 6/26/1962	
3	Joseph August Zaunbrecher	b: 8/28/1906		d: 1981
	+Anna Maria Dischler	b: 1904	m: 1925	d: 1977
4	Edna Augusta Zaunbrecher	b: 1926		
	+Claures Joseph Broussard	b: 1928	m: 1957	

Heinen

4	Leo Charles Zaunbrecher	b: 1927		
	+Stella Minnie Low	b: 1936	m: 1956	
4	Gerald Joseph Zaunbrecher	b: 1929		d: 1988
	+Shirley Mae Stark	b: 1937	m: 1956	d: 1994
4	Harold Joseph Zaunbrecher	b: 1929		d: 1999
	+Pauline Margaret Dupree	b: 1936	m: 1960	
4	Ferdinand Vincent Zaunbrecher	b: 1932		
	+Janet Louise Summers		m: 1960	

*2nd Wife of Ferdinand Vincent Zaunbrecher:

	+Jean Pascoe		m: 1980	
4	Genevieve Marie Zaunbrecher	b: 1934		
	+Gordon Edward Tate	b: 2/3/1934	m: 1963	d: 12/2004
4	Joyce Marie Zaunbrecher	b: 1935		
	+Howard Joseph Melancon	b: 1937	m: 1972	
4	Dorothy Ann Zaunbrecher	b: 1937		
4	Hilary Charles Zaunbrecher	b: 1939		
	+Suzanne Gayle Phillips	b: 1946	m: 1983	
4	Donald Louis Zaunbrecher	b: 1942		
	+Josephine Ann Busse	b: 1944	m: 1976	
3	Maria Gertrude Zaunbrecher	b: 1908		d: 1909

Heinen

3		Maria Leona Zaunbrecher	b: 7/17/1910		d: 12/2004
3		Joseph Anton Zaunbrecher	b: 1912		d: 1991
		+Marie Dischler	b: 1908		d: 1993
2		Elizabeth Augusta Heinen	b: 1/10/1871		d: 3/31/1944
		+Aloysuis Thevis	b: 1866	m: 2/18/1890	d: 1937
3		Jacob Andrew Thevis	b: 1890		d: 1903
3		Cornelia Josepha Thevis	b: 3/19/1894		d: 4/13/1971
		+Lawrence Edward Frey	b: 7/7/1890	m: 1912	d: 5/9/1922
	4	Elizabeth Frey	b: 1913		d: 1990
		+Elge Rasberry	b: 1909	m: 1934	d: Deceased
	4	Aloysuis Frey	b: 5/9/1915		
		+Marcella Rose Bollich	b: 1916	m: 1937	
3		Maria Walburga Thevis	b: 1896		d: 1984
		+Henry Joseph Ohlenforst	b: 2/25/1889	m: 1919	d: 8/20/1971
	4	Fr. William Ohlenforst	b: 11/5/1919		d: 1/3/1997
	4	Aloysius Ohlenforst	b: 1921		d: 1996
		+Micheline Courtat	b: 1929	m: 1946	
	4	George Lawrence Ohlenforst	b: 2/3/1923		d: 2/6/1923
	4	Gertrude Cecile Ohlenforst	b: 1924		d: 1994
		+Frank Bernard	b: 1920	m: 1946	d: 1984
	4	Thecla Theresa Ohlenforst	b: 2/28/1926		d: 4/21/1967
		+Lionel Paul Simoneaux, Jr.	b: 1923	m: 1951	d: 2005
	4	Andrew Lawrence Ohlenforst	b: 10/6/1928		d: 10/3/1983
		+Marcella Marie Leonards	b: 2/3/1934	m: 1/19/1955	

Heinen

4	Sr. Margaret Mary Ohlenforst	b: 10/20/1931		
4	Dorothy Ann Ohlenforst	b: 1933		
	+William Joseph Leger	b: 1928	m: 1953	d: 1992
4	Joseph Daniel Ohlenforst	b: 1935		
	+Brenda Marie Sonnier	b: 1946	m: 1965	
4	Saraphia Bernadette Ohlenforst	b: 1938		
	+Edlar Ronald Monte	b: 1938	m: 1959	
4	Francis Thomas Ohlenforst	b: 1940		
	+Jacquelyn Sue Dupont	b: 10/13/1942	m: 1969	d: 7/15/2005
3	William Ignatius Thevis	b: 1898		d: 1917
3	Lambertina Thecla Thevis	b: 9/23/1900		d: 2/27/1981
	+John Casper Berken	b: 7/6/1891	m: 6/18/1919	d: 1/30/1984
4	Herman Aloysius Berken	b: 3/5/1920		d: 2/18/1992
	+Elvina Bourque	b: 6/30/1930	m: 6/15/1950	d: 4/18/2000
4	Lawrence Herman Berken	b: 8/10/1921		d: 9/11/1996
	+Leona Hensgens	b: 5/6/1924	m: 1/30/1946	
4	Elizabeth Josephine Berken	b: 11/8/1922		d: 11/27/1995
	+Charles Klein	b: 8/8/1922	m: 11/20/1946	
4	Christina Marie Berken	b: 3/26/1924		
	+Simon Hornsby	b: 5/7/1925	m: 10/7/1950	d: 7/10/1978
4	Vincent Joseph Berken	b: 12/17/1925		d: 4/22/2005
	+Marie Louise Thevis	b: 2/19/1938	m: 10/24/1956	
4	Gertrude Angela Berken	b: 9/17/1927		
	+Robert Leger	b: 12/31/1927	m: 4/14/1951	d: 7/9/2003
4	Mary Agnes Berken	b: 11/30/1929		
	+Jesse Harrington	b: 10/1/1926	m: 6/21/1952	

Heinen

4	Anna Louise Berken	b: 1932		d: 1942	
4	Josephine Thecla Berken	b: 7/14/1934			
	+Anthony Thevis	b: 3/23/1928	m: 5/10/1955	d: 4/29/1992	
4	Reinhard John Berken	b: 8/4/1938		d: 10/3/2001	
	+Thelma Abshire	b: 10/26/1940	m: 1961	d: 4/6/2007	

*2nd Wife of Reinhard John Berken:

	+Brenda Credeur	b: 7/23/1949	m: 11/6/1982		
4	Rita Helena Berken	b: 3/23/1941			
	+Jesse Hoffpauir	b: 1/1/1941	m: 2/4/1961	d: 10/5/2002	
3	Maria Gertrude Thevis	b: 1903		d: 1993	
3	Anna Maria Thevis	b: 4/20/1905		d: 2/14/1973	
	+Frank Reiners	b: 9/8/1901	m: 2/12/1924	d: 9/25/1987	
4	Joseph Reiners	b: 4/9/1925		d: 2005	
	+Harriette Louise Klein	b: 10/13/1931	m: 11/9/1949		
4	Alois Andrew Reiners	b: 7/25/1926		d: 3/19/1999	
	+Lucille Clara Gossen	b: 11/11/1928	m: 11/25/1953		
4	Elizabeth Josephine Reiners	b: 10/16/1928		d: 4/17/2000	
4	Helen Marie Reiners	b: 9/20/1932			
	+Sylvester Lawrence Frey	b: 7/20/1930	m: 1954		
4	Anthony Francis Reiners	b: 11/18/1933			
	+Pauline Ann Habetz	b: 4/13/1934	m: 9/19/1957		
3	Elizabeth Anna Thevis	b: 3/12/1907		d: 1995	
	+Edward Frey	b: 10/14/1903	m: 1927	d: 8/8/1974	
4	Genevieve Frey	b: 11/11/1932			
	+Edwin Leonards	b: 9/21/1928	m: 7/9/1951	d: 4/21/2007	
4	Edward Frey	b: 3/7/1933			
	+D'uan Fontenot			d: 4/29/1987	

*2nd Wife of Edward Frey:

	+Pamela Schlicher		d: 7/28/2005

Heinen

4	Mildred Frey	b: 9/10/1935	
	+James Boudreax	b: 6/15/1932	
4	Rita Frey	b: 5/4/1937	
	+Lubert Reed		d: 4/10/1982
	*2nd Husband of Rita Frey:		
	+Harvey Hebert	b: 11/13/1921	
4	Frederick Frey	b: 9/15/1939	
	+Dorothy Vezinat		d: 12/9/1993
	*2nd Wife of Frederick Frey:		
	+Vicki Storer	m: 12/28/1997	
4	Sadie Frey	b: 2/20/1944	
	+Robert Thevis	b: 1/1/1942	
3	Maria Elizabeth Thevis	b: 1909	d: 1985
	+Christian Joseph Hensgens	b: 1907	m: 1928 d: 1972
4	Leonard Joseph Hensgens	b: 10/7/1929	
	+Sarah Ann Smith		m: 7/11/1950
4	Raymond Aloysious Hensgens	b: 7/22/1932	
	+Catherine "Kitty" Schneider		m: 10/20/1951
4	Lawrence Leo Hensgens	b: 4/1/1934	
	+Lula Link		m: 12/10/1953
4	Germaine Frances Hensgens	b: 12/14/1935	d: 2/2/1996
	+Frank J. Schneider		m: 10/25/1955
4	[2] Wilma Thecla Hensgens	b: 11/10/1937	d: 5/21/2006
	+[3] Henry Jerome Leonards	b: 9/13/1934	m: 1958
4	Alberta Gertrude Hensgens	b: 2/13/1940	

Heinen

		+Norwood Marcy Lyons		m: 5/25/1963	
2		William Michael Heinen	b: 9/29/1873		d: 9/3/1940
		+Barbara Hensgens	b: 8/6/1876	m: 1/2/1897	d: 5/21/1947
	3	Joseph Anton Heinen	b: 1898		d: 1955
		+Adele (Della) Naebors	b: 1895	m: 1918	d: 1956
	4	Wilfred Heinen	b: 5/7/1919		d: 1/10/1970
		+Maurine Muller	b: 5/5/1922	m: 1/11/1949	d: 8/21/2004
	4	Theodora Heinen	b: 7/14/1921		
		+Kenneth Faulk			
	4	Walter Heinen	b: 3/15/1924		d: 1/10/1985
		+Lorraine Frey	b: 9/30/1929	m: 4/28/1949	
	4	Wilhelmena "Wilma" Heinen	b: 12/28/1926		
		+Burton Cormier	b: 4/8/1923	m: 10/29/1947	d: 11/2/2005
	3	William Christian Heinen	b: 1900		d: 1957
		+Christina Margaret Naebers	b: 1901	m: 1926	d: 1965
	4	Charles Heinen	b: 11/17/1926		d: 6/16/1994
		+Lenora Trahan	b: 7/13/1935	m: 5/19/1956	d: 11/28/2001
	4	Hilda Heinen	b: 12/8/1928		
	4	Joseph Heinen	b: 10/16/1930		d: 10/16/1930
	4	Geraldine Heinen	b: 9/26/1931		d: 4/14/2001
		+Thomas Heard	b: 8/6/1927		d: 4/6/1984
	4	Josephine Regina Heinen	b: 6/27/1936		
		+Malcolm Millet	b: 4/8/1928	m: 6/1/1957	
	4	Lawrence William Heinen	b: 10/29/1938		d: 11/28/2005
		+Louise Regina Leonards	b: 1/9/1945	m: 6/27/1970	
	4	Annie Louise Heinen	b: 3/9/1941		d: 9/16/1995
		+Patrick Gautreaux	b: 5/24/1940	m: 6/10/1961	d: 4/26/2000
	4	[4] Arilda Gertrude Heinen	b: 3/16/1934		d: 5/8/1973

Heinen

	+[5] Benno Joseph Leonards	b: 6/16/1931	m: 11/16/1958	
3	Theodore Ignatius Heinen	b: 1902		d: 1962
	+Catherine Louise Gossen	b: 1905	m: 1927	d: 1996
3	Conrad Edward Heinen	b: 1904		d: 1924
3	Maria Gertrude Heinen	b: 1906		d: 2003
	+Henry John Naebers	b: 1904	m: 1928	d: 1972
3	Anthony Leo Heinen	b: 1909		d: 1924
3	Maria Regina Heinen	b: 1911		d: 1970
	+Wallace Joseph Link	b: 1909	m: 1935	d: 1953
4	Sylvia Link	b: 9/3/1936		d: 1/9/1996
	+Hershel Beard	b: 9/17/1928	m: 11/22/1953	
4	Barbara Ann Link	b: 9/17/1938		
	+Leonard "Buck" Leonards	b: 6/30/1937	m: 11/27/1958	
4	William Link	b: 10/6/1941		
	+Sylvia Simpson	b: 12/11/1943	m: 1/25/1964	
4	Wallace Link	b: 10/23/1944		
	+Marilyn Wright	b: 11/20/1952	m: 1/5/1974	
3	Lambertina Josepha Heinen	b: 1913		d: 1993
	+Joseph John Naebers	b: 1908	m: 1935	d: 1976
4	Jo Ann Naebers	b: 11/2/1935		
	+Al Claude Louviere	b: 9/6/1934	m: 7/1/1952	
4	Marlene Naebers	b: 9/20/1937		
	+Alvin Daigle	b: 12/12/1932	m: 1/9/1957	
4	Ronald Naebers	b: 4/25/1941		
	+Bobbie Sue Kratzer	b: 9/6/1940	m: 1/9/1960	
4	Gretchen Naebers	b: 10/24/1948		
	+Dallas Benoit II	b: 10/24/1947	m: 9/6/1965	
3	Annie Wilhelmena Heinen	b: 1915		d: 1958

Heinen

3		John Aloysius Heinen	b: 1919		d: 2004
		+Gertie Lou Leger	b: 1923	m: 1941	d: 2005
	4	John Aloysius Heinen II	b: 1/20/1943		
		+Jeannette Prather	b: 2/9/1943	m: 12/27/1961	
	4	William Heinen	b: 5/9/1944		
		+Jeanne Seaux	b: 10/11/1947	m: 2/12/1966	
	4	Cheryl Heinen	b: 8/8/1948		
		+Patrick Handley, Sr.	b: 6/11/1946	m: 2/17/1968	
	4	Barry Heinen	b: 2/14/1950		
		+Kathleen Kane	b: 5/10/1949	m: 9/3/1969	
	4	Debra Heinen	b: 2/1/1952		
		+Elliot Higginbotham	b: 7/9/1946	m: 8/18/1970	
	4	Paul Heinen	b: 10/15/1955		
		+Patricia Puissegur	b: 6/21/1958	m: 12/18/1976	
	4	Keith Heinen	b: 6/13/1957		
		+Dianna Hoffpauer	b: 3/10/1958	m: 1/16/1976	
	4	Sandra Heinen	b: 11/19/1963		
		+Bradley Lavergne	b: 1/23/1953	m: 8/18/1989	
2		Theodore Gregory Heinen	b: 5/9/1874		d: 11/9/1940
		+Rosa Neu	b: 1874	m: 1/13/1899	d: 1949
3		Placidus Joseph " Sam" Heinen	b: 1899		d: 1974
		+Anna Mathilda Dischler	b: 1900	m: 1921	d: 1989
	4	Dorothy Heinen	b: 1922		
	4	Henry Heinen	b: 1923		
		+Versie Fontenot		m: 1947	d: 1970
	4	Helen Heinen	b: 1925		d: 9/16/1991
		+Frank E. Landry II	b: 12/9/1920	m: 11/1946	
	4	James Heinen	b: 1928		
		+Bonita Rider		m: 1955	d: 1995
	4	Lillian Heinen	b: 1931		

Heinen

	+Norman "Bill" Barron		m: 1951	d: 2001
4	Beatrice Heinen	b: 1933		
	+John Burke Young	b: 1932	m: 1955	
4	Louis Heinen	b: 1935		
	+Marie Francois	b: 1945	m: 1977	
3	John Jacob Heinen	b: 1901		d: 1915
3	William Edward Heinen	b: 1903		d: 1982
	+Ethel Lafleur	b: 1908	m: 1927	d: 1972
4	Mary Rose Heinen	b: 11/16/1928		
	+Nathan Miller	b: 12/4/1926	m: 1/19/1947	
4	Dorothy Heinen	b: 12/30/1929		d: 8/25/1981
	+Joseph Toups	b: 3/10/1928	m: 9/12/1948	
4	Alberta Heinen	b: 1932		
	+Edmund Frey	b: 1926	m: 1950	
4	Raymond Heinen	b: 7/22/1938		
	+Dorothy Lanthier	b: 9/24/1938	m: 1/20/1956	
3	Joseph Anthony Heinen	b: 1905		d: 1927
3	Jacob Martin Heinen	b: 1907		d: 1987
	+Renola Hebert	b: 1910	m: 1927	d: 1940
4	Marguerite Heinen	b: 12/23/1927		
	+Dewey Constantin	b: 6/3/1923	m: 1946	d: 6/28/1982
4	Donald Heinen	b: 1929		d: 1930
4	Martin Jacob Heinen, Jr.	b: 5/30/1935		d: 4/3/2005
	+Evelyn Cunningham			
	*2nd Wife of Martin Jacob Heinen, Jr.:			
	+Dottie Jones			
3	Leo Ferdinand Heinen	b: 4/11/1909		d: 12/27/1959
	+Maria Catherine Hensgens	b: 2/8/1913	m: 1/25/1933	
4	Gwendolyn Heinen	b: 3/19/1934		
	+James Stewart	b: 7/29/1933	m: 9/19/1959	
4	Lowell Heinen	b: 1/2/1937		

Heinen

		+Catherine Davis	b: 11/22/1936	m: 12/27/1957	
	4	Dr. Brian Heinen	b: 8/12/1943		
		+Jennifer Guillory	b: 9/26/1945	m: 2/22/1963	
	4	Janet Heinen	b: 10/22/1946		
		+Donald Martel	b: 12/13/1944	m: 8/26/1967	
	4	Ferdinand Heinen	b: 9/8/1955		
		+Lori Gregory	b: 4/16/1959	m: 5/10/1996	
3		Aloyius Andrew Heinen	b: 1910		d: 1916
3		Othmar Gregory Heinen	b: 1912		d: 1938
2		Karl Joseph Heinen	b: 3/3/1876		d: 5/16/1876
2		Anton Joseph Heinen	b: 10/21/1877		d: 11/7/1929
		+Maria Josepha Ronkartz	b: 1889	m: 11/20/1907	d: 1972
3		Anna Marie Heinen	b: 1908		d: 1994
		+Roland Privat	b: 1906	m: 1931	d: 1963
	4	Louis Privat	b: 1932		
	4	Bobby Privat	b: 1933		d: 1993
		+Cindy Gardiner	b: 1934	m: 1956	
	4	Eddie Privat	b: 1936		
		+Gayle Arceneaux	b: 1937	m: 1958	
		*2nd Wife of Eddie Privat:			
		+Mary Ann Duzzer	b: 1939	m: 1983	
	4	Tommy Privat	b: 1940		
		+Pam Fontenot	b: 1941	m: 1964	
	4	Dan Privat	b: 1948		
		+Charlotte Simpson	b: 1946	m: 1968	
	4	Ann Marie Privat	b: 1948		
		+James Burch	b: 1949	m: 1982	
3		Maria Josepha Heinen	b: 1911		d: 2005
		+Clarence Dodd Daigle	b: 1909	m: 1934	d: 1974
	4	Freddie Daigle	b: 1936		
		+Sylvia Fontenot	b: 1934	m: 1955	
	4	Albert T. Daigle	b: 1936		

Heinen

		+Earlene Venable	b: 1938	m: 1957
	4	Janet Daigle	b: 1942	
		+James Ethridge	b: 1942	m: 1962
2		Maria Katharina Heinen	b: 1/12/1880	d: 1/25/1880
2		Katherina Lambertina Heinen	b: 5/20/1881	d: 12/30/1962
		+John Frey	b: 2/24/1876	m: 1/29/1902 d: 9/19/1957
3		Maria Josephine Frey	b: 11/28/1902	d: 1998
		+Nicholas Conrad Zaunbrecher	b: 9/21/1901	m: 1922 d: 12/29/1963
	4	Helen Zaunbrecher	b: 1923	
		+Joseph Thevis	b: 5/4/1919	m: 1946
	4	Lawrence Zaunbrecher	b: 4/12/1925	
		+Lucy Cramer	b: 7/30/1926	m: 1955
	4	Thelma "Tillie" Zaunbrecher	b: 7/30/1926	
		+Vincent Carl Leonards	b: 9/24/1924	m: 2/23/1949 d: 12/30/1998
	4	Laura Zaunbrecher	b: 3/6/1928	
		+Louis Bellard	b: 7/2/1924	m: 7/1948 d: 8/10/1996
	4	Louis Zaunbrecher	b: 8/30/1929	d: 9/12/2004
		+Helen Martell	b: 9/8/1931	m: 4/12/1953
	4	Jeanette Zaunbrecher	b: 9/24/1931	
		+Wayne Holtzapple	b: 6/12/1929	m: 11/28/1952
	4	Frances Zaunbrecher	b: 3/16/1933	
		+Jesse Paul Fruge	b: 12/12/1918	m: 11/29/1955 d: 11/30/1995
	4	Robert Zaunbrecher	b: 11/14/1934	
		+Claudette Johnson	b: 3/16/1938	m: 4/19/1958
	4	Stanley Zaunbrecher	b: 9/19/1936	
		+Lorette Langley	b: 6/18/1941	m: 4/2/1963 d: 1/26/1996
	4	Rodney Zaunbrecher	b: 5/8/1940	
		+Elaine Schneider	b: 3/16/1944	m: 1/26/1963

Heinen

4	Margaret Zaunbrecher	b: 5/18/1942		
	+Lawrence Leo "Larry" Regan		m: 11/18/1961	
4	Jo Ann Zaunbrecher	b: 7/22/1944		
	+Henry Leonard Meyer	b: 9/25/1940	m: 7/15/1964	
4	Edna Mae Zaunbrecher	b: 5/26/1946		
	+Michael Leger	b: 11/3/1949	m: 10/21/1972	
4	Lloyd Zaunbrecher	b: 6/4/1948		
	+Donna Lejeune	b: 3/30/1949	m: 2/18/1973	
3	Dorothy (Dora) Beatrice Frey	b: 1905		d: 1991
	+August Joseph Leonards	b: 9/25/1896	m: 1923	d: 5/3/1962
4	August Joseph Leonards, Jr.	b: 1/26/1924		d: 2/26/1988
	+Beatrice Aloysia Olinger	b: 8/13/1925	m: 8/20/1947	
4	Antoinette Beatrice Leonards	b: 9/5/1926		d: 4/16/2000
	+Ira Lawrence Miller	b: 7/3/1923	m: 5/7/1947	
4	Anthony J. Leonards	b: 12/20/1928		d: 12/20/1928
4	Alberta Genevieve Leonards	b: 3/25/1930		d: 6/17/1975
	+Elmen James Bergeron	b: 6/22/1923	m: 8/13/1947	d: 8/23/2000
4	Patricia Ann Leonards	b: 6/29/1933		
	+Adam Price Johnson	b: 3/5/1929	m: 11/27/1952	
4	Lloyd Phillip Leonards	b: 11/30/1935		
	+Constance Claire Ledoux	b: 1/28/1937	m: 5/2/1957	
3	Anna Barbara Frey	b: 1907		d: 2003
	+Charles Philip Zaunbrecher	b: 1908	m: 1924	d: 1984

Heinen

4	Bertha Zaunbrecher	b: 6/5/1927		
	+Paul Joseph Breaux	b: 1/9/1924	m: 5/20/1952	d: 4/12/2004
4	Augusta Agnes Zaunbrecher	b: 1/11/1928		
	+Elmo Joseph Bollich	b: 11/11/1924	m: 5/18/1947	
4	Edmond Charles Zaunbrecher		b: 8/25/1929	d: 4/2/1995
	+Ollie Marie Linscombe	b: 2/28/1931	m: 11/27/1952	
4	Vincent William Zaunbrecher		b: 12/22/1931	
	+Janet Benoit	b: 10/27/1936	m: 11/8/1955	
4	Raymond Joseph Zaunbrecher	b: 9/12/1932		d: 4/1/1954
4	Harry John Zaunbrecher	b: 6/3/1934		
	+Lucy Henry	b: 7/1/1938	m: 10/22/1959	
4	Ramona Marie Zaunbrecher	b: 1/14/1936		
	+Reno Paul Petry, Jr	b: 2/28/1933	m: 2/8/1958	
4	Nicholas Wayne Zaunbrecher		b: 4/25/1939	
	+Linda Faye Guidry	b: 12/26/1940	m: 11/5/1960	
4	Floyd Anthony Zaunbrecher	b: 9/8/1940		
	+Cene Mae Vidalier	b: 12/6/1942	m: 11/28/1962	
4	Carolyn Ann Zaunbrecher	b: 11/11/1943		
	+James Avert Guidry	b: 11/16/1942	m: 11/17/1965	
4	Barbara Ann Zaunbrecher	b: 7/8/1949		
	+William Joseph Leonards II	b: 12/12/1952	m: 6/28/1975	
4	Mary Jacqueline Zaunbrecher		b: 12/24/1951	

Heinen

		+Allen Ray Francois	b: 7/27/1949	m: 6/30/1973	
3		Marie Johanna Frey	b: 1/27/1910		d: 12/31/2005
		+Philip Joseph Leonards	b: 5/26/1908	m: 1928	d: 12/8/1973
	4	Gerald John Leonards	b: 8/10/1933		d: 5/23/1989
		+Shirley Mae Nickel	b: 4/15/1935	m: 11/24/1957	
	4	Elaine Leonards	b: 6/10/1938		
		+Herbert Gossen	b: 7/20/1936	m: 6/10/1958	
3		Joseph William Frey	b: 1/27/1919		d: 7/19/1943
3		Hilda Mathilda Frey	b: 8/19/1922		d: 6/11/2004
		+Franz "Frank" Zaunbrecher	b: 12/31/1914	m: 2/12/1941	d: 8/25/1984
	4	Loretta Ann Zaunbrecher	b: 11/11/1941		
		+Frederick Burns Leger	b: 12/1/1939	m: 5/10/1960	d: 11/28/1965

*2nd Husband of Loretta Ann Zaunbrecher:

		+John Kurta	b: 5/25/1930	m: 2/1/1975	
	4	Stephen Charles Zaunbrecher	b: 2/3/1943		
		+Shelby Jean Truax	b: 7/24/1945	m: 10/20/1962	

*2nd Wife of Stephen Charles Zaunbrecher:

		+Maxie Dale Darbonne	b: 8/18/1942	m: 8/10/1974	
	4	Linda Gayle Zaunbrecher	b: 2/1/1945		
		+Richard Belynn Frey	b: 7/12/1941	m: 2/8/1964	
	4	Joseph William Zaunbrecher	b: 3/27/1948		
		+Carol Louise Christ	b: 12/1/1948	m: 5/31/1973	
	4	Michael Wayne Zaunbrecher	b: 8/24/1949		
		+Blandina Leonards	b: 9/7/1950	m: 6/25/1972	
	4	Frank Dale Zaunbrecher	b: 10/8/1952		

Heinen

		+Gwendolyn Louise Leonards	b: 1/24/1956	m: 6/9/1973	
	4	Reginald Warren Zaunbrecher	b: 12/17/1954		
		+Joan Marie Heinen	b: 5/19/1957	m: 3/4/1978	
	4	John Lawrence Zaunbrecher	b: 9/23/1956		
		+Susan Elizabeth Craft	b: 5/6/1957	m: 1/17/1976	
		*2nd Wife of John Lawrence Zaunbrecher:			
		+Leslie Marie Soileau	b: 9/24/1963	m: 10/24/1986	
	4	Patrick August Zaunbrecher	b: 9/11/1958		d: 9/18/1973
	4	Lambertina Gertrude Zaunbrecher	b: 11/30/1960		
		+Mark Gerard Lahaye	b: 8/19/1960	m: 8/22/1981	
2		Anna Maria Heinen	b: 10/10/1884		d: 9/18/1962
		+Joseph Martin Neu	b: 6/9/1887	m: 11/24/1909	d: 9/4/1920
	3	Maria Josephine Neu	b: 8/30/1910		d: 1/6/1996
		+Robert Joseph Simoneaux, Sr.	b: 1910	m: 1935	d: 1952
	4	Lucille Ann Simoneaux	b: 10/4/1936		d: 2/28/1937
	4	Loretta Marie Simoneaux	b: 2/13/1938		
		+Ray Joseph Leblanc	b: 5/11/1937	m: 4/29/1961	
	4	Robert Joseph Simoneaux	b: 3/25/1940		
		+Shyra Marie Clement	b: 3/18/1942	m: 2/4/1967	
		*2nd Husband of Maria Josephine Neu:			
		+Kelly Zimmerman	b: 9/7/1917	m: 1954	d: 9/23/1988
	4	Diane Marie Zimmerman	b: 8/25/1955		
		+Jed Anthony Robinson	b: 12/2/1954	m: 11/8/1975	

Heinen

3	Maria Walburga Neu	b: 3/6/1912		d: 12/13/1994
	+Giles Joseph Arceneaux	b: 7/17/1909	m: 1932	d: 10/26/1950
4	Giles Joseph Arceneaux, Jr.	b: 1/28/1934		d: 6/4/1986
	+Burdell Marie Lawrent	b: 11/30/1938		
3	William Ambrose Neu	b: 12/7/1913		d: 11/27/1985
	+Esther Rose Patin	b: 6/13/1915	m: 4/18/1937	d: 6/5/1997
4	William Ambrose Neu, Jr.	b: 7/14/1939		
	+Alice Louise Powers			
4	Joseph Charles Neu	b: 7/28/1940		d: 1/30/2006
	+Amy Jacobson	b: 12/3/1954	m: 1/28/1984	
4	Jane Elizabeth Neu	b: 6/14/1942		
	+Gerald Lee Thibodeaux			
4	Thelma Rose Neu	b: 11/3/1944		
	+John Wayne Loper	b: 9/13/1942	m: 7/23/1966	
4	Mary Katherine Neu	b: 1/14/1948		
	+Dudley Scott Rollins	b: 12/26/1945	m: 9/10/1966	
4	James Michael Neu	b: 12/12/1950		
	+Karen Irene Tips	b: 12/28/1954	m: 2/9/1980	
4	Jacqueline Anna Neu	b: 2/1/1953		
	+Frederick Wentz Stumpf	b: 8/6/1948	m: 4/24/1999	
4	John Randolph Neu	b: 1/1/1956		
	+Kathryn Ann Smith Dipprey	b: 3/26/1948	m: 7/25/1972	
3	Raymond Jacob Neu	b: 11/12/1915		d: 5/9/1978
	+Zora Marie Lognion	b: 10/13/1927	m: 1946	
4	Charles Neu	b: 8/1947		d: 9/1947
4	Cynthia Neu	b: 11/30/1952		
	+George Munn			

Heinen

4	Ramona Neu	b: 1/29/1954		
	+Louis Adams			
	*2nd Husband of Ramona Neu:			
	+Tom Raise			
4	Barbara Neu	b: 9/24/1956		
	+Roy Olsen			
3	Rosa Dorothy Neu	b: 1/10/1917		d: 12/25/2001
	+Theodore Thevis	b: 2/15/1915	m: 1/4/1939	d: 7/5/2002
4	Jo Ann Thevis	b: 1/24/1940		
4	Louis Thevis	b: 1/29/1942		
	+Gail Rodrigue	b: 11/13/1949	m: 12/30/1967	
4	Benedict Joseph Thevis	b: 9/11/1943		
	+Deborah Rena Collins	b: 11/21/1953	m: 3/3/1977	
4	Mary Alice Thevis	b: 12/14/1944		
4	Mona Rae Thevis	b: 11/30/1947		
3	John Alexius Neu	b: 12/23/1918		d: 4/21/1996
	+Rita Credeur	b: 2/17/1925	m: 5/21/1946	
4	Linda Faye Neu	b: 2/27/1947		
	+Patrick Cormier	b: 10/8/1943	m: 3/18/1972	
4	Marlene Anna Neu	b: 12/4/1952		
	+Bryan Keith Fogleman	b: 5/12/1953	m: 1/8/1972	
4	Jay Anthony Neu	b: 11/12/1957		
	+Cherly Lynne Leger	b: 10/7/1958	m: 10/29/1983	
3	Anna Rita Neu		b: 2/9/1921	d: 12/26/2003
	+Nolton Herbert Menard	b: 9/29/1927	m: 1953	d: 8/5/1998
4	Connie Ann Menard	b: 6/11/1954		
	+Darryl Billiot		b: 12/24/1964	m: 10/7/1995
4	Susan Marie Menard	b: 2/17/1958		
	+Karl Anthony Henry	b: 12/7/1958	m: 10/14/1978	

Heinen

4	Wayne Herbert Menard	b: 9/29/1959	
4	Debra Lynn Menard	b: 9/17/1962	
	+Frederick Robinson	b: 2/27/1959	m: 2/12/1988

11. Heinen, Peter Wilhelm:

Peter Wilhelm Heinen b: 1836 d: 1908 from Schierwaldenrath was a brother of Gerhard Joseph Heinen. He never married and thus has no descendants (see Heinen family above).

12. Hensgens, Christian Joseph:

Christian Joseph Hensgens b: 12/24/1839 d: 7/6/1919 from Hastenrath was the son of Johann Christian Hensgens b: 12/31/1809 d: 3/25/1896 and Maria Katharina Dahlmans b: 10/30/1808 d: 1/24/1871. He married on 5/20/1871 to Maria Regina Tellers b: 9/7/1847 d: 11/27/1908 from Langbroich, who is the daughter of Johann Wilhelm Tellers b: 8/11/1813 d: ? and Maria Gertrude Ohlenforst b: 2/2/1814 d: ?.

2	Katharina Hensgens	b: 7/13/1872		d: 4/26/1955
	+Joseph Dischler	b: 5/6/1866	m: 5/8/1893	d: 6/18/1921
3	Maria Regina Dischler	b: 1894		d: 1977
	+Lambert Ronkartz	b: 1891	m: 1919	d: 1978
4	Josephine Marie Ronkartz	b: 1920		
	+Joseph John Burton	b: 1917	m: 1941	d: 2004
4	Joseph John Ronkartz	b: 1922		d: 1989
	+Rose Marie LeBlanc	b: 1926	m: 1946	d: 1989
4	John William Ronkartz	b: 1925		d: 2000
	+Effie Katherine Rogers	b: 1933	m: 1950	
4	Jeanette Juliana Ronkartz	b: 1929		
	+Ronald Gene Robinson	b: 1931	m: 1950	d: 1953
4	Louise Regina Ronkartz	b: 1932		
	+Daniel Hilarion Troyanowski	b: 1928	m: 1954	d: 1981
4	Jerome Lambert Ronkartz	b: 1933		
	+Jo Ann Zaunbrecher	b: 1934	m: 1956	
3	Joseph Dischler, Jr.	b: 1895		d: 1959
	+Louise Marie Fontenot	b: 1897	m: 1920	d: 1993
4	Lorraine Dischler			
	+Leon Rine			
4	Mary Belle Dischler			

Hensgens

	+Elmo Simon			
4	Johanna Dischler			
	+Edmond Dupre, Jr.			
4	Richard Dischler			
	+Sylvia Robinson			
3	Maria Gertrude Dischler	b: 1897		d: 1965
	+Ludwig (Louis) Leonards	b: 8/31/1899	m: 1922	d: 10/30/1978
4	Philomena Hedwig Leonards	b: 1923		
	+John Frank Ohlenforst	b: 1921	m: 1947	d: 1997
4	Blaise Philip Leonards	b: 3/21/1927		
	+Bernadine Marie Habetz	b: 6/9/1927	m: 10/27/1948	
4	Edwin Joseph Leonards	b: 9/21/1928		d: 4/21/2007
	+Genevieve Augusta Frey	b: 11/11/1932	m: 7/9/1951	
4	Eleanor Marie Leonards	b: 7/15/1930		
	+William A. Braun	b: 10/24/1922	m: 10/26/1950	
4	Dorothy Clara Leonards	b: 4/1/1932		
4	Marcella Marie Leonards	b: 2/3/1934		
	+Andrew Lawrence Ohlenforst	b: 10/6/1928	m: 1/19/1955	d: 10/3/1983
4	Louis Anthony Leonards	b: 1/14/1936		
	+Patricia Ann Spell	b: 1/21/1938	m: 12/28/1960	
4	[4] Leonard "Buck" Leonards	b: 6/30/1937		
	+[3] Barbara Ann Link	b: 9/17/1938	m: 11/27/1958	
4	Sylvia Jean Leonards	b: 2/24/1941		
	+Johnny Mack Frugé	b: 10/4/1939	m: 11/17/1962	
3	Charles Barromeo Dischler	b: 1898		d: 1986
	+Clara Julia Olinger	b: 1900	m: 1922	d: 1975

Hensgens

4	Barbara Catherine Dischler	b: 1923		d: 1993
	+William "Bill" Reed	b: 1920	m: 1952	
4	Charles Leo Dischler	b: 1924		
	+Carrie Mae Harmon	b: 1929	m: 1949	
4	Cecilia Madeline Dischler	b: 1926		
	+Daniel Landry	b: 1925	m: 1950	
4	Julia Theresa Dischler	b: 1928		
	+Sherril Thompson	b: 1928	m: 1957	d: 2002
4	Alvin Joseph Dischler	b: 1929		
	+Theresa Martarona	b: 1933	m: 1958	
4	Clarice Josephine Dischler	b: 1932		
	+Charles William Stewart	b: 1928	m: 1972	d: 1995
4	Ferdinand Louis Dischler	b: 1933		
	+Wanda George	b: 1933	m: 1956	
4	Robert Louis Dischler	b: 1935		d: 2003
	+Donna Sue Fast	b: 1941	m: 1964	
4	Thomas Anthony Dischler	b: 1938		
4	Marjorie Ann Dischler	b: 1940		
	+Robert Walker	b: 1940	m: 1959	
4	Michael Anthony Dischler	b: 1942		
	+Barbara Hazelton	b: 1948	m: 1973	
4	[8] Carol Bertha Dischler	b: 1/24/1945		
	+[7] Lawrence William Leonards	b: 2/4/1946	m: 6/7/1969	
3	Anthony Conrad Dischler	b: 9/2/1900		d: 1986
	+Maria Helena Zaunbrecher	b: 4/14/1896	m: 1923	d: 8/19/1952
4	Antonia Maria Dischler	b: 1926		

Hensgens

	Name	Born	Married	Died
	+John Clyde Leger	b: 1923	m: 1949	
4	Martin William Dischler	b: 1927		
	+Marcella Comeaux	b: 1928	m: 1949	
4	Pauline Bertha Dischler	b: 1929		d: 1/22/2006
	+Francis Charles Roy	b: 1929	m: 1949	d: 1993
4	Infant Dischler	b: 1931		d: 1931
4	Monica Ann "Mona" Dischler	b: 1934		
	+Ronald James Gossen	b: 1929	m: 1953	
4	Helena Marie Dischler	b: 1936		
	+Kenneth Jack Mantle		m: 1961	
	*2nd Husband of Helena Marie Dischler:			
	+Frank Robles	b: 1927	m: 1976	
3	Regina Josephine Dischler	b: 1902		d: 1997
	+Edward John Olinger	b: 1896	m: 1922	d: 1983
4	Ambrose Joseph Olinger	b: 1923		
	+Margaret Leonards	b: 1923	m: 1946	
4	Beatrice Aloysia Olinger	b: 1926		
	+August Joseph Leonards, Jr.	b: 1924	m: 1947	d: 1988
4	Irene Regina Olinger	b: 1927		
	+Ashton Simon Petitjean	b: 1914	m: 1951	d: 1979
4	Rose Marie Olinger	b: 1930		
	+John N. John III	b: 1929	m: 1950	d: 1983
4	Hilary Anthony Olinger	b: 1934		
	+Melba Dean Roy	b: 1937	m: 1955	
4	Mary Jo Olinger	b: 1938		
4	Ray Edward Olinger	b: 1942		
	+Johnnie Ruth Prather	b: 1941	m: 1966	
3	Anna Maria Dischler	b: 1904		d: 1977

Hensgens

	+Joseph August Zaunbrecher	b: 8/28/1906	m: 1925	d: 1981
4	Edna Augusta Zaunbrecher	b: 1926		
	+Claures Joseph Broussard	b: 1928	m: 1957	
4	Leo Charles Zaunbrecher	b: 1927		
	+Stella Minnie Low	b: 1936	m: 1956	
4	Gerald Joseph Zaunbrecher	b: 1929		d: 1988
	+Shirley Mae Stark	b: 1937	m: 1956	d: 1994
4	Harold Joseph Zaunbrecher	b: 1929		d: 1999
	+Pauline Margaret Dupree	b: 1936	m: 1960	
4	Ferdinand Vincent Zaunbrecher	b: 1932		
	+Janet Louise Sumners		m: 1960	
	*2nd Wife of Ferdinand Vincent Zaunbrecher:			
	+Jean Pascoe		m: 1980	
4	Genevieve Marie Zaunbrecher	b: 1934		
	+Gordon Edward Tate	b: 2/3/1934		d: 12/2004
4	Joyce Marie Zaunbrecher	b: 1935		
	+Howard Joseph Melancon	b: 1937	m: 1972	
4	Dorothy Ann Zaunbrecher	b: 1937		
4	Hilary Charles Zaunbrecher	b: 1939		
	+Suzanne Gayle Phillips	b: 1946	m: 1983	
4	Donald Louis Zaunbrecher	b: 1942		

Hensgens

	+Josephine Ann Busse	b: 1944	m: 1976	
3	Bertha Marie Dischler	b: 1905		d: 1990
	+Charles Joseph Zaunbrecher	b: 1905	m: 1929	d: 10/25/1972
4	Dolores Marie Zaunbrecher	b: 1930		
	+Philip Jacob Joseph Habetz	b: 3/19/1930	m: 1956	
4	Fr. Charles Zaunbrecher	b: 11/8/1931		d: 6/19/1996
4	Vincent William Zaunbrecher	b: 1933		
	+Genevieve Parrino	b: 1930	m: 6/14/1955	
4	Jane Frances Zaunbrecher	b: 1934		d: 1990
	+Wilvin LeLeux	b: 1935	m: 1958	
4	William "Billy" Zaunbrecher	b: 5/31/1938		d: 8/19/1997
	+Anna Margaret Cramer	b: 12/31/1938	m: 12/16/1963	
4	Stephen Joseph Zaunbrecher	b: 9/2/1940		
	+Rose Marie Reiners	b: 3/28/1942	m: 6/26/1962	
3	Marie Dischler	b: 1908		d: 1993
	+Anton Joseph Zaunbrecher	b: 1912	m: 1936	d: 1991
3	Francis Nicholas Dischler	b: 1910		d: 1983
	+Genevieve Clark	b: 1914	m: 1938	d: 1968
4	Kathleen Ann Dischler	b: 1941		
	+Daniel Peter Wilfrath	b: 1941	m: 1967	
4	Gretchen Solange Dischler	b: 1943		
	+Dalton John Istre	b: 1940	m: 1961	d: 1997
4	Nicholas Dischler II			
	+Tanya Firmin			

Hensgens

	4	Helen Manette Dischler	b: 1952		
		+Steven Paul Breaux	b: 1952	m: 1974	
		*2nd Husband of Helen Manette Dischler:			
		+Paul Keith Lopez	b: 1955	m: 1989	
2		Gertrude Hensgens	b: 9/7/1874		d: 11/8/1954
		+Lorenz Zaunbrecher	b: 10/23/1870	m: 1/23/1895	d: 10/26/1954
	3	Regina Marie Zaunbrecher	b: 12/5/1895		d: 10/26/1961
		+Joseph Andrew Klein	b: 7/19/1894	m: 2/20/1919	d: 4/16/1962
	4	Clara Regina Klein	b: 7/29/1921		d: 6/26/1990
	4	Hilda Marie Klein	b: 8/11/1923		d: 4/16/2004
		+Lloyd J. Simon	b: 10/19/1922	m: 11/29/1945	
	4	Gertrude Christine Klein	b: 9/15/1924		
		+Robert Jasper Labry		m: 7/31/1946	
	4	Anna Louise Klein	b: 3/15/1929		
		+Dewey Grant Heard	b: 5/17/1924	m: 11/19/1949	d: 6/12/1983
		*2nd Husband of Anna Louise Klein:			
		+Adam Warren DePerrodil	b: 1/22/1924	m: 12/9/1985	
	4	Lawrence Joseph Klein	b: 8/15/1932		d: 1/22/1957
		+Betty Jane Leger	b: 1/20/1935	m: 11/30/1955	
	3	Joseph Zaunbrecher	b: 11/19/1897		d: 2/13/1981
		+Mary Odilia Klein	b: 2/24/1898	m: 2/20/1919	d: 9/8/1979
	4	Mary Magdaline Zaunbrecher	b: 5/6/1920		d: 11/13/1982
		+Abdon Nolan Leblanc	b: 7/30/1911	m: 5/16/1950	d: 5/12/1978
	4	Philip Joseph Zaunbrecher	b: 11/4/1921		
		+Helen Toups	b: 4/24/1922	m: 7/5/1945	
	4	Wilfred Zaunbrecher	b: 10/19/1923		d: 4/10/1995
		+Bessie Istre	b: 1/22/1926	m: 8/22/1945	
	4	Antoinette Lucille Zaunbrecher	b: 2/13/1926		d: 10/15/1926

Hensgens

4	Frederick John Zaunbrecher	b: 2/24/1928		
	+Laura Belle Woods	b: 7/23/1932	m: 1/13/1954	
4	Dorothy Christina Zaunbrecher	b: 3/27/1930		
	+Ellis Jacob Toups, Sr.	b: 7/6/1928	m: 8/5/1953	
4	Julian George Zaunbrecher	b: 10/3/1932		
	+Laura May Broussard	b: 7/1/1933	m: 5/23/1953	d: 5/30/2002
4	Richard Lawrence Zaunbrecher	b: 11/1/1935		
	+June Mary Woods	b: 6/6/1936	m: 9/3/1958	
4	Charles Zaunbrecher	b: 10/19/1937		
4	Ronald Gregory Zaunbrecher	b: 5/10/1940		
	+Eldie Mary Bourque	b: 8/23/1942	m: 11/29/1961	
4	Francis William Zaunbrecher	b: 9/15/1946		
	+Nona Faye Petry	b: 2/19/1946	m: 10/7/1967	
3	William Joseph Zaunbrecher	b: 8/25/1899		d: 5/8/1930
3	Nicholas Conrad Zaunbrecher	b: 9/21/1901		d: 12/29/1963
	+Josephine Marie Frey	b: 11/28/1902	m: 1922	d: 1998
4	Helen Marie Zaunbrecher	b: 11/1/1923		
	+Joseph Herman Thevis	b: 5/4/1919	m: 1/23/1946	d: 12/20/2003
4	Lawrence Nicholas Zaunbrecher	b: 4/12/1925		
	+Lucy Theodora Cramer	b: 9/26/1922	m: 6/20/1955	
4	Thelma Regina Zaunbrecher	b: 7/30/1926		

Hensgens

	+Vincent Carl Leonards	b: 9/24/1924	m: 2/23/1949	d: 12/30/1998
4	Laura Lydia Zaunbrecher	b: 3/6/1928		
	+Louis Joseph Bellard	b: 7/2/1924	m: 1948	d: 8/10/1996
4	Louis John Zaunbrecher	b: 8/30/1929		d: 9/12/2004
	+Mary Helen Martell	b: 9/8/1931	m: 4/12/1953	
4	Jeanette Delores Zaunbrecher	b: 9/24/1931		
	+Wayne Elwood Holtzapple	b: 6/12/1929	m: 11/28/1952	
4	Frances Delores Zaunbrecher	b: 3/16/1933		
	+Jesse Paul Fruge	b: 12/12/1918	m: 11/29/1955	d: 11/30/1995
4	Robert Daniel Zaunbrecher	b: 11/14/1934		
	+Effie Claudette Johnson	b: 3/16/1938	m: 4/19/1958	
4	Stanley Joseph Zaunbrecher	b: 9/19/1936		
	+Loretta Louise Langley	b: 6/18/1941	m: 4/2/1963	d: 1/26/1996
4	Rodney William Zaunbrecher	b: 4/8/1940		
	+Mary Elaine Schneider	b: 1944	m: 1/26/1963	
4	Margaret Ann Zaunbrecher	b: 5/18/1942		
	+Lawrence Leo "Larry" Regan		m: 11/18/1961	
4	Jo Ann Zaunbrecher	b: 7/22/1944		
	+Henry Leonard Meyer	b: 9/25/1940	m: 7/15/1964	
4	Edna Mae Zaunbrecher	b: 5/26/1946		
	+Michael William Leger	b: 11/3/1949	m: 10/21/1973	

Hensgens

	4	Lloyd James Zaunbrecher	b: 6/4/1948		
		+Donna Claire Lejeune	b: 3/30/1949	m: 2/18/1973	
3		Barbara Marie Zaunbrecher	b: 11/26/1903		d: 11/8/1992
		+Franz Xavier Joseph Bollich	b: 10/29/1904	m: 1926	d: 2/9/1990
	4	Loretta Elaine Bollich	b: 11/7/1927		
		+Burnis Cooper	b: 10/19/1917	m: 9/11/1945	d: 6/26/1991
		*2nd Husband of Loretta Elaine Bollich:			
		+Louis C. Gaspard		m: 5/20/2000	
	4	Clara Louise Bollich	b: 3/23/1929		
		+Durland Joseph Miller	b: 8/25/1924	m: 11/24/1949	d: 2/10/2002
	4	Gerald Francis Bollich	b: 3/9/1930		
		+Delia Marie Breaux	b: 10/1/1931	m: 10/24/1953	d: 11/29/2003
	4	Donald Joseph Bollich	b: 3/26/1931		
		+Willie Dean Vidrine	b: 7/31/1934	m: 11/21/1953	
	4	Lawrence Charles Bollich	b: 6/21/1932		
		+Jacqueline Marie Brown	b: 8/2/1932	m: 4/12/1958	
	4	Austin William Bollich	b: 7/15/1933		
		+Sylvia Ann Stelly	b: 11/16/1934	m: 11/8/1953	
	4	Elmo Edward Bollich	b: 1/20/1935		d: 12/18/2005
		+Elrena Mary Manuel		m: 2/11/1956	
	4	Elaine Marie Bollich	b: 1/20/1935		
		+Carl Edward Turk	b: 2/1928	m: 6/5/1956	d: 11/23/1986
	4	Sylvia Ann Bollich	b: 6/21/1936		
		+John Luke Emery Lintzen	b: 3/22/1936	m: 4/8/1961	d: 1/13/1976
	4	Gregory Augustine Bollich	b: 11/28/1938		
		+Patricia Ann Sittig	b: 7/16/1940	m: 9/2/1961	
	4	Barbara Ann Bollich	b: 9/22/1942		
		+James Allen LeJeune	b: 9/19/1942	m: 10/27/1962	

Hensgens

4	Diane Louise Bollich	b: 2/10/1947		
	+Gary Layne Elkins	b: 12/13/1947	m: 7/3/1971	d: 6/17/2001
4	Judy Ann Bollich	b: 5/9/1949		
	+Kenneth Lee Joseph Hollier	b: 10/13/1949	m: 1/27/1973	
3	Anna Maria Zaunbrecher	b: 1/9/1906		d: 4/27/1990
	+Albert Harry Frey	b: 6/4/1904	m: 1928	d: 1/6/1973
4	[2] Lorraine Elaine Frey	b: 9/30/1929		
	+[1] Walter William Heinen	b: 3/15/1924	m: 4/28/1949	d: 1/10/1985
4	Reginald Lawrence Frey	b: 2/10/1931		d: 7/4/1982
	+Jo Ann Josephine Bollich	b: 10/6/1931	m: 1952	
4	Louellen Marie Frey	b: 12/3/1933		
	+Anthony Gerald Daigle	b: 12/29/1930	m: 10/1/1954	
4	Warren William Frey	b: 7/15/1937		
	+Verna Ellen Bankston	b: 12/5/1939	m: 9/3/1959	
4	Linda Ann Frey	b: 6/14/1943		
	+James Franklin Campbell III	b: 4/13/1940	m: 10/6/1962	
3	Charles Philip Zaunbrecher	b: 1908		d: 1984
	+Anna Barbara Frey	b: 1907	m: 1924	d: 2003
4	Bertha Zaunbrecher	b: 6/5/1926		
	+Paul Joseph Breaux	b: 1/9/1924	m: 5/20/1952	d: 4/12/2004
4	Augusta Agnes Zaunbrecher	b: 1/11/1928		
	+Elmo Joseph Bollich	b: 11/11/1924	m: 5/18/1947	
4	Edmond Charles Zaunbrecher	b: 8/25/1929		d: 4/2/1995
	+Ollie Marie Linscombe	b: 2/28/1931	m: 11/27/1952	

Hensgens

4	Vincent William Zaunbrecher		b: 12/22/1931	
	+Janet Benoit	b: 10/27/1936	m: 11/8/1955	
4	Raymond Joseph Zaunbrecher	b: 9/12/1932		d: 4/1/1954
4	Harry John Zaunbrecher	b: 6/3/1934		
	+Lucy Henry	b: 7/1/1938	m: 10/22/1959	
4	Ramona Marie Zaunbrecher	b: 1/14/1936		
	+Reno Paul Petry	b: 2/28/1933	m: 2/8/1958	
4	Nicholas Wayne Zaunbrecher		b: 4/25/1939	
	+Linda Fae Guidry	b: 12/26/1940	m: 11/5/1960	
4	Floyd Anthony Zaunbrecher	b: 9/8/1940		
	+Cene Mae Vidalier	b: 12/6/1942	m: 11/28/1962	
4	Carolyn Ann Zaunbrecher	b: 11/11/1943		
	+James Avert Guidry	b: 11/16/1942	m: 11/17/1965	
4	[10] Barbara Ann Zaunbrecher	b: 7/8/1949		
	+[9] William Joseph Leonards II	b: 12/12/1952	m: 6/28/1975	
4	Mary Jacqueline Zaunbrecher	b: 12/24/1951		
	+Allen Ray Francois	b: 7/27/1949	m: 6/30/1973	
3	August Zaunbrecher	b: 9/12/1910		d: 7/21/1993
	+Bobbie Gautreaux	b: 1912	m: 1938	d: 1998
4	Virginia Mary Zaunbrecher	b: 2/6/1950		
	+Dennis Lloyd West	b: 8/15/1950	m: 2/13/1971	
3	Marie Regina Zaunbrecher	b: 12/6/1912		d: 7/5/2006
3	Franz (Frank) Zaunbrecher	b: 12/31/1914		d: 8/25/1984

Hensgens

	+Hilda Mathilda Frey	b: 8/19/1922	m: 2/12/1941	d: 6/11/2004
4	Loretta Ann Zaunbrecher	b: 11/11/1941		
	+Frederick Burns Leger	b: 12/1/1939	m: 5/10/1960	d: 11/28/1965

*2nd Husband of Loretta Ann Zaunbrecher:

	+John Kurta	b: 5/25/1930	m: 2/1/1975	
4	Stephen Charles Zaunbrecher	b: 2/3/1943		
	+Shelby Jean Truax	b: 7/24/1945	m: 10/20/1962	

*2nd Wife of Stephen Charles Zaunbrecher:

	+Maxine Darbonne	b: 8/18/1942	m: 8/10/1974	
4	Linda Gayle Zaunbrecher	b: 2/1/1945		
	+Richard Belynn Frey	b: 7/12/1941	m: 2/8/1964	
4	Joseph William Zaunbrecher	b: 3/27/1948		
	+Carol Louise Christ	b: 12/1/1948	m: 5/31/1973	
4	Michael Wayne Zaunbrecher	b: 8/24/1949		
	+Blandina Gayle Leonards	b: 9/7/1950	m: 6/25/1972	
4	Frank Dale Zaunbrecher	b: 10/8/1952		
	+Gwendolyn Louise Leonards	b: 1/24/1956	m: 6/9/1973	
4	Reginald Warren Zaunbrecher	b: 12/17/1954		
	+Joan Marie Heinen	b: 5/19/1957	m: 3/4/1978	
4	John Lawrence Zaunbrecher	b: 9/23/1956		
	+Susan Elizabeth Craft	b: 5/6/1957	m: 1/17/1976	

*2nd Wife of John Lawrence Zaunbrecher:

	+Leslie Marie Soileau	b: 9/24/1963	m: 10/24/1986	
4	Patrick August Zaunbrecher	b: 9/11/1958		d: 9/18/1973

Hensgens

4	Lambertina Gertrude Zaunbrecher	b: 11/30/1960		
	+Mark Gerard Lahaye	b: 8/19/1960	m: 8/22/1981	
3	Clara Josephine Zaunbrecher	b: 1918		d: 1998
	+Benjamin Cullen Link	b: 1920	m: 1947	d: 1989
4	Rodney Lawrence Link	b: 9/22/1947		d: 6/7/1979
	+Judy Kay Woods	b: 2/15/1951	m: 2/2/1971	
4	Francis Eugene Link	b: 9/6/1948		
	+Sara Ruth Adams	b: 2/26/1949	m: 7/21/1968	
	*2nd Wife of Francis Eugene Link:			
	+Kathy Elaine Broussard	b: 11/6/1952	m: 10/10/2001	
4	Gerald Joseph Link	b: 9/2/1950		
	+Deborah Lynn Knuckles	b: 12/9/1952	m: 9/25/1971	
4	Thomas Carl Link	b: 10/10/1951		
	+Roxanne Matt	b: 2/27/1953	m: 8/14/1970	
	*2nd Wife of Thomas Carl Link:			
	+Dorothy Ann Boyd	b: 7/23/1954	m: 7/24/1987	
4	Arlene Claire Link	b: 8/6/1954		
	+John Edgar Bostich	b: 6/10/1955	m: 9/24/1977	
4	Richard James Link	b: 7/7/1955		
	+Rebecca Ann Trahan	b: 7/24/1957	m: 3/28/1980	
4	Suzanne Marie Link	b: 6/12/1957		
	+Paul Marvin Hollier	b: 2/3/1957	m: 6/15/1980	
3	Gertrude Anna Zaunbrecher	b: 1920		d: 2003
	+William Iglinsky, Jr.	b: 1919	m: 1946	d: 1989
4	Judy Ann Iglinsky	b: 9/30/1947		
	+James E. Tarver, Jr.	b: 6/20/1945	m: 8/13/1966	
4	William Lorenz Iglinsky	b: 7/12/1950		
	+Sandra Louise Gass	b: 2/19/1952	m: 6/24/1972	

Hensgens

4	Blanche Marie Iglinsky	b: 11/11/1951		
	+Leslie Joseph Waguespack	b: 10/19/1950	m: 12/14/1974	
4	Patrick Joseph Iglinsky	b: 12/10/1953		
	+Nina Marie Doonan	b: 1/13/1954	m: 7/19/1975	
4	Barbara Jean Iglinsky	b: 3/20/1956		
	+Ellis John Schwartzenburg	b: 1/21/1954	m: 5/22/1976	
2	Barbara Hensgens	b: 8/6/1876		d: 5/21/1947
	+William Michael Heinen	b: 9/29/1872	m: 1/2/1897	d: 3/9/1940
3	Joseph Anton Heinen	b: 1898		d: 1955
	+Adele "Della" Naebers	b: 1895	m: 1918	d: 1956
4	Wilfred Heinen	b: 5/7/1919		d: 1/10/1970
	+Maurine Muller	b: 5/5/1922	m: 1/11/1949	d: 8/21/2004
4	Theodora Heinen	b: 7/14/1921		
	+Kenneth Faulk			
4	[1] Walter William Heinen	b: 3/15/1924		d: 1/10/1985
	+[2] Lorraine Elaine Frey	b: 9/30/1929	m: 4/28/1949	
4	Wilhelmena "Wilma" Heinen	b: 12/28/1926		
	+Burton Cormier	b: 4/8/1923	m: 10/29/1947	d: 11/2/2005
3	William Christian Heinen	b: 1900		d: 1957
	+Christina Margaret Naebers	b: 1901	m: 1926	d: 1965
4	Charles Heinen	b: 11/17/1926		d: 6/16/1994
	+Lenora Trahan	b: 7/13/1935	m: 5/19/1956	d: 11/28/2001
4	Hilda Heinen	b: 12/8/1928		
4	Joseph Heinen	b: 10/16/1930		d: 10/16/1930
4	Geraldine Heinen	b: 9/26/1931		d: 4/14/2001
	+Thomas Heard	b: 8/6/1927		d: 4/6/1984
4	Arilda Heinen	b: 3/16/1934		d: 5/8/1973

Hensgens

	+Benno Leonards	b: 6/16/1931	m: 11/15/1958	
4	Josephine Regina Heinen	b: 6/27/1936		
	+Malcolm Millet	b: 4/8/1928	m: 6/1/1957	
4	[6] Lawrence William Heinen	b: 10/29/1938		d: 11/28/2005
	+[5] Louise Regina Leonards	b: 1/9/1945	m: 6/27/1970	
4	Annie Louise Heinen	b: 3/9/1941		d: 9/16/1995
	+Patrick Gautreaux	b: 5/24/1940	m: 6/10/1961	d: 4/26/2000
3	Theodore Ignatius Heinen	b: 1902		d: 1962
	+Catherine Louise Gossen	b: 1905	m: 1927	d: 1996
3	Conrad Edward Heinen	b: 1904		d: 1924
3	Maria Gertrude Heinen	b: 1906		d: 2003
	+Henry John Naebers	b: 1904	m: 1928	d: 1972
3	Anthony Leo Heinen	b: 1909		d: 1924
3	Maria Regina Heinen	b: 1911		d: 1970
	+Wallace Joseph Link	b: 1909	m: 1935	d: 1953
4	Sylvia Link	b: 9/3/1936		d: 1/9/1996
	+Hershel Beard	b: 9/17/1928	m: 11/22/1953	
4	[3] Barbara Ann Link	b: 9/17/1938		
	+[4] Leonard "Buck" Leonards	b: 6/30/1937	m: 11/27/1958	
4	William Link	b: 10/6/1941		
	+Sylvia Simpson	b: 12/11/1943	m: 1/25/1964	
4	Wallace Link	b: 10/23/1944		
	+Marilyn Wright	b: 11/20/1952	m: 1/5/1974	
3	Lambertina Josepha Heinen	b: 1913		d: 1993
	+Joseph John Naebers	b: 1908	m: 1935	d: 1976
4	Jo Ann Naebers	b: 11/2/1935		
	+Al Claude Louviere	b: 9/6/1934	m: 7/1/1952	
4	Marlene Naebers	b: 9/20/1937		

Hensgens

	+Alvin Daigle	b: 12/12/1932	m: 1/9/1957	
4	Ronald Naebers	b: 4/25/1941		
	+Bobbi Sue Kratzer	b: 9/6/1940	m: 1/9/1960	
4	Gretchen Naebers	b: 10/24/1948		
	+Dallas Benoit II	b: 10/24/1947	m: 9/6/1965	
3	Annie Wilhelmena Heinen	b: 1915		d: 1958
3	John Aloysius Heinen	b: 1919		d: 2004
	+Gertie Lou Leger	b: 1923	m: 1941	d: 2005
4	John Aloysius Heinen II	b: 1/20/1943		
	+Jeannette Prather	b: 2/9/1943	m: 12/27/1961	
4	William Heinen	b: 5/9/1944		
	+Jeanne Seaux	b: 10/11/1947	m: 2/12/1966	
4	Cheryl Heinen	b: 8/8/1948		
	+Patrick Handley, Sr.	b: 6/11/1946	m: 2/17/1968	
4	Barry Heinen	b: 2/14/1950		
	+Kathleen Kane	b: 5/10/1949	m: 9/3/1969	
4	Debra Heinen	b: 2/1/1952		
	+Elliot Higginbotham	b: 7/9/1946	m: 8/18/1970	
4	Paul Heinen	b: 10/15/1955		
	+Patricia Puissegur	b: 6/21/1958	m: 12/18/1976	
4	Keith Heinen	b: 6/13/1957		
	+Dianna Hoffpauer	b: 3/10/1958	m: 1/16/1976	
4	Sandra Heinen	b: 11/19/1963		
	+Bradley Lavergne	b: 1/23/1953	m: 8/18/1989	
2	Regina Hensgens	b: 7/19/1878		d: 11/19/1949
	+William Joseph Bollich, Sr.	b: 12/18/1877	m: 5/2/1902	d: 11/10/1966
3	Regina Bollich	b: 1902		d: 1903
3	Joseph Bollich	b: 1904		d: 1992
3	William Joseph Bollich, Jr.	b: 1906		d: 1986
	+Cecilia Theresa Zaunbrecher	b: 1911	m: 11/18/1931	d: 1983
4	Stanley Nicolas Bollich	b: 12/3/1932		d: 1/13/2005

Hensgens

		+Martha Gill	b: 10/5/1941	m: 9/3/1959	
	4	Fr. Ronald William Bollich	b: 5/12/1937		d: 8/7/1996
	4	Wilbur Anthony Bollich	b: 7/28/1938		
		+Betty Nesom	b: 7/19/1942	m: 6/4/1966	
	4	Hallet Joseph Bollich	b: 9/1/1940		
		+Gardlene Ann Trahan	b: 2/13/1958	m: 9/23/1972	
	4	James August Bollich	b: 2/14/1943		
		+Betty Ann Lemare	b: 12/29/1956	m: 3/12/1981	
	4	Mary Ann Bollich	b: 10/9/1945		
		+Robert Vincent Ogden		m: 8/11/1966	
3		Peter Joseph Bollich	b: 10/12/1907		d: 12/8/1986
		+Lottie Beatrice Frey	b: 6/26/1910	m: 1930	d: 2/27/2002
	4	Rodney Bollich	b: 4/19/1932		
		+Marie Louise Meyers	b: 2/1/1931	m: 6/20/1953	d: 12/13/1993
		*2nd Wife of Rodney Bollich:			
		+Judy W. Fisher	b: 10/10/1949	m: 6/4/1994	
	4	Winnie Rose Bollich	b: 10/24/1934		d: 4/22/1958
		+Bennon Price		m: 1950	
3		Marie Gertrude Bollich	b: 1910		d: 1994
		+Lawrence Henry Zaunbrecher	b: 1909	m: 1932	d: 1982
	4	Glenn Zaunbrecher	b: 11/21/1933		d: 11/7/1989
		+Margaret Pharr	b: 6/5/1936	m: 5/27/1956	
	4	Norma Zaunbrecher	b: 12/21/1934		d: 6/15/1995
		+Harold Prevost	b: 5/3/1932	m: 4/26/1958	
	4	Alfred Zaunbrecher	b: 5/28/1932		
		+Marceline Comeaux	b: 11/23/1937	m: 8/19/1956	
	4	Estelle Zaunbrecher	b: 1/24/1938		
		+Edwin Coy Wyatt	b: 11/18/1936	m: 1/14/1959	
	4	Irene Zaunbrecher	b: 8/22/1940		

Hensgens

	+Larry Fields	b: 3/26/1940	m: 4/22/1961	
4	Lois Zaunbrecher	b: 11/6/1949		
	+John Harpole, Jr.	b: 10/5/1948	m: 12/16/1972	
4	Janelle Zaunbrecher	b: 2/2/1954		
	+Wilbert J. Bourque, Sr.	b: 7/21/1951	m: 8/27/1971	
3	Mary Helen Bollich	b: 12/29/1912		d: 12/23/1994
	+Wilbert Paul Robichaux	b: 1909	m: 1937	d: 1948
4	Phyllis Helen Robichaux	b: 11/18/1939		
	+Dennis Louis Leonards	b: 5/24/1936	m: 1/14/1961	
4	Gerald Wilbert Robichaux	b: 12/15/1941		
	+Lela Mae Vidrine	b: 8/2/1948	m: 6/12/1971	
4	[12] Marjorie Ann Robichaux	b: 10/19/1943		
	+[11] John Herman Schultz	b: 9/6/1939	m: 11/10/1973	
4	Aline Emilda Robichaux	b: 12/25/1945		
	+Elwood Joseph Terro	b: 11/16/1933	m: 4/15/1977	
4	Denise Arlene Robichaux	b: 12/25/1945		
4	Jacqueline Wilma Robichaux	b: 4/4/1948		
	+Kenneth Joseph Benedik	b: 12/30/1946	m: 2/24/1990	
3	Anna Rosalie Bollich	b: 1913		d: 6/3/2006
	+Joseph Aloysius Olinger	b: 9/15/1894	m: 1947	d: 12/9/1968
4	Karen Marie Olinger	b: 9/15/1948		
	+Ellis Lesby Boyd, Jr.	b: 1946	m: 1968	
4	Janet Louise Olinger	b: 1/17/1950		
	+Kent Guy Hutslar	b: 1951	m: 1971	
	*2nd Husband of Janet Louise Olinger:			
	+Joseph Edward Landes	b: 12/30/1953	m: 11/12/1994	

4	Beverly Ann Olinger	b: 1/4/1951		
	+Louis Joseph Maloz, Sr.	b: 11/19/1947	m: 1/24/1970	
4	Charlotte Rose Olinger	b: 2/23/1952		
	+Oliver Kent Collins	b: 1951	m: 1976	
	*2nd Husband of Charlotte Rose Olinger:			
	+Kenneth LeBlanc	b: 8/11/1956	m: 12/9/1989	
4	Wayne Joseph Olinger	b: 8/4/1953		
	+Constance Anne Harding	b: 5/22/1955	m: 9/11/1976	
4	Charles William Olinger	b: 6/6/1955		
	+Jacqueline Marie Prejean	b: 12/3/1956	m: 8/30/1980	
4	Mary Regina Olinger	b: 7/2/1957		
	+Sidney James Broussard	b: 1956	m: 1982	
	*2nd Husband of Mary Regina Olinger:			
	+Phillip Landry	b: 9/24/1951	m: 6/11/1996	
3	Barbara Rose Bollich	b: 1913		d: 2004
	+William Joseph Leonards	b: 1917	m: 1940	d: 2000
4	Audrey Augusta Leonards	b: 9/4/1941		
	+Michael Henry McBride	b: 9/2/1941	m: 10/26/1963	
4	[14] Lucille Rose Leonards	b: 8/17/1942		
	+[13] Thomas Alvin Chisholm III	b: 7/6/1941	m: 9/17/1966	
4	Stephen Norbert Leonards	b: 11/20/1943		
	+Susan Landreneau	b: 4/19/1945	m: 1/2/1965	
4	[5] Louise Regina Leonards	b: 1/9/1945		

	+[6] Lawrence William Heinen	b: 10/29/1938	m: 6/27/1970	d: 11/28/2005
4	[7] Lawrence William Leonards	b: 2/4/1946		
	+[8] Carol Bertha Dischler	b: 1/24/1945	m: 6/7/1969	
4	Judith Josephine Leonards	b: 3/19/1948		
	+Cecil George Hoffpauir	b: 7/3/1946	m: 8/24/1968	
4	Gregory Joseph Leonards	b: 7/31/1949		
	+Sandra Meaux	b: 5/15/1951	m: 10/14/1972	

*2nd Wife of Gregory Joseph Leonards:

	+Vickie LeBlanc	b: 12/26/1950	m: 5/19/1984
4	Albert Joseph Leonards	b: 9/12/1950	
	+Brenda Chauvin	b: 9/17/1951	m: 5/20/1972
4	Alfred John Leonards	b: 9/12/1950	
4	[9] William Joseph Leonards II	b: 12/12/1952	
	+[10] Barbara Ann Zaunbrecher	b: 7/8/1949	m: 6/28/1975
3	Nicholas Joseph Bollich	b: 1916	d: 1995
	+Caroline Manuel	b: 1914	m: 1940	d: 1996
4	Elridge Nicholas Bollich	b: 9/10/1941	
	+Shirley Yackel	b: 7/3/1948	m: 7/14/1973
4	Sharon Bollich	b: 8/2/1943	
	+Daniel Pickett, Sr.	b: 7/13/1941	m: 7/14/1962
4	Larry Joseph Bollich	b: 9/16/1950	
	+Ann Rage	b: 4/25/1950	m: 7/1/1971
4	Barbara Bollich	b: 9/22/1954	
	+Patrick Ross		m: 10/12/1977

*2nd Husband of Barbara Bollich:

+Robert Reeser	b: 1/17/1954	m: 9/23/1989

Hensgens

3		Agnes Leona Bollich	b: 1918		d: 2002
		+Norbert Stephen Zaunbrecher	b: 1916	m: 1934	d: 1979
	4	Kenneth Zaunbrecher	b: 11/8/1936		
		+Gannol Richard	b: 11/5/1938	m: 9/30/1956	
		*2nd Wife of Kenneth Zaunbrecher:			
		+Suzanne Cheramie	b: 7/21/1939	m: 7/8/1983	
3		Hildegard (Hilda) Anna Bollich	b: 7/28/1920		
		+Francis Edgar Robichaux	b: 5/19/1916	m: 2/21/1946	d: 6/28/1980
	4	Diane Robichaux	b: 12/17/1946		
		+David Broussard, Sr.	b: 10/3/1943	m: 7/16/1966	
	4	Brenda Robichaux	b: 12/15/1947		
		+Doyle Maggard	b: 9/25/1948	m: 9/9/1967	
	4	Melba Robichaux	b: 4/11/1949		
		+Howard Spencer, Jr.	b: 3/21/1947	m: 8/14/1981	
	4	Lorraine Robichaux	b: 3/20/1951		
		+Terry Kostic	b: 8/5/1950	m: 4/7/1978	
	4	Donna Robichaux	b: 3/17/1952		
		+Donald Royer	b: 12/27/1946	m: 10/29/1994	
	4	Sandra Robichaux	b: 2/3/1954		
	4	Francis Robichaux, Jr.	b: 7/13/1955		
		+Debbie Heinen	b: 12/17/1959	m: 11/4/1983	
	4	Alvin Robichaux	b: 9/17/1956		
		+Lydia Trahan	b: 6/22/1959	m: 5/6/2000	
	4	Sharon Robichaux	b: 2/28/1962		
	4	Bryan Robichaux	b: 2/8/1964		
		+Leah Montfort	b: 2/4/1971	m: 5/26/2001	
2		Conrad Hensgens	b: 5/9/1880		d: 9/21/1956
		+Francesca Margaret Schatzle	b: 1887	m: 5/30/1905	d: 1975

Hensgens

3		Theresa Margaret Hensgens	b: 1906		d: 1995
		+Anton "Heinrich" Habetz	b: 12/10/1903	m: 2/3/1926	d: 4/18/1935
	4	James Leonard Habetz, Sr.	b: 12/13/1926		d: 2/18/1996
		+Mary Dean Breaux		m: 1/18/1950	d: 3/31/1989
	4	Henrietta Theresa Victoria Habetz	b: 6/1/1928		
		+Raymond N. Gossen		m: 2/3/1949	
	4	Leonard Conrad Habetz	b: 2/12/1931		d: 2/20/2006
		*2nd Husband of Theresa Margaret Hensgens:			
		+Henry Joseph Bollich	b: 1902	m: 1939	d: 1975
	4	Henry Joseph Bollich, Jr.	b: 1947		
		+Kathy Collins	b: 1952	m: 1973	
3		Joseph Hensgens	b: 1908		d: 1977
3		Regina Ida Hensgens	b: 9/23/1909		d: 1/26/1980
		+John Herman Schultz	b: 1/4/1911	m: 1/13/1937	d: 4/22/1963
	4	Charles Herman Schultz	b: 10/23/1937		
		+Geraldine Elaine Trumps	b: 5/20/1937	m: 11/9/1957	d: 12/4/1998
	4	[11] John Herman Schultz	b: 9/6/1939		
		+[12] Marjorie Ann Robichaux	b: 10/19/1943	m: 11/10/1973	
	4	Mary Frances Schultz	b: 1/13/1942		
		+Thomas Michael Wall	b: 12/4/1947	m: 7/17/1971	
	4	Patrick Leo Schultz	b: 2/16/1944		d: 9/1/1968
3		Catherine Hensgens	b: 1911		d: 1994
3		Annie Marie Hensgens	b: 1914		d: 1995
		+Lawrence William Dischler	b: 1910	m: 1933	d: 1991

Hensgens

4	Winona Frances Bertha Dischler	b: 1934		
	+Robert Cartwright	b: 1931	m: 1957	d: 1998
4	Carolyn Ann Dischler	b: 1940		
	+Herman F. "Freddie" Morgan, Jr.	b: 1936	m: 1958	
3	Gertrude Marie Hensgens	b: 1917		d: 1986
	+Louis Burton	b: 1919	m: 1940	d: 1998
4	Ramona Burton	b: 1940		
	+Lynn Boone	b: 1938	m: 1961	
4	Donald Burton	b: 1942		
	+Geraldine Fontenot	b: 1939	m: 1980	
4	Constance Burton	b: 1946		
	+Gerald Doucet	b: 1941	m: 1965	
4	Conrad Burton	b: 1946		
4	Randall Burton	b: 1949		
	+Diane Louviere	b: 1947	m: 1969	
4	Jude Burton	b: 1951		
	+Barbara Fontenot	b: 1952	m: 1971	
4	Judy Burton	b: 1951		
	+Adlas Herpin	b: 1950	m: 1971	
4	Margaret Burton	b: 1953		d: 2000
4	Gerald Burton	b: 1955		
4	Geraldine Burton	b: 1955		d: 1955
3	John Conrad Hensgens	b: 1919		d: 1992
	+Annie Gesina Thevis	b: 1917	m: 1946	
4	John Conrad Hensgens II	b: 1948		
	+Becky Collins	b: 1953	m: 1976	
3	Marie Barbara Hensgens	b: 1921		d: 1989
3	Henry William Hensgens	b: 1923		d: 1980
3	Elenora Beatrice Hensgens	b: 1924		d: 1997
	+George Annen Cart	b: 1922	m: 1944	

Hensgens

	4	George Annen Cart, Jr.	b: 1962		d: 1981
2		Johanna Maria Hensgens	b: 12/29/1882		d: 3/13/1930
		+Joseph G. Klauser	b: 1880	m: 10/17/1905	d: 1/2/1947
2		Joseph Hensgens	b: 2/24/1885		d: 10/6/1959
		+Gertrude Anna Reiners	b: 4/11/1885	m: 11/27/1906	d: 1/16/1969
	3	Christian Joseph Hensgens	b: 9/25/1908		d: 10/13/1972
		+Maria Elizabeth (Lizzie) Thevis	b: 10/24/1909	m: 11/19/1928	d: 1/3/1985
	4	Leonard (Lenny) Joseph Hensgens	b: 10/7/1929		
		+Sarah Ann Smith		m: 7/11/1950	
	4	Raymond (Ray) Aloysious Hensgens	b: 7/22/1932		
		+Catherine (Kitty) Schneider		m: 10/20/1951	
	4	Lawrence Leo Hensgens	b: 4/1/1934		
		+Lula Link		m: 12/10/1953	
	4	Germaine Francis Hensgens	b: 12/14/1935		d: 2/2/1996
		+Frank J. Schneider		m: 10/25/1955	
	4	Wilhelmina (Wilma) Thecla Hensgens	b: 11/10/1937		d: 5/21/2006
		+Henry Jerome Leonards	b: 9/13/1934	m: 1/26/1958	
	4	Alberta Gertrude Hensgens	b: 2/13/1940		
		+Norwood (Marcy) Lyons, Sr.		m: 5/25/1963	
	3	Regina Josepha Hensgens	b: 7/19/1909		d: 10/10/1909
	3	Catherine Frances Hensgens	b: 10/26/1916		d: 11/15/1997
		+Hubert Pirmin Habetz	b: 11/3/1911	m: 1/8/1936	d: 8/22/1970
	4	Laurentia (Sr. Lawrence) Frances Habetz	b: 1/21/1937		

Hensgens

4	Pirmin (Junior) Joseph Habetz	b: 6/4/1938		
	+Mary Lou Hebert		m: 5/16/1959	
4	Patricia Clara Habetz	b: 2/22/1940		
	+Bennett Augustine		m: 11/7/1959	
4	Marcella (Mel) Elizabeth Habetz	b: 4/16/1942		d: 5/22/1973
	+Ralph Gossen	b: 1934	m: 5/5/1962	
4	Patrick Conrad Habetz	b: 2/28/1944		
	+Marjorie (Margie) Granger		m: 4/11/1964	
4	Kathleen (Teemie) Habetz	b: 9/7/1945		
	+Cecil Compton		m: 8/21/1965	
3	Conrad Leo Hensgens	b: 1/25/1920		d: 4/22/1987
	+Marie Catherine (Gertie Mae) Theunissen	b: 1922	m: 11/29/1939	
4	Thomas Jude (Tommy) Hensgens	b: 11/2/1955		
	+JoAnn (Trina) Autin		m: 10/27/1989	
3	Anna Gertrude Hensgens	b: 12/27/1921		d: 11/28/2000
	+Lee Joseph Monlezun, Sr.	b: 4/24/1917	m: 8/13/1941	d: 7/31/1985
4	Lee Joseph Monlezun, Jr.	b: 1/20/1943		
	+Evelyn Anne Prague Gillett	b: 3/14/1947	m: 5/5/1979	
4	Robert Joseph Monlezun	b: 5/27/1944		
	+Wanda Lynn Womack	b: 7/23/1946	m: 11/6/1965	
4	Charles Joseph Monlezun	b: 9/29/1946		
	+Sharon Diane LeBleu	b: 12/22/1946	m: 8/9/1969	
4	Anna Bernadette Monlezun	b: 12/12/1947		

Hensgens

	+Col. Hector Rafael Ponton	b: 7/25/1936	m: 1/14/1978	
4	Constance Victoria Monlezun	b: 9/15/1950		
	+Victor Wayne Darbonne	b: 8/28/1948	m: 6/30/1973	
4	Malcolm Joseph Monlezun	b: 12/24/1952		
	+Ursula Ann Daigle	b: 2/25/1955	m: 12/27/1971	
4	Alvin Joseph Monlezun	b: 8/7/1954		d: 5/27/1965
4	Ione Marie Monlezun	b: 9/4/1956		
	+Whitney Broussard II			
4	Veronica Gertrude Monlezun	b: 2/7/1958		d: 5/27/1965
4	Dominique Joseph Monlezun	b: 9/20/1960		
	+Tina Louise King	b: 10/10/1961	m: 2/9/1980	
3	Barbara Leona Hensgens	b: 5/6/1924		
	+Herman Lawrence Berken	b: 8/10/1921	m: 1/30/1946	d: 9/11/1996
4	Charlotte Ann Berken	b: 2/15/1948		
	+George Kenneth "Ken" Connor		m: 1/25/1969	
4	Stephen Herman Berken	b: 5/5/1949		
	+Melanie Boutte		m: 12/16/1972	
4	Clarence Aloysius Berken	b: 12/22/1951		
	+Karen Berry		m: 1/6/1973	
4	Martha Elaine Berken	b: 3/26/1955		
	+Homer Stevens, II		m: 8/3/1974	
4	Rachel Lea Berken	b: 12/11/1957		
	+Tomas (Tom) Wayne Andrus		m: 9/4/1976	
4	Kevin Matthew Berken	b: 3/16/1961		
	+Shirley Hill		m: 12/14/1990	
4	Mary Gayle Berken	b: 3/18/1963		

Hensgens

    +Jay Womack
  *2nd Husband of Mary Gayle Berken:
    +Todd Moses   m: 6/12/1999
  *2nd Husband of Barbara Leona Hensgens:
    +Louis Smaihall   b: 10/1914   m: 7/6/2002   d: 1/20/2005

3   Nicholas Anthony (Tony) Hensgens   b: 12/6/1925   d: 12/6/1999
      +Gloria Theresa Deshotels   b: 3/12/1927   m: 11/16/1948   d: 2/5/1995

    4   Nicholas (Anthony) Hensgens, Jr.   b: 9/20/1949
        +Pamela (Pam) Boudreaux   m: 4/26/1980

    4   Stephanie Louise Hensgens   b: 4/27/1952
        +Ronald Berger   m: 8/17/1974

    4   Kenneth James Hensgens   b: 11/10/1954
        +Michelle Champagne

    4   Karl Joseph Hensgens   b: 3/26/1956
        +Melanie Hanks   m: 12/7/1984

3   Clarice Johanna Hensgens   b: 9/15/1929
      +Guy Gregory Gauthreaux, II   b: 1926   m: 4/23/1953

    4   Gwendolyn Clare Gauthreaux   b: 5/26/1954
        +Col. Charles (Brusle) Sherburne, Jr.   m: 5/21/1977

    4   Guy (G.G.) Gregoire Gauthreaux II   b: 4/16/1956
        +Debra Hinkle   m: 8/7/1976

    4   Kay Frances Gauthreaux
        +Dale Dugruise

    4   Joseph (Joey) Hensgens Gauthreaux
        +Chrystal Taylor   m: 10/9/2004

2   William Nicholas Hensgens   b: 12/26/1887   d: 10/4/1955

Hensgens

	+Maria Agnes Leonards	b: 11/12/1890	m: 1911	d: 7/24/1926
3	Maria Josepha Hensgens	b: 1911		d: 1998
	+Gilbert LeBlanc	b: 1909	m: 1934	d: 1999
4	Cynthia LeBlanc	b: 1938		
	+Joseph Kratzer	b: 1936	m: 1957	
3	Maria Catherine Hensgens	b: 2/8/1913		
	+Leo Ferdinand Heinen	b: 4/11/1909	m: 1/25/1933	d: 12/27/1959
4	Gwendolyn Heinen	b: 3/19/1934		
	+James Stewart	b: 7/29/1933	m: 9/19/1959	
4	Lowell Heinen	b: 1/2/1937		
	+Catherine Davis	b: 11/22/1936	m: 12/27/1957	
4	Dr. Brian Heinen	b: 8/12/1943		
	+Jennifer Guillory	b: 9/26/1945	m: 2/22/1963	
4	Janet Heinen	b: 10/22/1946		
	+Donald Martel	b: 12/13/1944	m: 8/26/1967	
4	Ferdinand Heinen	b: 9/8/1955		
	+Lori Gregory	b: 4/16/1959	m: 5/10/1996	
3	Regina Gertrude Hensgens	b: 1915		d: 2003
	+John Baptiste Duplechin	b: 1907	m: 1938	d: 1963
4	Baron Duplechin	b: 6/21/1943		
	+Carol Martin	b: 8/1/1944	m: 11/18/1967	
4	Sharon Duplechin	b: 9/7/1946		
4	Melanie Duplechin	b: 1/26/1949		
	+Donald Waters	b: 1/19/1949	m: 8/23/1970	d: 1/24/1999
3	Charles Nicholas Hensgens	b: 12/22/1916		d: 9/29/1995
	+Leola Landry	b: 9/17/1917	m: 11/9/1938	d: 6/2/1999
4	Charles Hensgens	b: 10/5/1939		d: 4/6/1985
	+Elizabeth Miller	b: 4/26/1940	m: 2/16/1963	
4	Mary Gayle Hensgens	b: 2/16/1941		
	+Lynn Iverson	b: 1/12/1942	m: 11/25/1967	d: 1/18/2004
4	Frank Eugene Hensgens	b: 9/4/1942		
	+Christine Broussard	b: 7/25/1945	m: 9/12/1970	

Hensgens

4	Warren Hensgens	b: 6/1/1944		
	+Cathy Williamson	b: 10/31/1950	m: 11/27/1974	
4	Charlotte Hensgens	b: 11/6/1945		
	+Glenn Valdetero	b: 9/19/1944	m: 8/8/1969	d: 2/4/2002
4	Beverly Hensgens	b: 1/25/1949		
	+George Dorr	b: 4/18/1948	m: 8/7/1970	
4	Dennis Hensgens	b: 6/21/1950		
	+Valerie Moody	b: 9/1/1952	m: 4/19/1974	
4	Jacqueline Hensgens	b: 10/2/1952		
	+John Keith Lambousy	b: 1/6/1951	m: 5/18/1973	
4	Gretchen Hensgens	b: 1/29/1957		
	+Cleveland Jackson Harrelson	b: 10/18/1956	m: 6/9/1990	
4	Geralyn Christine Hensgens	b: 3/18/1958		
	+Robert Vidrine	b: 12/4/1956	m: 1/6/1978	
3	Helen Agnes Hensgens	b: 1918		d: 1999
	+Sterling Boudreaux	b: 1914	m: 1938	d: 1993
4	Sandra Boudreaux	b: 1943		
	+Merlin Pritchard	b: 1941	m: 1981	
4	Sterling Boudreaux	b: 1947		
	+Dora Autin	b: 1949		
4	Nancy Boudreaux	b: 1953		
3	Christine Hensgens	b: 1919		d: 8/9/2006
	+Thomas Alvin Chisholm	b: 1918	m: 1940	d: 1991
4	[13] Thomas Alvin Chisholm III	b: 7/6/1941		
	+[14] Lucille Rose Leonards	b: 8/17/1942	m: 9/17/1966	
3	Annie Dorothy Hensgens	b: 1922		d: 2001
	+Cecil Joseph Hundley	b: 1922	m: 1949	d: 2002
4	Kelly Hundley	b: 10/27/1950		

Hensgens

	+Marian Trahan			
4	Debra Hundley	b: 2/10/1952		
	+Fred Stafford	b: 4/16/1952	m: 8/4/1973	
4	Nicholas Hundley	b: 4/12/1955		
	+Clara Cobena	b: 6/24/1955	m: 1/20/1973	
4	Douglas Hundley	b: 7/31/1956		
	+Cathy Moody	b: 11/30/1956	m: 5/30/1974	
4	James "Jimbo" Hundley	b: 8/3/1959		
	+Cathy Cook	b: 12/13/1959	m: 1/8/1982	
4	Michael Hundley	b: 5/9/1962		
	+Katherine John	b: 1/18/1963	m: 12/29/1984	
4	Rose Mary Hundley	b: 2/28/1966		
	+Randy Minch	b: 8/4/1955	m: 4/2/2001	
3	Louise Cecile Hensgens	b: 1/24/1924		
	+Gerard Lumodon Foley	b: 12/10/1920	m: 4/2/1945	d: 4/9/2005
4	Judy Foley	b: 7/25/1946		
	+Jerry Dibble II			
	*2nd Husband of Judy Foley:			
	+Bob King	b: 11/8/1930	m: 7/12/1990	
4	Donna Foley	b: 4/16/1949		
	+Bill Simpson			
4	Gerard Foley	b: 6/30/1950		
	+Susan Alexander	b: 4/14/1957	m: 12/23/2005	
4	Colleen Foley	b: 9/24/1952		
	+Randy Peacock	b: 6/5/1951	m: 2/2/1974	
4	Nichola Foley	b: 10/12/1953		
	+Darrell Lockridge	b: 2/13/1949	m: 8/11/1973	
4	Mary Foley	b: 5/7/1956		
	+Arlie Telschow	b: 5/14/1953	m: 12/30/1977	
4	Brigid Foley	b: 5/23/1958		
4	Jo Beth Foley	b: 11/18/1959		
	+Doug McLaughlin	b: 9/11/1957	m: 8/24/1985	

Hensgens

3	Nicholas Louis Hensgens	b: 1925		
	+Doris Landry	b: 1927	m: 1946	
4	Richard "Ricky" Hensgens	b: 1947		
4	Dale Hensgens	b: 1949		
	+Christina Baham	b: 1955	m: 1976	
4	Sheila Hensgens	b: 1951		
	+Calvin Hargrave	b: 1950	m: 1973	
4	Keith Hensgens	b: 1954		
	+Melanie Trahan	b: 1956	m: 1976	
	*2nd Wife of William Nicholas Hensgens:			
	+Lillian Miguez	b: 4/12/1891	m: 1927	d: 3/7/1987
3	Yvonne Hensgens	b: 1928		
	+Homer Istre	b: 1923	m: 1947	d: 1990
4	Gregory Istre	b: 1948		
	+Susan Smith	b: 1950	m: 1972	
4	Randall Istre	b: 1950		
	+Deborah Donchetz	b: 1952	m: 1973	

13. Huesers (Hüsers), Johann Heinrich:
Johann Heinrich Huesers b: 1855 d: 1931 from Meppen married in 1880 to Maria Margaretha Wilkens b: 1860 d: 10/29/1936, who is the daughter of Johann Herman Wilkens and Maria Helena Hilling.

2		Gesina Husers	b: 1881		d: 1/17/1933
		+Emile Joseph Thoman	b: 1882	m: 1908	d: 1958
3		Margaret Mary Thoman	b: 1908		d: 1985
		+George Leon Regan	b: 1906	m: 1927	d: 1986
	4	Clifford Leon Regan	b: 1928		
		+Lou Ella Daigle		m: 1955	
	4	Huey Patrick Regan	b: 1930		
		+Wilma Anna Zaunbrecher	b: 1928	m: 1950	
	4	Donald Lloyd Regan	b: 1932		
		+Doris Ann Dietz	b: 1933	m: 1953	
	4	Lois Elizabeth Regan	b: 1936		
		+Edward Marvin Dietz	b: 1929	m: 1954	
	4	Catherine Margaret Regan	b: 1938		
		+Floyd Louis LaCombe	b: 1932	m: 1956	d: 2005
	4	George Rodney Regan	b: 1940		d: 2003
		+Evaline Nell Dietz		m: 1961	
	4	James Richard Regan	b: 1944		d: 1993
		+Elizabeth Geer		m: 1966	
	4	Patricia Ann Regan	b: 1948		
		+Fred Delaney Stoute	b: 1937	m: 1967	
	4	David Wayne Regan	b: 1951		
		+Freddie Ann Toups	b: 1951	m: 1974	
3		Madeline Josephine Thoman	b: 1912		
		+Garland Durace Barras	b: 1912	m: 1933	d: 2001

Huesers

	4	Richard Garland Barras	b: 3/12/1934		
		+Glenda Landry	b: 1938	m: 10/9/1960	
	4	Robert Eward Barras	b: 10/3/1936		
		+Jeanette Edwards Francis	b: 11/14/1939	m: 8/22/1959	
	4	Donald Ray Barras	b: 7/14/1940		
		+Patricia Ann Johnson	b: 5/26/1942	m: 2/9/1966	
3		Joseph Bernard Thoman	b: 12/17/1914		
		+Mary Virginia Stewart	b: 3/30/1922	m: 1950	
3		Leon Albert Thoman	b: 8/17/1917		d: 12/13/1992
		+Leah Marie Chaisson	b: 1911	m: 10/16/1937	
3		Lawrence Edward Thoman	b: 1923		d: 1983
		+Betty Willis			
3		Marian Marguerite Thoman	b: 1924		d: 1929
3		Alma Marie Thoman	b: 1927		d: 1999
2		John Henry Husers, Jr.	b: 3/25/1885		d: 12/26/1935
		+Maria Agnes Gossen	b: 1885	m: 12/23/1908	d: 1929
3		Anna Margaret Husers	b: 3/20/1910		d: 1/30/1929
		+Earl Stakes	b: 1904	m: 12/22/1927	
	4	William Henry Stakes	b: 10/4/1928		d: 1/4/1929
3		Maria Elizabeth Husers	b: 6/11/1911		d: 1987
		+Foster Joseph Istre	b: 9/8/1905	m: 9/21/1929	d: 12/8/1963
	4	Joanna Istre	b: 9/21/1933		
		+Ervin J. Bourg	b: 9/3/1927	m: 6/2/1956	
	4	Maxine Elizabeth Istre	b: 9/19/1940		
		+Thomas L. Guerin	b: 8/19/1933	m: 9/5/1959	
		*2nd Husband of Maria Elizabeth Husers:			
		+Boyd Joseph Mayers	b: 3/5/1910	m: 9/4/1965	d: 1984
3		Hubert Henry Husers	b: 10/6/1913		d: 1988
		+Mary Lois Perry	b: 8/20/1922	m: 11/12/1938	
	4	Francis Husers			

Huesers

	4	Leroy Husers			
	4	Eddie Husers			
	4	Dean Husers			
	4	Oliver Husers			
	4	Jerry Husers			
	4	Glen Husers			
	4	? Husers			
3		Josephine Agnes Husers	b: 7/19/1915		d: 2000
		+Wilbur Abel Laine	b: 12/20/1914	m: 12/28/1937	d: 1998
	4	Priscilla Marie Laine	b: 2/18/1940		
		+Evans J. Richard	b: 8/8/1932	m: 9/8/1962	
3		Maria Gebina Husers	b: 12/24/1916		d: 2000
		+Placid Edwin Istre	b: 4/21/1914	m: 4/12/1935	d: 1988
	4	Judy Ann Istre	b: 6/14/1940		
		+Udell James LeJeune	b: 3/22/1939	m: 2/13/1959	
	4	Patricia Marie Istre	b: 9/29/1949		
		+Floyd Joseph Gotte	b: 3/7/1948	m: 6/28/1969	
	4	Fritz Henry Istre	b: 2/21/1951		
	4	Cynthia Agnes Istre	b: 1/4/1955		
		+Larry Dale Leckelt	b: 12/2/1945	m: 5/25/1973	
3		Anthony Bernard Husers	b: 1919		d: 1919
3		Martin Albert Husers	b: 8/3/1920		d: 7/3/1940
3		Maria Cecilia Husers	b: 1/31/1923		
		+Thomas Dodd Jenkins	b: 1922	m: 1/31/1943	d: 1997
	4	Cecilia Ann Jenkins	b: 4/19/1946		
	4	Dana Thomas Jenkins	b: 8/6/1959		
2		John Husers	b: 1888		d: 1965
		+Lilly Simpson/Simmons			
2		Bernard Joseph Husers	b: 1891		d: 9/19/1953
		+Mary Cecilia Regan	b: 1891	m: 1909	d: 1979
3		Thomas James Husers	b: 1910		d: 1985
		+Octavia Domingue	b: 1912	m: 1931	d: 2001

Huesers

4	Ronald Thomas Husers	b: 1936		
	+Benita Brasseaux		m: 1956	
4	Terrell David Husers	b: 1944		
4	Peggy Ann Husers	b: 1946		
	+Norman Ravia	b: 1949	m: 1990	
3	Jefferson Daniel Husers	b: 1912		d: 1984
	+Mathilda Marie Suire	b: 1913	m: 1934	d: 1987
3	Bernard George Husers	b: 1916		d: 1990
	+Lena Elena Aguillard	b: 1916	m: 1937	d: 1984
4	Dale Bernard Husers	b: 3/20/1938		
	+Catherine Mary Leonards	b: 7/19/1944	m: 5/9/1964	
4	Sylvia Marie Husers	b: 2/19/1942		
	+Phillip Otis DuBose	b: 7/16/1943	m: 1962	
3	Eugene Patrick Husers	b: 1918		d: 1/25/1935
3	Michael Joseph Husers	b: 1921		
	+Ruby Faulk	b: 1923	m: 1942	
4	Sandra Faye Husers	b: 9/11/1945		
	+John Ed Potier	b: 7/28/1944		
4	Patty Ann Husers	b: 8/26/1946		
	+Kenneth William Turner	b: 10/1/1938	m: 1/23/1976	d: 4/15/1991
4	Tommy Wade Husers	b: 1/16/1951		
	+Odile Dubey	b: 6/10/1958	m: 3/31/1983	
4	Joseph Michael Husers	b: 11/9/1953		
	+Joan Marie Guidry	b: 1/1/1954	m: 8/24/1974	
4	Mary Agnes Husers	b: 3/2/1959		
	+Jacob Davidson Stolzle	b: 12/4/1954	m: 7/3/1981	
3	Floyd Stephen Husers	b: 6/27/1923		d: 10/27/2002
	+Sylvia Mae Doucet	b: 1/25/1924	m: 12/13/1947	d: 8/18/2004
4	Celia LaVona Husers	b: 9/11/1948		

Huesers

	+Charles Joseph Taylor	b: 8/15/1945	m: 3/31/1967	
4	Molly Yolande Husers	b: 8/8/1950		
	+Norris Steven Benoit	b: 10/13/1948	m: 4/23/1976	
4	Steven Noel Husers	b: 10/22/1954		
	+Sheryl Elizabeth Perkins	b: 10/16/1957	m: 6/8/1979	
4	Elizabeth Ozea Husers	b: 7/20/1959		
	+Keith James Verret	b: 2/5/1959	m: 8/1/1981	
	*2nd Husband of Elizabeth Ozea Husers:			
	+Jerry Clark Tate	b: 8/12/1959	m: 8/10/2005	
3	Margaret Marie Husers	b: 1926		
	+Ray James Potier	b: 1922	m: 1943	d: 2005
4	Carol Marie Potier	b: 8/18/1944		
	+Don Amy	b: 1946	m: 1962	
	*2nd Husband of Carol Marie Potier:			
	+Wayne Belaire	b: 1955	m: Aft. 1962	d: Deceased
	*3rd Husband of Carol Marie Potier:			
	+Steve Beinvenu	b: 1948	m: 1986	
4	Bonnie Kathryn Potier	b: 9/10/1946		
	+Tommy Barousse	b: 1944	m: 1966	
4	David Ray Potier	b: 10/6/1950		
	+Dianna Richey	b: 1949	m: 1967	
4	Thaddeus James Potier	b: 2/22/1960		
	+Sonya Treadway	b: 8/1965	m: 1980	
4	Bridget Annette Potier	b: 8/13/1965		
	+Todd Venable	b: 1965	m: 4/6/1986	
4	Bridgette Ann Potier	b: 8/13/1965		
	+Mark Daigle	b: 1964	m: 1988	
3	Andrew Sullivan Husers	b: 1931		
	+Jacqueline Rita Miciotto	b: 1933	m: 1951	

Huesers

	4	Deborah Anne Husers	b: 1952		
		+Daniel J. Beggs	b: 1950	m: 1982	
	4	Bernard Joseph Husers	b: 1954		
		+Alicia Sonnier	b: 1956	m: 1974	
	4	Linda Marie Husers	b: 1958		
		+Ray Anthony Guidry	b: 1952	m: 1989	
	4	Mark Kevin Husers	b: 1961		d: 2003
		+Alisa Dugan	b: 1962	m: 1982	
	4	Charles Frederick Husers	b: 1969		
		+Chasity Schexnayder	b: 1974	m: 1993	
2		Albert Husers	b: 7/9/1894		d: 1/1979
		+Sarah Mitchell	b: 11/26/1893	m: 1914	d: 3/6/1926
3		Robert Louis Huser	b: 2/22/1915		d: 1/13/1998
		+Alice Ellen McCants	b: 6/20/1918	m: 1/23/1939	d: 11/25/1993
	4	Ellen Patricia Huser	b: 12/31/1939		
		+John Earl Taylor	b: 12/28/1933	m: 6/13/1964	
	4	Betty Louise Huser	b: 11/23/1945		
		+Dean Crawford			

*2nd Husband of Betty Louise Huser:

		+Judson Vosberg Kintner	b: 10/25/1933	m: 5/11/1982	
3		Charles Henry Husers	b: 1/9/1917		
		+Faye Berry	b: 1934		

*2nd Wife of Charles Henry Husers:

		+Delphia Reeves	b: 1/26/1925	m: 1950	d: 7/31/1992
	4	Rebekah Lynn Husers	b: 1/13/1954		
		+Kenny Hillman			

*2nd Husband of Rebekah Lynn Husers:

		+Roger Lee Wells	b: 7/19/1946	m: 3/14/1992	
	4	Charlene Husers	b: 2/24/1956		
		+Paul John Kaznowski	b: 11/13/1953	m: 5/17/1984	d: 7/10/2001

Huesers

3	Lloyd George Husers	b: 1/27/1920		d: 8/21/1995
	+Margaret Cornelia Bahnsen	b: 1924	m: 5/10/1946	
4	Dennis Lloyd Husers	b: 4/3/1947		
	+Linda Marie Self	b: 11/18/1949	m: 8/24/1968	
4	Jane Margaret Husers	b: 1/23/1949		
	+Joseph Wayne Gremillion	b: 5/20/1949	m: 12/20/1969	
4	Joyce Elaine Husers	b: 9/30/1952		
	+Michael Gilpin Miller	b: 3/1/1952	m: 7/24/1976	
4	Judy Ann Husers	b: 11/3/1957		d: 10/14/1981
4	Timothy Brian Husers	b: 6/27/1961		
	+Jacquelyn Nieto	b: 1964	m: 8/24/1994	
3	Albert Husers, Jr.	b: 3/1/1923		
	+Rosa Mae Vice	b: 8/3/1928	m: 3/5/1946	
4	Gary Lynn Husers	b: 7/22/1961		
	+Lou Dougat	b: 1994		
4	Angela Yvonne Husers	b: 2/10/1964		
	+Arthur "Butch" Dore, Jr.			
	*2nd Husband of Angela Yvonne Husers:			
	+Joseph Dauth	b: 3/30/1964	m: 10/26/1996	
3	Thelma Blanche Husers	b: 8/5/1925		
	+James Franklin Williams	b: 4/3/1917	m: 3/1/1941	d: 7/15/1975
4	Eugene Franklin Williams	b: 9/26/1944		
	+Sandra Ann Denton	b: 10/16/1944	m: 5/1/1965	
4	Sara Ella Williams	b: 7/16/1952		
	+Harrison Lee Root	b: 9/2/1947	m: 7/21/1972	
4	Martha Elizabeth Williams	b: 1/27/1954		

Huesers

		+Tyler Clark Caldwell	b: 10/15/1956	m: 7/7/1984	
	4	Joanne Williams	b: 9/6/1959		
		+Robert Mahlin Derouen	b: 5/29/1958	m: 5/24/1991	
		*2nd Husband of Thelma Blanche Husers:			
		+Robert McClelland	b: 1921	m: 1977	d: 1992
		*3rd Husband of Thelma Blanche Husers:			
		+Lee Howze	b: 1927	m: Aft. 1977	d: 2005
2		Maria Gebina Husers	b: 7/24/1898		d: 1984
		+William Augustus Sewe	b: 1892	m: 1918	d: 1976
3		Margaret Elizabeth Sewe	b: 1919		d: 1990
		+Paul Van Butaud	b: 1909	m: 1943	d: 2000
	4	Mary Margaret Butaud	b: 1950		
		+C.J. Guidry, Jr.		m: 1969	
		*2nd Husband of Mary Margaret Butaud:			
		+Michael Venable		m: 1972	
	4	Paula Marie Butaud	b: 1952		
		+Billy Gillette		m: 1990	
3		Helen Louise Sewe	b: 1921		
		+Woodrow Wilson Kloor	b: 1913	m: 1940	d: 1993
	4	Louis Woodrow Kloor	b: 1943		d: 2002
		+Betty Griffin	b: 1946	m: 1964	
	4	David Duane Kloor	b: 1945		
		+Lucercia Fagnil	b: 1955	m: 1978	
	4	Michael Fred Kloor	b: 1946		
		+Dinah Monic	b: 1948	m: 1967	
	4	Mary Susan Louise Kloor	b: 1953		
		+Terry Wayne Osborne	b: 1950	m: 1971	
3		William Sherrill Sewe	b: 1924		d: 1997

Huesers

*2nd Husband of Maria Gebina Husers:
 +William Henry   m: 1946   d: 1964
 Stalcup

14. Jabusch, Robert J.:

Robert J. Jabusch b: 1862 d: 1939 from East Prussia was the son of Gottlieh Jabusch b: ? d: ? and Amelia Paul b: ? d: ?. He married in 1880s to Magdalena Heintz b: 1862 d: 1940 from Alsace, Lorraine, the daughter of Jacob Heintz.

2		Robert Cornelius Jabusch	b: 1887		d: 1972
		+Mary Helena Thomas	b: 1892	m: 1910	d: 1975
3		Annie Magdelena Jabusch	b: 1911		d: 2004
		+Howard Allie Nunnery	b: 1903	m: 1938	d: 1961
	4	Buddy Nunnery			d: Deceased
		*2nd Husband of Annie Magdelena Jabusch:			
		+Enis Stutes	b: 1897	m: 1966	d: 1975
		*3rd Husband of Annie Magdelena Jabusch:			
		+Wilmer Elliot Chase	b: 1908	m: 1977	
3		Leo Robert Carl Jabusch	b: 1913		d: 1969
		+Mavis Hebert	b: 1918	m: 1937	
	4	Carolyn Jabusch			
3		Helen May Jabusch	b: 1914		d: 1984
		+Wilton Joseph Touchet	b: 1918	m: 1939	d: 2005
3		Robert Cornelius Jabusch, Jr.	b: 1915		d: 2004
		+Hilda Thibodeaux	b: 1915	m: 1944	
	4	Sybil Jabusch			
3		Katherine Josephine Jabusch	b: 1916		d: 2001
		+Perry Rue Milner	b: 1904	m: 1944	d: 1975
	4	Perry Rue Milner, Jr.			
		+Carolyn ?			
3		Joseph Herman Jabusch	b: 1917		d: 1984
3		Jacob Joseph Jabusch	b: 1920		d: 1997
		+Kathleen Margaret Fournet	b: 1924	m: 1945	d: 1992
	4	Robert "Robie" Jabusch	b: 1954		d: 2005
3		Lena Annie Jabusch	b: 1922		d: 2006

Jabusch

	+John Adams	b: 1922	m: 1945	d: 1967
4	Thomas Robert Adams	b: 1948		
4	Kathleen Adams	b: 1953		
4	Bronwyn Adams	b: 1963		
3	Willie Albert Jabusch	b: 1923		d: 1924
3	Emile Charles Jabusch	b: 1925		d: 2003
3	Mary Margaret Jabusch	b: 1927		d: 2004
3	Mildred Magdalen Jabusch	b: 1930		
	+Eugene Anthony Lemaire	b: 1929	m: 1949	d: 1992
4	Donna Marie Lemaire	b: 1951		
4	Raymond Paul Lemaire	b: 1954		
	+Marlene Broussard	b: 1955	m: 1973	
4	Anthony Eli Lemaire	b: 1955		
4	Frank Eugene Lemaire	b: 1959		
	+Penny Carter	b: 1962	m: 1984	
4	Mark David Lemaire	b: 1963		
	+Tricia Christine Woods	b: 1970	m: 1996	
2	Leo Jabusch	b: 1890		d: 1891
2	William Jabusch	b: 1890		d: 1891
2	Henry Joseph Jabusch	b: 12/7/1893		d: 3/27/1986
	+Mary Gertrude Wirtz	b: 1/22/1900	m: 11/4/1918	d: 10/3/1987
3	Annie Mae Jabusch	b: 11/28/1919		d: 5/31/2002
	+Rene Rollo Richard	b: 6/17/1907	m: 2/15/1942	d: 6/1/1982
4	Rene Rollo Richard, Jr.	b: 10/8/1943		
	+Renola Gilbert	b: 12/27/1943	m: 1964	d: 2002
4	Donald Wayne Richard	b: 3/14/1948		
	+Linda Karshaw	b: 7/1950	m: 1967	
4	Randall Gerard Richard	b: 2/11/1952		
	+Lois Boutte	b: 8/20/1954	m: 1982	
4	Steven Dale Richard	b: 1/10/1955		

Jabusch

	+Susan Spencer	b: 1957	m: 1982	
3	Fredrick Henry Jabusch	b: 8/21/1921		
	+Willa Elizabeth Duhon	b: 7/23/1925	m: 2/14/1947	
4	Sharon Ann Jabusch	b: 1950		
	+James W. Knight		m: 1970	
4	Stephanie Marie Jabusch	b: 1954		
3	Frank Conrad Jabusch	b: 11/26/1924		
	+Vera Marie Zaunbrecher	b: 11/6/1926	m: 2/17/1947	
4	Sandra Ann Jabusch	b: 1947		
	+Larry Eugene Walker	b: 1946	m: 1985	
4	Susan Elaine Jabusch	b: 1951		
	+Arnold Joseph LeBlanc	b: 1934		
4	Frank Conrad Jabusch, Jr.	b: 1952		
	+Deanne Lynn Daigle	b: 1959	m: 1977	
4	Patrick Keith Jabusch	b: 1953		
	+Melba Ann Richard	b: 1954	m: 1973	
4	Bryan Henry Jabusch	b: 1963		
	+Debra Louise Freeland	b: 1958	m: 1990	
4	Lorraine Marie Jabusch	b: 1964		
	+Richard John Breaux	b: 1963	m: 1989	
2	Maria Anna Jabusch	b: 1896		d: 1985
	+Peter Joseph Vondenstein	b: 1881	m: 1918	d: 1970
3	Josephine Ann Vondenstein	b: 4/6/1921		
	+Anthony Jacob Frey	b: 10/12/1919	m: 12/19/1946	
4	Stephen Joseph Frey	b: 9/6/1947		d: 5/27/1961
4	Leroy Vincent Frey	b: 12/18/1948		
	+Jo Anna Larson	b: 9/6/1951	m: 12/20/1976	
4	Patricia Ann Frey	b: 1/25/1952		

Jabusch

	+James T. Rainer	b: 1/11/1950	m: 8/3/1973
4	Sherri Lynn Frey	b: 4/9/1953	
	+Robert W. Steinriede	b: 5/5/1956	m: 10/3/1971
	*2nd Husband of Sherri Lynn Frey:		
	+Michael Tubertini	b: 4/12/1953	m: 11/3/1990
4	Tony Louis Frey	b: 8/14/1956	
	+Anna C. Hudson	b: 12/14/1965	m: 2/13/1988
4	Theresa Jo Frey	b: 11/9/1958	
	+John Austin Hord III	b: 3/14/1956	m: 3/10/1979
4	William Jude Frey	b: 11/2/1960	
	+Cashev Cetalu	b: 3/4/1959	m: 6/7/1980
4	Frances Elaine Frey	b: 5/3/1964	
	+Walter Lavch Muna	b: 7/3/1958	m: 3/7/1992
3	Joseph Robert Vondenstein	b: 1925	d: 1996

15. Jacobs, Arnold:

Arnold Jacobs b: 1859 d: 1936 from Langbroich was the son of Michael Jacobs and Katharina Teelen. He married in 1888 to Elizabeth Klumpp b: 1869 d: 1921, who is the daughter of Joseph Klumpp and Elizabeth Schmidt.

2		Maria Matilda Jacobs	b: 7/7/1890		d: 4/14/1968
		+Orville Gobert	b: 1885	m: 1908	d: 1952
3		Ruby Gobert	b: 1910		d: 1911
3		Willie Gobert	b: 1910		d: 1910
3		Adam Joseph Gobert	b: 1914		d: 4/1999
		+Beulah Sonnier	b: 1915	m: 1935	d: 1997
	4	Norma Faye Gobert	b: 2/27/1938		
		+Marvin Russell Munson, Sr.		m: 1958	d: 8/4/2004
		*2nd Husband of Norma Faye Gobert:			
		+Willard Harmon		m: 5/14/1965	d: 8/4/2003
	4	Adam Joseph Gobert, Jr.	b: 8/26/1942		
		+Garnette Fontenot	b: 7/4/1946	m: 7/23/1966	d: 7/6/2006
		*2nd Wife of Adam Joseph Gobert:			
		+Mae Craigen	b: 1915	m: 1969	d: 2006
		*3rd Wife of Adam Joseph Gobert:			
		+Aline		m: 1980	
3		[2] Milton Joseph Gobert	b: 1916		d: 1997
		+[1] Mary Elizabeth Jacobs	b: 1923	m: 1938	
3		Wilfred Henry Gobert	b: 10/31/1918		d: 1980
		+Erma June Frankenburger	b: 1923	m: 1944	
3		Wilbert Gobert	b: 10/31/1918		d: 7/1995
		+Mary Louise Elkins	b: 1918	m: 1944	d: 1965
3		Lilly Mae Gobert	b: 1/29/1921		
		+John Meaux	b: 2/3/1914	m: 5/31/1937	d: 1/27/1975
	4	Mary Lucy Meaux	b: 7/23/1938		

Jacobs

		+Lee Roy Joachim Dugas	b: 4/6/1932	m: 11/1/1959	
	4	Elizabeth Pearl Meaux	b: 9/30/1939		
		+Chester Francis Gonsoulin, Sr.	b: 2/24/1936	m: 6/11/1960	
	4	Walter Eugene Meaux	b: 9/17/1942		
		+Sandra Holcomb		m: 5/31/1967	
	4	John Dave Meaux	b: 11/18/1943		
		+Delores Theresa Barras	b: 2/1/1945		
3		Lillian Elizabeth Gobert	b: 1/29/1921		d: 10/11/1995
		+Edward William Beers	b: 6/2/1920	m: 5/10/1942	d: 12/22/1944
	4	Margaret Elizabeth Beers	b: 4/3/1939		d: 2/6/1994
		+Raymond Simon		m: 6/1958	
	4	Pearl Beers	b: 2/27/1944		
		+Gerald Jude Comeaux	b: 11/25/1939	m: 4/12/1960	
	4	Earl Beers	b: 2/27/1944		
		+Dianne G. Segura	b: 2/5/1946	m: 2/15/1964	
		*2nd Husband of Lillian Elizabeth Gobert:			
		+Louis Laviolette	b: 10/24/1918	m: 3/29/1957	d: 12/21/1979
3		Hazel Marie Gobert	b: 8/27/1922		d: 5/12/2003
		+Clayton Myers, Sr.	b: 1914	m: 1935	d: 1991
		*2nd Husband of Hazel Marie Gobert:			
		+Silton J. Ardoin	b: 1923	m: 1971	
3		Winnie Mae Gobert	b: 1924		d: 2004
		+Oliver Sterwerf	b: 10/10/1924	m: 1945	d: 4/1/1976
3		Mary Lorena Gobert	b: 2/15/1927		d: 8/24/2006
		+William John Kutta	b: 1906	m: 1949	d: 1975
	4	Matilda Kutta	b: 1950		
	4	William John Kutta	b: 1952		
	4	Paul Douglas Kutta	b: 1954		d: 2002

Jacobs

    *2nd Husband of Mary Lorena Gobert:
      +Lou Gene Gillie   m: 1976

3	Allen Joseph Gobert	b: 8/20/1929		d: 2002
	+Louise Bolden	b: 1932	m: 1949	
2	Henry Rudolf Jacobs	b: 1891		d: 1968
	+Marie Osa Wilfer	b: 1901	m: 1923	d: 1987
3	[1] Mary Elizabeth Jacobs	b: 1923		
	+[2] Milton Joseph Gobert	b: 1916	m: 1938	d: 1997
3	Willie Jacobs	b: 1925		d: 1926
3	Waverly Joseph Jacobs	b: 1928		d: 1972
	+Mary Ellen Rose	b: 1931	m: 1949	d: 1965
3	Dorothy Jacobs	b: 1931		
	+Dominick Martin	b: 1930	m: 1949	
2	Rosa Jacobs	b: 11/6/1893		d: 11/13/1893
2	Josef Arnold Jacobs	b: 1/7/1895		d: 1980
	+Lora Wilfer	b: 1906	m: 1924	d: 1987
3	Mary Ruby Jacobs	b: 1926		
	+Audrey Twain Stevens		m: 1950	
3	Willard Joseph Jacobs	b: 1933		
	+Laura Lee Dever	b: 1938	m: 1956	
3	Richard Jacobs	b: 1937		
	+Nelda House		m: 1959	
2	John Jacobs	b: 1898		d: 1985
	+Georgeanna Wilfer	b: 1913	m: 1930	
3	Elma Ruth Jacobs	b: 1932		
	+Wilfred Toups Jr.	b: 1930	m: 1951	
3	John James Jacobs	b: 1957		
	+Yanita Marie Stanley	b: 1958	m: 1978	
2	Arnold Jacobs, Jr.	b: 1901		d: 1961
	+Marie Babineaux	b: 1901	m: 1926	d: 1978
3	Joseph Clanny Jacobs	b: 1927		d: 1997

Jacobs

	+Evelyn Lee	b: 1932	m: 1954	d: 1968
4	Barbara Ann Jacobs	b: 1957		
	+? Washington			
4	Clarence Lawrence Jacobs	b: 1959		
4	Beverly Ann Jacobs	b: 1960		
	+Paul Joseph Adams	b: 3/6/1956	m: 1999	
4	Linda Gayle Jacobs	b: 1961		
4	David Lee Jacobs	b: 1963		
	+Marsha Turner	b: 1966		

*2nd Wife of Joseph Clanny Jacobs:

	+Patricia Diaz		m: Aft. 1968	
4	Christina Nicole Jacobs	b: 1979		
4	Patrick Lee Jacobs	b: 1980		d: 1998
3	Thelma Jacobs	b: 1929		
	+Leroy John Vige	b: 1929	m: 1954	
4	Catherine Marie Wayne	b: 1944		
	+James Merlin Fruge	b: 1939	m: 1962	
3	Clarence Joseph Jacobs	b: 1933		d: 1933
3	Lewis Jacobs	b: 1934		
	+Linda Mary Bellard	b: 1940	m: 1958	
4	Lawrence Ray Jacobs	b: 1959		d: 2004
	+Paula Ann Guidry			
4	Brenda Jacobs Jacobs	b: Aft. 1959		
4	Patricia Jacobs	b: Aft. 1959		
4	Belinda Sue Jacobs	b: 1965		
	+Berchman Ortego	b: 1961	m: 1992	
4	Russell Jacobs	b: Aft. 1965		
4	Tommy Keith Jacobs	b: Aft. 1965		
2	Agnes Kattie Jacobs	b: 1905		
	+Frank Joseph Perkins	b: 1886	m: 1925	d: 1964
3	Lee Perkins			

Jacobs

        +Della
3   Dorothy Perkins
        +? Richards
    *2nd Husband of Agnes Kattie Jacobs:
        +Sidney Lafleur Sr.   b: 1913   m: 1936
3   Sidney Lafleur Jr.

16. Janssen, Arnold Joseph:
Arnold Joseph Janssen b: 1868 d: 1956 from Birgden was the son of Mathias Cornelius Janssen b: 1829 d: ? and Barbara LeClerc. He married in 1903 to Elizabeth Klein b: 1881 d: 1974 from Busenberg, who is the daughter of Peter Klein, Sr. b: 1831 d: 1917 and Odilia Wegmann b: 1839 d: 1921.

2		Peter Joseph Janssen	b: 1903		d: 1986
		+Agnes Leger	b: 1917	m: 1933	
	3	Peter Joseph Janssen	b: 1934		d: 1942
	3	Judith Frances Janssen	b: 1943		
		+Thomas Ellyan Vincent	b: 3/2/1939	m: 1967	
	3	John Ray Janssen	b: 1946		
		+Sharon Lee Davidson Kampa	b: 9/18/1945	m: 1967	
		4	Jordan Joseph Janssen	b: 9/18/1984	
		4	Redmond Thomas Janssen	b: 9/29/1986	
	3	Janice Cheryl Janssen	b: 3/26/1951		
		+Michael Sperry	b: 1946		
		4	Christopher Peter Sperry	b: 3/10/1969	
			+Dacquiri Dee Bolch		m: 8/19/1995
		4	Amy Dineen Sperry	b: 9/2/1970	
			+Edward Hans Porner		
		*2nd Husband of Janice Cheryl Janssen:			
		+Ronald Vernon Overman, Sr.	b: 1951	m: 1976	
		4	Ronald Vernon Overman, Jr.	b: 7/19/1977	
		4	Sonja Reneé Overman		b: 9/20/1981
		*3rd Husband of Janice Cheryl Janssen:			
		+Ike Bartkowick	b: 3/10/1945	m: 1985	
	3	Veronica Louise Janssen	b: 1956		
2		Franz Joseph Janssen	b: 1907		d: 1976
		+Lela Miller	b: 1923	m: 1956	

Janssen

	3	Carmen Ruth Janssen	b: 1959		
2		Marie Odelia Janssen	b: 1909		d: 1975
		+David Luther Allen	b: 1893	m: 1936	d: 1968
	3	Thomas Daniel Allen	b: 1948		
		+Jacqueline Marie Benoit	b: 1954	m: 1970	
2		George Martin Janssen	b: 1912		d: 1985
		+Mary Frances Denton	b: 1923	m: 1940	
		*2nd Wife of George Martin Janssen:			
		+Irene Edith Faulk	b: 1915	m: 1954	
	3	George Martin Janssen, Jr	b: 1942		
		+Beatrice Darleen Broussard	b: 1944	m: 1962	
	4	Corby Layne Janssen	b: 5/27/1963		
	3	Marilyn Sue Janssen	b: 1949		
		+Williams Huggins	b: 1947		
2		Barbara Elizabeth Janssen	b: 1923		
		+Carlson Joseph Doucet	b: 1921	m: 1946	d: 1987
	3	Carl James Doucet	b: 1951		d: 1951
	3	Carolyn Ann Doucet	b: 1955		
		+Michael Bruce	b: 1956	m: 1979	
	3	Garry John Doucet	b: 1958		
2		Daniel Joseph Janssen	b: 1926		d: 3/8/1991
		+Patricia Ruth Miller	b: 1933	m: 1956	
	3	Bethany Anne Janssen	b: 11/19/1956		
		+Wendell James Fontenot	b: 10/22/1955	m: 1/22/1977	
	4	Joshua Ebra Fontenot	b: 10/3/1979		
		+Leslie Summer Maynor	b: 5/7/1985	m: 2/21/2004	
	3	Stephen William Janssen	b: 10/3/1959		
		+Tina Marie Galley		m: 1981	

Janssen

4	Jason Anthony Janssen	b: 9/29/1981	
	+Julie Nicole Maynor		m: 7/17/2004
	*2nd Wife of Stephen William Janssen:		
	+Janet Gayle Zaunbrecher	b: 2/11/1965	m: 10/14/2004
4	Seth William Janssen	b: 1/27/1995	
3	David Todd Janssen	b: 11/24/1964	
	+Pamela Ann Addison	b: 5/1970	m: 11/24/1989
4	Breanna Paige Janssen	b: 4/23/1991	
4	Trevor Daniel Joseph Janssen	b: 7/6/1993	

17. Knipping, Joseph Hubert:

Joseph Hubert Knipping b: 1857 d: 1934 from Heinsberg was the son of Reiner Joseph Hubert Knipping b: 1820 d: 1898 and Maria Louisa Puhlmann b: 1815 d: 1858. He married in 1886 to Maria Sophia Leonards b: 1861 d: 1922 from Pütt, the daughter of Johann Wilhelm Leonards b: 1819 d: 1900 and his second wife Anna Maria Friderichs b: 1819 d: 1898 from Langbroich. (Maria Sophia Leonards is a half-sister of Maria Helena Leonards, who married Nicholas Joseph Zaunbrecher (see Zaunbrecher family), and sisters to the Leonards brothers (see all the Leonards families).

2		Reiner Hubert Knipping	b: 1887		d: 1965
		+Rosa Hynson	b: 1887	m: 1916	
2		William Joseph Knipping	b: 1888		d: 1888
2		Deceased Infant Knipping	b: 1889		d: 1889
2		Helena Augusta Knipping	b: 1892		d: 1893
2		Charles Joseph Knipping	b: 8/22/1895		d: 1896
2		Joseph William Knipping	b: 1896		d: 1988
		+Anna Alleman	b: 1896	m: 1924	
	3	Mercedes Blythe Knipping	b: 1926		
		+Marius Mercier Hubbell	b: 1921	m: 1942	d: 1982
		*2nd Husband of Mercedes Blythe Knipping:			
		+George W. Britt	b: 1925	m: 1987	
	3	Carl George Knipping	b: 1928		
		+Betty Louise Spencer	b: 1927	m: 1949	
2		Henry Joseph Knipping	b: 1898		d: 1945
		+Lottie Kessler	b: 1900	m: 1926	d: 1981
2		Anna Bertha Knipping	b: 1904		d: 1999
		+Oscar Louis (Paco) Borne	b: 1901	m: 1925	d: 1984
	3	Gloria Joyce Borne	b: 1926		d: 1993
		+Aaron Perrodin	b: 1923	m: 1947	d: 2005
	4	Stephanie Perrodin			
	4	Trina Perrodin			

Knipping

3		Oscar Louis Borne, Jr.	b: 1928		d: 1991
		+Valrie Ann Guidry	b: 1927	m: 1948	
	4	Randall Louis Borne	b: 9/16/1949		
		+Pricilla Ann Lavergne	b: 8/25/1949	m: 9/21/1968	
	4	David Henry Borne	b: 1/15/1952		
		+Brenda Angelle		m: 1974	
		*2nd Wife of David Henry Borne:			
		+Judy Taggare		m: 9/1980	
		*3rd Wife of David Henry Borne:			
		+Laura Green		m: 4/13/2002	
	4	Cynthia Ann Borne	b: 5/30/1957		
		+Marcus Anthony Boudreaux	b: 4/3/1955	m: 8/9/1975	
		*2nd Husband of Cynthia Ann Borne:			
		+Fred Artin Marcantel	b: 7/16/1957	m: 10/20/1989	
	4	Oscar Louis Borne III	b: 1/5/1962		
		+Stephanie Fleffin		m: 6/1981	
		*2nd Wife of Oscar Louis Borne III:			
		+Cathy Harris		m: 6/1994	
3		Carol Richard Borne	b: 1930		d: 6/10/1989
		+Dorothy Ann Guidry	b: 1931	m: 1951	d: 1998
	4	Melissa Ann Borne	b: 7/8/1953		
		+Rick Davis			
	4	Bryan Borne	b: 2/14/1957		
	4	Carol Annette Borne	b: 11/10/1959		
		+Danny McAfee			
		*2nd Husband of Carol Annette Borne:			
		+Lynn Self			
	4	Angela Borne	b: 3/1/1963		d: 3/2005
		+Carl Giesie			
	4	Tobey James Borne	b: 12/1/1967		

		+Janice Michelle Buford		
	4	George Borne	b: Aft. 1967		d: Deceased
3		George Leonard Borne	b: 6/20/1935	
		+Patricia Ann Credeur	b: 11/20/1937	m: 6/22/1957
	4	Lisa Borne	b: 10/3/1958	
		+James Theodore Loftin	b: 6/2/1956	m: 6/25/1993
	4	Tammie Louise Borne	b: 1/1/1961	
		+Robert Benson Hunter	b: 5/10/1958	m: 1981	d: 1985
		*2nd Husband of Tammie Louise Borne:		
		+Lenis Cormier, Jr.	b: 8/13/1966	m: 4/27/1996
	4	Todd Patrick Borne	b: 2/1/1963	
		+Michele Fettinger	b: 11/23/1972	
3		Thomas Bradley Borne	b: 8/4/1941	
		+Sylvia White	b: 12/11/1942	m: 9/7/1978
	4	Melinda Ann Borne	b: 1/19/1980	
2		George Edward Knipping	b: 1906		d: 1967
		+Katherine Sanborn	b: 1914	m: 1935	d: 1990

18. Leonards, August:

August Leonards b: 1852 d: 1915 from Pütt was the son of Johann Wilhelm Leonards b: 4/26/1819 d: 3/10/1900 and his second wife Anna Maria Friedrichs b: 7/14/1819 d: 4/1/1898. He married on 11/29/1882 to Marie Olivia Fontenot b: 1862 d: 1915 from Grand Coteau, Louisiana, who is the daughter of Dul Fontenot and Mary Sanderson/Anderson. He returned to Germany and has no descendants. August Leonards is the brother of Maria Sophia Leonards (see Knipping family), Henry and Peter Joseph Leonards (see Leonards families below), and half-brother to Maria Helena Leonards, who married to Nicholas Joseph Zaunbrecher (see Zaunbrecher family).

19. Leonards, Henry:

Dr. Henry Leonards b: 2/24/1857 d: 3/29/1933 from Pütt was the brother of the other Leonards mentioned herein. He married in 1888 to Augusta Pfeuffer b: 1857 d: 1899 from New Braunfels, Texas.

2		Herbert William Leonards	b: 6/1889		d: 7/28/1915
2		Gertrude Leonards	b: 3/22/1892		d: 9/25/1974
		+Charles Arthur Wright		m: 1925	
	3	Henry Wright	b: 5/20/1926		d: 10/4/1986
		+Mildred Therese Murphy	b: 3/15/1927	m: Bef. 1986	
	4	Kelly Henry Wright	b: 11/9/1952		
	4	Dr. Palmer Patrick Wright	b: 3/28/1955		
		+Lizzy Enriques			
		*2nd Wife of Dr. Palmer Patrick Wright:			
		+Vickie Diane Voeller	b: 2/21/1952		
	4	Darrell Dennis Wright	b: 7/13/1956		
	4	Dr. Shauna Gertrude Wright	b: 1/17/1958		
		+Greg Chase			
2		Johanna Leonards	b: 1894		d: 1930

20. Leonards, Peter Joseph:

Peter Joseph Leonards b: 5/5/1859 d: 6/16/1924 from Pütt was a brother to August Leonards and other Leonards mentioned herein. He married on 3/9/1887 to Maria Josepha Gossen b: 12/17/1865 d: 1/18/1948, who is the daughter of Johann Peter Gossen b: 8/13/1815 d: 10/7/1882 from Gangelt and Maria Agnes Killen b: 3/3/1830 d: 1/2/1898 (see Gossen family).

2	Joseph William Leonards	b: 12/18/1887		d: 11/29/1888
2	Henry Leo Leonards	b: 7/17/1889		d: 3/18/1960
	+Mary Gertrude Olinger	b: 8/18/1891	m: 7/3/1912	d: 4/3/1978
3	Joseph Ferdinand Leonards	b: 3/13/1913		d: 7/14/1979
	+Alice Patin	b: 7/19/1914	m: 11/27/1935	d: 2004
4	Carolyn Leonards	b: 1936		
	+William Johnson		m: 1955	
	*2nd Husband of Carolyn Leonards:			
	+Jimmy Louviere	b: 1935	m: 1978	
4	Kathleen Leonards	b: 1940		
	+Richard Watkins		m: 1960	
	*2nd Husband of Kathleen Leonards:			
	+Milton Janise		m: 1990	
4	Jo Ann Leonards	b: 1942		
	+Phillip Watkins	b: 1942	m: 1964	
3	Ferdinand Joseph Leonards	b: 3/29/1914		d: 3/29/1914
3	Ferdinand Joseph Leonards	b: 4/12/1915		
	+Edna Mae Devillier	b: 10/18/1918	m: 2/18/1941	
3	Edmund Alois Leonards	b: 1/25/1917		d: 1/28/2006
	+Norma "Cookie" Ziegler	b: 2/25/1923	m: 6/25/1947	d: 1996
4	Mark Leonards	b: 1948		
3	Leo Charles Leonards	b: 7/28/1918		d: 1984
	+Mary Lee Dumesnil	b: 1/24/1930	m: 7/3/1950	
4	Mary Germaine Leonards	b: 1951		
	+Myron Ropp	b: 1954	m: 1986	
4	Leo Jerome Leonards	b: 1952		

Leonards

	+Anne Chappuis	b: 1953	m: 1973	
4	Mary Elizabeth Leonards	b: 1954		
	+James Bourgeois		m: 1979	
4	Bernadette Leonards	b: 1957		
	+Wayne Baronet	b: 1954	m: 1979	
4	Paul Joseph Leonards	b: 1959		
	+Lillie Harmon	b: 1959	m: 1978	
4	Mildred Leonards	b: 1962		
	+Terry D. Miller	b: 1965	m: 9/10/2005	
3	Rheinoldt John Leonards	b: 1/5/1920		d: 2003
3	Clara Marie Leonards	b: 10/29/1922		
	+Joseph Clemens Wilfert	b: 7/30/1914	m: 12/26/1944	d: 2001
4	Leonard Wilfert	b: 1946		
	+Rita Thenhaus		m: 1982	
	*2nd Wife of Leonard Wilfert:			
	+Theresa Zimmer	b: 1951	m: 1996	
4	Leobelle Wilfert	b: 1948		
	+William Nevitt	b: 1947	m: 1973	
4	Paula Ann Wilfert	b: 1952		
	+David Winzer	b: 1950	m: 1974	
4	Marian Wilfert	b: 1954		
	+Gary Beauchamp	b: 1949	m: 1986	
3	Henrietta Marcella Leonards	b: 10/10/1923		d: 1984
	+John Norbert Gayle	b: 11/25/1918	m: 11/20/1946	d: 3/3/1961
4	John Gayle	b: 1947		
	+Rita Barras	b: 1949	m: 1976	
4	William Gayle	b: 1949		
	+Alma Johnson	b: 1948	m: 1976	
4	Philip Anthony Gayle	b: 1952		
	+Nancy Johnson		m: 1978	
3	Alois Jerome Leonards	b: 12/28/1924		d: 1/21/1925

Leonards

3	Theresa Hilda Leonards	b: 11/8/1925		d: 1/6/1926
3	Sr. Mildred Gertrude Leonards	b: 10/27/1928		
3	Anthony Phillip Leonards	b: 12/31/1930		
	+Mary Theresa Carrothers	b: 5/15/1934	m: 8/15/1953	d: 1/14/1979
4	Thomas Leonards	b: 1954		
	+Patsy Suire	b: 1956	m: 1976	
4	Michael Leonards	b: 1955		
	+Maxine Miller	b: 1957	m: 1978	
4	Margaret Leonards	b: 1956		
	+Miguel DePuy	b: 1949	m: 1978	
4	Patricia Leonards	b: 1957		
	+Charles Benoit	b: 1957	m: 1988	
4	Robert Leonards	b: 1958		
	+Cindy Boulian	b: 1954	m: 1979	
4	Christopher Leonards	b: 1960		
	+Eliany Hernandez	b: 1978		
4	Andre Leonards	b: 1961		
	+Gil Guerriero	b: 1961	m: 1991	
4	Maria Leonards	b: 1962		
	+Nizar Abudiah	b: 1962	m: 1986	
	*2nd Wife of Anthony Phillip Leonards:			
	+Pamela Marie Mouton	b: 8/23/1955	m: 8/2/1976	
4	Ferdinand Leonards	b: 1977		
4	Natashia Leonards	b: 1979		
4	Christina Leonards	b: 1981		
4	Ann Bernadine Leonards	b: 1992		
4	Elizabeth Leonards	b: 1993		
4	Rachel Leonards	b: 1995		
3	James Leonards	b: 1932		d: 1932

Leonards

3		Sr. Bernadine Benedicta Leonards	b: 3/12/1934		d: 1986
2		Maria Agnes Leonards	b: 11/12/1890		d: 7/24/1926
		+William Nicholas Hensgens	b: 12/26/1887	m: 1911	d: 10/4/1955
	3	Maria Josepha Hensgens	b: 1911		d: 1998
		+Gilbert James LeBlanc	b: 1909	m: 1934	d: 1999
	4	Cynthia LeBlanc	b: 1938		
		+Joseph Kratzer	b: 1936	m: 1957	
	3	Catherine Maria Hensgens	b: 2/8/1913		
		+Leo Ferdinand Heinen	b: 4/11/1909	m: 1/25/1933	d: 12/27/1959
	4	Gwendolyn Heinen	b: 3/19/1934		
		+James M. Stewart	b: 7/29/1933	m: 9/19/1959	
	4	Lowell Heinen	b: 1/2/1937		
		+Catherine Davis	b: 11/22/1936	m: 12/27/1957	
	4	Dr. Brian Heinen	b: 8/12/1943		
		+Jennifer Guillory	b: 9/26/1945	m: 2/22/1963	
	4	Janet Heinen	b: 10/22/1946		
		+Donald Martel	b: 12/13/1944	m: 8/26/1967	
	4	Ferdinand Leo Heinen	b: 9/8/1955		
		+Lori Gregory	b: 4/16/1959	m: 5/10/1996	
	3	Gertrude Regina Hensgens	b: 1915		d: 2003
		+John Baptiste Duplechin	b: 1907	m: 1938	d: 1963
	4	Baron Duplechin	b: 6/21/1943		
		+Carol Martin	b: 8/1/1944	m: 11/18/1967	
	4	Sharon Duplechin	b: 9/7/1946		
	4	Melanie Duplechin	b: 1/26/1949		
		+Donald Waters	b: 1/19/1949	m: 8/23/1970	d: 1/24/1999
	3	Charles Nicholas Hensgens	b: 12/22/1916		d: 9/29/1995
		+Leola Landry	b: 9/17/1917	m: 11/9/1938	d: 6/2/1999
	4	Charles J. Hensgens	b: 10/5/1939		d: 4/6/1985
		+Elizabeth Miller	b: 4/26/1940	m: 2/16/1963	

Leonards

4	Mary Gayle Hensgens	b: 2/16/1941		
	+Lynn Iverson	b: 1/12/1942	m: 11/25/1967	d: 1/18/2004
4	Frank Eugene Hensgens	b: 9/4/1942		
	+Christine Broussard	b: 7/25/1945	m: 9/12/1970	
4	Warren Hensgens	b: 6/1/1944		
	+Kathy Williamson	b: 10/31/1950	m: 11/27/1974	
4	Charlotte Hensgens	b: 11/6/1945		
	+Glenn Alan Valdetero	b: 9/19/1944	m: 8/8/1969	d: 2/4/2002
4	Beverly Hensgens	b: 1/25/1949		
	+George Dorr III	b: 4/18/1948	m: 8/7/1970	
4	Dennis Hensgens	b: 6/21/1950		
	+Valerie Moody	b: 9/1/1952	m: 4/19/1974	
4	Jacqueline Hensgens	b: 10/2/1952		
	+John Keith Lambousy	b: 1/6/1951	m: 5/18/1973	
4	Gretchen Hensgens	b: 1/29/1957		
	+Cleveland Jackson Harrelson	b: 10/18/1956	m: 6/9/1990	
4	Geralyn Christine Hensgens	b: 3/18/1958		
	+Robert J. Vidrine	b: 12/4/1956	m: 1/6/1978	
3	Agnes Helen Hensgens	b: 1918		d: 1999
	+Sterling Morris Boudreaux	b: 1914	m: 1938	d: 3/1993
4	Sandra Boudreaux	b: 1943		
	+Merlin Pritchard	b: 1941	m: 1981	
4	Sterling Morris Boudreaux, Jr.	b: 1947		
	+Dora Autin	b: 1949		
4	Nancy Anne Boudreaux	b: 1953		
3	Maria Christine Hensgens	b: 1919		d: 8/9/2006
	+Thomas Alvin Chisholm, Jr.	b: 1918	m: 1940	d: 1991

Leonards

4	[2] Thomas Alvin Chisholm III	b: 7/6/1941		
	+[1] Lucille Rose Leonards	b: 8/17/1942	m: 9/17/1966	
3	Annie Dorothy Hensgens	b: 1922		d: 2001
	+Cecil Joseph Hundley	b: 1922	m: 1949	d: 2002
4	William Kelly Hundley	b: 10/27/1950		
	+Marian Trahan			
4	Deborah Hundley	b: 2/10/1952		
	+Fred Stafford	b: 4/16/1952	m: 8/4/1973	
4	Nicholas Hundley	b: 4/12/1955		
	+Clara Cobena	b: 6/24/1955	m: 1/20/1973	
4	Douglas Hundley	b: 7/31/1956		
	+Cathy Moody	b: 11/30/1956	m: 5/30/1974	
4	James Patrick "Jimbo" Hundley	b: 8/3/1959		
	+Cathy Cook	b: 12/13/1959	m: 1/8/1982	
4	Michael Charles Hundley	b: 5/9/1962		
	+Katherine Claire John	b: 1/18/1963	m: 12/29/1984	
4	Rosemary Hundley	b: 2/28/1966		
	+Randy Minch	b: 8/4/1955	m: 4/2/2001	
3	Louise Cecile Hensgens	b: 1/24/1924		
	+Gerard Lumodon Foley	b: 12/10/1920	m: 1945	d: 4/9/2005
4	Judith Foley	b: 7/25/1946		
	+Bob King	b: 11/8/1930	m: 7/12/1990	
4	Donna Foley	b: 4/16/1949		
4	Gerard Foley	b: 6/30/1950		
	+Susan Alexander	b: 4/14/1957	m: 12/23/2005	
4	Colleen Foley	b: 9/24/1952		
	+Randy Peacock	b: 6/5/1951	m: 2/2/1974	
4	Nichola Foley	b: 10/12/1953		
	+Darryll Lockridge	b: 2/13/1949	m: 12/30/1977	

Leonards

4	Mary Faith Foley	b: 5/7/1956		
	+Arlie Telschow	b: 5/14/1953	m: 12/30/1977	
4	Brigid Foley	b: 5/23/1958		
4	JoBeth Foley	b: 11/18/1959		
	+Doug McLaughlin	b: 9/11/1957	m: 8/24/1985	
3	Nicholas Louis Hensgens	b: 1925		
	+Doris Cecile Landry	b: 1927	m: 1946	
4	Richard Hensgens	b: 1947		
4	Dale Hensgens	b: 1949		
	+Christina Baham	b: 1955	m: 1976	
4	Sheila Hensgens	b: 1951		
	+Calvin Hargrave	b: 1950	m: 1973	
4	Keith Hensgens	b: 1954		
	+Melanie Trahan	b: 1956	m: 1976	
2	Charles Joseph Leonards	b: 2/3/1892		d: 9/23/1945
	+Maria Walburga Thevis	b: 12/20/1893	m: 1915	d: 10/20/1994
3	Gerhard Joseph Leonards	b: 10/21/1916		d: 2/20/1973
	+Victoria Ann Schatzle	b: 12/9/1921	m: 11/27/1940	
4	Fr. Martin Charles Leonards	b: 1/8/1942		
4	Theresa Ann Leonards	b: 1/9/1944		d: 6/15/1993
	+Alfred Matthew LeBlanc	b: 11/9/1938	m: 7/15/1972	
4	Charles Gerhard Leonards	b: 2/20/1946		d: 1/6/1997
4	Cecile Louise Leonards	b: 7/14/1948		
4	Barbara Mary Leonards	b: 5/12/1951		d: 6/21/2003
4	Jane Frances Leonards	b: 3/30/1954		
3	Josephine Anna Leonards	b: 2/16/1920		d: 3/14/1992
	+Anthony Joseph Ohlenforst	b: 6/28/1916	m: 1/31/1940	d: 8/26/1974
4	Juliana Ohlenforst	b: 1942		d: 9/6/1998

Leonards

	+Clyde W. Hoffpauir			
3	Agnes Elizabeth Leonards	b: 11/5/1921		
	+William Henry Habetz	b: 5/18/1918	m: 2/13/1946	
4	Carl William Habetz	b: 9/5/1951		
	+Deborah M. Darbonne		m: 1/12/1971	
4	Ronald Hubert Habetz	b: 4/2/1953		
	+Colleen Kennedy		m: 2/2/1974	
	*2nd Wife of Ronald Hubert Habetz:			
	+Deanna Faye Darbonne		m: 11/19/1993	
4	Marilyn Agnes Habetz	b: 1/28/1955		
4	David Wayne Habetz	b: 2/14/1956		
	+Andrea Elizabeth Bruce		m: 4/5/1975	
4	Janelle Mary Habetz	b: 10/30/1958		
	+Kenneth "Ted" Bruce		m: 4/21/1979	
4	Richard Joseph Habetz	b: 11/26/1959		
	+Darlene Tugwell		m: 1/22/1983	
4	Gregory Anthony Habetz	b: 9/1/1961		d: 9/5/1991
	+Deanna Faye Darbonne		m: 12/18/1982	
4	Loretta Ann Habetz	b: 12/29/1965		
	+Johnny Ray Darbonne, Jr.		m: 11/25/1989	
3	Margaret Mary Leonards	b: 7/15/1923		
	+Ambrose Joseph Olinger	b: 6/26/1923	m: 11/27/1946	
4	Charlene Anne Olinger	b: 1954		
	+Michael Olan Reynolds	b: 1955	m: 1980	
4	Gerard Joseph Olinger	b: 1955		

Leonards

		+Debbie Elizabeth Moreau	b: 1957	m: 1975	
	4	Dale Edward Olinger	b: 1958		
	4	Susan Marie Olinger	b: 1962		
	4	Laura Catherine Olinger	b: 1964		
		+Timothy Neal Burley	b: 1960	m: 1995	
	4	John Francis Olinger	b: 1965		
		+Leslie Michelle Johnson	b: 1965	m: 1995	
2		Lawrence Joseph Leonards	b: 2/24/1893		d: 8/5/1945
		+Elizabeth Augusta Zaunbrecher	b: 1/11/1898	m: 2/1917	d: 10/14/1924
	3	William Joseph Leonards	b: 12/12/1917		d: 8/24/2000
		+Barbara Rose Bollich	b: 1913	m: 11/20/1940	d: 5/11/2002
	4	Audrey Augusta Leonards	b: 9/4/1941		
		+Michael Henry McBride	b: 9/2/1941	m: 10/26/1963	
	4	[1] Lucille Rose Leonards	b: 8/17/1942		
		+[2] Thomas Alvin Chisholm III	b: 7/6/1941	m: 9/17/1966	
	4	Stephen Norbert Leonards	b: 11/20/1943		
		+Susan Landreneau	b: 4/19/1945	m: 1/2/1965	
	4	Louise Regina Leonards	b: 1/9/1945		
		+Lawrence William Heinen	b: 10/29/1938	m: 6/27/1970	d: 11/28/2005
	4	Lawrence William Leonards	b: 2/4/1946		
		+Carol Dischler	b: 1/24/1945	m: 6/7/1969	
	4	Judith Josephine Leonards	b: 3/19/1948		
		+Cecil George Hoffpauir	b: 7/3/1946	m: 8/24/1968	

Leonards

4	Gregory Joseph Leonards	b: 7/31/1949		
	+Sandra Meaux	b: 5/15/1951	m: 10/14/1972	
	*2nd Wife of Gregory Joseph Leonards:			
	+Vickie LeBlanc	b: 12/26/1950	m: 5/19/1984	
4	Albert Joseph Leonards	b: 9/12/1950		
	+Brenda Chauvin	b: 9/17/1951	m: 5/20/1972	
4	Alfred John Leonards	b: 9/12/1950		
4	William Joseph Leonards II	b: 12/12/1952		
	+Barbara Ann Zaunbrecher	b: 7/8/1949	m: 6/28/1975	
3	Josephine Leonards	b: 3/26/1919		d: 1/23/2002
	+Herman Aloyious Cramer	b: 12/5/1911		d: 11/10/1966
4	Lawrence Aloyious Cramer	b: 9/12/1941		
	+Mary Magdalene Reiners	b: 3/31/1944	m: 6/11/1963	
4	Louis Edward Cramer	b: 2/10/1943		
	+Katherine Carlson	b: 7/4/1945	m: 6/3/1973	
3	Rita Helen Leonards	b: 12/27/1920		
3	Norbert Nicholas Leonards	b: 9/12/1922		d: 4/13/1945
3	Vincent Carl Leonards	b: 9/24/1924		d: 12/30/1998
	+Thelma "Tillie" Zaunbrecher	b: 7/30/1926	m: 1949	
4	Norbert Leonards	b: 9/24/1952		
	+Vicki Broussard	b: 4/11/1954	m: 9/24/1972	
	*2nd Wife of Lawrence Joseph Leonards:			
	+Maria Anna Zaunbrecher	b: 11/1/1903	m: 6/15/1926	d: 9/4/1984
3	Raymond William Leonards	b: 1/19/1929		d: 4/22/1992
	+Louise Augusta Theunissen	b: 12/27/1932	m: 12/27/1952	

Leonards

4	Ramona Louise Leonards	b: 11/27/1953		
4	Randolph William Leonards	b: 4/4/1955		
	+Annette Patricia Barousse	b: 11/27/1954	m: 12/29/1973	
4	Adrian Paul Leonards	b: 8/14/1956		
	+Geronna Diedra Martin	b: 10/31/1960	m: 6/2/1979	
4	Michael Anthony Leonards	b: 12/30/1957		
	+Cynthia Breaux	b: 10/3/1956	m: 10/26/1979	
4	Rachel Ann Leonards	b: 9/5/1959		
	+Randal Chris Arceneaux	b: 8/10/1957	m: 8/2/1980	
4	Joan Maria Leonards	b: 9/25/1961		
	+John Ulyess Mouton	b: 5/22/1959	m: 7/10/1981	
4	Raymond William Leonards, Jr.	b: 5/22/1965		d: 4/17/1977
3	Benno Joseph Leonards	b: 6/16/1931		
	+Arilda Gertrude Heinen	b: 3/16/1934	m: 11/15/1958	d: 5/8/1973
4	Paul Lawrence Christian Leonards	b: 9/13/1965		
	+Wynelle Morgan	b: 9/18/1964	m: 12/17/1988	
4	Anne Christine Leona Leonards	b: 8/11/1967		
	+David Brian Cagle	b: 9/24/1968	m: 3/4/1995	
	*2nd Wife of Benno Joseph Leonards:			
	+Margaret Funk	b: 7/14/1930	m: 3/16/1974	
3	Johanna Augusta Leonards	b: 12/15/1932		d: 5/5/1993
3	Henry Jerome Leonards	b: 9/13/1934		
	+Wilhelmina (Wilma) Thecla Hensgens	b: 11/10/1937	m: 1/26/1958	d: 5/21/2006
4	Reginald "Jude" Leonards	b: 10/28/1958		

Leonards

	+Kelly Cart	b: 12/15/1959	m: 7/3/1981
4	Janet Marie Leonards	b: 3/31/1960	
	+David Grotefend	b: 10/20/1953	m: 3/16/1978
4	Jeffery Lawrence Leonards	b: 9/20/1961	
	+Debra Doucet	b: 8/15/1957	m: 11/12/1988
4	Donna Joan Leonards	b: 3/13/1963	
	+Brent Sarver	b: 8/27/1966	m: 6/3/1988
4	Elizabeth (Beth) Ann Leonards	b: 1/20/1965	
	+James Simon	b: 9/16/1956	m: 6/7/1995
4	Susan Clair Leonards	b: 7/21/1966	
	+Michael (Mike) Allbritton	b: 1/21/1965	
4	Kathrina Louise Leonards	b: 12/17/1969	
	+Dale Vidrine	b: 6/19/1972	m: 11/1/2001
3	Dennis Louis Leonards	b: 5/24/1936	
	+Phyllis Helen Robichaux	b: 11/18/1939	m: 1/14/1961
4	Denise Helen Leonards	b: 10/24/1961	
	+Hilton T. "Mack" Dumesnil III	b: 11/24/1959	m: 2/23/1985
4	John Lawrence "Bubba" Leonards	b: 10/18/1962	
	+Susan Marie Doucet	b: 5/21/1962	m: 2/23/1985
4	Angela Marie Leonards	b: 9/6/1964	
4	Nancy Ann Leonards	b: 4/23/1967	
	+Jeffery Jude Istre	b: 12/9/1966	m: 2/4/1989
4	Donald Anthony Leonards	b: 12/24/1969	
	+Angela Kay Johnson	b: 5/6/1970	m: 10/8/1994
4	James Paul Leonards	b: 7/28/1971	
	+Suzette Lee Benoit	b: 11/15/1970	m: 4/12/1997

Leonards

4	Robert William Leonards	b: 2/14/1973		
	+Winona Marie Braus	b: 12/20/1974	m: 8/2/1996	
4	Connie Christine Leonards	b: 9/4/1974	d: 2/3/2007	
3	Wilfred Charles Leonards	b: 7/3/1937		
	+Elaine Credeur	b: 11/12/1941	m: 7/1964	
4	Lisa Leonards	b: 6/6/1965		
	+Johnny McClelland	b: 11/8/1957	m: 6/29/1989	
4	Lorraine Louise Leonards	b: 7/5/1966		
	+Kent Gabriel Fontenot	b: 10/3/1962	m: 12/23/1988	
4	Damian Charles Leonards	b: 7/10/1967		
	+Marsha Dalgo	b: 9/29/1969	m: 9/10/1988	
4	Sarah Ann Leonards	b: 9/18/1968		
	+John David Ducote	b: 5/1/1962	m: 6/3/1989	
4	Stephanie Marie Leonards	b: 8/26/1969		
	+Edward Anthony Bartow	b: 7/31/1965	m: 5/22/1993	
4	Joel Martin Leonards	b: 10/22/1970		
	+Christie Guillory	b: 12/21/1971	m: 9/8/1990	
3	Mary Ann Leonards	b: 12/10/1938		
3	Lidwina Josephine Leonards	b: 7/20/1940		d: 3/9/1941
3	Catherine Mary Leonards	b: 7/19/1944		
	+Dale Bernard Huesers	b: 3/20/1938	m: 5/9/1964	
4	Christopher Scott Huesers	b: 8/4/1965		
4	Chad Lawrence Huesers	b: 10/11/1966		
	+Lisa Olivier	b: 4/3/1971	m: 2/24/1995	

*2nd Wife of Chad Lawrence Huesers:

Leonards

		+Danelle Roach Burch	b: 8/27/1971	m: 8/5/2005
	4	Karen Anne Huesers	b: 9/30/1968	
		+Troy Dale Perry	b: 12/10/1966	m: 9/7/1990
	4	Julie Adelle Huesers	b: 11/25/1969	
		+Gregory Joseph Nolan	b: 2/22/1965	m: 4/21/1990
2		Maria Theresa Leonards	b: 6/7/1894	d: 11/30/1894
2		August Joseph Leonards	b: 9/25/1896	d: 5/3/1962
		+Dorothy "Dora" Beatrice Frey	b: 3/5/1905	m: 1923 / d: 10/14/1991
	3	August Joseph Leonards, Jr.	b: 1/26/1924	d: 2/26/1988
		+Beatrice Aloysia Olinger	b: 8/13/1926	m: 1947
	4	August Leonards III	b: 1948	
		+Myrtis Thibodeaux	b: 1948	m: 1973
	4	Don Edward Leonards	b: 1952	
		+Deborah Gayle Brunet	b: 1951	m: 1978
	4	Gene John Leonards	b: 1956	
		+Sharon Ruppert	b: 1963	m: 1982
	3	Antoinette Beatrice Leonards	b: 9/5/1926	d: 4/16/2000
		+Ira Lawrence Miller	b: 7/3/1923	m: 1947
	4	Beatrice Miller	b: 2/19/1948	
		+Roy Sattler		m: 8/6/1969
	4	Stephen Miller	b: 3/22/1949	
		+Sue Hallum	b: 1/1/1952	m: 2/16/1970
	4	Jude Miller	b: 6/21/1952	
		+Ann McGee	b: 3/10/1954	m: 9/30/1972
	4	Richard Miller	b: 2/9/1955	
		+Delana Marcantel	b: 9/30/1958	m: 9/12/1980
		*2nd Wife of Richard Miller:		
		+Peggy Doucet	b: 5/20/1955	m: 6/20/2005

Leonards

4	Arlene Miller	b: 12/3/1959		
	+Donald Trahan	b: 1962	m: 8/12/1983	
3	Anthony Leonards	b: 12/20/1928		d: 12/20/1928
3	Alberta Genevieve Leonards	b: 3/25/1930		d: 6/17/1975
	+Elmen James Bergeron	b: 6/22/1923	m: 1947	d: 8/28/2000
4	Elmen Bergeron, Jr	b: 7/13/1948		
	+Jan Baker	b: 8/21/1948	m: 11/25/1974	
4	Glenn Bergeron	b: 8/7/1949		
	+Mary Ann Burke	b: 2/9/1954	m: 7/1/1978	
4	Diana Bergeron	b: 10/17/1950		
4	Kenneth Bergeron	b: 10/27/1952		
	+Kim Burnette	b: 1/9/1954		d: 11/29/1991
4	Randall Bergeron	b: 5/14/1954		
	+Robin Comeaux		m: 11/1974	
	*2nd Wife of Randall Bergeron:			
	+Deborah Carona		m: 9/1984	
	*3rd Wife of Randall Bergeron:			
	+Kim Calendar		m: 9/1998	
3	Patricia Ann Leonards	b: 6/29/1933		
	+Adam Price Johnson	b: 3/5/1929	m: 1952	
4	Melinda Johnson	b: 12/1/1953		
	+Ronnie Valenta	b: 9/9/1949	m: 5/29/1977	
4	Mary Ann Johnson	b: 1962		d: 1962
4	Colleen Johnson	b: 3/5/1961		
	+Roy Van Gustin	b: 9/27/1956	m: 9/27/1981	
	*2nd Husband of Colleen Johnson:			
	+Didier Clay Ardoin	b: 12/29/1960	m: 2/9/1996	
4	Michelle Johnson	b: 6/9/1964		
	+Jeffery DeRouen	b: 7/25/1958	m: 1983	
3	Lloyd Phillip Leonards	b: 11/30/1935		

Leonards

		+Constance Claire Ledoux	b: 1/28/1937	m: 1957	
	4	Lloyd Philip Leonards, Jr.	b: 3/12/1958		
		+Shelia Manual	b: 10/27/1955	m: 9/16/1978	
	4	Denise Leonards	b: 7/29/1959		
		+Bernard Lebouef	b: 8/29/1959	m: 10/12/1979	
	4	Kimberly Leonards	b: 4/9/1962		
		+Kenneth Gaspard	b: 10/4/1960	m: 4/27/1984	
	4	Yvette Leonards	b: 8/2/1968		
		+Dirk Ortego	b: 11/15/1966	m: 5/11/1990	
2		William Joseph Leonards	b: 1/6/1898		d: 5/21/1898
2		Ludwig (Louis) Leonards	b: 8/31/1899		d: 10/30/1978
		+Maria Gertrude Dischler	b: 1897	m: 1922	d: 1965
3		Philomena Hedwig Leonards	b: 1923		
		+John Francis Ohlenforst	b: 1921	m: 1947	d: 1997
	4	Maria Goretti Ohlenforst	b: 6/20/1951		
		+Joseph James Kracher	b: 1/10/1948	m: 5/29/1976	
	4	Dorita Lois Ohlenforst	b: 12/4/1952		
		+Richard Dalton Comeaux	b: 9/24/1947	m: 1/13/1996	
	4	Jude Anthony Ohlenforst	b: 10/28/1955		
		+Gretchen Louise Gray	b: 2/4/1957	m: 6/27/1986	
3		Blaise Philip Leonards	b: 3/21/1927		
		+Bernadine Marie Habetz	b: 6/9/1927	m: 10/27/1948	
	4	Sylvester Guy Leonards	b: 8/30/1949		
		+Eugenie Marie Forstall (Cassie) Colomb	b: 10/14/1951	m: 7/13/1974	
	4	Blandina Gayle Leonards	b: 9/7/1950		

Leonards

	+Michael Wayne Zaunbrecher	b: 8/23/1950	m: 6/22/1972	
4	Ludwig Joseph Leonards	b: 1/30/1952		
	+Eula Theresa Devall	b: 9/8/1956	m: 6/22/1974	
4	Ignatius William Leonards	b: 9/6/1953		
	+Janet Esther Lawrence	b: 4/13/1951	m: 10/27/1979	
4	Gwendolyn Leonards	b: 1/24/1956		
	+Frank Dale Zaunbrecher	b: 10/8/1952	m: 6/9/1973	
4	Daniel Lawrence Leonards	b: 3/16/1957		
	+Rita Elaine Lejeune	b: 7/10/1958	m: 11/19/1977	
4	Caroline Anne Leonards	b: 9/5/1958		
	+Eddie James Fontenot	b: 9/2/1958	m: 11/18/1978	d: 9/27/1984
	*2nd Husband of Caroline Anne Leonards:			
	+Ellis Michael Trahan	b: 11/20/1959	m: 10/26/2002	
4	Joan Dione Leonards	b: 6/8/1960		
	+Robert Joseph Douget	b: 7/18/1957	m: 6/10/1978	
4	Marie Elaine Leonards	b: 12/10/1961		
	+Ronald James Fontenot	b: 1/9/1956	m: 7/19/1983	
4	Paul Brent Leonards	b: 2/21/1966		
	+Connie Marie Rabalais	b: 3/10/1966	m: 8/10/1990	
3	Edwin Joseph Leonards	b: 9/21/1928		d: 4/21/2007
	+Genevieve Augusta Frey	b: 11/11/1932	m: 7/9/1951	
4	Kenneth Stephen Leonards	b: 3/3/1954		
	+Reba Debetaz	b: 10/21/1954	m: 1/12/1974	
4	Keith Anthony Leonards	b: 9/2/1955		

Leonards

4	Karl Michael Leonards	b: 10/19/1956		
	+Terry Ann Grezaffi	b: 9/19/1957	m: 2/4/1981	
4	Kevin James Leonards	b: 2/20/1958		
	+Tammy Kaye Grezaffi	b: 9/26/1960	m: 7/7/1979	
4	Katherine Marie Leonards	b: 6/19/1959		
	+James Alvin Laurent	b: 5/19/1956	m: 10/21/1977	
4	Karen Anne Leonards	b: 3/15/1963		
	+Merle Gregory Bazer	b: 11/19/1957	m: 4/3/1982	
3	Eleanor Marie Leonards	b: 7/15/1930		
	+William Anton Braun	b: 10/24/1922	m: 10/26/1950	
4	Constance Louise Braun	b: 10/21/1951		
	+Robert James Wheeler	b: 10/4/1951	m: 7/1/1972	
4	Robert William Braun	b: 11/10/1954		
	+Janine Tara Matzke	b: 7/16/1962	m: 9/27/1986	
4	Cynthia Anne Braun	b: 3/3/1959		
	+James Lee Hasz	b: 10/9/1957	m: 9/2/1972	
3	Dorothy Clara Leonards	b: 4/1/1932		
3	Marcella Marie Leonards	b: 2/3/1934		
	+Andrew Lawrence Ohlenforst	b: 10/6/1928	m: 1/19/1955	d: 10/3/1983
4	Monika Joan Ohlenforst	b: 10/31/1955		
	+Kermit Pierre Arceneaux	b: 6/28/1955	m: 7/5/1975	
4	Stephen Charles Ohlenforst	b: 7/1958		d: 7/1958
4	Timothy Paul Ohlenforst	b: 1/17/1960		
	+Rebecca Sue Foux	b: 1/24/1961	m: 6/7/1985	
4	Philip Leo Ohlenforst	b: 5/13/1961		
	+Yvette Marie Richard	b: 4/10/1961	m: 10/18/1980	
4	Martin Louis Ohlenforst	b: 6/16/1965		
	+Dana Nelson	b: 7/25/1969	m: 10/25/1997	

Leonards

4	Marian Clare Ohlenforst	b: 12/17/1968		
	+Brian David Broussard	b: 1/9/1965	m: 4/28/1990	
3	Louis Anthony Leonards	b: 1/14/1936		
	+Patricia Ann Spell	b: 1/21/1938	m: 12/28/1960	
4	Trudy Ellen Leonards	b: 3/22/1963		
	+Charles Andrew Bergeron	b: 6/9/1963	m: 6/2/1984	

*2nd Husband of Trudy Ellen Leonards:

	+Duane Murray Huffty	b: 7/9/1965	m: 8/2/1999	
4	Heidi Ruth Leonards	b: 11/28/1964		
4	Kurt Louis Leonards	b: 9/7/1966		
	+Dana Lynn Chapman	b: 8/28/1972	m: 7/16/1994	
3	Leonard Lawrence "Buck" Leonards	b: 6/30/1937		
	+Barbara Ann Link	b: 9/17/1938	m: 11/27/1958	
4	Bryan Gregory Leonards	b: 2/17/1960		
	+Charolette Anne Moody	b: 5/26/1961	m: 3/28/1979	
4	David John Leonards	b: 11/22/1964		
	+Kim Soileau	b: 9/17/1965	m: 5/6/1988	
4	Gretchen Ann Leonards	b: 3/3/1966		
	+Karl Thomas Venable	b: 3/9/1965	m: 12/29/1983	

*2nd Husband of Gretchen Ann Leonards:

	+Thomas Alan Faulk	b: 12/10/1959	m: 11/6/1996	
4	Douglas William Leonards	b: 6/15/1968		
	+Julia Mary Guidry	b: 3/21/1964	m: 12/2/1993	
4	Julie Regina Leonards	b: 4/25/1970		
	+Stephen Mitchell	b: 7/13/1970	m: 12/29/2001	
3	Sylvia Jean Leonards	b: 2/24/1941		
	+Johnny Mack Frugé	b: 10/4/1939	m: 11/17/1962	
4	Janice Marie Frugé	b: 9/22/1963		

Leonards

		+Jeffery Charles Guidry	b: 1/16/1962	m: 6/1/1985	
	4	Suzanne Lynn Frugé	b: 2/18/1965		
	4	Sara Jean Frugé	b: 10/4/1966		
		+Byron Paul Stephens	b: 11/5/1966	m: 8/10/1990	
		*2nd Wife of Ludwig (Louis) Leonards:			
		+Ella Elizabeth Cobena	b: 1903	m: 1968	d: 1982
2		Maria Anna Leonards	b: 1/20/1901		d: 3/22/1975
		+William Frederick Zaunbrecher	b: 12/19/1899	m: 1/18/1922	d: 12/6/1972
	3	Paul William Zaunbrecher	b: 6/10/1923		d: 9/20/1982
		+Cecilia Augusta Habetz	b: 12/6/1921	m: 2/13/1946	
	4	Timothy Daniel Zaunbrecher	b: 12/12/1946		
		+Judy Cluchey	b: 9/20/1947	m: 5/29/1971	
	4	Godfrey William Zaunbrecher	b: 2/21/1948		
		+Anagail Mitchell	b: 1948	m: 7/27/1968	
		*2nd Wife of Godfrey William Zaunbrecher:			
		+Gail Cemer	b: 2/21/1952	m: 2/20/1981	
		*3rd Wife of Godfrey William Zaunbrecher:			
		+Kathleen Rae Reiftroffer		m: 2000	
	4	Gwendolyn Zaunbrecher	b: 1/8/1950		d: 1/8/1950
	4	Gerard Joseph Zaunbrecher	b: 1/24/1952		
		+Marsha Ann Sanchez	b: 6/1/1952	m: 1/10/1976	
	3	Richard Andrew Zaunbrecher, Sr	b: 11/30/1924		
		+Verna Mary Johnson	b: 12/18/1925	m: 6/19/1946	
	4	Katherine Marie Zaunbrecher	b: 12/29/1947		

Leonards

	+Robert Dennis Reischman	b: 5/30/1941	m: 2/22/1968	d: 5/7/1996
4	Edwin Jerome Zaunbrecher	b: 3/1/1950		
	+Neil Ann Puryear		m: 6/19/1971	
	*2nd Wife of Edwin Jerome Zaunbrecher:			
	+Bobbi Mckinney	b: 12/10/1952	m: 4/10/1982	
4	Richard Andrew Zaunbrecher, Jr	b: 12/18/1952		
	+Judy Rockel	b: 1/8/1952	m: 5/9/1976	
4	Alan Anthony Zaunbrecher	b: 6/23/1954		
	+Susan Lynch	b: 7/10/1954	m: 2/23/1980	
4	Don Thomas Zaunbrecher	b: 3/4/1957		
	+Susan Buonocore	b: 7/28/1959	m: 4/24/1982	
4	Anne Louise Zaunbrecher	b: 8/11/1959		
	+René Ledet	b: 12/2/1958	m: 6/19/1982	
3	Felix Leo Zaunbrecher	b: 12/30/1926		
	+Hilda Mary Broussard	b: 5/17/1929	m: 1/27/1948	
4	Thomas James Zaunbrecher	b: 11/13/1948		
	+Rosemary Giuffre	b: 11/4/1951	m: 2/24/1973	
4	Cynthia Louise Zaunbrecher	b: 7/14/1950		
	+Albon "Bud" Young	b: 1/2/1948	m: 1971	d: 1/24/1987
4	Robert Leo Zaunbrecher	b: 9/2/1951		
	+Jacqueline Stemmans	b: 9/12/1952	m: 12/23/1972	
4	Karl Isadore Zaunbrecher	b: 11/18/1953		
	+Lynda Kirkpatrick	b: 2/26/1946	m: 10/29/1977	
4	Michael William Zaunbrecher	b: 3/6/1957		

Leonards

	+Deborah Falcon	b: 8/25/1958	m: 5/30/1981	
4	David Zaunbrecher	b: 9/2/1960		
	+Lynette Landry	b: 4/16/1959	m: 5/25/1979	
4	Julie Marie Zaunbrecher	b: 4/16/1962		
	+Russell Champagne	b: 12/6/1959	m: 8/5/1983	
3	William Zaunbrecher	b: 4/13/1928		d: 4/13/1928
3	Mary Agnes Zaunbrecher	b: 2/21/1930		
	+Clarence Albert Fabacher	b: 3/17/1931	m: 2/4/1956	
4	Philip Jules Fabacher	b: 4/1/1957		
4	William Frederick Fabacher	b: 8/13/1958		
	+Emily Marie Seilhan	b: 4/18/1965	m: 1/27/1984	
4	Andre Paul Fabacher	b: 6/21/1962		
	+Nadenia Marie Louviere	b: 6/10/1963	m: 4/7/1990	
3	Theresa Marie Zaunbrecher	b: 9/28/1931		
	+Jean Edwin Broussard	b: 1/24/1926	m: 11/26/1953	
4	Stephanie Ann Broussard	b: 8/28/1955		
4	Claire Helena Broussard	b: 11/2/1956		
	+Earnest Hebert	b: 4/5/1956	m: 9/2/1983	
4	Donna Broussard	b: 11/15/1957		
	+Jack Arceneaux		m: 1980	
	*2nd Husband of Donna Broussard:			
	+Gary Nance		m: 5/22/1998	
4	Geralyn Christine Broussard	b: 7/10/1959		
	+Alfred Oscar "Trey" Beidiger III	b: 9/27/1957	m: 8/19/1980	
4	Brian Gerard Broussard	b: 9/21/1961		
	+Donna Menard	b: 4/19/1958	m: 3/1/1985	
4	Kevin Gerard Broussard	b: 10/30/1962		
	+Rechelle Simon	b: 8/19/1967	m: 10/22/1988	

Leonards

4	Karen Broussard	b: 10/30/1962		
	+Arthur "Rocky" Rabalais	b: 10/3/1960	m: 6/19/1993	
3	Josephine Ann Zaunbrecher	b: 8/6/1934		
	+Jerome Ronkartz	b: 2/16/1933	m: 8/20/1956	
4	Gwendolyn Ronkartz	b: 8/17/1957		
	+Harry Heinen	b: 6/8/1954	m: 11/10/1978	
4	Gregory Martin Ronkartz	b: 9/5/1958		
	+Dianne Hornsby	b: 11/6/1956	m: 6/28/1980	
4	Christopher Ronkartz	b: 1/30/1960		d: 1/30/1960
4	Stephen Mark Ronkartz	b: 8/26/1961		
	+Patricia Payne	b: 8/15/1960	m: 6/9/1989	
3	William Francis Zaunbrecher	b: 9/18/1935		d: 9/18/1935
3	Willietta Dorothy Zaunbrecher	b: 9/6/1938		
	+Urban Anderson Phillips	b: 10/8/1933	m: 8/29/1959	d: 5/18/1998
4	John Terrell Phillips	b: 10/31/1963		
	+Valerie Elaine Long	b: 10/30/1964	m: 11/10/1990	
4	Kelly Marie Phillips	b: 6/23/1969		
	+Jose Adamé	b: 6/27/1957	m: 3/19/1988	
3	Francis Martin "Bud" Zaunbrecher	b: 11/11/1943		
	+Hannah Casselman		m: 1963	
4	Dwayne Zaunbrecher	b: 5/24/1964		
	+June Lowe	b: 8/26/1966	m: 7/14/1992	
4	Douglas Zaunbrecher	b: 7/19/1967		
	+Marla Joubert	b: 1/7/1972	m: 11/18/1995	
	*2nd Wife of Francis Martin "Bud" Zaunbrecher:			
	+Judy Craighead	b: 6/16/1945	m: 2/9/1973	

Leonards

4	Amy Marie Zaunbrecher	b: 10/17/1974			
4	Martin Zaunbrecher	b: 8/11/1976			

*3rd Wife of Francis Martin "Bud" Zaunbrecher:
+Christine Schroeder   b: 7/25/1937   m: 10/19/1983   d: 11/23/1984

*4th Wife of Francis Martin "Bud" Zaunbrecher:
+Bertha Jane Doucet   b: 10/26/1941   m: 3/8/1990   d: 5/20/2007

2	Philip Joseph Leonards	b: 5/26/1908		d: 12/8/1973
	+Marie Johanna Frey	b: 1/27/1910	m: 1928	d: 12/31/2005
3	Gerald John Lawrence Leonards	b: 1933		d: 1989
	+Shirley Mae Nickel	b: 1935	m: 11/1957	
4	Sheryl Leonards	b: 11/9/1958		
	+Kurt Venable	b: 11/19/1958	m: 11/14/1980	
4	Gerald Leonards, Jr.	b: 5/21/1960		
	+Karen Pousson	b: 12/12/1963	m: 11/12/1983	
4	Velma Leonards	b: 5/8/1961		
	+Wayne Gautreaux	b: 5/17/1959	m: 2/9/1980	

*2nd Husband of Velma Leonards:
+Terry Faul   b: 2/26/1960   m: 12/29/1989

4	Donna Leonards	b: 5/25/1962		
	+Michael Lejeune	b: 10/9/1962		

*2nd Husband of Donna Leonards:
+Henry "Bubba" Spaetgens   b: 5/25/1962   m: 4/1/2000

4	Glenn Leonards	b: 5/11/1963		
	+Monique Leger	b: 6/5/1964	m: 1/29/1988	

*2nd Wife of Glenn Leonards:
+Ann Dill   b: 11/7/1963   m: 6/16/2001

4	Todd Leonards	b: 6/18/1964		
	+Priscilla Richard	b: 2/17/1967	m: 7/25/1986	
4	Marietta Leonards	b: 3/8/1967		
	+Doug Sikat	b: 10/25/1961	m: 7/8/1995	

Leonards

4	Stephanie Leonards	b: 7/12/1968		
	+Chad Miller	b: 2/8/1968	m: 7/8/1988	
	*2nd Husband of Stephanie Leonards:			
	+Lee Venable	b: 2/12/1957	m: 6/30/2001	
3	Elaine Lorraine Leonards	b: 6/10/1938		
	+Herbert Joseph Gossen	b: 7/20/1936	m: 6/1958	
4	Diane Gossen	b: 1959		
	+Clyde Comeaux	b: 1958	m: 1977	
4	Cynthia Gossen	b: 1960		
	+Ferdara Hubbard	b: 1958		
	*2nd Husband of Cynthia Gossen:			
	+Paul Gibson	b: 1953	m: 1998	
4	Philip Gossen	b: 1961		
	+Jennifer Colligan	b: 1963	m: 1986	
4	Saundra Gossen	b: 1962		
	+Anthony Cook	b: 1959	m: 1982	
4	Darlene Gossen	b: 1964		
	+Kent Smith	b: 1962	m: 1985	
4	Dwayne Gossen	b: 1965		
	+Carla Clayton	b: 1968	m: 1987	
4	Bonnie Gossen	b: 1966		
	+John Foreman	b: 1962	m: 1988	
4	Keith Gossen	b: 1968		
	+Julie Johnson	b: 1968	m: 1990	
4	Charlene Gossen	b: 1970		
	+Lynn Boone	b: 1968	m: 1989	
4	Paul Gossen	b: 1971		
	+Danielle Constantin	b: 1973	m: 1993	
4	Herbert Gossen II	b: 1973		
	+Nanette Monceaux	b: 8/20/1964		
4	Infant Gossen	b: 1975		d: 1975

21. Meyer, Johann Bernard:

Johann Bernard Meyer b: 1872 d: 1964 from Hebelermeer was the son of Bernard Heinrich Meyer b: ? d: 1891 and Anna Helena Berken b: 1846 d: 1926. He married on 1/21/1896 to Johanna Katharina Achten b: 6/18/1874 d: 1/24/1929, daughter of Heinrich Joseph Achten b: 6/19/1834 d: 8/5/1902 from Breberen and Maria Josepha Piepers b: 8/20/1833 d: 5/14/1904 (see Achten family). His second marriage in 1943 to Rosa Rine b: 1880 d: 1968, who is the daughter of Mr. Rine and Sarah Meranda Thrailkill b: 1854 d: 1930.

2		Anna Helena Meyer	b: 9/2/1896		d: 10/19/1988
		+Danial Joseph Theunissen	b: 1/19/1892	m: 1918	d: 7/2/1985
3		Maria Catharine Theunissenv	b: 12/16/1918		d: 10/14/1989
		+Ralius Paul Dupuis	b: 4/14/1924	m: 1949	d: 6/21/1993
	4	Ralius Paul Dupuis, Jr.	b: 1/20/1950		
		+JoAnn Chatlain	b: 5/25/1951	m: 1/12/1970	
	4	Larry James Dupuis	b: 9/2/1951		
		+Janet Trahan		m: 1970	
	4	Wayne Michael Dupuis	b: 7/21/1953		d: 8/30/1992
	4	Ray Dupuis	b: 2/22/1958		
		+Josette Habetz	b: 2/25/1961	m: 1/23/1982	
3		Joseph Peter Theunissen	b: 1921		d: 1956
		+Eva Gertrude Leblanc	b: 1923	m: 1947	
	4	Steven Joseph Theunissen	b: 12/4/1947		
		+Gail LaBauve	b: 10/21/1953	m: 2/23/1974	
	4	Lucille Helen Theunissen	b: 6/20/1949		
		+Joseph Preston Guidry	b: 2/1/1950	m: 7/13/1973	
	4	Samuel William Theunissen	b: 9/6/1951		
		+Kathy Sensat	b: 12/27/1955	m: 6/21/1974	
	4	Dexter Leo Theunissen	b: 10/28/1952		
		+Yvonne Cahanan	b: 11/29/1953	m: 11/7/1975	
	4	Mary Beth Theunissen	b: 10/6/1955		

Meyer

	+Karl Louis Boudreaux	b: 11/5/1956	m: 7/20/1979	
3	Annie Louise Theunissen	b: 3/21/1923		d: 3/16/1991
	+John Daniel Klein	b: 12/30/1924	m: 2/5/1947	d: 8/6/1964
4	Paul Charles Klein	b: 8/13/1948		
	+Sylvia Jane Lavergne		m: 11/18/1967	
4	Catherine Annie Klein	b: 12/31/1950		
	+Jimmy Joseph Frugé	b: 9/9/1948	m: 2/7/1970	
4	Susan Marie Klein	b: 7/7/1953		
	+Don Charles Wilhelmi	b: 10/27/1951	m: 10/31/1974	
4	Patricia Lynn Klein	b: 9/25/1956		
	+Jesse Chuck Greene	b: 3/17/1952	m: 9/20/1980	
4	Cynthia Louise Klein	b: 8/26/1961		
	+John Bradley Wartelle	b: 8/30/1957	m: 10/10/1987	
3	Joseph Hubert Theunissen	b: 1925		d: 1993
	+Audrey Hope Billeaudeau	b: 1929	m: 1949	d: 1992
4	Joseph Daniel Theunissen	b: 3/19/1952		
	+Janet Parr	b: 1/1/1948	m: 1/17/1970	
4	Hubert Bernard Theunissen	b: 8/25/1953		
	+Thelma Siddon	b: 6/30/1947	m: 6/23/1975	
4	Donald John Theunissen	b: 6/18/1955		
	+Judy Chandler	b: 12/18/1956	m: 10/10/1978	
4	Bill Hampton Theunissen	b: 8/27/1956		
	+Kathy Hogue	b: 8/7/1960	m: 12/1/1979	
4	Stacy Ann Theunissen		b: 7/8/1958	
	+Mark Walker	b: 8/6/1955	m: 8/27/1983	d: 10/23/1999
4	Michael James Theunissen	b: 10/17/1960		
	+Lisa Portwood	b: 4/19/1962	m: 5/5/1989	
4	Faye Ann Theunissen	b: 10/9/1962		

Meyer

	+Scott Brown	b: 3/7/1961	m: 5/19/1984
4	Joseph Hubert Theunissen, Jr.	b: 4/22/1966	
	+Davenderjit Jasuja Dimple	b: 12/7/1967	m: 12/6/1993
3	Mathilda Theunissen	b: 10/15/1929	
	+Paul Jasper Johnson	b: 6/11/1922	m: 1/19/1950
4	Kenneth Daniel Johnson	b: 11/3/1951	
	+Jeannie Bearb	b: 11/18/1953	m: 11/18/1972
4	Albert Michael Johnson	b: 10/31/1953	
	+Bonnie Rita Melancon	b: 5/27/1955	m: 3/12/1977
4	Helen Marie Johnson	b: 2/6/1955	
4	Brenda Louise Johnson	b: 2/8/1958	
	+Robert C. Hooper	b: 9/24/1958	m: 11/4/1978
4	Mary Augusta Johnson	b: 7/20/1960	
	+Wayne Bingham	b: 12/6/1946	m: 7/19/1987
4	Edward Joseph Johnson	b: 12/26/1965	
	+Tina Daigle	b: 12/30/1969	m: 6/9/1989
3	Hilda Helena Theunissen	b: 10/15/1929	
	+James Curney Haure	b: 1930	m: 10/1952
4	Kim James Haure	b: 10/2/1953	
	+Myrtis Ann Judice	b: 1/4/1956	m: 4/11/1974
4	Vanessa Ann Haure	b: 3/5/1955	
	+Terry Comeaux	b: 12/1/1952	m: 10/30/1971
4	Terri Judith Haure	b: 10/30/1958	
	+Ricky Guilbeaux	b: 3/18/1955	m: 3/14/1980
	*2nd Husband of Terri Judith Haure:		
	+Victor Matt	b: 8/20/1971	m: 9/15/1993
4	Pierre Haure II	b: 7/18/1965	
	+Theresa Reyes	b: 6/5/1960	m: 2/12/1988
3	Louise Augusta Theunissen	b: 12/27/1932	

Meyer

	+Raymond William Leonards	b: 1/19/1929	m: 12/27/1952	d: 4/22/1992
4	Ramona Louise Leonards	b: 11/27/1953		
4	Randolph William Leonards	b: 4/4/1955		
	+Annette Patricia Barousse	b: 11/27/1954	m: 12/29/1973	
4	Adrian Paul Leonards	b: 8/14/1956		
	+Geronna Diedra Martin	b: 10/31/1960	m: 6/2/1979	
4	Michael Anthony Leonards	b: 12/30/1957		
	+Cynthia Breaux	b: 10/3/1956	m: 10/26/1979	
4	Rachel Ann Leonards	b: 9/5/1959		
	+Randal Chris Arceneaux	b: 8/10/1957	m: 8/2/1980	
4	Joan Maria Leonards	b: 9/25/1961		
	+John Ulyess Mouton	b: 5/22/1959	m: 7/10/1981	
4	Raymond William Leonards, Jr.	b: 5/22/1965		d: 4/17/1977
	*2nd Husband of Louise Augusta Theunissen:			
	+F.E. Landry	b: 12/9/1920	m: 5/20/1994	
3	William Richard (Preacher) Theunissen	b: 11/30/1935		d: 1993
	+Anna Mae Simon	b: 1937	m: 1954	
4	Debbie Theunissen	b: 1/15/1955		
	+Ricky Matt	b: 11/16/1955	m: 9/14/1974	
	*2nd Husband of Debbie Theunissen:			
	+Patrick Nutt	b: 7/12/1966	m: 8/6/1988	
4	Jennifer Theunissen	b: 8/30/1956		
	+Saul Broussard	b: 9/22/1952	m: 8/28/1986	
4	Mitchel Theunissen	b: 10/9/1957		
	+Pam Wilkinson			

Meyer

    *2nd Wife of Mitchel Theunissen:
    +Roxanne Broussard

4	Connie Theunissen	b: 5/7/1961		
	+Charles John Trahan	b: 12/24/1960	m: 2/23/1981	
4	William Theunissen, Jr.	b: 3/8/1962		
4	Scott Theunissen	b: 10/18/1963		
4	Lisa Theunissen	b: 5/4/1965		
	+Ted Duplichan	b: 7/7/1959	m: 10/30/1987	
3	Frances Margaret (Poochie) Theunissen	b: 6/15/1939		
	+Edward Joseph Benoit	b: 3/28/1939	m: 5/19/1960	
4	Trudy Benoit	b: 4/19/1961		
	+Donald Hooper	b: 9/30/1959	m: 7/12/1980	
4	Troy Benoit	b: 3/22/1963		
	+Wanda Thibodeaux			

*2nd Husband of Frances Margaret (Poochie) Theunissen:

	+Melford Primeaux	b: 1935	m: 1979	
2	Herman Joseph Meyer	b: 1899		d: 1919
2	Henry Joseph Meyer	b: 1901		d: 1983
	+Elna Lafleur	b: 1906	m: 1927	d: 1994
3	Ben Anthony Meyer	b: 1/9/1929		
	+Virginia Rita Falcon	b: 3/11/1930	m: 4/17/1951	d: 4/16/1994
4	Susan Marie Meyer	b: 10/13/1952		
	+Richard Dale Latiolais	b: 2/28/1952	m: 9/18/1976	

    *2nd Husband of Susan Marie Meyer:

	+Steve Dollison	b: 10/14/1945	m: 11/15/2003	
4	Ben Anthony Meyer, Jr.	b: 9/16/1953		
	+Clair Emily Cormier	b: 6/27/1965	m: 5/8/2004	
4	Phyllis Claire Meyer	b: 9/4/1954		
	+Wilson Jean Hebert	b: 8/1/1952	m: 8/3/1974	
4	Dora Ann Meyer	b: 7/13/1958		
4	Cynthia Faye Meyer	b: 11/5/1959		

Meyer

	+Charles Earl Vondenstein, Jr.	b: 9/17/1958	m: 10/21/1978	
4	Billie Joan Meyer	b: 2/25/1961		
	+James R. Lewis		m: 12/27/1985	
4	Daniel Joseph Meyer	b: 11/27/1962		
	+Angela Reneé Deville	b: 5/15/1971	m: 12/29/1995	
4	Donald James Meyer	b: 2/1/1966		
3	Clara Marjorie Meyer	b: 8/12/1930		
	+Louis J. Simar	b: 11/18/1934	m: 8/5/1961	
4	Geraldine Ann Simar	b: 9/9/1961		
	+Daniel Ray Simoneaux	b: 11/5/1960	m: 3/5/1982	
3	Gerald James Meyer	b: 4/18/1933		d: 8/10/1951
3	Sylvia Marie Meyer	b: 1/30/1936		
	+Jay Istre	b: 4/21/1935	m: 11/8/1955	
	*2nd Husband of Sylvia Marie Meyer:			
	+Claude D. Cochran	b: 12/13/1935	m: 9/4/1991	
3	Anna Lois Meyer	b: 11/7/1937		
	+Francis Ray Lormand, Sr.	b: 3/23/1935	m: 11/23/1961	
4	Gregory Paul Lormand	b: 2/14/1962		
	+Rebecca Melancon	b: 11/9/1954	m: 12/20/1986	
4	Jeffery Mark Lormand	b: 3/30/1963		
	+Lisa Falconer			
	*2nd Wife of Jeffery Mark Lormand:			
	+Melanie Simmons	b: 3/15/1967	m: 2/8/1997	
4	Raymond Lee Lormand	b: 11/30/1964		
	+Tiffany Faulk	b: 3/12/1970	m: 5/16/1992	
4	Francis Ray Lormand, Jr.	b: 3/23/1966		
	+Michelle Doré	b: 3/11/1963	m: 11/5/1988	
4	Mary Ann Lormand	b: 3/31/1967		
	+Ricky Reed	b: 2/8/1966	m: 9/2/1996	

Meyer

3	Doris Mildred Meyer	b: 1/20/1940		
	+Robert Guilbeau	b: 2/21/1939	m: 6/4/1960	
4	Gerald Guilbeau	b: 10/18/1961		
	+Cindy L. Hebert	b: 1/3/1964		
4	Rebecca Ann Guilbeau	b: 10/10/1962		
	+Wayne Lanerie	b: 2/27/1961	m: 9/1/1981	

*2nd Husband of Rebecca Ann Guilbeau:

	+Kenneth Leger	b: 5/14/1957	m: 12/26/1995	

*2nd Husband of Doris Mildred Meyer:

	+Farol Wade Guidry	b: 5/14/1934	m: 4/4/1969	
4	Wade Christopher Guidry	b: 8/14/1972		
	+Naomi LeJeune	b: 1/2/1976	m: 1/18/2003	
3	Henry Joseph Meyer, Jr.	b: 2/5/1942		d: 6/25/2004
3	Lee Leonard Meyer	b: 3/3/1944		
	+Shirley Broussard	b: 9/20/1951	m: 10/28/1967	
4	Marcus Lee Meyer	b: 11/26/1970		
	+Rachel Bellon	b: 4/4/1971	m: 10/18/2003	
4	Lisa Ann Meyer	b: 3/3/1974		
4	Todd Allen Meyer	b: 8/25/1975		
	+Nora Nicole Leger	b: 8/20/1975	m: 2/11/1994	
4	Chad Jude Meyer	b: 1/30/1977		
4	Brandi Lynn Meyer	b: 9/15/1979		
3	Harold Phillip Meyer, Sr.	b: 12/7/1946		
	+Carol Lejeune	b: 7/15/1952	m: 12/7/1968	
4	Katherine Ann Meyer	b: 3/19/1969		
	+John Leonard Andre, Jr.	b: 6/27/1967	m: 11/24/1990	
4	Angela Ann Meyer	b: 11/10/1975		
	+James Breaux	b: 12/13/1974	m: 4/19/1997	
4	Harold Phillip Meyer, Jr.	b: 6/24/1971		d: 6/24/1971
3	Gerald Meyer	b: 1947		d: 1951

Meyer

3		Ronald William Meyer	b: 1/18/1949		
		+Jessie Lynn Hawkins	b: 5/5/1948	m: 8/2/1969	
	4	Alva Dan Meyer	b: 12/13/1969		
		+Sherri Goodknight	b: 11/5/1972	m: 4/12/1989	
		*2nd Wife of Ronald William Meyer:			
		+Loretta Mae Elliot	b: 12/3/1948	m: 10/25/1976	d: 10/25/1999
2		Josephine Meyer	b: 1903		d: 1993
		+Heinrich Leonard Habetz	b: 3/3/1874	m: 1943	d: 6/9/1958
3		Johanna Habetz	b: 10/6/1944		
		+Carrol Wayne Sittig		m: 6/29/1968	
	4	Kye Christopher Sittig	b: 11/4/1969		
		+Kenya Trahan	b: 1/8/1969		
	4	Jude Christian Sittig	b: 12/13/1971		
		+Anne Schneider	b: 9/7/1975		
3		Henry Clemens Habetz	b: 3/5/1947		d: 8/8/2003
3		Leonard Paul Habetz	b: 9/2/1950		
		+Brenda Rose Dartez		m: 2/28/1970	
	4	Traci Paulette Estella Habetz	b: 11/13/1970		
		+Nathan Joseph Leblanc		m: 6/25/1993	
2		Mathias Joseph Meyer	b: 1905		d: 1979
		+Maria Catherine Scheufens	b: 1912	m: 1932	d: 1988
3		Charles Joseph Meyer, Sr.	b: 2/8/1933		
		+Agnes Ruth McCown	b: 10/19/1938	m: 5/25/1956	d: 2005
	4	Anthony Wayne Meyer	b: 7/18/1957		d: 12/3/1979
	4	Darrell Louis Meyer	b: 1/13/1959		
		+Bernadetta F. Meche	b: 7/10/1957	m: 7/28/1979	
	4	Debra Ann Meyer	b: 3/5/1960		
		+Quentin E. Callaway	b: 5/18/1962	m: 9/28/1984	
	4	Kenneth Joseph Meyer	b: 9/13/1961		

Meyer

	+Rhonda Crochet	b: 12/25/1968	m: 10/12/1989	d: 1/1/1992

*2nd Wife of Kenneth Joseph Meyer:

	+Pamela Gail Hanks	b: 10/20/1972	m: 12/18/1998	
4	Charles Joseph Meyer, Jr.	b: 2/13/1965		
	+Halissa Barnes		m: 10/27/1989	

*2nd Wife of Charles Joseph Meyer, Jr.:

	+Djuana Gary	b: 8/9/1964	m: 8/3/1996	
3	Arnold Remy "Ray" Meyer, Sr.	b: 5/23/1934		d: 11/13/2006
	+Geneva Viola Louviere	b: 12/10/1935	m: 6/4/1959	
4	Arnold Remy Meyer, Jr.			d: 8/12/1974
4	Donna Marie Meyer	b: 9/10/1961		
	+Tony Boudreaux	b: 8/15/1961	m: 11/21/1980	
3	John Allen Meyer	b: 3/7/1936		d: 7/17/2005
	+Sandra McCown	b: 1/15/1947	m: 4/11/1969	
4	Allen Wade Meyer	b: 11/17/1969		
	+Melinda "Mindy" Duhon	b: 12/8/1971	m: 12/12/1992	
4	Shelly Renee Meyer	b: 11/14/1974		
	+Gregory Simmons	b: 10/10/1965	m: 5/22/1996	
3	Louis Theodore Meyer	b: 11/26/1937		
	+Jean Pitre	b: 8/29/1942	m: 12/29/1962	
4	Rachael Ann Meyer	b: 11/15/1970		
	+Neil Marshall Larriviere	b: 1/4/1967		

*2nd Husband of Rachael Ann Meyer:
  +Todd Benoit

*3rd Husband of Rachael Ann Meyer:

	+David Grant		m: 8/4/1989	
4	Louis Theodore "Ted" Meyer, Jr.	b: 6/9/1974		
	+Angelique Elaine Monju	b: 11/27/1979	m: 7/28/2001	

Meyer

3	Edwin Frank Meyer	b: 9/21/1939		
	+Bobbie Jane Caswell	b: 4/19/1941	m: 6/15/1963	
4	Angela Kay Meyer	b: 6/30/1964		
	+Steven Crispino	b: 6/3/1961	m: 1/7/1989	
4	James Douglas Meyer	b: 7/13/1968		
	+Angelia Eve LeComp	b: 11/10/1971	m: 5/2/1998	
3	Johanna Catherine Meyer	b: 2/19/1941		
	+Leland Cormier	b: 8/19/1936	m: 7/15/1962	
4	Stephanie Catherine Cormier	b: 1/7/1963		
	+Mark Allan Fontenot	b: 11/9/1959	m: 8/7/1982	
4	Leland "Buddy" Cormier, Jr.	b: 1/18/1965		
	+Carla Ann Denison	b: 1/11/1968	m: 11/20/2004	
4	Terri Jo Cormier	b: 7/28/1969		
	+Dowd Gemeth Dietrich	b: 11/16/1969	m: 5/29/1993	
3	Clyde Joseph Meyer	b: 4/15/1942		d: 3/17/2003
	+Alice Faye Miguez	b: 2/16/1948		
3	Frances Jane Meyer	b: 8/24/1943		
	+Clyde Coble	b: 5/8/1942	m: 3/8/1972	
4	Jacqueline Yvette Coble	b: 7/2/1979		
	+Dallas Steven Stark	b: 4/2/1979	m: 4/16/2005	
3	Matthias Joseph Meyer, Jr.	b: 5/25/1946		d: 9/29/1995
	+Dolores Ann Richard	b: 9/17/1945	m: 5/10/1966	
4	Farrah Ann Meyer	b: 11/8/1976		
	+Dexter Fountain	b: 2/9/1971	m: 8/8/1998	
3	Steven James Meyer	b: 11/16/1947		
	+Eloise Joan Richard	b: 1/15/1950	m: 2/14/1969	
4	Tara Yvonne Meyer	b: 6/27/1970		
	+Troy Hebert			

*2nd Husband of Tara Yvonne Meyer:

Meyer

		+Selwyn January	b: 2/19	m: 7/11/2003	
	4	Gisele Lynn Meyer	b: 1/22/1974		
		+Joseph Michael Weber	b: 7/12/1973	m: 9/11/1999	
		*2nd Wife of Steven James Meyer:			
		+Sharon Gayle Galley	b: 1953	m: 1973	
	3	Michael Lawrence Meyer	b: 4/1/1951		
		+Susan Matt	b: 10/30/1952	m: 10/17/1970	
	4	Kayla Renee Meyer	b: 8/25/1985		
	3	Thomas Larry Meyer	b: 7/6/1953		
		+Bridgett Ann Hoffpauir	b: 8/31/1955	m: 8/16/1975	
	4	Jill Nicole Meyer	b: 6/9/1978		
		+Ross Meche Key			
		*2nd Wife of Thomas Larry Meyer:			
		+Sarah Frances Kennedy	b: 1/2/1958	m: 4/19/1990	
	4	Thomas Lane Meyer	b: 1/16/1992		
2		Maria Gebina Meyer	b: 1908		d: 1929
2		Gerhard Aloysuis Meyer	b: 1910		d: 1975
		+Antoinette Dischler	b: 1911	m: 1933	d: 1998
	3	Melvin Meyer	b: 1941		
		+Audrey Dommert	b: 1940	m: 1975	d: 1996
2		John Kasper Meyer	b: 1912		d: 7/25/1987
		+Anna Marie Habetz	b: 6/28/1910	m: 6/7/1937	d: 5/9/1990
	3	Leonard John Meyer	b: 1/31/1938		d: 3/2/1938
	3	Leonard "John" Meyer	b: 3/28/1939		
		+Pearl Ann Watson	b: 1940	m: 11/26/1966	
	4	Stephanie Marie Meyer	b: 10/9/1968		
		+Chad Thevenot	b: 7/1966	m: 9/1999	
	4	Mary Elizabeth Meyer	b: 12/2/1970		
		+Thomas Barrett Harrington II	b: 1/1961	m: 5/2001	
	4	Maria Therese Meyer	b: 1/27/1973		

Meyer

	+Michael Brian Cardiff	b: 8/1972	m: 9/24/1994	
4	Johnette Rosa Meyer	b: 12/20/1976		
	+Jason Hanemann	b: 3/1974	m: 7/1998	
4	Laurie Ann Meyer	b: 10/31/1979		
	+Nakia Lantz	b: 5/1975		
4	Jerard J. Meyer	b: 7/23/1982		
3	Henry Leonard Meyer	b: 9/25/1940		
	+Jo Ann Zaunbrecher	b: 7/22/1944	m: 7/15/1964	
4	Conrad Meyer	b: 2/17/1965		
4	Rebecca Meyer	b: 12/16/1969		
	+Dale James Guidroz	b: 12/1962	m: 12/1998	
4	Gerald Kasper Meyer	b:	11/24/1971	
	+Monica Leger	m:	9/15/1993	
3	Mary Ann Meyer	b: 2/2/1942		
	+John Herman Reiners	b: 10/19/1938	m: 4/8/1961	
4	John Herman Reiners III	b: 8/26/1961		d: 8/31/1961
4	Cynthia Ann Reiners	b: 9/10/1962		
	+Fred Allen Schexnider	b: 10/1955	m: 9/18/1984	
4	Susan Ann Reiners	b: 7/3/1964		
	+Bobby Ray Kibodeaux, Jr.	b: 3/1962	m: 6/24/1981	
4	Lisa Ann Reiners	b: 4/2/1966		
	+Nelson Joseph Leleux	b: 7/1964	m: 2/10/1990	
4	John Constant Reiners		b: 9/9/1967	
	+Goldie Marie Monceaux	b: 5/1968	m: 7/10/1986	
4	Dwayne John Reiners	b: 11/3/1968		
4	Donna Ann Reiners	b: 3/6/1970		
	+Michael Gerard Legnion	b: 5/1968	m: 4/28/1990	
4	Karen Ann Reiners	b: 8/20/1972		

Meyer

	+Kevin Scott Hanks	b: 8/1969	m: 11/10/1986	
4	Kevin John Reiners	b: 8/17/1974		
	+Tekoah Anne Broussard	b: 8/1975	m: 2/19/1994	
4	Keith John Reiners	b: 9/19/1976		
4	Kristie Ann Reiners	b: 3/14/1979		
3	Margaret Mary Meyer	b: 7/31/1943		
	+Charles Herbert Simpson	b: 9/1942	m: 5/12/1964	
4	Timothy Jude Simpson	b: 1/3/1965		
	+Chantelle Alleman	b: 5/1977	m: 7/2005	
4	Cheryl Ann Simpson	b: 12/17/1965		
	+Jimmy Joseph Smith, Jr.	b: 1/1965	m: 7/10/1987	
4	Sadie Ann Simpson	b: 7/14/1970		
	+Glen Richard	b: 6/1975	m: 12/2002	
3	Joseph Bernard Meyer	b: 8/27/1944		d: 8/23/1989
	+Betty Ann Gould	b: 4/1946	m: 4/28/1966	
4	Todd Joseph Meyer	b: 1/23/1967		
	+Lisa Ann Desormeaux	b: 5/1964	m: 8/10/1990	
4	Stacy Leonie Meyer	b: 12/21/1968		
	+Darrel Billiot	b: 7/1968	m: 5/1987	
	*2nd Husband of Stacy Leonie Meyer:			
	+Joey Monceaux	b: 3/1964	m: 2/14/1996	
4	Leslie Ann Meyer	b: 9/17/1971		
	+Jeffery Wilfert Comeaux	b: 2/1967	m: 4/20/1996	
3	Kathleen Marie Meyer	b: 11/19/1947		
	+Larry John Viator	b: 1947	m: 6/6/1970	
4	Andrea Claire Viator	b: 3/5/1971		
	+Johnny Johnson	b: 9/1960	m: 4/2003	
4	Chad Anthony Viator	b: 2/10/1972		

Meyer

	+Amy Barras	b: 5/1975	m: 8/25/1995	
4	Michelle Lynn Viator	b: 7/1/1975		
	+Kendal Matassa	b: 3/1974		
4	Eryn Kathleen Viator	b: 10/26/1984		
3	Marie Antoinette Meyer	b: 12/19/1950		d: 6/8/1951
3	James Anthony Meyer	b: 10/22/1955		
	+Patricia A. Meche	b: 9/1962	m: 10/26/1991	
4	Lauren Marie Meyer	b: 8/18/1995		
4	Lindsey Marie Meyer	b: 8/1996		
2	Maria Frances Meyer	b: 1914		d: 1986
	+Leonard Alphonse Sr. Habetz	b: 1916	m: 1941	d: 1974
3	Henry Bernard Habetz	b: 12/19/1941		d: 1/7/1986
	+Laura Sonnier	b: 1943	m: 11/28/1963	d: 8/11/2006
4	Gregory Jude Habetz	b: 7/24/1967		d: 7/25/1967
4	Dwight Bernard Habetz	b: 1/4/1969		
	+Giselle LeBlanc	b: 8/5/1967	m: 5/16/1997	
4	Ashley Aline Habetz	b: 11/20/1981		
3	Leonard "Alphonse" Habetz, Jr.	b: 6/23/1943		
	+Carolyn Spell	b: 1948	m: 6/5/1965	
4	Shannon Claire Habetz	b: 9/28/1966		
	+John Guglielmo	b: 2/27/1965	m: 4/8/1989	
4	Jeremy Leonard Habetz	b: 10/2/1973		
4	Blanche Margaret Habetz	b: 2/5/1975		
4	Heath Leonard Habetz	b: 9/1/1976		
3	Alberta Habetz	b: 2/21/1945		
	+Johnny Winn Barlow	b: 8/9/1953	m: 2/2/1974	
4	Christopher John Barlow	b: 7/15/1977		
	+Heather Lee Higbee	b: 9/21/1976	m: 1/3/2004	
3	Charles Joseph Habetz	b: 9/6/1946		
	+Katherine Link	b: 1/22/1948	m: 4/27/1968	

Meyer

4	Charles "Chuck" Joseph Habetz, Jr.	b: 10/28/1968		
	+Sarah Mary Zaunbrecher	b: 8/22/1969	m: 6/23/1995	
4	Annette Christine Habetz	b: 11/2/1970		
	+Marshall Creigh Rosinski	b: 10/7/1969	m: 11/4/1995	
4	Jason Christopher Habetz	b: 1/4/1972		
	+Jessica Rae Guidry	b: 11/19/1973	m: 6/20/1997	
3	Lucille Marie Habetz	b: 4/2/1948		
	+Norman Jean Borne, Jr.	b: 9/15/1946	m: 6/12/1976	
4	Eric Scott Borne	b: 9/23/1978		
4	Melissa Ann Borne	b: 6/26/1980		
4	Michelle Ann Borne	b: 5/27/1983		
3	Catherine Helen Habetz	b: 6/25/1949		
	+Hugh Fred "Pudgy" O'Connor, Jr.	b: 3/31/1938	m: 8/21/1982	d: 3/4/2002
3	Henrietta Louise Habetz	b: 7/28/1951		
3	Ralph Mark Habetz	b: 2/16/1953		
	+Katherine Sudwischer	b: 1/16/1957	m: 7/15/1983	
4	Nicholas Mark Habetz	b: 1/13/1984		
4	Mitchell Mark Habetz	b: 11/22/1992		
3	Frances Adelieth Habetz	b: 8/10/1954		d: 2004
	+Dan R. Hooten	b: 2/4/1944	m: 12/4/1982	d: 1/2002
3	Claire Marie Habetz	b: 9/22/1957		
3	Pauline Margaret Habetz	b: 1/5/1960		
	*2nd Wife of Johann Bernard Meyer:			
	+Rosa Rine	b: 1880	m: 1943	d: 1968

22. Moeder, Joseph:
Joseph Moeder b: 1949 d: 1936 from Bavaria never married and thus has no descendants.

23. Neu, Jacob:

Jacob Neu, Jr. b: 3/25/1841 d: 11/25/1926 and his sister Anna Neu b: 1845 d: 1920 were the children of Jacob Neu, Sr b: 12/17/1813 d: 1874 and Angelia Festor b: 1811 d: 1875. Jacob Neu, Jr. married on 8/6/1861 to Barbara Zarn b: 1841 d: 5/31/1915, who is the daughter of Blaise Zarn from Ems, Switzerland.

2		Michael Neu	b: 9/29/1863		d: 3/29/1898
		+Mary Wissel	b: 10/10/1865	m: 1/1887	d: 9/14/1958
3		Rosa Mary Neu	b: 1888		d: 7/12/1946
		+Karl Christopher Schnellenburger	b: 1888		d: 5/31/1955
3		Magdelena Mary Neu	b: 1890		d: 2/26/1932
		+Albert Becher	b: 1888	m: 1914	d: 4/3/1953
	4	Amanda Becher			
		+Roy Kunkler			
	4	Ambrose Becher			
		+Mary Catherine Barkman			
	4	Harold Becher			
		+Lucille Tretter			
	4	Mildred Becher			
		+Arthur Balte			
	4	Roman Becher			
		+Leona Mehling			
	4	Irma Becher			
		+Frank Fisher			
	4	Anna Mae Becher			
		+John Kunkler			
3		William Jacob Neu	b: 1893		d: 1/26/1958
		+Mayme Scholastica Hoge	b: 1897	m: 1917	d: 8/15/1971
	4	William Jacob Neu, Jr.			d: 2/2/1960
		+Leona Waldeir			
	4	Michael Neu			

Neu

	4	Patrick Neu			
		+Pat Schum			
	4	John Neu			
		+Karen Snyder			
3		Regina Mary Neu	b: 1895		d: 7/16/1947
		+Frank Brackman	b: 1888		d: 1/11/1976
	4	Mervyn Brackman			
		+Dorothy Ballard			
	4	Renola Brackman			
		+Francis Nord			
	4	James Brackman			
		+Mary Lee Gardner			
	4	Edna Brackman			
		+David Eger			
3		Mary Katherina Neu	b: 1897		d: 1987
2		Barbara Neu	b: 12/24/1866		d: 1/30/1919
		+Ferdinand Olinger	b: 7/2/1861	m: 10/21/1890	d: 1942
3		Mary Gertrude Olinger	b: 8/18/1891		d: 4/3/1978
		+Henry Leo Leonards	b: 7/17/1889	m: 7/3/1912	d: 3/18/1960
	4	Joseph Ferdinand Leonards	b: 3/13/1913		d: 7/14/1979
		+Alice Patin	b: 7/19/1914	m: 11/27/1935	d: 2004
	4	Ferdinand Joseph Leonards	b: 3/29/1914		d: 3/29/1914
	4	Ferdinand Joseph Leonards	b: 4/12/1915		
		+Edna Mae Devillier	b: 10/18/1918	m: 2/18/1941	
	4	Edmund Alois Leonards	b: 1/25/1917		d: 1/28/2006
		+Norma Elizabeth "Cookie" Ziegler	b: 2/25/1923	m: 6/25/1947	d: 1996
	4	Leo Charles Leonards	b: 7/28/1918		d: 1984
		+Mary Lee Dumesnil	b: 1/24/1930	m: 7/3/1950	

Neu

4	Rheinoldt John Leonards	b: 1/5/1920		d: 2003
4	Clara Marie Leonards	b: 10/29/1922		
	+Joseph Clemens Wilfert	b: 7/30/1914	m: 12/26/1944	d: 2001
4	Henrietta Marcella Leonards	b: 10/10/1923		d: 1984
	+John Norbert Gayle	b: 11/25/1918	m: 11/20/1946	d: 3/3/1961
4	Alois Jerome Leonards	b: 12/28/1924		d: 1/21/1925
4	Theresa Hilda Leonards	b: 11/8/1925		d: 1/6/1926
4	Sr. Mildred Gertrude Leonards	b: 10/27/1928		
4	Anthony Philip Leonards	b: 12/31/1930		
	+Mary Theresa Carrothers	b: 5/15/1934	m: 8/15/1953	d: 1/14/1979
	*2nd Wife of Anthony Philip Leonards:			
	+Pamela Marie Mouton	b: 8/23/1955	m: 8/2/1976	
4	James Leonards	b: 1932		d: 1932
4	Sr. Bernadine Benedicta Leonards	b: 3/12/1934		d: 1986
3	Joseph Olinger	b: 1893		d: 1894
3	Joseph Aloysius Olinger	b: 9/15/1894		d: 12/9/1968
	+Anna Rosalie Bollich	b: 1913	m: 1947	d: 6/3/2006
4	Karen Marie Olinger	b: 9/15/1948		
	+Ellis Lesby Boyd, Jr.	b: 1946	m: 1968	
4	Janet Louise Olinger	b: 1/17/1950		
	+Kent Guy Hutslar	b: 1951	m: 1971	
	*2nd Husband of Janet Louise Olinger:			
	+Joseph Edward Landes	b: 12/30/1953	m: 11/12/1994	
4	Beverly Ann Olinger	b: 1/4/1951		
	+Louis Joseph Maloz, Sr.	b: 11/19/1947	m: 1/24/1970	

Neu

4	Charlotte Rose Olinger	b: 2/23/1952		
	+Oliver Kent Collins	b: 1951	m: 1976	
	*2nd Husband of Charlotte Rose Olinger:			
	+Kenneth LeBlanc	b: 8/11/1956	m: 12/9/1989	
4	Wayne Joseph Olinger	b: 8/4/1953		
	+Constance Anne Harding	b: 5/22/1955	m: 9/11/1976	
4	Charles William Olinger	b: 6/6/1955		
	+Jacqueline Marie Prejean	b: 12/3/1956	m: 8/30/1980	
4	Mary Regina Olinger	b: 7/2/1957		
	+Sidney James Broussard	b: 1956	m: 1982	
	*2nd Husband of Mary Regina Olinger:			
	+Phillip Landry	b: 9/24/1951	m: 6/11/1996	
3	Edward John Olinger	b: 1896		d: 1983
	+Regina Josephine Dischler	b: 1902	m: 1922	d: 1997
4	Ambrose Joseph Olinger	b: 1923		
	+Margaret Leonards	b: 1923	m: 1946	
4	Beatrice Aloysia Olinger	b: 1926		
	+August Joseph Leonards, Jr.	b: 1924	m: 1947	d: 1988
4	Irene Regina Olinger	b: 1927		
	+Ashton Simon Petitjean	b: 1914	m: 1951	d: 1979
4	Rose Marie Olinger	b: 1930		
	+John N. John III	b: 1929	m: 1950	d: 1983
4	Hilary Anthony Olinger	b: 1934		
	+Melba Dean Roy	b: 1937	m: 1955	
4	Mary Jo Olinger	b: 1938		
4	Ray Edward Olinger	b: 1942		
	+Johnnie Ruth Prather	b: 1941	m: 1966	

Neu

3		Anthony Dominic Olinger	b: 1898		d: 1974
		+Frieda Mary Boeglin	b: 1909	m: 1933	d: 1982
	4	James Ferdinand Olinger	b: 1934		
		+Shirley Schenell	b: 1937	m: 1963	
	4	Robert Andrew Olinger	b: 1935		
		+Nancy Gerber	b: 1942	m: 1961	
	4	Mary Lee Olinger	b: 1937		
		+Joe Meyer	b: 1931	m: 1966	d: 2002
	4	Jerome "Jerry" Alphonse Olinger	b: 1938		
		+Julie Krueger	b: 1941	m: 1962	
	4	Barbara Ann Olinger	b: 1940		
		+Gerald Herbig	b: 1937	m: 1960	
	4	Norma Jane Olinger	b: 1941		
		+Del Steinhart	b: 1941	m: 1962	
3		Clara Julia Olinger	b: 1900		d: 1975
		+Charles Barromeo Dischler	b: 1898	m: 1922	d: 1986
	4	Barbara Catherine Dischler	b: 1923		d: 1993
		+William "Bill" Reed	b: 1920	m: 1952	
	4	Charles Leo Dischler	b: 1924		
		+Carrie Mae Harmon	b: 1929	m: 1949	
	4	Cecilia Madeline Dischler	b: 1926		
		+Daniel Landry	b: 1925	m: 1950	
	4	Julia Theresa Dischler	b: 1928		
		+Sherril Thompson	b: 1928	m: 1957	d: 2002
	4	Alvin Joseph Dischler	b: 1929		
		+Theresa Martarona	b: 1933	m: 1958	
	4	Clarice Josephine Dischler	b: 1932		

Neu

	+Charles William Stewart	b: 1928	m: 1972	d: 1995
4	Ferdinand Louis Dischler	b: 1933		
	+Wanda George	b: 1933	m: 1956	
4	Robert Louis Dischler	b: 1935		d: 2003
	+Donna Sue Fast	b: 1941	m: 1964	
4	Thomas Anthony Dischler	b: 1938		
4	Marjorie Ann Dischler	b: 1940		
	+Robert Walker	b: 1940	m: 1959	
4	Michael Anthony Dischler	b: 1942		
	+Barbara Hazelton	b: 1948	m: 1973	
4	Carol Bertha Dischler	b: 1945		
	+Lawrence Leonards	b: 1946	m: 1969	
3	Rt. Rev. Msgr. Aloysius Odilon Olinger	b: 8/18/1902		d: 6/18/1969
3	Julia Rosa Olinger	b: 1904		d: 1991
	+Henry Peter Gossen	b: 1903	m: 1929	d: 1982
4	Henrietta Anna Gossen	b: 1929		
	+Julian A. Didier	b: 1928	m: 1949	
4	Gilbert William Gossen	b: 1931		
	+Florence Gonsonlin	b: 1935	m: 1955	
4	Ralph Alois Gossen	b: 1934		
	+Marcella Habetz	b: 1942	m: 1962	d: 1973
	*2nd Wife of Ralph Alois Gossen:			
	+Marjorie Devillier	b: 1937	m: 1977	
4	Herbert Joseph Gossen	b: 1936		
	+Elaine Leonards	b: 1938	m: 1958	
4	Donald Charles Gossen	b: 1941		
	+Henrietta Breaux	b: 1947	m: 1967	
4	Flavia Diane Gossen	b: 1943		d: 1946

Neu

3		Emil Franz Olinger	b: 1910		d: 1988
		+Mary Elizabeth "Alice" Laake	b: 1913	m: 1936	
	4	Rita Ann Olinger	b: 1937		
		+Wayne Anthony Jones, Sr.	b: 1934	m: 1960	
	4	John Lee Olinger	b: 1939		
		+Pierette Denise Berbeu	b: 1937	m: 1969	
	4	Mary Ellen Olinger	b: 1942		
		+Leo Sylvester Will	b: 1937	m: 1964	
	4	Joseph Aloysius Olinger	b: 1942		d: 1979
	4	Martha Jane Olinger	b: 1944		
	4	Stephen Linus Olinger	b: 1952		
		+Karen Lynn Collins	b: 1954	m: 1977	
	4	Thomas Paul Olinger	b: 1958		
		+Sandra Lee Benson	b: 1957		
2		Rosa Neu	b: 1874		d: 1949
		+Theodore Gregory Heinen	b: 1874	m: 1/13/1899	d: 1940
3		Placidus Joseph Sam Heinen	b: 1899		d: 1974
		+Anna Mathilda Dischler	b: 1900	m: 1921	d: 1989
	4	Dorothy Heinen	b: 1922		
	4	Henry Heinen	b: 1923		
		+Versie Fontenot		m: 1947	d: 1970
	*2nd Wife of Henry Heinen:				
		+Lilly Landreneaux		m: 1973	d: 1981
	4	Helen Heinen	b: 1925		d: 9/16/1991
		+Frank E. Landry II	b: 12/9/1920	m: 11/1946	
	4	James Heinen	b: 1928		
		+Bonita Rider		m: 1955	d: 1995

Neu

4	Lillian Heinen	b: 1931		
	+Norman "Bill" Barron		m: 1951	d: 2001
4	Beatrice Heinen	b: 1933		
	+John Burke Young	b: 1932	m: 1955	
4	Louis Heinen	b: 1935		
	+Marie Francois	b: 1945	m: 1977	
3	John Jacob Heinen	b: 1901		d: 1915
3	William Edward Heinen	b: 1903		d: 1982
	+Ethel Lafleur	b: 1908	m: 1927	d: 1972
4	Mary Rose Heinen			
	+Nathan Miller			
4	Dorothy Heinen			
	+Joseph Toups			
4	Alberta Heinen			
	+Edmund Frey			
4	Raymond Heinen			
	+Dorothy Lanthier			
3	Joseph Anthony Heinen	b: 1905		d: 1927
3	Jacob Martin Heinen	b: 1907		d: 1987
	+Renola Hebert	b: 1910	m: 1927	d: 1940
4	Marguerite Heinen	b: 12/23/1927		
	+Dewey Constantin	b: 6/3/1923	m: 1946	d: 6/28/1982
4	Donald Heinen	b: 1929		d: 1930
4	Martin Jacob Heinen, Jr.	b: 5/30/1935		d: 4/3/2005
	+Evelyn Cinningham			
	*2nd Wife of Martin Jacob Heinen, Jr.:			
	+Dottie Jones			
3	Leo Ferdinand Heinen	b: 4/11/1909		d: 12/27/1959
	+Maria Catherine Hensgens	b: 2/8/1913	m: 1/25/1933	
4	Gwendolyn Heinen	b: 3/19/1934		
	+James Stewart	b: 7/29/1933	m: 9/19/1959	

Neu

	4	Lowell Heinen	b: 1/2/1937		
		+Catherine Davis	b: 11/22/1936	m: 12/27/1957	
	4	Dr. Brian Heinen	b: 8/12/1943		
		+Jennifer Guillory	b: 9/26/1945	m: 2/22/1963	
	4	Janet Heinen	b: 10/22/1946		
		+Donald Martel	b: 12/13/1944	m: 8/26/1967	
	4	Ferdinand Heinen	b: 9/8/1955		
		+Lori Gregory	b: 4/16/1959	m: 5/10/1996	
3		Aloysius Andrew Heinen	b: 1910		d: 1916
3		Othmar Gregory Heinen	b: 1912		d: 1938
2		Clara (Sister Agnes) Neu	b: 1876		d: 1920
2		Louisa (Sister Flavia) Neu	b: 2/15/1879		d: 10/30/1970
2		Philomena (Sister Ambrose) Neu	b: 12/14/1884		d: 4/15/1976
2		Joseph Martin Neu	b: 6/9/1887		d: 9/4/1920
		+Anna Maria Heinen	b: 10/10/1884	m: 1909	d: 9/18/1962
3		Marie Josephine Neu	b: 8/30/1910		d: 1/6/1996
		+Robert Joseph Simoneaux, Sr.	b: 1910	m: 1935	d: 1952
	4	Lucille Ann Simoneaux	b: 10/4/1936		d: 2/28/1937
	4	Loretta Marie Simoneaux	b: 2/13/1938		
		+Ray Joseph Leblanc	b: 5/11/1937	m: 4/29/1961	
	4	Robert Joseph Simoneaux	b: 3/25/1940		
		+Shyra Marie Clement	b: 3/18/1942	m: 2/4/1967	
		*2nd Husband of Marie Josephine Neu:			
		+Kelly Zimmerman	b: 9/7/1917	m: 1954	d: 9/23/1988
	4	Diane Marie Zimmerman	b: 8/25/1955		
		+Jed Anthony Robinson	b: 12/2/1954	m: 11/8/1975	
3		Maria Walburga Neu	b: 3/6/1912		d: 12/13/1994

Neu

	+Giles Joseph Arceneaux	b: 7/17/1909	m: 1932	d: 10/26/1950
4	Giles Joseph Arceneaux, Jr.	b: 1/28/1934		d: 6/4/1986
	+Burdell Marie Laurent	b: 11/30/1938		
3	William Ambrose Neu	b: 12/7/1913		d: 11/27/1985
	+Esther Rose Patin	b: 6/13/1915	m: 4/18/1937	d: 6/5/1997
4	William Ambrose Neu, Jr.	b: 7/14/1939		
	+Alice Louise Powers			
4	Joseph Charles Neu	b: 7/28/1940		d: 1/30/2006
	+Amy Jacobson	b: 12/3/1954	m: 1/28/1984	
4	Jane Elizabeth Neu	b: 6/14/1942		
	+Gerald Lee Thibodeaux			
4	Thelma Rose Neu	b: 11/3/1944		
	+John Wayne Loper	b: 9/13/1943	m: 7/23/1966	
4	Mary Katherine Neu	b: 1/14/1948		
	+Dudley Scott Rollins	b: 12/26/1945	m: 9/10/1966	
4	James Michael Neu	b: 12/12/1950		
	+Karen Irene Tips	b: 12/28/1954	m: 2/9/1980	
4	Jacqueline Anna Neu	b: 2/1/1953		
	+Frederick Wentz Stumpf	b: 8/6/1948	m: 4/24/1999	
4	John Randolph Neu	b: 1/1/1956		
	+Kathryn Ann Smith Dipprey	b: 3/26/1948	m: 7/25/1972	
3	Raymond Jacob Neu	b: 11/12/1915		d: 5/9/1978
	+Zora Marie Lognion	b: 10/13/1927	m: 1946	
4	Charles Neu	b: 8/1947		d: 9/1947
4	Cynthia Neu	b: 11/30/1952		
	+George Munn			
4	Ramona Neu	b: 1/29/1954		

Neu

	+Tom Raise			
4	Barbara Neu	b: 9/24/1956		
	+Roy Olsen			
3	Rosa Dorothy Neu	b: 1/10/1917		d: 12/25/2001
	+Theodore Thevis	b: 2/15/1915	m: 1/4/1939	d: 7/2/2002
4	Jo Ann Thevis	b: 1/24/1940		
4	Louis Thevis	b: 1/29/1942		
	+Gail Rodrigue	b: 11/13/1949	m: 12/30/1967	
4	Benedict Joseph Thevis	b: 9/11/1943		
	+Deborah Rena Collins	b: 11/21/1953	m: 3/3/1977	
4	Mary Alice Thevis	b: 12/14/1944		
4	Mona Ray Thevis	b: 11/30/1947		
3	John Alexius Neu	b: 12/23/1918		d: 4/21/1996
	+Rita Credeur	b: 2/17/1925	m: 5/21/1946	
4	Linda Faye Neu	b: 2/27/1947		
	+Patrick Cormier	b: 10/8/1943	m: 3/18/1972	
4	Marlene Anna Neu	b: 12/4/1952		
	+Bryan Keith Fogleman	b: 5/12/1953	m: 1/8/1972	
4	Jay Anthony Neu	b: 11/12/1957		
	+Cherly Lynne Leger	b: 10/7/1958	m: 10/29/1983	
3	Anna Rita Neu	b: 2/9/1921		d: 12/26/2003
	+Nolton Herbert Menard	b: 9/29/1927	m: 1953	d: 8/5/1998
4	Connie Ann Menard	b: 6/11/1954		
	+Darryl Billiot		b: 12/24/1964	m: 10/7/1995
4	Susan Marie Menard	b: 2/17/1958		
	+Karl Anthony Henry	b: 12/7/1958	m: 10/14/1978	
4	Wayne Herbert Menard	b: 9/29/1959		
4	Debra Lynn Menard	b: 9/17/1962		
	+Fredrick Robinson	b: 2/27/1959	m: 2/12/1988	

Neu

2 Peter Neu
2 Agnes Neu

24. Ohlenforst, Johann Wilhelm:

Johann Wilhelm Ohlenforst b: 1841 d: 1925 from Nachbarheid was the son of Johann Peter Ohlenforst b: 1805 d: 1896 and Maria Katharina Rulands of Gangelt. He married in 1867 to Anna Maria Koch b: 1848 d: 1927, daughter of Johann George Koch and Eva Theresia Shram.

2		Eva Theresia Ohlenforst	b: 1869		d: 1870
2		John George Ohlenforst	b: 1871		d: 1939
2		Anna Margaretha Ohlenforst	b: 1874		d: 2/9/1918
		+Heinrich Leonard Habetz	b: 3/3/1874	m: 2/20/1895	d: 6/9/1958
3		Maria Katharina Habetz	b: 12/5/1895		d: 1/1/1896
3		Maria (Mae) Katharina Habetz	b: 1/27/1897		d: 6/1/1988
3		Gertrude Victoria Habetz	b: 6/7/1899		d: 7/16/1965
		+William Joseph Schneider		m: 1943	
3		Herman Joseph Habetz	b: 11/16/1901		d: 2/6/1966
		+[1] Anna Gesina Cramer	b: 1908	m: 1/30/1929	d: 2000
	4	Lawrence Joseph Habetz	b: 12/27/1929		
		+Marie Legnon	b: 12/27/1933	m: 2/10/1957	
	4	Leonard Joseph Habetz	b: 4/11/1932		
		+Deanna Dean Hoffpauir		m: 6/29/1957	
	4	Clementine Anna Habetz	b: 10/27/1934		
		+Huey Pierre Kirsch	b: 9/17/1935	m: 6/7/1958	
	4	Bernadine Anna Habetz	b: 2/7/1937		d: 7/6/1994
	4	Bernard Joseph Habetz	b: 1/19/1939		
		+Patricia Ann Molbert	b: 10/8/1939	m: 11/17/1962	d: 7/15/2004
	4	Albert Joseph Habetz	b: 2/10/1942		
		+Brenda Fay Ruppert		m: 5/29/1965	
	4	Robert Joseph Habetz	b: 2/1/1944		
		+Priscilla Vera Keigley	b: 10/13/1946	m: 7/15/1967	

Ohlenforst

4	Josephine Anna (Joann) Habetz	b: 1/28/1947		
	+Fredrick Ledoux	b: 8/9/1947	m: 9/4/1971	
4	Anna Agnes Habetz	b: 10/15/1949		
	+Thomas Michael Jones	b: 2/9/1949	m: 6/21/1969	
3	Anton Heinrich Habetz	b: 12/8/1903		d: 4/18/1935
	+Theresa Hensgens	b: 5/22/1906	m: 2/3/1926	d: 6/26/1995
4	James Leonard Habetz, Sr.	b: 12/13/1926		d: 2/18/1996
	+Mary Dean Breaux	b: 1/1/1929	m: 1/18/1950	d: 3/31/1989
4	Henrietta Theresa Victoria Habetz	b: 6/1/1928		
	+Raymond N. Gossen	b: 4/3/1927	m: 2/3/1949	
4	Leonard Conrad Habetz	b: 2/12/1931		d: 2/20/2006
3	Mary Magdalena Habetz	b: 1/5/1906		d: 12/30/1995
	+Jacob Herman Cramer	b: 4/7/1910	m: 1/7/1936	d: 1/28/1973
4	Anna Marie "Sr. Mary Clare" Cramer	b: 10/16/1936		
4	Angelina Maria Cramer	b: 1/5/1938		
	+Ralph Gonthier	b: 8/7/1934	m: 6/20/1964	d: 6/25/2001
4	Leonard "Jake" Jacob Cramer	b: 2/17/1939		
	+Catherine Gossen	b: 8/4/1939	m: 11/9/1961	
4	Barbara Anna Cramer	b: 12/18/1940		
	+Stephen Edmund Dubose	b: 8/2/1938	m: 6/25/1960	
4	Alberta Gertrude Cramer	b: 8/16/1942		d: 12/11/1993
	+Leland Paul Hebert, Jr.	b: 11/6/1943	m: 2/16/1963	
4	Bernadette Rose Cramer	b: 11/7/1943		
	+Douglas Guidry	b: 7/16/1942	m: 8/29/1964	

Ohlenforst

4	Anthony Edward Cramer	b: 2/20/1945		
	+Rhena Joan Vienne	b: 11/11/1946	m: 4/23/1966	
4	Michael John Cramer	b: 10/14/1946		
	+Yvonne Alice Prather		m: 9/4/1965	
4	Theresa Marie Cramer	b: 6/21/1948		
	+Lawrence Wayne Doucet	b: 2/13/1947	m: 1/31/1970	d: 12/21/1993
4	Loretta Clementine Cramer	b: 1/10/1952		
	+Glenn Michael Boudreaux	b: 12/27/1948	m: 1/8/1977	
3	Rev. Msgr. Leonard (Clement) Habetz	b: 1/21/1908		d: 9/16/1968
3	Anna Marie Habetz	b: 6/28/1910		d: 5/9/1990
	+John Kasper Meyer	b: 1912	m: 6/7/1937	d: 7/25/1987
4	Leonard John Meyer	b: 1/31/1938		d: 1/31/1938
4	Leonard "John" Meyer	b: 3/28/1939		
	+Pearl Ann Watson	b: 11/1939	m: 11/26/1966	
4	Henry Leonard Meyer	b: 9/25/1940		
	+Jo Ann Zaunbrecher	b: 7/22/1944	m: 7/15/1964	
4	Mary Ann Meyer	b: 2/2/1942		
	+John Herman Reiners, Jr.	b: 10/19/1938	m: 4/8/1961	
4	Margaret Mary Meyer	b: 7/31/1943		
	+Charles Herman Simpson	b: 9/1942	m: 5/12/1964	
4	Joseph Bernard Meyer	b: 8/27/1944		d: 8/23/1989
	+Betty Ann Gould	b: 4/1946	m: 4/28/1966	
4	Kathleen Marie Meyer	b: 11/19/1947		
	+Larry John Viator	b: 2/1947	m: 6/6/1970	
4	Marie Antoinette Meyer	b: 12/19/1950		d: 6/8/1951
4	James Anthony Meyer	b: 10/22/1955		

Ohlenforst

		+Patricia A. Meche	b: 9/1962	m: 10/26/1991	
3		Heinrich Leonard (Leo) Habetz, Jr.	b: 5/11/1912		d: 9/16/1985
		+Mary Leona Cramer	b: 6/11/1912	m: 2/3/1937	d: 7/1/1981
	4	Leonard Jerome "Jack" Habetz	b: 4/16/1938		
		+Sylvia Bigelow	b: 7/3/1940	m: 1/4/1964	
	4	Donald Bernard Habetz	b: 9/25/1940		d: 10/24/2004
		+Patricia Anne Istre	b: 3/27/1940	m: 8/24/1963	
	4	Edmund "E.L." Leonard Habetz	b: 11/6/1949		
		+Cheryl Anne Hoffpauir	b: 1/15/1948	m: 5/1/1971	
	4	Allan Norbert Habetz	b: 9/7/1952		
		+Gwendolyn Marie Truax	b: 1/6/1952	m: 9/21/1973	
	4	Kenneth Michael Habetz	b: 11/13/1955		
		+Penny Anne Hargroder	b: 8/3/1958	m: 11/7/1980	
3		Felicitas Gertrude Habetz	b: 5/25/1914		
		+John Herman Cramer	b: 1909	m: 2/23/1938	d: 1980
	4	Anna Margaret Cramer	b: 12/31/1938		
		+William "Billy" Louis Zaunbrecher	b: 5/31/1938	m: 12/16/1963	d: 8/19/1997
	4	Bernard Cramer	b: 9/25/1942		d: 9/25/1942
	4	Patricia Marie Cramer	b: 2/21/1947		d: 2004
	4	Carolyn Clementine Cramer	b: 7/6/1950		
	4	Ignatius John Cramer	b: 4/5/1952		d: 7/23/1982
		+Kathleen Marie Gros		m: 7/11/1975	
3		Leonard Alphonse Habetz, Sr.	b: 5/12/1916		d: 4/9/1974
		+Frances Meyer	b: 7/30/1914	m: 1/8/1941	d: 8/13/1986

Ohlenforst

	4	Henry Bernard Habetz	b: 12/19/1941		d: 1/7/1986
		+Laura Sonnier	b: 1/2/1943	m: 11/28/1963	d: 8/11/2006
	4	Leonard "Alphonse" Habetz, Jr.	b: 6/23/1943		
		+Carolyn Spell	b: 9/23/1940	m: 6/5/1965	
	4	Alberta Habetz	b: 2/21/1945		
		+Johnny Winn Barlow	b: 8/9/1953	m: 2/2/1974	
	4	Charles Joseph Habetz	b: 9/6/1946		
		+Katherine Link	b: 1/22/1948	m: 4/27/1968	
	4	Lucille Marie Habetz	b: 4/2/1948		
		+Norman Jean Borne, Jr.	b: 9/15/1946	m: 6/12/1976	
	4	Catherine Helen Habetz	b: 6/25/1949		
		+Hugh Fred "Pudgy" O'Connor, Jr.	b: 3/31/1938	m: 8/21/1982	d: 3/4/2002
	4	Henrietta Louise Habetz	b: 7/28/1951		
	4	Ralph Mark Habetz	b: 2/16/1953		
		+Katherine Sudwischer	b: 1/16/1957	m: 7/15/1983	
	4	Frances Adelieth Habetz	b: 8/10/1954		d: 10/30/2004
		+Dan R. Hooten	b: 2/4/1944	m: 12/4/1982	d: 1/2002
	4	Claire Marie Habetz	b: 9/22/1957		
	4	Pauline Margaret Habetz	b: 1/5/1960		
2		Maria Victoria Ohlenforst	b: 1876		d: 1889
2		Peter Anton Ohlenforst	b: 1878		d: 1944
		+Catherine Josepha Reiners	b: 1881	m: 1903	d: 1938
3		Maria Frances Ohlenforst	b: 7/6/1904		d: 2/14/1988
		+Hubert Joseph Thevis	b: 8/16/1899	m: 1923	d: 5/24/1988
	4	Antonia Josephine Thevis	b: 3/1/1928		
		+Lloyd Lynn Hoffpauir	b: 5/30/1926	m: 11/23/1948	d: 7/5/2006
	4	Herbert Joseph Thevis	b: 3/13/1933		d: 9/16/1945

Ohlenforst

4	Raymond Gerhard Thevis	b: 4/13/1934		
	+Eunice Marie Abshire	b: 10/9/1935	m: 2/11/1956	
4	Norbert Anthony Thevis	b: 1/18/1938		
	+Betty Jean Norman	b: 10/4/1941	m: 1/18/1964	
4	Edward Daniel Thevis	b: 10/1/1941		
	+Selma Marie Touchet	b: 4/4/1942	m: 12/1/1961	
3	Veronica Wilhelmena Ohlenforst	b: 6/7/1907		d: 12/25/1975
	+Gerhard John Thevis	b: 6/30/1901	m: 11/17/1926	d: 4/27/1971
4	Anthony Joseph Thevis	b: 3/23/1928		d: 4/29/1992
	+Josephine Thecla Berken	b: 7/14/1934	m: 5/10/1955	
4	Ferdinand Thevis	b: 7/19/1930		
	+Wilda Ann LeJeune	b: 7/14/1933	m: 8/8/1953	
4	Lionel Edward Thevis	b: 10/25/1934		
	+Barbara Nell Monte	b: 2/14/1938	m: 9/29/1956	
3	Anna Josepha Ohlenforst	b: 8/10/1913		d: 2/29/1980
	+Leonard Joseph Thevis	b: 3/19/1906	m: 11/17/1931	d: 3/17/1969
4	James Thomas Thevis	b: 12/22/1933		
	+Normalie Blanchard	b: 3/18/1941	m: 5/19/1959	
3	Anthony Joseph Ohlenforst	b: 6/28/1916		d: 8/26/1974
	+Josephine Anna Leonards	b: 1920	m: 1940	d: 1992
4	Juliana Ohlenforst	b: 1942		d: 9/6/1998
	+Clyde W. Hoffpauir			
3	Catherine Margaret (Dollie) Ohlenforst	b: 4/29/1919		d: 4/14/1987
3	John Francis Ohlenforst	b: 2/12/1921		d: 1997
	+Philomena Hedwig Leonards	b: 4/3/1923	m: 1/4/1947	

Ohlenforst

4	Maria Goretti Ohlenforst	b: 6/20/1951		
	+Joseph James Kracher	b: 1/10/1948	m: 5/29/1976	
4	Dorita Lois Ohlenforst	b: 12/4/1952		
	+Richard Dalton Comeaux	b: 9/24/1947	m: 1/13/1996	
4	Jude Anthony Ohlenforst	b: 10/28/1955		
	+Gretchen Louise Gray	b: 2/4/1957	m: 6/27/1986	
3	Rita Victoria Ohlenforst	b: 1924		d: 1999
	+Joseph Peter Habetz	b: 1920	m: 1946	d: 7/25/2006
4	Flavia Ann Habetz	b: 1946		
	+Glenn John Eldridge		m: 1969	
4	Michael Anthony Habetz	b: 1948		
	+Cynthia Scott		m: 1970	
4	Bruno Joseph Habetz	b: 1950		
	+Debra Judice		m: 1975	
	*2nd Wife of Bruno Joseph Habetz:			
	+Mary Katherine Derouen		m: 1984	
	*3rd Wife of Bruno Joseph Habetz:			
	+Linda Leeper		m: 1992	
4	Tedmund Daniel Habetz	b: 1953		
	+Kay Voohries		m: 1980	
4	Joline Rita Habetz	b: 1955		d: 1955
2	John Martin Ohlenforst	b: 1880		d: 1884
2	Anna Martha Ohlenforst	b: 1883		d: 1937
	+Joseph August Habetz	b: 8/30/1880	m: 12/11/1902	d: 12/21/1972
3	Leonard August Habetz	b: 8/28/1903		d: 11/29/1978

Ohlenforst

	+[1] Anna Gesina Cramer	b: 1908	m: 11/28/1934	d: 2000
4	Margaret Mary Habetz	b: 9/24/1935		
	+Wesley Boullion	b: 2/26/1936	m: 11/13/1955	d: 11/8/1990
4	Geraldine A. Habetz	b: 5/25/1937		
	+Sherman J. Trahan	b: 2/26/1939	m: 3/17/1962	
4	Louise Gertrude Habetz	b: 1/6/1939		
	+Johnny Wade Meche	b: 12/25/1939	m: 11/4/1961	
4	Edward Joseph Habetz	b: 2/7/1941		
	+Marlene Miller	b: 1/10/1946	m: 11/3/1962	
4	Daniel Leo Habetz	b: 1/3/1943		
	+Judy Savoy	b: 12/19/1943	m: 11/2/1962	
4	Gerhard Raymond Habetz	b: 12/31/1944		
	+Brenda Gale Guidry		m: 11/12/1966	
	*2nd Wife of Gerhard Raymond Habetz:			
	+Gloria Higginbotham	b: 8/2/1945	m: 4/17/1985	
4	Charles Herman Habetz	b: 5/22/1946		
	+Pattie L. Beard	b: 3/31/1949	m: 10/11/1970	
4	Robert John Habetz	b: 5/13/1948		
	+Amber Thomas		m: 4/4/1969	
4	Rose Marie Habetz	b: 4/20/1950		d: 9/1/1951
3	Marie Henrietta Habetz	b: 4/15/1905		d: 10/12/1988
	+Stephen Matthew Foytlin	b: 1900	m: 10/22/1940	d: 1967
4	Mary Magdalene Foytlin	b: 10/25/1943		d: 12/1/1943
4	Stephen August Foytlin	b: 2/26/1945		
	+Rebecca Jane Amie		m: 11/19/1969	
4	Joseph John Foytlin	b: 3/16/1949		
	+Romona St. Amand		m: 5/3/1969	
3	John Ferdinand Habetz	b: 12/27/1906		d: 8/24/1963
	+Anna Gertrude Thevis	b: 1908	m: 1/21/1931	d: 1982

Ohlenforst

4	Vincent John Habetz	b: 10/17/1931			
	+Louella Rita Dronet Greene		m: 9/26/1970		
4	Theresa Margaret Habetz	b: 6/25/1933			
4	Lawrence "Jerome" Habetz	b: 8/12/1935			
4	Florence Marie Habetz	b: 3/15/1939			
	+Paul Edward Russell		m: 3/1959		
4	Annie Louise Habetz	b: 7/29/1942			
	+Elby Joseph Pellerin		m: 5/4/1963		
3	William Andrew Habetz, Sr.	b: 2/4/1909		d: 4/17/1979	
	+Clothilde Borne	b: 1912	m: 6/6/1939	d: 1998	
4	William Andrew Habetz, Jr.	b: 8/13/1940			
	+Jeanette Marie Richard		m: 10/20/1972		
4	Harold Joseph Habetz, Sr.	b: 11/26/1942			
	+Barbara A. Mouton		m: 10/12/1963		
	*2nd Wife of Harold Joseph Habetz, Sr.:				
	+Priscilla A. Savoie		m: 7/27/1974		
4	Martha Anna Habetz	b: 4/23/1944			
	+Paul Pierret, Jr.		m: 2/20/1976		
4	Doris Marie Habetz	b: 5/31/1945			
	+Isaac Miller, Jr.		m: 3/8/1973		
	*2nd Husband of Doris Marie Habetz:				
	+Henry Purvis Carmouche III		m: 7/3/1980		
4	Louetta Gertrude Habetz	b: 12/15/1946		d: 7/15/1993	
	+Robert L. Richard		m: 11/30/1968		
4	Mary Alice Habetz	b: 4/22/1949			

Ohlenforst

	+Michael James Pastor		m: 11/16/1974	
4	Mildred Jane Habetz	b: 2/5/1951		
	+Roland Leo Matte		m: 5/31/1972	
4	Milton James Habetz	b: 2/5/1951		
	+Jeanette Bourque		m: 6/17/1972	
	*2nd Wife of Milton James Habetz:			
	+Karen Ruth Faulk		m: 7/23/1983	
4	Janet Louise Habetz	b: 3/18/1956		
	+Joey Paul Fontenot		m: 9/18/1978	
3	Herman Joseph Habetz	b: 5/29/1911		d: 1/25/1991
3	William Raymond Habetz	b: 8/30/1913		d: 2004
	+Maria Adelheid Cramer	b: 8/30/1915	m: 8/17/1950	
4	May Rose Habetz	b: 1/3/1954		
	+Anthony Bourgeois	b: 1/1/1955	m: 8/17/2000	
3	Anna Franziska Habetz	b: 3/12/1916		d: 2005
3	Gertrude Mathilda Habetz	b: 3/12/1916		d: 6/18/1994
3	Wenzel Henry Habetz	b: 5/24/1918		
	+Marie Menard	b: 1930	m: 11/8/1947	
3	Helen Walburga Habetz	b: 5/22/1921		
3	Josepha Habetz	b: 5/22/1921		d: 5/22/1921
3	Rita Martha Habetz	b: 6/14/1923		d: 2001
3	Benedict George Habetz	b: 3/21/1926		d: 2/20/1996
	+Rita Barbier	b: 1942	m: 9/11/1962	
4	Christine Ann Habetz	b: 12/16/1963		
	+Greg P. Benoit		m: 1985	
4	George John Habetz	b: 1/29/1965		
	+Judy Peacock		m: 1987	
3	Paul Anton Habetz	b: 10/27/1928		d: 10/29/1928
2	Wenzeslaus John Ohlenforst	b: 1885		d: 1920
	+Mary Frances (Mamie) Mayor		m: 1914	d: 1957

Ohlenforst

3		Aloysius William Ohlenforst	b: 1916		d: 1994
		+Victoria Victerine Leitell	b: 1919	m: 1937	
	4	John Roland Ohlenforst, Sr.			
		+Lena Hocke			
2		Henry Joseph Ohlenforst	b: 2/25/1889		d: 8/20/1971
		+Maria Walburga Thevis	b: 1896	m: 1919	d: 1984
3		Fr. John William Ohlenforst	b: 11/5/1919		d: 1/3/1997
3		Aloysius Joseph (Alois) Ohlenforst	b: 1921		d: 1996
		+Micheline "Mickie" Courtat	b: 1929	m: 1946	
	4	Patrick Michael Ohlenforst	b: 12/10/1948		
		+Cinthia Morgan		m: 6/12/1971	
	4	Marie Claire Ohlenforst	b: 7/24/1952		
		+James Edward Tirres		m: 7/13/1974	
	4	Michelle Ohlenforst	b: 10/6/1959		
		+John Graham III		m: 8/21/1982	
	4	Christian Jon Ohlenforst	b: 9/19/1968		
		+Pamela Tschirhart		m: 8/12/2000	
3		George Lawrence Ohlenforst	b: 2/3/1923		d: 2/6/1923
3		Gertrude Cecilia Ohlenforst	b: 1924		d: 1994
		+Frank Joseph Bernard	b: 1920	m: 1946	d: 1984
	4	Linda Bernard	b: 10/16/1947		
		+Richard Crum		m: 1967	
	4	Frank Joseph Bernard II	b: 11/29/1953		
		+Stacey Simmons		m: 10/5/1984	
	4	Dennis Joseph Bernard	b: 8/17/1956		d: 9/2006
		+Penny Nichols			

Ohlenforst

3	Thecla Theresa Ohlenforst	b: 2/28/1926		d: 4/21/1967
	+Lionel Paul Simoneaux, Jr.	b: 1923	m: 1951	d: 2005
4	Fr. Jody Jude Simoneaux	b: 11/17/1955		
4	James Dale Simoneaux	b: 3/20/1957		
	+Danette Bergeron		m: 7/8/1978	
4	Jerald John Simoneaux	b: 6/24/1958		
	+Donna Oubre		m: 1978	
	*2nd Wife of Jerald John Simoneaux:			
	+Tina Ammann		m: 9/22/2001	
4	Jules Andrew Simoneaux	b: 4/19/1960		
	+Gina Mula			
3	Andrew Lawrence Ohlenforst	b: 10/6/1928		d: 10/3/1983
	+Marcella Marie Leonards	b: 2/3/1934	m: 1/19/1955	
4	Monika Joan Ohlenforst	b: 10/31/1955		
	+Kermit Pierre Arceneaux	b: 6/28/1955	m: 7/5/1975	
4	Stephen Charles Ohlenforst	b: 7/1958		d: 7/1958
4	Timothy Paul Ohlenforst	b: 1/17/1960		
	+Rebecca Sue Foux	b: 1/24/1961	m: 6/7/1985	
4	Philip Leo Ohlenforst	b: 5/13/1961		
	+Yvette Marie Richard	b: 4/10/1961	m: 10/18/1980	
4	Martin Louis Ohlenforst	b: 6/16/1965		
	+Dana Nelson	b: 7/25/1969	m: 10/25/1997	
4	Marian Clare Ohlenforst	b: 12/17/1968		
	+Brian David Broussard	b: 1/9/1965	m: 4/28/1990	
3	Sr. Margaret Mary Ohlenforst	b: 10/20/1931		

Ohlenforst

3	Dorothy Ann Ohlenforst	b: 1933		
	+William Joseph Leger	b: 1928	m: 1953	d: 1992
4	David B. Leger	b: 1/11/1955		
	+Cynthia Gautreaux		m: 8/1978	
4	Margaret Mary Leger	b: 3/8/1956		
	+Malcolm Doucet		m: 3/22/1980	
4	Mark A. Leger	b: 11/10/1957		
	+Christina Spaetgens			
	*2nd Wife of Mark A. Leger:			
	+Debra Vincent		m: 8/25/1985	
4	Wayne J. Leger	b: 8/18/1961		
	+Stephanie Naquin		m: 11/3/1984	
3	Joseph Daniel Ohlenforst	b: 1935		
	+Brenda Marie Sonnier	b: 1946	m: 1965	
4	Dwayne Joseph Ohlenforst	b: 12/15/1965		
	+Vicky A. Vail		m: 2/7/1991	
4	Darren K. Ohlenforst	b: 12/3/1966		
4	Darrell L. Ohlenforst	b: 12/3/1966		
4	Daniel S. Ohlenforst	b: 6/29/1968		
	+Brandi Maturin		m: 4/13/2003	
4	Amy Ohlenforst	b: 4/15/1972		
3	Saraphia Bernadette Ohlenforst	b: 1938		
	+Edlar Ronald Monte	b: 1938	m: 1959	
4	Mona Ann Monte	b: 2/16/1960		
	+Marc Mouton, Jr.		m: 10/12/1980	
4	Gregory John Monte	b: 7/10/1961		
	+Terrie Volenweider		m: 10/29/1983	
4	Marlene Monte	b: 11/27/1963		
	+Michael Patin		m: 12/20/1986	
4	Glen Paul Monte	b: 9/26/1966		

Ohlenforst

	+Michelle Lavergne		m: 2/20/1988	
3	Francis Thomas Ohlenforst	b: 1940		
	+Jacquelyn Sue Dupont	b: 10/13/1942	m: 1969	d: 7/15/2005
4	Annette Ohlenforst	b: 6/27/1970		
	+Randy Simon		m: 6/17/1989	
4	Thomas Joseph Ohlenforst	b: 8/18/1971		
	+Susan Lynn Bellard		m: 4/8/1994	
4	Marcus Ohlenforst	b: 10/22/1974		
	+Brenda Bailey		m: 9/13/1994	

25. Ohlenforst, Theodore:
Theodore Ohlenforst b:1832 d: 1918 was a brother of Johann Wilhelm Ohlenforst (see above). He never married, thus there are no descendants.

For the St. Leo IV Annex groundbreaking ceremony on March 6, 1995 were members of the building committee (left to right), Lawrence Habetz, Shirley Leonards, Julian Didier, Mary Jo Olinger, Father Francis Bourgeois, E.L. Habetz, Contractor, Robert Barras, Architect, and committee members, Louis Cramer and Jerry Leonards.

The completed annex next to the St. Leo IV Catholic Church.

The original Germanfest Steering Committee that planned the first festival in 1995 were (front row, left to right), Susan Olinger, Rusty Leonards, Kay Habetz, Gwen Thevis (back row), Bubba Spaetgens, Michael Leonards, Lawrence Habetz, Louis Cramer.

The Germanfest crowd under the big tent dancing to the chicken dance.

Alpenfest band playing the alpine horn. The Alpenfest band has provided entertainment every year since the first festival in 1995.

The Kinder Auftrit "children of Robert's Cove" perform each day at the annual Germanfest festival.

The Germanfest Folk Singers, a very popular group at the Germanfest festivals and other invites presenting cultural presentations. They sing many of the old traditional German songs that were sung by the ancestors at the family gatherings and reunions.

Shelby and Zachry Istre in their German costumes for the festival.

Threshing demonstration presented each day at the Germanfest festival.

You cannot have Germanfest without bratwurst and sauerkraut.

Tommy Benoit and Jeramie Hebert enjoying the German beer "Warsteiner."

The Robert's Cove German Heritage Museum completed and officially opened on September 16, 2002.

The Museum provides a permanent display of all the immigrants and their families. There are also pictures of the original homes of the immigrants in Robert's Cove.

For the 2005 Germanfest and several months in 2006, a room presented statues, pictures, and other wall-hangings of angels. Many were on loan from families of the original immigrants.

The "Wallfahrtskappelle" or Pilgrimage Chapel was rebuilt in 2004, having been substantially destroyed by Hurricane Lili in 2002.

The Pilgrimage Chapel, also known as Wallfahrtskappelle, was blessed and rededicated during a ceremony at 11 a.m. Mass at St. Leo IV Catholic Church in Robert's Cove. *Pictured in front:* Stephen Benoit and Phillip Reiners; *second row,* Father Thomas Habatz, Ambrose Olinger, Sr. Margaret Ohlenforst, Sr. Claire Cramer, Father Francis Bourgeois; *third row,* Father Paul Thibodeaux, Father George Hefner, and Daniel Reynolds; *back row,* Michael Legnion, Zachary Benoit, John Leonards and John Reynolds. (*Acadiana Tribune* Photo by Josie Henry)

Inside the Pilgrimage Chapel is the statue "Piata" that was totally restored after the hurricane damage in 2002.

Father Charles Zaunbrecher
Born: 11/8/1931 Died: 6/19/1996
The Genealogical Pillar of the Robert's Cove Community

Clara Habetz
Born: 10/4/1914 Died: 8/22/2006
The Heart and Soul of Robert's Cove

Catholic Pilgrimage to Europe June 10-28, 1965 – *Front Left to Right:* Barbara F. Zaunbrecher, Clara Habetz, Leona Zaunbrecher, Louise G. Heinen, Alberta L. Bergeron, Antoinette L. Miller, Rosa B. Leonards, Tillie Z. Leonards, Dora F. Leonards, Mary O. Leonards, Carolyn Zaunbrecher. *Back Left to Right:* Rita Leonards, Mae T. Zaunbrecher, Patricia Zaunbrecher, Dot Leonards, Joe Zaunbrecher, Elmen Bergeron, Father Charles Zaunbrecher, C.P. (Charlie) Zaunbrecher and William Leonards.

1981 Centennial European Excursion – *First Row Right to Left:* Josephine L. (Sis) Cramer, Hilda Heinen, Frances (Poochie) T. Premeaux, Mel Premeaux. *Second row:* Sadie F. Thevis, Paul Zaunbrecher, Cecilia H. Zaunbrecher, Jo Ann Z. Ronkartz, Fred Frey, Louise Z. Carpenter, Rita O. Habetz, Dot V. Frey, Mary Agnes Z. Fabacher, Josephine (Phenie) L. Ohlenforst, Lee Monlezun. *Back Row:* Genevieve F. Leonards, Edwin Leonards, Dot O. Leger, William (Fats) Leger, Doris L. Hensgens, Father Charles Zaunbrecher, Jerome Ronkartz, Edwin (Bruce) Broussard, John Ohlenforst. *Not pictured:* Philip Fabacher, Nick Hensgens, Leonard (Buck) Leonards, Barbara L. Leonards, Philo L. Ohlenforst, Louis Privat, Glen Zaunbrecher, Margaret P. Zaunbrecher.

European Trip taken with Father Charles Zaunbrecher June 10 – 27, 1985. This photo was taken in Florence, Italy. *Left to Right*: Annette, Fred and Marianne Gossen, Peggy Gossen, Father Charles Zaunbrecher, Benno and Margaret Leonards, Genny Dischler, Helen and F.E. Landry, Mary Ann (Rusty) Leonards, Josie Thevis, Lois Bennett, Jack (Ferdinand) Thevis, Carl (Bus Driver), Rita B. Hoffpauir, Heloise G. Dischler, Wilda Thevis and Anna Rosa Rohrer (American Express Tour Manager).

Robert's Cove Heritage Tour June 27 – July 14, 1985- This photo was taken at Heidelberg Castle, Germany. *Top Row Left to Right:* Dorita Ohlenforst, Father Charles Zaunbrecher, Keith Leonards, Dot Leonards, Yvonne Simon, Gerry H. Heard, Mac Millet. *Second Row:* Annie H. Gautreaux, Tour Manager Jenny Bruce, Pat Gautreaux, Theodora H. Faulk, Wilma H. Cormier, Josie H. Millet. *Third Row:* Loretta Z. Kurta, Louis Privat, Juliana O. Hoffpauir, Linda Gayle Z. Frey. *Front Row:* Anne Leger, Josephine (Sis) L. Cramer, Peter Arta (Bus Driver), Lambertina Z. LaHaye, Josephine (Phenie) L. Ohlenforst.

1990 Robert's Cove Heritage Tour – *Left to Right back:* Joe Benechek, Shirley and Bill Winchester, Wilma leonards, Guy Gautreaux, Henry Leonards, Clarice Gautreaux, Father Charles Zaunbrecher, Leona Berken, Lloyd Hoffpauir, Jill Habetz, Gertrude Monlezun, Joe Neu, Sylvia Daigle, Wilda Babineaux, Marilyn Vidrene and Antonia Hoffpauir.

1995 Robert's Cove Heritage Tour, the last with Father Charles Zaunbrecher. June 24 – July 11, 1995. This picture was taken in front of St. Leo IV Altar in St. Peter's Basilica, Rome, Italy. Members were: Fred and Annette Gossen, Jason and Amy Gossen, Madeline Gossen, Leona Berken, Christina Hornsby, Josie, Gwen and Trudy Thevis, Mildred Boudreaux, Sadie and Kirk Thevis, Carmen Sims, Elridge (Nick) and Shirley Bollich, Jennifer, Brian and Sandra Bollich, Daniel and Sharon Bollich Pickett, Mary Ann Leonards, Joan L. Mouton, Anne L. Cagle, Audrey L. McBride, Helen Maraist and Yvonne M. Simon, Bonnie Heinen, James and Eloise Brewer, James and Stella Z. Doucet, Ann Gallagher, Lois Hakanson, Linda Salter, Joseph Benichuk, Dr. Philip J. Fabacher and Father Charles Zaunbrecher (Tour Escort).

2000 Trip – Father Charles Zaunbrecher's Memorial Trip to Europe: Members were: Philip Fabacher, Jenny Lejeune, Donald and Henrietta Gossen, Angela Boudreaux, Carolyn Morgan, Winona Cartwright, Julius Ballinger, III, Frances Bahlinger, Willietta Phillips, Mary Ann Leonards, Ann, Renee and Casey Leger, Loretta Kurta, Cecillia Zaunbrecher, Kendra Zaunbrecher, Elaine Leger, Linda Frey, Peter Bahlinger, Harold Bahlinger, Bonnie Heinen, Mary Heinen, Catherine Fabacher, Blaise and Bernadine Leonards, Ignatius, Janet, Ashley, Lacey and Ingram Leonards, Jeff Fabacher.

2005 Robert's Cove Heritage Tour – Philip Fabacher, Tour Director. June 14 –July 1, 2005, Celebrating 125th Anniversary of the Robert's Cove Settlement. *Back Row Left to Right:* Louis Cramer, Philip Fabacher, Charles Habetz, Jennifer Habetz, Leo Thevis, Cheryl Habetz, Clara T. Savoy, Leona H. Berken, Lawrence Cramer, Cathy H. O'Conner, Ed Habetz, Claire Habetz, Pauline Habetz and Harold Bahlinger. *Front row:* Evelyn Stoute, Peter Bahlinger, Jan Thevis, Jenny Lejeune, Madeline Fockens, Kay Habetz, Carl Cramer, Ann Robique, Beulah (Doo) Bischoff Amy, and Loretta Z. Kurta.

26. Olinger, Ferdinand:

Ferdinand Olinger b: 7/2/1861 d: 1/10/1942 was the son of Matthias Olinger b: 1810 d: 1893 from Faha, Germany, and Margaret Seunnen b: 1820 d: 1908 from Wellenstein, Luxembourg. He first married on 10/21/1890 to Barbara Neu b: 12/24/1866 d: 1/30/1919, daughter of Jacob Neu, Jr. b: 3/25/1841 d: 11/25/1926 and Barbara Zarn b: 1841 d: 1915 from Ems, Switzerland (see Neu family). His second marriage in 1921 was to Anna Schum Abbott b: 1869 d: 1965.

2		Mary Gertrude Olinger	b: 8/18/1891		d: 4/3/1978	
		+Henry Leo Leonards	b: 7/17/1889	m: 7/3/1912	d: 3/18/1960	
3		Joseph Ferdinand Leonards	b: 3/13/1913		d: 7/14/1979	
		+Alice Helen Patin	b: 7/19/1914	m: 11/27/1935	d: 2004	
	4	Carolyn Leonards	b: 1936			
		+William Johnson		m: 1955		
		*2nd Husband of Carolyn Leonards:				
		+Jimmy Louviere	b: 1935	m: 1978		
	4	Kathleen Leonards	b: 1940			
		+Richard Watkens		m: 1960		
		*2nd Husband of Kathleen Leonards:				
		+Milton Janise		m: 1990		
	4	Jo Ann Leonards	b: 1942			
		+Phillip Watkins	b: 1942	m: 1964		
3		Ferdinand Joseph Leonards	b: 3/29/1914		d: 3/29/1914	
3		Ferdinand Joseph Leonards	b: 4/12/1915			
		+Edna Mae Devillier	b: 10/18/1918	m: 2/18/1941		
3		Edmund Alois Leonards	b: 1/25/1917		d: 1/28/2006	
		+Norma Elizabeth Ziegler	b: 2/25/1923	m: 6/25/1947	d: 1996	
	4	Mark Leonards	b: 1948			
3		Leo Charles Leonards	b: 7/28/1918		d: 1984	
		+Mary Lee Dumesnil	b: 1/24/1930	m: 7/3/1950		

4	Mary Germaine Leonards	b: 1951		
	+Myron Ropp	b: 1954	m: 1986	
4	Leo Jerome Leonards	b: 1952		
	+Anne Chappuis	b: 1953	m: 1973	
4	Mary Elizabeth Leonards	b: 1954		
	+James Bourgeois		m: 1979	
4	Bernadette Leonards	b: 1957		
	+Wayne Baronet	b: 1954	m: 1979	
4	Paul Joseph Leonards	b: 1959		
	+Lillie Harmon	b: 1959	m: 1978	
4	Mildred Leonards	b: 1962		
	+Terry D. Miller	b: 2/21/1965	m: 9/10/2005	
3	Rheinholdt John Leonards	b: 1/5/1920		d: 2003
3	Clara Marie Leonards	b: 10/29/1922		
	+Joseph Clemens Wilfert	b: 7/30/1914	m: 12/26/1944	d: 2001
4	Leonard Wilfert	b: 1946		
	+Rita Thenhaus		m: 1982	
	*2nd Wife of Leonard Wilfert:			
	+Theresa Zimmer	b: 1951	m: 1996	
4	Leobelle Wilfert	b: 1948		
	+William Nevitt	b: 1947	m: 1973	
4	Paula Ann Wilfert	b: 1952		
	+David Winzer	b: 1950	m: 1974	
4	Marian Wilfert	b: 1954		
	+Gary Beauchamp	b: 1949	m: 1986	
3	Henrietta Marcella Leonards	b: 10/10/1923		d: 1984
	+John Norbert Gayle	b: 11/25/1918	m: 11/20/1946	d: 3/3/1961
4	John Gayle	b: 1947		

Olinger

	+Rita Barras	b: 1949	m: 1976	
4	William Joseph Gayle	b: 1949		
	+Alma Johnson	b: 1948	m: 1976	
4	Philip Anthony Gayle	b: 1952		
	+Nancy Johnson		m: 1978	
3	Alois Jerome Leonards	b: 12/28/1924		d: 1/21/1925
3	Theresa Hilda Leonards	b: 11/8/1925		d: 1/6/1926
3	Sister Mildred Gertrude Leonards	b: 10/27/1928		
3	Anthony Philip Leonards	b: 12/31/1930		
	+Mary Theresa Carrothers	b: 5/15/1934	m: 8/15/1953	d: 1/14/1979
4	Thomas Leonards	b: 1954		
	+Patsy Suire	b: 1956	m: 1976	
4	Michael Leonards	b: 1955		
	+Maxine Miller	b: 1957	m: 1978	
4	Margaret Leonards	b: 1956		
	+Miguel DePuy	b: 1949	m: 1978	
4	Patricia Leonards	b: 1957		
	+Charles Benoit	b: 1957	m: 1988	
4	Robert Leonards	b: 1958		
	+Cindy Boulian	b: 1954	m: 1979	
4	Christopher Leonards	b: 1960		
	+Eliany Hernandez	b: 1978	m: 1999	
4	Andre Leonards	b: 1961		
	+Gil Guerriero		b: 1961	m: 1991
4	Maria Leonards	b: 1962		
	+Nizar Abudiah	b: 1962	m: 1986	
	*2nd Wife of Anthony Philip Leonards:			
	+Pamela Marie Mouton	b: 8/23/1955	m: 8/2/1976	
4	Ferdinand Leonards	b: 1977		

Olinger

	4	Natashia Leonards	b: 1979		
	4	Christina Leonards	b: 1981		
	4	Ann Bernadine Leonards	b: 1992		
	4	Elizabeth Leonards	b: 1993		
	4	Rachel Leonards	b: 1995		
3		James Leonards	b: 1932		d: 1932
3		Sister Bernadine Benedicta Leonards	b: 3/12/1934		d: 1986
2		Joseph Olinger	b: 1893		d: 1894
2		Joseph Aloysius Olinger	b: 9/15/1894		d: 12/9/1968
		+Anna Rosalie Bollich	b: 1913	m: 1947	d: 6/3/2006
3		Karen Marie Olinger	b: 9/15/1948		
		+Ellis Lesby Boyd, Jr.	b: 1946	m: 1968	
	4	Laurie Ann Boyd	b: 6/17/1969		
		+Tony Vice	b: 1968	m: 1993	

*2nd Husband of Laurie Ann Boyd:

		+Keith Moreaux	b: 6/26/1971	m: 6/11/2004
	4	Ellis Joseph Boyd	b: 5/8/1974	
		+Andrea Leah McCall	b: 7/13/1977	m: 12/6/1997
3		Janet Louise Olinger	b: 1/17/1950	
		+Kent Guy Hutslar	b: 1951	m: 1971
	4	Charles Scott Hutslar	b: 6/17/1972	
		+Teresa Freeman	b: 8/22/1973	m: 3/6/1993
	4	Michelle Renee Hutslar	b: 2/26/1974	
		+Todd Pourciaux	b: 1969	m: 1993

*2nd Husband of Michelle Renee Hutslar:

		+Robert Thomas Bruce	b: 7/30/1970	m: 5/22/2005
	4	Kellie Ann Hutslar	b: 4/23/1976	

*2nd Husband of Janet Louise Olinger:

+Joseph Edward Landes	b: 12/30/1953	m: 11/12/1994

Olinger

3		Beverly Ann Olinger	b: 1/4/1951	
		+Louis Joseph Maloz, Sr.	b: 11/19/1947	m: 1/24/1970
	4	Louis Joseph "Joey" Maloz, Jr.	b: 11/26/1970	
		+Michelle LaPointe	b: 4/21/1972	m: 5/22/1993
	4	Amy Katherine Maloz	b: 10/29/1972	
	4	Christina Lynn Maloz	b: 2/4/1976	
	4	Brad Anthony Maloz	b: 6/12/1977	
		+Nicole Habetz	b: 8/29/1976	m: 3/31/2001
3		Charlotte Rose Olinger	b: 2/23/1952	
		+Oliver Kent Collins	b: 1951	m: 1976
	4	Oliver Kent Collins, Jr.	b: 7/22/1977	
		+Elana Smith	b: 1/2/1979	m: 7/2/2004
	4	Melanie Michelle Collins	b: 12/16/1978	
	4	Valerie Lynn Collins	b: 3/23/1980	
		+Randy Seidel	b: 4/8/1974	m: 8/29/1999
		*2nd Husband of Charlotte Rose Olinger:		
		+Kenneth LeBlanc	b: 8/11/1956	m: 12/9/1989
3		Wayne Joseph Olinger	b: 8/4/1953	
		+Constance Anne Harding	b: 5/22/1955	m: 9/11/1976
	4	Jason Michael Olinger	b: 3/13/1978	
		+Angel Stafford	b: 6/28/1973	m: 6/1/2005
	4	Jessica Marie Olinger	b: 7/30/1979	
		+James Bradshaw	b: 10/19/1978	m: 7/28/2000
	4	Jarrold Wayne Olinger	b: 11/1/1983	
3		Charles William Olinger	b: 6/6/1955	
		+Jacqueline Marie Prejean	b: 12/3/1956	m: 8/30/1980
	4	Nicholas Paul Olinger	b: 11/1/1984	
	4	Brian James Olinger	b: 2/6/1987	

Olinger

3		Mary Regina Olinger	b: 7/2/1957		
		+Sidney James Broussard	b: 1956	m: 1982	
	4	Ryan Mark Broussard	b: 5/15/1985		
	4	Allison Claire Broussard	b: 10/30/1988		
		*2nd Husband of Mary Regina Olinger:			
		+Phillip Landry	b: 9/24/1951	m: 6/11/1996	
2		Edward John Olinger	b: 1896		d: 1983
		+Regina Josephine Dischler	b: 1902	m: 1922	d: 1997
	3	Ambrose Joseph Olinger	b: 1923		
		+Margaret Mary Leonards	b: 1923	m: 1946	
	4	Charlene Anne Olinger	b: 1954		
		+Michael Olan Reynolds	b: 1955	m: 1980	
	4	Gerard Joseph Olinger	b: 1955		
		+Debbie Elizabeth Moreau	b: 1957	m: 1975	
	4	Dale Edward Olinger	b: 1958		
	4	Susan Marie Olinger	b: 1962		
	4	Laura Catherine Olinger	b: 1964		
		+Timothy Neal Burley	b: 1960	m: 1995	
	4	John Francis Olinger	b: 1965		
		+Leslie Michelle Johnson	b: 1965	m: 1995	
	3	Beatrice Aloysia Olinger	b: 1925		
		+August Joseph Leonards, Jr.	b: 1924	m: 1947	d: 1988
	4	August Joseph Leonards III	b: 1948		
		+Myrtis Thibodeaux	b: 1948	m: 1973	
	4	Don Edward Leonards	b: 1952		

Olinger

	Name	Birth	Marriage	Death
	+Deborah Gayle Burnet	b: 1951	m: 1978	
4	Gene John Leonards	b: 1956		
	+Sharon Ruppert	b: 1963	m: 1982	
3	Irene Regina Olinger	b: 1927		
	+Ashton Simon Petitjean	b: 1914	m: 1951	d: 1979
4	Charlotte Anne Petitjean	b: 1951		
	+Charles Gulotta	b: 1949	m: 1974	
4	Darlene Marie Petitjean	b: 1959		
	+Charles Russell	b: 1957	m: 1993	
4	Annette Louise Petitjean	b: 1963		
	+John Ebert	b: 1968	m: 1995	
3	Rose Marie Olinger	b: 1930		
	+John N. John III	b: 1929	m: 1950	d: 1983
4	John N. John IV	b: 1951		
	+Melanie Melancon	b: 1957	m: 1983	
4	Joseph Allen John	b: 1954		
	+Connie Marie Arabie	b: 1955	m: 1977	
4	William Mark John	b: 1955		
	+Patricia Roberts	b: 1954	m: 1978	
4	Michelle Ann John	b: 1958		
	+Brian Rasmussen		m: 1979	
	*2nd Husband of Michelle Ann John:			
	+Van Landry	b: 1949	m: 1999	
4	Christopher Charles John	b: 1960		
	+Payton Smith	b: 1967	m: 1992	
4	Katherine Claire John	b: 1963		
	+Michael Charles Hundley	b: 1962	m: 1984	
3	Hilary Anthony Olinger	b: 1934		
	+Melba Dean Roy	b: 1937	m: 1955	

Olinger

	4	Rhonda Olinger	b: 1957		
		+Thomas Broussard	b: 1957	m: 1979	
	4	Hilary Anthony "Tony" Olinger	b: 1963		
		+Verna Begnaud	b: 1972	m: 1998	
3		Mary Jo Olinger	b: 1938		
3		Ray Edward Olinger	b: 1942		
		+Johnnie Ruth Prather	b: 1941	m: 1966	
	4	Jude Anthony Olinger	b: 2/11/1967		
		+Erika Schroder	b: 11/18/1968	m: 9/13/2003	
	4	Yvette Barbara Olinger Plaisance	b: 9/25/1971		
	4	Nancy Lucille Olinger	b: 1/9/1981		
		+Stephen Gregory Choate	b: 1/11/1979	m: 3/31/2000	
2		Anthony Dominic Olinger	b: 1898		d: 1974
		+Frieda Mary Boeglin	b: 1909	m: 1933	d: 1982
3		James Ferdinand Olinger	b: 1934		
		+Shirley Rose Schness	b: 1937	m: 1963	
	4	Marilyn Olinger	b: 1967		
		+Jay Leonard	b: 1963	m: 1987	
	4	Becky Olinger	b: 1972		
3		Robert Andrew Olinger	b: 1935		
		+Nancy Gerber	b: 1942	m: 1961	
	4	Kelly Olinger	b: 1962		
		+Louis Hildenbrand	b: 1959	m: 1982	
	4	Kristy Olinger	b: 1965		
		+Chris Dilger	b: 1963	m: 1986	
	4	Nick Olinger	b: 1968		
	4	Amy Olinger	b: 1970		
		+Jason Stamm	b: 1967	m: 2000	
3		Mary Lee Olinger	b: 1937		

Olinger

	+Earl Sylvester Meyer	b: 1931	m: 1966	d: 2002
4	Max Meyer	b: 1969		
4	Maria Meyer	b: 1972		
	+Keith Sander	b: 1970	m: 1992	
3	Jerome "Jerry" Alphonse Olinger	b: 1938		
	+Julie Ann Krueger	b: 1941	m: 1962	
4	Jan Olinger	b: 1963		
	+Cecilia Mullen	b: 1966	m: 1992	
4	Jennifer Olinger	b: 1965		
	+Mike Deckwith	b: 1964	m: 1990	
4	Jane Olinger	b: 1966		
	+Scott Altmeyer	b: 1965	m: 1989	
	*2nd Husband of Jane Olinger:			
	+Mike Fritch	b: 1959	m: 1999	
4	Jill Olinger	b: 1969		
	+Tim Tretter	b: 1966	m: 1991	
4	Jody Olinger	b: 1972		
	+Ray Burdette	b: 1975	m: 1995	
3	Barbara Ann Olinger	b: 1940		
	+Gerald Wayne Herbig	b: 1937	m: 1960	
4	Rick Herbig	b: 1961		
	+Ava ?	b: 1960	m: 1987	
4	Debbie Herbig	b: 1962		
	+Phil Hoffman	b: 1959	m: 1984	
4	Sue Herbig	b: 1966		
3	Norma Jane Olinger	b: 1941		
	+Del Steinhart	b: 1941	m: 1962	
4	John Steinhart	b: 1970		
	+Sandy Sturgun	b: 1973	m: 1997	
4	Michael Steinhart	b: 1973		
	+Vicki Borden	b: 1970	m: 1998	

Olinger

2		Clara Julia Olinger	b: 1900			d: 1975
		+Charles Barromeo Dischler	b: 1898	m: 1922		d: 1986
	3	Barbara Catherine Dischler	b: 1923			d: 1993
		+Willard Paul Reed	b: 1920	m: 1952		
		4 Patricia Lois Reed	b: 1953			
		+Warren Hotard	b: 1952	m: 1977		
		4 Mary Lucille Reed	b: 1954			
		+Norm Cornilius	b: 1957	m: 1981		
		*2nd Husband of Mary Lucille Reed:				
		+Michael Gott	b: 1951	m: 1992		
		4 Donald Paul Reed	b: 1956			
		+Jeannie Bello	b: 1961	m: 1982		
		4 Kathleen Ann Reed	b: 1959			
		+Robert Telatovich	b: 1956	m: 1981		
		4 Joan Marie Reed	b: 1963			
		+Eric Lauber	b: 1960	m: 1986		
	3	Charles Leo Dischler	b: 1924			
		+Carrie Mae Harmon	b: 1930	m: 1949		
	3	Cecilia Madelene Dischler	b: 1926			
		+Daniel Nicholas Landry	b: 1925	m: 1950		
		4 Mary Claire Landry	b: 1951			
		+John Ledlow	b: 1946	m: 1991		
		4 Daniel Nicholas Landry, Jr.	b: 1952			
		+Alice Ziegler	b: 1956	m: 1983		
		4 Kenneth O'Neil Landry	b: 1956			
	3	Julia Theresa Dischler	b: 1928			
		+Sherril Paul Thompson	b: 1926	m: 1957		d: 2002
		4 Gregory Scott Thompson	b: 1958			

Olinger

		+Shelly Savoie	b: 1959	m: 1984	
	4	Charles Allen Thompson	b: 1960		
		+Lori Jones	b: 1963	m: 1987	
	4	Rhonda Claire Thompson	b: 1962		
		+Shane LaHood	b: 1970	m: 1994	
3		Alvin Joseph Dischler	b: 1929		
		+Theresa Nartarona	b: 1933	m: 1958	
	4	Stephen Jude Dischler	b: 1964		
		+Kelly Colburn	b: 1973	m: 1997	
	4	Jennifer Dischler	b: 1965		
		+Michael Bennefield	b: 1964	m: 1985	
	4	Dean Charles Dischler	b: 1968		
		+Paula Stoudt	b: 1968	m: 1996	
	4	Janet Marie Dischler	b: 1971		
		+William Maunel	b: 1970	m: 1994	
3		Clarice Josephine Dischler	b: 1932		
		+William Charles Stewart	b: 1928	m: 1972	d: 1995
3		Ferdinand Louis Dischler	b: 1933		
		+Wanda Jane George	b: 1933	m: 1956	
	4	Ronald Charles Dischler	b: 1957		
		+Jean McClelland		m: 1984	
		*2nd Wife of Ronald Charles Dischler:			
		+Marcia Landry	b: 1955	m: 1993	
	4	Pamela Ann Dischler	b: 1958		
		+Steve Celestin	b: 1960	m: 1988	
	4	Gregory Jude Dischler	b: 1960		
		+Joy Bender	b: 1966	m: 1991	
	4	Angela Melita Dischler	b: 1961		
		+David Lippman	b: 1960	m: 1984	

Olinger

4	Timothy Irvin Dischler	b: 1962		
	+Becky Landry	b: 1966	m: 1998	
4	Stephanie Lucille Dischler	b: 1965		
	+Dwayne Misita	b: 1959	m: 1995	
3	Robert Louis Dischler	b: 1935		d: 2003
	+Donna Sue Fast	b: 1941	m: 1964	
4	Christopher Dischler	b: 1965		
4	Jason Dischler	b: 1968		
4	Kelli Dischler	b: 1970		
	+David Cochran	b: 1969	m: 1994	
4	Stacy Dischler	b: 1974		
3	Thomas Anthony Dischler	b: 1938		
3	Marjorie Ann Dischler	b: 1940		
	+Robert Joseph Walker	b: 1940	m: 1959	
4	Stephen Charles Walker	b: 1960		
	+Monica Sittig	b: 1964	m: 1991	
4	Carmen Mary Walker	b: 1961		
	+David Speer	b: 1955	m: 1989	
4	Michael Gerard Walker	b: 1963		
	+Deborah Dalme	b: 1955	m: 1988	
4	Mary Elizabeth "Beth" Walker	b: 1964		
	+Zan Trahan	b: 1965	m: 1985	
4	Mark Robert Walker	b: 1969		
	+Kimberly Fruge	b: 1970	m: 1990	
4	Ann Catherine Walker	b: 1973		
	+Jerry Pickett	b: 1970	m: 1992	
3	Michael Anthony Dischler	b: 1942		
	+Barbara Hazelton	b: 1948	m: 1973	
4	Krista Dischler	b: 1968		
4	Jill Dischler	b: 1970		

Olinger

		+Danny Baber	b: 1963	m: 1990	
	4	Michael Anthony Dischler, Jr.	b: 1975		
3		Carol Bertha Dischler	b: 1945		
		+Lawrence William Leonards	b: 1946	m: 1969	
	4	Karl William Leonards	b: 1970		
	4	Kenneth Charles Leonards	b: 1970		
		+Tonya Miller	b: 1971	m: 1994	
	4	Lisa Ann Leonards	b: 1972		
		+Jason Guy Turner		m: 6/7/2003	
	4	Bryan Lawrence Leonards	b: 1973		
		+Nancy McDaniel	b: 1975	m: 1999	
2		Rev. Msgr. Aloysius Odilon Olinger	b: 8/18/1902		d: 6/18/1969
2		Julia Rosa Olinger	b: 1904		d: 1991
		+Henry Peter Gossen	b: 1903	m: 1929	d: 1982
3		Henrietta Ann Gossen	b: 1929		
		+Julian A. Didier	b: 1928	m: 1949	
	4	Barbara Ann Didier	b: 1951		
	4	Mary Ellen Didier	b: 1953		
		+Richard Duhon	b: 1952	m: 1974	
	4	Ronald Didier	b: 1954		
		+Kim Aucoin	b: 1961	m: 1982	
	4	Daniel Didier	b: 1955		
		+Jennifer Hebert	b: 1958	m: 1979	
	4	Stephen Didier	b: 1957		
		+Annette Rogers	b: 1959	m: 1979	
	4	Thomas Didier	b: 1958		
		+Rebecka Nolan	b: 1965	m: 1979	
	4	Judy Didier	b: 1962		

Olinger

	+John Bonin	b: 1960	m: 1990	
4	Leo Didier	b: 1963		
	+Claire Clayton		m: 1990	
3	Gilbert William Gossen	b: 1931		
	+Florence Rita Gonsoulin	b: 1935	m: 1955	
4	David William Gossen	b: 1957		
4	Jeannie Marie Gossen	b: 1957		
	+Kirk James Thibodeaux	b: 1959	m: 1983	
4	Leonard Brian Gossen	b: 1960		
	+Leslie Loran Lasseigne	b: 1959	m: 1991	
4	Lynette Ann Gossen	b: 1963		
	+William Harrison Perry	b: 1962	m: 1986	
4	Kathryn Aileen Gossen	b: 1972		
	+Jean Paul Theriot	b: 1970	m: 1994	
3	Ralph Aloysius Gossen	b: 1934		
	+Marcella Elizabeth Habetz	b: 1942	m: 1962	d: 1973
4	Randall Joseph Gossen	b: 1963		
	+Mary Elizabeth Broussard	b: 1973	m: 1993	
4	John William Gossen	b: 1966		
	+Fay Ann Fruge	b: 1969	m: 1994	
	*2nd Wife of Ralph Aloysius Gossen:			
	+Marjorie Marie Devillier	b: 1937	m: 1977	
3	Herbert Joseph Gossen	b: 1936		
	+Elaine Leonards	b: 1938	m: 1958	
4	Diane Gossen	b: 1959		
	+Clyde Comeaux	b: 1958	m: 1977	

Olinger

	4	Cynthia Gossen	b: 1960	
		+Ferdara Hubbard	b: 1958	
		*2nd Husband of Cynthia Gossen:		
		+Paul Gibson	b: 1953	m: 1998
	4	Philip Gossen	b: 1961	
		+Jennifer Colligan	b: 1963	m: 1986
	4	Saundra Gossen	b: 1962	
		+Anthony Cook	b: 1959	m: 1982
	4	Darlene Gossen	b: 1964	
		+Kent Smith	b: 1962	m: 1985
	4	Dwayne Gossen	b: 1965	
		+Carla Clayton	b: 1968	m: 1987
	4	Bonnie Gossen	b: 1966	
		+John Foreman	b: 1962	m: 1988
	4	Keith Gossen	b: 1968	
		+Julie Johnson	b: 1968	m: 1990
	4	Charlene Gossen	b: 1970	
		+Lynn Boone	b: 1968	m: 1989
	4	Paul Gossen	b: 1971	
		+Danielle Constantin	b: 1973	m: 1993
	4	Herbert Gossen II	b: 1973	
		+Nanette Monceaux	b: 8/20/1964	
	4	Deceased Infant Gossen	b: 1975	
3		Donald Charles Gossen	b: 1941	
		+Henrietta Breaux	b: 1948	m: 1967
	4	Angela Claire Gossen	b: 1967	
		+Edwin Daniel Boudreaux	b: 1970	m: 1991
	4	Lisa Ann Gossen	b: 1970	
		+Robert Jules Romero	b: 1968	m: 1988
3		Flavia Diane Gossen	b: 1943	d: 1946
2		Emil Franz Olinger	b: 1910	d: 1988

Olinger

	+Alice Mary Laake	b: 1913	m: 1936	
3	Rita Ann Olinger	b: 1937		
	+Wayne Anthony Jones	b: 1934	m: 1960	
4	Wayne Anthony "Tony" Jones	b: 1961		
4	Lori Suzanne Jones	b: 1962		
	+Anthony Robert Petrucciani	b: 1964	m: 1989	
4	Weston Andrew Jones	b: 1965		
4	Benjamin Scott Jones	b: 1968		
4	Bryant Stephen Jones	b: 1969		
	+Laura Kay Huter	b: 1970	m: 1998	
3	John Leo Olinger	b: 1939		
	+Pierrette Denise Berbeu	b: 1937	m: 1969	
4	Karen Ann Olinger	b: 1972		
	+Benjamin Richmond	b: 1971	m: 1997	
4	Philip Thomas Olinger	b: 1973		
	+Christy Deberry	b: 1975	m: 1998	
4	Nicole Marie Olinger	b: 1975		
4	Mary Beth Olinger	b: 1976		
3	Mary Ellen Olinger	b: 1942		
	+Leo Sylvester Will	b: 1937	m: 1964	
4	Eric John Will	b: 1965		
	+Alice Marie Aydt	b: 1966	m: 1988	
4	Dianne Lynn Will	b: 1967		
	+Christopher James Thomas	b: 1964	m: 1993	
4	Julie Marie Will	b: 1973		
	+Todd Preston Yunker	b: 1974	m: 1997	
3	Joseph Aloysius Olinger	b: 1942		d: 1979
3	Martha Jane Olinger	b: 1944		

Olinger

4	John Paul Olinger	b: 1976	
3	Stephen Linus Olinger	b: 1952	
	+Karen Collins	b: 1954	m: 1977
4	Jill Marie Olinger	b: 1981	
3	Thomas Paul Olinger	b: 1958	
	+Sandra Benson	b: 1957	
4	Christian Andrew Olinger	b: 1989	
4	Elizabeth Margrethe Olinger	b: 1991	

27. Reiners, Franz Anton:

Franz Anton Reiners b: 7/3/1846 d: 1907 from Braunsrath was the son of Peter Leonard Reiners b: 5/5/1816 d: 7/2/1870 and Anna Gertrude Mertens b: 1811 d: 11/22/1856. He married on 6/30/1872 to Maria Veronika Knoben b: 10/17/1847 d: 1928, the daughter of Lambert Arnold Knoben b: 9/17/1811 d: 1/19/1904 and Anna Mechtilde Oidtmann b: 1812 d: 3/11/1901.

2		Peter Joseph Reiners	b: 1/11/1874		d: 5/13/1936
		+Anna Helena Berken	b: 4/24/1880	m: 2/14/1900	d: 9/8/1968
	3	Frank Reiners	b: 9/8/1901		d: 9/25/1987
		+Anna Maria Thevis	b: 4/20/1905	m: 2/12/1924	d: 2/14/1973
	4	Joseph Reiners	b: 4/9/1925		d: 11/16/2005
		+Harriette Louise Klein	b: 10/13/1931	m: 11/9/1949	
	4	Alois Andrew Reiners	b: 7/25/1926		d: 3/19/1999
		+Lucille Clara Gossen	b: 11/11/1928	m: 11/25/1953	
	4	Elizabeth Reiners	b: 10/16/1928		d: 4/17/2000
	4	Helen Marie Reiners	b: 9/20/1932		
		+Sylvester Lawrence Frey	b: 7/20/1930	m: 1/20/1954	
	4	Anthony Francis Reiners	b: 11/18/1933		
		+Pauline Ann Habetz	b: 4/14/1934	m: 9/19/1957	
	3	John Herman Reiners	b: 1904		d: 1904
	3	Maria Adelheid Reiners	b: 1907		d: 1907
	3	Adelheid Reiners	b: 11/24/1907		d: 12/15/1975
	3	John Herman Reiners Sr.	b: 6/27/1915		d: 11/1/1991
		+Willie Mae Reed	b: 2/16/1916	m: 11/10/1937	d: 7/17/1945
	4	John Herman Reiners Jr.	b: 10/19/1938		
		+Mary Ann Meyer	b: 2/2/1942	m: 4/8/1961	
	4	Rose Marie Reiners	b: 3/28/1942		
		+Stephen Joseph Zaunbrecher	b: 9/2/1940	m: 6/26/1962	
	4	Mary Magdalene Reiners	b: 3/31/1944		

Reiners

	+Lawrence Aloyious Cramer, Sr.	b: 9/12/1941	m: 6/11/1963	
4	Anna Marie Reiners	b: 7/17/1945		d: 7/17/1945
4	[2] William Joseph Reiners, Sr.	b: 8/7/1940		d: 11/28/1999
	+[1] Elizabeth Magdalene Thevis	b: 3/1/1942	m: 11/11/1961	
	*2nd Wife of John Herman Reiners Sr.:			
	+Agnes Ancelet	b: 8/17/1925	m: 7/26/1971	
3	Anna Helena Reiners	b: 1918		d: 1918
3	Anna Maria Reiners	b: 1918		d: 1918
3	Helena Veronica Reiners	b: 3/9/1919		
	+Camile Richard	b: 11/7/1914	m: 8/28/1940	d: 5/10/1999
4	Joseph Richard	b: 7/6/1941		
	+Rose Marie Robicheaux			
4	Theresa Marie Richard	b: 10/6/1942		
	+Wilbert Thevis Sr.	b: 8/27/1940	m: 1/24/1961	
2	William Joseph Reiners	b: 1876		d: 1930
	+Maria Elizabeth Scheufens	b: 1884	m: 1907	d: 1940
3	Theodore Reiners	b: 1907		d: 1907
3	Maria Catherine Reiners	b: 1909		d: 1986
	+Anatole Gary	b: 1897	m: 1940	d: 1973
4	Wilton Joseph Gary	b: 9/1/1944		
	+Marcella Faye Vaughn	b: 8/18/1945	m: 2/27/1965	
4	Marie Anne Gary	b: 2/6/1946		
	+Obrey "Toboy" Benoit, Jr.	b: 2/4/1944	m: 10/24/1964	
4	Bertha Marie Gary	b: 7/13/1949		
	+Joseph Velior LaCombe	b: 8/14/1946	m: 11/22/1969	

Reiners

3	Maria Veronica Reiners	b: 1911		d: 1911
3	Veronica Reiners	b: 3/3/1912		
	+Peter Jacob Thevis	b: 2/26/1911	m: 11/11/1936	d: 10/13/1998
4	Marie Louise Thevis	b: 2/19/1938		
	+Vincent Joseph Berken	b: 12/17/1925	m: 10/24/1956	d: 4/22/2005
4	Wilbert Thevis	b: 8/27/1940		
	+Theresa Marie Richard	b: 10/9/1942	m: 1/24/1961	
4	Mary Kathleen Thevis	b: 10/7/1946		d: 10/19/2001
	+Glyn Roy Hoffpauir	b: 8/9/1945	m: 10/15/1966	d: 2/26/2003
4	[1] Elizabeth Magdalene Thevis	b: 3/1/1942		
	+[2] William Joseph Reiners, Sr.	b: 8/7/1940	m: 11/11/1961	d: 11/28/1999
3	Anthony Reiners	b: 1914		d: 1914
3	Agnes Columba Reiners	b: 1/31/1920		
	+William John Thevis	b: 3/4/1917	m: 11/26/1940	d: 8/11/1985
4	Frank William Thevis	b: 8/18/1941		
	+Nora Lou Bellard	b: 8/7/1941	m: 5/11/1963	d: 12/30/2004
4	Leo Joseph Thevis	b: 9/8/1946		
	+Jeanette Marie Daigle	b: 8/4/1950	m: 12/31/1974	
4	Clara Marie Thevis	b: 9/28/1949		
	+John Michael Savoy	b: 11/9/1949	m: 7/26/1969	
4	Paul Daniel Thevis	b: 1/2/1954		
	+Veronica Fuselier	b: 5/13/1953	m: 11/3/1973	
4	Rose Marie Thevis	b: 5/9/1957		
	+Ronald Kenneth Hornsby	b: 5/13/1956	m: 2/19/1976	
4	Andrew John Thevis	b: 4/6/1960		
	+Connie Dee LaCombe	b: 11/16/1960	m: 2/2/1980	
4	Loretta Ann Thevis	b: 3/30/1961		

Reiners

		+Harlan David Kebodeaux	b: 8/8/1965	m: 9/8/1990
	4	Arnold Stephen Thevis	b: 8/16/1964	
		+Kathleen Meche	b: 5/18/1959	m: 1/16/1988
3		Dorothy Josephine Reiners	b: 1921	
		+Deynoodt John Richard	b: 1922	d: 2003
	4	Margaret Donotel Richard	b: 7/25/1942	
		+James Harry Comeaux	b: 2/27/1936	m: 5/4/1963 d: 4/5/1999
	4	David William Richard	b: 8/7/1948	
		+Katherine Elizabeth Guidry	b: 6/2/1951	m: 9/2/1974
	4	Nancy Elizabeth Richard	b: 1/10/1953	
		+Marshall Glenn Pousson	b: 2/13/1953	m: 6/10/1972
	4	Simon James Richard	b: 9/4/1954	
		+Barbara Suiter	b: 9/6/1951	m: 8/26/1978
	4	George John Richard	b: 6/24/1956	
	4	Joyce Marie Richard	b: 6/14/1959	
		+Barry Paul Chaisson	b: 4/12/1955	m: 6/18/1977
	4	Yvonne Marie Richard	b: 4/10/1961	
		+Harold Clarke Bullock	b: 1/6/1961	m: 8/9/1980
	4	Yvette Marie Richard	b: 4/10/1961	
		+Philip Leo Ohlenforst	b: 5/13/1961	m: 10/18/1980
2		Catherine Josepha Reiners	b: 1881	d: 1938
		+Peter Anton Ohlenforst	b: 1878	m: 1903 d: 1944
3		Maria Frances Ohlenforst	b: 7/6/1904	d: 2/14/1988
		+Hubert Joseph Thevis	b: 8/16/1899	m: 11/28/1923 d: 5/24/1988
	4	Antonia Josephine Thevis	b: 3/1/1928	
		+Lloyd Lynn Hoffpauir	b: 5/30/1926	m: 11/23/1948 d: 7/5/2006

Reiners

4	Herbert Joseph Thevis	b: 3/13/1933		d: 9/16/1945
4	Raymond Gerhard Thevis	b: 4/13/1934		
	+Eunice Marie Abshire	b: 10/9/1935	m: 2/11/1956	
4	Norbert Anthony Thevis	b: 1/18/1938		
	+Betty Jean Norman	b: 10/4/1941	m: 1/18/1964	
4	Edward Daniel Thevis	b: 10/1/1941		
	+Selma Marie Touchet	b: 4/4/1942	m: 12/1/1961	
3	Veronica Wilhelmena Ohlenforst	b: 6/7/1907		d: 12/25/1975
	+John Gerhard Thevis	b: 6/30/1901	m: 11/17/1926	d: 4/27/1971
4	Anthony Joseph Thevis	b: 3/23/1928		d: 4/29/1992
	+Josephine Thecla Berken	b: 7/14/1934	m: 5/10/1955	
4	Ferdinand Thevis	b: 7/19/1930		
	+Wilda Ann LeJeune	b: 7/14/1933	m: 8/8/1953	
4	Lionel Edward Thevis	b: 10/25/1934		
	+Barbara Nell Monte	b: 2/14/1938	m: 9/29/1956	
3	Anna Josepha Ohlenforst	b: 8/10/1913		d: 2/29/1980
	+Leonard Joseph Thevis	b: 3/19/1906	m: 11/17/1931	d: 3/17/1969
4	James Thomas Thevis	b: 12/22/1933		
	+Normalie Blanchard	b: 3/18/1941	m: 5/19/1959	
3	Anthony Joseph Ohlenforst	b: 6/28/1916		d: 8/26/1974
	+Josephine Anna Leonards	b: 2/16/1920	m: 1940	d: 3/14/1992
4	Juliana Ohlenforst	b: 1942		d: 9/6/1998
	+Clyde W. Hoffpauir			
3	Catherine Margaret (Dollie) Ohlenforst	b: 1919		d: 1987
3	John Francis Ohlenforst	b: 1921		d: 1997
	+Philomena Hedwig Leonards	b: 1923	m: 1947	
4	Maria Goretti Ohlenforst	b: 6/20/1951		

Reiners

	+Joseph Kracher	b: 1/10/1948	m: 5/29/1976	
4	Dorita Lois Ohlenforst	b: 12/4/1952		
	+Richard Dalton Comeaux	b: 9/24/1947	m: 1/13/1996	
4	Jude Anthony Ohlenforst	b: 10/28/1955		
	+Gretchen Louise Gray	b: 2/4/1957	m: 6/27/1986	
3	Rita Victoria Ohlenforst	b: 1924		d: 1999
	+Joseph Peter Habetz	b: 1920	m: 1946	d: 7/25/2006
4	Flavia Ann Habetz	b: 1946		
	+Glenn John Eldridge		m: 11/27/1969	
4	Michael Anthony Habetz	b: 1948		
	+Cynthia Scott		m: 7/25/1970	
4	Bruno Joseph Habetz	b: 1950		
	+Debra Judice		m: 5/24/1975	
	*2nd Wife of Bruno Joseph Habetz:			
	+Mary Katherine Derouen		m: 10/27/1984	
	*3rd Wife of Bruno Joseph Habetz:			
	+Linda Leeper		m: 10/9/1992	
4	Tedmund Daniel Habetz	b: 1953		
	+Kay Voohries		m: 1980	
4	Joline Rita Habetz	b: 1955		d: 1955
2	Gertrude Anna Reiners	b: 4/11/1885		d: 1/16/1969
	+Joseph Hensgens	b: 2/24/1885	m: 11/27/1906	d: 10/6/1959
3	Christian Joseph Hensgens	b: 9/25/1908		d: 10/13/1972
	+Maria Elizabeth Thevis	b: 10/24/1909	m: 11/19/1928	d: 1/3/1985
4	Leonard Joseph Hensgens	b: 10/7/1929		
	+Sarah Ann Smith		m: 7/11/1950	
4	Raymond Aloysious Hensgens	b: 7/22/1932		

Reiners

	+Catherine (Kitty) Schneider		m: 10/20/1951	
4	Lawrence Leo Hensgens	b: 4/1/1934		
	+Lula Link		m: 12/10/1953	
4	Germaine Frances Hensgens	b: 12/14/1935		d: 2/2/1996
	+Frank J. Schneider		m: 10/25/1955	
4	Wilhelmina Thecla (Wilma) Hensgens	b: 11/10/1937		d: 5/21/2006
	+Henry Jerome Leonards	b: 9/13/1934	m: 1/26/1958	
4	Alberta Gertrude Hensgens	b: 2/13/1940		
	+Joseph Norwood (Marcy) Lyons		m: 5/25/1963	
3	Josepha Regina Hensgens	b: 7/19/1909		d: 10/10/1909
3	Catherine Frances Hensgens	b: 10/26/1916		d: 11/15/1997
	+Pirmin Hubert Habetz	b: 11/3/1911	m: 1/8/1936	d: 8/22/1970
4	Laurentia Frances (Sr. Lawrence) Habetz	b: 1/21/1937		
4	Pirmin Joseph (Junior) Habetz	b: 6/4/1938		
	+Mary Lou Hebert		m: 5/16/1959	
4	Patricia Clara Habetz	b: 2/22/1940		
	+Bennett Augustine		m: 11/7/1959	
4	Marcella Elizabeth (Mel) Habetz	b: 4/16/1942		d: 5/22/1973
	+Ralph Alois Gossen	b: 1934	m: 5/5/1962	
4	Patrick Conrad Habetz	b: 2/28/1944		
	+Marjorie Granger		m: 4/11/1964	
4	Kathleen Gertrude (Teemie) Habetz	b: 9/7/1945		
	+Cecil Compton		m: 8/21/1965	
3	Conrad Leo Hensgens	b: 1/25/1920		d: 4/22/1987

Reiners

	+Marie Catherine (Gertie Mae) Theunissen	b: 1922	m: 11/29/1939	
4	Thomas Jude (Tommy) Hensgens	b: 1955		
	+Jo Ann (Trina) Autin		m: 10/27/1989	
3	Anna Gertrude Hensgens	b: 12/27/1921		d: 11/28/2000
	+Lee Joseph Monlezun, Sr.	b: 4/24/1917	m: 8/13/1941	d: 7/31/1985
4	Lee Joseph Monlezun, Jr.	b: 1/20/1943		
	+Evelyn Anne Prague Gillett	b: 3/14/1947	m: 5/5/1979	
4	Robert Joseph Monlezun	b: 5/27/1944		
	+Wanda Lynn Womack	b: 7/23/1946	m: 11/6/1965	
4	Charles Joseph Monlezun	b: 9/29/1946		
	+Sharon Diane LeBleu	b: 12/22/1946	m: 8/9/1969	
4	Anna Bernadette Monlezun	b: 12/12/1947		
	+Col. Hector Rafael Ponton	b: 7/25/1936	m: 1/14/1978	
4	Constance Victoria Monlezun	b: 9/15/1950		
	+Victor Wayne Darbonne	b: 8/28/1948	m: 6/30/1973	
4	Malcolm Joseph Monlezun	b: 12/24/1952		
	+Ursula Ann Daigle	b: 2/25/1955	m: 12/27/1971	
4	Alvin Joseph Monlezun	b: 8/7/1954		d: 5/27/1965
4	Ione Marie Monlezun	b: 9/4/1956		
	+Whitney Broussard II			
4	Veronica Gertrude Monlezun	b: 2/7/1958		d: 5/27/1965

Reiners

4	Dominique Joseph Monlezun	b: 9/20/1960		
	+Tina Louise King	b: 10/10/1961	m: 2/9/1980	
3	Barbara Leona Hensgens	b: 5/6/1924		
	+Lawrence Herman Berken	b: 8/10/1921	m: 1/30/1946	d: 9/11/1996
4	Charlotte Ann Berken	b: 2/15/1948		
	+George Kenneth Connor	b: 4/23/1948	m: 1/25/1969	
4	Stephen Herman Berken	b: 5/5/1949		
	+Melanie Boutte	b: 7/21/1953	m: 12/16/1972	
4	Clarence Aloysius Berken	b: 12/12/1951		
	+Karen Berry		m: 1/6/1973	
4	Martha Elaine Berken	b: 3/26/1955		
	+Homer Stevens II		m: 8/3/1974	
4	Rachel Lea Berken	b: 12/1/1957		
	+Tomas (Tom) Wayne Andrus		m: 9/4/1976	
4	Kevin Matthew Berken	b: 3/16/1961		
	+Shirley Hill		m: 12/14/1990	
4	Mary Gayle Berken	b: 3/18/1963		
	+Jay Womack			
	*2nd Husband of Mary Gayle Berken:			
	+Todd Moses		m: 6/12/1999	
	*2nd Husband of Barbara Leona Hensgens:			
	+Lewis Smaihall	b: 10/1914	m: 7/6/2002	d: 1/20/2005
3	Nicholas Anthony Hensgens	b: 12/6/1925		d: 12/6/1999
	+Gloria Theresa Deshotels	b: 3/12/1927	m: 11/16/1948	d: 2/5/1995
4	Nicholas Anthony Hensgens, Jr.	b: 9/20/1949		

Reiners

	+Pamala Marie Boudreaux		m: 4/26/1980	
4	Stephanie Louise Hensgens	b: 4/27/1952		
	+Ronald Berger		m: 8/17/1974	
4	Kenneth James Hensgens	b: 11/10/1954		
	+Michelle Champagne			
4	Karl Joseph Hensgens	b: 3/26/1956		
	+Melanie Hanks		m: 12/7/1984	
3	Clarice Johanna Hensgens	b: 9/15/1929		
	+Guy Gregory Gauthreaux	b: 1926	m: 4/23/1953	
4	Gwendolyn Clare Gauthreaux	b: 5/26/1954		
	+Charles (Brusle) Sherburne, Jr.		m: 5/21/1977	
4	Guy Gregoire (G.G.) Gauthreaux II	b: 4/16/1956		
	+Deborah (Debbie) Hinkle		m: 8/7/1976	
4	Kay Frances Gauthreaux			
	+Dale Dugruise			
4	Joseph Hensgens (Joey) Gauthreaux			
	+Chrystal Taylor		m: 10/9/2004	
2	Maria Catherine Reiners	b: 1889		d: 1966
	+Arnold Joseph Scheufens	b: 1886	m: 1910	d: 1967
3	Maria Veronica Scheufens	b: 1910		d: 1996
3	Maria Catherine Scheufens	b: 1912		d: 1988
	+Matthias Joseph Meyer	b: 1905	m: 1932	d: 1979
4	Charles Joseph Meyer, Sr.	b: 2/8/1933		
	+Agnes Ruth McCown	b: 10/19/1938	m: 5/25/1956	d: 2005
	*2nd Wife of Charles Joseph Meyer, Sr.:			
	+Djuana Gary	b: 1964	m: 1996	

Reiners

4	Arnold Remy "Ray" Meyer, Sr.	b: 5/23/1934		d: 11/13/2006
	+Geneva Viola Louviere	b: 12/10/1935	m: 6/4/1959	
4	John Allen Meyer	b: 3/7/1936		d: 7/17/2005
	+Sandra McCown	b: 1/15/1947	m: 4/11/1969	
4	Louis Theodore Meyer	b: 11/26/1937		
	+Jean Pitre	b: 8/29/1942	m: 12/29/1962	
4	Edwin Frank Meyer	b: 9/21/1939		
	+Bobbie Jane Caswell	b: 4/19/1941	m: 6/15/1963	
4	Johanna Catherine Meyer	b: 2/19/1941		
	+Leland Cormier	b: 8/19/1936	m: 7/15/1962	
4	Clyde Joseph Meyer	b: 4/15/1942		d: 3/17/2003
	+Alice Faye Miguez	b: 2/16/1948		
4	Frances Jane Meyer	b: 8/24/1943		
	+Clyde Coble	b: 5/8/1942	m: 3/8/1972	
4	Matthias Joseph Meyer, Jr.	b: 5/25/1946		d: 9/29/1995
	+Dolores Ann Richard	b: 9/17/1945	m: 5/10/1966	
4	Stephen James Meyer	b: 11/16/1947		
	+Eloise Joan Richard	b: 1/15/1950	m: 2/14/1969	
	*2nd Wife of Stephen James Meyer:			
	+Sharon Gayle Galley	b: 1953	m: 1973	
4	Michael Lawrence Meyer	b: 4/1/1951		
	+Susan Matt	b: 10/30/1952	m: 10/17/1970	
4	Thomas Larry Meyer	b: 7/6/1953		
	+Bridgett Ann Hoffpauir	b: 8/31/1955	m: 8/16/1975	
	*2nd Wife of Thomas Larry Meyer:			
	+Sarah Frances Kennedy	b: 1/2/1958	m: 4/19/1990	

Reiners

3	Theodor Scheufens	b: 1/14/1916		d: 1991
	+Estelle Boudreaux	b: 8/17/1916	m: 1937	
4	Mary Genevieve Scheufens	b: 1/5/1938		
	+Gordon Ray Franklin	b: 8/14/1933		
4	Barbara Scheufens	b: 9/29/1939		d: 9/29/1939
4	Theodor Joseph Scheufens, Jr.	b: 10/22/1942		
	+Deborah Sharp	b: 9/23/1953	m: 10/22/1980	
4	Clyde Joseph Scheufens	b: 4/2/1944		
4	Frank Homer Scheufens	b: 1/9/1946		
	+Sallye Frances Guthrey	b: 8/29/1948	m: 5/31/1968	
3	Francis Joseph Scheufens	b: 1918		d: 1985
3	Hubert Joseph Scheufens	b: 1920		d: 1921
3	Anna Antoinette Scheufens	b: 9/10/1925		d: 10/12/1999
	+Arnold Rubin Hicks	b: 1925	m: 1951	
4	Janice Marie Hicks	b: 4/28/1953		
	+Floyd LeBlanc	b: 9/16/1956	m: 1/24/1981	
4	Larry James Hicks	b: 9/20/1954		
	+Deborah Soileau	b: 8/10/1959	m: 11/7/1983	
	*2nd Wife of Larry James Hicks:			
	+Tina Crowder	b: 5/7/1966	m: 5/12/2006	
3	Elizabeth Marie Margaret Scheufens	b: 1928		
	+Nolton Paul Broussard	b: 1921	m: 1947	d: 1971
4	Pamela Ann Broussard	b: 1949		
	+Michael Earl Fontenot	b: 1949	m: 1969	
4	Randall Paul Broussard	b: 1950		
	+Ann Richard	b: 1949	m: 1969	
4	Blaine Patrick Broussard	b: 1957		

Reiners

	+Celeste Hilda Comeaux	b: 1960	m: 1979

*2nd Husband of Elizabeth Marie Margaret Scheufens:

	+Floyd Silvia	b: 1925	m: 1975
3	Henry Charles Vincent Scheufens	b: 1930	
	+Billye Jewell Lyle	b: 1939	m: 1958
4	William Arnold Scheufens	b: 1962	
	+Susan Hollister Hall	b: 1965	m: 1986
4	Gregory Vincent Scheufens	b: 1964	
	+Susan Michelle Bryeans Welsh	b: 1965	m: 1996
4	Trecia Denise Scheufens	b: 1965	
	+Kevin Roy Quebodeaux	b: 1966	m: 1987

28. Ronkartz, Johann:

Johann Ronkartz b: 1862 d: 1907 from Schierwaldenrath was the son of Johann Lambert Ronkartz and Maria Lucia Peters. He married in 1889 to Maria Anna Vondenstein b: 1870 d: 1920, the daughter of Wilhelm Joseph Vondenstein b: 1831 d: 1901 from Langbroich and Maria Josepha Killen b: 1842 d: 1913 from Hastenrath (see Vondenstein family).

2	Maria Josepha Ronkartz	b: 1889		d: 1972	
	+Anton Joseph Heinen	b: 1877	m: 1907	d: 1929	
3	Anna Marie Heinen	b: 1908		d: 1994	
	+Roland Privat	b: 1906	m: 1931	d: 1963	
4	Louis Privat	b: 1932			
4	Bobby Privat	b: 1933		d: 1993	
	+Cindy Gardiner	b: 1934	m: 1956		
4	Eddie Privat	b: 1936			
	+Gayle Arceneaux	b: 1937	m: 1958		
	*2nd Wife of Eddie Privat:				
	+Mary Ann Duzzer	b: 1939	m: 1983		
4	Tommy Privat	b: 1940			
	+Pam Fontenot	b: 1941	m: 1964		
4	Dan Privat	b: 1948			
	+Charlotte Simpson	b: 1946	m: 1968		
4	Ann Marie Privat	b: 1948			
	+James Burch	b: 1949	m: 1982		
3	Maria Josepha Heinen	b: 1911		d: 2005	
	+Clarence Dodd Daigle	b: 1909	m: 1934	d: 1974	
4	Freddie Daigle	b: 1936			
	+Sylvia Fontenot	b: 1934	m: 1955		
4	Albert T. Daigle	b: 1936			
	+Earlene Venable	b: 1938	m: 1957		
4	Janet Daigle	b: 1942			
	+James Ethridge	b: 1942	m: 1962		
2	Lambert Ronkartz	b: 1891		d: 1978	

Ronkartz

	+Regina Maria Dischler	b: 1894	m: 1919	d: 1977
3	Josephine Marie Ronkartz	b: 1920		
	+Joseph John Burton	b: 1917	m: 1941	d: 2004
4	Charles Donahue Burton	b: 1941		
	+Marie Louise Stephanie Menou	b: 1942	m: 1961	
4	Jo Ann Burton	b: 1943		d: 1943
4	Thomas Miles Burton	b: 1946		
	+Donita Lane Grey		m: 1967	
4	Wayne John Burton	b: 1948		
	+Sandra Claire Daigle	b: 1950	m: 1972	
4	Carl Mitchell Burton	b: 1949		
	+Keta Fontenot	b: 1952	m: 1988	
4	James Lambert Burton	b: 1951		
	+Judy Marie Lejeune	b: 1956	m: 1978	
4	Deborah Burton	b: 1953		
	+Robert McDaniel			
	*2nd Husband of Deborah Burton:			
	+Steve Joseph Longenbaugh	b: 1948	m: 1981	
4	Dale Anthony Burton	b: 1957		
	+Shelia Faye Mayberry	b: 1956	m: 1985	
4	Joseph Damian Burton	b: 1959		
	+Cecile Johnson			
	*2nd Wife of Joseph Damian Burton:			
	+Vanessa Jane Fontenot	b: 1959	m: 1996	
4	Josette Marie Burton	b: 1961		
	+Charles David Pruitt	b: 1960	m: 1983	d: 2003
3	Joseph John Ronkartz	b: 1922		d: 1989
	+Rose Marie Leblanc	b: 1926	m: 1946	d: 1989
4	Russel James Ronkartz	b: 1948		

Ronkartz

	+Julie Michelle Chappuis	b: 1948	m: 1969	
	*2nd Wife of Russel James Ronkartz:			
	+Anita Boulanger	b: 1952	m: 1978	
	*3rd Wife of Russel James Ronkartz:			
	+Sheila Estrello	b: 1945	m: 1982	d: 1982
	*4th Wife of Russel James Ronkartz:			
	+Trudy Fay Osterhause	b: 1952	m: 1987	
4	Byron Joseph Ronkartz	b: 1949		
	+Bernadine Trappey	b: 1957		
	*2nd Wife of Byron Joseph Ronkartz:			
	+Janet Gilbert	b: 1952	m: 1971	
4	Jo Ann Ronkartz	b: 1952		
	+Jerry Marvin Boberts	b: 1951	m: 1971	
	*2nd Husband of Jo Ann Ronkartz:			
	+William Charles Plitt, Jr.	b: 1939	m: 1982	
4	Judith Anne Ronkartz	b: 1955		
	+Joe David Milian	b: 1943	m: 1987	
4	Warren Mark Ronkartz	b: 1956		d: 1965
4	Rose Mary Ronkartz	b: 1959		
	+George Dainel Parker	b: 1957	m: 1986	
3	John William Ronkartz	b: 1925		d: 2000
	+Effie Katherine Rogers	b: 1933	m: 1950	
4	John William Ronkartz, Jr.	b: 1951		
	+Nancy Williams	b: 1958	m: 1993	
4	Sheila Ronkartz	b: 1952		
	+Edward Ray Hughes	b: 1947		
4	Karen Sue Ronkartz	b: 1954		
4	Donald Wayne Ronkartz	b: 1957		d: 1957
4	Wendy Ronkartz	b: 1959		

Ronkartz

		+Donnie Ray Cooper	b: 1955		
	3	Jeanette Juliana Ronkartz	b: 1929		
		+Ronald Gene Robinson	b: 1931	m: 1950	d: 1953
	3	Louise Regina Ronkartz	b: 1932		
		+Daniel Hilarion Troyanowski	b: 1928	m: 1954	d: 1981
4		Larry Daniel Troyanowski	b: 1956		
		+Kathryn de Valcourt	b: 1956	m: 1979	
	3	Jerome Lambert Ronkartz	b: 1933		
		+Josephine Ann Zaunbrecher	b: 1934	m: 1956	
4		Gwendolyn Ann Ronkartz	b: 8/17/1957		
		+Harry Heinen	b: 1954		
4		Gregory Paul Ronkartz	b: 9/5/1958		
		+Diane Hornsby	b: 1956	m: 1980	
4		Christopher Ronkartz	b: 1/30/1960		d: 1/30/1960
4		Stephen Mark Ronkartz	b: 8/26/1961		
		+Patricia Ann Payne		m: 1989	
2		Maria Agnes Ronkartz	b: 1894		d: 1969
		+Peter Leonard Thevis	b: 1891	m: 1916	d: 1987
	3	Leonard Gerhard Thevis	b: 1917		
	3	John Joseph Thevis	b: 1920		d: 1993
		+Nancee Ruth Andrew		m: 1969	
		*2nd Wife of John Joseph Thevis:			
		+Ouida Mae Spell		m: 1977	
	3	Mary Anna Thevis	b: 1922		
	3	Anna Josephine Thevis	b: 1925		
	3	Leona Walburga (Sister Agnes Leonard) Thevis	b: 1927		
	3	Lawrence Vincent Thevis	b: 1929		d: 1995
		+Betty Jane Henderson	b: 1929	m: 1980	

Ronkartz

3 Louise Helen Thevis b: 1931
3 Dorothy Agnes Thevis b: 1934

29. Schaffhausen, Joseph Hubert:

Joseph Hubert Schaffhausen b: 1855 d: 1938 from Gillrath was the son of Johann Schaffhausen and Anna Katharina Krückels. He first married in 1893 to Sophia Dischler b: 1873 d: 1893, the daughter of Franz Xavier Dischler and Carolina Niederst (see Dischler family). His second marriage in 1904 was to Katharina Agnes Scheufens b: 1881 d: 1964, who is the daughter of Johann Theodor Scheufens b: 2/13/1841 d: 2/7/1903 from Hastenrath and Maria Katharina Janssen b: 9/18/1843 d: 9/19/1933 from Birgden (see Scheufens family).

2		Mary Catherine Schaffhausen	b: 1906		d: 2005
2		Elizabeth Mary Schaffhausen	b: 1907		d: 1984
2		Josephine Catherine Schaffhausen	b: 1909		d: 1991
		+Leo Gunby Bird	b: 1895	m: 1943	d: 1949
3		Julie Agnes Bird	b: 8/27/1943		
		+Charles DeLacerda	b: 12/1/1939	m: 7/15/1961	
	4	Lisa Marie DeLacerda	b: 4/22/1962		
	4	Charles Leo DeLacerda	b: 2/13/1965		
		+Kelly Moncrief	b: 10/25/1968	m: 8/6/1994	
	4	Kimberly Clare DeLacerda	b: 11/21/1965		
		+René Kent Grossman	b: 8/16/1965	m: 10/21/1995	
3		Jo Ann Bird	b: 1/12/1945		
		+Harvey James Dugas	b: 11/17/1942	m: 9/3/1966	
	4	Natalie Dugas	b: 1/11/1968		
		+Dennis Beam	b: 9/3/1956	m: 12/12/1987	
	4	Joel Luke Dugas	b: 7/15/1970		
	4	Nicole Katherine Dugas	b: 9/28/1975		
3		Jude Richard Bird	b: 1947		
		+Susan Guidry		m: 1986	
	4	Phillip Jude Bird	b: 7/5/1987		
3		James Bernard Bird	b: 1949		
		+Cynthia Lynn Hamilton	b: 1954	m: 1976	

Schaffhausen

	4	Christina Elaine Bird	b: 7/6/1978		d: 9/16/1981
		*2nd Wife of James Bernard Bird:			
		+Sonya Marie Demourella		m: 1987	
	4	Allison Marie Bird	b: 11/27/1987		
		+Tim Pousson		m: 2/2006	
	4	Darren James Bird	b: 10/18/1989		
2		Catherine Frances (Sister Claire) Schaffhausen	b: 1913		d: 2003
2		Anna Katrina Schaffhausen	b: 1915		d: 1984

30. Schatzle, Florenz Christian:

Florenz Christian Schatzle b: 1865 d: 1938 from Ferdinand, Indiana was the son of Jacob Schatzle and Angela Kasper. He married in 1886 to Margaret Ann Simon b: 1868 d: 1937 from Fulda, Indiana, who is the daughter of Martin Simon and Margaret Roth.

2		Francesca Margaret Schatzle	b: 3/10/1887		d: 10/26/1975
		+Conrad Hensgens	b: 5/9/1880	m: 5/30/1905	d: 9/21/1956
3		Theresa Margaret Hensgens	b: 5/22/1906		d: 6/26/1995
		+Anton Heinrich Habetz	b: 12/10/1903	m: 2/3/1926	d: 4/18/1935
	4	James Leonard Habetz	b: 12/13/1927		d: 2/18/1996
		+Mary Dean Breaux	b: 1/1/1929	m: 1/18/1950	d: 3/31/1989
	4	Henrietta Theresa Victoria Habetz	b: 6/1/1928		
		+Raymond Nicholas Gossen	b: 4/3/1927	m: 2/3/1949	
	4	Leonard Conrad Habetz	b: 2/12/1931		d: 2/20/2006
		*2nd Husband of Theresa Margaret Hensgens:			
		+Henry Joseph Bollich	b: 1902	m: 1939	d: 1975
	4	Henry Joseph Bollich, Jr.	b: 1947		
		+Kathy Collins	b: 1952	m: 1973	
3		Lawrence Joseph Hensgens	b: 1908		d: 1977
3		Regina Ida Hensgens	b: 9/23/1909		d: 1/26/1980
		+John Herman Schultz	b: 1/4/1911	m: 1/13/1937	d: 4/22/1963
	4	Charles Herman Schultz	b: 10/23/1937		
		+Geraldine Elaine Trumps	b: 5/20/1937	m: 11/9/1957	d: 12/4/1998
	4	John Herman Schultz	b: 9/6/1939		
		+Marjorie Ann Robicheaux	b: 10/19/1943	m: 11/10/1973	
	4	Mary Frances Schultz	b: 1/13/1942		
		+Thomas Michael Wall	b: 12/4/1947	m: 7/17/1971	

Schatzle

4	Patrick Leo Schultz	b: 2/16/1944		d: 9/1/1968
3	Catherine Hensgens	b: 1911		d: 1994
3	Annie Marie Hensgens	b: 1914		d: 1995
	+Lawrence William Dischler	b: 1910	m: 1933	d: 1991
4	Winona Frances Bertha Dischler	b: 1934		
	+Robert Cartwright	b: 1931	m: 1957	d: 1998
4	Carolyn Ann Dischler	b: 1940		
	+Herman F. "Freddie" Morgan, Jr.	b: 1936		
3	Gertrude Marie Hensgens	b: 1917		d: 1986
	+Louis Burton	b: 1919	m: 1940	d: 1998
4	Ramona Burton	b: 1940		
	+Lynn Boone	b: 1938	m: 1961	
4	Donald Burton	b: 1942		
	+Geraldine Fontenot	b: 1939	m: 1980	
4	Constance Burton	b: 1946		
	+Gerald Doucet	b: 1941	m: 1965	
4	Conrad Burton	b: 1946		
4	Randall Burton	b: 1949		
	+Diane Louviere	b: 1947	m: 1969	
4	Jude Burton	b: 1951		
	+Barbara Fontenot	b: 1952	m: 1971	
4	Judy Burton	b: 1951		
	+Adlas Herpin	b: 1950	m: 1971	
4	Margaret Burton	b: 1953		d: 2000
4	Gerald Burton	b: 1955		
4	Geraldine Burton	b: 1955		d: 1955
3	John Conrad Hensgens	b: 1919		d: 1992
	+Annie Gesina Thevis	b: 1917	m: 1946	

Schatzle

	4	John Conrad Hensgens II	b: 1948		
		+Becky Collins	b: 1953	m: 1976	
	3	Marie Barbara Hensgens	b: 1921		d: 1989
	3	Henry William Hensgens	b: 1923		d: 1980
	3	Elenora Beatrice Hensgens	b: 1924		d: 1997
		+George Annen Cart	b: 1922	m: 1944	
	4	George Annen Cart, Jr.	b: 1962		d: 1981
2		Catherine Mary Schatzle	b: 1889		d: 1976
		+Joseph Theophile Mehling	b: 1880	m: 1907	d: 1947
	3	Mitchell Florenz Mehling	b: 1908		d: 1962
		+Nola Broussard	b: 1910	m: 1950	
	3	Josephine Ida Mehling	b: 1911		d: 1989
		+Willie Morgan	b: 1904	m: 1935	d: 1974
	4	Anthony Mehling LeJeune	b: 1929		d: 1981
		+Rosa Richard	b: 1924		
	4	Clarice Mehling	b: 1932		
		+Hilton Alter	b: 1929		
	4	Anna Grace Morgan	b: 1937		d: 2001
		+Gary Dowden	b: 1939		
	4	Alvin Morgan	b: 1939		d: 1999
		+Vera Ardoin			
	4	Francis Morgan	b: 1940		
		+Judy Cormier	b: 1953		
	4	Harry Morgan	b: 1943		d: 2004
		+Melba Holcomb	b: 1946		
	4	Helen Morgan	b: 1946		
		+Wilson East	b: 1943		
	4	Clifton Morgan	b: 1948		
	4	Betty Morgan	b: 1949		
		+Buddy Baumgarten	b: 1946		

Schatzle

3		Mary Ann Mehling	b: 1920		d: 2000
		+Lee Roy Hebert	b: 1917	m: 1937	d: 1966
	4	Joseph Emile Hebert	b: 1938		
		+Norma Jean Miley	b: 1039		
	4	Loretta Catherine Hebert	b: 1940		
		+Donald Spellmeyer	b: 1934		
		*2nd Husband of Mary Ann Mehling:			
		+Odes Elmo Hopkins	b: 1923	m: 1960	
2		Martin Joseph Schatzle	b: 7/30/1891		d: 11/27/1966
		+Francisca Louisa Schneider	b: 4/8/1895	m: 1917	d: 3/7/1980
3		Joseph Florenz Schatzle	b: 1917		d: 1993
		+Margaret Catherine Klein	b: 2/1/1921	m: 10/8/1947	
	4	Fr. Michael Schatzle	b: 8/10/1948		
	4	Katherine Schatzle	b: 4/7/1952		
3		Sophie Schatzle	b: 1919		
		+Gerhard Cramer	b: 8/22/1917	m: 1946	d: 11/28/1978
	4	Jacquline Cramer	b: 10/24/1948		
		+Darrell LeBlanc	b: 3/26/1946	m: 1/11/1966	
	4	Mary Frances Cramer	b: 12/22/1950		d: 4/6/1957
	4	Elizabeth "Betty" Cramer	b: 7/13/1952		
		+Michael Bellard	b: 5/8/1949	m: 10/14/1972	
	4	Cynthia Cramer	b: 6/23/1956		
		+Cody Miller	b: 6/4/1950	m: 6/13/1981	
	4	Josie Cramer	b: 11/3/1958		
		+Benny Stelly			
3		Victoria Annie Schatzle	b: 12/9/1921		
		+Gerhard Joseph Leonards	b: 10/21/1916	m: 11/27/1940	d: 2/20/1973
	4	Fr. Martin Charles Leonards	b: 1/8/1942		

Schatzle

	4	Theresa Ann Leonards	b: 1/9/1944		d: 6/15/1993
		+Alfred Matthew LeBlanc	b: 11/9/1938	m: 7/15/1972	
	4	Charles Gerhard Leonards	b: 2/20/1946		d: 1/6/1997
	4	Cecile Louise Leonards	b: 7/14/1948		
	4	Barbara Mary Leonards	b: 5/12/1951		d: 6/21/2003
	4	Jane Frances Leonards	b: 3/30/1954		
2		Ida Susan Schatzle	b: 3/14/1893		d: 10/13/1957
		+Henry Joseph Vondenstein	b: 1/24/1887	m: 1915	d: 1/3/1971
	3	Charles Earl Vondenstein	b: 7/2/1933		d: 4/18/1999
	4	Charles Earl Vondenstein, Jr.	b: 1958		
		+Cynthia Faye Meyer	b: 1959		
2		Florenz Christian Schatzle	b: 1895		d: 1966
		+Ella Chachere	b: 1892	m: 1922	d: 1986
	3	Rosalie Ida Schatzle	b: 1923		d: 2006
		+Michael A. Page	b: 1919	m: 1946	
	4	Michael Nicholas Page	b: 1947		d: 1985
	4	Rosalie Suzanne Page	b: 1948		
		+Steven Mobbs			
		*2nd Husband of Rosalie Suzanne Page:			
		+Wayne Ensign	b: 1945	m: 1967	
	3	Bernard Joseph Schatzle	b: 1924		
		+Joyce Mae Fontenot	b: 1927	m: 1950	d: 1975
	4	Patricia Ann Schatzle	b: 1950		
		+Ovie Vance McGlothlin	b: 1948	m: 1972	
	4	Constance Marie Schatzle	b: 1958		
		+John Hubert Fontenot	b: 1953	m: 1975	

Schatzle

4	Joseph Steven Schatzle	b: 1964			
	+Jennifer Veillon	b: 1966	m: 1986		
	*2nd Wife of Bernard Joseph Schatzle:				
	+Nettie L. Lafleur	b: 1917	m: 1976		
3	Jacob Conrad Schatzle	b: 1926		d: 2005	
	+Mildred Christ	b: 1931	m: 1950		
4	Paula Schatzle	b: 1951			
	+James C. Dischler	b: 1950	m: 1972		
4	Delores Schatzle	b: 1954			
	+Craig Olivier	b: 1952	m: 1973		
4	Julia Schatzle	b: 1958			
	+David Doyle				
	*2nd Husband of Julia Schatzle:				
	+Donald Patin				
4	David Schatzle	b: 1961			
	+Melissa Duplichin	b: 1963	m: 1986		
2	Aloysius Theophile Schatzle	b: 1897		d: 1973	
	+Mildred Gibson	b: 1898	m: 1948	d: 1972	
2	Mary Margaret Schatzle	b: 1901		d: 1984	
	+Dallas Bourgeois	b: 1907	m: 1933	d: 1994	
2	Annie Schatzle	b: 1903		d: 1911	
2	John Joseph Schatzle	b: 1905		d: 1969	
	+Ida Marie Fontenot	b: 1909	m: 1930	d: 1994	
3	Joyce Schatzle	b: 1931		d: 1986	
	+Ralph Young	b: 1932	m: 1954	d: 2006	
4	Robert Eugene Young	b: 1956			
	+Suzette Kockler	b: 1957			
4	Lisa Kay Young	b: 1957			
	+Randall H. Lormand	b: 1966	m: 1988		
3	Joan Theresa Schatzle	b: 1940			
	+Vernon Charles McManus	b: 1938	m: 1960		

Schatzle

	4	Hilton Charles McManus	b: 1961		
		+Blanche Freund	b: 1969	m: 1994	
	4	Erin Elizabeth McManus	b: 1963		
		+Robert Perik	b: 1961	m: 1994	
	4	Kelly Susan McManus	b: 1964		
		+Russel Buettner	b: 1961	m: 1988	
	4	Brian Charles McManus	b: 1972		
2		Margaret Amelia Schatzle	b: 1907		d: 1970
		+Jesse E. Morgan	b: 1907	m: 1929	d: 1954
3		Wanda Ruth Morgan	b: 1930		d: 1969
		+Willie Joseph Jones	b: 1929	m: 1946	d: 1957
	4	Larry Paul Jones	b: 1951		
		+Kathleen Whelan	b: 1955	m: 1982	
	4	Carol Ann Jones	b: 1952		
		+Jerry DiBenedetto	b: 1947	m: 1975	
		*2nd Husband of Wanda Ruth Morgan:			
		+James Marion Hurst	b: 1920	m: 1958	
	4	Katherine Lynn Hurst	b: 1958		
3		Patricia Ann Morgan	b: 1940		
		+James Hiram Dorton, Jr.	b: 1942	m: 1965	
	4	Stephan Patrick Dorton	b: 1966		
		+Shannon Marie Maher	b: 1975	m: 2006	
	4	Linda Faye Dorton	b: 1968		
		+David Watso	b: 1963	m: 2000	
	4	Sandra Gail Dorton	b: 1971		
	4	Nancy Jean Dorton	b: 1974		
		+Joseph Bement	b: 1971	m: 2003	
2		Conrad Joseph Schatzle	b: 1909		d: 1995
		+Anna Marie Fontenot	b: 1912	m: 1932	d: 1995
3		Joseph Donald Schatzle	b: 1934		d: 1998

Schatzle

		+Leana Marie Fruge	b: 1942	m: 1960
	4	Erick Joseph Schatzle	b: 1961	
		+Suzanne Smith	b: 1962	m: 1990
	4	Stephanie Schatzle	b: 1962	
		+Brett Sprague		
	4	Melinda Schatzle	b: 1964	
		+Brian Scott Vincent	b: 1962	m: 1983
	4	Darlene Schatzle	b: 1966	
		+Byron McPherson		m: 2005
	4	Edmund Paul Schatzle	b: 1967	
		+Elizabeth Davlos	b: 1968	m: 1989
		*2nd Wife of Joseph Donald Schatzle:		
		+Judy Melford		m: 1984
		*3rd Wife of Joseph Donald Schatzle:		
		+Gerlinol Perkins		m: 1996
3		Conrad Joseph Schatzle	b: 1940	
		+Carol Marie Strack	b: 1940	m: 1962
	4	John Schatzle	b: 1963	
		+Ann Richard	b: 1963	m: 1984
	4	Lucia Schatzle	b: 1965	
3		Jacqueline Anne Schatzle		
		+Shelby Wayne Newcomer		m: 1946
		*2nd Husband of Jacqueline Anne Schatzle:		
		+Harry John Daniel Halliburton	b: 1942	m: 1969
	4	John Thomas "Sparky" Halliburton	b: 1970	
	4	William Kane Halliburton	b: 1973	
2		Leopold Schatzle	b: 1/29/1912	d: 1987
		+Eva Louise Esters	b: 9/7/1914	m: 7/4/1934

Schatzle

3	Jeanette Lorene Schatzle	b: 3/3/1938			
	+Everett Stanfield	b: 8/26/1934	m: 1/25/1955		
4	David Stanfield	b: 9/15/1956			
	+Darlene Janes				
4	Terry Stanfield	b: 10/11/1957			
	+Kathy Morgan				
4	Rhonda Stanfield	b: 1/2/1959			
	+Lester Floyd	b: 4/29/1955			
4	Lorie Stanfield	b: 2/17/1960			
	+Gary Hailey				
4	Tina Stanfield	b: 9/2/1966			
	+Bobby Creel				
3	Charles Eugene Schatzle	b: 6/30/1939			
	+Dorothy McCright	b: 9/15/1938	m: 1/19/1958	d: 1/1/1985	
4	Randy Lee Schatzle	b: 11/30/1958			
	+Adrie Murdock	b: 4/16/1960	m: 5/12/1984		
4	Kenneth Michael Schatzle	b: 8/21/1962			
	+Lisa Benton		m: Bef. 1987		
	*2nd Wife of Kenneth Michael Schatzle:				
	+Michele Schick	b: 11/5/1962	m: 2/9/1998		
4	Kevin C. Schatzle	b: 4/2/1968		d: 6/30/1995	
	*2nd Wife of Charles Eugene Schatzle:				
	+Sue Stringer Cooper	b: 11/23/1938	m: 3/4/2000		
3	Barbara Ann Schatzle	b: 3/6/1941			
	+Ernest McClendon	b: 10/11/1937	m: 2/9/1960	d: 12/27/1996	
4	Denise McClendon	b: 1/18/1961			
	+Dean Cockerham	b: 6/25/1957	m: 6/10/1977		
4	Renee McClendon	b: 11/14/1963			
	+Jeffrey LeGrande	b: 3/18/1965	m: 9/12/1987		
	*2nd Husband of Renee McClendon:				
	+Herman Jackson	b: 5/17/1954	m: 12/9/2000		

Schatzle

4	Eva McClendon	b: 2/1/1969	
	+Timothy Williamson		
3	Betty Jane Schatzle	b: 1942	
	+Oliver Louis Bohannon	b: 1936	m: 1956
4	Oliver Leo Bohannon	b: 1958	
	+Tammi Ann Cockerham		m: Bef. 1981

*2nd Wife of Oliver Leo Bohannon:

	+Cheryl Lou Morgan	b: 1966	m: Aft. 1981
4	Ronald Bohannon	b: 1960	
	+Toni Taylor		m: Bef. 1982

*2nd Wife of Ronald Bohannon:

	+Jacki Cecil Gulde	b: 1964	m: Aft. 1982
4	Mary Jean Bohannon	b: 1962	
	+Lewis Franklin Martin, Jr.		m: Bef. 1984

*2nd Husband of Mary Jean Bohannon:

	+Blain LaBorde	b: 1963	m: Aft. 1984
4	Kimberly Ann Bohannon	b: 1966	
	+Bruce McMurray		m: Bef. 1991

*2nd Husband of Kimberly Ann Bohannon:

	+Donnie Ogden	b: 1955	m: Aft. 1991

*2nd Husband of Betty Jane Schatzle:

	+Grady Burl Hortman	b: 1930	m: Aft. 1956

*3rd Husband of Betty Jane Schatzle:

	+Henry Ross Brown		m: Aft. 1956

31. Scheufens, Johann Theodor:
Johann Theodor Scheufens b: 2/13/1841 d: 2/7/1903 from Hastenrath was the son of Gerhard Arnold Scheufens b: 1813 d: 1897 and Maria Katharina Sentis b: 1810 d: 1887. He married on 10/7/1873 to Maria Katharina Janssen b: 9/18/1843 d: 9/19/1933 from Birgden, the daughter of Peter Joseph Janssen b: 1793 d: 1865 and Maria Elizabeth Schaps b: 1799 d: 1863.

2		Gerhard Arnold Scheufens	b: 9/17/1875		d: 6/30/1880
2		Maria Katharina (Sister Columba) Scheufens	b: 8/1/1877		d: 7/17/1945
2		Maria Christina Elizabeth Scheufens	b: 4/27/1880		d: 12/24/1880
2		Katharina Agnes Scheufens	b: 10/15/1881		d: 1/21/1964
		+Joseph Hubert Schaffhausen	b: 1855	m: 1904	d: 1938
3		Mary Catherine Schaffhausen	b: 1906		d: 2005
3		Elizabeth Marie Schaffhausen	b: 1907		d: 1984
3		Josephine Catherine Schaffhausen	b: 1909		d: 1991
		+Leo Gunby Bird	b: 1895	m: 1943	d: 1949
	4	Julie Agnes Bird	b: 8/27/1943		
		+Charles DeLacerda	b: 12/1/1939	m: 7/15/1961	
	4	Jo Ann Bird	b: 1/12/1945		
		+Harvey James Dugas	b: 11/17/1942	m: 9/3/1966	
	4	Jude Richard Bird	b: 1947		
		+Susan Guidry		m: 1986	
	4	James Bernard Bird	b: 1949		
		+Cynthia Lynn Hamilton	b: 1954	m: 1976	
		*2nd Wife of James Bernard Bird:			
		+Sonya Marie Demourella		m: 1987	

Scheufens

3	Catherine Frances(Sister Claire) Schaffhausen	b: 1913		d: 2003
3	Anna Katrina Schaffhausen	b: 1915		d: 1984
2	Maria Elizabeth Scheufens	b: 1/11/1884		d: 8/6/1940
	+William Joseph Reiners	b: 1876	m: 1907	d: 1930
3	Theodore Reiners	b: 1907		d: 1907
3	Maria Catherine "Katie" Reiners	b: 1909		d: 1986
	+Anatole Gary	b: 1897	m: 1940	d: 1973
4	Wilton Joseph Gary	b: 9/1/1944		
	+Marcella Faye Vaughn	b: 8/18/1945	m: 2/27/1965	
4	Marie Anna Gary	b: 2/6/1946		
	+Obrey "Toboy" Benoit, Jr.	b: 2/4/1944	m: 10/24/1964	
4	Bertha Marie Gary	b: 7/13/1949		
	+Joseph Velior LaCombe	b: 8/14/1946	m: 11/22/1969	
3	Maria Veronica Reiners	b: 1911		d: 1911
3	Veronica Reiners	b: 3/3/1912		
	+Peter Jacob Thevis	b: 2/26/1911	m: 11/11/1936	d: 10/13/1998
4	Marie Louise Thevis	b: 2/19/1938		
	+Vincent Joseph Berken	b: 12/17/1925	m: 10/24/1956	d: 4/22/2005
4	Wilbert Thevis	b: 8/27/1940		
	+Theresa Marie Richard	b: 10/9/1942	m: 1/24/1961	
4	Elizabeth Magdalene Thevis	b: 3/1/1942		
	+William Joseph Reiners	b: 8/7/1940	m: 11/11/1960	d: 11/28/1999
4	Mary Kathleen Thevis	b: 10/7/1946		d: 10/19/2001
	+Glyn Roy Hoffpauir	b: 8/9/1945	m: 10/15/1966	d: 2/26/2003

Scheufens

3	Anthony Reiners	b: 1914		d: 1914
3	Agnes Columba Reiners	b: 1/31/1920		
	+William John Thevis	b: 3/4/1917	m: 11/26/1940	d: 8/11/1985
4	Frank William Thevis	b: 8/18/1941		
	+Nora Lou Bellard	b: 8/7/1941	m: 5/11/1963	d: 12/30/2004
4	Leo Joseph Thevis	b: 9/8/1946		
	+Jeanette Marie Daigle	b: 8/4/1950	m: 12/31/1974	
4	Clara Marie Thevis	b: 9/28/1949		
	+John Michael Savoy	b: 11/9/1949	m: 7/26/1969	
4	Paul Daniel Thevis	b: 1/2/1954		
	+Veronica Fuselier	b: 5/13/1953	m: 11/3/1973	
4	Rose Marie Thevis	b: 5/9/1957		
	+Ronald Kenneth Hornsby	b: 5/13/1956	m: 10/2/1976	
4	Andrew John Thevis	b: 4/6/1960		
	+Connie Dee LaCombe	b: 11/16/1060	m: 2/2/1980	
4	Loretta Ann Thevis	b: 3/30/1961		
	+Harlan David Kebodeaux	b: 8/8/1965	m: 9/8/1990	
4	Arnold Stephen Thevis	b: 8/16/1964		
	+Kathleen Meche	b: 5/18/1959	m: 1/16/1988	
3	Dorothy Josephine Reiners	b: 1921		
	+Deynoodt John Richard	b: 1922		d: 2003
4	Margaret Donotel Richard	b: 7/25/1942		
	+James Harry Comeaux	b: 2/27/1936	m: 5/4/1963	d: 4/5/1999
4	David William Richard	b: 8/7/1948		
	+Katherine Elizabeth Guidry	b: 6/2/1951	m: 9/2/1974	
4	Nancy Elizabeth Richard	b: 1/10/1953		

Scheufens

		+Marshall Glenn Pousson	b: 2/13/1953	m: 6/10/1972	
	4	Simon James Richard	b: 9/4/1954		
		+Barbara Suiter	b: 9/6/1951	m: 8/26/1978	
	4	George John Richard	b: 6/24/1956		
	4	Joyce Marie Richard	b: 6/14/1959		
		+Barry Paul Chaisson	b: 4/12/1955	m: 6/18/1977	
	4	Yvonne Marie Richard	b: 4/10/1961		
		+Harold Clarke Bullock	b: 1/6/1961	m: 8/9/1980	
	4	Yvette Marie Richard	b: 4/10/1961		
		+Philip Leo Ohlenforst	b: 5/13/1961	m: 10/18/1980	
2		Arnold Joseph Scheufens	b: 2/1/1886		d: 5/30/1967
		+Maria Catherine Reiners	b: 1889	m: 1910	d: 1966
	3	Maria Veronica Scheufens	b: 1910		d: 1996
	3	Maria Catherine Scheufens	b: 1912		d: 1988
		+Matthias Joseph Meyer	b: 1905	m: 1932	d: 1979
	4	Charles Joseph Meyer, Sr.	b: 2/8/1933		
		+Agnes Ruth McCown	b: 10/19/1938	m: 5/25/1956	d: 2005
	4	Arnold Remy "Ray" Meyer, Sr.	b: 5/23/1934		d: 11/13/2006
		+Geneva Viola Louviere	b: 12/10/1935	m: 6/4/1959	
	4	John Allen Meyer	b: 3/7/1936		d: 7/17/2005
		+Sandra McCown	b: 1/15/1947	m: 4/11/1969	
	4	Louis Theodore Meyer	b: 11/26/1937		
		+Jean Pitre	b: 8/29/1942	m: 12/29/1962	
	4	Edwin Frank Meyer	b: 9/21/1939		
		+Bobbie Jane Caswell	b: 4/19/1941	m: 6/15/1963	
	4	Johanna Catherine Meyer	b: 2/19/1941		
		+Leland Cormier	b: 8/19/1936	m: 7/15/1962	
	4	Clyde Joseph Meyer	b: 4/15/1942		d: 3/17/2003

Scheufens

	+Alice Faye Miguez	b: 2/16/1948		
4	Frances Jane Meyer	b: 8/24/1943		
	+Clyde Coble	b: 5/8/1942	m: 3/8/1972	
4	Matthias Joseph Meyer, Jr.	b: 5/25/1946		d: 9/29/1995
	+Dolores Ann Richard	b: 9/17/1945	m: 5/10/1966	
4	Steven James Meyer	b: 11/16/1947		
	+Eloise Joan Richard	b: 1/15/1950	m: 2/14/1969	
	*2nd Wife of Steven James Meyer:			
	+Sharon Gayle Galley	b: 1953	m: 1973	
4	Michael Lawrence Meyer	b: 4/1/1951		
	+Susan Matt	b: 10/30/1952	m: 10/17/1970	
4	Thomas Larry Meyer	b: 7/6/1953		
	+Bridgett Ann Hoffpauir	b: 8/31/1955	m: 8/16/1975	
	*2nd Wife of Thomas Larry Meyer:			
	+Sarah Frances Kennedy	b: 1/2/1958	m: 4/19/1990	
3	Theodor Joseph Scheufens	b: 1/14/1916		d: 1991
	+Estelle Boudreaux	b: 8/17/1916	m: 4/8/1937	
4	Mary Genevieve Scheufens	b: 1/5/1938		
	+Gordon Ray Franklin	b: 8/14/1933	m: 5/19/1956	
4	Barbara Scheufens	b: 9/28/1940		d: 9/28/1940
4	Theodor Joseph Scheufens, Jr.	b: 10/22/1942		
	+Deborah Sharp	b: 9/23/1953	m: 10/22/1980	
4	Clyde Joseph Scheufens	b: 4/2/1944		
4	Frank Homer Scheufens	b: 1/9/1946		
	+Sallye Frances Guthrey	b: 8/29/1948	m: 5/31/1968	
3	Francis Joseph Scheufens	b: 1918		d: 1985

Scheufens

3	Hubert Joseph Scheufens	b: 1920		d: 1921
3	Anna Antoinette Scheufens	b: 9/10/1925		d: 10/12/1999
	+Arnold Rubin Hicks	b: 1925	m: 1951	
4	Janice Marie Hicks	b: 4/28/1953		
	+Floyd LeBlanc	b: 9/16/1956	m: 1/24/1981	
4	Larry James Hicks	b: 9/20/1954		
	+Deborah Soileau	b: 8/10/1959	m: 11/7/1983	
	*2nd Wife of Larry James Hicks:			
	+Tina Crowder	b: 5/7/1966	m: 5/12/2006	
3	Elizabeth Marie Margaret Scheufens	b: 1928		
	+Nolton Paul Broussard	b: 1921	m: 1947	d: 1971
4	Pamela Ann Broussard	b: 1949		
	+Michael Earl Fontenot	b: 1949	m: 1969	
4	Randall Paul Broussard	b: 1950		
	+Ann Richard	b: 1949	m: 1969	
4	Blaine Patrick Broussard	b: 1957		
	+Celeste Hilda Comeaux	b: 1960	m: 1979	
	*2nd Husband of Elizabeth Marie Margaret Scheufens:			
	+Floyd Silvia	b: 1925	m: 1975	
3	Henry Charles Vincent Scheufens	b: 1930		
	+Billye Jewell Lyle	b: 1939	m: 1958	
4	William Arnold Scheufens	b: 1962		
	+Susan Hollister Hall	b: 1965	m: 1986	
4	Gregory Vincent Scheufens	b: 1964		
	+Susan Michelle Bryeans Welch	b: 1965	m: 1996	
4	Trecia Denise Scheufens	b: 1965		

Scheufens

	+Kevin Roy Quebodeaux	b: 1966	m: 1987	
2	Wilhelm Joseph Scheufens	b: 1/20/1888		d: 9/26/1939
2	Franz (Frank) Scheufens	b: 11/5/1890		d: 6/24/1943

32. Schlicher, Johann Lambert:

Johann Lambert Schlicher b: 4/20/1856 d: 11/1/1929 from Schierwaldenrath was the brother of Johann Peter Schlicher (see below). He married in 1880 to Maria Gertrude Ohlenforst b: 1/3/1853 d: 8/21/1916 from Schierwaldenrath, who is the daughter of Jacob Franz Ohlenforst b: 1828 d: ? and Mary Agnes Melgiers b: 1826 d: ?.

2		Maria Agnes Corgubertinn Schlicher	b: 2/18/1881		d: 4/13/1971
		+Rufus Mires	b: 11/28/1878	m: 1/30/1902	d: 10/6/1955
	3	Bertha Gertrude Mires	b: 1902		d: 1987
	3	Katie Mires	b: 1903		d: 1903
	3	Joseph Mires	b: 1904		d: 1904
	3	John (Bo) William Mires	b: 8/10/1906		d: 2/22/1970
		+Lou Plaisance			
2		Wilhelm Joseph Schlicher	b: 5/5/1882		d: 1957
		+Mary Lejeune	b: 10/8/1882	m: 1906	d: 7/24/1952
	3	Eva Schlicher	b: 12/12/1898		
	3	Wiley F. Miles Schlicher	b: 8/7/1894		
2		Maria Johanna Lutimilla Schlicher	b: 7/15/1883		d: 3/19/1952
		+Aurelien Breaux	b: 1872	m: 1915	d: 1966
	3	Bertha Breaux	b: 1903		d: 1976
		+Mayo Dupre	b: 1897	m: 1924	d: 1973
	3	Grace Gertrude Breaux	b: 1905		
		+Morris Dugas	b: 1899	m: 1922	d: 2/2/1992
		4 Ethel Dugas			
		4 Clifton Dugas			
		4 Margie Dugas			
	3	Amy Breaux	b: 1909		
		+Willie Louis James	b: 1892	m: 1926	d: 1967
		4 Bernice James			
		+Clayton Cormier			

*2nd Husband of Amy Breaux:

Schlicher

		+Ervin Camile Laughlin	b: 7/18/1907	m: 1930	d: 12/7/1956
	3	Alberta Breaux	b: 4/21/1911		d: 1914
	3	Lambert Joseph (Buster) Breaux	b: 2/12/1915		d: 1989
		+Verna Mae Prejean	b: 9/27/1918	m: 1933	d: 8/14/1976
	3	Edward Solomon Breaux	b: 1917		d: 7/24/1972
		+Nina Tarpley	b: 1927	m: 1942	
	3	Clara Isabelle Breaux	b: 1919		d: 1945
		+Austin Alleman	b: 1921	m: 1937	
	4	Gladys Alleman			d: 1983
	3	Earl Aurelien Breaux	b: 1921		d: 1969
		+Rose Mary Adamo	b: 1929	m: 1947	
	3	Emma Louise (Dolly) Breaux	b: 1922		d: 9/26/1991
		+Daniel Vasco Laughlin	b: 1915	m: 1942	
	4	Wilefer Laughlin			
	3	Juanita Gladys Breaux	b: 5/29/1929		d: 11/21/1929
2		Henry Schlicher	b: 1885		d: 1885
2		Peter John Schlicher	b: 12/24/1887		d: 1887
2		Gerhard (Garrett) Joseph Schlicher	b: 11/1/1889		d: 1968
		+Alice East	b: 1900	m: 1912	d: 1946
	3	Gertie Mae Schlicher	b: 1913		
		+Clovis Albertice Morgan	b: 1908	m: 1930	d: 1977
	4	Albertice Coy Morgan	b: 1931		
		+Cupal Jeanet Carpenter	b: 1936	m: 1956	
	4	Elmer Ray Morgan	b: 1933		d: 2000
		+Carol Jean Trahan	b: 1934	m: 1958	d: 1994
		*2nd Wife of Elmer Ray Morgan:			
		+Eileen Stell Landry	b: 1938	m: 1970	d: 1997
	4	Mary Elizabeth Morgan	b: 1935		

Schlicher

	+James O. Jones	b: 1922	m: 1953	d: 1989
4	Carolyn Alice Morgan	b: 1945		
	+Chester Minshew	b: 1933	m: 1970	
	*2nd Husband of Carolyn Alice Morgan:			
	+Chester Williams	b: 1934	m: 1980	
3	Joseph Lambert Schlicher	b: 2/10/1916		d: 9/11/1992
	+Frances Anna Hardin	b: 1922	m: 1939	d: 1999
4	Cynthia Kay Schlicher	b: 1954		
	+Howard Dobson	b: 1952	m: 1986	d: 2004
	*2nd Husband of Cynthia Kay Schlicher:			
	+Travis Rost	b: 1952	m: 2005	
4	Kenneth Lee Schlicher	b: 1940		
	+Barbara Guther	b: 1941	m: 1961	
4	Bobby Carol Schlicher	b: 1947		d: 1979
	+Camil Compton	b: 1947	m: 1973	
3	Lawrence Garrett Schlicher	b: 1926		d: 1993
	+Nora Jeanita Sittig	b: 1926	m: 1944	
4	Lawrence Garrett Schlicher	b: 1950		d: 2002
3	Garrett Joseph Schlicher	b: 1924		d: 1979
	+Margaret Evelyn Abbott	b: 1928	m: 1947	
4	Gary Wayne Schlicher	b: 1952		
	+Delores Bertrand		m: 1972	
4	Debbie Elaine Schlicher	b: 1957		
3	Lloyd Sidney Schlicher	b: 1926		d: 2003
	+Pearl Jean Hebert	b: 1927	m: 1949	d: 1/20/1994
2	Heinrich Jacob (Jake) Schlicher	b: 12/29/1891		d: 12/21/1965
	+Jenna Myers	b: 2/15/1896	m: 4/12/1911	d: 2/14/1976
3	Katie Mae Schlicher	b: 9/8/1915		d: 1/4/1993

Schlicher

3	Joseph William (Tip) Schlicher	b: 5/29/1918		d: 1994
	+Annabelle Lang	b: 8/6/1924	m: 4/1943	
4	Freda Ann Schlicher	b: 8/10/1942		
	+Robert Garrison		m: 8/29/1964	
4	Cherie Jean Schlicher	b: 7/20/1946		
	+Michael James McNeal, Sr.		m: 12/1/1962	

*2nd Husband of Cherie Jean Schlicher:

	+Westly Schull		m: Aft. 1962	
4	Deborah Ann Schlicher	b: 1/11/1951		
	+Harold Deloach, Sr.			
3	Alberta Mary (Sing) Schlicher	b: 6/4/1920		
	+Clytis Lee Savoit	b: 6/15/1920	m: 3/1942	d: 10/17/1996
4	John Michael Savoit	b: 1/26/1943		
	+Jeanette Dronette		m: 6/15/1963	
4	Paul Allen Savoit	b: 5/25/1965		
	+Taina Judice			
4	Timothy Paul Savoit	b: 1/26/1948		
	+Sandra Hebert		m: 4/6/1968	
3	Hardy Howard (BeBe) Schlicher	b: 3/25/1924		d: 2/9/1987
	+Emmadel Quinn	b: 10/23/1930	m: 8/23/1949	
4	Robert Wayne Schlicher	b: 9/6/1950		
	+Annette Keisler	b: 1/9/1949		

*2nd Wife of Robert Wayne Schlicher:

	+Sharon Ann Vice	b: 5/18/1954	m: 7/18/1971	
4	Beverly Gale Schlicher	b: 12/13/1954		
	+Allen Dale Duhon	b: 11/5/1954	m: 12/16/1972	
4	Teresa Dale Schlicher	b: 12/13/1954		
	+George Joseph Luquette	b: 11/21/1954	m: 9/15/1973	

Schlicher

4	Jena Frances Schlicher	b: 11/24/1956		
	+John Clifford Bourque, Jr.	b: 7/20/1955	m: 2/23/1973	d: 2/1/1976
	*2nd Husband of Jena Frances Schlicher:			
	+Mark Anthony Renard	b: 9/3/1955	m: 9/6/1978	
3	Roy Lambert (Snake) Schlicher	b: 7/31/1928		d: 2/8/1996
	+Bernice Chaisson	b: 8/11/1928	m: 11/1955	

33. Schlicher, Johann Peter:
Johann Peter Schlicher b: 8/14/1860 d: 1942 from Schierwaldenrath is the son of Peter Gerhard Schlicher b: 1/17/1821 d: ? and Maria Agnes Ronkartz b: 1/5/1819 d: 11/26/1876. He married in 1887 to Sarah Meranda Thrailkill (the widow of Mr. Rine) b: 1854 d: 1930, the daughter of William C. Thrailkill and Sarah Langs.

2	Mary Agnes Schlicher	b: 4/14/1889		d: 12/29/1982
	+George Eli Taylor	b: 12/31/1879	m: 6/1/1907	d: 1964
3	Thornwell Francis Taylor	b: 3/10/1908		d: 2/8/1995
	+Hollis Mabel Reed	b: 5/9/1913	m: 9/14/1935	
4	Janet Frances Taylor	b: 4/23/1941		
	+Jerry R. Morris			
	*2nd Husband of Janet Frances Taylor:			
	+Sherwood Swain		m: 6/23/1990	
4	Joan Evelyn Taylor	b: 9/2/1944		
	+Robert William Cameron, Sr.			
4	Thomas Arthur Taylor	b: 2/14/1947		
	+Marilyn Mills		m: 7/2/1971	
4	Jane Ella Taylor	b: 9/21/1942		d: 10/5/1942
3	Lloyd Jacob Taylor	b: 12/21/1912		
	+Ellen Hope Baker	b: 7/19/1921	m: 6/6/1939	d: 12/23/1985
3	Georgia Evelyn Taylor	b: 6/6/1916		
	+Charles Rufus Hull	b: 2/6/1902	m: 1944	d: 5/28/1975
4	Sharon Ruth Hull	b: 1/14/1945		
	+Robert Nelson Rosemont		m: 7/14/1967	
3	Robert Raymond Taylor	b: 1918		
	+Jane Ella Morgan	b: 1918	m: 1935	
4	Roberta Taylor	b: 5/9/1936		
	+David Carl Baggett			
4	Lloyd Raymond Taylor	b: 10/1/1938		
	+Betty Ruth Meadors		m: 9/28/1959	

Schlicher

	4	Michael Byron Taylor	b: 2/19/1953		
		+Gale Paige Schmidt		m: 7/5/1974	
	4	Pat Taylor	b: 2/19/1953		
2		Gertrude Wilhelmena (Minnie) Schlicher	b: 2/22/1891		d: 6/1/1976
		+David Levy Murrell	b: 1888	m: 1917	d: 1966
	3	Marjorie Winona Murrell	b: 12/12/1917		d: 2/16/1983
		+Herman Frank Hayes	b: 1/1/1900	m: 1939	d: 2/24/1993
	4	Barbara Lucille Hayes	b: 11/4/1940		
	4	Michael David Hayes	b: 4/5/1941		
		+Dulcy Randolph	b: 4/3/1940	m: 1/5/1955	
	4	Martha Fann Hayes	b: 9/15/1943		
		+Mac Beckham			
	4	Lynn Ellen Hayes	b: 5/11/1945		
		+Jimmy Ray Shrum	b: 12/18/1942	m: 6/15/1968	
	4	Henry William "Chip" Hayes	b: 5/11/1950		d: 8/10/1996
	3	Earline Davidee Murrell	b: 9/15/1919		d: 9/2004
	3	David Levy Murrell Jr.	b: 1921		d: 1921
	3	Gertrude Lenor Murrell	b: 8/11/1923		d: 5/8/1981
		+Eugene Adrian "Bud" East	b: 2/14/1922	m: 1948	
	4	David Eugene East	b: 8/17/1948		
	4	Rebecca Earlene East	b: 8/21/1949		
		+Louis Thomas III	b: 6/30/1948	m: 11/16/1967	
	4	Debra East	b: 9/1/1950		
		+John Chabreck		m: 11/1970	
	4	Catherine Gale East	b: 8/29/1951		
		+John Blackwell			
	4	Rheba Elizabeth East	b: 9/24/1952		
	3	Samara Maxine Murrell	b: 12/19/1924		
	3	Darold Lloyd Murrell	b: 12/30/1926		d: 11/4/1976

Schlicher

	+Juanita Lucille Robichaux	b: 9/19/1928	m: 11/10/1947	
4	Darold Lloyd "Bubba" Murrell, Jr.	b: 8/4/1948		
	+Donna Marie Duhon	b: 1/15/1948	m: 6/5/1981	
4	Cynthia Louise Murrell	b: 7/29/1949		d: 9/4/2004
	+Leroy Abshire			d: 9/5/1973
	*2nd Husband of Cynthia Louise Murrell:			
	+Ronald Wayne Benoit	b: 2/6/1950	m: 8/4/1974	d: 12/2/2000
4	Roberta Lynn Murrell	b: 7/2/1951		
	+William Leonard Schmaltz	b: 7/4/1948	m: 6/11/1977	
4	John Larry Murrell	b: 1/4/1954		
	+Shirley Ann Broussard	b: 6/13/1953	m: 5/31/1974	
4	Marlene Ann Murrell	b: 3/30/1956		
	+Edwin Burton Prather	b: 1/4/1955	m: 4/20/1974	
4	David Wayne Murrell	b: 7/6/1957		
	+Wilma Kathleen Nelson	b: 7/28/1959	m: 11/10/1978	
4	Jeffery James Murrell	b: 7/28/1961		
	+Debra Ann Oliver	b: 4/8/1963	m: 4/11/1981	
4	Bernadette Murrell	b: 2/18/1965		
	+Carl Frederick Moeller	b: 9/23/1960	m: 7/17/1987	
4	Mary Martha Murrell	b: 6/4/1966		
	+Jackie Lawrence Abshire	b: 6/23/1965	m: 2/9/1985	
2	William Gerard Schlicher	b: 5/3/1893		d: 10/8/1936
	+Lucille Grant	b: 1894	m: 1918	d: 1955

Schlicher

	3	William Gerard Schlicher Jr.	b: 1920		d: 1959
2		Robert Edward Schlicher Sr.	b: 9/25/1895		d: 1/26/1962
		+Daisy Louise Weekly	b: 1895	m: 1922	d: 1983
	3	Robert Edward Schlicher, Jr.	b: 1922		d: 11/15/2002
		+Rose Mary Fremeaux	b: 1923	m: 1946	d: 2003
	4	Robert Edward (Bob) Schlicher III	b: 1947		
		+Sharon Ann Olson	b: 1948		
	4	Clifton David (Cliff) Schlicher	b: 1948		
		+Laura Elizabeth Castile	b: 1951		
	4	Virginia Judith (Judy) Schlicher	b: 1951		
		+Kenneth Paul Mayeaux	b: 1949		
		*2nd Husband of Virginia Judith (Judy) Schlicher:			
		+William Amos Ponder	b: 1951		
	4	Charles Louis (Cholly) Schlicher	b: 1959		
		+Tammy Ray Holbrook	b: 1959		
	4	Margaret Mary Schlicher	b: 1961		
		+Jesse Bond			
	3	Daniel Wilburn Schlicher	b: 1925		
		+Lucille Euphrosyne Craig	b: 1929	m: 1949	d: 1998
	4	Dan Wilburn Schlicher, Jr.	b: 1951		
		+Lori Ann Cline	b: 1958		d: 2005
	4	Susan Euphrosyne Schlicher	b: 1953		

Schlicher

	+Kenny Neumann	b: 1952		
4	Craig Erle Schlicher	b: 1956		
	+Cecilia Cowart	b: 1956		
4	Russell Edward Schlicher	b: 1960		
3	Jane Pamela Schlicher	b: 1937		d: 2005
	+Vivion Peter Hanagriff, Jr.	b: 1933	m: 1955	d: 1987
4	Richard Glenn Hanagriff			
	+Ida Marie Schexnayder			

*2nd Husband of Jane Pamela Schlicher:
+Edward Frey Jr.   b: 1934   m: 198070

34. Spaetgens, Heinrich Joseph:

Heinrich Joseph Spaetgens b: 3/19/1861 d: 6/21/1904 from Hastenrath is the son of Johann Spaetgens b: 1815 d: 1881 and Agnes Scheufens b: 1822 d; 1871. He married on 1/24/1889 to Maria Dilger b: 10/2/1855 d: 1909 from St. Maergen, Baden, who is the daughter of Lorenz Dilger b: 1801 d: 1858 and Catherina Schertzinger b: 1808 d: 1867.

2	John Lawrence Spaetgens	b: 4/6/1892		d: 8/19/1909
2	Hubert Leo Spaetgens	b: 5/9/1894		d: 8/10/1981
	+Josepha Elizabeth Gossen	b: 1891	m: 1915	d: 1975
3	Henry Joseph Spaetgens	b: 1916		d: 1996
	+Bertha Ewing	b: 6/26/1923	m: 1/7/1941	
4	Leona Jane Spaetgens	b: 11/12/1941		
	+Luther William Wright	b: 1938	m: 2/20/1965	d: 1993
4	Barbara Ann Spaetgens	b: 7/31/1946		
	+Allen Ray Comeaux	b: 9/24/1943	m: 8/14/1965	d: 2002
4	Catherine Marie Spaetgens	b: 7/30/1950		
	+Harvey Dale Schexnider	b: 1/9/1949	m: 12/19/1969	
4	Henry Joseph Spaetgens, Jr.	b: 2/14/1952		
	+Mary Etta Morgan	b: 6/8/1953	m: 2/10/1973	d: 1993
	*2nd Wife of Henry Joseph Spaetgens, Jr.:			
	+Donna Leonards	b: 1962	m: 2000	
4	Kristina Elizabeth Spaetgens	b: 9/4/1958		
	+Mark Leger	b: 1957	m: 1979	
	*2nd Husband of Kristina Elizabeth Spaetgens:			
	+Michael Thibodeuax	b: 1963	m: 1985	d: 1985
	*3rd Husband of Kristina Elizabeth Spaetgens:			
	+Jon Martin	b: 1962	m: 1988	

Spaetgens

4	JoAnn Celeste Spaetgens	b: 5/15/1963		
	+Russell Alan Gout	b: 1964	m: 1993	
3	John Hubert Spaetgens	b: 1919		d: 1919
3	Anna Marie Spaetgens	b: 1920		
	+Joseph M. Broussard	b: 2/12/1919	m: 11/28/1945	
4	Faye Ann Broussard	b: 1948		
	+James Cecil Blankenship	b: 12/6/1945	m: 5/30/1970	
4	Betty Joan Broussard	b: 1949		
	+Anthony Laperous	b: 11/1/1946	m: 11/28/1970	
4	Laura Marie Broussard	b: 1957		
	+Kevin Russell	b: 1955	m: 1980	
4	Elaine Agnes Broussard	b: 1959		
	+Dempsey Thibodeaux	b: 1959	m: 1981	
4	Judy Clare Broussard	b: 1961		
	+Bennett Dugas	b: 1962	m: 1992	
3	William Leo Spaetgens	b: 1922		
	+Ruby Marie Faulk	b: 1/22/1937	m: 2/1/1958	
4	Michael John Spaetgens	b: 12/13/1958		
	+Charlotte Istre	b: 1963	m: 1980	
4	Jackie Paul Spaetgens	b: 9/24/1963		
	+Evelyn Lambert	b: 1963	m: 1982	
	*2nd Wife of Jackie Paul Spaetgens:			
	+Renee Bertrand	b: 1963	m: 1997	
3	Anthony Leonard Spaetgens	b: 1924		
	+Mae Joyce Hoffpauir	b: 8/7/1926	m: 1/11/1947	
4	Karen Marie Spaetgens	b: 10/27/1948		
	+Wayne Paul Blanchard	b: 5/1/1945	m: 8/14/1971	
4	Ramona Ann Spaetgens	b: 3/29/1952		
	+James Gross	b: 1955	m: 1980	

Spaetgens

	4	Melanie Jean Spaetgens	b: 1/25/1963	
		+Richard Comeaux	b: 1963	m: 1988
3		Lawrence Anthony Spaetgens	b: 1926	
		+Carol Jean Linscombe	b: 1/28/1937	m: 8/29/1956
	4	Lawrence Anthony Spaetgens, Jr.	b: 2/25/1958	
		+Karen Badon	b: 1959	m: 1981
	4	Darla Kay Spaetgens	b: 11/21/1962	
	4	Sherry Gail Spaetgens	b: 1/27/1965	
		+Hugh Zaunbrecher	b: 1963	m: 1988
	4	Jana Lynn Spaetgens	b: 2/5/1968	
		+Jason Zaunbrecher	b: 1968	m: 1996
3		Charles Joseph Spaetgens	b: 1928	
		+Barbara Ann Perry	b: 8/28/1934	m: 6/18/1956 d: 1989
	4	Cheryl Ann Spaetgens	b: 4/1/1957	
		+Douglas Short	b: 1959	m: 1978
	4	Ella Marie Spaetgens	b: 6/3/1958	
		+James Thevis	b: 1961	m: 1982
	4	Stella Elizabeth Spaetgens	b: 6/3/1958	
	4	Susan Lynn Spaetgens	b: 10/23/1959	
		+Wayne Michael Guidry	b: 1959	m: 1979
		*2nd Husband of Susan Lynn Spaetgens:		
		+Wendell Wayne Guillot	b: 1956	m: 2003
	4	Anna Maria Spaetgens	b: 2/21/1964	
		+Kevin Benoit	b: 1961	m: 1991
	4	Mary Louise Spaetgens	b: 8/7/1969	
		+Adam Soileaux	b: 1968	m: 1989
		*2nd Husband of Mary Louise Spaetgens:		
		+Rodney Dean	b: 1959	m: 2001

Spaetgens

*2nd Wife of Charles Joseph Spaetgens:
+Virginia Gautreaux m: Aft. 1989
*3rd Wife of Charles Joseph Spaetgens:
+Ethel Broussard b: 1931 m: 1994

3	Allie Agnes Spaetgens	b: 1931		
	+James Calvin Caillier	b: 1/20/1931	m: 4/4/1951	d: 1993
4	Carolyn Elizabeth Caillier	b: 8/16/1954		
	+Lawrence Arthur Dyer	b: 1955	m: 1995	
4	Arlene Marie Caillier	b: 10/4/1960		
	+Thomas Cary Chachere	b: 1959	m: 1982	
4	Cynthia Ann Caillier	b: 7/29/1964		
	+Robert Chet Oliver	b: 1964	m: 1990	
4	Annette Theresa Caillier	b: 7/20/1967		
	+Bryan Lynn Corzine	b: 1970	m: 1989	
4	Cathleen Mary Caillier	b: 8/11/1972		
	+Daniel Andre Bedel	b: 1968	m: 1994	

35. Stamm, John Ferdinand:
John Ferdinand Stamm b: 1836 d: 1909 from Hannover, Germany married in 1865 to Bernadine Kesse b: 1843 d: 1920 from Essen, Germany.

2		John Ferdinand Stamm	b: 1865			d: 1937
		+Maria Tietjen	b: 1865		m: 18v90	d: 1940
3		Arnold Ferdinand Stamm	b: 1890			d: 1969
		+Mary Cora Morales	b: 1893		m: 1915	d: 1974
	4	Arnold Ferdinand Stamm, Jr.	b: 3/3/1916			d: 8/24/1997
		+Jeanette Wolfe	b: 1/30/1932			
	4	Aurelita Stamm	b: 4/15/1917			d: 8/5/2002
		+Daniel H. McLendon	b: 9/4/1915			d: 1/5/1977
	4	Eliska Stamm	b: 4/15/1917			d: 9/27/2004
		+J. Albert Zock				d: 1995
	4	Jocelyn Stamm	b: 11/29/1920			d: 12/16/1995
		+J.L. Page	b: 9/4/1913			
	4	Joy Stamm	b: 11/29/1920			
		+Lemuel L. Leach, Jr.	b: 10/24/1918			d: 11/22/1998
	4	Stephen Morales Stamm	b: 8/20/1923			
		+Catherine Toon	b: 3/28/1922			d: 5/18/2005
	4	Paula Stamm	b: 3/18/1927			d: 1959
3		Adeline Bernadine Stamm	b: 1893			d: 1967
		+Anthony Etienne Raymond	b: 1893		m: 1912	d: 1938
	4	John Raymond				
		+Lucille ?				
	4	Sylvia Raymond				
		+Henry Bergeaux				
	4	Mona Raymond	b: 1917			
		+John D. Hunter				
	4	Anthony Raymond				
		+Jerry McBride				

Stamm

3		Maria Henrietta Stamm	b: 1898		d: 1983
		+Bertrand Nash Sweeney, Sr.	b: 1894	m: 1918	d: 1943
	4	Mary Etta Sweeney	b: 5/9/1921		d: 3/5/2000
		+Guy Hamilton Johnston	b: 3/14/1920		d: 7/5/1977
	4	Bertrand Nash Sweeney, Jr.			
		+Jane Schexneider			
	4	Kevin "Woody" Sweeney			
3		Catherine Eleanor Stamm	b: 1900		d: 1983
		+Laurent Joseph Guidry	b: 1896	m: 1922	d: 1987
	4	John Stamm Guidry	b: 6/18/1923		d: 6/18/2002
		+Montez Tassin			
	4	Warren Guidry			
2		Alice Alvina Stamm	b: 1867		d: 1931
		+Henry Scheele	b: 1861		d: 1932
3		Charlotte Scheele	b: 1888		d: 1902
3		Ferdinand Scheele	b: 1890		d: 1894
3		Adelaide Scheele	b: 1892		d: 1896
2		Josephine Stamm	b: 1871		d: 1872
2		Caroline Stamm	b: 1872		d: 1933
		+Henry Peter Bohmann	b: 1866	m: 1894	d: 1948
3		Marcella Bohmann	b: 1893		d: 1894
3		Carola Lorraine Bohmann	b: 1895		d: 1984
		+Arthur Theodore Karow	b: 1896	m: 1919	d: 1973
3		Edgar Herbert Bohmann	b: 1899		
2		Anna Stamm	b: 1873		d: 1948
		+Hubert S. Kopmeier			
3		Theodora Mary Kopmeier	b: 1892		
		+Albert Peter Schloegel	b: 1890	m: 1912	d: 1960
3		Leonie Helen Kopmeier	b: 1899		d: 1973

Stamm

		+Stephen Tully		m: 1917	
	3	Hubert Arnold Kopmeier	b: 1904		d: 1961
		+Lorraine			
2		Maria Elizabeth Stamm	b: 1874		d: 1955
		+Charles Clemmens Schutten	b: 1867	m: 1896	d: 1946
	3	Maria Bernadine Schutten	b: 1898		
		+Robert Eugene Young Sr.	b: 1895	m: 1922	d: 1983
	3	Bernadine Catherine Schutten	b: 1900		d: 1900
	3	Rev. Msgr. Carl Jacob Schutten	b: 1902		d: 1979
	3	Adelaide Marie Schutten	b: 1904		d: 1966
		+Robert Joseph Elliot		m: 1926	d: 1957
		*2nd Husband of Adelaide Marie Schutten:			
		+Louis Joseph Pujoe	b: 1902	m: 1938	d: 1979
	3	Reginald John Schutten	b: 1906		
		+Ellen Landry		m: 1943	
	3	Ferdinand Henry Schutten	b: 1909		
		+Pearl Jarona	b: 1917	m: 1962	
	3	Philomena Schutten	b: 1911		d: 1912
2		Alphonse Stamm	b: 1878		d: 1880
2		Helena Stamm	b: 4/5/1882		d: 9/30/1956
		+Henry Zaunbrecher	b: 9/17/1875	m: 1/22/1902	d: 6/16/1944
	3	Bernadine Stephania Zaunbrecher	b: 1902		d: 1979
		+Charles Percy Dubose	b: 1905	m: 1928	d: 1996
	4	Michael Dubose	b: 9/24/1936		d: 4/20/1944
	4	Stephen Dubose	b: 8/2/1938		
		+Barbara Ann Cramer	b: 12/18/1940	m: 6/25/1960	
	3	Ferdinand Nicholas Zaunbrecher	b: 1904		d: 1966

Stamm

	+Thelma Eve Hines	b: 1905	m: 1922	d: 1955
4	Infant Zaunbrecher	b: 1925		d: 1925
4	Reginald Zaunbrecher	b: 7/15/1926		d: 4/2004
	+Marion Trahan	b: 7/31/1924	m: 2/14/1945	
4	Infant Zaunbrecher	b: 1928		d: 1928
4	Infant Zaunbrecher	b: 1929		d: 1929
4	Malcolm Zaunbrecher	b: 10/15/1931		
	+Mona Jane Smith	b: 12/24/1930	m: 6/19/1948	
3	Johann Edward Zaunbrecher	b: 3/17/1906		d: 1992
3	William Alton Zaunbrecher	b: 1907		d: 1989
	+Monique Petitjean	b: 1909	m: 1928	d: 1968
4	Joyce Zaunbrecher	b: 9/5/1929		
	+Stanley Faulk	b: 10/18/1926	m: 6/10/1948	d: 11/30/1996
	*2nd Wife of William Alton Zaunbrecher:			
	+Odille Guillot Navarre	b: 1910	m: 1969	d: 2005
3	Lawrence Henry Zaunbrecher		b: 1909	d: 1982
	+Marie Gertrude Bollich	b: 1910	m: 1932	d: 1994
4	Glenn Zaunbrecher	b: 11/21/1933		d: 11/7/1989
	+Margaret Pharr	b: 6/5/1936	m: 5/27/1956	
4	Norma Zaunbrecher	b: 12/21/1934		d: 6/15/1995
	+Harold Prevost	b: 5/3/1932	m: 4/26/1958	
4	Alfred Zaunbrecher	b: 5/28/1932		
	+Marceline Comeaux	b: 11/23/1937	m: 8/19/1956	
4	Estelle Zaunbrecher	b: 1/24/1938		
	+Edwin Coy Wyatt	b: 11/18/1936	m: 1/14/1959	
4	Irene Zaunbrecher	b: 8/22/1940		
	+Larry Fields	b: 3/26/1940	m: 4/22/1961	
4	Lois Zaunbrecher	b: 11/6/1949		
	+John D. Harpole, Jr.	b: 10/5/1948	m: 12/16/1972	
4	Janelle Zaunbrecher	b: 2/2/1954		

Stamm

		+Wilbert J. Bourque	b: 7/21/1951	m: 8/27/1971	
3		Raymond Carl Zaunbrecher	b: 1911		d: 1982
		+Anita Marie Perrodin	b: 1921	m: 1940	
	4	Sylvia Zaunbrecher	b: 8/29/1941		
		+Ray Robichaux	b: 11/3/1939	m: 7/9/1959	
	4	Russell Zaunbrecher	b: 12/25/1950		
		+Mary Shea	b: 7/8/1953	m: 9/10/1976	
3		Henrietta Mary Zaunbrecher	b: 1913		d: 1993
		+Murphy Byrun Owens	b: 1904	m: 1936	d: 1975
	4	Infant Owens	b: 1937		d: 1937
	4	Patrick Owens	b: 12/27/1938		
	4	Patricia Owens	b: 12/27/1938		d: 9/11/1994
		+Benjamin Cogburn		m: 1/30/1965	
3		Arnold Martin Zaunbrecher	b: 1915		d: 1975
		+Beatrice Clark	b: 1916	m: 8/8/1942	
	4	Dr. Frederick Martin Zaunbrecher	b: 9/27/1943		
		+Michele Dufilho	b: 7/15/1947	m: 12/30/1972	
	4	Martin Zaunbrecher, Jr.	b: 1/24/1947		
		+Lucille Ann Fontenot	b: 7/5/1944	m: 8/1/1969	
	4	Michael Henry Zaunbrecher	b: 3/29/1948		
		+Claudia Cansler		m: 7/10/1971	
	4	Nanette Helen Daboval Zaunbrecher	b: 1/3/1950		
		+Peter Grojean	b: 11/1950	m: 11/15/1979	
3		Norbert Stephen Zaunbrecher	b: 1916		d: 1979
		+Agnes Leona Bollich	b: 1918	m: 1934	d: 2002
	4	Kenneth Zaunbrecher	b: 11/8/1936		

Stamm

	+Gannol Richard	b: 11/5/1938	m: 9/30/1956	
	*2nd Wife of Kenneth Zaunbrecher:			
	+Suzanne Cheramic	b: 7/21/1939	m: 7/8/1983	
3	Hildegard (Hilda) Marie Zaunbrecher	b: 1918		d: 2005
	+Leland Paul Hebert, Sr.	b: 1918	m: 1/13/1939	d: 1963
4	Helen Rita Hebert	b: 10/27/1939		
	+James Carol Menard	b: 8/12/1939	m: 2/7/1959	
4	Mary Ann Hebert	b: 1941		d: 1941
4	Leland Paul Hebert, Jr.	b: 11/6/1942		
	+Alberta Gertrude Cramer	b: 8/16/1942	m: 2/16/1963	d: 12/11/1993
	*2nd Wife of Leland Paul Hebert, Jr.:			
	+Camella Borne	b: 11/20/1942	m: 10/2/2004	
4	Infant Hebert	b: 1944		d: 1944
4	Raymond Hebert	b: 4/14/1947		
	+Karen Credeur	b: 9/8/1947	m: 8/21/1965	
4	Gregory Lewis Hebert	b: 1/2/1949		
	+Susan Petitjean	b: 11/27/1950	m: 2/14/1968	
	*2nd Wife of Gregory Lewis Hebert:			
	+Sheila Richard Matte	b: 11/2/1959	m: 3/31/1990	
4	Geoffrey Joseph Hebert, Sr.	b: 8/1/1950		
	+Kathy Plattsmier	b: 10/30/1952	m: 6/23/1972	
	*2nd Wife of Geoffrey Joseph Hebert, Sr.:			
	+Sheila Hargrave		m: 1983	
	*3rd Wife of Geoffrey Joseph Hebert, Sr.:			
	+Mona Vincent Veazey	b: 12/8/1953	m: 3/31/2000	
4	Theresa Kay Hebert	b: 10/4/1951		
	+Timothy Paul Cronan	b: 12/22/1950	m: 6/16/1973	
4	Elizabeth Hebert	b: 1956		

Stamm

4	Timothy James Hebert, Sr.	b: 8/30/1958		
	+Deborah Jean Cox	b: 11/16/1957	m: 12/11/1982	
3	Marcella Marie Zaunbrecher	b: 1921		d: 1929
2	Adelhaide Stamm	b: 1884		d: 1930

36. Theunissen, Hubert Josef:

Hubert Josef Theunissen b: 1842 d: 1908 from Langbroich is the son of Johann Leonard Theunissen b: 1814 d: 1904 and Elizabeth Katharina Thewissen b: 1818 d: 1881. He married in 1873 to Maria Katharina Kerres b: 1849 d: 1942, who is the daughter of Peter Joseph Kerres b: 1821 d: 1905 and Maria Elizabeth Merx b: 1822 d: 1907.

2	Maria Elizabeth Dionysia Theunissen	b: 1873		d: 1949
2	Maria Katharina Theunissen	b: 1875		d: 5/27/1958
	+Theodore Vondenstein	b: 1872	m: 1902	d: 7/26/1946
3	Maria Catherina Vondenstein	b: 1/11/1903		d: 5/3/1985
	+Elridge Francis Humble	b: 12/20/1904	m: 1926	d: 11/1/1980
4	Edward Arthur Humble	b: 8/4/1929		d: 11/30/1968
4	Anna Mae Humble	b: 12/8/1927		d: 6/21/1997
4	Margie Mary Humble	b: 11/24/1933		
3	Hubert Joseph Vondenstein	b: 4/5/1904		d: 5/4/1971
	+Donatile Leboeuf	b: 2/8/1900	m: 1925	d: 10/9/1999
4	Joseph Daniel Vondenstein	b: 9/22/1927		d: 3/29/2001
4	Hebert A. Vondenstein	b: 1931		d: 6/6/1993
4	Alma Vondenstein			
3	Helena Josepha Vondenstein	b: 9/22/1905		d: 3/26/1953
3	Mary Elizabeth Vondenstein	b: 6/12/1907		d: 3/3/1992
	+Adam Leboeuf	b: 2/17/1911	m: 1932	d: 10/25/1987
4	Adair Leboeuf			d: 3/31/2001
4	Norris Leboeuf			d: 7/23/1984
3	Mary Augusta Vondenstein	b: 6/12/1907		d: 6/12/1907
3	Peter Joseph Vondenstein	b: 4/29/1909		d: 2/15/1987
	+Elta Theriot	b: 3/29/1913	m: 1934	d: 8/1/1982
4	Lawrence Vondenstein	b: 7/13/1937		

Theunissen

3	William Joseph Vondenstein	b: 12/23/1911			d: 10/16/1992
	+Necez Primeaux	b: 4/16/1918	m: 1936		d: 12/4/1991
4	Charles Vondenstein	b: 2/2/1944			d: 1/26/1964
4	Winston Vondenstein	b: 7/14/1945			
3	Bernard Johann Vondenstein	b: 3/12/1913			d: 11/17/1997
	+Ella Leboeuf	b: 12/3/1916	m: 1936		d: 5/30/1989
4	James Bernard Vondenstein	b: 5/30/1939			
4	Velma Marie Vondenstein	b: 12/17/1941			
4	Mildred Ann Vondenstein	b: 9/6/1950			
3	Daniel Joseph Vondenstein	b: 7/23/1915			d: 12/24/1985
	+Zulma Broussard	b: 9/20/1920	m: 1938		d: 7/15/2003
4	John Edward Vondenstein	b: 3/26/1940			
4	Shirley Rose Vondenstein	b: 9/7/1941			
4	Anna Belle Vondenstein	b: 6/24/1943			
4	Pirmin Dean Vondenstein	b: 4/22/1947			
2	Maria Magdelena Theunissen	b: 10/10/1876			d: 2/22/1975
	+Peter Joseph Thevis	b: 9/21/1868	m: 1/27/1897		d: 6/7/1955
3	Maria Catherina Thevis	b: 11/12/1897			d: 4/19/1981
3	Hubert Joseph Thevis	b: 8/16/1899			d: 4/24/1988
	+Maria Frances Ohlenforst	b: 7/6/1904	m: 11/28/1923		d: 2/14/1988
4	Antonia Josephine Thevis	b: 3/1/1928			
	+Lloyd Lynn Hoffpauir	b: 5/30/1926	m: 11/23/1948		d: 7/5/2006
4	Herbert Joseph Thevis	b: 3/13/1933			d: 9/16/1945

Theunissen

4	Raymond Gerhard Thevis	b: 4/13/1934		
	+Eunice Marie Abshire	b: 10/9/1935	m: 2/11/1956	
4	Norbert Anthony Thevis	b: 1/18/1938		
	+Betty Jean Norman	b: 10/4/1941	m: 1/18/1964	
4	Edward Daniel Thevis	b: 10/1/1941		
	+Selma Marie Touchet	b: 4/4/1942	m: 12/1/1961	
3	Gerhard John Thevis	b: 6/30/1901		d: 4/27/1971
	+Veronica Wilhelmena Ohlenforst	b: 1907	m: 1926	d: 12/25/1975
4	Anthony Joseph Thevis	b: 3/23/1928		d: 4/29/1992
	+Josephine Thecla Berken	b: 7/14/1934	m: 5/10/1955	
4	Ferdinand Thevis	b: 7/19/1930		
	+Wilda Ann LeJeune	b: 7/14/1933	m: 8/8/1953	
4	Lionel Edward Thevis	b: 10/25/1934		
	+Barbara Nell Monte	b: 2/14/1938	m: 9/29/1956	
3	Daniel Aloysius Thevis	b: 4/4/1904		d: 4/27/1958
3	Leonard Joseph Thevis	b: 3/19/1906		d: 3/17/1969
	+Anna Josepha Ohlenforst	b: 1913	m: 1931	d: 1980
4	James Thomas Thevis	b: 12/22/1933		
	+Normalie Blanchard	b: 3/18/1941	m: 5/19/1959	
3	Anna Gertrude Thevis	b: 2/13/1908		d: 4/24/1982
	+Ferdinand John Habetz	b: 1906	m: 1931	d: 1963
4	Vincent John Habetz	b: 10/17/1931		d: 9/5/2001
	+Louella Rita Dronet	b: 8/15/1931	m: 9/26/1970	
4	Theresa Margaret Habetz	b: 6/25/1933		d: 6/24/1999
4	Lawrence Jerome Habetz	b: 8/12/1935		d: 10/20/2004
4	Florence Marie Habetz	b: 3/15/1939		
	+Paul Edward Russell	b: 6/4/1935	m: 3/28/1959	d: 5/7/1995
4	Anna Louise Habetz	b: 7/29/1942		

Theunissen

		+Elby Joseph Pellerin	b: 1/23/1939	m: 5/4/1963	
3		Peter Jacob Thevis	b: 2/26/1911		d: 10/13/1998
		+Veronica Maria Reiners	b: 1912	m: 11/11/1936	
	4	Marie Louise Thevis	b: 2/19/1938		
		+Vincent Joseph Berken	b: 12/17/1925	m: 10/24/1956	d: 4/22/2005
	4	Wilbert Thevis	b: 8/27/1940		
		+Theresa Marie Richard	b: 10/9/1942	m: 1/24/1961	
	4	Elizabeth Magdaline Thevis	b: 3/1/1942		
		+William Joseph Reiners	b: 8/7/1940	m: 11/11/1960	d: 11/28/1999
	4	Mary Kathleen Thevis	b: 10/7/1946		d: 10/19/2001
		+Glyn Roy Hoffpauir	b: 8/9/1945	m: 10/15/1966	d: 2/26/2003
3		Martin Thevis	b: 2/20/1913		d: 4/26/1989
		+Mary Ellen Schneider	b: 1921	m: 1940	d: 1982
	4	Patricia Ann Thevis	b: 12/14/1940		
		+Thomas Mitchell Marshburn	b: 7/2/1935	m: 1/15/1966	
	4	Margaret Mary Thevis	b: 8/17/1943		
		+Alvin Joseph Benoit	b: 7/28/1941	m: 6/10/1961	
	4	Arlene Ruth Thevis	b: 3/4/1945		
		+Rene Joseph Daboval	b: 12/11/1944	m: 6/26/1965	
	4	Dorothy Jane Thevis	b: 11/20/1947		
		+Gaylan LeBlanc	b: 1/11/1944	m: 7/15/1967	
		*2nd Husband of Dorothy Jane Thevis:			
		+Norman James Lapoint	b: 11/6/1943	m: 4/30/1982	
3		Theodore Thevis	b: 2/15/1915		d: 7/5/2002
		+Rosa Dorothy Neu	b: 1917	m: 1939	d: 2001
	4	Jo Ann Thevis	b: 1/24/1940		
	4	Louis Thevis	b: 1/29/1942		

Theunissen

	+Gail Rodrigue	b: 11/13/1949	m: 12/30/1967	
4	Benedict Joseph Thevis	b: 9/11/1943		
	+Deborah Rena Collins	b: 11/21/1953	m: 3/3/1977	
4	Mary Alice Thevis	b: 12/14/1944		
4	Mona Rae Thevis	b: 11/30/1947		
3	William John Thevis	b: 3/4/1917		d: 8/11/1985
	+Agnes Columba Reiners	b: 1920	m: 1940	
4	Frank William Thevis	b: 8/18/1941		
	+Nora Lou Bellard	b: 8/7/1941	m: 4/11/1963	d: 12/30/2004
4	Leo Joseph Thevis	b: 9/8/1946		
	+Jeanette Marie Daigle	b: 8/4/1950	m: 12/31/1974	
4	Clara Marie Thevis	b: 9/28/1949		
	+John Michael Savoy	b: 11/9/1949	m: 7/26/1969	
4	Paul Daniel Thevis	b: 1/2/1954		
	+Veronica Fuselier	b: 4/13/1953	m: 11/3/1973	
4	Rose Marie Thevis	b: 4/9/1957		
	+Ronald Kenneth Hornsby	b: 4/13/1956	m: 10/2/1976	
4	Andrew John Thevis	b: 4/6/1960		
	+Connie Dee LaCombe	b: 11/16/1960	m: 2/2/1980	
4	Loretta Ann Thevis	b: 3/30/1961		
	+Harlan David Kebodeaux	b: 8/8/1965	m: 9/8/1990	
4	Arnold Stephen Thevis	b: 8/16/1964		
	+Kathleen Meche	b: 4/18/1959	m: 1/16/1988	
3	Frances Helena Thevis	b: 1/7/1920		d: 2/28/2005
	+Alphonse Melancon	b: 1914	m: 1948	d: 1966
4	Russell Billui Melancon	b: 10/14/1950		
	+Mary Frances Guidry	b: 8/16/1957	m: 12/18/1976	
4	Mary Magdalene Melancon	b: 6/9/1952		

Theunissen

	+John Wesley Raine IV	b: 3/16/1950	m: 7/27/1974	
2	Peter Joseph Theunissen	b: 1878		d: 1880
2	Johann Theunissen	b: 1881		d: 1882
2	Julius Joseph Theunissen	b: 1884		d: 1884
2	Maria Augusta Helena Theunissen	b: 9/8/1885		d: 11/14/1967
2	Maria Josefa "Franziska" Theunissen	b: 3/9/1889		d: 3/13/1980
	+Joseph Wilhelm Habetz	b: 8/24/1887	m: 1/18/1911	d: 12/9/1968
3	Hubert "Pirmin" Habetz	b: 11/3/1911		d: 8/22/1970
	+Catherine Frances Hensgens	b: 1916	m: 1/8/1936	d: 1997
4	Sr. Lawrence Laurentia (Loraine) Habetz	b: 1/21/1937		
4	Pirmin "Junior" Joseph Habetz	b: 6/4/1938		
	+Mary Lou Hebert		m: 5/16/1959	
4	Patricia Clara Habetz	b: 2/22/1940		
	+Bennett Augustine		m: 11/7/1959	
4	Marcella Elizabeth Habetz	b: 4/16/1942		d: 5/22/1973
	+Ralph Gossen	b: 1934	m: 5/5/1962	
4	Patrick Conrad Habetz	b: 2/28/1944		
	+Margie Granger		m: 4/11/1964	
4	Kathleen Gertrude Habetz	b: 9/7/1945		
	+Cecil Compton		m: 8/21/1965	
3	Msgr. Daniel Habetz	b: 2/10/1913		d: 9/27/1977
3	Maria "Clara" Habetz	b: 10/4/1914		d: 8/22/2006
3	Sr. Anna "Maria" Habetz	b: 7/31/1916		
3	William Henry Habetz	b: 5/18/1918		
	+Agnes Leonards	b: 1921	m: 2/13/1946	
4	Carl William Habetz	b: 9/5/1951		

Theunissen

		+Deborah M. Darbonne		m: 1/12/1974
	4	Ronald Hubert Habetz	b: 4/2/1953	
		+Colleen A. Kennedy		m: 2/2/1974
		*2nd Wife of Ronald Hubert Habetz:		
		+[1] Deanna Faye Darbonne		m: 11/19/1993
	4	Marilyn Agnes Habetz	b: 1/28/1955	
	4	David Wayne Habetz	b: 2/14/1956	
		+Andrea E. Bruce		m: 4/5/1975
	4	Janelle Mary Habetz	b: 10/30/1958	
		+Ted Bruce		m: 4/21/1979
	4	Richard Joseph Habetz	b: 11/26/1959	
		+Darlene Tugwell		m: 1/22/1983
	4	Gergory Anthony Habetz	b: 9/1/1961		d: 9/5/1991
		+[1] Deanna Faye Darbonne		m: 12/18/1982
	4	Loretta Ann Habetz	b: 12/29/1965	
		+Johnny Ray Darbonne, Jr.		m: 11/25/1989
3		Joseph Peter Habetz	b: 3/8/1920		d: 7/25/2006
		+Rita Ohlenforst	b: 1924	m: 1/2/1946	d: 1999
	4	Flavia Ann Habetz	b: 11/1/1946	
		+Glenn John Eldridge		m: 11/27/1969
	4	Michael Anthony Habetz	b: 1/5/1948	
		+Cynthia Scott		m: 7/25/1970
	4	Bruno Joseph Habetz	b: 6/20/1950	
		+Debra Judice		m: 5/24/1975
		*2nd Wife of Bruno Joseph Habetz:		
		+Mary Katherine Derouen		m: 10/27/1984
		*3rd Wife of Bruno Joseph Habetz:		

Theunissen

	+Linda Leeper		m: 10/9/1992	
4	Tedmund Daniel Habetz	b: 1/4/1953		
	+Kay Voohries		m: 2/29/1980	
4	Joline Rita Habetz	b: 8/3/1955		d: 8/3/1955
3	Cecilia Augusta Habetz	b: 12/6/1921		
	+Paul Zaunbrecher	b: 1923	m: 2/13/1946	d: 9/20/1982
4	Timothy Daniel Zaunbrecher	b: 12/12/1946		
	+Judy Cluchey		m: 5/29/1971	
4	Godfrey William Zaunbrecher	b: 2/21/1948		
	+Annagail Mitchell		m: 7/27/1968	
	*2nd Wife of Godfrey William Zaunbrecher:			
	+Gail Gregory		m: 2/20/1982	
	*3rd Wife of Godfrey William Zaunbrecher:			
	+Kathleen Rae Reiftroffer		m: 2000	
4	Gwendolyn Marie Zaunbrecher	b: 1/8/1950		d: 1/8/1950
4	Gerard Joseph Zaunbrecher	b: 1/24/1952		
	+Marsha Ann Sanchez		m: 1/10/1976	
3	Hilda Helena Habetz	b: 8/23/1923		d: 10/23/1924
3	Anton Theodore Habetz	b: 6/7/1925		d: 2/12/2004
	+Jose "Joyce" Lynn Leleux	b: 1937	m: 2/24/1960	
4	[3] Josette Marie Habetz	b: 2/25/1961		
	+Ray Anthony Dupuis		b: 2/22/1958	m: 1/23/1982
4	Monica Lynn Habetz	b: 1/28/1962		
	+Charles Miller		m: 8/10/1985	
4	Martin Anthony Habetz	b: 12/14/1962		
	+Tammy Sue Castille		m: 4/9/1983	
	*2nd Wife of Martin Anthony Habetz:			
	+Jennifer Hildalgo		m: Aft. 1983	

Theunissen

4	Nicholas William Habetz	b: 11/14/1964	
	+Cynthia Ann Dartez		m: 7/10/1987
4	Barbara Ann Habetz	b: 11/29/1965	
	+Carl Stephen Cramer	b: 9/10/1967	m: 6/13/1987
4	Dennis Joseph Habetz	b: 11/1/1967	
	+Antoinette "Toni" Lavergne		m: 5/12/1990
4	Dewayne Paul Habetz	b: 11/7/1968	
	+Tasca White		m: 11/7/1992
	*2nd Wife of Dewayne Paul Habetz:		
	+Michelle Renee Henry		m: Aft. 1992
	*3rd Wife of Dewayne Paul Habetz:		
	+Christa Leger		m: 7/22/2006
4	Alois Philip Habetz	b: 11/7/1969	
	+Gaylin Ann Vice		
4	Rev. Thomas Edmund Habetz	b: 11/5/1971	
4	Hilary Wayne Habetz	b: 8/28/1973	
3	Bernardine Marie Habetz	b: 6/9/1927	
	+Blaise Philip Leonards	b: 1927	m: 10/27/1948
4	Sylvester Guy Leonards	b: 8/29/1949	
	+Eugenie Marie Forstall (Cassie) Colomb		m: 7/13/1974
4	Blandina Gayle Leonards	b: 9/7/1950	
	+Michael Zaunbrecher		m: 6/25/1972
4	Ludwig Joseph Leonards	b: 1/31/1952	
	+Theresa Devall		m: 6/22/1974
4	Ignatius William Leonards	b: 9/6/1953	
	+Janet Lawrence		m: 10/27/1979
4	Gwendolyn Louise Leonards	b: 1/24/1956	

Theunissen

	+Dale Zaunbrecher		m: 6/9/1973	
4	Daniel Lawrence Leonards	b: 3/16/1957		
	+Rita Elaine Lejeune		m: 11/19/1977	
4	Caroline Anne Leonards	b: 9/5/1958		
	+Eddie James Fontenot		m: 11/18/1978	d: 9/27/1984
4	Joan Dione Leonards	b: 6/8/1960		
	+Robert Joseph Douget		m: 6/10/1978	
4	Marie Elaine Leonards	b: 12/10/1961		
	+Ronald James Fontenot		m: 7/19/1983	
4	Paul Brent Leonards	b: 2/21/1966		
	+Connie Rabalais		m: 8/10/1990	
3	Martin Habetz	b: 5/20/1929		d: 5/20/1929
3	Bertha Catherine Habetz	b: 10/31/1930		
	+Gerard Owen	b: 1917	m: 8/4/1957	d: 12/27/1987
4	Eileen Owen	b: 10/30/1957		
4	Yvette Owen	b: 12/5/1960		
	+Sergio Garcia		m: 6/17/1983	
2	Daniel Joseph Theunissen	b: 1/19/1892		d: 7/2/1985
	+Anna Helena Meyer	b: 9/2/1896	m: 1918	d: 10/19/1988
3	Marie Catherine Theunissen	b: 12/16/1918		d: 10/14/1989
	+Ralius Paul Dupuis	b: 4/14/1924	m: 1949	d: 6/21/1993
4	Ralius Paul Dupuis, Jr.	b: 1/20/1950		
	+Jo Ann Chatlain	b: 5/25/1951	m: 1/12/1970	
4	Larry James Dupuis	b: 9/2/1951		
	+Janet Trahan		m: 1970	
4	Wayne Michael Dupuis	b: 7/21/1953		d: 8/30/1992
4	[2] Ray Dupuis	b: 2/22/1958		
	+[3] Josette Marie Habetz	b: 2/25/1961	m: 1/23/1982	

Theunissen

3		Joseph Peter Theunissen	b: 1921		d: 1956
		+Eva Gertrude Leblanc	b: 1923	m: 1947	
	4	Steven Joseph Theunissen	b: 12/4/1947		
		+Gail LaBauve	b: 10/21/1953	m: 2/23/1974	
	4	Lucille Helen Theunissen	b: 6/20/1949		
		+Joseph Preston Guidry	b: 2/1/1950	m: 7/13/1973	
	4	Samuel William Theunissen	b: 9/6/1951		
		+Kathy Sensat	b: 12/27/1955	m: 6/21/1974	
	4	Dexter Leo Theunissen	b: 10/28/1952		
		+Yvonne Cahanan	b: 11/29/1953	m: 11/7/1975	
	4	Mary Beth Theunissen	b: 10/6/1955		
		+Karl Louis Boudreaux	b: 11/5/1956	m: 7/20/1979	
3		Annie Louise Theunissen	b: 3/21/1923		d: 3/16/1991
		+John Daniel Klein	b: 12/30/1924	m: 2/5/1947	d: 8/6/1964
	4	Paul Charles Klein	b: 8/13/1948		
		+Sylvia Jane Lavergne		m: 11/18/1967	
	4	Catherine Annie Klein	b: 12/31/1950		
		+Jimmy Joseph Frugé	b: 9/9/1948	m: 2/7/1970	
	4	Susan Marie Klein	b: 7/7/1953		
		+Don Charles Wilhelmi	b: 10/27/1951	m: 10/31/1974	
	4	Patricia Lynn Klein	b: 9/25/1956		
		+Jessie Chuck Greene	b: 3/17/1952	m: 9/20/1980	
	4	Cynthia Louise Klein	b: 8/26/1961		
		+John Bradley Wartelle	b: 8/30/1957	m: 10/10/1987	
3		Joseph Hubert Theunissen	b: 1925		d: 1993
		+Audrey Hope Billeaudeau	b: 1929	m: 1949	d: 1992
	4	Joseph Daniel Theunissen	b: 3/19/1952		

Theunissen

	+Janet Parr	b: 1/1/1948	m: 1/17/1970	
4	Hubert Bernard Theunissen	b: 8/25/1953		
	+Thelma Siddon	b: 6/30/1947	m: 6/23/1975	
4	Donald John Theunissen	b: 6/18/1955		
	+Judy Chandler	b: 12/18/1956	m: 10/10/1978	
4	Bill Hampton Theunissen	b: 8/27/1956		
	+Kathy Hogue	b: 8/7/1960	m: 12/1/1979	
4	Stacy Ann Theunissen	b: 7/8/1958		
	+Mark Walker	b: 8/6/1955	m: 8/27/1983	d: 10/23/1999
4	Michael James Theunissen	b: 10/17/1960		
	+Lisa Portwood	b: 4/19/1962	m: 5/5/1989	
4	Faye Ann Theunissen	b: 10/9/1962		
	+Scott Brown	b: 3/7/1961	m: 5/19/1984	
4	Joseph Hubert Theunissen, Jr.	b: 4/22/1966		
	+Davenderjit Jasuja Dimple	b: 12/7/1967	m: 12/6/1993	
3	Mathilda Josephine Theunissen	b: 10/15/1929		
	+Paul Jasper Johnson	b: 6/11/1922	m: 1/19/1950	
4	Kenneth Daniel Johnson	b: 11/3/1951		
	+Jeannie Bearb	b: 11/18/1953	m: 11/18/1972	
4	Albert Michael Johnson	b: 10/31/1953		
	+Bonnie Rita Melancon	b: 5/27/1955	m: 3/12/1977	
4	Helen Marie Johnson	b: 2/6/1955		
4	Brenda Louise Johnson	b: 2/8/1958		
	+Robert C. Hooper	b: 9/24/1958	m: 11/4/1978	
4	Mary Augusta Johnson	b: 7/20/1960		
	+Wayne Bingham	b: 12/6/1946	m: 7/19/1987	
4	Edward Joseph Johnson	b: 12/26/1965		

Theunissen

	+Tina Daigle	b: 12/30/1969	m: 6/9/1989	
3	Hilda Helena Theunissen	b: 10/15/1929		
	+James Curney Haure	b: 1930	m: 10/1952	
4	Kim James Haure	b: 10/2/1953		
	+Myrtis Ann Judice	b: 1/4/1956	m: 4/11/1974	
4	Vanessa Ann Haure	b: 3/5/1955		
	+Terry Comeaux	b: 12/1/1952	m: 10/30/1971	
4	Terri Judith Haure	b: 10/30/1958		
	+Ricky Guilbeaux	b: 3/18/1955	m: 3/14/1980	
	*2nd Husband of Terri Judith Haure:			
	+Victor Matt	b: 8/20/1971	m: 9/15/1993	
4	Pierre Haure II	b: 7/18/1965		
	+Theresa Reyes	b: 6/5/1960	m: 2/12/1988	
3	Louise Augusta Theunissen	b: 12/27/1932		
	+Raymond William Leonards	b: 1/19/1929	m: 12/27/1952	d: 4/22/1992
4	Ramona Louise Leonards	b: 11/27/1953		
4	Randolph William Leonards	b: 4/4/1955		
	+Annette Patricia Barousse	b: 11/27/1954	m: 12/29/1973	
4	Adrian Paul Leonards	b: 8/14/1956		
	+Geronna Diedra Martin	b: 10/31/1960	m: 6/2/1979	
4	Michael Anthony Leonards	b: 12/30/1957		
	+Cynthia Breaux	b: 10/3/1956	m: 10/26/1979	
4	Rachel Ann Leonards	b: 9/5/1959		
	+Randal Chris Arceneaux	b: 8/10/1957	m: 8/2/1980	
4	Joan Maria Leonards	b: 9/25/1961		
	+John Ulyess Mouton	b: 5/22/1959	m: 7/10/1981	

Theunissen

4	Raymond William Leonards, Jr.	b: 5/22/1965		d: 4/17/1977

*2nd Husband of Louise Augusta Theunissen:
+Frank E. Landry   b: 12/9/1920   m: 5/20/1994

3 William Richard (Preacher) Theunissen   b: 11/30/1935   d: 1993
　　+Anna Mae Simon   b: 1937   m: 1954
4 Debbie Theunissen   b: 1/15/1955
　　+Ricky Matt   b: 11/16/1955   m: 9/14/1974
　*2nd Husband of Debbie Theunissen:
　　+Patrick Nutt   b: 7/12/1966   m: 8/6/1988
4 Jennifer Theunissen   b: 8/30/1956
　　+Saul Broussard   b: 9/22/1952   m: 8/28/1986
4 Mitchel Theunissen   b: 10/9/1957
　　+Pam Wilkinson
　*2nd Wife of Mitchel Theunissen:
　　+Roxanne Broussard
4 Connie Theunissen   b: 5/7/1961
　　+Charles John Trahan   b: 12/24/1960   m: 2/23/1981
4 William Theunissen, Jr.   b: 3/8/1962
4 Scott Theunissen   b: 10/18/1963
4 Lisa Theunissen   b: 5/4/1965
　　+Ted Duplichan   b: 7/7/1959   m: 10/30/1987
3 Frances Margaret "Poochie" Theunissen   b: 6/15/1939
　　+Edward Joseph Benoit   b: 3/28/1939   m: 5/19/1960
4 Trudy Benoit   b: 4/19/1961
　　+Donald Hooper   b: 9/30/1959   m: 7/12/1980
4 Troy Benoit   b: 3/22/1963
　　+Wanda Thibodeaux
　*2nd Husband of Frances Margaret "Poochie" Theunissen:
　　+Milford Primeaux   b: 1935   m: 1979

Theunissen

2		Peter Joseph Theunissen	b: 1897			d: 1970
		+Lillian Green	b: 1902	m: 1919		d: 1992
	3	Marie Catherine (Gertie Mae) Theunissen	b: 1922			
		+Conrad Leo Hensgens	b: 1920	m: 1939		d: 1987
		4	Thomas Jude Hensgens	b: 1955		
			+Trina Ann Autin	b: 1962	m: 1989	
	3	Daisy Deen Theunissen	b: 1924			d: 1936
	3	Peter Joseph Theunissen, Jr.	b: 1926			d: 1990
		+Jacqueline Marie Reaud	b: 1932	m: 1951		
		4	Peter Jules Theunissen	b: 1952		
			+Martha Broussard	b: 1953		
		*2nd Wife of Peter Jules Theunissen:				
			+Karen Colhour	b: 1952	m: 1993	
		4	Richard Dean Theunissen	b: 1953		d: 1991
		4	Trudy Lynn Theunissen	b: 1954		
			+William Reeves	b: 1951	m: 1978	d: 1995
		4	Cheryl Ann Theunissen	b: 1956		
			+Frank Dennis	b: 1960		
		4	Kathy Marie Theunissen	b: 1962		
			+Broussard	b: 1961	m: 1986	
	3	Bernan Hubert Theunissen	b: 1929			
		+Anna Carol Bryan	b: 1932	m: 1951		
		4	Bernan Hubert Theunissen, Jr.	b: 1952		
			+Elizabeth A. Roy	b: 1955	m: 1971	
		*2nd Wife of Bernan Hubert Theunissen, Jr.:				
			+Jamie M. Broussard	b: 1958	m: 1979	
		4	Randall Theunissen	b: 1953		
			+Cathy Ann Nuzum	b: 1954		
		*2nd Wife of Randall Theunissen:				

Theunissen

	+Laura K. Austin	b: 1960	m: 1996
4	Kendall Theunissen	b: 1958	
	+Katherine D.	b: 1967	m: 1994
4	Marcus Kade Theunissen	b: 1974	
	+Jeri Landry	b: 1970	m: 1998
3	Gerald Joseph Theunissen	b: 1933	
	+Patricia Ann Reaud	b: 1929	m: 1956
4	Terry Sue Theunissen	b: 1958	
	+David Denson Persac	b: 1957	m: 1981
4	Julie Ann Theunissen	b: 1959	
	+John Martin	b: 1955	m: 1985
	*2nd Husband of Julie Ann Theunissen:		
	+Bruce McDonald	b: 1956	m: 2002
4	Gerald Joseph "Jay" Theunissen, Jr.	b: 1960	
	+Tiffany Frey Leger	b: 1968	m: 2001
3	Pirmin James Theunissen	b: 1935	
	+Velda Lea Guidry	b: 1936	m: 1958
4	Daisy Denise Theunissen	b: 1959	
4	Stephen Glen Theunissen	b: 1961	
	+Carole Denise Conner	b: 1963	m: 1983
4	Mary Catherine Theunissen	b: 1962	
	+Bentley LaFleur	b: 1962	m: 1982
4	David Wayne Theunissen	b: 1966	
	+Angela Sue Bourque	b: 1960	m: 1985
4	Ann Louise Theunissen	b: 1969	
	+Joseph Jay Johnson	b: 1969	m: 1992
4	Michael Pirmin Theunissen	b: 1973	
	+Maria Kimberly Coung Nguyen	b: 1970	m: 1998

Theunissen

3		Daniel Theunissen	b: 1938		d: 1938
3		Julo Conrad Theunissen	b: 1943		
		+Cheryl Jane Boudreaux	b: 1945	m: 1965	
	4	Michele Aline Theunissen	b: 1967		
		+Andrew John Timmer	b: 1963	m: 2001	
	4	Natalie Angela Theunissen	b: 1970		
		+David Michael Byrnes	b: 1964	m: 1995	

37. Thevis, Jacob:

Jacob Thevis b: 1830 d: 1907 from Langbroich was the son of Johann Daniel Thevis b: 5/28/1795 d: 2/27/1845 and Maria Barbara Janssen b: 3/13/1799 d: 1/22/1867. He married in 1855 to Maria Gertrude Mertens b: 1832 d: 1882, the daughter of Johann Mertens and Maria Cornelia Houben.

2		Maria Thevis	b: 1856		
2		Johann Gerhard Thevis	b: 12/9/1857		d: 3/12/1934
		+Anna Maria Klein	b: 1865	m: 11/17/1884	d: 10/13/1895
3		Marie Odelia Thevis	b: 1886		d: 1984
		+John Herman Cramer II	b: 1882	m: 1909	d: 1970
	4	Anna Marie Cramer	b: 1910		d: 2005
	4	Maria Gesina Cramer	b: 5/20/1914		d: 8/29/2000
		+Lawrence Xavier Schultz	b: 9/1/1912	m: 1/17/1934	d: 10/21/1975
	4	Adelheid Walburga Cramer	b: 1920		d: 1937
3		Peter Reinhard Thevis	b: 1887		d: 1904
3		Peter Joseph Thevis	b: 1889		d: 1969
		+Anna Maria Cramer	b: 1893	m: 1912	d: 1980
	4	John Gerhard Thevis	b: 7/28/1914		d: 1983
		+Martha Frances Burton	b: 11/15/1920	m: 12/31/1940	d: 1999
	4	Annie Gesina Thevis	b: 1917		
		+John Conrad Hensgens	b: 1919	m: 1946	d: 1992
	4	Joseph Herman Thevis	b: 1919		d: 2003
		+Helen Marie Zaunbrecher	b: 1924	m: 1946	
	4	Mary Agnes Thevis	b: 7/14/1921		
		+Paul Doucet	b: 8/17/1919	m: 1945	
3		Peter Leonard Thevis	b: 1891		d: 1987
		+Maria Agnes Ronkartz	b: 1894	m: 1916	d: 1969
	4	Leonard Gerhard Thevis	b: 1917		

Thevis

4	John Joseph Thevis	b: 1920		d: 1993
	+Nancee Ruth Andrew		m: 1969	
	*2nd Wife of John Joseph Thevis:			
	+Ouida Mae Spell		m: 1977	
4	Mary Anna Thevis	b: 1922		
4	Anna Josephine Thevis	b: 1925		
4	"Sister Agnes" Leona Walburga Thevis	b: 1927		
4	Lawrence Vincent Thevis	b: 1929		d: 1995
	+Betty Jane Henderson	b: 1929	m: 1980	
4	Louise Helen Thevis	b: 1931		
4	Dorothy Agnes Thevis	b: 1934		
3	Maria Walburga Thevis	b: 1893		d: 1994
	+Charles Joseph Leonards	b: 1892	m: 1915	d: 1945
4	Gerhard Joseph Leonards	b: 1916		d: 1973
	+Victoria Ann Schatzle	b: 1921	m: 11/27/1940	
4	Josephine Anna Leonards	b: 1920		d: 1992
	+Anthony Joseph Ohlenforst	b: 1916	m: 1/31/1940	d: 1974
4	Agnes Elizabeth Leonards	b: 1921		
	+William Henry Habetz	b: 1918	m: 2/13/1946	
4	Margaret Mary Leonards	b: 1923		
	+Ambrose Joseph Olinger	b: 1923	m: 11/27/1946	
2	Cornelia Thevis	b: 1862		d: 1950
2	Katharina Gertrude Thevis	b: 11/15/1863		d: 2/29/1964
	+Peter Klein, Jr	b: 3/16/1863	m: 2/8/1886	d: 9/21/1942

Thevis

3	Peter Jacob Klein	b: 11/18/1886		d: 3/4/1902
3	Peter Leonard Klein	b: 6/16/1888		d: 5/26/1962
	+Katherine Maria Isenberg	b: 11/4/1889	m: 11/22/1916	d: 1/4/1949
4	Gertrude Barbara Klein	b: 5/8/1919		
	+Claude Boudreaux, Jr.			d: 1/19/1962
	*2nd Husband of Gertrude Barbara Klein:			
	+Clifford Trahan		m: Aft. 1962	d: 1983
4	Margaret Klein	b: 2/1/1921		
	+Joseph Schatzle	b: 11/29/1917	m: 10/8/1947	d: 7/14/1993
4	John Daniel Klein	b: 12/30/1924		d: 8/6/1964
	+Annie Theunissen	b: 3/21/1923	m: 2/5/1947	
4	Dorothy Klein	b: 2/10/1928		d: 5/1928
4	Peter Joseph Klein	b: 11/7/1931		d: 3/26/1996
4	[2] Charles Klein	b: 8/8/1922		
	+[1] Elizabeth Josephine Berken	b: 11/8/1922	m: 11/20/1946	d: 11/27/1995
3	John Joseph Klein	b: 1/4/1892		d: 1987
	+Gertrude Mildred Nungesser	b: 12/2/1899	m: 2/19/1919	d: 1983
4	Mary Magdalene Klein	b: 1920		d: 12/11/2002
	+Raymond Hotard		m: 2/19/1949	d: 1/28/2004
4	Mildred Gertrude Klein	b: 10/16/1922		
	+George Stanley Southerland			
4	Edmund Joseph Klein	b: 3/16/1924		
	+Jo Ann Hebert	b: 2/3/1929	m: 11/30/1957	
4	Catherine Claire Klein	b: 2/10/1928		
	+Harvey Broussard	b: 4/10/1924	m: 2/19/1946	d: 1/13/2004
3	Finton John George Klein	b: 2/17/1894		d: 1986
	+Kate Sullivan	b: 1/15/1905	m: 1925	d: 11/22/1970
4	Cecelia Klein	b: 12/16/1925		
	+Leroy Labbie			

Thevis

4	Finton John George Klein, Jr.	b: 6/26/1927		
	+Aileen Cowart	b: 12/27/1933	m: 12/18/1954	
4	Marie Louise Klein	b: 3/13/1929		d: 6/22/2004
	+Charles Atchison	b: 4/5/1925		d: 3/15/2001
4	Daniel Klein	b: 5/1/1931		
4	John Harold Klein	b: 8/19/1935		d: 7/25/1987
	+Margaret Ann Koulise	b: 8/13/1936		
4	Francis Joseph Klein	b: 3/28/1938		d: 2/15/1998
	+Barbara Lee	b: 1/12/1942	m: 9/3/1960	
4	Rachel Gertrude Klein	b: 7/12/1939		
	+Deward Comeaux		m: 2/20/1960	
4	Reginald Thomas Klein	b: 2/14/1941		
	+Janice Lee			
3	Maria Gertrude Klein	b: 5/31/1895		d: 4/19/1972
	+Marvin Peter Young, Sr	b: 7/29/1894	m: 6/29/1921	d: 1/4/1963
4	Marie Young			
	+Howard J. Caillouet			
4	Marvin Peter Young, Jr.			d: 8/12/1979
	+Ruby D.			
4	Winnie Young			
	+Hugh G. Fontenot, Sr.			
3	Anna Maria Klein	b: 7/4/1897		d: 1981
3	John Daniel Klein	b: 2/1/1900		d: 6/10/1923
3	Anna Odilia Klein	b: 7/31/1905		d: 5/13/1906
2	Aloysuis Thevis	b: 1866		d: 1937
	+Elizabeth Augusta Heinen	b: 1871	m: 1890	d: 1944
3	Jacob Andrew Thevis	b: 1890		d: 1903
3	Cornelia Josepha Thevis	b: 3/19/1894		d: 4/13/1971
	+Lawrence Edward Frey	b: 7/7/1890	m: 1912	d: 5/9/1922
4	Elizabeth Frey	b: 1913		d: 1990

Thevis

	+Elge Rasberry	b: 1909	m: 1934	
4	Aloysuis Frey	b: 5/9/1915		
	+Marcella Rose Bollich	b: 1916	m: 1937	
3	Maria Walburga Thevis	b: 1896		d: 1984
	+Henry Joseph Ohlenforst	b: 2/25/1889	m: 1919	d: 8/20/1971
4	Fr. John William Ohlenforst	b: 11/5/1919		d: 1/3/1997
4	Aloysius Ohlenforst	b: 1921		d: 1996
	+Micheline Courtat	b: 1929	m: 1946	
4	George Lawrence Ohlenforst	b: 2/3/1923		d: 2/6/1923
4	Gertrude Cecilia Ohlenforst	b: 1924		d: 1994
	+Frank Joseph Bernard	b: 1920	m: 1946	d: 1984
4	Thecla Theresa Ohlenforst	b: 2/28/1926		d: 4/21/1967
	+Lionel Paul Simoneaux, Jr.	b: 1923	m: 1951	d: 2005
4	Andrew Lawrence Ohlenforst	b: 10/6/1928		d: 10/3/1983
	+Marcella Marie Leonards	b: 2/3/1934	m: 1/19/1955	
4	Sister Margaret Mary Ohlenforst	b: 10/20/1931		
4	Dorothy Ann Ohlenforst	b: 1933		
	+William Joseph Leger	b: 1928	m: 1953	d: 1992
4	Joseph Daniel Ohlenforst	b: 1935		
	+Brenda Marie Sonnier	b: 1946	m: 1965	
4	Saraphia Bernadette Ohlenforst	b: 1938		
	+Edlar Ronald Monte	b: 1938	m: 1959	

Thevis

	4	Francis Thomas Ohlenforst	b: 1940		
		+Jacquelyn Sue Dupont	b: 10/13/1942	m: 1969	d: 7/15/2005
3		William Ignatius Thevis	b: 1898		d: 1917
3		Lambertina Thecla Thevis	b: 1900		d: 1981
		+Johan Casper Berken	b: 7/6/1891	m: 6/18/1919	d: 1/30/1984
	4	Herman Aloysius Berken	b: 3/5/1920		d: 2/18/1992
		+Elvina Bourque	b: 6/30/1930	m: 6/15/1950	d: 4/18/2000
	4	Lawrence Herman Berken	b: 8/10/1921		d: 9/11/1996
		+Leona Hensgens	b: 5/6/1924	m: 1/30/1946	
	4	[1] Elizabeth Josephine Berken	b: 11/8/1922		d: 11/27/1995
		+[2] Charles Klein	b: 8/8/1922	m: 11/20/1946	
	4	Christina Marie Berken	b: 3/26/1924		
		+Simon Hornsby	b: 5/7/1925	m: 10/7/1950	d: 7/10/1978
	4	[6] Vincent Joseph Berken	b: 12/17/1925		d: 4/22/2005
		+[5] Marie Louise Thevis	b: 2/19/1938	m: 10/24/1956	
	4	Gertrude Angela Berken	b: 9/17/1927		
		+Robert Leger	b: 12/31/1927	m: 4/14/1951	d: 7/9/2003
	4	Mary Agnes Berken	b: 11/30/1929		
		+Jesse Harrington	b: 10/1/1926	m: 6/21/1952	
	4	Anna Louise Berken	b: 1932		d: 1942
	4	[4] Josephine Thecla Berken	b: 7/14/1934		
		+[3] Anthony Joseph Thevis	b: 3/23/1928	m: 5/10/1955	d: 4/29/1992
	4	Reinhard John Berken	b: 8/4/1938		d: 10/3/2001
		+Thelma Abshire	b: 10/26/1940	m: 1961	d: 4/6/2007

*2nd Wife of Reinhard John Berken:

Thevis

	+Brenda Credeur	b: 7/23/1949	m: 11/6/1982	
4	Rita Helena Berken	b: 3/23/1941		
	+Jesse Hoffpauir	b: 1/1/1941	m: 2/4/1961	d: 10/5/2002
3	Maria Gertrude Thevis	b: 1903		d: 1993
3	Anna Maria Thevis	b: 4/20/1905		d: 2/14/1973
	+Frank Reiners	b: 9/8/1901	m: 2/12/1924	d: 9/25/1987
4	Joseph Reiners	b: 4/9/1925		d: 2005
	+Harriette Louise Klein	b: 10/13/1931	m: 11/9/1949	
4	Alois Andrew Reiners	b: 7/25/1926		d: 3/19/1999
	+Lucille Clara Gossen	b: 11/11/1928	m: 11/25/1953	
4	Elizabeth Josephine Reiners	b: 10/16/1928		d: 4/17/2000
4	Helen Marie Reiners	b: 9/20/1932		
	+Sylvester Lawrence Frey	b: 7/20/1930	m: 1/20/1954	
4	Anthony Francis Reiners	b: 11/18/1933		
	+Pauline Ann Habetz	b: 4/14/1934	m: 9/19/1957	
3	Elizabeth Anna Thevis	b: 3/12/1907		d: 1995
	+Edward Frey	b: 10/14/1903	m: 1927	d: 8/8/1974
4	Genevieve Frey	b: 11/11/1932		
	+Edwin Leonards	b: 1928	m: 1948	d: 4/21/2007
4	Edward Frey	b: 3/7/1933		
	+D'uan Fontenot			d: 4/29/1987
	*2nd Wife of Edward Frey:			
	+Pamela Schlicher			d: 7/28/2005
4	Mildred Frey	b: 9/10/1935		
	+James Boudreax	b: 6/15/1932		
4	Rita Frey	b: 5/4/1937		
	+Lubert Reed			d: 4/10/1982
	*2nd Husband of Rita Frey:			
	+Harvey Hebert	b: 11/13/1921		

Thevis

	4	Frederick Frey	b: 9/15/1939		
		+Dorothy Vezinat			d: 12/9/1993
		*2nd Wife of Frederick Frey:			
		+Vicki Storer		m: 12/28/1997	
	4	Sadie Frey	b: 2/20/1944		
		+Robert Thevis	b: 1/1/1942		
3		Maria Elizabeth Thevis	b: 10/24/1909		d: 1/3/1985
		+Christian Joseph Hensgens	b: 9/25/1907	m: 11/19/1928	d: 10/13/1972
	4	Leonard Joseph (Lenny) Hensgens	b: 10/7/1929		
		+Sarah Ann Smith		m: 7/11/1950	
	4	Raymond Aloysious Hensgens, Sr.	b: 7/22/1932		
		+Catherine (Kitty) Schneider		m: 10/20/1951	
	4	Lawrence Leo Hensgens	b: 4/1/1934		
		+Lula Link		m: 12/10/1953	
	4	Germaine Frances Hensgens	b: 12/14/1935		d: 2/2/1996
		+Frank J. Schneider		m: 10/25/1955	
	4	Wilhelmina (Wilma) Thecla Hensgens	b: 11/10/1937		d: 5/21/2006
		+Henry Jerome Leonards	b: 9/13/1934	m: 1/26/1958	
	4	Alberta Gertrude Hensgens	b: 2/13/1940		
		+Joseph Norwood Marcy Lyons		m: 5/25/1963	
2		Peter Joseph Thevis	b: 9/21/1868		d: 6/7/1955
		+Maria Magdelena Theunissen	b: 10/10/1876	m: 1/27/1897	d: 2/22/1975
	3	Maria Catherina Thevis	b: 11/12/1897		d: 4/19/1981
	3	Hubert Joseph Thevis	b: 8/16/1899		d: 5/24/1988

Thevis

	+Maria Frances Ohlenforst	b: 7/6/1904	m: 11/28/1923	d: 2/14/1988
4	Antonia Josephine Thevis	b: 3/1/1928		
	+Lloyd Lynn Hoffpauir	b: 5/30/1926	m: 11/23/1948	d: 7/5/2006
4	Herbert Joseph Thevis	b: 3/13/1933		d: 9/16/1945
4	Raymond Gerhard Thevis	b: 4/13/1934		
	+Eunice Marie Abshire	b: 10/9/1935	m: 2/11/1956	
4	Norbert Anthony Thevis	b: 1/18/1938		
	+Betty Jean Norman	b: 10/4/1941	m: 1/18/1964	
4	Edward Daniel Thevis	b: 10/1/1941		
	+Selma Maie Touchet	b: 4/4/1942	m: 12/1/1961	
3	Gerhard John Thevis	b: 6/30/1901		d: 4/27/1971
	+Veronica Wilhelmena Ohlenforst	b: 6/7/1907	m: 11/17/1926	d: 12/25/1975
4	[3] Anthony Joseph Thevis	b: 3/23/1928		d: 4/29/1992
	+[4] Josephine Thecla Berken	b: 7/14/1934	m: 5/10/1955	
4	Ferdinand Joseph Thevis	b: 7/19/1930		
	+Wilda Ann LeJeune	b: 7/14/1933	m: 8/8/1953	
4	Lionel Edward Thevis	b: 10/25/1934		
	+Barbara Nell Monte	b: 2/14/1938	m: 9/29/1956	
3	Daniel Aloysius Thevis	b: 5/4/1904		d: 5/27/1958
3	Leonard Joseph Thevis	b: 3/19/1906		d: 3/17/1969
	+Anna Josepha Ohlenforst	b: 8/10/1913	m: 11/17/1931	d: 2/29/1980
4	James Thomas Thevis	b: 12/22/1933		
	+Normalie Blanchard	b: 3/18/1941	m: 5/19/1959	
3	Anna Gertrude Thevis	b: 2/13/1908		d: 4/24/1982
	+Ferdinand John Habetz	b: 12/27/1906	m: 1/21/1931	d: 8/24/1963
4	Vincent John Habetz	b: 10/17/1931		d: 9/5/2001

Thevis

	+Louella Rita Dronet	b: 8/15/1931	m: 9/26/1970	
4	Theresa Margaret Habetz	b: 6/25/1933		d: 6/24/1999
4	Lawrence Jerome Habetz	b: 8/12/1935		d: 10/20/2004
4	Florence Marie Habetz	b: 3/15/1939		
	+Paul Edward Russell	b: 6/4/1935	m: 3/28/1959	d: 5/7/1995
4	Anna Louise Habetz	b: 7/29/1942		
	+Elby Joseph Pellerin	b: 1/23/1939	m: 5/4/1963	
3	Peter Jacob Thevis	b: 2/26/1911		d: 10/13/1998
	+Veronica Maria Reiners	b: 3/3/1912	m: 11/11/1936	
4	[5] Marie Louise Thevis	b: 2/19/1938		
	+[6] Vincent Joseph Berken	b: 12/17/1925	m: 10/24/1956	d: 4/22/2005
4	Wilbert Thevis	b: 8/27/1940		
	+Theresa Marie Richard	b: 10/9/1942	m: 1/24/1961	
4	Elizabeth Magdaline Thevis	b: 3/1/1942		
	+William Joseph Reiners	b: 8/7/1940	m: 11/11/1960	d: 11/28/1999
4	Mary Kathleen Thevis	b: 10/7/1946		d: 10/19/2001
	+Glyn Roy Hoffpauir	b: 8/9/1945	m: 10/15/1966	d: 2/26/2003
3	Martin Thevis	b: 2/20/1913		d: 4/26/1989
	+Mary Ellen Schneider	b: 5/5/1921	m: 1/24/1940	d: 2/23/1982
4	Patricia Ann Thevis	b: 12/14/1940		
	+Thomas Mitchell Marshburn	b: 7/2/1935	m: 1/15/1966	
4	Margaret Mary Thevis	b: 8/17/1943		
	+Alvin Joseph Benoit	b: 7/28/1941	m: 6/10/1961	
4	Arlene Ruth Thevis	b: 3/4/1945		
	+Rene Joseph Daboval	b: 12/11/1944	m: 6/26/1965	
4	Dorothy Jane Thevis	b: 11/20/1947		
	+Gaylan LeBlanc	b: 1/11/1944	m: 7/15/1967	

*2nd Husband of Dorothy Jane Thevis:

Thevis

		+Norman James Lapoint	b: 11/6/1943	m: 4/30/1982	
3		Theodore Thevis	b: 2/15/1915		d: 7/5/2002
		+Rosa Dorothy Neu	b: 1/10/1917	m: 1/4/1939	d: 12/25/2001
	4	Jo Ann Thevis	b: 1/24/1940		
	4	Louis Thevis	b: 1/29/1942		
		+Gail Rodrigue	b: 11/13/1949	m: 12/30/1967	
	4	Benedict Joseph Thevis	b: 9/11/1943		
		+Deborah Rena Collins	b: 11/21/1953	m: 3/3/1977	
	4	Mary Alice Thevis	b: 12/14/1944		
	4	Mona Rae Thevis	b: 11/30/1947		
3		William John Thevis	b: 3/4/1917		d: 8/11/1985
		+Agnes Columba Reiners	b: 1/31/1920	m: 11/26/1940	
	4	Frank William Thevis	b: 8/18/1941		
		+Nora Lou Bellard	b: 8/7/1941	m: 4/11/1963	d: 12/30/2004
	4	Leo Joseph Thevis	b: 9/8/1946		
		+Jeanette Marie Daigle	b: 8/4/1950	m: 12/31/1974	
	4	Clara Marie Thevis	b: 9/28/1949		
		+John Michael Savoy	b: 11/9/1949	m: 7/26/1969	
	4	Paul Daniel Thevis	b: 1/2/1954		
		+Veronica Fuselier	b: 4/13/1953	m: 11/3/1973	
	4	Rose Marie Thevis	b: 4/9/1957		
		+Ronald Kenneth Hornsby	b: 4/13/1956	m: 10/2/1976	
	4	Andrew John Thevis	b: 4/6/1960		
		+Connie Dee LaCombe	b: 11/16/1960	m: 2/2/1980	
	4	Loretta Ann Thevis	b: 3/30/1961		
		+Harlan David Kebodeaux	b: 8/8/1965	m: 9/8/1990	
	4	Arnold Stephen Thevis	b: 8/16/1964		

Thevis

		+Kathleen Meche	b: 4/18/1959	m: 1/16/1988	
3		Frances Helena Thevis	b: 1/7/1920		d: 2/28/2005
		+Alphonse Melancon	b: 6/26/1914	m: 7/17/1949	d: 11/22/1966
	4	Russell Billui Melancon	b: 10/14/1950		
		+Mary Frances Guidry	b: 8/16/1957	m: 12/18/1976	
	4	Mary Magdalene Melancon	b: 6/9/1952		
		+John Wesley Raine IV	b: 3/16/1950	m: 7/27/1974	
2		(Reverend) John Daniel Thevis	b: 1871		d: 1899
2		Anna Maria Thevis	b: 6/13/1880		d: 9/30/1957
		+Everhard Cramer	b: 1/8/1879	m: 1907	d: 6/27/1961
3		Anna Gesina Cramer	b: 10/2/1908		d: 4/18/2002
		+Leonard August Habetz	b: 8/28/1903	m: 1934	d: 11/22/1978
	4	Margaret Mary Habetz	b: 9/24/1935		
		+Wesley Bouillion	b: 2/26/1936	m: 11/13/1955	d: 11/8/1990
	4	Geraldine Habetz	b: 5/25/1937		
		+Sherman Trahan	b: 2/26/1939	m: 3/17/1962	
	4	Louise Habetz	b: 1/6/1939		
		+Johnny Meche	b: 12/25/1939	m: 11/4/1961	
	4	Edward Habetz	b: 2/7/1941		
		+Marlene Miller	b: 1/10/1946	m: 11/3/1962	
	4	Daniel Habetz	b: 1/3/1943		
		+Judy Savoy	b: 12/19/1943	m: 11/2/1962	
	4	Gerhard Habetz	b: 12/31/1944		
		+Brenda Gale Guidry		m: 11/12/1966	
		*2nd Wife of Gerhard Habetz:			
		+Gloria Higginbotham	b: 8/2/1945	m: 4/17/1985	
	4	Charles Habetz	b: 5/22/1946		
		+Patty Beard	b: 3/31/1949	m: 10/11/1970	
	4	Robert Habetz	b: 5/13/1948		

Thevis

		+Amber Thomas		m: 4/4/1969	
	4	Rose Marie Habetz	b: 4/20/1950		d: 9/1951
3		Jacob Cramer	b: 4/7/1910		d: 1/28/1973
		+Mary Magdalena Habetz	b: 1/5/1906	m: 1/7/1936	d: 12/30/1995
	4	Anna Marie "Sr. Mary Clare" Cramer	b: 10/16/1936		
	4	Angelina Cramer	b: 1/5/1938		
		+Ralph Gonthier	b: 8/7/1934	m: 6/20/1964	d: 6/25/2001
	4	Leonard "Jake" Jacob Cramer	b: 2/17/1939		
		+Catherine Gossen	b: 8/4/1939	m: 11/9/1961	
	4	Barbara Anna Cramer	b: 12/18/1940		
		+Stephen Dubose	b: 8/4/1938	m: 6/25/1960	
	4	Alberta Cramer	b: 8/16/1942		d: 12/11/1993
		+Leland Paul "T-Boy" Hebert	b: 11/7/1943	m: 2/16/1963	
	4	Bernadette Cramer	b: 11/7/1943		
		+Douglas Guidry	b: 7/16/1942	m: 8/29/1964	
	4	Anthony Edward Cramer	b: 2/20/1945		
		+Rhena Vienne	b: 11/11/1946	m: 4/23/1966	
	4	Michael John Cramer	b: 10/14/1946		
		+Yvonne Prather	b: 11/11/1946	m: 9/4/1965	
	4	Theresa Cramer	b: 6/21/1948		
		+Lawrence Doucet	b: 2/13/1947	m: 1/31/1970	d: 12/21/1993
	4	Loretta Cramer	b: 1/10/1952		
		+Glenn Michael Boudreaux	b: 12/27/1948	m: 1/8/1977	
3		Herman Aloyious Cramer	b: 12/5/1911		d: 11/10/1966
		+Josephine Leonards	b: 3/26/1919		d: 1/23/2002
	4	Lawrence Aloyious Cramer	b: 9/12/1941		

Thevis

	+Mary Magdalene Reiners	b: 3/31/1944	m: 6/11/1963	
4	Louis Edward Cramer	b: 2/10/1943		
	+Katherine Carlson	b: 7/4/1945	m: 6/3/1973	
3	Gertrude Cramer	b: 10/2/1913		d: 7/1996
3	Adeline "Addie" Cramer	b: 8/30/1915		
	+William "Raymond" Habetz	b: 8/30/1913	m: 8/17/1950	d: 2004
4	May Rose Habetz	b: 1/3/1954		
	+Anthony Bourgeois	b: 1/1/1955	m: 8/17/2000	
3	Gerhard Cramer	b: 8/22/1917		d: 11/28/1978
	+Sophie Schatzle	b: 1920	m: 1946	
4	Jacquline Cramer	b: 10/24/1948		
	+Darrell LeBlanc	b: 3/26/1946	m: 1/11/1966	
4	Mary Frances Cramer	b: 12/22/1950		d: 4/6/1957
4	Elizabeth "Betty" Cramer	b: 7/13/1952		
	+Michael Bellard	b: 5/8/1949	m: 10/14/1972	
4	Cynthia Cramer	b: 6/23/1956		
	+Cody Miller	b: 6/4/1950	m: 6/13/1981	
4	Josie Cramer	b: 11/3/1958		
	+Benny Stelly			
3	Marie Rose Cramer	b: 3/11/1920		
	+Leo Mouton	b: 4/19/1919	m: 2/12/1941	d: 12/9/1981
4	Johnny Mouton	b: 1/6/1942		d: 10/10/2005
	+Virlee Mier	b: 12/24/1941		
4	Edwin Mouton	b: 10/17/1944		
	+Ann Burnett	b: 11/27/1943	m: 2/8/1964	
4	James Mouton	b: 7/30/1946		
	+Judy Bearb	b: 12/11/1946	m: 4/15/1967	
4	Genevieve Mouton	b: 2/16/1949		
	+Ronald Melancon	b: 12/21/1949	m: 6/14/1969	
4	Patricia Mouton	b: 2/13/1951		

Thevis

	+Leonard Breaux	b: 1/25/1949	m: 3/7/1970	
4	Mary Jo Mouton	b: 4/30/1953		
	+Patrick Boudreaux	b: 1/18/1949		d: 6/14/1977
4	Gregory Mouton	b: 3/12/1955		
	+Sherry Myers	b: 8/13/1957	m: 8/17/1974	
4	Dianna Mouton	b: 9/4/1957		d: 9/4/1957
4	Linda Mouton	b: 11/17/1959		

38. Thevis, Peter Joseph:
Peter Joseph Thevis b: 1843 d: 10/4/1913 from Langbroich was a brother of Jacob Thevis (see above). He married on 3/22/1881 to Johanna Katharina Piepers b: 10/6/1845 d: 5/6/1905, who is the daughter of Matthias Piepers and Agnes Kreckelberg. Johanna Katharina Piepers was a sister to Maria Josepha Piepers who married Heinrich Joseph Achten (see Achten family). Peter Joseph Thevis and his wife returned to Germany.

2		Maria Cornelia Thevis	b: 1888		d: 1933
		+Wilhelm Ohlenforst	b: 1878	m: 1920	d: 1955
3		Christian "Herbert" Ohlenforst	b: 1921		d: 1981
		+Helene Hulton Schmidt	b: 1932	m: 1959	
	4	Hans Ohlenforst			
	4	Ralf Ohlenforst			
3		Ludwig "Hans" Ohlenforst	b: 1924		d: 2000
		+Johanna		m: 1953	
	4	Willie Ohlenforst			
	4	Bernard Ohlenforst			

39. Vondenstein, Wilhelm Joseph:

Wilhelm Joseph Vondenstein b: 1/7/1831 d: 3/23/1901 from Langbroich was the son of Johann Peter Vondenstein b: 1799 d: 1850 and Maria Gertrude Hallmanns b: 1794 d: 1876. He married in 1867 to Maria Josepha Killen b: 8/17/1842 d: 12/19/1913 from Kreuzrath, who is the daughter of Johann Arnold Killen b: 1800 d: 4/10/1857 from Hastenrath and his second wife, Maria Elizabeth Schoeffelen b: 1802 d: 1857. Maria Josepha Killen was a half-sister to Maria Agnes Killen, who married Johann Peter Gossen (see Gossen family).

2		Maria Anna Vondenstein	b: 1870		d: 1920
		+Johann Ronkartz	b: 1862	m: 1889	d: 1907
3		Maria Josepha Ronkartz	b: 1889		d: 1972
		+Anton Joseph Heinen	b: 1877	m: 1907	d: 1929
	4	Anna Marie Heinen	b: 1908		d: 1994
		+Roland Privat	b: 1906	m: 1931	d: 1963
	4	Maria Josepha Heinen	b: 1911		d: 2005
		+Clarence Dodd Daigle	b: 1904	m: 1934	d: 1974
3		Lambert Ronkartz	b: 1891		d: 1978
		+Maria Regina Dischler	b: 1894	m: 1919	d: 1977
	4	Josephine Marie Ronkartz	b: 1920		
		+Joseph John Burton	b: 1917	m: 1941	d: 2004
	4	Joseph John Ronkartz	b: 1922		d: 1989
		+Rose Marie Leblanc	b: 1926	m: 1946	d: 1989
	4	John William Ronkartz	b: 1925		d: 2000
		+Effie Katharine Rogers	b: 1933	m: 1950	
	4	Jeanette Juliana Ronkartz	b: 1929		
		+Ronald Gene Robinson	b: 1931	m: 1950	d: 1953
	4	Louise Regina Ronkartz	b: 1932		
		+Daniel Hilarion Troyanowski	b: 1928	m: 1954	d: 1981

Vondenstein

	4	Jerome Lambert Ronkartz	b: 1933		
		+Josephine Ann Zaunbrecher	b: 1934	m: 1956	
3		Marie Agnes Ronkartz	b: 1894		d: 1969
		+Peter Leonard Thevis	b: 1891	m: 1916	d: 1987
	4	Leonard Gerhard Thevis	b: 1917		
	4	John Joseph Thevis	b: 1920		
		+Nancee Ruth Andrew		m: 1969	
		*2nd Wife of John Joseph Thevis:			
		+Ouida Mae Spell		m: 1977	
	4	Mary Anna Thevis	b: 1922		
	4	Anna Josephine Thevis	b: 1925		
	4	Leona Walburga (Sister Agnes Leonard) Thevis	b: 1927		
	4	Lawrence Vincent Thevis	b: 1929		d: 1995
		+Betty Jane Henderson	b: 1929	m: 1980	
	4	Louise Helen Thevis	b: 1931		
	4	Dorothy Agnes Thevis	b: 1934		
2		Theodore Vondenstein	b: 1872		d: 1946
		+Maria Katharina Theunissen	b: 1875	m: 1902	d: 1958
3		Maria Catherina Vondenstein	b: 1/11/1903		d: 5/3/1985
		+Elridge Francis Humble	b: 12/20/1904	m: 1926	d: 11/1/1980
	4	Edward Arthur Humble	b: 8/4/1929		d: 11/30/1968
	4	Anna Mae Humble	b: 12/8/1927		d: 6/21/1997
	4	Margie Mary Humble	b: 11/24/1933		
3		Hubert Joseph Vondenstein	b: 4/5/1904		d: 5/4/1971
		+Donatile LeBoeuf	b: 2/8/1900	m: 1925	d: 10/9/1999
	4	Joseph Daniel Vondenstein	b: 9/22/1927		d: 3/29/2001
	4	Hebert A. Vondenstein	b: 1931		d: 6/6/1993

Vondenstein

4	Alma Vondenstein			
3	Helena Josepha Vondenstein	b: 9/22/1905		d: 3/26/1953
3	Mary Elizabeth Vondenstein	b: 6/12/1907		d: 3/3/1992
	+Adam LeBoeuf	b: 2/17/1911	m: 1932	d: 10/25/1987
4	Adair LeBoeuf			d: 3/31/2001
4	Norris LeBoeuf			d: 7/23/1984
3	Mary Augusta Vondenstein	b: 6/12/1907		d: 1907
3	Peter Joseph Vondenstein	b: 4/29/1909		d: 2/15/1987
	+Elta Theriot	b: 3/29/1913	m: 1934	d: 8/1/1982
4	Lawrence Vondenstein	b: 7/13/1937		
3	William Joseph Vondenstein	b: 12/23/1911		d: 10/16/1992
	+Necez Primeaux	b: 4/16/1918	m: 1936	d: 12/4/1991
4	Charles Vondenstein	b: 2/2/1944		d: 1/26/1964
4	Winston Vondenstein	b: 7/14/1945		
3	Bernard Johann Vondenstein	b: 3/12/1913		d: 11/17/1997
	+Ella LeBoeuf	b: 12/3/1916	m: 1936	d: 5/30/1989
4	James Bernard Vondenstein	b: 5/30/1939		
4	Velma Marie Vondenstein	b: 12/17/1941		
4	Mildred Ann Vondenstein	b: 9/6/1950		
3	Daniel Joseph Vondenstein	b: 7/23/1915		d: 12/24/1985
	+Zulma Broussard	b: 9/20/1920	m: 1938	d: 7/15/2003
4	John Edward Vondenstein	b: 3/26/1940		
4	Shirley Rose Vondenstein	b: 9/7/1941		
4	Anna Belle Vondenstein	b: 6/24/1943		

Vondenstein

	4	Pirmin Dean Vondenstein	b: 4/22/1947		
2		Maria Agnes (Sister Mary Leona) Vondenstein	b: 1876		d: 1922
2		Peter Joseph Vondenstein	b: 4/10/1878		d: 2/18/1963
		+Helena Wirtz	b: 1895	m: 1/3/1917	d: 1970
	3	Mary Helen Vondenstein	b: 1/15/1918		
		+Henry Fontenot	b: 8/18/1914	m: 4/13/1941	d: 9/16/1979
	4	Lucille Ann Fontenot	b: 7/5/1944		
		+Martin Arnold Zaunbrecher, Jr.	b: 1/24/1947	m: 8/1/1969	
	4	Mary Diane Fontenot	b: 10/7/1947		
		+James Cecil Patterson	b: 6/29/1945	m: 8/12/1969	
		*2nd Husband of Mary Diane Fontenot:			
		+Thomas Taylor Church	b: 4/14/1948	m: 4/29/1990	
	4	Helen Suzanne Fontenot	b: 3/25/1952		
		+Jimmy Paul Ramsey	b: 9/26/1947	m: 4/16/1972	
	4	Rita Kay Fontenot	b: 2/25/1954		
		+Roger Bedell Patterson	b: 6/27/1951	m: 9/17/1971	
	4	Margaret Rose Fontenot	b: 8/28/1959		
		+Michael Harrison Baker	b: 4/30/1952	m: 4/24/1988	
	3	Annie Vondenstein	b: 6/15/1919		
		+Henry Schultz, Jr.	b: 9/21/1918	m: 1/8/1941	d: 11/1/1983
	4	Carol Jean Schultz	b: 3/28/1944		
	4	Donald James Schultz	b: 10/16/1947		
		+Carla Claire Gilmore	b: 12/20/1954	m: 7/12/1980	
	4	Barbara Lynn Schultz	b: 6/11/1949		
		+Ronald Lee Miller	b: 1/10/1949	m: 6/15/1969	
	4	Patricia Ann Schultz	b: 1/31/1955		d: 9/18/1998

Vondenstein

		+Raymond Kenneth Fielder	b: 11/4/1959	m: 6/23/1979	
		*2nd Husband of Patricia Ann Schultz:			
		+Thomas Winfred Bruner	b: 4/23/1956	m: 2/20/1993	
3		John Joseph Vondenstein	b: 5/23/1921		
		+Lorraine Pearl Miller	b: 8/17/1923	m: 12/9/1944	d: 9/17/2000
	4	John Darrell Vondenstein	b: 10/28/1945		d: 4/15/2005
		+Colleen Mary Kennedy	b: 11/28/1947	m: 7/3/1971	
	4	Janet Marie Vondenstein	b: 3/6/1947		
		+John Dale Trahan	b: 12/17/1947	m: 8/25/1968	
	4	Wayne Maurice Vondenstein	b: 7/19/1950		
		+Jan Marie Fuller	b: 8/23/1950	m: 12/30/1972	
	4	Steven Peter Vondenstein	b: 1/11/1953		
		+Jacqueline Simon	b: 2/25/1953	m: 11/23/1974	
	4	Elaine Theresa Vondenstein	b: 12/26/1955		
		+Daniel Edward Rogers, Jr.	b: 3/22/1955	m: 4/23/1976	
		*2nd Husband of Elaine Theresa Vondenstein:			
		+Gary Randolph Bell	b: 7/8/1950	m: 12/9/1990	
	4	Larry Paul Vondenstein	b: 4/2/1958		
		+Marie Ann Gossen	b: 3/19/1958	m: 8/11/1979	
	4	Lisa Ann Vondenstein	b: 10/11/1961		
		+Thomas Ludlow McNeely III	b: 5/9/1960	m: 2/25/1984	
3		William Anthony Vondenstein	b: 2/7/1924		d: 1/30/2004
		+Dorothy Theresa Prather	b: 10/19/1930	m: 8/2/1950	

Vondenstein

	4	William Anthony Vondenstein, Jr.	b: 6/15/1951		
		+Jean Renee Chappius	b: 3/25/1952	m: 8/11/1973	
	4	Mary Kathleen Vondenstein	b: 7/10/1956		
		+Michael Edward Shetler	b: 7/14/1955	m: 11/26/1976	
	3	Rita Cecelia Vondenstein	b: 5/6/1928		
		+Henry Wilbert Foret, Jr.	b: 6/22/1924	m: 6/29/1947	
	4	Cynthia Ann Foret	b: 3/30/1948		
		+Samuel Kent McDaniel	b: 8/10/1947	m: 6/1/1969	
	4	Lynell Claire Foret	b: 3/31/1952		
		+Randy James Meaux	b: 9/11/1950	m: 12/12/1970	
	4	Elise Foret	b: 5/1953		d: 5/1953
	4	Tracie Marie Foret	b: 2/7/1966		
		+Raphael Dupre	b: 11/27/1963	m: 9/20/1986	
2		Anna Catharina (Sr Mary Lucy) Vondenstein	b: 1879		d: 1920
2		Infant Girl Vondenstein	b: 1880		d: 1881
2		Joseph Vondenstein	b: 1881		d: 1970
		+Maria Anna Jabusch	b: 1896	m: 1918	d: 1985
	3	Josephine Ann Vondenstein	b: 4/6/1921		
		+Anthony Jacob Frey	b: 10/12/1919	m: 12/19/1946	
	4	Stephen Joseph Frey	b: 9/6/1947		d: 5/27/1961
	4	Leroy Vincent Frey	b: 12/18/1948		
		+Jo Anna Larson	b: 9/6/1951	m: 12/20/1976	
	4	Patricia Ann Frey	b: 1/25/1952		
		+James T. Rainer	b: 1/11/1950	m: 8/3/1973	
	4	Sherri Lynn Frey	b: 4/9/1953		
		+Robert W. Steinriede	b: 5/5/1956	m: 10/3/1971	

*2nd Husband of Sherri Lynn Frey:

Vondenstein

		+Michael Tubertini	b: 4/12/1953	m: 11/3/1990	
	4	Tony Louis Frey	b: 8/14/1956		
		+Anna C. Hudson	b: 12/14/1965	m: 2/13/1988	
	4	Theresa Jo Frey	b: 11/9/1958		
		+John Austin Hord III	b: 3/14/1956	m: 3/10/1979	
	4	William Jude Frey	b: 11/2/1960		
		+Cashev Cetalu	b: 3/4/1959	m: 6/7/1980	
	4	Frances Elaine Frey	b: 5/3/1964		
		+Walter Lavch Muna	b: 7/3/1958	m: 3/7/1992	
3		Joseph Robert Vondenstein	b: 1925		d: 1996
2		Anna Katharina Vondenstein	b: 1884		d: 1968
		+John Bernard Cramer	b: 1876	m: 1905	d: 1933
3		Maria Josephine Cramer	b: 1906		d: 2000
		+Nicholas Martin Zaunbrecher	b: 1893	m: 1927	d: 1975
	4	Wilma Anna Zaunbrecher	b: 12/6/1928		
		+Huey Patrick Regan	b: 9/7/1930	m: 4/25/1950	
	4	William Joseph Zaunbrecher	b: 7/16/1931		d: 4/1/1990
		+Laurea Marie James	b: 11/15/1939	m: 12/10/1963	d: 9/17/1992
	4	Clarice Ann Zaunbrecher	b: 9/26/1933		
		+Rodney William LeJeune	b: 11/27/1930	m: 4/15/1953	
	4	Otto Bernard Zaunbrecher	b: 8/22/1935		
		+Sylvia Jean Armstrong	b: 9/18/1943	m: 2/8/1964	
	4	Elaine Marie Zaunbrecher	b: 11/25/1937		d: 10/25/2001
		+Carl Barry Leger	b: 8/25/1936	m: 2/1/1958	
	4	Mary Jo Zaunbrecher	b: 1/27/1940		

Vondenstein

	+Carl Jerome Foreman	b: 2/29/1940	m: 11/28/1964	
4	Wanda Ann Zaunbrecher	b: 12/2/1941		
	+Shelton Eugene Launey	b: 2/9/1937	m: 11/4/1961	
3	Anna Gesina Cramer	b: 1908		d: 2000
	+Herman Joseph Habetz	b: 11/16/1901	m: 1/30/1929	d: 2/6/1966
4	Lawrence Joseph Habetz	b: 12/27/1929		
	+Marie Legnon	b: 12/27/1933	m: 2/10/1957	
4	Leonard Joseph Habetz	b: 4/11/1932		
	+Deanna Dean Hoffpauir		m: 6/29/1957	
4	Clementine Anna Habetz	b: 10/27/1934		
	+Huey Pierre Kirsch	b: 9/17/1935	m: 6/7/1958	
4	Bernadine Anna Habetz	b: 2/7/1937		d: 7/6/1994
4	Bernard Joseph Habetz	b: 1/19/1939		
	+Patricia Ann Molbert	b: 10/8/1939	m: 11/17/1962	d: 7/15/2004
4	Albert Joseph Habetz	b: 2/10/1942		
	+Brenda Fay Ruppert		m: 5/29/1965	
4	Robert Joseph Habetz	b: 2/1/1944		
	+Priscilla Vera Keigley	b: 10/13/1946	m: 7/15/1967	
4	Josephine Anna "Joann" Habetz	b: 1/28/1947		
	+Fredrick Ledoux	b: 8/9/1947	m: 9/4/1971	
4	Anna Agnes Habetz	b: 10/15/1949		
	+Thomas Michael Jones	b: 2/9/1949	m: 6/21/1969	
3	John Herman Cramer	b: 1909		d: 1980
	+Gertrude Felicitas Habetz	b: 5/25/1914	m: 2/23/1938	
4	Anna Margaret Cramer	b: 12/31/1938		

Vondenstein

	+William "Billy" Louis Zaunbrecher	b: 5/31/1938	m: 12/16/1963	d: 8/19/1997
4	Bernard Cramer	b: 9/25/1942		d: 9/25/1942
4	Patricia Marie Cramer	b: 2/21/1947		d: 2004
4	Carolyn Clementine Cramer	b: 7/6/1950		
4	Ignatius John Cramer	b: 4/5/1952		d: 7/23/1982
	+Kathleen Marie Gros		m: 7/11/1975	
3	Mary Leona Cramer	b: 6/11/1912		d: 7/1/1981
	+Heinrich "Leo" Leonard Habetz, Jr.	b: 5/11/1912	m: 2/3/1932	d: 9/16/1985
4	Leonard Jerome "Jack" Habetz	b: 4/16/1938		
	+Sylvia Dawn Bigelow	b: 7/3/1940	m: 1/4/1964	
4	Donald Bernard Habetz	b: 9/25/1940		d: 10/24/2004
	+Patricia Anne Istre	b: 3/27/1940		
4	Edmund "E.L." Leonard Habetz	b: 11/6/1949		
	+Cheryl Anne Hoffpauir	b: 1/15/1948	m: 5/1/1971	
4	Allan Norbert Habetz	b: 9/7/1952		
	+Gwendolyn Marie Truax	b: 1/6/1952	m: 9/21/1973	
4	Kenneth Michael Habetz	b: 11/13/1955		
	+Penny Anne Hargroder	b: 8/3/1958	m: 11/7/1980	
3	Adelheid Helen Cramer	b: 1914		d: 2/24/2007
3	William Joseph Cramer, Sr.	b: 1917		d: 2000
	+Fannie Mary Primeaux	b: 8/10/1922	m: 1943	d: 11/22/1995
4	Jerri Cramer			
	+Les Dolph			
4	Jimmy Dale Cramer			
	+Vickie Denison			

Vondenstein

	4	Jolene Cramer			
		+Charles Raymond Williams			
	4	William Joseph Cramer, Jr.			d: 1989
		+Anna Bouillion			
3		Joseph Bernard Cramer	b: 1920		d: 1992
3		Theodora Lucy Cramer	b: 9/26/1922		
		+Lawrence Nicholas Zaunbrecher	b: 4/12/1925	m: 6/20/1955	
	4	Elwin Zaunbrecher	b: 8/19/1957		
	4	Eugene Zaunbrecher	b: 1/10/1964		
3		Henry Norbert Cramer	b: 1925		
		+Carrie Amelia Leleux	b: 1922	m: 1950	
3		Mary Cecilia (Sister Mary Lucy) Cramer	b: 1927		d: 1965
2		Henry Joseph Vondenstein	b: 1/24/1887		d: 1/3/1971
		+Ida Susan Schatzle	b: 3/14/1893	m: 1915	d: 10/13/1957
3		Charles Earl Vondenstein	b: 7/2/1933		d: 4/18/1999
	4	Charles Earl Vondenstein, Jr.	b: 9/17/1958		
		+Cynthia Faye Meyer	b: 11/5/1959	m: 10/21/1978	

40. Wirtz, Hubert Nikolaus:

Hubert Nikolaus Wirtz b: 1847 d: 1929 from Langbroich was the son of Karl Joseph Wirtz b: 1817 d: 1864 and Maria Joseph Schröder. His first marriage in the 1870s was to Ludmilla Schmitz b: 1842 d: 1883 from Langbroich. His second marriage in 1884 was to Margaret Ann McCormach b: 1860 d: 1919, the daughter of Robert McCormack b: 1841 d: 1904 and Mary Ann Kennater.

2	Alphonse Karl Wirtz		b: 1875		d: 1952
	+Carolina Jane Iona Killmer		b: 1875	m: 1897	d: 1950
3	Annie Mae Wirtz		b: 9/8/1898		d: 7/26/1990
	+Walter D. Sutherland		b: 1893	m: 11/1933	d: 1/11/1940
	4	Barbara Ann Sutherland	b: 11/4/1937		
		+John Paul Chavers	b: 7/19/1922	m: 1973	d: 9/6/1979
	*2nd Husband of Annie Mae Wirtz:				
	+Willis Leger		b: 1895	m: 1944	d: 1972
3	Mary Gertrude Wirtz		b: 1/22/1900		d: 10/3/1987
	+Henry Jacob Jabusch		b: 12/7/1893	m: 11/4/1918	d: 3/27/1986
	4	Annie Mae Jabusch	b: 11/28/1919		d: 5/31/2002
		+Rene Rolo Richard	b: 6/17/1907	m: 2/15/1942	d: 6/1/1982
	4	Fredrick Henry Jabusch	b: 8/21/1921		
		+Willa Duhon	b: 7/23/1925	m: 2/14/1947	
	4	Frank Jabusch	b: 11/26/1924		
		+Vera Zaunbrecher	b: 11/6/1926	m: 2/17/1947	
3	Catherine Viola Wirtz		b: 9/18/1901		d: 9/11/1982
	+Louie Phillip Kotz		b: 4/30/1890	m: 1926	d: 2/4/1966
	4	Louie Charles Kotz	b: 2/2/1928		d: 12/11/1995
		+Margie Bernice Kuykendall	b: 7/16/1930	m: 1/29/1949	d: 9/14/1991
	4	Edward Roy Kotz	b: 3/24/1930		d: 7/15/2001
		+Elizabeth Ann Fortenberry	b: 3/30/1933	m: 3/27/1953	
	4	Alvin Donald Kotz	b: 2/18/1932		
		+Eugenia "Cookie" Arrendondo	b: 6/23/1947	m: 6/6/1970	

Wirtz

4	Raymond Phillip Kotz	b: 4/4/1935		
	+Pat Mae Braley	b: 12/11/1939	m: 1/21/1960	
3	Joseph William Wirtz	b: 1/16/1904		d: 2/4/1983
	+Nedia Monceaux	b: 11/12/1908	m: 12/29/1928	d: 12/30/1995
4	Joseph William Wirtz, Jr.	b: 12/25/1929		d: 1/22/2000
	+Edna Bourque			
	*2nd Wife of Joseph William Wirtz, Jr.:			
	+Marie Simar	b: 7/23/1934	m: 10/10/1953	
4	Betty Lou Wirtz	b: 6/28/1931		d: 7/12/1994
	+Percy Joseph Gautreaux			
	*2nd Husband of Betty Lou Wirtz:			
	+Preston Joseph Guidry, Sr.	b: 9/25/1928	m: 3/12/1949	d: 9/21/1967
4	Thelma Wirtz	b: 10/15/1932		
	+Joseph Dupre Kibodeaux	b: 2/18/1932	m: 10/23/1948	d: 7/31/1967
	*2nd Husband of Thelma Wirtz:			
	+Ulyses Girard, Jr.		m: 6/12/1976	
4	Ruby Dean Wirtz	b: 2/14/1936		
	+Richard Lee Cart	b: 8/30/1930	m: 6/5/1954	d: 11/19/1992
4	James Dudley Wirtz	b: 3/5/1941		
	+Eva Dell Gautreaux	b: 2/15/1947	m: 6/4/1968	
4	Raymond Lee Wirtz	b: 6/13/1945		
	+Earleen Dugar		m: 12/19/1964	
3	Edith Iona Wirtz	b: 7/20/1906		d: 10/3/1980
	+William Gautreaux	b: 12/12/1907	m: 12/19/1928	d: 10/4/1978
4	William Charles Gautreaux, Sr.	b: 7/13/1930		d: 4/18/1995
	+Sylvia Marie Sensat	b: 9/2/1937	m: 1/20/1955	d: 10/28/1992
4	Hurley Gautreaux	b: 4/30/1932		
	+Leartice Ann Simar	b: 4/28/1940	m: 4/24/1957	
4	Gloria Iona Gautreaux	b: 8/13/1934		d: 12/20/1995

Wirtz

	+Milton Joseph LeBlanc	b: 2/16/1937	m: 5/13/1961	d: 1/15/1989
4	Jeanette Gautreaux	b: 9/30/1936		
	+Joseph Curley Sensat	b: 5/23/1935	m: 1/29/1955	d: 3/24/1963

*2nd Husband of Jeanette Gautreaux:

	+Allen James Stutes	b: 11/8/1931	m: 4/3/1965	
4	Ralph Joseph Gautreaux	b: 8/12/1938		
	+Delores Ann Myers			

*2nd Wife of Ralph Joseph Gautreaux:

	+Judith Amanda Fontenot		m: 12/3/1960	
4	Velma Lorraine Gautreaux	b: 12/31/1942		
	+Earl Vincent Kibodeaux	b: 3/8/1938	m: 8/23/1958	
4	Richard Wayne Gautreaux	b: 7/25/1948		
	+Velma Jane Thibodeaux	b: 7/9/1953	m: 3/11/1972	
3	Julia Esther Wirtz	b: 4/11/1909		d: 9/8/1968
	+Howard Lawrence Sensat	b: 8/29/1909	m: 12/7/1929	d: 1/4/1992
3	Lula Belle Wirtz	b: 1912		
	+Buddy Stewart	b: 1913	m: 1934	d: 1995
4	Shirley Jean Stewart	b: 9/21/1935		
	+George Allen Hebert	b: 4/18/1935	m: 6/4/1955	d: 4/13/2000
4	Buddy Roger Stewart	b: 8/13/1941		
	+Patrica Webb	b: 9/24/1944	m: 9/5/1964	
4	Charles Fredrich Stewart	b: 1/10/1945		
	+Laurie Jean Breaux	b: 9/26/1947	m: 12/31/1966	

*2nd Wife of Charles Fredrich Stewart:

+Sharon Ann Thibodeaux Cramer	b: 6/15/1954	m: 11/18/1995	

Wirtz

	4	Anthony Norman Stewart	b: 9/29/1947		
		+Emily Thibodeaux	b: 11/29/1948	m: 7/25/1970	
3		Alfred Charles Wirtz	b: 1914		d: 2001
2		Bernard Wirtz	b: 1878		d: 1883
2		Gertrude Wirtz	b: 2/8/1881		d: 3/28/1961
		+August Zaunbrecher	b: 1883	m: 1907	d: 1919
3		Joseph Nicholas Zaunbrecher	b: 3/23/1910		d: 1/31/1980
3		Cecilia Theresa Zaunbrecher	b: 9/7/1911		d: 8/3/1983
		+William Joseph Bollich, Jr.	b: 11/22/1905	m: 11/18/1931	d: 3/9/1986
	4	Stanley Nicolas Bollich	b: 12/3/1932		d: 1/13/2005
		+Martha Gill	b: 10/5/1941	m: 9/3/1959	
	4	Fr. Ronald William Bollich	b: 5/12/1937		d: 8/7/1996
	4	Wilbur Anthony Bollich	b: 7/28/1938		
		+Betty Nesom	b: 7/19/1942	m: 6/4/1966	
	4	Hallet Joseph Bollich	b: 9/1/1940		
		+Gardlene Ann Trahan	b: 2/13/1958	m: 9/23/1972	
	4	James August Bollich	b: 2/14/1943		
		+Betty Ann Lemare	b: 12/29/1956	m: 3/12/1981	
	4	Mary Ann Bollich	b: 10/9/1945		
		+Robert Vincent Ogden		m: 8/11/1966	
3		Anthony Martin Zaunbrecher	b: 5/10/1913		d: 10/27/1966
		+Vernell Hoffpauir	b: 7/18/1922	m: 12/28/1938	
	4	Lawrence Anthony Zaunbrecher	b: 12/11/1939		d: 7/10/1940

Wirtz

	4	Richard Aaron Zaunbrecher	b: 3/12/1941		d: 9/4/1996
		+Winnie Hebert			
	4	Gerald Benedict Zaunbrecher	b: 9/27/1942		d: 1/23/1943
3		Rose Helen Zaunbrecher	b: 11/5/1915		d: 2/22/1993
		+James Dallas Schneider	b: 10/6/1919	m: 2/24/1941	d: 11/26/1988
	4	Barbara Ann Schneider	b: 2/28/1942		
		+David Lee McDaniel	b: 9/11/1941	m: 10/29/1960	
	4	Mary Elaine Schneider	b: 3/16/1944		
		+Rodney William Zaunbrecher	b: 5/8/1940	m: 1/26/1963	
	4	Stephen Joseph Schneider	b: 9/13/1945		
		+Rita Diane LaCombe	b: 5/19/1947	m: 4/16/1966	
	4	Michael Glen Schneider	b: 10/2/1957		
		+Carol Ann Blood	b: 12/16/1960	m: 7/2/1982	

*2nd Wife of Hubert Nikolaus Wirtz:

		+Margaret Ann McCormack	b: 1860	m: 1884	d: 1919
2		Magdalena Wirtz	b: 9/10/1886		d: 9/12/1952
		+Philemon H. Fox	b: 1/31/1868	m: 9/10/1904	d: 12/28/1950
3		Albert Joseph Fox, Sr.	b: 1/28/1907		d: 7/17/1980
		+Ernestine Gillard	b: 1908	m: 7/9/1927	d: 1941
	4	Albert Joseph (Buster) Fox, Jr.	b: 1/27/1930		d: 8/25/1990
	4	GeorgeAnna Fox			
	4	Roy Lee Fox			
	4	Floyd Fox	b: 7/19/1931		d: 6/20/1997
	4	Curly James (Dutch) Fox	b: 12/24/1936		
		+Verna Lonaner		m: 1/12/1971	
	4	Melvin Fox	b: 8/11/1939		

*2nd Wife of Albert Joseph Fox, Sr.:

		+Geneva Roy	b: 3/8/1927	m: 11/1/1945
	4	Robert L. Fox	b: 3/18/1947	
	4	Connie Sue Fox	b: 3/30/1949	d: 6/20/1977
	4	Dianne Fox	b: 4/10/1950	
3		George Fox	b: 11/24/1909	d: 8/15/1976
		+Ludy Rose Lejeune	b: 10/26/1917	m: 8/26/1938 d: 9/15/2003
	4	George Ervin Fox	b: 9/16/1939	
		+Mattie Susan Peveto	b: 3/1/1944	m: 5/13/1961
		*2nd Wife of George Ervin Fox:		
		+Bernice E. Lesmister	b: 8/29/1938	m: 5/1988
		*3rd Wife of George Ervin Fox:		
		+Eve Lorraine Breaux Marks	b: 8/3/1937	m: 11/26/1993
	4	Margaret Agnes Fox	b: 10/5/1940	
		+M.J. Breaux		m: 1958
	4	JoAnn Catherine Fox	b: 2/5/1944	
		+Vick Ledeaux		m: 1960
	4	Clifford Darrell Fox	b: 11/3/1946	
		+Angie Castalaw		m: 1961
	4	David Lynn Fox	b: 11/3/1954	
		+Cindy Townsend		m: 6/14/1976
3		Allen Fox	b: 12/25/1911	d: 4/11/1979
		+Amy Norma Lejeune	b: 11/18/1920	m: 10/1938 d: 1/25/1991
	4	John Allen Fox	b: 10/12/1939	
		+Carolyn Garrett		m: 6/25/1990
	4	Linda Ruth Fox	b: 12/1/1941	
		+Terry McClanahan		m: 1962
	4	Philip Henry Fox	b: 12/29/1943	
	4	Wanda M. Fox	b: 1/6/1945	
		+Harry Venable		m: 1/22/1969 d: 7/24/1999
	4	Leo J. Fox	b: 12/20/1947	d: 10/6/1997
		+Nelda Sinks		m: 1967

4	Michael W. Fox	b: 11/1948		d: 1/1949
4	Agnes Anne Fox	b: 2/15/1961		
3	Etta Fox	b: 3/13/1913		d: 3/13/1994
	+August Albert Frey	b: 6/12/1913	m: 12/5/1933	d: 1998
4	Martha Elaine Frey	b: 9/7/1935		
	+Richard Reed	b: 1/7/1932	m: 11/6/1954	d: 2/25/2005
4	Alberta Antoinette Frey	b: 11/18/1937		
	+Louis Hubert Green, Jr.	b: 1/19/1933	m: 6/9/1956	d: 5/13/2003
3	Clifford Fox	b: 1918		d: 1942
3	Ambrose Fox	b: 4/9/1920		d: 7/18/2006
	+Johnnie Smith Jackson	b: 1931	m: 12/9/1952	
4	Debra Ann Fox	b: 2/25/1955		
	+Paul Stacey		m: 1990	
4	James Cliff (Butch) Fox	b: 1/17/1957		
	+Janice Martin		m: 2005	
4	Gerald Keith Fox	b: 11/25/1959		
	+Debra L. Sharo		m: 2005	
4	Pamala Kay Fox	b: 10/27/1962		
	+George Schulte		m: 1990	
3	Sadie Fox	b: 1/8/1922		d: 3/18/2006
	+William Seaborn Howell	b: 1921	m: 1946	
4	Carolyn Joyce Howell	b: 4/14/1945		
	*2nd Husband of Sadie Fox:			
	+Charles Edward McCormick	b: 1921	m: 1956	
4	Charles Edward McCormick, Jr.	b: 10/11/1957		d: 1/20/1996
	*3rd Husband of Sadie Fox:			
	+Hayden Charles Willis	b: 1910	m: 1969	
3	Anna Mae Fox	b: 7/9/1930		d: 10/30/2001

Wirtz

		+Lowell Oren Nations	b: 1926	m: 1950	
	4	Ronald Oren Nations	b: 9/13/1950		
		+Jessie Blackman		m: 1971	
	4	Janis Nations	b: 9/5/1957		d: 3/7/2006
	4	Raymond Nations	b: 11/4/1954		
	4	Mona Nations	b: 2/20/1960		
2		Martin Andrew Wirtz	b: 1888		d: 1890
2		Anna Marie Wirtz	b: 1890		d: 1890
2		Martin Hubert Wirtz	b: 6/24/1891		d: 3/27/1947
2		William Hubert Wirtz	b: 1893		d: 1918
		+Emma Helen Regan	b: 1894	m: 1915	d: 1918
3		Ruby Mary Wirtz	b: 1916		d: 1986
		+Elvin Matthew Trumps	b: 1913	m: 1934	d: 1973
		*2nd Husband of Ruby Mary Wirtz:			
		+Needham Brantly Taylor	b: 1921	m: 1981	
2		Helena Wirtz	b: 1895		d: 1970
		+Peter Joseph Vondenstein	b: 1878	m: 1/3/1917	d: 1963
3		Mary Helen Vondenstein	b: 1/15/1918		d: 1986
		+Henry Fontenot	b: 8/18/1914	m: 4/13/1941	d: 9/16/1979
	4	Lucille Ann Fontenot	b: 7/5/1944		
		+Martin Arnold Zaunbrecher, Jr.	b: 1/24/1947	m: 8/1/1969	
	4	Mary Diane Fontenot	b: 10/7/1947		
		+James Cecil Patterson	b: 6/29/1945	m: 8/12/1969	
		*2nd Husband of Mary Diane Fontenot:			
		+Thomas Taylor Church	b: 4/14/1948	m: 4/29/1990	
	4	Helen Suzanne Fontenot	b: 3/25/1952		
		+Jimmy Paul Ramsey	b: 9/26/1947	m: 4/16/1972	
	4	Rita Kay Fontenot	b: 2/25/1954		

Wirtz

	+Roger Bedell Patterson	b: 6/27/1951	m: 9/17/1971	
4	Margaret Rose Fontenot	b: 8/28/1959		
	+Michael Harrison Baker	b: 4/30/1952	m: 4/24/1988	
3	Annie Vondenstein	b: 6/15/1919		
	+Henry Schultz, Jr.	b: 9/21/1918	m: 1/8/1941	d: 11/1/1983
4	Carol Jean Schultz	b: 3/28/1944		
4	Donald James Schultz	b: 10/16/1947		
	+Carla Claire Gilmore	b: 12/20/1954	m: 7/12/1980	
4	Barbara Lynn Schultz	b: 6/11/1949		
	+Ronald Lee Miller	b: 1/10/1949	m: 6/15/1969	
4	Patricia Ann Schultz	b: 1/31/1955		d: 9/18/1998
	+Raymond Kenneth Fielder	b: 11/4/1959	m: 6/23/1979	
	*2nd Husband of Patricia Ann Schultz:			
	+Thomas Winfred Bruner	b: 4/23/1956	m: 2/20/1993	
3	John Joseph Vondenstein	b: 5/23/1921		
	+Lorraine Pearl Miller	b: 8/17/1923	m: 12/9/1944	d: 9/17/2000
4	John Darrell Vondenstein	b: 10/28/1945		d: 4/15/2005
	+Colleen Mary Kennedy	b: 11/28/1947	m: 7/3/1971	
4	Janet Marie Vondenstein	b: 3/6/1947		
	+John Dale Trahan	b: 12/17/1947	m: 8/25/1968	
4	Wayne Maurice Vondenstein	b: 7/19/1950		
	+Jan Marie Fuller	b: 8/23/1950	m: 12/30/1972	
4	Steven Peter Vondenstein	b: 1/11/1953		
	+Jacqueline Simon	b: 2/25/1953	m: 11/23/1974	
4	Elaine Theresa Vondenstein	b: 12/26/1955		

Wirtz

		+Daniel Edward Rogers, Jr.	b: 3/22/1955	m: 4/23/1976
		*2nd Husband of Elaine Theresa Vondenstein:		
		+Gary Randolph Bell	b: 7/8/1950	m: 12/9/1990
	4	Larry Paul Vondenstein	b: 4/2/1958	
		+Marie Ann Gossen	b: 3/19/1958	m: 8/11/1979
	4	Lisa Ann Vondenstein	b: 10/11/1961	
		+Thomas Ludlow McNeely III	b: 5/9/1960	m: 2/25/1984
3		William Anthony Vondenstein	b: 2/7/1924	d: 1/30/2004
		+Dorothy Theresa Prather	b: 10/19/1930	m: 8/2/1950
	4	William Anthony Vondenstein, Jr.	b: 6/15/1951	
		+Jean Renee Chappius	b: 3/25/1952	m: 8/11/1973
	4	Mary Kathleen Vondenstein	b: 7/10/1956	
		+Michael Edward Shetler	b: 7/14/1955	m: 11/26/1976
3		Rita Cecilia Vondenstein	b: 5/6/1928	
		+Henry Wilbert Foret, Jr.	b: 6/22/1924	m: 6/29/1947
	4	Cynthia Ann Foret	b: 3/30/1948	
		+Samuel Kent McDaniel	b: 8/10/1947	m: 6/1/1969
	4	Lynell Claire Foret	b: 3/31/1952	
		+Randy James Meaux	b: 9/11/1950	m: 12/12/1970
	4	Elise Foret Foret	b: 5/1953	d: 5/1953
	4	Tracie Marie Foret	b: 2/7/1966	
		+Raphael Dupre	b: 11/27/1963	m: 9/20/1986
2		Henry Joseph Wirtz	b: 3/10/1898	d: 2/10/1962
2		Robert Wirtz	b: 1900	d: 1919
2		John Joseph Wirtz	b: 1903	d: 1970

Wirtz

	+Evelyn Marie Meadus	b: 1910	m: 1925	d: 1978
3	John Henry Wirtz	b: 1926		
	+Margery Ackley	b: 1923	m: 1975	
3	Hubert Curtis Wirtz	b: 1930		
	+Dorothy Jean Wilson	b: 1931	m: 1950	

41. Zaunbrecher, Nicholas Joseph:

Nicholas Joseph Zaunbrecher b: 11/9/1846 d: 3/30/1918 from Nierstrass was the son of Johann Joseph Zaunbrecker b: 2/24/1809, d: 1866 and Helena Katharina Schiffers b: 11/25/1810 d: 2/2/1864. He married on 11/13/1865 to Maria Helena Leonards b: 3/17/1844 d: 5/6/1926 from Pütt, who is the daughter of Johann Wilhelm Leonards b: 4/26/1819 d: 3/10/1900 and his first wife Katharina Agnes Gielen b: 8/24/1823 d: 3/21/1844. Maria Helena Leonards is a half-sister to August, Henry, and Peter Joseph Leonards (see Leonards families).

2		Wilhelm Joseph Zaunbrecher	b: 10/3/1867		d: 3/11/1922
		+Maria Walburga Heinen	b: 5/1/1869	m: 11/19/1892	d: 1/25/1959
	3	Martin Nicholas Zaunbrecher	b: 11/10/1893		d: 3/26/1975
		+Maria Josephine Cramer	b: 1/6/1906	m: 1/11/1928	d: 2000
	4	Wilma Anna Zaunbrecher	b: 12/6/1928		
		+Huey Patrick Regan	b: 9/7/1930	m: 4/25/1950	
	4	William Joseph Zaunbrecher	b: 7/16/1931		d: 4/1/1990
		+Laurea Marie James	b: 11/15/1939	m: 2/10/1963	d: 9/17/1992
	4	Clarice Ann Zaunbrecher	b: 9/26/1933		
		+Rodney William LeJeune	b: 11/27/1930	m: 4/15/1953	
	4	Otto Bernard Zaunbrecher	b: 8/22/1935		
		+Sylvia Jean Armstrong	b: 9/18/1943	m: 2/8/1964	
	4	Elaine Marie Zaunbrecher	b: 11/25/1937		d: 10/25/2001
		+Carl Barry Leger	b: 8/25/1936	m: 2/1/1958	
	4	Mary Jo Zaunbrecher	b: 1/27/1940		
		+Carl Jerome Foreman	b: 2/29/1940	m: 11/28/1964	

Zaunbrecher

4	Wanda Ann Zaunbrecher	b: 12/2/1941		
	+Shelton Eugene Launey	b: 2/9/1937	m: 11/4/1961	
3	Maria Helena Zaunbrecher	b: 4/14/1896		d: 8/19/1952
	+Anthony Conrad Dischler	b: 9/2/1900	m: 1923	d: 1996
4	Antonia Maria Dischler	b: 1926		
	+John Clyde Leger	b: 1923	m: 1949	
4	Martin William Dischler	b: 1927		
	+Marcella Comeaux	b: 1928	m: 1949	
4	Pauline Bertha Dischler	b: 1929		d: 1/22/2006
	+Francis Charles Roy	b: 1929	m: 1949	d: 1993
4	[3] Monica Ann "Mona" Dischler	b: 1934		
	+[2] Ronald James Gossen	b: 1929	m: 1953	
4	Helen Marie Dischler	b: 1936		
	+Kenneth Jack Mantle		m: 1961	
	*2nd Husband of Helen Marie Dischler:			
	+Frank Robles	b: 1927	m: 1976	
3	Elizabeth Augusta Zaunbrecher	b: 1898		d: 1924
	+[1] Lawrence Joseph Leonards	b: 2/24/1893	m: 2/1917	d: 8/5/1945
4	William Joseph Leonards	b: 12/12/1917		d: 8/24/2000
	+Barbara Rose Bollich	b: 1913	m: 11/20/1940	d: 5/11/2002
4	Josephine Marie Leonards	b: 3/26/1919		d: 1/23/2002
	+Herman Aloyious Cramer	b: 1911	m: 11/13/1940	d: 11/10/1966
4	Rita Helen Leonards	b: 12/27/1920		

Zaunbrecher

4	Norbert Nicholas Leonards	b: 9/12/1922		d: 4/13/1945
4	Vincent Karl Leonards	b: 9/24/1924		d: 12/30/1998
	+Thelma "Tillie" Zaunbrecher	b: 7/30/1926	m: 1949	
3	William Frederick Zaunbrecher	b: 12/19/1899		d: 12/6/1972
	+Maria Anna Leonards	b: 1/20/1901	m: 1/18/1922	d: 3/22/1975
4	Paul William Zaunbrecher	b: 6/10/1923		d: 9/20/1982
	+Cecilia Augusta Habetz	b: 12/6/1921	m: 2/13/1946	
4	Richard Andrew Zaunbrecher, Sr.	b: 11/30/1924		
	+Verna Mary Johnson	b: 12/18/1925	m: 6/19/1946	
4	Felix Leo Zaunbrecher	b: 12/30/1926		
	+Hilda Mary Broussard	b: 5/17/1929	m: 1/27/1948	
4	William Zaunbrecher	b: 4/13/1928		d: 4/13/1928
4	Mary Agnes Zaunbrecher	b: 2/21/1930		
	+Clarence Albert Fabacher	b: 3/17/1931	m: 2/4/1956	
4	Theresa Marie Zaunbrecher	b: 9/28/1931		
	+Jean Edwin Broussard	b: 1/24/1926	m: 11/26/1953	
4	Josephine Ann Zaunbrecher	b: 8/6/1934		
	+Jerome Ronkartz	b: 2/16/1933	m: 8/20/1956	
4	William Francis Zaunbrecher	b: 9/18/1935		d: 9/18/1935
4	Willietta Dorothy Zaunbrecher	b: 9/6/1938		

Zaunbrecher

	+Urban Anderson Phillips	b: 10/8/1933	m: 8/29/1959	d: 5/18/1998
4	Francis Martin "Bud" Zaunbrecher	b: 11/11/1943		
	+Hannah Casselman		m: 1963	

*2nd Wife of Francis Martin "Bud" Zaunbrecher:

	+Judy Craighead	b: 1945	m: 2/9/1973	

*3rd Wife of Francis Martin "Bud" Zaunbrecher:

	+Christine Schroeder	b: 7/25/1937	m: 10/19/1983	d: 11/23/1984

*4th Wife of Francis Martin "Bud" Zaunbrecher:

	+Bertha Jane Doucet	b: 10/26/1941	m: 3/8/1990	d: 5/20/2007
3	Henry Joseph Zaunbrecher	b: 11/19/1901		d: 3/26/1993
	+Annie Caroline Bollich	b: 4/10/1906	m: 1/20/1926	
4	Vera Marie Zaunbrecher	b: 11/6/1926		
	+Frank Conrad Jabusch	b: 1924	m: 1947	
4	Stella Josephine Zaunbrecher	b: 5/5/1928		
	+James William Doucet	b: 1928	m: 1951	d: 3/2005
4	Leroy Francis Zaunbrecher	b: 8/1/1929		d: 10/2003
	+Sammie Jane Meaux	b: 1931	m: 1950	
4	James Anthony Zaunbrecher	b: 8/3/1931		
	+Helen Joy Martin	b: 1934	m: 1954	
4	Louise Frances Zaunbrecher	b: 9/1/1933		
	+Aubrey DeCuir Caffery	b: 5/21/1923	m: 6/1/1957	d: 7/5/1999
4	Lorraine Marie Zaunbrecher	b: 1/9/1935		d: 11/1962
	+John Joseph Gordon	b: 1926	m: 1956	d: 2004

Zaunbrecher

4	Suzanne Zaunbrecher	b: 5/21/1936		
	+Howard "Boochie" Duncan	b: 1927	m: 1958	d: 2004
4	Dennis Henry Zaunbrecher	b: 12/1938		d: 1991
	+Gerry Broussard	b: 1938	m: 1961	
4	Leonard Anthony Zaunbrecher	b: 8/31/1943		
	+Charlotte Joan Sittig	b: 1942	m: 1964	
3	Maria Anna Zaunbrecher	b: 11/1/1903		d: 9/5/1984
	+[1] Lawrence Joseph Leonards	b: 2/24/1893	m: 6/15/1926	d: 8/5/1945
4	Raymond William Leonards	b: 1/29/1929		d: 4/22/1992
	+Louise Augusta Theunissen	b: 12/27/1932	m: 12/27/1952	
4	Benno Joseph Leonards	b: 6/16/1931		
	+Arilda Gertrude Heinen	b: 3/16/1934	m: 11/15/1958	d: 5/8/1973
	*2nd Wife of Benno Joseph Leonards:			
	+Margaret Funk	b: 7/14/1930	m: 3/16/1974	
4	Johanna Augusta Leonards	b: 12/15/1932		d: 5/5/1993
4	Henry Jerome Leonards	b: 9/13/1934		
	+Wilma Thecla Hensgens	b: 11/10/1937	m: 1958	d: 5/21/2006
4	Dennis Louis Leonards	b: 5/24/1936		
	+Phyllis Helen Robicheaux	b: 11/18/1939	m: 1/14/1961	
4	Wilfred Charles Leonards	b: 4/3/1937		
	+Elaine Credeur	b: 11/12/1941	m: 7/1964	
4	Mary Ann Leonards	b: 12/10/1938		

Zaunbrecher

	4	Lidwina Josephine Leonards	b: 7/20/1940		d: 3/9/1941
	4	Catherine Mary Leonards	b: 7/19/1944		
		+Dale Bernard Huesers	b: 3/20/1938	m: 5/9/1964	
3		Charles Joseph Zaunbrecher	b: 1905		d: 10/25/1972
		+Maria Bertha Dischler	b: 1905	m: 1929	d: 1990
	4	Dolores Marie "Bubbles" Zaunbrecher	b: 1930		
		+Phillip Jacob Joseph Habetz	b: 3/19/1930	m: 1956	
	4	Fr. Charles Zaunbrecher	b: 11/8/1931		d: 6/19/1996
	4	Vincent Zaunbrecher	b: 1933		
		+Genevieve Parrino	b: 1930	m: 6/14/1955	
	4	Jane Zaunbrecher	b: 1934		d: 1990
		+Wilvin Charles Leleux	b: 1935	m: 1958	
	4	William "Billy" Zaunbrecher	b: 5/31/1938		d: 8/19/1997
		+Anna Margaret Cramer	b: 12/31/1938	m: 12/16/1963	
	4	Stephen Zaunbrecher	b: 9/2/1940		
		+Rose Marie Reiners	b: 3/28/1942	m: 6/26/1962	
3		Joseph August Zaunbrecher	b: 8/28/1906		d: 2/10/1981
		+Anna Maria Dischler	b: 1904	m: 1925	d: 1977
	4	Edna Augusta Zaunbrecher	b: 1926		
		+Claures Joseph Broussard	b: 1928	m: 1957	
	4	Leo Charles Zaunbrecher	b: 1927		

Zaunbrecher

	+Stella Minnie Lowe	b: 1936	m: 1956	
4	Gerald Joseph Zaunbrecher	b: 1929		d: 1988
	+Shirley Mae Stark	b: 1937	m: 1956	d: 1994
4	Harold Joseph Zaunbrecher	b: 1929		d: 1999
	+Pauline Margaret Dupree	b: 1936	m: 1960	
4	Ferdinand Vincent Zaunbrecher	b: 1932		
	+Janet Louise Summers		m: 1960	

*2nd Wife of Ferdinand Vincent Zaunbrecher:

	+Jean Pascoe		m: 1980	
4	Genevieve Marie Zaunbrecher	b: 1934		
	+Gordon Edward Tate	b: 2/3/1934	m: 1963	d: 12/2004
4	Joyce Marie Zaunbrecher	b: 1935		
	+Howard Joseph Melancon	b: 1937	m: 1972	
4	Dorothy Ann Zaunbrecher	b: 1937		
4	Hilary Charles Zaunbrecher	b: 1939		
	+Snzanne Gayle Phillips	b: 1946	m: 1983	
4	Donald Louis Zaunbrecher	b: 1942		
	+Josephine Ann Busse	b: 1944	m: 1976	
3	Maria Gertrude Zaunbrecher	b: 1908		d: 1909
3	Maria Leona Zaunbrecher	b: 7/17/1910		d: 12/2004
3	Joseph Anton Zaunbrecher	b: 1912		d: 1991

Zaunbrecher

		+Marie Dischler	b: 1908		d: 1993
2		Theresa Zaunbrecher	b: 1869		d: 1933
		+Peter Joseph Gossen	b: 1862	m: 1/4/1890	d: 1945
	3	Marie Agnes Gossen	b: 1891		d: 1893
	3	Maria Helena Gossen	b: 1893		d: 1894
	3	William Joseph Gossen	b: 1894		d: 1974
		+Edmae Servat	b: 3/6/1906		d: 11/17/1985
		*2nd Wife of William Joseph Gossen:			
		+Della Marie Petitjean	b: 1898	m: 1916	d: 1947
	4	Louetta Josephine Gossen	b: 1917		
		+Louis Clarence Butaud, Sr.	b: 1913	m: 1936	
	4	Edward Joseph Gossen	b: 4/8/1920		d: 5/1/2003
		+Bobbie Louise Hains	b: 1/22/1924	m: 6/8/1946	
	4	Richard Nicholas Gossen	b: 9/10/1922		
		+Sarah Ann Tobey	b: 6/28/1923	m: 1/26/1942	
	4	Francis Allen Gossen	b: 5/8/1928		d: 8/7/1989
		+Lois Trahan	b: 7/13/1928	m: 5/5/1948	d: 6/22/1964
		*2nd Wife of Francis Allen Gossen:			
		+Billie Jean Long	b: 2/28/1944	m: 3/6/1965	
		*3rd Wife of William Joseph Gossen:			
		+Beulah Marie Hebert	b: 1905	m: 1959	d: 1972
	3	Maria Josepha Gossen	b: 1895		d: 1990
		+William Livingston Larcade	b: 1891	m: 1918	d: 1951
	4	Harold William Larcade	b: 1/16/1920		d: 8/31/1997
		+Louise Isabel Marchant	b: 8/18/1905	m: 10/20/1950	d: 1/19/1985
		*2nd Wife of Harold William Larcade:			
		+Stella Dupont	b: 10/1/1923	m: 1991	d: 5/4/2001
	4	Rita Leona Larcade	b: 10/19/1923		d: 1/18/2005

Zaunbrecher

		+James Howard Booksh, Jr.	b: 1/19/1922	m: 2/4/1947	
3		William Leo Gossen	b: 1897		d: 1897
3		Maria Helena Gossen	b: 1898		d: 1982
		+Austin Peter Landry	b: 1891	m: 1916	d: 1922
	4	Vincent Joseph Landry	b: 1917		d: 1968
		+Ruby Mae Dubus	b: 12/19/1918	m: 1938	
	4	Cecilia Elizabeth Landry	b: 7/31/1919		d: 1998
		+Samuel David Wilder, Sr.	b: 11/7/1914	m: 1937	d: 2002

*2nd Husband of Maria Helena Gossen:

		+Adolph Paul Frank	b: 1896	m: 1925	d: 1959
3		Peter Joseph Gossen Jr.	b: 1902		d: 1981
		+Sadie Marie Breaux	b: 1904	m: 1924	d: 1990
	4	Gerald Gossen	b: 1/8/1927		
		+Alberta Broussard	b: 1928	m: 1947	
	4	Peter Joseph Gossen III	b: 1933		
		+Dorotha Jim Alverson	b: 1935	m: 1956	
	4	Stephen Drozin Gossen	b: 7/20/1939		
		+Judith Martin	b: 1939	m: 6/6/1959	

*2nd Wife of Stephen Drozin Gossen:

		+Kathryn Lagarde	b: 4/22/1949	m: 1/26/1980	
	4	[2] Ronald James Gossen	b: 1929		
		+[3] Monica Ann "Mona" Dischler	b: 8/29/1934	m: 3/15/1954	

*2nd Wife of [2] Ronald James Gossen:

		+Peggy L. Dufour	b: 1929	m: 2/18/1993	
3		Henry Joseph Gossen	b: 1904		d: 1998
		+Rita Aline Hebert	b: 1907	m: 4/28/1925	d: 1990
	4	Lois Elaine Gossen	b: 7/24/1926		
		+Harrison Freeman Bennett, Jr.	b: 11/22/1920	m: 3/2/1947	d: 3/9/1973

Zaunbrecher

	4	Conrad Joseph Gossen	b: 11/2/1930		
		+Barbara Roussel	b: 4/12/1933	m: 10/8/1952	
	4	Peggy Ann Gossen	b: 3/1/1935		
		+George Bradford Ware	b: 1/13/1931	m: 2/1/1958	
	4	Frederick Joseph Gossen, Sr.	b: 11/21/1940		
		+Annette Marie Larriviere	b: 12/2/1941	m: 8/10/1963	
3		Marie Elizabeth (Sister Ann Pauline) Gossen	b: 1907		d: 1989
2		Lorenz Zaunbrecher	b: 10/23/1870		d: 10/26/1954
		+Gertrude Hensgens	b: 7/9/1874	m: 1/23/1895	d: 8/11/1954
3		Regina Marie Zaunbrecher	b: 12/5/1895		d: 10/26/1961
		+Joseph Andrew Klein	b: 7/19/1894	m: 2/20/1919	d: 4/26/1962
	4	Clara Regina Klein	b: 7/29/1921		d: 6/26/1990
	4	Hilda Marie Klein	b: 8/11/1923		d: 4/16/2004
		+Lloyd J. Simon	b: 10/19/1922	m: 11/29/1945	
	4	Gertrude Christine Klein	b: 9/15/1924		
		+Robert Jasper Labry		m: 7/31/1946	
	4	Anna Louise Klein	b: 3/15/1929		
		+Dewey Grant Heard	b: 5/17/1924	m: 11/19/1949	d: 6/12/1983
		*2nd Husband of Anna Louise Klein:			
		+Adam Warren DePerrodil	b: 1/22/1924	m: 12/9/1985	
	4	Lawrence Joseph Klein	b: 8/15/1932		d: 1/22/1957
		+Betty Jane Leger	b: 1/20/1935	m: 11/30/1955	
3		Joseph Zaunbrecher	b: 11/19/1897		d: 2/13/1981
		+Mary Odilia Klein	b: 2/24/1898	m: 2/20/1919	d: 9/8/1979
	4	Mary Magdalene Zaunbrecher	b: 5/6/1920		d: 11/13/1982
		+Abdon Nolan Leblanc	b: 7/30/1911	m: 5/16/1950	d: 5/12/1978

Zaunbrecher

4	Philip Joseph Zaunbrecher	b: 11/4/1921		
	+Helen Toups	b: 4/24/1922	m: 7/5/1945	
4	Wilfred Zaunbrecher	b: 10/19/1923		d: 4/10/1995
	+Bessie Istre	b: 1/22/1926	m: 8/22/1945	
4	Antoinette Lucille Zaunbrecher	b: 2/13/1926		d: 10/15/1926
4	Frederick John Zaunbrecher	b: 2/24/1928		
	+Laura Belle Woods	b: 7/23/1932	m: 1/13/1954	
4	Dorothy Christina Zaunbrecher	b: 3/27/1930		
	+Ellis Jacob Toups, Sr.	b: 7/6/1928	m: 8/5/1953	
4	Julian George Zaunbrecher	b: 10/3/1932		
	+Laura May Broussard	b: 7/1/1933	m: 5/23/1953	d: 5/30/2002
4	Richard Lawrence Zaunbrecher	b: 11/1/1935		
	+June Mary Woods	b: 6/6/1936	m: 9/3/1958	
4	Charles Anthony Zaunbrecher	b: 10/19/1937		
4	Ronald Gregory Zaunbrecher	b: 5/10/1940		
	+Eldie Mary Bourque	b: 8/23/1942	m: 11/29/1961	
4	Francis William Zaunbrecher	b: 9/15/1946		
	+Nona Faye Petry	b: 2/19/1946	m: 10/7/1967	
3	William Joseph Zaunbrecher	b: 8/25/1899		d: 5/8/1930
3	Nicholas Conrad Zaunbrecher	b: 9/21/1901		d: 12/29/1963
	+Maria Josephine Frey	b: 11/28/1902	m: 1922	d: 1998
4	Helen Marie Zaunbrecher	b: 11/1/1923		

Zaunbrecher

	+Joseph Herman Thevis	b: 5/4/1919	m: 11/23/1946	d: 12/20/2003
4	Lawrence Nicholas Zaunbrecher	b: 4/12/1925		
	+Lucy Theodora Cramer	b: 9/26/1922	m: 6/20/1955	
4	Thelma Regina "Tillie" Zaunbrecher	b: 7/30/1926		
	+Vincent Carl Leonards	b: 9/24/1924	m: 2/23/1949	d: 12/30/1998
4	Laura Lydia Zaunbrecher	b: 3/6/1928		
	+Louis Joseph Bellard	b: 7/2/1924	m: 7/1948	d: 8/10/1996
4	Louis John Zaunbrecher	b: 8/30/1929		d: 9/12/2004
	+Mary Helen Martell	b: 9/8/1931	m: 4/12/1953	
4	Jeanette Delores Zaunbrecher	b: 9/24/1931		
	+Wayne Elwood Holtzapple	b: 6/12/1929	m: 11/28/1952	
4	Frances Delores Zaunbrecher	b: 3/16/1933		
	+Jesse Paul Fruge	b: 12/12/1918	m: 11/29/1955	d: 11/30/1995
4	Robert Daniel Zaunbrecher	b: 11/14/1934		
	+Effie Claudette Johnson	b: 3/16/1938	m: 4/19/1958	
4	Stanley Joseph Zaunbrecher	b: 9/19/1936		
	+Lorette Louise Langley	b: 6/18/1941	m: 4/2/1963	d: 1/26/1996
4	[5] Rodney William Zaunbrecher	b: 5/8/1940		
	+[4] Mary Elaine Schneider	b: 3/16/1944	m: 1/26/1963	

Zaunbrecher

- 4   Margaret Ann Zaunbrecher   b: 5/18/1942
  - +Lawrence Leo "Larry" Regan   m: 11/18/1961
- 4   Jo Ann Zaunbrecher   b: 7/22/1944
  - +Henry Leonard Meyer   b: 9/25/1940   m: 7/15/1964
- 4   Edna Mae Zaunbrecher   b: 5/26/1946
  - +Michael William Leger   b: 11/3/1949   m: 10/21/1973
- 4   Lloyd James Zaunbrecher   b: 6/4/1948
  - +Donna Claire Lejeune   b: 3/30/1949   m: 2/18/1973
- 3   Barbara Marie Zaunbrecher   b: 11/26/1903   d: 11/8/1992
  - +Franz Xavier Joseph Bollich   b: 10/29/1904   m: 1926   d: 2/9/1990
  - 4   Loretta Elaine Bollich   b: 11/7/1927
    - +Burnis Cooper   b: 10/19/1917   m: 9/11/1945   d: 6/26/1991
  - *2nd Husband of Loretta Elaine Bollich:
    - +Louis C. Gaspard   m: 5/20/2000
  - 4   Clara Louise Bollich   b: 3/23/1929
    - +Durland Joseph Miller   b: 8/25/1924   m: 11/24/1949   d: 2/10/2002
  - 4   Gerald Francis Bollich   b: 3/9/1930
    - +Delia Marie Breaux   b: 10/1/1931   m: 10/24/1953   d: 11/29/2003
  - 4   Donald Joseph Bollich   b: 3/26/1931
    - +Willie Dean Vidrine   b: 7/31/1934   m: 11/21/1953
  - 4   Lawrence Charles "Larry" Bollich   b: 6/21/1932
    - +Jacqueline Marie Brown   b: 8/2/1932   m: 4/12/1958
  - 4   Austin William Bollich   b: 7/15/1933

Zaunbrecher

	+Sylvia Ann Stelly	b: 11/16/1934	m: 11/8/1953	
4	Elaine Marie Bollich	b: 1/20/1935		
	+Carl Edward Turk	b: 2/1/1928	m: 6/5/1956	d: 11/23/1986
4	Elmo Edward Bollich	b: 1/20/1935		
	+Elrena Manuel		m: 2/11/1956	
4	Sylvia Ann Bollich	b: 6/21/1936		
	+John Luke Emery Lintzen	b: 3/22/1936	m: 4/8/1961	d: 1/13/1976
4	Gregory Augustine Bollich	b: 11/28/1938		
	+Patricia Ann Sittig	b: 7/16/1940	m: 9/2/1961	
4	Barbara Ann Bollich	b: 9/22/1942		
	+James Allen "Tank" Lejeune	b: 9/19/1942	m: 10/27/1962	
4	Diane Louise Bollich	b: 2/10/1947		
	+Gary Layne Elkins	b: 12/13/1947	m: 7/3/1971	d: 6/17/2001
4	Judy Ann Bollich	b: 5/9/1949		
	+Kenneth Lee Joseph Hollier	b: 10/13/1949	m: 1/27/1973	
3	Anna Maria Zaunbrecher	b: 1/9/1906		d: 4/27/1990
	+Albert Harry Frey	b: 6/4/1904	m: 1928	d: 1/6/1973
4	Lorraine Elaine Frey	b: 9/30/1929		
	+Walter William Heinen	b: 3/15/1924	m: 4/25/1948	d: 4/10/1985
4	Reginald Lawrence Frey	b: 2/10/1931		d: 7/4/1982
	+Jo Ann Josephine Bollich	b: 10/6/1931	m: 1952	
4	Louellen Marie Frey	b: 12/3/1933		
	+Anthony Gerald Daigle	b: 12/29/1930	m: 10/1/1954	
4	Warren William Frey	b: 7/15/1937		
	+Verna Ellen Bankston	b: 12/5/1939	m: 9/3/1959	
4	Linda Ann Frey	b: 6/14/1943		

Zaunbrecher

	+James Franklin Campbell III	b: 4/13/1940	m: 10/6/1962	
3	Charles Philip Zaunbrecher	b: 1908		d: 1984
	+Anna Barbara Frey	b: 1907	m: 1924	d: 2003
4	Bertha Zaunbrecher	b: 6/5/1926		
	+Paul Joseph Breaux	b: 1/9/1924	m: 5/20/1952	d: 4/12/2004
4	Augusta Agnes Zaunbrecher	b: 1/11/1928		
	+Elmo Joseph Bollich	b: 11/11/1924	m: 5/18/1947	
4	Edmond Charles Zaunbrecher	b: 8/25/1929		d: 4/2/1995
	+Ollie Marie Linscombe	b: 2/28/1931	m: 11/27/1952	
4	Vincent William Zaunbrecher	b: 12/22/1931		
	+Janet Benoit	b: 10/27/1936	m: 11/8/1955	
4	Raymond Joseph Zaunbrecher	b: 9/12/1932		d: 4/1/1954
4	Harry John Zaunbrecher	b: 6/3/1934		
	+Lucy Henry	b: 7/1/1038	m: 10/22/1959	
4	Ramona Marie Zaunbrecher	b: 1/14/1936		
	+Reno Paul Petry	b: 2/28/1933	m: 2/8/1958	
4	Nicholas Wayne Zaunbrecher	b: 4/25/1939		
	+Linda Faye Guidry	b: 12/26/1940	m: 11/5/1960	
4	Floyd Anthony Zaunbrecher	b: 9/8/1940		
	+Cene Mae Vidalier	b: 12/6/1942	m: 11/28/1962	
4	Carolyn Ann Zaunbrecher	b: 11/11/1943		
	+James Avert Guidry	b: 11/16/1942	m: 11/17/1965	
4	Barbara Ann Zaunbrecher	b: 7/8/1949		

Zaunbrecher

	+William Joseph Leonards II	b: 12/12/1952	m: 6/28/1975	
4	Mary Jacqueline Zaunbrecher	b: 12/24/1951		
	+Allen Ray Francois	b: 7/27/1949	m: 6/30/1973	
3	August Zaunbrecher	b: 9/12/1910		d: 7/21/1993
	+Bobbie Gautreaux	b: 1912	m: 1938	d: 1998
4	Virginia Mary Zaunbrecher	b: 2/6/1950		
	+Dennis Lloyd West	b: 8/15/1950	m: 2/13/1971	
3	Regina Marie Zaunbrecher	b: 12/6/1912		d: 7/5/2006
3	Franz "Frank" Zaunbrecher	b: 12/31/1914		d: 8/25/1984
	+Hilda Mathilda Frey	b: 8/19/1922	m: 2/12/1941	d: 6/11/2004
4	Loretta Ann Zaunbrecher	b: 11/11/1941		
	+Frederick Burns Leger	b: 12/1/1939	m: 5/10/1960	d: 11/28/1965
	*2nd Husband of Loretta Ann Zaunbrecher:			
	+John Kurta	b: 5/25/1930	m: 2/1/1975	
4	Stephen Charles Zaunbrecher	b: 2/3/1943		
	+Shelby Jean Truax	b: 7/24/1945	m: 10/20/1962	
	*2nd Wife of Stephen Charles Zaunbrecher:			
	+Maxie Dale Darbonne	b: 8/18/1942	m: 8/10/1974	
4	Linda Gayle Zaunbrecher	b: 2/1/1945		
	+Richard Belynn Frey	b: 7/12/1941	m: 2/8/1964	
4	Joseph William Zaunbrecher	b: 3/27/1948		
	+Carol Louise Christ	b: 12/1/1948	m: 5/31/1973	
4	Michael Wayne Zaunbrecher	b: 8/24/1949		

Zaunbrecher

	+Blandina Leonards	b: 9/7/1950	m: 6/25/1972	
4	Frank Dale Zaunbrecher	b: 10/8/1952		
	+Gwendolyn Louise Leonards	b: 1/24/1956	m: 6/9/1973	
4	Reginald Warren Zaunbrecher	b: 12/17/1954		
	+Joan Marie Heinen	b: 5/19/1957	m: 3/4/1978	
4	John Lawrence Zaunbrecher	b: 9/23/1956		
	+Susan Elizabeth Craft	b: 5/6/1957	m: 1/17/1976	
	*2nd Wife of John Lawrence Zaunbrecher:			
	+Leslie Marie Soileau	b: 9/24/1963	m: 10/24/1986	
4	Patrick August Zaunbrecher	b: 9/11/1958		d: 9/18/1973
4	Lambertina Gertrude Zaunbrecher	b: 11/30/1960		
	+Mark Gerard Lahaye	b: 8/19/1960	m: 8/22/1981	
3	Clara Josephine Zaunbrecher	b: 1918		d: 1998
	+Benjamin Cullen Link	b: 1920	m: 1947	d: 1989
4	Rodney Lawrence Link	b: 9/22/1947		d: 6/7/1979
	+Judy Kay Woods	b: 2/15/1951	m: 2/2/1971	
4	Francis Eugene Link	b: 9/6/1948		
	+Sara Ruth Adams	b: 2/26/1949	m: 9/21/1968	
	*2nd Wife of Francis Eugene Link:			
	+Kathy Elaine Broussard	b: 11/6/1952	m: 10/10/2001	
4	Gerald Joseph Link	b: 9/2/1950		
	+Deborah Lynn Knuckles	b: 12/9/1952	m: 9/25/1971	
4	Thomas Carl Link	b: 10/10/1951		
	+Roxanne Matt	b: 2/27/1953	m: 8/14/1970	

Zaunbrecher

	*2nd Wife of Thomas Carl Link:			
	+Dorothy Ann Boyd	b: 7/23/1954	m: 7/24/1987	
4	Arlene Claire Link	b: 8/6/1954		
	+John Edgar Bostick	b: 6/10/1955	m: 9/24/1977	
4	Richard James Link	b: 7/7/1955		
	+Rebecca Ann Trahan	b: 7/24/1957	m: 3/28/1980	
4	Suzanne Marie Link	b: 6/12/1957		
	+Paul Marvin Hollier	b: 2/3/1957	m: 6/15/1980	
3	Gertrude Anna Zaunbrecher	b: 1920		d: 2003
	+Dr. William Iglinsky, Jr.	b: 1919	m: 1946	d: 1989
4	Judy Ann Iglinsky	b: 9/30/1947		
	+James E. Tarver Jr.	b: 6/20/1945	m: 8/13/1966	
4	William Lorenz Iglinsky	b: 7/12/1950		
	+Sandra Louise Gass	b: 2/19/1952	m: 6/24/1972	
4	Blanche Marie Iglinsky	b: 11/11/1951		
	+Leslie Joseph Waguespack	b: 10/19/1950	m: 12/14/1974	
4	Patrick Joseph Iglinsky	b: 12/10/1953		
	+Nina Marie Doonan	b: 1/13/1954	m: 7/19/1975	
4	Barbara Jean Iglinsky	b: 3/20/1956		
	+Ellis John Schwartzenburg	b: 1/21/1954	m: 5/22/1976	
2	Maria Katharina Zaunbrecher	b: 2/1872		d: 8/18/1872
2	Deceased Infant	b: 6/17/1873		d: 6/17/1873
2	Johann Jacob Zaunbrecher	b: 6/25/1874		d: 10/26/1874
2	Henry Zaunbrecher	b: 9/17/1875		d: 1944
	+Helena Stamm	b: 1882	m: 1902	d: 1956
3	Bernadine Stephania Zaunbrecher	b: 1902		d: 1979
	+Charles Percy Dubose	b: 1905	m: 1928	
4	Michael Dubose	b: 9/24/1936		d: 4/20/1944

Zaunbrecher

4	Stephen Dubose	b: 8/2/1938		
	+Barbara Cramer	b: 12/18/1940	m: 6/25/1960	
3	Ferdinand Nicholas Zaunbrecher	b: 1904		d: 1966
	+Thelma Eve Hines	b: 1905	m: 1922	d: 1955
4	Deceased Infant Zaunbrecher	b: 1925		d: 1925
4	Reginald Zaunbrecher	b: 7/15/1926		d: 4/2004
	+Marion Trahan	b: 7/31/1924	m: 2/14/1945	
4	Infant Zaunbrecher	b: 1928		d: 1928
4	Infant Zaunbrecher	b: 1929		d: 1929
4	Malcolm Anthony Zaunbrecher	b: 10/15/1931		d: 9/23/2006
	+Mona Jane Smith	b: 12/24/1930	m: 6/19/1948	
3	Johann Edward Zaunbrecher	b: 3/17/1906		d: 1992
3	William Alton Zaunbrecher	b: 1907		d: 1989
	+Monique Petitjean	b: 1909	m: 1928	d: 1968
4	Joyce Zaunbrecher	b: 9/5/1929		
	+Stanley Faulk	b: 10/18/1926	m: 6/10/1948	d: 11/30/1996
	*2nd Wife of William Alton Zaunbrecher:			
	+Odille Guillot Navarre	b: 1910	m: 1969	d: 2005
3	Lawrence Henry Zaunbrecher	b: 1909		d: 1982
	+Marie Gertrude Bollich	b: 1910	m: 1932	d: 1994
4	Glenn Zaunbrecher	b: 11/21/1933		d: 11/7/1989
	+Margaret Pharr	b: 6/5/1936	m: 5/27/1956	
4	Norma Zaunbrecher	b: 12/21/1934		d: 6/15/1995
	+Harold Prevost	b: 5/3/1932	m: 4/26/1958	
4	Alfred Zaunbrecher	b: 5/28/1932		
	+Marceline Comeaux	b: 11/23/1937	m: 8/19/1956	
4	Estelle Zaunbrecher	b: 1/24/1938		

Zaunbrecher

	+Edwin Coy Wyatt	b: 11/18/1936	m: 1/14/1959	
4	Irene Zaunbrecher	b: 8/22/1940		
	+Larry Fields	b: 3/26/1940	m: 4/22/1961	
4	Lois Zaunbrecher	b: 11/6/1949		
	+John D. Harpole, Jr.	b: 10/5/1948	m: 12/16/1972	
4	Janelle Zaunbrecher	b: 2/2/1954		
	+Wilbert J. Bourque, Sr.	b: 7/21/1951	m: 8/27/1971	
3	Raymond Carl Zaunbrecher	b: 1911		d: 1982
	+Anita Marie Perrodin	b: 1921	m: 1940	
4	Sylvia Zaunbrecher	b: 8/29/1941		
	+Ray Robicheaux	b: 11/3/1939	m: 7/9/1959	
4	Russell Zaunbrecher	b: 12/25/1950		
	+Mary Shea	b: 7/8/1953	m: 9/10/1976	
3	Henrietta Mary Zaunbrecher	b: 1913		d: 1993
	+Murphy Byrun Owens	b: 1904	m: 1936	d: 1975
4	Infant Owens	b: 1937		d: 1937
4	Patrick Owens	b: 12/27/1938		
4	Patricia Owens	b: 12/27/1938		d: 9/11/1994
	+Benjamin Cogburn		m: 1/30/1965	
3	Arnold Martin Zaunbrecher	b: 1915		d: 1975
	+Beatrice Clark	b: 1916	m: 8/8/1942	
4	Dr. Frederick Martin Zaunbrecher	b: 9/27/1943		
	+Michelle Dufilho	b: 7/15/1947	m: 12/30/1972	
4	Martin Zaunbrecher, Jr.	b: 1/24/1947		
	+Lucille Anne Fontenot	b: 7/5/1944	m: 8/1/1969	
4	Michael Henry Zaunbrecher	b: 3/29/1948		

Zaunbrecher

	+Claudia Cansler		m: 7/10/1971	
4	Nanette Helen Daboval Zaunbrecher	b: 1/3/1950		
	+Peter Grojean	b: 11/1950	m: 11/15/1979	
3	Norbert Stephen Zaunbrecher	b: 1916		d: 1979
	+Agnes Leona Bollich	b: 1918	m: 1934	d: 2002
4	Kenneth Zaunbrecher	b: 11/8/1936		
	+Gannol Richard	b: 11/5/1938	m: 9/30/1956	
	*2nd Wife of Kenneth Zaunbrecher:			
	+Suzanne Cheramie	b: 7/21/1939	m: 7/8/1983	
3	Hildegard (Hilda) Mary Zaunbrecher	b: 1918		d: 2005
	+Leland Paul Hebert Sr.	b: 1918	m: 1/13/1939	d: 1963
4	Helen Rita Hebert	b: 10/27/1939		
	+James Carol Menard	b: 8/12/1939	m: 2/7/1959	
4	Mary Ann Hebert	b: 1941		d: 1941
4	Leland Hebert, Jr.	b: 11/6/1942		
	+Alberta Cramer	b: 8/16/1942	m: 2/16/1963	d: 12/11/1993
	*2nd Wife of Leland Hebert, Jr.:			
	+Camella Borne	b: 11/20/1942	m: 10/2/2004	
4	Infant Hebert	b: 1944		d: 1944
4	Raymond Phillip Hebert	b: 4/14/1947		
	+Karen Credeur	b: 9/8/1947	m: 8/21/1965	
4	Gregory Lewis Hebert	b: 1/2/1949		
	+Susan Petitjean	b: 11/27/1950	m: 2/14/1968	
	*2nd Wife of Gregory Lewis Hebert:			
	+Sheila Richard Matte	b: 11/2/1959	m: 3/31/1990	
4	Geoffery Joseph Hebert, Sr.	b: 8/1/1950		
	+Kathy Plattsmier	b: 10/30/1952	m: 6/23/1972	
	*2nd Wife of Geoffery Joseph Hebert, Sr.:			

Zaunbrecher

		+Sheila Hargrave		m: 1983	
		*3rd Wife of Geoffery Joseph Hebert, Sr.:			
		+Mona Vincent Veazey	b: 12/8/1953	m: 3/31/2000	
	4	Theresa Kay Hebert	b: 10/4/1951		
		+Timothy Paul Cronan	b: 12/22/1950	m: 6/16/1973	
	4	Elizabeth Hebert	b: 3/9/1956		
	4	Timothy James Hebert, Sr.	b: 8/30/1958		
		+Deborah Jean Cox	b: 11/16/1957	m: 12/11/1982	
3		Marcella Marie Zaunbrecher	b: 1921		d: 1929
2		Karl Frederick Zaunbrecher	b: 10/20/1876		d: 1950
		+Helena Louise Frey	b: 6/3/1887	m: 1/16/1906	d: 1969
3		Stephanie Marie Zaunbrecher	b: 12/26/1906		d: 1988
3		John Nicholas Zaunbrecher	b: 1908		d: 1969
		+Thelma Prather	b: 1914	m: 1942	d: 2006
3		Theresa Helen Zaunbrecher	b: 1909		d: 2004
		+Benjamin Hillman Bailey	b: 1908	m: 1932	d: 1997
	4	Kathleen Bailey	b: 1938		
		+Robert Burk		m: 1965	
	4	Karl Bailey	b: 1942		
		+Joy Nell Brewton		m: 1972	
	4	David Bailey	b: 1945		
		+Martha Hughes		m: 1969	
3		Julia Leona Zaunbrecher	b: 1911		
3		Karl Zaunbrecher, Jr	b: 1913		d: 4/23/2007
		+Lucy Buller	b: 1914	m: 1936	d: 1995
3		Louise Marie Zaunbrecher	b: 1915		

Zaunbrecher

		+Leonard Barber Carpenter	b: 1912		d: 1975
	4	Barbara Carpenter	b: 1955		
		+Darrell Miller		m: 1978	
	3	Hubert William Zaunbrecher	b: 1917		d: 1976
		+Edna Mae Theriot	b: 1919	m: 1946	d: 2004
	3	Eleanor Elizabeth Zaunbrecher	b: 1919		d: 2004
		+Wallace Raymond Ousse	b: 1920	m: 1949	d: 2005
	4	Helena Ousse	b: 1951		
		+Calvin Long		m: 1977	
	4	Wallace Ousse II	b: 1954		
		+Debra Shablow		m: 1978	
	4	Anne Marie Ousse	b: 1957		
	3	Mary Zaunbrecher	b: 1921		d: 1921
	3	Bernard Frederick Zaunbrecher	b: 1924		
	3	Thomas Philip Zaunbrecher	b: 1926		
	3	Patricia Ann Zaunbrecher	b: 1931		
2		Anna Maria Zaunbrecher	b: 10/10/1878		d: 1955
		+William Joseph Gossen	b: 1871	m: 1/7/1901	d: 1963
	3	Nicholas Joseph Gossen	b: 1901		d: 1990
		+Mary Magdelena "Mitch" Bollich	b: 1904		d: 1995
	4	Antoinette Gossen	b: 12/18/1923		
		+William Puissegur	b: 4/21/1922	m: 11/5/1947	
	4	Edna Gossen	b: 7/10/1925		
		+W.J. Palttsmier	b: 8/3/1921	m: 10/19/1948	d: 7/22/1996
	4	Raymond Gossen	b: 4/3/1927		
		+Henrietta Habetz	b: 6/1/1928	m: 2/3/1949	

Zaunbrecher

4	Lucille Gossen	b: 11/11/1928			
	+Alois Andrew Reiners	b: 7/25/1926	m: 11/25/1953	d: 3/19/1999	
4	Robert Gossen	b: 10/1/1933	d: 11/3/2006		
	+Jeanne Privat		b: 3/15/1937	m: 5/6/1956	
4	Helen Gossen	b: 8/14/1936			
	+Clarence Arsement	b: 9/15/1932	m: 10/15/1956		
4	Catherine Gossen	b: 8/4/1939			
	+Leonard Jacob Cramer	b: 2/17/1939	m: 11/9/1961		
3	Henry Peter Gossen	b: 1903		d: 1982	
	+Julia Rosa Olinger	b: 1904	m: 1929	d: 1991	
4	Henrietta Ann Gossen	b: 1929			
	+Julian Didier	b: 1928	m: 1949		
4	Gilbert William Gossen	b: 1931			
	+Florence Rita Gonsoulin	b: 1935	m: 1955		
4	Ralph Aloysius Gossen	b: 1934			
	+Marcella Elizabeth Habetz	b: 1942	m: 1962	d: 1973	
	*2nd Wife of Ralph Aloysius Gossen:				
	+Margorie Marie Devillier	b: 1937	m: 1977		
4	Herbert Joseph Gossen	b: 1936			
	+Elaine Leonards	b: 1938	m: 1958		
4	Donald Charles Gossen	b: 1941			
	+Henrietta Breaux	b: 1948	m: 1967		
4	Flavia Diane Gossen	b: 1943		d: 1946	
3	Catherine Louise Gossen	b: 1905		d: 1996	
	+Theodore Ignatius Heinen	b: 1902	m: 1927	d: 1962	
	*2nd Husband of Catherine Louise Gossen:				
	+Raoul Hebert	b: 1907	m: 1966		

Zaunbrecher

3		Charles Joseph Gossen	b: 1907		d: 1992
		+Helen Marie Dawson	b: 1914		d: 1987
	4	Timothy Gossen	b: 1952		
3		Clara Josepha Gossen	b: 1909		d: 2000
		+Eugene Joseph Caillouet	b: 1905	m: 1943	d: 1979
3		Agnes Elizabeth Gossen	b: 1911		d: 1987
		+Elbert Arnold	b: 1911	m: 1938	d: 1966
	4	Arleen Arnold	b: 1939		
		+Ralph Stutes		m: 1957	
	4	Wade Arnold	b: 1940		d: 1941
	4	Ione Arnold	b: 1943		
		+Henry Reed		m: 1964	
2		Edward Zaunbrecher	b: 6/8/1880		d: 1880
2		August Zaunbrecher	b: 1883		d: 1919
		+Gertrude Wirtz	b: 2/8/1881	m: 11/4/1907	d: 3/28/1961
3		Joseph Nicholas Zaunbrecher	b: 3/23/1910		d: 1/31/1980
3		Cecilia Theresa Zaunbrecher	b: 9/7/1911		d: 8/3/1983
		+William Joseph Bollich, Jr.	b: 11/22/1905	m: 11/18/1931	d: 3/9/1986
	4	Stanley Nicolas Bollich	b: 12/3/1932		d: 1/13/2005
		+Martha Gill	b: 10/5/1941	m: 9/3/1959	
	4	Fr. Ronald William Bollich	b: 5/12/1937		d: 8/7/1996
	4	Wilbur Anthony Bollich	b: 7/28/1938		
		+Betty Nesom	b: 7/19/1942	m: 6/4/1966	
	4	Hallet Joseph Bollich	b: 9/1/1940		
		+Gardlene Ann Trahan	b: 2/13/1958	m: 9/23/1972	
	4	James August Bollich	b: 2/14/1943		
		+Betty Ann Lemare	b: 12/29/1956	m: 3/12/1981	

Zaunbrecher

4	Mary Ann Bollich	b: 10/9/1945		
	+Robert Vincent Ogden		m: 8/11/1966	
3	Anthony Martin Zaunbrecher	b: 5/10/1913		d: 10/27/1966
	+Vernell Hoffpauir	b: 7/18/1922	m: 12/28/1938	
4	Lawrence Anthony Zaunbrecher	b: 12/11/1939		d: 7/10/1940
4	Richard Aaron Zaunbrecher	b: 3/12/1941		d: 9/4/1996
	+Winnie Hebert			
	*2nd Wife of Richard Aaron Zaunbrecher:			
	+Georganna Barry			
4	Gerald Benedict Zaunbrecher	b: 9/27/1942		d: 1/23/1943
3	Rose Helen Zaunbrecher	b: 11/5/1915		d: 2/22/1993
	+James Dallas Schneider	b: 10/6/1919	m: 2/24/1941	d: 11/26/1988
4	Barbara Ann Schneider	b: 2/28/1942		
	+David Lee McDaniel	b: 9/11/1941	m: 10/29/1960	
4	[4] Mary Elaine Schneider	b: 3/16/1944		
	+[5] Rodney William Zaunbrecher	b: 5/8/1940	m: 1/26/1963	
4	Stephen Joseph Schneider	b: 9/13/1945		
	+Rita Diane Lacombe	b: 5/19/1947	m: 4/16/1966	
4	Michael Glen Schneider	b: 10/2/1957		
	+Carol Ann Blood	b: 12/16/1960	m: 7/2/1982	

Bibliography

Primary Sources
Archival Collections

Archives of the Diocese of Lafayette, Lafayette, Louisiana (1985).

Archives of St. Joseph's Catholic Church, Rayne, Louisiana (1881-1882).

Archives of St. Leo's Catholic Church, Roberts Cove, Louisiana (1883-1985).

Official Documents

Schuler, Charles. *Ackerbau Gelegenheiten in Tangipahoa Parish, Louisiana.* New Orleans, 1907.

———. *Karte von Louisiana.* New Orleans, 1907.

———. *Ouachita Parish im Staate Louisiana: Was die Gegend den deutschen Ansiedlern bietet.* New Orleans, 1907.

———. *Schweinezucht in Louisiana.* New Orleans, 1907.

———. *Tensas Parish im Staate Louisiana.* New Orleans, 1907.

State of Louisiana. *Official Journal of the House of Representatives, 1st Regular Session, 1916.* Baton Rouge, 1916.

———. *Official Journal of the House of Representatives, 1st Extra Session, 1917.* Baton Rouge, 1917.

———. *Official Journal of the House of Representatives, 2nd Regular Session, 1918.* Baton Rouge, 1918.

United States Army, Office of Judge Advocate General. *Compilation of War Laws of the Various States and Possessions.* Washington, D.C., 1919.

United States Bureau of the Census. *Statistics for Louisiana: Thirteenth Census of the United States Taken in the Year, 1910.* Washington, D.C., 1916.

United States Customs Bureau. *Passenger Lists of Vessels Arriving in New*

Bibliography

Orleans. Microfilm Reel Nos. 63 and 64, University of Louisiana at Lafayette.

Philip Fabacher Collection.

"Fabacher Family Records and Genealogy."

"Obituary of Joseph Fabacher."

Father Charles Zaunbrecher Collection

"Begrüssung von Grete Esserheim," June 27, 1981, Köln (welcoming address).

Dahlen, Josef. "Begrüssung an Pater Zaunbrecher und Gäste," June 1981, Geilenkirchen, Germany (welcoming address).

"Die Deutsche Katolische Colonie St. Leo bei Rayne, Parish Acadia" (book excerpt).

Duson, W.W. "German Farmers of Southwest Louisiana."

"Fr. Zaunbrecher Sets Anniversary Fete."

"German Hymns Sung at Roberts Cove."

"History of St. Joseph's Catholic Church."

"History of St. Leo."

Lentzen, Herman-Josef. "35 Amerikaner auf den Spuren ihrer Ahnen; Schamlz, Apfelmus und Schwarzbrot Serviert," June 27, 1981 (newspaper article).

"Life of St. Leo IV" (book excerpt).

Fontenot, Mary Alice. "German Settlement Is 100 Years Old" (newspaper clipping).

"Medical Student [Philip Fabacher] Traces Family History from 16" (newspaper clipping).

"Notes About St. Leo."

"Recollections of William Gossen and Gertrude Thevis Klein, 1954."

Bibliography

"Schatzle Book."

"Some Pastors of St. Leo" (book excerpt).

"Specifications and Contract of St. Leo's Church, November 8, 1893."

"The Reverend Peter Leonhard Thevis" (excerpt from article).

Toups, Kathleen. "St. Nickolas Visits Roberts Cove" (newspaper clipping).

Vincent, Eva. "St. Nickolas Visits Robert Cove" (newspaper clipping).

Vincent, Keith L. *A Century of Catholic Life, 1885-1985: St. Leo IV Catholic Church, Roberts Cove, Louisiana, St. Leo IV Day, 17 July 1985* (pamphlet).

Voelker, Bill. "Kulturkampf Drove Germans to Acadia" (newspaper clipping).

Zaunbrecher, Charles. "Experiences of St. Nicholas' Visit Recounted by Father Charles Zaunbrecher" (newspaper clipping).

———. "German Centennial, 1880-1980."

———. "German Centennial Newsletter No. 1."

———. "German Centennial Newsletter No. 2."

———. "German Centennial Newsletter No. 3."

———. "German Colonists of Roberts Cove, Louisiana: Their Ancestors, Children and Grandchildren."

———. "In Roberts Cove: A Special Celebration" (newspaper clipping).

———. Letter to the author, May 11, 1977.

———. "Letter to the Descendants of the Original Passengers of the *S.S. Mississippi*," November 7, 1981.

Interviews

Interview with N.J. Gossen, December 7, 1977, Rayne, Louisiana.

Interview with Professor Matthew Schott, May 21, 1984, Lafayette, Louisiana.

Bibliography

Interviews with Charles Zaunbrecher, April 14, 1975, October 5, 1980, January 3, 1983, October 22, 1985, Roberts Cove, Louisiana.

Newspapers

Baton Rouge *Morning Advocate*, 1980.

Crowley *Daily Signal*, 1899-1980.

Crowley *Daily Signal: Golden Anniversary Edition, 1899-1949. An Album of Acadia Parish and Neighboring Communities*, 1949.

Das Echo von New Orleans, July 31, 1870.

Der Südliche Pionier, May 31, 1893.

Eunice *News*, August 26, 1965.

Lafayette *Daily Advertiser*, 1980.

Lafayette *Morning Star*, 1980.

New Orleans *Times-Picayune*, March 4, 1897.

Ozone Pelican, 1908.

Rayne *Acadian Tribune*, 1974, 1980.

Rayne *Free Press*, 1980.

Rayne *Independent*, 1980.

Rayne *Signal*, August 28, 1886.

St. Landry Democrat, September 18, 1880.

Secondary Sources
Books

Baudier, Roger. *The Catholic Church in Louisiana*. New Orleans, 1972.

Brown, David H. *A History of Who's Who in Louisiana Politics in 1916*. New Orleans, 1916.

Bibliography

Davis, Ellis Arthur, ed. *The Historical Encyclopedia of Louisiana*. Baton Rouge, 1940.

Deiler, J. Hanno. *Geschichte der deutschen Gesellschaft von New Orleans*. New Orleans, 1897.

———. *Geschichte der New Orleanser deutschen Presse*. New Orleans, 1901.

———. *Louisiana, Ein Heim für deutsche Ansiedler*. New Orleans, 1895.

———. *Zur Geschichte der deutschen Kirchengemeinden im Staate Louisiana*. New Orleans, 1894.

Duson, W.W. *Deutsche Landwirte von Südwest Louisiana*. Crowley, LA, 1907.

Fontenot, Mary Alice, and Paul B. Freeland. *Acadia Parish, Louisiana: A History to 1900*. Baton Rouge, 1976.

Harris, William H. *Louisiana: Products Resources and Attractions*. New Orleans, 1881.

Kleber, Albert. *History of St. Meinard Archabbey, 1854-1954*. St. Meinard, Ind., 1954.

Luebke, Frederick C. *Bonds of Loyalty: German-Americans and World War I*. Dekalb, IL, 1974.

Mönckmeier, Wilhelm. *Die deutsche überseeische Auswanderung: Ein Beitrag zur deutschen Wanderungsgeschichte*. Jena, Germany, 1912.

Nau, John Frederick. *The German People of New Orleans, 1850-1900*. Leiden, 1958.

Palmer, R.R., and Joel Colton. *A History of the Modern World*. New York, 1984.

Perrin, William Henry, ed. *Southwest Louisiana Biographical und Historical*. New Orleans, 1891.

Timpe, Georg. *Katholisches Deutschtum in den Vereinigten Staaten von Amerika*. Freiburg, Germany, 1937.

Voss, Louis. *Louisianas Einlaudung an Deutsche Landwirte and Kolonisten*.

Bibliography

New Orleans, 1907.

Wittke, Carl. *German-Americans and the World War.* Columbus, Ohio, 1936.

Articles

Boudreaux, Florence. "German Customs Still Retained in Roberts Cove," *Attakapas Gazette,* 3 (1968).

Clark, Robert T. "Reconstruction and the New Orleans German Colony," *Louisiana Historical Quarterly,* 23 (1940), 501-524.

———. "The German Liberals in New Orleans, 1840-1860," *Louisiana Historical Quarterly,* 20 (1937), 137-151.

———. "The New Orleans German Colony in the Civil War," *Louisiana Historical Quarterly,* 20 (1937), 990-1015.

Ginn, Mildred K. "A History of Rice Production in Louisiana to 1896," *Louisiana Historical Quarterly,* 23 (1940), 544-588.

Hair, Velma Lea. "The History of Crowley, Louisiana," *Louisiana Historical Quarterly,* 27 (1944), 1119-1225.

Kondert, Reinhart. "Les Allemands en Louisiane de 1721 à 1732," *Revue d'Histoire de l'Amérique française,* 33 (1979), 51-65.

———. "The Germans of Acadia Parish," *Louisiana Review/Revue de Louisiane,* 6 (1977), 19-37.

Konrad, William. "The Diminishing Influence of German Culture in New Orleans Life Since 1865," *Louisiana Historical Quarterly,* 24 (1941), 127-167.

Moehlenbrock, Arthur H. "The German Drama on the New Orleans Stage," *Louisiana Historical Quarterly,* 26 (1943), 361-627.

Palmer, Jean M. "The Impact of World War One on Louisiana's Schools and Community Life," *Louisiana History,* 7 (1966), 323-331.

Reinartz, Werner, and S. Corsten. "Von der Frankenzeit bis zur Gegenwart," *Unsere Heimat,* (1963), 84-96.

Bibliography

Dissertations, Theses, and Papers

Kaiser, T.E. "Yellow Fever in 19th Century New Orleans." M.A. thesis, Tulane University, 1941.

Kondert, Reinhart. "The New Orleans German Society, 1847-1927. Paper read before the Southwestern Social Science Association, Fort Worth, Texas, March 23, 1984.

McCord, Stanley Joseph. "A Historical and Linguistic Study of the German Settlement at Roberts Cove." Ph.D. dissertation, Louisiana State University, 1969.

Index

Achten, Joseph, 10, 29
Achten, Matthew, 29

Barras, Robert, 62
Begnaud, Stanley (Father), 61
Benoit, Zachary, 72
Berken, John, 20
Bessler, Francis (Brother), 24
Bismarck, Otto von, xi, 2
Bogaerts, John (Father), 24
Bourgeois, Francis (Father), 61-64, 72-73
Buschor, Sylvan (Father), 22-24

Cramer, Clare (Sister), 63, 72
Cramer, Felicitas, 65
Cramer, Kay, 67, 69
Cramer, Lawrence, 62, 65
Cramer, Louis, 62-67

Das Echo von New Orleans, 4-5
Deiler, J. Hanno, 19, 34
Der Südliche Pionnier, 18
Didier, Julian, 62-63
Dischler, Xavier, 18
Duson, W.W., 14, 21, 32-34

Fabacher, Ignatius (Father), 54
Fabacher, Joseph, 5-6, 54
Fabacher, Philip, 65, 73-75

Frey, Anton, 5, 7-8, 10-11, 23
Frey, Gerard (Bishop), 54, 59
Frey, John, 45

Geilenkirchen, 1-3, 7-8, 20, 53, 56-58, 74-75
Germanfest, 63-64, 66-72, 75-76; Germanfests, 21, 36
German Heritage Museum, 63-66, 68, 76
German Society, 8, 19-20, 34, 37-40
Gielen, Johann, 18, 29
Gielen, John, 9
Gielen, Magelena, 12
Gossen, Herbie, 65
Gossen, Jerry, 73
Gossen, Joseph, 16, 18, 29, 33, 36, 73
Gossen, Peter, 9, 11-12, 17
Gossen, William, 30, 38, 53
Grein, Herman, 7-8, 11, 29
Gruwe, Luke (Father), 24-25
Guidry, Mitchell (Deacon), 63

Habetz, Clara, 55, 60, 65, 69-71
Habetz, Edmund, 62
Habetz, E.L., 62-63
Habetz, Kay, 64-65, 67
Habetz, Lawrence, 62-63, 65, 67
Habetz, Marie (Sister), 63-65
Habetz, Thomas (Father), 63, 72
Habetz, Wilhelm, 70
Hefner, George (Father), 63, 72
Heinen, Gerhard Joseph. *See* Joseph

Index

Heinen
Heinen, Johnny, Sr., 65
Heinen, Joseph, 11, 16-17, 25, 29, 33, 36-37
Heinen, Peter William, 11
Heinen, Theodore, 15
Heinen, William, 29-30, 32, 35, 45, 50
Hennemann, Aegidius (Father), 21-23, 36
Hensgens, Christian, 5, 9, 11-12, 18, 29, 36
Hensgens, Gertrude, 26
Hensgens, Raymond, 65
Hoffpauir, Joshua, 64
Huber, Zeno, 5

Jacobs, Arnold, 11, 29

Kedinger, Paul, 64-65
Kögl, Johann (Brother), 21, 23
Kulturkampf, xi, 2-3, 9, 21-22
Kurta, Loretta, 65

Leger, Don (Father), 62
Leger, Dorothy "Dot" O., 63, 65
Legnion, Michael, 72
Leo IV, ix, 23, 59-63, 67, 69-70, 72-73, 75
Leonards, August, 8, 16, 29
Leonards, Heinrich, 8
Leonards, Jerry, 62-63
Leonards, John, 72
Leonards, Joseph, 9, 15-16, 18, 30, 33, 38
Leonards, Mary Ann, 67
Leonards, Mike, 67

Leonards, Peter J., 29
Leonards, Shirley, 62, 65
Leo XIII, 22-23
Louis XIV, 1-2

McCord, Stanley Joseph, xiii, 11, 16

New Orleans German Society, 8, 19-20, 34

Odin, Jean-Marie (Archbishop), 3-4
O'Donnell, Edward (Bishop), 62
Ohlenforst, Dawn, 62
Ohlenforst, Margaret (Sister), 63, 72
Ohlenforst, William "Bill," 63
Olinger, Ambrose, 72-73
Olinger, Ferdinand, 45
Olinger, Gerard, 65
Olinger, Mary Jo, 62-63
Olinger, Susan, 67

Piepers, Johanna, 8
Provost, Glen (Monsignor), 63

Rayne *Acadian Tribune*, 62, 64, 68, 71
Reiners, Franz, 9, 11, 15, 18, 29
Reynolds, Daniel, 72
Reynolds, John, 72
Reznicek, Alois (Father), 61
Rhineland, 1-2
Rimmer, Matt, 73
Ronkartz, Jerome, 65

Index

Ronkartz, Johann, 11
Rumpf, Felix (Father), 24-25

St. Leo the Great, 22
St. Meinard Abbey, 21, 23, 49
St. Nickolas' Day, 58
Schaffhausen, Joseph, 20, 45
Scheuffens, Theodore, 18-19, 29
Schexnayder, Maurice (Bishop), 54, 62, 73
Schlicher, Johann P., 9, 16, 29
Schlicher, Lambert, 9, 12, 16-18, 29
Schlicher, Marie, 12
Schwab, Leo (Father), 35, 49
Seichler, Clement (Brother), 22-23
Spaetgens, Joseph, 11, 17, 29
Speyer, Jude (Bishop), 54
S.S. Frankfurt, 8
S.S. Mississippi, 5, 9-10
Stamm, Johann, 45
Stark, Leonard, 47-48

Theunissen, Franziska, 71
Theunissen, Hubert, 11-12, 16, 29
Theunissen, Maria Catherina, 11
Thevis, Daniel, 10
Thevis, Gerhard, 8, 16-17
Thevis, Gwen, 67
Thevis, Jacob, 9, 16-18, 36
Thevis, John Gerhard, 7
Thevis, Josephine "Josie" B., 63, 65
Thevis, Magdelena Gertrude, 12
Thevis, Peter Joseph, 8, 16-17, 25
Thevis, Peter Leonhard (Father), 3-10, 21-22
Thibodeaux, Paul, 72
Thibodeaux, Paul (Father), 72

Vincent, Keith (Father), 59, 61, 63
Vondenstein, Joseph, 8
Vondenstein, Josepha, 8
Vondenstein, Peter Joseph, 12

Wirtz, Hubert, 9, 11, 15-16, 29
Wolbers, Gerard (Father), xii

Zarn, Placidus (Father), 26, 35
Zaunbrecher, August, 47
Zaunbrecher, Bertha Dischler, 69
Zaunbrecher, Charles, 69
Zaunbrecher, Charles Joseph (Father), xii, 55-56, 59, 69-70, 73-75
Zaunbrecher, Lawrence, 26, 30, 32, 35
Zaunbrecher, Lorenz, 10, 15, 18
Zaunbrecher, Nicholas Joseph, 9, 11, 15-17, 25, 29-30, 33
Zaunbrecher, Vincent, 65
Zaunbrecher, William Joseph, 15-16, 29-33, 40, 46-48, 53

Addendum
Religious Vocations from the Descendants of the Original German Families
Compiled by Clara Habetz

Sisters
Columba Scheufens, O.S.B.
Mary Leona Vondenstein, O.S.B.
Mary Lucy Vondenstein, O.S.B.
Ann Pauline Gossen, C.D.P.
Marie Habetz, C.D.P.
M. Lawrence Habetz, O'Carm.
Margaret Mary Ohlenforst, M.H.S.
Mary Clare Cramer, O'Carm.
Lucy Cramer, C.D.P.
Clare Schaffhausen, H.C.
Mildred Leonards, C.D.P.
Bernadine Leonards, C.D.P.
Agnes Leonards Thevis, C.D.P.
Linda Constantin, O.S.F.
Theresa Marie Gossen, C.D.P.
Marie Therese Hebert, P.C.P.A.

Priests
Rev. Daniel Thevis
Rt. Rev. Msgr. Alois Olinger
R. Rev. Msgr. Leonard Clement Habetz
R. Rev. Msgr. Daniel Habetz
Rev. John William Ohlenforst
Rev. Charles Joseph Zaunbrecher
Rev. Jody Simoneaux
Rev. Charles Thevis
Rev. Thomas E. Habetz
Rev. Martin Leonards
Rev. Michael Schatzle
Rev. Ronald Bollich
Rev. Gerard Young
Rev. Carl J. Schutten
Rt. Rev. Msgr. Carl Jacob

www.ingramcontent.com/pod-product-compliance
Lightning Source LLC
Chambersburg PA
CBHW071113080526
44587CB00013B/1330